IBM® PC ASSEMBLY LANGUAGE AND PROGRAMMING

Third Edition

Peter Abel

*British Columbia
Institute of Technology*

PRENTICE HALL, Upper Saddle River, New Jersey 07458

Library of Congress Cataloging-in-Publication Data

Abel, Peter, 1932-
IBM PC assembly language and programming / by Peter Abel. — 3rd
  ed.
      p.   cm.
   Includes index.
   ISBN 0-13-124603-8
      1. IBM Personal Computer—Programming.   2. Assembler language
(Computer program language)   3. IBM Personal System/2 (Computer
system)   I. Title.
QA76.8.I2594A236   1994
005.265—dc20

94-40847
CIP

Pre-press/Manufacturing buyer: BILL SCAZZERO
Acquisitions editor: MARCIA HORTON
Editorial/production supervision
   and interior design: RICHARD DeLORENZO
Copy editor: BRIAN BAKER
Editorial assistant: DOLORES MARS
Supplement editor: ALICE DWORKIN

© 1995 by Prentice-Hall, Inc.
A Simon & Schuster Company
Upper Saddle River, New Jersey 07458

The author and publisher of this book have used their best efforts in preparing this book. These efforts include the development, research, and testing of the theories and programs to determine their effectiveness. The author and publisher make no warranty of any kind, expressed or implied, with regard to these programs or the documentation contained in this book. The author and publisher shall not be liable in any event for incidental or consequential damages in connection with, or arising out of, the furnishing, performance, or use of these programs.

Printed in the United States of America

10   9   8   7   6   5   4   3

ISBN   0-13-124603-8

Prentice-Hall International (UK) Limited, London
Prentice-Hall of Australia Pty. Limited, Sydney
Prentice-Hall Canada Inc., Toronto
Prentice-Hall Hispanoamericana, S.A., Mexico
Prentice-Hall of India Private Limited, New Delhi
Prentice-Hall of Japan, Inc., Tokyo
Simon & Schuster Asia Pte. Ltd., Singapore
Editora Prentice-Hall do Brasil, Ltda., Rio de Janeiro

Contents

Preface

The heart of a computer is a microprocessor, which handles the computer's requirements for arithmetic, logic, and control. The microprocessor had its origin in the 1960s, when research designers devised the integrated circuit (IC) by combining various electronic components into a single component on a silicon "chip." The manufacturers set this tiny chip into a device resembling a centipede and connected it into a functioning system. In the early 1970s, Intel introduced the 8008 chip, which, installed in a computer terminal, ushered in the first generation of microprocessors.

By 1974, the 8008 had evolved into the 8080, a popular second-generation microprocessor with general-purpose use. In 1978, Intel produced the third-generation 8086 processor, which provided some compatibility with the 8080 and represented a significant advance on its design. Next, Intel developed a variation of the 8086 to provide a slightly simpler design and compatibility with then-current input/output devices. This new processor the 8088, was selected by IBM for its forthcoming personal computer in 1981. An enhanced version of the 8088 is the 80188, and enhanced versions of the 8086 are the 80186, 80286, 80386, 80486, and Pentium (also known as P5), each of which provides additional operations and processing power.

The spread of microcomputers also caused a renewed interest in assembly language, whose use provides a number of advantages:

- A program written in assembly language requires considerably less memory and execution time than a program written in what are known as high-level languages, such as Pascal and C.
- Assembly language gives a programmer the ability to perform highly technical tasks that would be difficult, if not impossible, in a high-level language.

- A knowledge of assembly language provides an understanding of machine architecture that no high-level language can ever provide.
- Although most software specialists develop new applications in high-level languages, which are easier to write and maintain, a common practice is to recode in assembly language those routines that have caused processing bottlenecks.
- Resident programs and interrupt service routines are almost always developed in assembly language.

High-level languages were designed to eliminate the technicalities of a particular computer, whereas an assembly language is designed for a specific computer or, more accurately, for a specific family of processors. The following is required for learning PC assembly language:

- Access to an IBM personal computer (any model) or equivalent compatible.
- A copy of the MS-DOS or PC-DOS operating system (preferably, a recent version) and familiarity with its use.
- A copy of an assembler translator program (again, preferably, a recent version). The Microsoft versions are called MASM and QuickAssembler, Borland's is TASM, and SLR System's is OPTASM.

The following are not required for learning assembly language:

- Prior knowledge of a programming language, although such knowledge may help you grasp some programming concepts more readily.
- Prior knowledge of electronics or circuitry. This book provides all the information about PC architecture that you require for programming in assembly language.

OPERATING SYSTEMS

The major purposes of an operating system are (1) to allow users to instruct a computer regarding actions it is to take (such as executing a particular program) and (2) to provide means of storing ("cataloging") information on disk and of accessing it.

The most common operating system for the PC and its compatibles is MS-DOS from Microsoft, known as PC-DOS on the IBM PC. Each version of DOS has provided additional features that have extended the capability of the PC. A discussion of such advanced operating systems as OS/2 and UNIX is outside the scope of this book.

FOCUS OF THE BOOK

The primary aim of this book is to assist readers in learning assembly language programming. To this end, the book first covers the simpler aspects of the hardware and the language and then introduces instructions as they are needed. As well, the text emphasizes clarity in program examples. Thus the examples use those instructions and approaches that are the easiest to understand, even though a professional programmer would solve similar problems with more sophisticated—but less clear—code.

The programs also omit macro instructions (explained in Chapter 22); although professional programmers use macros extensively, their appearance in a book of this nature would interfere with learning the principles of the language. Once these principles are learned, a programmer can adopt the clever techniques of the professional.

THE APPROACH TO TAKE

This book can act as both a tutorial and a permanent reference. To make the most effective use of your investment in a microcomputer and software, work through each chapter carefully, and reread any material that is not immediately clear. Key the program examples into your computer, convert them into executable "modules," and get them to execute (or "run"). Also, be sure to work through the exercises at the end of each chapter.

The first nine chapters furnish the foundation material for the book and for assembly language. After studying these chapters, you can proceed with Chapters 12, 13, 15, 16, 20, 21, or 22. Chapters 25, 26, 27, and 28 are intended as references. Chapters related to each other are:

- 9 through 11 (on screen and keyboard operations)
- 13 and 14 (on arithmetic operations)
- 16 through 19 (on disk processing)
- 23 and 24 (on subprograms and memory management)

On completing this book, you will be able to:

- Understand the hardware of the personal computer.
- Understand machine-language code and hexadecimal format.
- Understand the steps involved in assembling, linking, and executing a program.
- Write programs in assembly language to handle the keyboard and screen, perform arithmetic, convert between ASCII and binary formats, perform table searches and sorts, and handle disk input and output.
- Trace machine execution as an aid in program debugging.
- Write your own macro instructions to facilitate faster coding.
- Link separately assembled programs into one executable program.

Learning assembly language and getting your programs to work is an exciting and challenging experience. For the time and effort invested, the rewards are sure to be great.

NOTES ON THE THIRD EDITION

This third edition reflects a considerable number of enhancements to the previous edition, some of which are the following:

- The inclusion of, and more emphasis on, additional functions in more recent versions of DOS
- Programming for mouse operations

- Features of the Intel 80486 and Pentium processors
- The inclusion of material on the upper memory area and the high memory area
- The inclusion of material on more recent assembler versions
- More coverage of disk processing for DOS functions, the file allocation table, and random processing
- Thorough details of the extended keyboard's key combinations and scan codes.
- Considerable reorganization and revision of explanations throughout the text.

ACKNOWLEDGMENTS

The author is grateful for the assistance and cooperation of all those who contributed suggestions for, reviews of, and corrections to earlier editions. For this third edition, a special thanks to Brian R. Anderson of the British Columbia Institute of Technology for inputs on mouse and C programming

CHAPTER 1 ————————————

Introduction to PC Hardware

OBJECTIVE

To explain the basic features of microcomputer hardware
and program organization.

INTRODUCTION

Writing a program in assembly language requires knowledge of the computer's hardware (or architecture), its instruction set, and the rules for using that instruction set. An explanation of the basic hardware—bits, bytes, registers, memory, the processor, and the data bus—is provided in this chapter. The instruction set and its use are developed throughout the book.

The fundamental building blocks of a computer are the *bit* and the *byte*. These supply the means by which a computer can represent data and instructions in memory.

The main internal hardware features of a computer are a microprocessor, memory, and registers; external hardware features are the computer's input/output devices such as the keyboard, monitor, and disk. Software consists of the various programs and data files (including the operating system), stored on the disk. To execute (or run) a program, the system copies it from disk into internal memory. (Internal memory is what people mean when they claim that their computer has, for example, 8 megabytes of memory.) The microprocessor executes the program instructions, and the registers handle arithmetic, data movement, and addressing.

An assembly language program consists of one or more *segments* for defining data and for storing machine instructions and a segment named the *stack* that contains stored addresses.

BITS AND BYTES

The smallest unit of data in a computer is a *bit*. A bit may be unmagnetized, or *off*, so that its value is zero, or it may be magnetized, or *on*, so that its value is one. A single bit doesn't provide much information, but it is surprising what a bunch of them can do.

Bytes

A group of nine bits is called a *byte*, which represents storage locations both in internal memory and on external disk. In memory, each byte has a unique address, beginning with zero for the first byte. Each byte consists of eight bits for data and one bit for parity:

0	0	0	0	0	0	0	0	1

|———————————————— data bits ————————————————| parity |

The eight data bits provide the basis for binary arithmetic and for representing such characters as the letter A and the asterisk symbol (*). Eight bits allow 256 different combinations of on-off conditions, from all bits off (00000000) through all bits on (11111111). For example, a representation of the bits for the letter A is 01000001 and for the asterisk is 00101010, although you don't have to memorize such facts.

Parity requires that in each byte, the number of bits that are on is always *odd*. Since the letter A contains two bits that are on, the processor automatically sets its parity bit on also (01000001-1), to force odd parity. Similarly, since the asterisk contains three bits that are on, the processor sets its parity bit off (00101010-0), to maintain odd parity. When an instruction references a byte in internal storage, the processor checks its parity. If its parity is even, the system assumes that a bit is "lost" and displays an error message. A parity error may be a result of a hardware fault or an electrical disturbance; either way, it is a rare event.

You may have wondered how a computer "knows" that bit value 01000001 represents the letter A. When you key in A on the keyboard, the system delivers a signal from that particular key into memory and sets a byte (in an input location) to the bit value 01000001. You can move the contents of this byte about in memory as you will, and you can even print it or display it on the screen as the letter A.

For reference purposes, the bits in a byte are numbered 0 to 7 from right to left, as shown here for the letter A (we no longer need be concerned with the parity bit):

Bit number:	7	6	5	4	3	2	1	0
Bit contents for A:	0	1	0	0	0	0	0	1

Related Bytes

A program can treat a group of bytes as a unit of data, such as time or distance. A group of one or more bytes that defines a particular value is commonly known as a *field*. A computer also supports certain sizes that are natural to it:

- *Word.* A 2-byte (16-bit) field. Bits in a word are numbered 0 through 15 from right to left, as shown here for the letters 'PC':

Bit number:	15	14	13	12	11	10	9	8	7	6	5	4	3	2	1	0
Bit contents (PC):	0	1	0	1	0	0	0	0	0	1	0	0	0	0	1	1

- *Doubleword.* A 4-byte (32-bit) field.
- *Quadword.* An 8-byte (64-bit) field.
- *Paragraph.* A 16-byte (128-bit) field.
- Kilobyte (KB). The number 2^{10} equals 1,024, which happens to be the value K, for kilobytes. Thus a computer with 640K memory has 640 × 1,024, or 655,360, bytes.
- Megabyte (MB). The number 2^{20} equals 1,048,576, or one megabyte.

BINARY NUMBERS

Because a computer can distinguish only between 0 and 1 bits, it works in a base-2 numbering system known as binary. In fact, the word "bit" is a contraction of "Binary digIT."

A collection of bits can represent any numeric value. The value of a binary number is based on the relative positions of the bits and whether each is a zero or a one. Just as in decimal numbers, the positions represent ascending powers (but of 2, not 10) from right to left. In the following eight-bit number, all bits are set to one (on):

Position:	7	6	5	4	3	2	1	0
Bit value:	1	1	1	1	1	1	1	1
Position value:	128	64	32	16	8	4	2	1

The rightmost bit assumes the value 1 (2^0), the next digit to the left assumes the value 2 (2^1), the next the value 4 (2^2), and so forth. The value of the binary number in this case is $1 + 2 + 4 + \ldots + 128 = 255$ (or 2^8-1).

In a similar manner, the value of the binary number 01000001 is calculated to be 1 plus 64, or 65:

Bit value:	0	1	0	0	0	0	0	1
Position value:	128	64	32	16	8	4	2	1

But isn't 01000001 the letter A? Indeed, it is. The bits 01000001 can represent either the number 65 or the letter A, as follows:

- If a program defines the data for arithmetic purposes, then 01000001 represents a binary number equivalent to the decimal number 65.
- If a program defines the data for descriptive purposes, such as a heading, then 01000001 represents an alphabetic character.

When you start programming, you will see this distinction more clearly, because you define and use each data item for a specific purpose; in practice, the two uses are rarely a source of confusion.

A binary number is not limited to 8 bits. A processor that uses 16-bit (or 32-bit) architecture handles 16-bit (or 32-bit) numbers automatically. For 16 bits, $2^{16} - 1$ provides values up to 65,535, and for 32 bits, $2^{32} - 1$ provides values up to 4,294,967,295.

Binary Arithmetic

A microcomputer performs arithmetic only in *binary* format. Consequently, an assembly language programmer has to be familiar with binary format and binary addition. The following examples illustrate binary addition:

$$
\begin{array}{cccc}
0 & 0 & 1 & 1 \\
+0 & +1 & +1 & +1 \\
\hline
0 & 1 & 10 & +1 \\
 & & & \hline
 & & & 11
\end{array}
$$

Note the carry of a 1-bit in the last two examples. Now, let's add 01000001 and 00101010. Are we adding the letter A and an asterisk? No, they are the decimal values 65 and 42:

Decimal	Binary
65	01000001
+42	+00101010
107	01101011

Check that the binary sum 01101011 is actually 107. As another example, add the decimal values 60 and 53:

Decimal	Binary
60	00111100
+53	+00110101
113	01110001

Negative Numbers

The preceding binary numbers are all positive values because in each the leftmost bit is a zero. A negative binary number contains a 1-bit in its leftmost position. However, it's not as simple as changing the leftmost bit to 1, such as 01000001 (+65) to 11000001. A negative value is expressed in *two's complement notation*; that is, to represent a binary number as negative, the rule is: Reverse the bits and add 1. Let's find the two's complement of 01000001 (or 65) as an example:

```
Number +65:        01000001
Reverse bits:      10111110
Add 1:                    1
                   _____
Number −65:        10111111
```

A binary number is negative if its leftmost bit is 1, but if you add the 1-bit values to convert the number 10111111 to decimal, you won't get 65. To determine the absolute value of a negative binary number, simply repeat the previous operation; that is, reverse the bits and add 1:

```
Number −65:        10111111
Reverse bits:      01000000
Add 1:                    1
                   _____
Number +65:        01000001
```

The sum of +65 and −65 should be zero. Let's try it:

```
+65         01000001
−65       +10111111
           _____
 00       (1)00000000
```

In the sum, the 8-bit value is all zeros, and the carry of the 1-bit on the left is lost. But because there is a carry into the sign bit and a carry out, the result is correct.

Binary subtraction is a simple matter: Convert the number being subtracted to two's complement format, and add the numbers. Let's subtract 42 from 65. The binary representation for 42 is 00101010, and its two's complement is 11010110:

```
   65         01000001
+(−42)      +11010110
            _____
   23       (1)00010111
```

The result, 23, is correct. Once again, there is a valid carry into the sign bit and a carry out.

If the justification for two's complement notation isn't immediately clear, consider the following question: What value would you have to add to binary 00000001 to make it equal to 00000000? In terms of decimal numbers, the answer would be −1. The two's complement of 1 is 11111111. So we add +1 and −1 as follows:

```
    1          00000001
 +(−1)         11111111
               _____
Result:       (1)00000000
```

Ignoring the carry of 1, you can see that the binary number 11111111 is equivalent to decimal −1. You can also see a pattern form as the binary numbers decrease in value:

```
+3        00000011
+2        00000010
+1        00000001
 0        00000000
−1        11111111
−2        11111110
−3        11111101
```

In fact, the 0-bits in a negative binary number indicate its (absolute) value: Treat the positional value of each 0-bit as if it were a 1-bit, sum the values, and add 1.

You'll find this material on binary arithmetic and negative numbers particularly relevant when you get to Chapters 12 and 13 on arithmetic.

HEXADECIMAL REPRESENTATION

Imagine that you want to view the contents of a binary value in four adjacent bytes (a doubleword) in memory. Although a byte may contain any of the 256 bit combinations, there is no way to display or print many of them as standard ASCII characters. (Examples of such characters include the bit configurations for Tab, Enter, Form Feed, and Escape.) Consequently, computer designers developed a shorthand method of representing binary data. The method divides each byte in half and expresses the value of each half-byte. As an example, consider the following four bytes:

Binary:	0101	1001	0011	0101	1011	1001	1100	1110
Decimal:	5	9	3	5	11	9	12	14

Since the numbers 11, 12, and 14 require two digits, let's extend the numbering system so that 10 = A, 11 = B, 12 = C, 13 = D, 14 = E, and 15 = F. Here's the revised shorthand number that represents the contents of the bytes just given:

59   35   B9   CE

The numbering system thus involves the "digits" 0 through F and, since there are 16 such digits, the system is known as *hexadecimal* (or *hex*) representation. Figure 1–1 shows the decimal numbers 0 through 15 along with their equivalent binary and hexadecimal values.

Binary	Decimal	Hexadecimal	Binary	Decimal	Hexadecimal
0000	0	0	1000	8	8
0001	1	1	1001	9	9
0010	2	2	1010	10	A
0011	3	3	1011	11	B
0100	4	4	1100	12	C
0101	5	5	1101	13	D
0110	6	6	1110	14	E
0111	7	7	1111	15	F

Figure 1–1   Binary, Decimal, and Hexadecimal Representation

Assembly language makes considerable use of hexadecimal format. A listing of an assembled program shows, in hexadecimal, all addresses, machine-code instructions, and the contents of data constants. For debugging your programs, you can use the DOS DEBUG program, which also displays the addresses and contents of bytes in hexadecimal format.

You'll soon get used to working in hexadecimal format. Keep in mind that the hex number immediately following hex F is hex 10, which is decimal value 16. Following are some simple examples of hex arithmetic:

$$\begin{array}{cccccc}
6 & 5 & F & F & 10 & FF \\
+4 & +8 & +1 & +F & +30 & +\ 1 \\
\hline
A & D & 10 & 1E & 40 & 100
\end{array}$$

Note also that hex 40 equals decimal 64, hex 100 is decimal 256, and hex 1,000 is decimal 4,096.

To indicate a hex number in a program, code an "H" immediately after the number; thus 25H = decimal 37. By convention, a hex number always begins with a decimal digit 0-9, so you should code B8H as 0B8H. In this book, we indicate a hexadecimal value with the word "hex" or an "H" following the number (such as hex 4C or 4CH); a binary value with the word binary or a "B" following the number (such as binary 01001100 or 01001100B); and a decimal value simply by a number (such as 76). An occasional exception occurs where the base is obvious from the context.

Appendix A gives an explanation of how to convert hex numbers to decimal and vice versa.

ASCII CODE

To standardize the representation of characters, microcomputer manufacturers have adopted the ASCII (American National Standard Code for Information Interchange) code. A standard code facilitates the transfer of data between different computer devices. The 8-bit extended ASCII code that the PC uses provides 256 characters, including symbols for foreign alphabets. For example, the combination of bits 01000001 (hex 41) indicates the letter A. Appendix B provides a list of the 256 ASCII characters, and Chapter 8 shows how to display most of them on the screen.

THE PROCESSOR

An important hardware element of the PC is the system unit, which contains a system board, power supply, and expansion slots for optional boards. Features of the system board are an Intel (or equivalent) microprocessor, read-only memory (ROM), and random access memory (RAM).

The brain of the PC and compatibles is a *microprocessor* based on the Intel 8086 family that performs all processing of instructions and data. Processors vary in their speed and capacity of memory, registers, and data bus. A *data bus* transfers data between the processor, memory, and external devices, in effect, managing data traffic. Following is a brief description of various Intel processors:

8088/80188. These processors have 16-bit registers and an 8-bit data bus and can address up to 1 million bytes of internal memory. The registers can process two bytes at a time, whereas the data bus can transfer only one byte at a time. The 80188 is a souped-up 8088 with a few additional instructions. Both types of processor run in what is known as *real mode*, that is, one program at a time.

8086/80186. These processors are similar to the 8088/80188, but have a 16-bit data bus and can run faster. The 80186 is a souped-up 8086 with a few additional instructions.

80286. This processor can run faster than the preceding processors and can address up to 16 million bytes. It can run in real mode or in protected mode for multitasking.

80386. This processor has 32-bit registers and a 32-bit data bus and can address up to 4 billion bytes of memory. It can run in real mode or in protected mode for multitasking.

80486. This processor also has 32-bit registers and a 32-bit data bus (although some clones have a 16-bit data bus) and is designed for enhanced performance. It can run in real mode or in protected mode for multitasking.

Pentium (or P5). This processor has 32-bit registers and a 64-bit data bus and can execute more than one instruction per clock cycle. (Intel adopted the name "Pentium" because, in contrast to numbers, names can be copyrighted.)

Execution Unit and Bus Interface Unit

The processor is partitioned into two logical units: an execution unit (EU) and a bus interface unit (BIU), as illustrated in Figure 1–2. The role of the EU is to execute instructions, whereas the BIU delivers instructions and data to the EU. The EU contains an arithmetic and logic unit (ALU), a control unit (CU), and a number of registers. These features provide for execution of instructions and arithmetic and logical operations.

The most important function of the BIU is to manage the bus control unit, segment registers, and instruction queue. The BIU controls the buses that transfer data to the EU, to

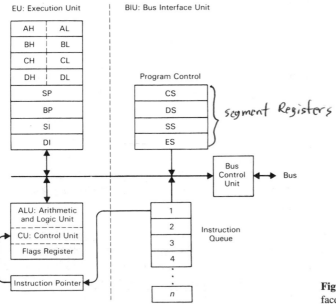

Figure 1–2 Execution Unit and Bus Interface Unit

memory, and to external input/output devices, whereas the segment registers control memory addressing.

Another function of the BIU is to provide access to instructions. Since the instructions for a program that is executing are in memory, the BIU must access instructions from memory and place them in an *instruction queue.* Because this queue is from 4 to 32 bytes in size, depending on the processor, the BIU is able to look ahead and prefetch instructions so that there is always a queue of instructions ready to execute.

The EU and BIU work in parallel, with the BIU keeping one step ahead. The EU notifies the BIU when it needs access to data in memory or an I/O device. Also, the EU requests machine instructions from the BIU instruction queue. The top instruction is the currently executable one, and while the EU is occupied executing an instruction, the BIU fetches another instruction from memory. This fetching overlaps with execution and speeds up processing.

Processors up through the 80486 have what is known as a *single pipeline,* which restricts them to completing one instruction before starting the next. The Pentium and later processors have a *dual pipeline* structure that enables it to run many operations in parallel.

INTERNAL MEMORY

A microcomputer contains two types of internal memory: *random access memory* (RAM) and *read-only memory* (ROM). Bytes in memory are numbered consecutively, beginning with 00, so that each location has a uniquely numbered address.

Figure 1–3 shows a physical memory map of an 8086-type PC. Of the first megabyte of memory, the first 640K is RAM, most of which is available for your own use.

ROM. ROM is a special memory chip that (as the full name suggests) can only be read. Since instructions and data are permanently "burned into" a ROM chip, they cannot be altered. The ROM Basic Input/Output System (BIOS) begins at address 768K and handles input/output devices, such as a hard disk controller. ROM beginning at 960K controls the computer's basic functions, such as the power-on self-test, dot patterns for graphics, and the disk self-loader. When you switch on the power, ROM performs various check-outs and loads special system data from disk into RAM.

```
     Start Address              Purpose

      Dec      Hex                                  - - - - - - - - - -
      960K    F0000    |   64K base system ROM     |
                       | - - - - - - - - - - - - - - - |
                       |   192K memory expansion   |    upper
      768K    C0000    |   area (ROM)              |    memory
                       | - - - - - - - - - - - - - - - |
                       |   128K video display      |
      640K    A0000    |   area (RAM)              |   - - - - - - - - -
                       | - - - - - - - - - - - - - - - |
                       |                           |
                       |                           |    conventional
                       |   640K memory (RAM)       |    memory
                       |                           |
      zero    00000    |                           |
                       |                           |   - - - - - - - - -
```

Fig. 1–3   Map of Physical Memory

RAM.   A programmer is mainly concerned with RAM, which would be better named "read-write memory." RAM is available as a "worksheet" for temporary storage and execution of programs.

Since the contents of RAM are lost when you turn off the power, you need separate, external storage for keeping programs and data. If you have a DOS diskette inserted or a hard disk installed when you turn on the power, the ROM boot-up procedure loads the DOS COMMAND.COM program into RAM. You then request COMMAND.COM to perform actions, such as loading a program from a disk into RAM. Since COMMAND.COM occupies only a small part of RAM, there is space for other programs as well. Your program executes in RAM and normally produces output on the screen, printer, or disk. When finished, you may ask COMMAND.COM to load another program into RAM, an action that overwrites the previous program. All further discussions of RAM will use the general term "memory."

Addressing Memory Locations

Depending on the model, the processor can access one or more bytes of memory at a time. Consider the decimal number 1,025. The hex representation of this value, 0401H, requires two bytes, or one word, of memory. It consists of a high-order (most significant) byte, 04, and a low-order (least significant) byte, 01. The system stores these in memory in *reverse-byte sequence*: the low-order byte in the low memory address and the high-order byte in the high memory address. For example, the processor would transfer 0401H from a register into memory locations 5612 and 5613 like this:

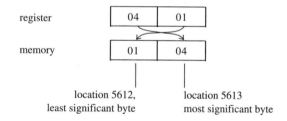

register | 04 | 01 |

memory | 01 | 04 |

location 5612,   location 5613
least significant byte   most significant byte

The processor expects numeric data in memory to be in reverse-byte sequence and processes such data accordingly. When the processor retrieves the word from memory, it again reverses the bytes, restoring them correctly in the register as hex 04 01. Although this feature is entirely automatic, you have to be alert to it when programming and debugging assembly language programs.

An assembly language programmer has to distinguish clearly between the *address* and the *contents* of a memory location. In the preceding example, the contents of location 5612 is 01, and the contents of location 5613 is 04.

SEGMENTS AND ADDRESSING

A *segment* is a special area in a program that begins on a *paragraph boundary*, that is, at a location evenly divisible by 16, or hex 10. Although a segment may be located almost anywhere in memory and may be up to 64K bytes in real mode, it requires only as much space as the program requires for its execution.

A segment in real mode can be up to 64K bytes. There may be any number of segments; to address a particular segment, it is necessary only to change the address in the appropriate segment register. The three main segments are the *code*, *data*, and *stack* segments.

Code Segment

The *code segment* contains the machine instructions that are to execute. Typically, the first executable instruction is at the start of this segment, and the operating system links to that location to begin program execution. As the name implies, the code segment (CS) register addresses the code segment. If your code area requires more than 64K, your program may need to define more than one code segment.

Data Segment

The *data segment* contains a program's defined data, constants, and work areas. The data segment (DS) register addresses the data segment. If your data area requires more than 64K, your program may need to define more than one data segment.

Stack Segment

In simple terms, the *stack* contains any data and addresses that you need to save temporarily or for use by your own "called" subroutines. The stack segment (SS) register addresses the stack segment.

Segment Boundaries

The segment registers contain the starting address of each segment. Figure 1–4 presents a graphic view of the CS, DS, and SS registers; the registers and segments are not necessarily in the order shown. Other segment registers are the ES (extra segment) and, on the 80386 and later processors, the FS and GS registers, which have specialized uses.

As discussed earlier, a segment begins on a paragraph boundary, which is an address evenly divisible by decimal 16, or hex 10. Assume that a data segment begins at memory location 045F0H. Since in this and all other cases the rightmost hex digit is zero, the computer designers decided that it would be unnecessary to store the zero digit in the segment register. Thus 045F0H is stored as 045F, with the rightmost zero understood. Where appropriate, the text refers to the rightmost zero through the use of square brackets, such as in 045F[0].

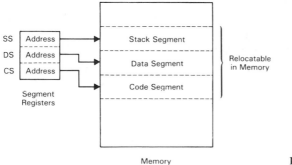

Figure 1–4   Segments and Registers

Segment Offsets

Within a program, all memory locations are relative to a segment's starting address. The distance in bytes from the segment address is expressed as an *offset* (or displacement). A two-byte (16-bit) offset can range from 0000H through FFFFH, or zero through 65,535. Thus the first byte of the code segment is at offset 00, the second byte is at offset 01, and so forth, through to offset 65,535. To reference any memory address in a segment, the processor combines the segment address in a segment register with an offset value.

In the following example, the DS register contains the segment address of the data segment at hex 045F[0], and an instruction references a location with an offset of 0032H bytes within the data segment.

segment address 045F0H   offset 32H

The actual memory location of the byte referenced by the instruction is therefore 04622H:

DS segment address:	045F0H
Offset:	+ 0032H
Actual address:	04622H

Note that a program contains one or more segments, which may begin almost anywhere in memory, may vary in size, and may be in any sequence.

Addressing Capacity

The PC series has used a number of Intel processors that provide different addressing capabilities.

8086/8088 Addressing.   The registers of the 8086/8088 processors provide 16 bits. Since a segment address is on a paragraph boundary, the rightmost 4 bits of its address are zero. As discussed earlier, an address is stored in a segment register, and the computer assumes four rightmost zero bits (one hex digit), as hex nnnn[0]. Now, FFFF[0]H allows addressing up to 1,048,560 bytes. If you are uncertain, decode each hex F as binary 1111, allow for the four rightmost 0-bits, and add the values for the 1-bits.

80286 Addressing.   In real mode, the 80286 processor handles addressing the same as an 8086 does. In protected mode, the processor uses 24 bits for addressing, so that FFFFF[0] allows addressing up to 16 million bytes. The segment registers act as selectors for accessing a 24-bit segment address from memory and add this value to a 16-bit offset address:

Segment register:	16 bits [0000]
Segment address:	24 bits

80386/486/586 Addressing.   In real mode, these processors also handle addressing much the same as an 8086 does. In protected mode, the processors use 48 bits for addressing, which allows addressing segments up to 4 billion bytes. The 16-bit segment registers act as selectors for accessing a 32-bit segment address from memory and add this value to a 32-bit offset address:

Segment register:	16 bits [0000]
Segment address:	32 bits

REGISTERS

The processor's *registers* are used to control instructions being executed, to handle addressing of memory, and to provide arithmetic capability. The registers are addressable by name. Bits are conventionally numbered from right to left, as in

. . .   15   14   13   12   11   10   9   8   7   6   5   4   3   2   1   0

Segment Registers

A *segment register* is 16 bits long and provides for addressing an area of memory known as the current segment. As discussed earlier, a segment aligns on a paragraph boundary, and its address in a segment register assumes four 0-bits to its right.

CS register.   DOS stores the starting address of a program's code segment in the CS register. This segment address, plus an offset value in the instruction pointer (IP) register, indicates the address of an instruction to be fetched for execution. For normal programming purposes, you need not reference the CS register.

DS register.   The starting address of a program's data segment is stored in the DS register. In simple terms, this address, plus an offset value in an instruction, causes a reference to a specific byte location in the data segment.

SS register.   The SS register permits the implementation of a stack in memory, used for temporary storage of addresses and data. DOS stores the starting address of a program's stack segment in the SS register. This segment address, plus an offset value in the stack pointer (SP) register, indicates the current word in the stack being addressed. For normal programming purposes, you need not directly reference the SS register.

ES register.   Some string (character data) operations use the extra segment register to handle memory addressing. In this context, the ES register is associated with the DI (index) register. A program that requires the use of the ES register may initialize it with an appropriate segment address.

FS and GS Registers.   These are additional extra segment registers on the 80386 and later processors.

Instruction Pointer Register

The 16-bit IP register contains the offset address of the next instruction that is to execute. The IP is associated with the CS register in that the IP indicates the current instruction within the currently executing code segment. You would not normally reference the IP register in a program, but you can change its value when using the DOS DEBUG program to test a program. The 80386 and later processors have an extended 32-bit IP called the EIP.

In the following example, the CS register contains 25A4[0]H, and the IP contains 412H. To find the next instruction to be executed, the processor combines the addresses in the CS and IP:

Segment address in CS register:	25A40H
Offset address in IP register:	+ 412H
Address of next instruction:	25E52H

Pointer Registers

The SP (stack pointer) and BP (base pointer) registers are associated with the SS register and permit the system to access data in the stack segment.

SP register.   The 16-bit stack pointer is associated with the SS register and provides an offset value that refers to the current word being processed in the stack. The 80386 and later processors have an extended 32-bit stack pointer, the ESP register. The system automatically handles these registers.

In the following example, the SS register contains segment address 27B3[0]H, and the SP contains offset 312H. To find the current word being processed in the stack, the computer combines the addresses in the SS and SP:

Segment address in SS register:	27B30H
Offset in SP register:	+ 312H
Address in stack:	27E42H

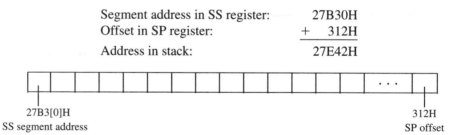

27B3[0]H   312H
SS segment address   SP offset

BP register.   The 16-bit BP facilitates referencing parameters, which are data and addresses passed via the stack. The 80386 and later processors have an extended 32-bit BP called the EBP register.

General-Purpose Registers

The AX, BX, CX, and DX general-purpose registers are the workhorses of the system. They are unique in that you can address them as one word or as a one-byte portion. The leftmost byte is the "high" portion and the rightmost byte is the "low" portion. For example, the CX register consists of a CH (high) and a CL (low) portion, and you can reference any portion by its name. The following instructions move zeros to the CX, CH, and CL registers, respectively:

```
MOV    CX,00

MOV    CH,00

MOV    CL,00
```

The 80386 and later processors support all the general-purpose registers, plus 32-bit extended versions of them: the EAX, EBX, ECX, and EDX.

AX register.   The AX register, the primary accumulator, is used for operations involving input/output and most arithmetic. For example, multiply, divide, and translate instructions assume the use of the AX. Also, some instructions generate more efficient code if they reference the AX rather than another register.

BX register.   The BX is known as the base register since it is the only general-purpose register that can be used as an index to extend addressing. Another common purpose of the BX is for computations.

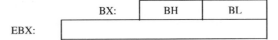

CX register.   The CX is known as the count register. It may contain a value to control the number of times a loop is repeated or a value to shift bits left or right. The CX is also used for many computations.

DX register.   The DX is known as the data register. Some input/output operations require its use, and multiply and divide operations that involve large values assume the DX and AX together as a pair.

You may use any of the general-purpose registers for addition and subtraction of 8-bit, 16-bit, or 32-bit values.

Index Registers

The SI and DI registers are available for indexed addressing and for use in addition and subtraction.

SI register.   The 16-bit source index register is required for some string (character) operations. In this context, the SI is associated with the DS register. The 80386 and later processors support a 32-bit extended register, the ESI.

DI register.   The 16-bit destination index register is also required for some string operations. In this context, the DI is associated with the ES register. The 80386 and later processors support a 32-bit extended register, the EDI.

Flags Register

Of the 16 bits of the flags register, 9 are common to all 8086-family processors to indicate the current status of the machine and the results of processing. Many instructions involving comparisons and arithmetic change the status of the flags, which some instructions may test to determine subsequent action.

Briefly, the common flag bits are as follows:

OF (overflow).   Indicates overflow of a high-order (leftmost) bit following arithmetic.

DF (direction).   Designates left or right direction for moving or comparing string (character) data.

IF (interrupt).   Indicates that an external interrupt, such as keyboard entry, is to be processed or ignored.

TF (trap).   Permits operation of the processor in single-step mode. Debugger programs such as DEBUG set the trap flag so that you can step through execution a single instruction at a time to examine the effect on registers and memory.

SF (sign).   Contains the resulting sign of an arithmetic operation (0 = positive and 1 = negative).

ZF (zero).   Indicates the result of an arithmetic or comparison operation (0 = nonzero and 1 = zero result).

AF (auxiliary carry).   Contains a carry out of bit 3 on eight-bit data, for specialized arithmetic.

PF (parity).   Indicates even or odd parity of a low-order (rightmost) eight-bit data operation.

CF (carry).   Contains carries from a high-order (leftmost) bit following an arithmetic operation; also, contains the contents of last bit of a shift or rotate operation.

The flags are in the flags register in the following locations:

Bit no.:	15	14	13	12	11	10	9	8	7	6	5	4	3	2	1	0
Flag:					O	D	I	T	S	Z		A		P		C

The flags most relevant to assembly programming are O, S, Z, and C for comparisons and arithmetic operations, and D for the direction of string operations. The 80286 and later processors have some flags used for internal purposes, concerned primarily with protected mode. The 80386 and later processors have a 32-bit extended flags register known as Eflags. Chapter 8 contains more details about the flags register.

KEY POINTS

- The computer distinguishes only between bits that are 0 (off) and 1 (on) and performs arithmetic only in binary format.
- The value of a binary number is determined by the placement of its bits. Thus binary 1101 equals $2^3 + 2^2 + 0^1 + 2^0$, or 13.
- A negative binary number is represented in two's complement notation: Reverse the bits of its positive representation and add 1.
- A single character of memory is a byte, comprised of eight data bits and one parity bit. Two adjacent bytes comprise a word, and four adjacent bytes comprise a doubleword.
- The value K equals 2^{10}, or 1,024 bytes.
- Hexadecimal format is a shorthand notation for representing groups of four bits. Hex digits 0–9 and A–F represent the binary values 0000 through 1111.
- The representation of character data is done in ASCII format.
- The heart of the PC is a microprocessor. The processor stores numeric data in words in memory in reverse-byte sequence.
- The two types of internal memory are ROM and RAM.
- An assembly language program consists of one or more segments: a stack segment for maintaining return addresses, a data segment for defined data and work areas, and a code segment for executable instructions. Locations in a segment are expressed as an offset relative to the segment's starting address.
- The CS, DS, and SS registers provide for addressing the code, data, and stack segments, respectively.
- The IP register contains the offset address of the next instruction that is to execute.
- The SP and BP pointer registers are associated with the SS register and permit the system to access data in the stack segment.
- The AX, BX, CX, and DX general-purpose registers are the system's workhorses. The leftmost byte is the "high" portion, and the rightmost byte is the "low" portion. The AX (primary accumulator) is used for input/output and most arithmetic. The BX (base register) can be used as an index to extend addressing. The CX is known as the count register, and the DX is known as the data register.
- The SI and DI index registers are available for extended addressing and for use in addition and subtraction. These registers are also required for some string (character) operations.

- The flags register indicates the current status of the computer and the results of executing instructions.

QUESTIONS

1–1. Provide the binary bit configuration for the following numbers: (a) 6; (b) 14; (c) 22; (d) 28; (e) 30.

1–2. Add the following binary numbers:

(a) 00010101	(b) 00111101	(c) 00011101	(d) 01010111
00001101	00101010	00000011	00111101

1–3. Determine the two's complement of the following binary numbers: (a) 00010110; (b) 00111101; (c) 00111100.

1–4. Determine the positive (absolute) value of the following negative binary numbers: (a) 11001000; (b) 10111101; (c) 11111110; (d) 11111111.

1–5. Determine the hex representation of the following values: (a) ASCII letter Q; (b) ASCII number 7; (c) binary 01011101; (d) binary 01110111.

1–6. Add the following hex numbers:

(a) 23A6	(b) 51FD	(c) 7779	(d) EABE	(e) FBAC
+0022	+0003	+0887	+26C4	+0CBE

1–7. Determine the hex representation of the following decimal numbers. Refer to Appendix A for the conversion method. You could also check your result by converting the hex to binary and adding the 1-bits. (a) 19; (b) 33; (c) 89; (d) 255; (e) 4095; (f) 63,398.

1–8. Provide the ASCII bit configuration for the following one-byte characters. Use Appendix B as a guide: (a) P; (b) p; (c) #; (d) 5.

1–9. What is the purpose of the processor?

1–10. What are the two main kinds of memory on the PC, and what are their main purposes?

1–11. Show how the system stores hex 012345 as a value in memory.

1–12. Explain the following: (a) segment; (b) offset; (c) address boundary.

1–13. What are (a) the three kinds of segments, (b) their maximum size, and (c) the address boundary on which they begin?

1–14. Explain the purpose of each of the three segment registers.

1–15. Explain which registers are used for the following purposes: (a) addition and subtraction; (b) counting for looping; (c) multiplication and division; (d) addressing segments; (e) indication of a zero result; (f) offset address of an instruction that is to execute.

1–16. Show the EAX register and the size and position of the AH, AL, and AX within it.

1–17. Code the assembly language instructions to move the value 25 to the following registers: (a) CH; (b) CL; (c) CX; (d) ECX.

CHAPTER 2 ————————————

PC Software Requirements

```
┌─────────────────────────────────────────────────────────┐
│                                                           │
│                        OBJECTIVE                          │
│                                                           │
│   To explain the general software environment for the PC. │
│                                                           │
└─────────────────────────────────────────────────────────┘
```

INTRODUCTION

In this chapter, we describe the PC software environment: the functions of DOS and its main components. We examine the boot process (how the system loads itself when you power up the computer), and consider how the system loads a program for execution, how the system uses the stack, and how an instruction in the code segment addresses data in the data segment.

The chapter completes the basic explanations of the PC's hardware and software and enables us to proceed to Chapter 3, where we take up keying programs into memory and executing them step by step.

OPERATING SYSTEM CHARACTERISTICS

DOS is an operating system that provides general, device-independent access to the resources of a computer. The devices it supports include keyboards, screens, and disk drives. "Device independence" means that you don't have to address devices specifically, since DOS and its device drivers can handle the operations at the device level.

Among the DOS functions that concern us in this book are the following:

- *File management*. DOS maintains the directories and files on the system's disks. Programs create and update files, but DOS bears the responsibility of managing their location on disk.
- *Input/output*. Programs request input data from DOS or deliver such data to DOS by means of interrupts. DOS relieves the programmer of coding at the I/O level.
- *Program loading*. A user or program requests execution of a program; DOS handles the steps involved in accessing the program from disk, placing it in memory, and initializing it for execution.
- *Memory management*. When DOS loads a program for execution, it allocates a large enough space in memory for the program code and its data. Programs can process data within their memory area, can release unwanted memory, and can request additional memory.
- *Interrupt handling*. DOS allows users to install resident programs that attach themselves to the interrupt system to perform special functions.

Organization of DOS

The three major components of DOS are IO.SYS, MSDOS.SYS, and COMMAND.COM.

IO.SYS performs initialization functions at bootup time and also contains important input/output functions and device drivers that supplement the primitive I/O support in ROM BIOS. This component is stored on disk as a hidden system file and is known under PC-DOS as IBMBIO.COM.

MSDOS.SYS acts as the DOS kernel and is concerned with file management, memory management, and input/output. This component is stored on disk as a hidden system file and is known under PC-DOS as IBMDOS.COM.

COMMAND.COM is a command processor or shell that acts as the interface between the user and the operating system. It displays the DOS prompt, monitors the keyboard, and processes user commands such as deleting a file or loading a program for execution.

THE BOOT PROCESS

Turning on the computer's power causes a "cold boot." The processor enters a reset state, clears all memory locations to zero, performs a parity check of memory, and sets the CS register to segment address FFFF[0]H and the IP register to offset zero. The first instruction to execute, therefore, is at the address formed by the CS:IP pair, which is FFFF0H, the entry point to BIOS in ROM.

The BIOS routine beginning at FFFF0H checks the various ports to identify and initialize devices that are attached to the computer. BIOS then establishes two data areas:

1. An *interrupt service table* that begins in low memory at location 0 and contains addresses for interrupts that occur.
2. A *BIOS data area* beginning at location 40[0], largely concerned with attached devices.

```
640K
      ┌─────────────────────────────────────────────────────────┐
      │ COMMAND.COM transient portion                           │
      │ (executing programs may erase it)                       │
      │ ------------------------------------------------------- │
      │ Available for programs' use                             │
      │ ------------------------------------------------------- │
      │ COMMAND.COM resident portion (resides permanently)      │
      │ ------------------------------------------------------- │
      │ System files IO.SYS and MSDOS.SYS                       │
      │ ------------------------------------------------------- │
      │ BIOS data area                                          │
      │ ------------------------------------------------------- │
 0K   │ Interrupt services table                                │
      └─────────────────────────────────────────────────────────┘
```

Figure 2–1   Map of Conventional Memory

BIOS next determines whether a disk containing the DOS system files is present and, if so, it accesses the bootstrap loader from the disk. This program loads system files IO.SYS and MSDOS.SYS from the disk into memory and transfers control to the entry point of IO.SYS, which contains device drivers and other hardware-specific code. IO.SYS relocates itself in memory and transfers control in its turn to MSDOS.SYS. This module initializes internal DOS tables and the DOS portion of the interrupt table. It also reads the CONFIG.SYS file and executes its commands. Finally, MSDOS.SYS passes control to COMMAND.COM, which processes the AUTOEXEC.BAT file, displays its prompt, and monitors the keyboard for input.

At this point, conventional memory up to 640K appears as shown in Figure 2–1. Under memory management, part of DOS may be relocated into high memory.

DOS-BIOS INTERFACE

BIOS contains a set of routines in ROM to provide device support. BIOS tests and initializes attached devices and provides services that are used for reading to and for writing from the devices. One task of DOS is to interface with BIOS when there is a need to access its facilities.

When a user program requests a service of DOS, it may transfer the request to BIOS, which in its turn accesses the requested device. Sometimes, however, a program makes requests directly to BIOS, especially for keyboard and screen services. And at other times—although rarely and not recommended—a program can bypass both DOS and BIOS to access a device directly. Figure 2–2 shows these alternative paths.

SYSTEM PROGRAM LOADER

DOS supports two types of executable programs: .COM and .EXE. A .*COM program* consists of one segment that contains code, data, and the stack. You would write a .COM program if you wanted a small utility program or a resident program (one that is installed permanently and is available while other programs run). An .*EXE program* consists of separate code, data, and stack segments and is the method used for more serious programs. This book makes use of both types of programs.

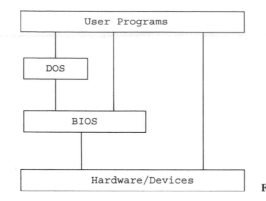

Figure 2–2 DOS-BIOS Interface

When you request DOS to load an .EXE program from disk into memory for execution, the loader performs the following operations:

1. Accesses the .EXE program from disk.
2. Constructs a 256-byte (100H) program segment prefix (PSP) on a paragraph boundary in available internal memory.
3. Stores the program in memory immediately following the PSP.
4. Loads the address of the PSP in the DS and ES registers.
5. Loads the address of the code segment in the CS and sets the IP to the offset of the first instruction (usually zero) in the code segment.
6. Loads the address of the stack in the SS and sets the SP to the size of the stack.
7. Transfers control to the program for execution, beginning (usually) with the first instruction in the code segment.

In the foregoing way, the DOS loader correctly initializes the CS:IP and SS:SP registers. But note that the loader program stores the address of the PSP in both the DS and ES registers, although your program normally needs the address of the data segment in these registers. As a consequence, your programs have to initialize the DS with the address of the data segment, as you'll see in Chapter 4.

We'll now examine the stack and then the code and data segments.

THE STACK

Both .COM and .EXE programs require an area in the program reserved as a *stack*. The purpose of the stack is to provide a space for the temporary storage of addresses and data items.

DOS automatically defines the stack for a .COM program, whereas you must explicitly define a stack for an .EXE program. Each data item in the stack is one word (two bytes). The SS register, as initialized by DOS, contains the address of the beginning of the stack. Initially, the SP contains the size of the stack, a value that points to the byte past the end of the stack. The stack differs from other segments in its method of storing data: It begins at the highest location and stores data downward through memory.

SS
segment address of stack

SP
top of stack

The PUSH instruction (among others) decrements the SP by 2 to the next lower storage word in the stack and stores (or pushes) a value there. The POP instruction (among others) returns a value from the stack and increments the SP by 2 to the next higher storage word.

The following example illustrates pushing the contents of the AX and BX registers
onto the stack and then subsequently popping them off. Assume that the AX contains
015AH, the BX contains 03D2H, and the SP contains 28H. (The address in the SS does not
concern us here.)

1. Initially, the stack is empty and looks like this:

SS
segment address of stack

SP = 28
top of stack

2. PUSH AX: Decrements the SP by 2 (to 26H) and stores the contents of the AX,
   015AH, in the stack. Note that the operation reverses the sequence of the stored bytes,
   so that 015A becomes 5A01:

SS
segment address of stack

SP = 26
top of stack

3. PUSH BX: Decrements the SP by 2 (to 24H) and stores the contents of the BX,
   03D2H, in the stack:

SS
segment address of stack

SP = 24
top of stack

4. POP BX: Restores the word from where the SP points in the stack to the BX register
   and increments the SP by 2 (to 26H). The BX now contains 03D2H, with the bytes
   correctly reversed:

SS
segment address of stack

SP = 26
top of stack

5. POP AX: Restores the word from where the SP points in the stack to the AX register and increments the SP by 2 (to 28H). The AX now contains 015AH, with the bytes correctly reversed:

SS   SP = 28
segment address of stack   top of stack

Note that POP instructions are coded in reverse sequence from PUSH instructions. Thus the example pushed the AX and BX, but popped the BX and AX, in that order. Also, the values pushed onto the stack are still there, although the SP no longer points to them.

You should always ensure that your program coordinates pushing values onto the stack with popping them off of it. Although this is a fairly straightforward requirement, an error can result in a program crash. Also, for an .EXE program, you have to define a stack that is large enough to contain all values that could be pushed onto it.

Other related instructions that push values onto the stack and pop them off of it are:

- PUSHF and POPF: Save and restore the status of the flags.
- PUSHA and POPA (for the 80286 and later): Save and restore the contents of all the general-purpose registers.

PROGRAM ADDRESSING

Normally, programmers write in *symbolic* code and use the assembler to translate it into *machine code*. For program execution, DOS loads only machine code into memory. Every instruction consists of at least an operation, such as move, add, or return. Depending on the operation, an instruction may also have one or more operands that reference the data the operation is to process.

As discussed in Chapter 1, the CS register provides the address of the beginning of a program's code segment, and the DS register provides the address of the beginning of the data segment. The code segment contains instructions that are to be executed, whereas the data segment contains data that the instructions reference. The IP register indicates the offset address of the current instruction in the code segment that is to be executed. An instruction operand indicates an offset address in the data segment that is to be referenced.

Consider an example in which DOS has determined that it is to load an .EXE program into memory, beginning at location 04AF0H. DOS accordingly sets the CS register with segment address 04AF[0]H and the DS with, say, segment address 04B1[0]H. The program has already begun executing, and the IP currently contains the offset 0013H. The CS:IP together determine the address of the next instruction to execute, as follows:

CS segment address:	4AF0H
IP offset:	+ 0013H
Instruction address:	4B03H

Let's say that the instruction beginning at 04B03H copies the contents of a byte in memory into the AL register; the byte is at offset 0012H in the data segment. Here are both the machine code and the symbolic code for this operation:

```
            A01200     MOV     AL,[0012]
               |
      Location 04B03H
```

Memory location 04B03H contains the first byte (A0) of the instruction the processor is to access. The second and third bytes contain the offset value, in reversed-byte sequence (0012 becomes 1200). To access the data item, the processor determines its location from the segment address in the DS register plus the offset (0012H) in the instruction operand. Since the DS contains 04B1[0]H, the actual location of the referenced data item is

DS segment address:	4B10H
Segment offset:	+ 0012H
Address of data item:	4B22H

Let's say that location 04B22H contains 1BH. Then the processor extracts the 1BH at location 04B22H and copies it into the AL register, as shown in Figure 2–3.

As the processor fetches each byte of the instruction, it increments the IP register so that the IP contains the offset (0016H) for the next instruction. The processor is now ready to execute the next instruction, which it derives once again from the segment address in the CS (04AF0H) plus the current offset in the IP (0016H)—in effect, 04B06H.

An instruction may also access more than one byte at a time. For example, suppose an instruction is to store the contents of the AX register (0567H) in two adjacent bytes in the data segment beginning at offset 0012H. The symbolic code is MOV [0012],AX. The operand [0012] in square brackets (an index operator) indicates a memory location, to distinguish it from simply the number 12. The processor loads the two bytes in the AX in reversed-byte sequence as

```
      Contents of bytes:           67  05
                                    |   |
      Offset in data segment:     0012  0013
```

Another instruction, MOV AX,[0012], subsequently could retrieve these bytes by copying them from memory back into the AX. The operation reverses (and corrects) the bytes in the AX as 05 67.

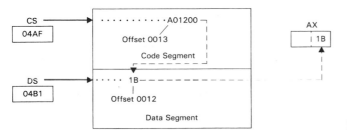

Figure 2 3   Segments and Offsets

MEMORY AND REGISTER REFERENCES

One feature to get clear is the use in instruction operands of names, of names in square brackets, and of numbers. In the following examples, WORDA is defined as a word (two bytes) in memory:

```
WORDA      DW       0                ;Define word

           ...

           MOV      AX,BX            ;Move contents of BX to AX

           MOV      AX,WORDA         ;Move contents of WORDA to AX

           MOV      AX,25            ;Move value 25 to AX

           MOV      AX,[BX]          ;Move contents of location specified by BX
```

The square brackets in the fourth example define an *index operator* that means: Use the offset address in the BX (combined with the segment address in the DS, as DS:BX) to locate a word in memory, and move its contents to the AX. Compare the effect of this instruction with that of the first example, which simply moves the contents of the BX to the AX.

KEY POINTS

- The three major components of DOS are IO.SYS, MSDOS.SYS, and COMMAND.COM.
- Turning on the computer's power causes a "cold boot." The processor enters a reset state, clears all memory locations to zero, performs a parity check of memory, and sets the CS register and the IP register to the entry point of BIOS in ROM.
- The two types of DOS programs are .COM and .EXE.
- When you request DOS to load an .EXE program for execution, DOS constructs a 256-byte (100H) PSP on a paragraph boundary in memory and stores the program immediately following the PSP. It then loads the address of the PSP in the DS and ES registers, loads the address of the code segment in the CS, sets the IP to the offset of the first instruction in the code segment, loads the address of the stack in the SS, and sets the SP to the size of the stack. Finally, the loader transfers control to the program for execution.
- The purpose of the stack is to provide a space for the temporary storage of addresses and data items. Each data item in the stack is one word (two bytes).
- DOS defines the stack for a .COM program, whereas you must explicitly define a stack for an .EXE program.
- As the processor fetches each byte of an instruction, it increments the IP register so that the IP contains the offset for the next instruction.

QUESTIONS

2–1. What are the five main functions of DOS?

2–2. What are the three main components of DOS, and what is the purpose of each?

2–3. What steps does the system take on a "cold boot"?

2–4. (a) What data area does DOS construct and store in front of an executable module when the module is loaded for execution? (b) What is the size of this data area?

2–5. DOS performs certain operations when it loads an .EXE program for execution. What values does DOS initialize (a) in the CS and IP registers? (b) in the SS and SP registers? (c) in the DS and ES registers?)

2–6. What is the purpose of the stack?

2–7. In what way is the stack defined for (a) a .COM program and (b) an .EXE program? (That is, who or what defines the stack?)

2–8. (a) What is the size of each entry in the stack? (b) Where initially is the top of the stack, and how is it addressed?

2–9. During execution of a program, the CS contains 5A2B[0], the SS contains 5B53[0], the IP contains 52H, and the SP contains 48H. (Values are shown in normal, not reversed-byte, sequence.) Calculate the addresses of (a) the instruction to execute and (b) the top (current location) of the stack.

2–10. The DS contains 5B24[0], and an instruction that moves data from memory to the AL is A03A01 (where A0 means "move"). Calculate the referenced memory address.

CHAPTER 3 ——————————————

Execution of Instructions

```
┌─────────────────────────────────────────────┐
│                  OBJECTIVE                    │
│                                               │
│  To introduce the entering and executing of   │
│  programs in memory.                          │
└─────────────────────────────────────────────┘
```

INTRODUCTION

This chapter uses a DOS program named DEBUG that allows you to view memory, to enter programs in memory, and to trace their execution. The text describes how you can enter these programs directly into memory in a code segment and provides an explanation of each execution step. Some readers may have access to sophisticated debuggers such as CODEVIEW or TurboDebugger; however, we'll use DEBUG since it is simple to use and universally available.

In the initial exercises, you get to inspect the contents of particular areas of memory. The first program example uses "immediate" data defined within the instructions for loading data into registers and performing arithmetic. The second program example uses data defined separately in the data segment. Tracing these instructions as they execute provides insight into the operation of a computer and the role of the registers.

You can start right in with no prior knowledge of assembly language or even of programming. All you need is an IBM PC or equivalent computer and a disk containing the DOS operating system. We do assume, however, that you are familiar with booting up a computer, handling diskettes, and selecting disk drives and files.

THE DEBUG PROGRAM

The DOS system comes with a program named DEBUG that is used for testing and debugging executable programs. A feature of DEBUG is that it displays all program code and data in hexadecimal format, and any data that you enter into memory is also in hex format. Another feature is that DEBUG allows you to execute a program in *single-step mode*, so that you can view the effect of each instruction on memory locations and registers.

DEBUG Commands

DEBUG provides a set of commands that lets you perform a number of useful operations. The commands that concern us at this point are the following:

A	Assemble symbolic instructions into machine code
D	Display the contents of an area of memory
E	Enter data into memory, beginning at a specific location
G	Run the executable program in memory (G means "go")
N	Name a program
P	Proceed, or execute a set of related instructions
Q	Quit the DEBUG session
R	Display the contents of one or more registers
T	Trace the execution of one instruction
U	"Unassemble" (really, disassemble) machine code into symbolic code
W	Write a program onto disk

Rules of DEBUG Commands

For its own purposes, DEBUG does not distinguish between lowercase and uppercase letters, so you may enter commands either way. Also, you enter a space only where it is needed to separate parameters in a command. The following three examples use DEBUG's D command to display the same area of memory, beginning at offset 200H in the data segment (DS):

```
        D DS:200      (command in uppercase, space following)

        DDS:200       (command in uppercase, no space following)

        dds:200       (command in lowercase, no space following)
```

Note that you specify segments and offsets with a colon, in the form segment:offset. Also, DEBUG assumes that all numbers are in hexadecimal format.

The DEBUG Display

The DEBUG display consists of three parts. To the left is the hex address of the leftmost displayed byte, in segment:offset format. The wide area in the center is the hex representation of the displayed area. To the right is the ASCII representation of bytes that contain displayable characters, which can help you interpret the hex area. Diagrammatically, we have:

```
Address   |<-------- Hexadecimal representation -------->|<--ASCII-->|

xxxx:xx10  xx ............... xx-xx ............... xx x.........x

xxxx:xx20  xx ............... xx-xx ............... xx x.........x

xxxx:xx30  xx ............... xx-xx ............... xx x.........x
```

Each line displays 16 bytes of memory. The address to the left refers only to the leftmost byte, in segment:offset format; you can count across the line to determine the position of each byte. The hex representation area shows two hex characters for each byte, followed by a space for readability. Also, a hyphen separates the second eight bytes from the first eight, again for readability. Thus if you want to locate the byte at offset xx13H, start with xx10H, and count three bytes successively to the right.

This book makes considerable use of DEBUG and explains details of its commands as they are needed. Appendix E provides a full description of DEBUG commands.

Starting DEBUG

To start DEBUG, set the system to the directory on hard disk containing DEBUG, or insert a DOS diskette containing DEBUG in the default drive. To initiate the program, key in the word DEBUG and press Enter. DEBUG should load from disk into memory. When DEBUG's prompt, a hyphen (-), appears on the screen, DEBUG is ready to accept your commands. (That *is* a hyphen, although it resembles the cursor.) Let's now use DEBUG to snoop about in memory.

VIEWING MEMORY LOCATIONS

In our first exercise, you will use DEBUG to view the contents of selected memory locations. The only command with which this exercise is concerned is D (Display), which lists eight lines of 16 bytes each and shows both their hex and their ASCII representations.

Checking System Equipment

Let's first see what BIOS has determined is your installed equipment. An equipment status word in the BIOS data area provides a primitive indication of installed devices. This word is at locations 410H–411H, which you can view from DEBUG by means of a two-part address: 40 for the segment address (the last zero is assumed) and 10 for the offset from the segment address. Read the address 40:10 as segment 40[0]H plus offset 10H. Key in the following exactly as you see it:

```
D 40:10 [and press Enter]
```

The display should begin like this:

```
0040:0010 63 44 .. .. ..
```

In this example, the two bytes in the equipment status word contain the hex values 63 and 44. We reverse the bytes (44 63) and convert them to binary:

Bit:	15	14	13	12	11	10	9	8	7	6	5	4	3	2	1	0
Binary:	0	1	0	0	0	1	0	0	0	1	1	0	0	0	1	1

Here's an explanation of the hex code:

BITS	DEVICE
15,14	Number of parallel printer ports attached = 1 (binary 01)
11–9	Number of serial ports attached = 2 (binary 010)
7,6	Number of diskette devices = 2 (where 00 = 1, 01 = 2, 10 = 3, and 11 = 4)
5,4	Initial video mode = 10 (where 01 = 40 × 25 color, 10 = 80 × 25 color, and 11 = 80 × 25 monochrome)
1	1 = math coprocessor is present
0	1 = diskette drive is present

Unreferenced bytes are not used.

You can stay in DEBUG for the next exercise or enter Q to quit.

Checking Memory Size

The next step is to examine the amount of memory that DOS "thinks" you have installed. Depending on the computer model, the value may be based on switches set internally and may indicate less memory than is actually installed. The value is in the BIOS data area at locations 413H and 414H. Key in the following exactly as you see it:

```
D 40:13 [and press Enter]
```

The display should begin like this:

```
0040:0013 .. .. .. xx xx . . .
```

The first two bytes displayed at offset 0013H are kilobytes of memory size in hexadecimal, with the bytes in reverse sequence. Here are two examples showing reversed hex, corrected hex, and the decimal equivalent:

REVERSED HEX	CORRECTED HEX	DECIMAL (K)
00 02	02 00	512
80 02	02 80	640

Checking Serial Number and Copyright Notice

The computer's serial number is embedded in ROM BIOS at location FE000H. To view it, type

```
D FE00:0 [and press Enter]
```

The screen should display a seven-digit serial number followed, on conventional machines, by a copyright notice. The serial number is viewable as hex numbers, whereas the copyright notice is more recognizable from the ASCII area to the right. The copyright notice may continue past what is already displayed; to view it, simply press D followed by the Enter key.

Checking ROM BIOS Date

The date of manufacture of your ROM BIOS begins at location FFFF5H, recorded as mm/dd/yy. To view it, type

```
D FFFF:5 [and press Enter]
```

Knowing this date could be useful for determining a computer's age and model.

Checking Model ID

Immediately following the ROM BIOS manufacture date is the model ID at location FFF-FEH, or FFFF:E. Here are a number of model IDs:

CODE	MODEL
F8	PS/2 models 70 and 80
F9	PC convertible
FA	PS/2 model 30
FB	PC-XT (1986)
FC	PC-AT (1984), PC-XT model 286, PS/2 models 50 and 60, etc.
FE	PC-XT (1982), portable (1982)
FF	Original IBM PC

Now that you know how to use the display command, you can view the contents of any storage location. You can also step through memory simply by pressing D repeatedly—DEBUG displays eight lines successively, continuing from the last D operation.

When you've completed poking about, enter Q (for quit) to exit from DEBUG, or continue with the next exercise.

MACHINE LANGUAGE EXAMPLE I: IMMEDIATE DATA

Let's now use DEBUG to enter the first of two programs directly into memory and trace its execution. Both programs illustrate simple machine language code as it appears in main storage and the effect of its execution. For this purpose, we'll begin with the DEBUG E (Enter) command. Be especially careful in its use, since entering data at a wrong location or entering incorrect data may cause unpredictable results. You are not likely to cause any damage, but you may get a bit of a surprise and may lose data that you entered during the DEBUG session.

The first program uses *immediate data—data defined as part of an instruction*. We show both the machine language in hexadecimal format and, for readability, the symbolic code, along with an explanation. For the first instruction, the symbolic code is MOV AX,0123, which moves (or copies) the value 0123H to the AX register. (You don't have to define an immediate value in reverse-byte sequence.) MOV is the instruction, the AX register is the first operand, and the immediate value 0123H is the second operand.

MACHINE INSTRUCTION	SYMBOLIC CODE	EXPLANATION
B82301	MOV AX,0123	Move value 0123H to AX.
052500	ADD AX,0025	Add value 0025H to AX.
8BD8	MOV BX,AX	Move contents of AX to BX.
03D8	ADD BX,AX	Add contents of AX to BX.
8BCB	MOV CX,BX	Move contents of BX to CX.
2BC8	SUB CX,AX	Subtract contents of AX from CX.
2BC0	SUB AX,AX	Subtract AX from AX (clear AX).
90	NOP	No operation (do nothing).

You may have noticed that machine instructions may be one, two, or three bytes in length. The first byte is the actual operation, and any other bytes that are present are operands—references to an immediate value, a register, or a memory location. Program execution begins with the first machine instruction and steps through each instruction, one after another. At this point do not expect to make much sense of the machine code. For example, in one case the machine code (the first byte) for move is hex B8, and in another case the code for move is hex 8B.

Entering Program Instructions

Begin this exercise just as you did the preceding one: Key in the command DEBUG and press Enter. When DEBUG is fully loaded, it displays its prompt (-). To enter this program directly into memory, just type in the machine language portion, but not the symbolic code or explanation. Key in the following E (Enter) command, including the blanks, where indicated:

```
E CS:100 B8 23 01 05 25 00 [press Enter]
```

CS:100 indicates the starting memory address at which the data is to be stored—100H (256) bytes following the start of the code segment (the normal starting address for machine code under DEBUG). The E command causes DEBUG to store each pair of hexadecimal digits into a byte in memory, from CS:100 through CS:105.

The next E command stores six bytes, starting at CS:106 through 107, 108, 109, 10A, and 10B:

```
E CS:106 8B D8 03 D8 8B CB [followed by Enter]
```

The last E command stores five bytes, starting at CS:10C through 10D, 10E, 10F, and 110:

```
E CS:10C 2B C8 2B C0 90 [followed by Enter]
```

If you key in an incorrect command, simply repeat it with the correct values.

```
-E CS:100 B8 23 01 05 25 00
-E CS:106 8B D8 03 D8 8B CB
-E CS:10C 2B C8 2B C0 90
-R
AX=0000  BX=0000  CX=0000  DX=0000  SP=FFEE  BP=0000  SI=0000  DI=0000
DS=21C1  ES=21C1  SS=21C1  CS=21C1  IP=0100   NV UP EI PL NZ NA PO NC
21C1:0100 B82301        MOV     AX,0123
-T

AX=0123  BX=0000  CX=0000  DX=0000  SP=FFEE  BP=0000  SI=0000  DI=0000
DS=21C1  ES=21C1  SS=21C1  CS=21C1  IP=0103   NV UP EI PL NZ NA PO NC
21C1:0103 052500        ADD     AX,0025
-T

AX=0148  BX=0000  CX=0000  DX=0000  SP=FFEE  BP=0000  SI=0000  DI=0000
DS=21C1  ES=21C1  SS=21C1  CS=21C1  IP=0106   NV UP EI PL NZ NA PE NC
21C1:0106 8BD8          MOV     BX,AX
-T

AX=0148  BX=0148  CX=0000  DX=0000  SP=FFEE  BP=0000  SI=0000  DI=0000
DS=21C1  ES=21C1  SS=21C1  CS=21C1  IP=0108   NV UP EI PL NZ NA PE NC
21C1:0108 03D8          ADD     BX,AX
-T

AX=0148  BX=0290  CX=0000  DX=0000  SP=FFEE  BP=0000  SI=0000  DI=0000
DS=21C1  ES=21C1  SS=21C1  CS=21C1  IP=010A   NV UP EI PL NZ AC PE NC
21C1:010A 8BCB          MOV     CX,BX
-T

AX=0148  BX=0290  CX=0290  DX=0000  SP=FFEE  BP=0000  SI=0000  DI=0000
DS=21C1  ES=21C1  SS=21C1  CS=21C1  IP=010C   NV UP EI PL NZ AC PE NC
21C1:010C 2BC8          SUB     CX,AX
-T

AX=0148  BX=0290  CX=0148  DX=0000  SP=FFEE  BP=0000  SI=0000  DI=0000
DS=21C1  ES=21C1  SS=21C1  CS=21C1  IP=010E   NV UP EI PL NZ AC PE NC
21C1:010E 2BC0          SUB     AX,AX
-T

AX=0000  BX=0290  CX=0148  DX=0000  SP=FFEE  BP=0000  SI=0000  DI=0000
DS=21C1  ES=21C1  SS=21C1  CS=21C1  IP=0110   NV UP EI PL ZR NA PE NC
21C1:0110 90            NOP
-
```

Figure 3–1   Trace of Machine Instructions

Executing Program Instructions

Now it's a simple matter to execute the preceding instructions one at a time. Figure 3–1 shows all the steps, including the E commands. Your screen should display similar results as you enter each DEBUG command. At the same time, you can view the contents of the registers after each instruction. The DEBUG commands that concern us here are R (Register) and T (Trace).

To view the initial contents of the registers and flags, key in the R command, followed by the Enter key. DEBUG displays the contents of the registers in hexadecimal format, for example, as

AX=0000 BX=0000 . . .

Because of differences in the various DOS versions, some register contents on your screen may differ from those shown in Figure 3–1. The IP register displays IP=0100, indicating that execution of instructions is to begin 100H bytes past the start of the code segment. (That is why you used E CS:100 to enter the start of the program.)

The flags register in Figure 3–1 shows the following settings:

```
NV UP EI PL NZ NA PO NC
```

These settings mean no overflow, up (or right) direction, enable interrupt, plus sign, nonzero, no auxiliary carry, parity odd, and no carry, respectively. At this time, none of these settings is important to us.

The R command also displays at offset 0100H the first instruction to be executed. Note that in the figure the CS register contains 21C1. Since your CS segment address is sure to differ from this, we'll show it as xxxx for the instructions:

```
xxxx:0100 B82301 MOV AX,0123
```

- xxxx indicates the start of the code segment as xxxx[0]. The value xxxx:0100 means offset 100H bytes following the CS segment address xxxx[0].
- B82301 is the machine code that you entered at CS:100.
- MOV AX,0123 is the symbolic assembly instruction for the machine code. This instruction means, in effect, move the immediate value 0123H into the AX register. DEBUG has "unassembled" the machine instructions so that you may interpret them more easily. In later chapters, you will code assembly instructions exclusively.

At this point, the MOV instruction has not executed. For that purpose, key in T (Trace) and press the Enter key. The machine code is B8 (move to AX register) followed by 2301. The operation moves the 23 to the low half (AL) of the AX register and the 01 to the high half (AH) of the AX register:

```
        AH   AL
AX:    | 01 | 23 |
```

DEBUG displays the results in the registers. The contents of the IP register is 0103H, to indicate the offset location in the code segment of the next instruction to be executed, namely:

```
xxxx:0103 052500 ADD AX,0025
```

To execute this instruction, enter another T. The ADD instruction adds 25H to the low half (AL) of the AX register and 00H to the high half (AH), in effect adding 0025H to the AX. AX now contains 0148H, and IP contains 0106H for the next instruction to be executed:

```
xxxx:0106 8BD8 MOV BX,AX
```

Key in another T command. The MOV instruction moves the contents of the AX register to the BX register. Note that after the move the BX contains 0148H. AX still contains 0148H because MOV *copies* rather than actually moves the data from one location to another.

Now key in successive T commands to step through the remaining instructions. The ADD instruction adds the contents of AX to BX, giving 0290H in BX. Then the program moves (copies) the contents of BX into CX, subtracts AX from CX, and subtracts AX from itself. After this last operation, the zero flag is changed from NZ (nonzero) to ZR (zero), to indicate that the result of the last operation was zero. (Subtracting AX from itself cleared it to zero.)

If you want to reexecute these instructions, reset the IP register to 100H and trace through them again. Enter R IP, enter 100, and then enter R and the required number of T commands, all followed by the Enter key.

Displaying Memory Contents

Although you can also press T for the last instruction, NOP (no-operation), this instruction doesn't perform anything. Instead, to view the machine language program in the code segment, request a display as follows:

D CS:100

DEBUG now displays 16 bytes (32 hex digits) of data on each line. To the right is the ASCII representation (if printable) of each byte (pair of hex digits). In the case of machine code, the ASCII representation is meaningless and may be ignored. Later sections discuss the right side of the display in more detail.

The first line of the display begins at offset 100H of the code segment and represents the contents of locations CS:100 through CS:10F. The second line represents the contents of CS:110 through CS:11F. Although your program ends at CS:110, the D command automatically displays eight lines from CS:100 through CS:170.

Figure 3–2 shows the results of the D CS:100 command. Expect only the machine code from CS:100 through 110 to be identical to that of your own display; the bytes that follow could contain anything. Also, the figure shows that the DS, ES, SS, and CS registers all contain the same address. This is because DEBUG happens to treat the program area as one segment, with code and data (if any) in the same segment, although you must keep them separated.

Enter Q (Quit) to end the DEBUG session, or continue with the next exercise.

```
-D CS:100
21C1:0100  B8 23 01 05 25 00 8B D8-03 D8 8B CB 2B C8 2B C0  .#..%.......+.+.
21C1:0110  90 C3 8D 46 14 50 51 52-FF 76 28 E8 74 00 8B E5  ...F.PQR.v(.t...
21C1:0120  B8 01 00 50 FF 76 32 FF-76 30 FF 76 2E FF 76 28  ...P.v2.v0.v..v(
21C1:0130  E8 88 15 8B E5 FF 36 18-12 FF 36 16 12 8B 76 28  ......6...6...v(
21C1:0140  FF 74 3A 89 46 06 E8 22-CE 8B E5 30 E4 3D 0A 00  .t:.F.."...0.=..
21C1:0150  75 32 A1 16 12 2D 01 00-8B 1E 18 12 83 DB 00 53  u2...-.........S
21C1:0160  50 8B 76 28 FF 74 3A A3-16 12 89 1E 18 12 E8 FA  P.v(.t:.........
21C1:0170  CD 8B E5 30 E4 3D 0D 00-74 0A 83 06 16 12 01 83  ...0.=..t.......
-
```

Figure 3–2   Dump of the Code Segment

Correcting an Entry

If you enter an incorrect value in the data segment or code segment, reenter the E command to correct it. Also, to resume execution at the first instruction, set the IP register to 0100. Key in the R command followed by the designated register, that is, R IP [Enter]. DEBUG displays the contents of the IP and waits for an entry. Key in the value 0100 (followed by Enter). Next, key in an R command (without the IP). DEBUG displays the registers, flags, and first instruction to be executed. You can now use T to retrace the instruction steps. If your program accumulates totals, you may have to clear some memory locations and registers. But be sure not to change the contents of the CS, DS, SP, and SS registers, all of which have specific purposes.

MACHINE LANGUAGE EXAMPLE II: DEFINED DATA

The preceding example used immediate values defined directly within MOV and ADD instructions. We next illustrate a similar example that defines the data values (or constants) 0123H and 0025H as separate data items within the program. The program is to access the memory locations that contain these values.

Working through this example should give you an insight into how a computer accesses data by means of an address in the DS register and offset addresses. The example defines the following data items and contents:

DS OFFSET	HEX CONTENTS
0200H	2301H
0202H	2500H
0204H	0000H
0206H	2A2A2AH

Remember that a hex digit occupies a half-byte, so that, for example, 23H is stored in offset 0200H (the first byte) of the data area, and 01H is stored in offset 0201H (the second byte). Here are the machine language instructions that process these data items:

INSTRUCTION	EXPLANATION
A10002	Move the word (two bytes) beginning at DS offset 0200H into the AX register.
03060202	Add the contents of the word (two bytes) beginning at DS offset 0202H into the AX register.
A30402	Move the contents of the AX register to the word beginning at DS offset 0204H.
90	No operation.

You may have noticed that the two move instructions have different machine codes: A1 and A3. The actual machine code is dependent on the registers that are referenced, the size of data (byte or word), the direction of data transfer (from or to a register), and the reference to immediate data or memory.

Entering Program Instructions

Again, you can use DEBUG to enter the program and to watch its execution. First, use E (Enter) commands for defining data, beginning at DS:0200:

```
E  DS:0200  23  01  25  00  00  00  [press Enter]

E  DS:0206  2A  2A  2A  [press Enter]
```

Now use the E command to key in the instructions, again beginning at CS:100:

```
E  CS:100  A1  00  02  03  06  02  02  [press Enter]

E  CS:107  A3  04  02  90  [press Enter]
```

The first E command stores the three words (six bytes) at the start of the data area, DS:0200. Note that you have to enter these words with the bytes reversed, so that 0123 is 2301 and 0025 is 2500. When a MOV instruction subsequently accesses these words and loads them into a register, it "unreverses" the bytes, so that 2301 becomes 0123 and 2500 becomes 0025.

The second E command stores three asterisks (***), defined as 2A2A2A, so that you can view them later using the D (Display) command. Otherwise, these asterisks serve no particular purpose in the data segment.

Figure 3–3 shows all the steps in the program, including the E commands. Your screen should display similar results, although the addresses in the CS and DS probably differ. To examine the stored data (at DS:200H through 208H) and the instructions (at CS:100H through 10AH), key in the following D commands:

```
To view the data:   D  DS:200,208  [press Enter]

To view the code:   D  CS:100,10A  [press Enter]
```

Check that the contents of both areas (other than segment addresses) are identical to what is shown in Figure 3–3.

Executing Program Instructions

You can execute the instructions shown just as you did earlier. Press R to view the contents of the registers and flags and to display the first instruction. The registers contain the same values as at the start of the first example. The first displayed instruction is

```
xxxx:0100 A10002 MOV AX,[0200]
```

CS:0100 references your first instruction, A10002. DEBUG interprets this instruction as a MOV and has determined that the reference is to the first location [0200H] in the data area. The square brackets are to tell you that this reference is to a memory address and

```
-E DS:200 23 01 25 00 00 00
-E DS:206 2A 2A 2A
-E CS:100 A1 00 02 03 06 02 02
-E CS:107 A3 04 02 90
-D DS:200,208
21C1:0200  23 01 25 00 00 00 2A 2A-2A                      #.%...***
-D CS:100,10A
21C1:0100  A1 00 02 03 06 02 02 A3-04 02 90                ...........
-R
AX=0000  BX=0000  CX=0000  DX=0000  SP=FFEE  BP=0000  SI=0000  DI=0000
DS=21C1  ES=21C1  SS=21C1  CS=21C1  IP=0100  NV UP EI PL NZ NA PO NC
21C1:0100 A10002       MOV    AX,[0200]                    DS:0200=0123
-T

AX=0123  BX=0000  CX=0000  DX=0000  SP=FFEE  BP=0000  SI=0000  DI=0000
DS=21C1  ES=21C1  SS=21C1  CS=21C1  IP=0103  NV UP EI PL NZ NA PO NC
21C1:0103 03060202      ADD    AX,[0202]                   DS:0202=0025
-T

AX=0148  BX=0000  CX=0000  DX=0000  SP=FFEE  BP=0000  SI=0000  DI=0000
DS=21C1  ES=21C1  SS=21C1  CS=21C1  IP=0107  NV UP EI PL NZ NA PE NC
21C1:0107 A30402        MOV    [0204],AX                    DS:0204=0000
-T

AX=0148  BX=0000  CX=0000  DX=0000  SP=FFEE  BP=0000  SI=0000  DI=0000
DS=21C1  ES=21C1  SS=21C1  CS=21C1  IP=010A  NV UP EI PL NZ NA PE NC
21C1:010A 90           NOP
-D DS:0200,0208
21C1:0000  23 01 25 00 48 01 2A 2A-2A                      #.%.H.***
-Q
```

Figure 3–3 Trace of Machine Instructions

not an immediate value. (An immediate value for moving 0200H to the AX register would appear as MOV AX,0200.)

Now key in the T (Trace) command. The instruction MOV AX,[0200] moves the contents of the word at offset 0200H to the AX register. The contents are 2301H, which the operation reverses in the AX as 0123H.

Enter another T command to cause execution of the next instruction, ADD. The operation adds the contents of the word in memory at DS offset 0202 to the AX register. The result in the AX is now the sum of 0123H and 0025H, or 0148H.

The next instruction is MOV [0204],AX. Key in a T command for it to execute. The instruction moves the contents of the AX register to the word in memory at DS offset 0204H. To view the changed contents of the data from 200H through 208H, key in

```
D DS:200,208 [Enter]
```

The displayed values should be:

```
Value in data area:  23   01   25   00   48   01   2A   2A   2A
                      |    |    |    |    |    |    |    |    |
       Offset :      200  201  202  203  204  205  206  207  208
```

The value 0148H is moved from the AX register to the data area at offsets 204H and 205H and is reversed as 4801H. The left side of the display shows the actual machine code as it appears in memory. The right side simply helps you locate character data more easily. Note that these hex values are represented on the right of the screen by their ASCII equivalents. Thus 23H generates a number (#) symbol, and 25H generates a percent (%) symbol, while the three 2AH bytes generate asterisks (*).

Since there are no more instructions to execute, enter Q (Quit) to end the DEBUG session, or continue with the next exercise (and remember to reset the IP to 100).

ENTERING A SYMBOLIC ASSEMBLY PROGRAM

Although to this point the program examples have been in machine language format, you can also use DEBUG to enter symbolic assembly language statements. You may find occasions to use both methods. Let's now examine entering assembly language statements.

The A Command

The A (Assemble) command tells DEBUG to begin accepting symbolic assembly instructions and to convert them into machine language. Initialize the starting address in the code segment at offset 100H for your instructions as

```
          A 100 [Enter]
```

DEBUG displays the value of the code segment and the offset as xxxx:0100. Type in each instruction, followed by the Enter key. Try entering the following program:

```
          MOV    AL,25    [Enter]

          MOV    BL,32    [Enter]

          ADD    AL,BL    [Enter]

          NOP             [Enter, Enter]
```

When you've keyed in the program, press Enter again to exit from the A command. That's one extra Enter, which tells DEBUG you have no more symbolic instructions to enter. On completion, DEBUG should display the following:

```
          xxxx:0100         MOV    AL,25

          xxxx:0102         MOV    BL,32

          xxxx:0104         ADD    AL,BL

          xxxx:0106         NOP
```

You can see that DEBUG has determined the starting location of each instruction. But before executing the program, let's use DEBUG's U (Unassemble) command to examine the generated machine language.

The U (Unassemble) Command

DEBUG's U command displays the machine code for your assembly language instructions. You can use this command to tell DEBUG the locations of the first and last instructions that you want to see, in this case, 100H and 106H. Key in

```
U 100,106 [Enter]
```

The screen should display columns for the location, machine code, and symbolic code:

```
xxxx:0100   B025        MOV   AL,25

xxxx:0102   B332        MOV   BL,32

xxxx:0104   00D8        ADD   AL,BL

xxxx:0106   90          NOP
```

Now trace the execution of the program—the machine code is what actually executes. Begin by entering R to display the registers and the first instruction, and then T successively to trace subsequent instructions. When you get to the NOP at location 106H, continue with the next exercise or press Q to quit execution.

You can now see how to enter a program in either machine or assembly language. However, DEBUG is really intended for what its name implies—debugging programs—and most of your efforts will involve the use of conventional assembly language, which is not associated with DEBUG.

USING THE INT INSTRUCTION

The following three examples show how to access DOS and BIOS to deliver information about the system. To this end, you use the INT (interrupt) instruction, which exits from your program, enters a DOS or BIOS routine, performs the requested function, and returns to your program. Rather than single-stepping, we'll use the DEBUG P (Proceed) command to execute through the whole interrupt routine.

Getting the Version Number of DOS

There are times when a program needs to know which version of DOS the computer is running, since each version has made new functions available. The instruction that delivers the version number is DOS INT 21H, function 30H; that is, load 30H in the AH register and request INT 21H. To try this, enter the DEBUG A 100 command and these assembler instructions:

```
MOV   AH,30

INT   21

NOP   (followed by an additional Enter)
```

To trace execution of the instructions, first enter R to view the registers and T to trace the MOV. Instead of tracing the INT instruction, enter P (Proceed) to execute through the entire DOS routine. Processing stops at the NOP instruction. You can now view the AL for the DOS major version number, such as the X in DOS X.20, and the AH for the minor number, such as 14H (or 20) in DOS X.20.

Press Q to quit, or continue with the next exercise (and reset the IP to 100).

Getting the Current Date

Now that you know how to access the DOS version number, you can use a similar approach to access the current date. The instruction for this purpose is DOS INT 21H, function 2AH. Once again, enter the DEBUG command A 100 and then the following assembly program:

```
MOV     AH,2A

INT     21

NOP
```

Enter R to display the registers and T to execute the MOV. Then enter P to proceed through the interrupt routine; the operation stops at the NOP instruction. The registers display this information:

- · AL: Day of the week (where 0 = Sunday)
- · CX: Year (in hex; for example, 07CDH = 1997)
- · DH: Month (01 through 12)
- · DL: Day of the month (01 through 31)
- · Press Q to quit, or continue with the next exercise.

Determining the Size of Memory

In an early exercise in this chapter, you checked locations 413H and 414H for the amount of memory (RAM) that your computer contains. BIOS also provides an interrupt routine, INT 12H, that delivers the size of memory. Enter the DEBUG command A 100 and then these instructions:

```
INT     12

NOP
```

Enter R to display the registers and the first instruction. The instruction, INT 12H, passes control to a routine in BIOS that delivers the size of memory to the AX. Press T (and Enter) repeatedly to see each BIOS instruction execute. (Yes, we are violating a rule against tracing through an interrupt, but this time it works all right.)

The actual instructions in your BIOS may differ somewhat from these, depending on the version installed (the comments to the right are the author's):

```
STI                        ;Set interrupt

PUSH    DS                 ;Save DS address in stack

MOV     AX,0040            ;Segment 40[0]H

MOV     DS,AX              ; plus

MOV     AX,[0013]          ; offset 0013H

POP     DS                 ;Restore address in DS

IRET                       ;Return from interrupt
```

If you survived this adventure into BIOS, the AX contains the size of memory, in 1K bytes. The last T command exits from BIOS and returns to DEBUG. The displayed instruction is the NOP that you entered. Press Q to quit or continue with the next exercise (and reset the IP to 100).

SAVING A PROGRAM FROM WITHIN DEBUG

You may use DEBUG to save a program on disk under two circumstances:

1. To read the program, modify it, and then save it, follow these steps:
   - Read the program under its name: DEBUG n:filename.
   - Use the D command to view the machine language program and E to enter changes.
   - Use the W (Write) command to write the revised program.
2. To use DEBUG to write a very small machine language program that you now want to save, follow these steps:
   - Request the DEBUG program.
   - Use A (Assemble) and E (Enter) to create the program.
   - Name the program: N filename.COM. The program extension must be .COM. (See Chapter 7 for details of .COM files.)
   - Since only you know where the program really ends, tell DEBUG the size of the program in bytes. Consider this example:

```
xxxx:0100   MOV AL,25

xxxx:0102   MOV BL,32

xxxx:0104   ADD AL,BL

xxxx:0106   NOP
```

Since the last instruction, NOP, is one byte, the program size is 100H through 106H inclusive, or 7.
   - First use R BX to display the BX, and enter 0 to clear it.
   - Next use R CX to display the CX register. DEBUG replies with CX 0000 (zero value), and you reply with the program size, 7.
   - Write the revised program: W [Enter].

The reason for clearing the BX is because the program length is in the BX:CX pair, although the CX is adequate for our purposes.

DEBUG displays a message, "Writing nnnn bytes." If the number is zero, you have failed to enter the program length; try again. Watch out for the size of the program, since the last instruction could be longer than one byte.

ASSEMBLY LANGUAGE EXAMPLE: THE PTR OPERATOR

Let's now examine another program that introduces some new features. In this example, we move and add data between registers and memory locations. Here are the instructions for that purpose:

```
100     MOV     AX,[11A]

103     ADD     AX,[11C]

107     ADD     AX,25

10A     MOV     [11E],AX

10D     MOV     WORD PTR [120],25

113     MOV     BYTE PTR [122],30

118     NOP

119     NOP

11A     DB      14 23

11C     DB      05 00

11E     DB      00 00

120     DB      00 00 00
```

An explanation of the instructions is as follows:

100: Move the contents of memory locations 11AH–11BH to the AX. The square brackets indicate a memory address rather than an immediate value.

103: Add the contents of memory locations 11CH–11DH to the AX.

107: Add the immediate value 25H to the AX.

10A: Move the contents of the AX to memory locations 11EH–11FH.

10D: Move the immediate value 25H to memory locations 120H–121H. Note the use of the WORD PTR operator, which tells DEBUG that the 25H is to move into a *word* in memory. If you were to code the instruction as MOV [120],25, DEBUG would have no way of determining what length is intended and would display an ERROR message. Although you will seldom need to use the PTR operator, it's vital to know when it is needed.

113: Move the immediate value 30H to memory location 122H. This time, we want to move a byte, and the BYTE PTR operator indicates this length.

11A: Define the byte values 14H and 23H. DB here means "define byte(s)" and allows you to define data items that your instructions (such as the one at 100) are to reference.

11C, 11E, and 120: Define other byte values for use in the program.

To run this program, first type in A 100 [Enter], and then key in each symbolic instruction (but not the location). At the end, key in an additional Enter to exit from the A command. Begin by entering R to display the registers and the first instruction; then enter successive T commands. Quit execution when you get to the NOP at 118. Key in D 110 to view the changed contents of the AX (233E) and of locations 11EH–11FH (3E23), 120H–121H (2500), and 122H (30).

KEY POINTS

- The DOS DEBUG program is useful for testing and debugging machine language and assembly language programs.
- DEBUG provides a set of commands that lets you perform a number of useful operations, such as display, enter, and trace.
- Since DEBUG does not distinguish between lowercase and uppercase letters, you may enter commands either way.
- DEBUG assumes that all numbers are in hexadecimal format.
- If you enter an incorrect value in the data segment or code segment, reenter the E command to correct it.
- To resume execution at the first instruction, set the instruction pointer (IP) register to 0100. Key in the R (Register) command, followed by the designated register, as R IP [Enter]. DEBUG displays the contents of the IP and waits for an entry. Key in the value 0100 (followed by Enter).

QUESTIONS

3–1. What is the purpose of each of the following DEBUG commands? (a) A; (b) D; (c); E; (d) P; (e) Q; (f) R; (g) T; (h) U.

3–2. Provide the DEBUG commands for the following requirements.

   (a) Display the memory beginning at offset 264H in the data segment.

   (b) Display the memory beginning at location 410H. (Note: Separate this address into its segment and offset values.)

   (c) Enter the hex value A8B364 into the data segment beginning at location 200H.

   (d) Display the contents of (*i*) all registers and (*ii*) the IP register only.

   (e) Unassemble the machine code in locations 100H through 11EH.

3–3. Provide the machine code instructions for the following operations: (a) Move the hex value 4629 to the AX register; (b) add the hex value 036A to the AX register.

3–4. Assume that you have used DEBUG to enter the following E command:

E CS:100 B8 45 01 05 25 00

The hex value 45 was supposed to be 54. Code another E command to correct only the one byte that is incorrect; that is, change the 45 to 54 directly.

3–5. Assume that you have used DEBUG to enter the following E command:

E CS:100 B8 04 30 05 00 30 90

(a) What are the three symbolic instructions represented here? (The first program in this chapter gives a clue.)

(b) On executing this program, you discover that the AX register ends up with 6004 instead of the expected 0460. What is the error, and how would you correct it?

(c) Having corrected the instructions, you now want to reexecute the program from the first instruction. What two DEBUG commands are required?

3–6. Consider the machine language program

B0 25 D0 E0 B3 15 F6 E3 90

This program performs the following:

- Moves the hex value 25 to the AL register.
- Shifts the contents of the AL one bit left. (The result is 4A.)
- Moves the hex value 15 to the BL register.
- Multiplies the AL by the BL.

  Use DEBUG's E command to enter the program beginning at CS:100. Remember that these are hexadecimal values. After entering the program, key in D CS:100 to view it. Then key in R and enough successive T commands to step through the program until reaching the NOP. What is the final product in the AX register?

3–7. Use DEBUG's E command to enter the following machine language program:

```
Machine code (at 100H):   A0  00  02  D0  E0  F6  26  01  02  A3  02  02  90

        Data (at 200H):   25  15  00  00
```

This program performs the following:

- Moves the contents of the one byte at DS:0200 (25) to the AL register.
- Shifts the AL contents one bit left. (The result is 4A.)
- Multiplies the AL by the one-byte contents at DS:0201 (15).
- Moves the product from the AX to the word beginning at DS:0202.

  After entering the program, key in D commands to view the code and the data. Then key in R and enough successive T commands to step through the program until reaching the NOP. At this point, the AX should contain the product in memory at 0612H. Key in another D DS:0200, and note that the product at DS:0202 is stored as 1206H.

3–8. For Question 3–7, code the commands that write the program on disk under the name TRIAL.COM.

3–9. Use DEBUG's A command to enter the following instructions:

```
                MOV    BX,25

                ADD    BX,30
```

```
SHL    BX,01

SUB    BX,22

NOP
```

Unassemble the instructions and trace their execution through to the NOP, and check the value in the BX after each instruction.

3–10. What is the purpose of the INT instruction?

CHAPTER 4 ——————————————————

Assembly Language Requirements

OBJECTIVE

To cover the basic requirements for coding an assembly
language program and defining data items.

INTRODUCTION

Chapter 3 showed how to use DEBUG for keying in and executing machine language programs. No doubt, you were very aware of the difficulty in deciphering the machine code, even for a small program. Probably no one seriously codes in machine language other than for the smallest programs. A higher level of coding is the assembly level, in which a programmer uses symbolic instructions in place of machine instructions and descriptive names for data items and memory locations. You write an assembly program according to a strict set of rules and then use the assembler translator program to convert the assembly program into machine code.

In this chapter, we explain the basic requirements for developing an assembly program: the use of comments, the general coding format, the directives for printing a program listing, and the directives for defining segments and procedures. We also cover the general organization of a program, including initializing the program and ending its execution. Finally, we cover the requirements for defining data items.

ASSEMBLERS AND COMPILERS

Let's first identify two classes of programming languages: *high level* and *low level*. Programmers writing in a high-level language such as C and Pascal code powerful commands, each of which may generate many machine language instructions. Programmers writing in a low-level assembly language, on the other hand, code symbolic instructions, each of which generates one machine language instruction. Despite the fact that coding in a high-level language is more productive, some advantages to coding in assembly language are that it

- Provides more control over handling particular hardware requirements.
- Generates smaller, more compact executable modules.
- More likely results in faster execution.

A common practice is to combine the benefits of both programming levels: Code the bulk of a project in a high-level language, and code critical modules (those that cause noticeable delays) in assembly language.

Regardless of the programming language you use, it is still a symbolic language that has to be translated into a form the computer can execute. A high-level language uses a *compiler* to translate the source code into machine code (technically, object code). A low-level language uses an *assembler* to perform the translation. A *linker* program for both high and low levels completes the process by converting the object code into executable machine language.

ASSEMBLY LANGUAGE COMMENTS

The use of comments throughout a program can improve its clarity, especially in assembly language, where the purpose of a set of instructions is often unclear. A comment begins with a semicolon (;), and wherever you code it, the assembler assumes that all characters on the line to its right are comments. A comment may contain any printable character, including a blank.

A comment may appear on a line by itself or following an instruction on the same line, as the following two examples illustrate:

```
1. ;This entire line is a comment

2.   ADD AX,BX ;Comment on same line as instruction
```

Since a comment appears only on a listing of an assembled source program and generates no machine code, you may include any number of comments without affecting the assembled program's size or execution. In this book, assembly instructions are in uppercase letters and comments are in lowercase, only as a convention and to make the programs more readable. Technically, you can freely use upper- or lowercase for instructions and comments.

Another way to provide comments is by means of the COMMENT directive, described in Chapter 27.

RESERVED WORDS

Certain words in assembly language are *reserved* for its own purposes, to be used only under special conditions. By category, reserved words include

- instructions, such as MOV and ADD, which are operations that the computer can execute;
- directives, such as END or SEGMENT, which you use to provide commands to the assembler;
- operators, such as FAR and SIZE, which you use in expressions; and
- predefined symbols, such as @Data and @Model, which return information to your program.

Using a reserved word for a wrong purpose causes the assembler to generate an error message. Appendix C provides a list of assembly language reserved words.

IDENTIFIERS

An *identifier* is a name that you apply to items in your program. The two types of identifier are *name*, which refers to the address of a data item, and *label*, which refers to the address of an instruction. The same rules apply to both names and labels. An identifier can use the following characters:

- Alphabetic letters: A through Z and a through z
- Digits: 0 through 9 (may not be the first character)
- Special characters: question mark (?)
                        underline (_)
                        dollar ($)
                        at (@)
                        period (.) (may not be the first character)

The first character of an identifier must be an alphabetic letter or a special character, except for the period. Since the assembler uses some special words that begin with the @ symbol, you should avoid using it for your own definitions.

The assembler treats uppercase and lowercase letters the same. The maximum length of an identifier is 31 characters (247 since MASM 6.0). Examples of valid names are COUNT, PAGE25, and $E10. Descriptive, meaningful names are recommended. The names of registers, such as AX, DI, and AL, are reserved for referencing those registers. Consequently, in an instruction such as

```
ADD AX,BX
```

the assembler automatically knows that AX and BX refer to registers. However, in an instruction such as

```
MOV REGSAVE,AX
```

the assembler can recognize the name REGSAVE only if you define it elsewhere in the program.

STATEMENTS

An assembly language program consists of a set of *statements*. The two types of statements are:

1. **instructions** such as MOV and ADD, which the assembler translates to object code; and
2. **directives,** which tell the assembler to perform a specific action, such as define a data item.

Here is the general format for a statement, where square brackets indicate an optional entry:

[identifier]	operation	[operand(s)] [;comment]

An identifier (if any), operation, and operand (if any) are separated by at least one blank or tab character. There is a maximum of 132 characters on a line (512 since MASM 6.0), although most programmers prefer to stay within 80 characters because that is the maximum number the screen will accomodate. Two examples of statements are the following:

IDENTIFIER	OPERATION	OPERAND	COMMENT
Directive: COUNT	DB	1	;Name, operation, operand
Instruction:	MOV	AX,0	;Operation, two operands

The identifier, operation, and operand may begin in any column. However, consistently starting at the same column for these entries makes a more readable program. Also, most editor programs provide useful tab stops every eight positions to facilitate spacing.

Identifier

As described earlier, the term *name* applies to the name of a defined item or directive, whereas the term *label* applies to the name of an instruction; we'll use these terms from now on.

Operation

The *operation*, which must be coded, is most commonly used for defining data areas and coding instructions. For a data item, an operation such as DB or DW defines a field, work area, or constant. For an instruction, an operation such as MOV or ADD indicates an action to perform.

Operand

The *operand* (if any) provides information for the operation to act on. For a data item, the operand defines its initial value. For example, in the following definition of a data item named COUNTER, the operation DB means "define byte," and the operand initializes its contents with a zero value:

NAME	OPERATION	OPERAND	COMMENT
COUNTER	DB	0	;Define byte (DB) with 0 value

For an instruction, an operand indicates where to perform the action. An instruction's operand may contain one, two, or even no entries. Here are three examples:

OPERATION	OPERAND	COMMENT	OPERANDS
RET		;Return	None
INC	CX	;Increment CX register	One
ADD	AX,12	;Add 12 to AX register	Two

DIRECTIVES

Assembly language supports a number of statements that enable you to control the way in which a program assembles and lists. These statements, called *directives*, act only during the assembly of a program and generate no machine-executable code. The most common directives are explained in the next few sections. Chapter 27 covers all of the directives in detail; you may use that chapter as a reference any time.

Listing Directives: PAGE and TITLE

The PAGE and TITLE directives help to control the format of a listing of an assembled program. This is their only purpose, and they have no effect on subsequent execution of the program.

PAGE.   At the start of a program, the PAGE directive designates the maximum number of lines to list on a page and the maximum number of characters on a line. Its general format is

```
PAGE [length] [,width]
```

The following common example provides 60 lines per page and 132 characters per line:

```
PAGE 60,132
```

The number of lines per page may range from 10 through 255, and the number of characters per line may range from 60 through 132. Omission of a PAGE statement causes the assembler to default to PAGE 50,80.

Suppose that the line count for PAGE is defined as 60. Then, when the assembled program has listed 60 lines, it ejects the forms to the top of the next page and increments a page count. You may also want to force a page to eject at a specific line in the program listing, such as the end of a segment. At the required line, simply code PAGE with no operand. On encountering PAGE, the assembler automatically ejects the page and resumes printing at the top of the next page.

TITLE. You can use the TITLE directive to cause a title for a program to print on line 2 of each page of the program listing. You may code TITLE once, at the start of the program. Its general format is

```
TITLE text
```

For the text operand, a recommended technique is to use the name of the program, as cataloged on disk. For example, if you named the program ASMSORT, code that name plus an optional descriptive comment, all up to 60 characters in length, like this:

```
TITLE ASMSORT Assembly program to sort customer names
```

SEGMENT Directive

An assembly program in .EXE format consists of one or more segments. A stack segment defines stack storage, a data segment defines data items, and a code segment provides for executable code. The directives for defining a segment, SEGMENT and ENDS, have the following format:

```
NAME      OPERATION      OPERAND        COMMENT

name        SEGMENT      [options]     ;Begin segment
  .
  .
  .
name        ENDS                       ;End segment
```

The SEGMENT statement defines the start of a segment. The segment name must be present, must be unique, and must follow the naming conventions of the language. The ENDS statement indicates the end of the segment and contains the same name as the SEGMENT statement. The maximum size of a segment is 64K. The operand of a SEGMENT statement may contain three types of options: alignment, combine, and class, coded in this format:

```
name   SEGMENT   align   combine   'class'
```

Alignment type. The align entry indicates the boundary on which the segment is to begin. For the typical requirement, PARA, the segment aligns on a paragraph boundary, so that the starting address is evenly divisible by 16, or 10H. Omission of an operand causes the assembler to default to PARA.

Combine type. The combine entry indicates whether to combine the segment with other segments when they are *linked* after assembly (explained later under "Linking the Program"). Combine types are STACK, COMMON, PUBLIC, and AT expression. For example, the stack segment is commonly defined as

```
name   SEGMENT   PARA   STACK
```

You may use PUBLIC and COMMON where you intend to combine separately assembled programs when linking them. Otherwise, where a program is not to be combined with other programs, you may omit this option or code NONE.

Class type.   The class entry, enclosed in apostrophes, is used to group related segments when linking. This book uses the classes 'code' for the code segment (recommended by Microsoft), 'data' for the data segment, and 'stack' for the stack segment.

The following example defines a stack segment with alignment, combine, and class types:

```
name  SEGMENT  PARA  STACK  'Stack'
```

The partial program in Figure 4–1 illustrates SEGMENT statements with various options.

PROC Directive

The code segment contains the executable code for a program. It also contains one or more *procedures*, defined with the PROC directive. A segment that contains only one procedure would appear as follows:

NAME	OPERATION	OPERAND	COMMENT
segname	SEGMENT	PARA	
procname	PROC	FAR	;One
.			;procedure
.			;within
.			;the code
procname	ENDP		;segment
segname	ENDS		

The procedure name must be present, must be unique, and must follow naming conventions for the language. The operand FAR in this case is related to program execution. When you request execution of a program, the DOS program loader uses this procedure name as the entry point for the first instruction to execute.

The ENDP directive indicates the end of a procedure and contains the same name as the PROC statement to enable the assembler to relate the two. Since procedures must be fully contained within segments, ENDP defines the end of the procedure before ENDS defines the end of the segment.

The code segment may contain any number of procedures used as subroutines, each with its own set of PROC and ENDP statements. Each additional PROC is usually coded with (or defaults to) the NEAR operand; Chapter 7 covers this situation.

ASSUME Directive

A program uses the SS register to address the stack, the DS register to address the data segment, and the CS register to address the code segment. To this end, you have to tell the assembler the purpose of each segment in the program. The directive for this purpose is ASSUME, coded in the code segment as follows:

OPERATION	OPERAND
ASSUME	SS:stackname,DS:datasegname,CS:codesegname, ...

SS:stackname means that the assembler is to associate the name of the stack segment with the SS register, and similarly for the other operands shown. The operands may appear in any sequence. ASSUME may also contain an entry for the ES, such as ES:datasegname; if your program does not use the ES register, you may omit its reference or code ES:NOTH-ING. (Since MASM 6.0, the assembler automatically generates an ASSUME for the code segment.)

Like other directives, ASSUME is just a message to help the assembler convert symbolic code to machine code; you may still have to code instructions that physically load addresses in segment registers at execution time.

END Directive

As already mentioned, the ENDS directive ends a segment, and the ENDP directive ends a procedure. An END directive ends an entire program. Its general format is:

OPERATION	OPERAND
END	[procname]

The operand may be blank if the program is not to execute; for example, you may want to assemble only data definitions, or you may want to link the program with another (main) module. In most programs, the operand contains the name of the first or only PROC designated as FAR, where program execution is to begin.

INITIALIZING A PROGRAM FOR EXECUTION

The two basic types of executable programs are .EXE and .COM. We'll develop the requirements for .EXE programs first and leave .COM programs for Chapter 7. Figure 4–1 provides a skeleton of an .EXE program showing the stack, data, and code segments.

Let's examine the program statements by line number:

LINE	EXPLANATION
1	The PAGE directive for this listing establishes 60 lines and 132 columns per page.
2	The TITLE directive identifies the program's name as P04ASM1.
3	Lines 3, 7, and 11 are comments that clearly set out the defined segments.
4–6	These statements define the stack segment, STACKSG (but not its contents in this example).
8–10	These statements define the data segment, DATASG (but not its contents).
12–21	These statements define the code segment, CODESG.
13–20	These statements define the code segment's only procedure, named BEGIN. This procedure illustrates common initialization and exit requirements for an .EXE program. The two requirements for initializing are (1) notify the

```
 1               PAGE    60,132
 2               TITLE   P04ASM1 Skeleton of an .EXE Program
 3     ;-------------------------------------------------------------
 4     STACKSG SEGMENT PARA STACK 'Stack'
 5               ...
 6     STACKSG ENDS
 7     ;-------------------------------------------------------------
 8     DATASG  SEGMENT PARA 'Data'
 9               ...
10     DATASG  ENDS
11     ;-------------------------------------------------------------
12     CODESG  SEGMENT PARA 'Code'
13     BEGIN   PROC    FAR
14               ASSUME  SS:STACKSG,DS:DATASG,CS:CODESG
15               MOV     AX,DATASG   ;Get address of data segment
16               MOV     DS,AX       ;Store address in DS
17               ...
18               MOV     AX,4C00H    ;Request
19               INT     21H         ;  exit to DOS
20     BEGIN   ENDP
21     CODESG  ENDS
22               END     BEGIN
```

Figure 4–1   Skeleton of an .EXE Program

assembler which segments to associate with segment registers and (2) load
the DS with the address of the data segment.

14   The ASSUME directive notifies the assembler to associate certain segments with certain segment registers, in this case, STACKSG with the SS,
DATASG with the DS, and CODESG with the CS:

```
        ASSUME  SS:STACKSG,DS:DATASG,CS:CODESG
```

By associating segments with segment registers, the assembler can determine offset addresses for items in the stack, for data items in the data segment, and for instructions in the code segment. For example, each machine
instruction in the code segment is a specific length. The first instruction in
machine language would be at offset 0, and if it is two bytes long, the second instruction would be at offset 2, and so forth.

15, 16   Two instructions initialize the address of the data segment in the DS register:

```
    MOV   AX,DATASG      ;Get address of data segment

    MOV   DS,AX          ;Store address in DS
```

The first MOV loads the address of the data segment into the AX register, and
the second MOV copies the address from the AX into the DS. Two MOVs
are required because no instruction can move data directly from memory to
a segment register; you have to move the address from another register to the
segment register. Thus the statement MOV DS,DATASG would be illegal.
Chapter 5 discusses initializing segment registers in more detail.

18, 19   These two instructions request an end to program execution and a return to
          DOS. A later section discusses them in more detail.

22   The END statement tells the assembler that this is the end of the program,
          and the BEGIN operand provides the entry point for subsequent program
          execution.

The sequence in which you define segments is usually unimportant. Figure 4–1 defines them as follows:

```
STACKSG    SEGMENT    PARA    STACK    'Stack'

DATASG     SEGMENT    PARA    'Data'

CODESG     SEGMENT    PARA    'Code'
```

Keep this point in mind: The program in the figure is coded in *symbolic language*. To execute it, you have to use an assembler program and a linker to translate it into executable machine code. In that case, it would become an .EXE program.

As described in Chapter 2, when DOS loads an .EXE program from disk into memory for execution, it constructs a 256-byte (100H) PSP on a paragraph boundary in available internal memory and stores the program immediately following the boundary. DOS then

- loads the address of the code segment in the CS;
- loads the address of the stack in the SS; and
- loads the address of the PSP in the DS and ES registers.

The DOS loader initializes the CS:IP and SS:SP registers, but not the DS and ES registers. However, your program normally needs the address of the data segment in the DS (and often in the ES as well). As a consequence, you have to initialize the DS with the address of the data segment, as shown by the two MOV instructions in Figure 4–1.

Now, even if this initialization is not clear at this point, take heart: Every .EXE program has virtually identical initialization steps that you can duplicate each time you code an assembly program.

ENDING PROGRAM EXECUTION

INT 21H is a common DOS interrupt operation that uses a function code in the AH register to specify an action to be performed. The many functions of INT 21H include keyboard input, screen handling, disk I/O, and printer output. The function that concerns us here is 4CH, which INT 21H recognizes as a request to end program execution. You can also use this operation to pass a return code in the AL for subsequent testing in a batch file (via the IF ERRORLEVEL statement), as follows:

```
MOV AH,4CH          ;Request end

MOV AL,retcode      ;Return code (optional)

INT 21H             ;Exit to DOS
```

The return code for normal completion of a program is usually 0 (zero). You may also code the two MOVs as one statement (as shown in Figure 4–1):

```
MOV AX,4C00H      ;Request normal exit
```

DOS function 4CH has superseded the original end operations INT 20H and INT 21H, function 00H.

EXAMPLE OF A SOURCE PROGRAM

Figure 4–2 combines the preceding information into a simple but complete assembly source program that adds two data items in the AX register.

STACKSG contains one entry, DW (Define Word), that defines 32 words initialized to zero, an adequate size for most programs.

DATASG defines three data words named FLDA, FLDB, and FLDC.

CODESG contains the executable instructions for the program, although the first statement, ASSUME, generates no executable code.

The ASSUME directive performs these operations:

- Assigns STACKSG to the SS register, so that the system uses the address in the SS register for addressing STACKSG.

- Assigns DATASG to the DS register, so that the system uses the address in the DS register for addressing DATASG.

- Assigns CODESG to the CS register, so that the system uses the address in the CS register for addressing CODESG.

```
            page 60,132
   TITLE    P04ASM1 (EXE)  Move and add operations
   ; ---------------------------------------------------
   STACKSG  SEGMENT PARA STACK 'Stack'
            DW       32 DUP(0)
   STACKSG  ENDS
   ; ---------------------------------------------------
   DATASG   SEGMENT PARA 'Data'
   FLDA     DW       250
   FLDB     DW       125
   FLDC     DW       ?
   DATASG   ENDS
   ; ---------------------------------------------------
   CODESG   SEGMENT PARA 'Code'
   BEGIN    PROC     FAR
            ASSUME   SS:STACKSG,DS:DATASG,CS:CODESG
            MOV      AX,DATASG      ;Set address of DATASG
            MOV      DS,AX          ;    in DS register

            MOV      AX,FLDA        ;Move 0250 to AX
            ADD      AX,FLDB        ;Add  0125 to AX
            MOV      FLDC,AX        ;Store sum in FLDC
            MOV      AX,4C00H       ;Exit to DOS
            INT      21H
   BEGIN    ENDP                    ;End of procedure
   CODESG   ENDS                    ;End of segment
            END      BEGIN          ;End of program
```

Figure 4–2   .EXE Source Program With Conventional Segments

When loading a program from disk into memory for execution, the system loader sets the actual addresses in the SS and CS registers, but, as shown by the first two MOV instructions, you have to initialize the DS (and ES) register.

We'll trace the assembly, linkage, and execution of this program in Chapter 5.

INITIALIZING FOR PROTECTED MODE

In protected mode under the 80386 and later processors, a program may address up to 16 megabytes of memory. The use of DWORD to align segments on a doubleword address speeds up accessing memory for 32-bit data buses. In the following code, the .386 directive tells the assembler to accept instructions that are unique to these processors; the USE32 use type tells the assembler to generate code appropriate to 32-bit protected mode:

```
.386

segname SEGMENT   DWORD USE32
```

Initialization of the data segment register could look like this, since on these processors the DS register is still 16 bits in size:

```
MOV      EAX,DATASEG   ;Get address of data segment

MOV      DS,AX         ;Load 16-bit portion
```

The STI, CLI, IN, and OUT instructions, available in real mode, are not allowed in protected mode.

SIMPLIFIED SEGMENT DIRECTIVES

The Microsoft and Borland assemblers provide some shortcuts in defining segments. To use the shortcuts, you initialize the *memory model* before defining any segment. The general format (including the leading period) is

The memory model may be TINY, SMALL, MEDIUM, COMPACT, or LARGE. (Another model, HUGE, need not concern us here.) The requirements for each model are:

MODEL	NUMBER OF CODE SEGMENTS	NUMBER OF DATA SEGMENTS
TINY	*	*
SMALL	1	1
MEDIUM	More than 1	1
COMPACT	1	More than 1
LARGE	More than 1	More than 1

You may use any of these models for a stand-alone program (that is, a program that is not linked to another program). The TINY model is intended for the exclusive use of .COM programs, which have their data, code, and stack in one segment. The SMALL model requires that code fits within a 64K segment and data fit within another 64K segment; this model is suitable for most of the examples in the book. The .MODEL directive automatically generates the required ASSUME statement.

The general formats (including the leading period) for the directives that define the stack, data, and code segments are:

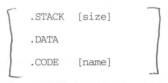

```
.STACK  [size]

.DATA

.CODE   [name]
```

Each of these directives causes the assembler to generate the required SEGMENT statement and its matching ENDS. The default segment names (which you don't have to define) are STACK, _DATA, and _TEXT (for the code segment). The underline (or break) character at the beginning of _DATA and _TEXT is intended. As the coding format indicates, you may override the default name for the code segment. The default stack size is 1,024 bytes, which you may also override. You use these directives to identify where in the program the three segments are to be located. Note, however, that the instructions you now use to initialize the address of data segment in the DS are:

```
MOV     AX,@data

MOV     DS,AX
```

Figure 4–2 gave an example of a program using conventionally defined segments. Figure 4–3 provides the same example, but this time using the simplified segment directives

```
            page    60,132
    TITLE   P04ASM2 (EXE)  Move and add operations
    ;---------------------------------------------------------
            .MODEL  SMALL
            .STACK  64                      ;Define stack
            .DATA                           ;Define data
    FLDA    DW      250
    FLDB    DW      125
    FLDC    DW      ?
    ;---------------------------------------------------------
            .CODE                           ;Define code segment
    BEGIN   PROC    FAR
            MOV     AX,@data                ;Set address of DATASG
            MOV     DS,AX                   ;   in DS register

            MOV     AX,FLDA                 ;Move 0250 to AX
            ADD     AX,FLDB                 ;Add  0125 to AX
            MOV     FLDC,AX                 ;Store sum in FLDC

            MOV     AX,4C00H                ;Exit to DOS
            INT     21H
    BEGIN   ENDP                            ;End of procedure
            END     BEGIN                   ;End of program
```

Figure 4–3   .EXE Source Program with Simplified Segment Directives

.STACK, .DATA, and .CODE. The memory model is specified as SMALL in the fourth line. The stack is defined as 64 bytes (32 words). Note that the assembler does not generate conventional SEGMENT and ENDS statements, and you also don't code an ASSUME statement.

As you'll see in the next chapter, the assembler handles programs coded with simplified segment directives slightly differently from those using conventional segment directives.

The .STARTUP and .EXIT Directives

MASM 6.0 introduced the .STARTUP and .EXIT directives to simplify program initialization and termination. .STARTUP generates the instructions to initialize the segment registers, whereas .EXIT generates the INT 21H function 4CH instructions for exiting the program. For purposes of learning assembly language, examples in this text code the full sets of instructions and leave shortcuts to more experienced programmers.

DATA DEFINITION

As already discussed, the purpose of the data segment in an .EXE program is to define constants, work areas, and input/output areas. The assembler permits definitions of items in various lengths according to a set of directives that defines data. For example, DB defines a byte and DW defines a word. A data item may contain an *undefined* (that is, uninitialized) *value*, or it may contain a *constant*, defined either as a character string or as a numeric value. Here is the general format for data definition:

Name.   A program that references a data item does so by means of a name. The name of an item is otherwise optional, as indicated by the square brackets. The earlier section, "Statements," provides the rules for names.

Directive.   The directives that define data items are DB (byte), DW (word), DD (doubleword), DF (farword), DQ (quadword), and DT (tenbytes), each of which explicitly indicates the length of the defined item.

Expression.   The expression in an operand may contain a question mark to indicate an uninitialized item, such as

```
        FLD1   DB   ?        ;Uninitialized item
```

In this case, when your program begins execution, the initial value of FLD1 is unknown to you. The normal practice before using this item is to move some value into it (any at all, but it must fit the defined size).

You can also use the operand to define a constant, such as

```
        FLD2   DB   25       ;Initialized item
```

You can freely use this initialized value throughout your program and can even change the contents of FLD2.

An expression may contain multiple constant values separated by commas and limited only by the length of the line, as follows:

```
FLD3   DB   11,  12,  13,  14,  15,  16,  ...
```

The assembler defines these constants in adjacent bytes. A reference to FLD3 is to the first one-byte constant, 11 (you could think of the first byte as FLD3+0), and a reference to FLD3+1 is to the second constant, 12. For example, the instruction

```
MOV   AL,FLD3+3
```

loads the value 14 (0EH) into the AL register. The expression also permits duplication of constants in a statement of the general form

```
[name]  Dn  repeat-count DUP(expression)  ...
```

The following examples illustrate duplication:

```
DW   10 DUP(?)              ;Ten words, uninitialized

DB   5 DUP(14)             ;Five bytes containing hex 0E0E0E0E0E

DB   3 DUP(4 DUP(8))   ;Twelve 8s
```

The third example generates four copies of the digit 8 (8888) and duplicates that value three times, giving twelve 8s in all.

An expression may define and initialize a character string or a numeric constant.

Character Strings

Character strings are used for descriptive data such as people's names and page titles. The string is defined within single quotes, such as 'PC', or within double quotes, such as "PC". The assembler translates character strings into object code in normal ASCII format.

Strangely, DB is the only format that defines a character string exceeding two characters and stores the characters in normal left-to-right sequence. Consequently, DB is the conventional format for defining character data of any length. An example is

```
DB 'Character string'
```

The assembler stores the characters in ASCII format, without the apostrophes. If the string must contain a single or double quote, you can define it in one of these ways:

```
DB   "Honest Ed's PC Emporium"    ;Double quotes for string,

                                    single quote for apostrophe

DB   'Honest Ed''s PC Emporium'   ;Single quotes for string, two

                                    single quotes for apostrophe
```

Numeric Constants

Numeric constants are used to define arithmetic values and memory addresses. The constant is not defined within quotes, but is followed by an optional *radix specifier*, such as H in the hexadecimal value 12H. For most of the data definition directives, the assembler converts defined numeric constants to hexadecimal and stores the generated bytes in object code in reverse sequence—from right to left. Following are the various numeric formats.

Decimal.   Decimal format permits defining the decimal digits 0 through 9, optionally followed by the radix specifier D, such as 125 or 125D. Although the assembler allows you to define values in decimal format as a coding convenience, it converts your decimal values to binary object code and represents them in hex. For example, a definition of decimal 125 becomes hex 7D.

Hexadecimal.   Hex format permits defining the hex digits 0 through F, followed by the radix specifier H, which you can use to define binary values. Since the assembler expects that a reference beginning with a letter is a symbolic name, the first digit of a hex constant must be 0 to 9. Examples are 2EH and 0FD8H, which the assembler stores as 2E and D80F, respectively. Note that the bytes in the second example are stored in reverse sequence.

Binary.   Binary format permits defining the binary digits 0 and 1, followed by the radix specifier B. The normal use for binary format is to distinguish values for the bit-handling instructions AND, OR, XOR, and TEST.

Since the assembler converts all numeric values to binary (and represents them in hex), definitions of decimal 12, hex C, and binary 1100 all generate the same value: binary 00001100 or hex 0C, depending on how you view the contents of the byte.

Because the letters D and B act as both radix specifiers and hex digits, they may cause some confusion. As a solution, MASM 6.0 introduced the use of T (as in *ten*) and Y (as in *binary*) as radix specifiers for decimal and binary, respectively.

Real.   The assembler converts a given real value—a decimal or hex constant followed by the radix specifier R—into floating-point format for use with a numeric coprocessor.

Be sure to distinguish between the use of character and numeric constants. A character constant defined as DB '12' generates two ASCII characters, represented as hex 3132. A numeric constant defined as DB 12 generates a binary number, represented as hex 0C.

DIRECTIVES FOR DEFINING DATA

The conventional directives used to define data, along with the names introduced by MASM 6.0, are:

DESCRIPTION	CONVENTIONAL DIRECTIVES	MASM 6.0 DIRECTIVES
Define byte	DB	BYTE
Define word	DW	WORD

Define doubleword	DD	DWORD
Define farword	DF	FWORD
Define quadword	DQ	QWORD
Define tenbytes	DT	TBYTE

This text uses the conventional directives because of their commonly accepted usage.

The assembled program in Figure 4–4 provides examples of directives that define character strings and numeric constants, with the generated object code on the left, which

```
                                    page 60,132
                          TITLE     P04DEFIN (EXE)   Define data items
                                    .MODEL   SMALL
                                    .DATA
                          ;         Define Byte - DB:
                          ;         ----------------
0000 00                   FLD1DB    DB   ?              ;Uninitialized
0001 20                   FLD2DB    DB   32             ;Decimal constant
0002 20                   FLD3DB    DB   20H            ;Hex constant
0003 59                   FLD4DB    DB   01011001B      ;Binary constant
0004 000A[ 00 ]           FLD5DB    DB   10 DUP(0)      ;Ten zeros
000E 50 65 72 73 6F 6E    FLD6DB    DB   'Personal Computer'
     61 6C 20 43 6F 6D                                  ;Character string
     70 75 74 65 72
001F 33 32 36 35 34       FLD7DB    DB   '32654'        ;Numbers as chars
0024 01 4A 61 6E 02 46    FLD8DB    DB   01,'Jan',02,'Feb',03,'Mar'
     65 62 03 4D 61 72                                  ;Table of months

                          ;         Define Word - DW:
                          ;         ----------------
0030 FFF0                 FLD1DW    DW   0FFF0H         ;Hex constant
0032 0059                 FLD2DW    DW   01011001B      ;Binary constant
0034 001F R               FLD3DW    DW   FLD7DB         ;Address constant
0036 0003 0004 0007       FLD4DW    DW   3,4,7,8,9      ;Table of five
     0008 0009                                          ;   constants
0040 0005[ 0000 ]         FLD5DW    DW   5 DUP(0)       ;Five zeros

                          ;         Define Doubleword - DD:
                          ;         ----------------------
004A 00000000             FLD1DD    DD   ?              ;Uninitialized
004E 00007F3C             FLD2DD    DD   32572          ;Decimal value
0052 0000000E 00000031    FLD3DD    DD   14,49          ;Two constants
005A 00000001             FLD4DD    DD   FLD3DB - FLD2DB  ;Difference
                                                        ;   between addresses
005E 00005043             FLD5DD    DD   'PC'           ;Character string

                          ;         Define Quadword - DQ:
                          ;         --------------------
0062 0000000000000000     FLD1DQ    DQ   ?              ;Uninitialized
006A 474D000000000000     FLD2DQ    DQ   04D47H         ;Hex constant
0072 3C7F000000000000     FLD3DQ    DQ   32572          ;Decimal constant

                          ;         Define Tenbytes - DT:
                          ;         --------------------
007A 000000000000000000   FLD1DT    DT   ?              ;Uninitialized
     00
0084 563412000000000000   FLD2DT    DT   123456         ;Decimal constant
     00
008E 435000000000000000   FLD3DT    DT   'PC'           ;Character string
     00
```

Figure 4–4   Definitions of Character Strings and Numeric Values (Part 1 of 2)

```
Segments and Groups:
              N a m e        Length    Align      Combine    Class
DGROUP  . . . . . . . .   GROUP
  _DATA  . . . . . . .    0098       WORD       PUBLIC     'DATA'
_TEXT  . . . . . . . .    0000       WORD       PUBLIC     'CODE'

Symbols:
              N a m e        Type       Value      Attr
FLD1DB  . . . . . . . .   L BYTE      0000       _DATA
FLD1DD  . . . . . . . .   L DWORD     004A       _DATA
FLD1DQ  . . . . . . . .   L QWORD     0062       _DATA
FLD1DT  . . . . . . . .   L TBYTE     007A       _DATA
FLD1DW  . . . . . . . .   L WORD      0030       _DATA
FLD2DB  . . . . . . . .   L BYTE      0001       _DATA
FLD2DD  . . . . . . . .   L DWORD     004E       _DATA
FLD2DQ  . . . . . . . .   L QWORD     006A       _DATA
FLD2DT  . . . . . . . .   L TBYTE     0084       _DATA
FLD2DW  . . . . . . . .   L WORD      0032       _DATA
FLD3DB  . . . . . . . .   L BYTE      0002       _DATA
FLD3DD  . . . . . . . .   L DWORD     0052       _DATA
FLD3DQ  . . . . . . . .   L QWORD     0072       _DATA
FLD3DT  . . . . . . . .   L TBYTE     008E       _DATA
FLD3DW  . . . . . . . .   L WORD      0034       _DATA
FLD4DB  . . . . . . . .   L BYTE      0003       _DATA
FLD4DD  . . . . . . . .   L DWORD     005A       _DATA
FLD4DW  . . . . . . . .   L WORD      0036       _DATA
FLD5DB  . . . . . . . .   L BYTE      0004       _DATA    Length - 000A
FLD5DD  . . . . . . . .   L DWORD     005E       _DATA
FLD5DW  . . . . . . . .   L WORD      0040       _DATA    Length = 0005
FLD6DB  . . . . . . . .   L BYTE      000E       _DATA
FLD7DB  . . . . . . . .   L BYTE      001F       _DATA
FLD8DB  . . . . . . . .   L BYTE      0024       _DATA

       0 Warning Errors
       0 Severe  Errors
```

Figure 4–4   (continued)

you are urged to examine. Note that the object code for uninitialized values appears as hex zeros. Since this program consists of only a data segment, it is not suitable for execution.

Define Byte: DB or BYTE

Of the directives that define data items, one of the most useful is DB (Define Byte).

A DB (or BYTE) numeric expression may define one or more one-byte constants. The maximum of one byte means two hex digits. With the leftmost bit acting as the sign, the largest positive one-byte hex number is 7F; all "higher" numbers, 80 through FF (where the sign bit is 1), represent negative values. In terms of decimal numbers, these limits are +127 and −128. The assembler converts numeric constants to binary object code (represented in hex). In Figure 4–4, numeric DB constants are FLD2DB, FLD3DB, FLD4DB, and FLD5DB.

A DB character expression may contain a string of any length up to the end of the line. For example, see FLD6DB and FLD7DB in the figure. The object code shows the ASCII character for each byte in normal left-to-right sequence; 20H represents a blank character.

FLD8DB shows a mixture of numeric and string constants suitable for defining a table.

Define Word: DW or WORD

The DW directive defines items that are one word (two bytes) in length. A DW (or WORD) numeric expression may define one or more one-word constants. The largest positive one-word hex number is 7FFF; all "higher" numbers, 8000 through FFFF (where the sign bit is 1), represent negative values. In terms of decimal numbers, the limits are +32,767 and −32,768.

The assembler converts DW numeric constants to binary object code (represented in hex), but stores the bytes in reverse sequence. Consequently, a decimal value defined as 12345 converts to hex 3039, but is stored as 3930.

In Figure 4–4, FLD1DW and FLD2DW define DW numeric constants. FLD3DW defines the operand as an address—in this case, the offset address of FLD7DB. The generated object code is 001F (the R to the right means *relocatable*), and a check of the figure shows that the offset address of FLD7DB (the leftmost column) is indeed 001F.

A DW character expression is limited to two characters, which the assembler reverses in the object code, so that 'PC' would become 'CP.' If you think that DW is of limited use for defining character strings, you're right.

FLD4DW defines a table of five numeric constants. Note that the length of each constant is one word (two bytes).

Define Doubleword: DD or DWORD

The DD directive defines items that are a doubleword (four bytes) in length. A DD (or DWORD) numeric expression may define one or more constants, each with a maximum of four bytes (eight hex digits). The largest positive doubleword hex number is 7FFFFFFF; all "higher" numbers, 80000000 through FFFFFFFF (where the sign bit is 1), represent negative values. In terms of decimal numbers, these maximums are +2,147,483,647 and −2,147,483,648.

The assembler converts DD numeric constants to binary object code (represented in hex), but stores the bytes in reverse sequence. Consequently, a decimal value defined as 12345678 converts to 00BC614EH, but is stored as 4E61BC00H.

In Figure 4–4, FLD2DD defines a DD numeric constant, and FLD3DD defines two numeric constants. FLD4DD generates the numeric difference between two defined addresses; in this case, the result is the length of FLD2DB.

A DD character expression is also limited to two characters and is as trivial as those for DW. The assembler reverses the characters and left-adjusts them in the four-byte doubleword, as shown in the object code for FLD5DD.

Define Farword: DF or FWORD

The DF directive defines a farword as six bytes. Its normal use is for the 80386 and later processors.

Define Quadword: DQ or QWORD

The DQ directive defines items that are four words (eight bytes) in length. A DQ (or QWORD) numeric expression may define one or more constants, each with a maximum of eight bytes, or 16 hex digits. The largest positive quadword hex number is 7 followed by

15 Fs. As an indication of the magnitude of this number, hex 1 followed by 15 0s equals the decimal number 1,152,921,504,606,846,976.

The assembler handles DQ numeric values and character strings just as it does DD and DW numeric values. In Figure 4–4, FLD2DQ and FLD3DQ illustrate only numeric values.

Define Tenbytes: DT or TBYTE

The DT directive defines data items that are 10 bytes long. Its purpose is related to packed BCD (binary-coded decimal) numeric values, which are more useful for numeric co-processors than for standard arithmetic operations. A BCD number is packed with two dec-imal digits per byte, with the leftmost bit as the sign (0 or 1). For a constant defined as 12345678, the assembler stores the bytes in reverse sequence as 78 56 34 12 00 00 00 00 00 00. Note that DT (or TBYTE), unlike the other data directives, stores numeric constants as decimal rather than hexadecimal values.

Figure 4–4 illustrates DT for an uninitialized item, a numeric value, and a two-character constant.

Display of the Data Segment

The program in Figure 4–4 contains only a data segment. Although the assembler gener-ated no error messages, the link map displayed "Warning: No STACK Segment," and the linker displayed "There were 1 errors detected." Despite the warning, you can still use DE-BUG to view the object code, which is shown in Figure 4–5.

Assemble and link the program, use DEBUG to load the .EXE file, and enter D DS:100 for a display of the data. The right side of the display shows the ASCII representa-tion, such as "Personal Computer," whereas the hexadecimal values on the left indicate the actual stored contents. Your display should be identical to Figure 4–5 for offsets 0000 through 0097. Expect your segment address (0F07 in the figure) and data following offset 0097 to differ.

```
0F07:0000   00 20 20 59 00 00 00 00-00 00 00 00 00 00 50 65     .  Y.........Pe
0F07:0010   72 73 6F 6E 61 6C 20 43-6F 6D 70 75 74 65 72 33     rsonal Computer3
0F07:0020   32 36 35 34 01 4A 61 6E-02 46 65 62 03 4D 61 72     2654.Jan.Feb.Mar
0F07:0030   F0 FF 59 00 1F 00 03 00-04 00 07 00 08 00 09 00     ..Y.............
0F07:0040   00 00 00 00 00 00 00 00-00 00 00 00 00 00 3C 7F     ..............<.
0F07:0050   00 00 0E 00 00 00 31 00-00 00 01 00 00 00 43 50     ......1.......CP
0F07:0060   00 00 00 00 00 00 00 00-00 00 47 4D 00 00 00 00     ..........GM....
0F07:0070   00 00 3C 7F 00 00 00 00-00 00 00 00 00 00 00 00     ..<.............
-D
0F07:0080   00 00 00 00 56 34 12 00-00 00 00 00 00 00 43 50     ....V4........CP
0F07:0090   00 00 00 00 00 00 00 00-72 03 E9 6B 01 2B C0 50     ........r..k.+.P
0F07:00A0   50 FF 76 04 E8 F5 5D 83-C4 06 0B D0 74 03 E9 57     P.v..]....t..W
0F07:00B0   01 B8 FF FF 50 2B C0 50-FF 76 04 E8 DE 5D 83 C4     ....P+.P.v...]..
0F07:00C0   06 8B 1E A4 43 FF 06 A4-43 D1 E3 D1 E3 A1 0E 3C     ....C...C......<
0F07:00D0   8B 16 10 3C 89 87 8A 32-89 97 8C 32 5E 8B E5 5D     ...<...2...2^..]
0F07:00E0   C3 90 B8 05 00 50 B8 CC-07 50 8D 46 80 50 E8 23     .....P...P.F.P.#
0F07:00F0   6C 83 C4 06 FF 76 04 8D-46 80 50 E8 98 0D 83 C4     l....v..F.P.....

            <─────── hexadecimal representation ───────>    <─── ASCII ───>
```

Figure 4–5 Display of the Data Segment

You issued DS:100 for the display because the loader set the DS with the address of the PSP, and the data segment for this program is 100 bytes after that address. Later, when you use DEBUG for .EXE programs that initialize the DS to the address of the data segment, you'll use DS:0 for displaying it.

THE EQU DIRECTIVE

The EQU directive does not define a data item. Instead, it defines a value that the assembler can use to substitute in other instructions. Consider the following EQU statement coded in the data segment:

```
TIMES  EQU  10
```

The name, in this case TIMES, may be any name acceptable to the assembler. Now whenever the word TIMES appears in an instruction or another directive, the assembler substitutes the value 10. For example, the assembler converts the directive

```
FIELDA  DB  TIMES  DUP(?)
```

to its equivalent value

```
FIELDA  DB  10  DUP(?)
```

An instruction may also contain an equated operand, as in the following:

```
COUNTR  EQU  05

         . . .

MOV  CX,COUNTR
```

The assembler replaces COUNTR in the MOV operand with the value 05, making the operand an immediate value, as if it were coded

```
MOV  CX,05       ;Assembler substitutes 05
```

The advantage of EQU is that many statements may use the value defined by COUNTR. If the value has to be changed, you need change only the EQU statement. Needless to say, you can use an equated value only where a substitution makes sense to the assembler. You can also equate symbolic names, as in the following code:

```
TOTALPAY DW    0

         . . .

TP        EQU    TOTALPAY

MPY       EQU    MUL
```

The first EQU equates the nickname TP to the defined item TOTALPAY. For any instruction that contains the operand TP, the assembler replaces it with the address of TOTAL-

PAY. The second EQU enables a program to use the word MPY in place of the regular symbolic instruction MUL.

MASM 6.0 introduced a TEXTEQU directive for text data with the format

```
name   TEXTEQU   <text>
```

KEY POINTS

- A semicolon precedes a comment on a line.
- Reserved words in assembly language are used for its own purposes, only under special conditions.
- An identifier is a name that you apply to items in your program. The two types of identifiers are *name*, which refers to the address of a data item, and *label*, which refers to the address of an instruction.
- An operation is commonly used for defining data areas and coding instructions. An operand provides information for the operation to act on.
- A program consists of one or more segments, each of which begins on a paragraph boundary.
- The ENDS directive ends each segment, ENDP ends each procedure, and END ends the program.
- The ASSUME directive associates segment registers CS, DS, and SS with their appropriate segment names.
- .EXE programs (but not .COM programs) should provide at least 32 words for stack addressing.
- For an .EXE program, you normally initialize the DS register with the address of the data segment.
- For the simplified segment directives, you initialize the memory model before defining any segment. Options are SMALL (one code segment and one data segment), MEDIUM (any number of code segments and one data segment), COMPACT (one code segment and any number of data segments), and LARGE (any number of code segments and data segments).
- INT 21H, function 4CH, is the standard instruction for exiting a program.
- Names of data items should be unique and descriptive. For example, an item for an employee's wage could be named EMPWAGE.
- DB is the preferred format for defining character strings, since it permits strings longer than two bytes and converts them to normal left-to-right sequence.
- Decimal and binary (hex) constants generate different values. Consider the effect of adding decimal 25 versus that of adding hex 25:

```
ADD   AX,25      ;Add 25

ADD   AX,25H     ;Add 37
```

- DW, DD, and DQ store numeric values in object code with the bytes in reverse sequence.
- DB items are used for processing half registers (AL, BL, etc.), DW for full registers (AX, BX, etc.), and DD for extended registers (EAX, EBX, etc.). Longer numeric items require special handling.

QUESTIONS

4–1. Distinguish between a compiler and an assembler.

4–2. What is a reserved word in assembler language? Give two examples.

4–3. What are the two types of identifiers?

4–4. Determine which of the following names are valid: (a) PC_AT; (b) $50; (c) @$_Z; (d) 34B7; (e) AX.

4–5. Distinguish between a directive and an instruction.

4–6. What commands cause the assembler (a) to print a heading at the top of a page of the program listing and (b) to eject to a new page?

4–7. What is the purpose of each of the three segments described in this chapter?

4–8. The format for the SEGMENT directive is

```
name SEGMENT align combine 'class'
```

Explain the purpose of (a) align; (b) combine; (c)'class'.

4–9. (a) What is the purpose of a procedure? (b) How do you define the beginning and the end of a procedure? (c) When would you define a procedure as FAR and when as NEAR?

4–10. Explain what particular END statements are concerned with ending (a) a program; (b) a procedure; (c) a segment.

4–11. Distinguish between the statement that ends an assembly and the statements that end execution.

4–12. Given the names STKSEG, DATSEG, and CDSEG for the stack, data segment, and code segment, respectively, code the required ASSUME.

4–13. Consider the instruction MOV AX,4C00H used with INT 21H. (a) What does the instruction perform? (b) What is the purpose of the 4C and the 00?

4–14. For the simplified segment directives, the .MODEL directive provides for TINY, SMALL, MEDIUM, COMPACT, and LARGE models. Under what circumstances would you use each model?

4–15. Give the lengths in bytes generated by the following data directives: (a) DD; (b) DW; (c) DT; (d) DQ; (e) DB.

4–16. Define a character string named TITLE1 containing the constant RGB Electronics.

4–17. Define the following numeric values in data items named FIELDA through FIELDE, respectively:

(a) A four-byte item containing the hex equivalent of decimal 215.

(b) A one-byte item containing the hex equivalent of decimal 35.

(c) A two-byte item containing an undefined value.

(d) A one-byte item containing the binary equivalent of decimal 25.

(e) A DW containing the consecutive values 17, 19, 21, 26, and 31.

4–18. Show the generated hex object code for (a) DB '28'; (b) DB 28.

4–19. Determine the assembled hex object code for (a) DB 28H; (b) DW 2845H; (c) DD 28733AH; (d) DQ 28733AH.

CHAPTER 5 —————————

Assembling, Linking, and Executing a Program

OBJECTIVE

To cover the steps in assembling, linking, and executing an assembly language program.

INTRODUCTION

This chapter explains the procedure for keying in an assembly language program and for assembling, linking, and executing it. The symbolic instructions that you code in assembly language are known as the *source program*. You use the assembler program to translate the source program into machine code, known as the *object program*. Finally, you use the linker program to complete the machine addressing for the object program, generating an *executable module*.

The sections on assembling explain how to request execution of the assembler program, which provides diagnostics (including any error messages) and generates the object program. Also explained are details of the assembler listing and, in general terms, how the assembler processes a source program.

The sections on linking explain how to request execution of the linker program so that you can generate an executable module. Also explained are details of the generated link map, as well as the diagnostics. Finally, a section explains how to request execution of the executable module.

PREPARING A PROGRAM FOR EXECUTION

Figure 4–2 illustrated only the source code for a program not yet in executable format. For keying in this program, you could use an editor program such as the one supplied with DOS. In the following examples of DOS commands, substitute the appropriate drive for your system. You can also gain a lot of productivity by loading your programs and files into a RAM disk. Call up your editor program, key in the statements for the program in Figure 4–2, and name the resulting file P05ASM1.ASM.

Although spacing is not important to the assembler, a program will be more readable if you keep the name, operation, operand, and comments consistently aligned on columns. Most editors have tab stops every eight positions to facilitate aligning columns.

Once you have entered all the statements for the program, check the code for accuracy. Most editors have a print facility, but if yours does not, turn on your printer, and request the DOS PRINT program:

```
PRINT n:P05ASM1.ASM [Enter]
```

As it stands, the program is just a text file that cannot execute—you must first assemble and link it.

1. The *assembly* step involves translating the source code into object code and generating an intermediate .OBJ (object) file, or module. (You have already seen examples of machine code and source code in earlier chapters.) One of the assembler's tasks is to calculate the offset for every data item in the data segment and every instruction in the code segment. The assembler also creates a header immediately ahead of the generated .OBJ module; part of the header contains information about incomplete addresses. The .OBJ module is not quite in executable form.
2. The *link* step involves converting the .OBJ module to an .EXE (executable) machine code module. One of the linker's tasks is to combine separately assembled programs into one executable module.
3. The last step is to *load* the program for execution. Since the loader knows where the program is about to load, it is able to complete any addresses indicated in the header that were left incomplete. The loader drops the header and creates a PSP immediately before the program loaded in memory.

Figure 5–1 provides a chart of the steps involved in assembling, linking, and executing a program.

ASSEMBLING A SOURCE PROGRAM

The Microsoft assembler program (up to version 5.x) is MASM.EXE, whereas the Borland Turbo program is TASM.EXE. Since version 6.0, Microsoft assembler normally uses the ML command, but also accepts MASM for compatibility with earlier versions.

You can key in the command to run MASM or TASM with a command line or by means of prompts. This section shows how to use the command line; see Appendix D for the prompt method. The general format for a command line to assemble a program is

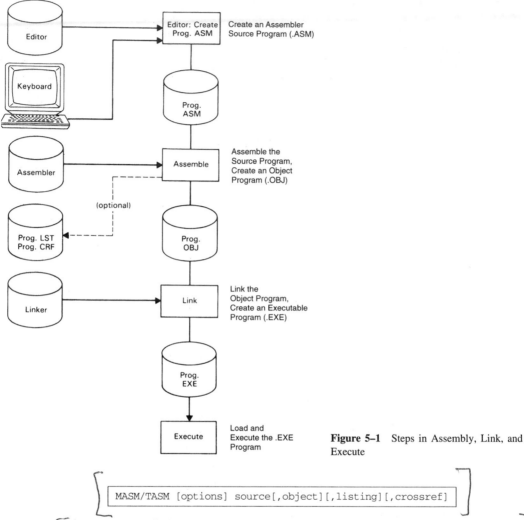

Figure 5–1   Steps in Assembly, Link, and Execute

```
MASM/TASM [options] source[,object][,listing][,crossref]
```

- *Options* provides for such features as setting levels of warning messages and is explained in Appendix D. Since the assembler's defaults are usually adequate, you'll seldom need to use options.
- *Source* identifies the name of the source program, such as P05ASM1. The assembler assumes the extension .ASM, so you need not enter it. You can also enter a disk drive number if you don't want to accept the current default drive.
- *Object* provides for a generated .OBJ file. The drive, subdirectory, and filename may be the same as or different from those in the source.
- *Listing* provides for a generated .LST file that contains both the source and object code. The drive, subdirectory, and filename may be the same as or different from those in the source.

- *Crossref* generates a cross-reference file containing the symbols used in the program, which you can use for a cross-reference listing. The extension is .CRF for MASM and .XRF for TASM. The drive, subdirectory, and filename may be the same as or different from those in the source.

You always enter the name of the source file, and you usually request an .OBJ file, which is required for linking a program into executable form. You'll probably often request .LST files, especially when you want to examine the generated machine code. A .CRF file is useful for very large programs where you want to see which instructions reference which data items. Also, the .CRF request causes the assembler to generate line numbers for statements in the .LST file to which the .CRF file refers. Later sections cover .LST and .CRF files in detail.

Example 1: Specify source file P05ASM1 on drive D, and generate object, listing, and cross-reference files. If a filename is to be the same as the one in the source, you need not repeat it; a reference to drive number is sufficient to indicate a request for a file:

```
MASM/TASM D:P05ASM1,D:,D:,D:
```

Example 2: Generate only an object file. In this case, you may omit the reference to the listing and cross-reference files and simply enter the command

```
MASM/TASM D:P05ASM1,D:
```

The assembler converts your source statements into machine code and displays any errors on the screen. Typical errors include a name that violates naming conventions, an operation that is spelled incorrectly (such as MOVE instead of MOV), and an operand containing a name that is not defined. There are about 100 error messages, explained in the assembler manual. Since there are many different assembler versions, we won't attempt to list the errors. The assembler attempts to correct some errors, but in any event, you should reload your editor, correct the .ASM source program, and reassemble it.

ASSEMBLER LISTING OF CONVENTIONAL SEGMENT DEFINITIONS

Figure 5–2 provides the listing that the assembler produced under the name P05ASM1.LST. The line width is 132 positions because of the PAGE entry. You can also print this listing if your printer can compress the print line. Many impact printers have a switch that will force compressed printing, or you could request your editor or word processor to print in compressed mode. Another way is to use the DOS MODE command; for 132 characters per inch and six lines per inch, turn on the printer, key in the command MODE LPT1:132,6, and request DOS PRINT.

Note at the top of the listing how the assembler has acted on the PAGE and TITLE directives. None of the directives, including SEGMENT, PROC, ASSUME, and END, generates machine code, since they are just messages to the assembler.

At the extreme left is the number for each line. The second column shows the hex addresses of data fields and instructions. The third column shows the translated machine code in hexadecimal format. To the right is the original source code.

```
P05ASM1 (EXE)  Move and add operations                       Page   1-1

   1                       page 60,132
   2              TITLE     P05ASM1 (EXE)  Move and add operations
   3              ; ------------------------------------------------
   4 0000         STACKSG   SEGMENT PARA STACK 'Stack'
   5 0000  0020[            DW      32 DUP(0)
   6        0000
   7           ]
   8
   9 0040         STACKSG   ENDS
  10              ; ------------------------------------------------
  11 0000         DATASG    SEGMENT PARA 'Data'
  12 0000  00FA   FLDA      DW      250
  13 0002  007D   FLDB      DW      125
  14 0004  0000   FLDC      DW      ?
  15 0006         DATASG    ENDS
  16              ; ------------------------------------------------
  17 0000         CODESG    SEGMENT PARA 'Code'
  18 0000         BEGIN     PROC    FAR
  19                        ASSUME  SS:STACKSG,DS:DATASG,CS:CODESG
  20 0000 B8 ---- R         MOV     AX,DATASG   ;Set address of DATASG
  21 0003 8E D8             MOV     DS,AX       ;   in DS register
  22
  23 0005 A1 0000 R         MOV     AX,FLDA     ;Move 0250 to AX
  24 0008 03 06 0002 R      ADD     AX,FLDB     ;Add  0125 to AX
  25 000C A3 0004 R         MOV     FLDC,AX     ;Store sum in FLDC
  26 000F B8 4C00           MOV     AX,4C00H    ;Exit to DOS
  27 0012 CD 21             INT     21H
  28 0014         BEGIN     ENDP                ;End of procedure
  29 0014         CODESG    ENDS                ;End of segment
  30                        END     BEGIN       ;End of program
```

```
Segments and Groups:
            N a m e              Length   Align    Combine   Class
CODESG . . . . . . . . . . . .   0014     PARA     NONE      'CODE'
DATASG . . . . . . . . . . . .   0006     PARA     NONE      'DATA'
STACKSG  . . . . . . . . . . .   0040     PARA     STACK     'STACK'

Symbols:
            N a m e              Type     Value    Attr
BEGIN  . . . . . . . . . . . .   F PROC   0000     CODESG    Length = 0014

FLDA . . . . . . . . . . . . .   L WORD   0000     DATASG
FLDB . . . . . . . . . . . . .   L WORD   0002     DATASG
FLDC . . . . . . . . . . . . .   L WORD   0004     DATASG

@CPU . . . . . . . . . . . . .   TEXT     0101h
@FILENAME  . . . . . . . . . .   TEXT     p05asm1
@VERSION . . . . . . . . . . .   TEXT     510

      27 Source  Lines
      27 Total   Lines
      15 Symbols
  0 Warning Errors
  0 Severe  Errors
```

Figure 5–2   Assembled Program with Conventional Segments

For each of the three segments, the SEGMENT directive notifies the assembler to align the segment on an address that is evenly divisible by hex 10—the statement itself generates no machine code. Theoretically, each segment address begins at offset location

0000. Actually, when the program begins execution, the segment is stored in memory according to an address that DOS loads in the segment register and is offset zero bytes from that address.

Note that the stack, data segment, and code segment are separate areas, each with its own offset value for data or instructions.

Stack Segment

The stack segment contains a DW (Define Word) directive that defines 32 words, each generating a zero value designated by (0). This definition of 32 words is a realistic size for a stack because a large program may require many interrupts for input/output and calls to subprograms, all involving use of the stack. The stack segment ends at offset 0040H, which is equivalent to decimal value 64 (32 words × 2 bytes).

If the stack size is too small to contain all the items pushed onto it, neither the assembler nor the linker warns you, and the executing program may crash in an unpredictable way.

Data Segment

The program defines a data segment, DATASG, containing three defined values, all in DW (Define Word) format. FLDA defines a word (two bytes) initialized with decimal value 250, which the assembler has translated to 00FAH (shown on the left). FLDB defines a word initialized with decimal value 125, assembled as 007DH. The actual storage values of these two constants are, respectively, FA00 and 7D00, which you can check with DEBUG.

FLDC is coded as a DW with ? in the operand to define a word with an uninitialized constant.

Code Segment

The program defines a code segment, CODESG, which contains the program's executable code, all in one procedure (PROC).

Three statements establish the addressability of the data segment:

```
            ASSUME SS:STACKSG,DS:DATASG,CS;CODESG

0000  B8 ---- R      MOV AX,DATASG

0003  8E D8          MOV DS,AX
```

- The ASSUME directive relates DATASG to the DS register. Note that the program does not require the ES register, but some programmers define it as a standard practice. ASSUME simply provides information to the assembler, which generates no machine code for it.
- The first MOV instruction "stores" DATASG in the AX register. Now, an instruction cannot actually store a segment in a register—the assembler simply recognizes an attempt to load the address of DATASG. Note the machine code to the left: B8 ——R. The four hyphens mean that at this point the assembler cannot determine the address of DATASG; the system determines this address only when the object program is linked and loaded for execution. Since the system loader may locate a program

anywhere in memory, the assembler leaves the address open and indicates the fact with an R; the DOS loader program is to replace (or relocate) the incomplete address with the actual one.

- The second MOV instruction moves the contents of the AX register to the DS register. Since there is no valid instruction for a direct move from memory to the DS register, you have to code two instructions to initialize the DS.

The DOS loader automatically initializes the SS and CS when it loads a program for execution, but it is your responsibility to initialize the DS, and the ES if required.

For the simplified segment directives, initialize the DS like this:

```
MOV   AX,@data
MOV   DS,AX
```

While all this business may seem unduly involved, at this point you really don't have to understand it. All programs in this book use a standard definition and initialization, and you simply have to reproduce this code for each of your programs. To this end, store a skeleton assembly program on disk, and for each new program that you want to create, COPY the skeleton program into a file with its correct name, and use your editor to complete the additional instructions.

The first instruction after initializing the DS register is MOV AX,FLDA, which begins at offset location 0005 and generates machine code A1 0000. The space between A1 (the operation) and 0000 (the operand) is only for readability. The next instruction is ADD AX,FLDB, which begins at offset location 0008 and generates four bytes of machine code. In this example, machine instructions are two, three, or four bytes in length.

The last statement in the program, END, contains the operand BEGIN, which relates to the name of the PROC at offset 0000. This is the location in the code segment where the program loader is to transfer control for execution.

Following the program listing are a Segments and Groups table and a Symbols table.

Segments and Groups Table

The first table at the end of the assembled listing shows any defined segments and groups. Note that segments are not listed in the same sequence as they are coded; the assembler lists them in alphabetic sequence by name. (This program contains no groups, which is a later topic.) The table provides the length in bytes of each segment, the alignment (both are paragraphs), the combine type, and the class. The assembler has converted the class names to uppercase.

Symbols Table

The second table provides the names of data fields in the data segment (FLDA, FLDB, and FLDC) and the labels applied to instructions in the code segment. For BEGIN (the only entry in the example), Type F PROC means far procedure. The Value column gives the offset for the beginning of the segment for names, labels, and procedures. The column headed Attr (for attribute) provides the segment in which the item is defined.

Appendix D explains all the options for these tables. To cause the assembler to omit the tables, code a /N option following the MASM command, that is, MASM /N.

As for the last three entries, @CPU identifies the processor, @FILENAME gives the name of the program, and @VERSION shows the assembler version in the form n.nn.

ASSEMBLER LISTING OF SIMPLIFIED SEGMENT DIRECTIVES

Figure 4–3 showed how to code a program using the simplified segment directives. Figure 5–3 provides the assembled listing of that program. The first part of the symbol table under "Segments and Groups" shows the three segments renamed by the assembler and listed alphabetically:

- _DATA, with a length of 6 bytes
- STACK, with a length of 40H (64 bytes)
- _TEXT, for the code segment, with a length of 14H (20 bytes)

Under the heading "Symbols" are names defined in the program or default names. The simplified segment directives provide a number of predefined equates, which begin with an @ symbol and which you are free to reference in a program. As well as @data, they are:

@CODE	Equated to the name of the code segment, _TEXT
@CODESIZE	Set to zero for the small and medium models
@CPU	Model of processor
@DATASIZE	Set to zero for the small and medium models
@FILENAME	Name of the program
@VERSION	Version of assembler (n.nn)

You may use @code and @data in ASSUME and executable statements, such as MOV AX,@data.

TWO-PASS ASSEMBLER

Many assemblers make two passes through a source program in order to resolve forward references to addresses not yet encountered in the program. During pass 1, the assembler reads the entire source program and constructs a symbol table of names and labels used in the program, that is, names of data fields and program labels and their relative locations (offsets) within the segment. You can see such a symbol table immediately following the assembled program in Figure 5–3, where the offsets for FLDA, FLDB, and FLDC are 0000, 0002, and 0004 bytes, respectively. Although the program defines no instruction labels, they would appear in the code segment with their own offsets. Pass 1 determines the amount of code to be generated for each instruction. MASM starts generating object code in pass 1, whereas TASM does it in pass 2.

During pass 2, the assembler uses the symbol table that it constructed in pass 1. Now that it "knows" the length and relative position of each data field and instruction, it can

```
P05ASM2 (EXE)  Move and add operations                    Page    1-1

                              page    60,132
                    TITLE     P05ASM2 (EXE)  Move and add operations
                    ;----------------------------------------------------
                              .MODEL  SMALL
                              .STACK  64              ;Define stack
                              .DATA                   ;Define data
0000  00FA          FLDA      DW      250
0002  007D          FLDB      DW      125
0004  0000          FLDC      DW      ?
                    ;----------------------------------------------------
                              .CODE                   ;Define code segment
0000                BEGIN     PROC    FAR
0000  B8 ---- R               MOV     AX,@data        ;Set address of DATASG
0003  8E D8                   MOV     DS,AX           ;   in DS register

0005  A1 0000 R               MOV     AX,FLDA         ;Move 0250 to AX
0008  03 06 0002 R            ADD     AX,FLDB         ;Add  0125 to AX
000C  A3 0004 R               MOV     FLDC,AX         ;Store sum in FLDC

000F  B8 4C00                 MOV     AX,4C00H        ;Exit to DOS
0012  CD 21                   INT     21H
0014                BEGIN     ENDP                    ;End of procedure
                              END     BEGIN           ;End of program
```

```
Segments and Groups:
                  N a m e         Length    Align     Combine Class
DGROUP . . . . . . . . . . . .GROUP
  _DATA  . . . . . . . . . .0006      WORD      PUBLIC    'DATA'
  STACK  . . . . . . . . . .0040      PARA      STACK     'STACK'
_TEXT  . . . . . . . . . . .0014      WORD      PUBLIC    'CODE'

Symbols:
                  N a m e         Type      Value     Attr
BEGIN  . . . . . . . . . . . .F PROC     0000      _TEXT     Length = 0014

FLDA . . . . . . . . . . . .L WORD    0000      _DATA
FLDB . . . . . . . . . . . .L WORD    0002      _DATA
FLDC . . . . . . . . . . . .L WORD    0004      _DATA

@CODE  . . . . . . . . . . .TEXT      _TEXT
@CODESIZE  . . . . . . . . .TEXT      0
@CPU . . . . . . . . . . . .TEXT      0101h
@DATASIZE  . . . . . . . . .TEXT      0
@FILENAME  . . . . . . . . .TEXT      p05asm2

        0 Warning Errors
        0 Severe  Errors
```

Figure 5–3   Assembled Program with Simplified Segment Directives

complete the object code for each instruction. It then produces, if requested, the various object (.OBJ), list (.LST), and cross-reference (.REF) files.

A potential problem in pass 1 is *forward references*: A jump instruction in the code segment may reference a label, but the assembler has not yet encountered its definition. MASM constructs object code based on what it supposes is the length of each generated machine language instruction. If there are any differences between pass 1 and pass 2 concerning instruction lengths, MASM issues an error message "Phase error between passes." Such errors are relatively rare, and if one appears, you'll have to trace its cause and correct it.

Since version 6.0, MASM does a more effective job of handling instruction lengths, taking as many passes through the file as necessary.

LINKING AN OBJECT PROGRAM

Once your program is free of error messages, your next step is to link the object module, P05ASM1.OBJ, that was produced by the assembler and that contains only machine code. The linker performs the following functions:

- Combines, if requested, more than one separately assembled module into one executable program, such as two or more assembly programs or an assembly program with a C program.
- Generates an .EXE module and initializes it with special instructions to facilitate its subsequent loading for execution.

Once you have linked one or more .OBJ modules into an .EXE module, you may execute the .EXE module any number of times. But whenever you need to make a change in the program, you must correct the source program, assemble it into another .OBJ module, and link the .OBJ module into an .EXE module. Even if initially these steps are not entirely clear, you will find that with only a little experience, they become automatic.

You may convert many .EXE programs to .COM programs. See Chapter 7 for details.

The linker version for Microsoft is LINK, whereas the Borland version is TLINK. You can key in LINK or TLINK with a command line or by means of prompts. (Since MASM 6.0, the ML command provides for both assembling and linking.) This section shows how to link using a command line; see Appendix D for using prompts. The command line for linking is

```
LINK/TLINK objfile,exefile[,mapfile][,libraryfile]
```

- *Objfile* identifies the object file generated by the assembler. The linker assumes the extension .OBJ, so you need not enter it. The drive, subdirectory, and filename may be the same as or different from those in the source.
- *Exefile* provides for generating an .EXE file. The drive, subdirectory, and filename may be the same as or different from those in the source.
- *Mapfile* provides for generating a file with an extension .MAP that indicates the relative location and size of each segment and any errors that LINK has found. A typical error is the failure to define a stack segment. Entering CON (for console) tells the linker to display the map on the screen (instead of writing it on disk) so that you can view the map immediately for errors.
- *Libraryfile* provides for the libraries option, which you don't need at this early stage of assembly language programming.

This example links the object file P05ASM1.OBJ that was generated by the earlier assembly. The linker is to write the .EXE file on drive D, display the map, and ignore the library option:

```
LINK D:P05ASM1,D:,CON
```

If the filename is to be the same as that of the source, you need not repeat it: the reference to drive number is sufficient to indicate a request for the file. Appendix D supplies other options.

Link Map for the First Program

For the program P05ASM1, LINK produced this map:

START	STOP	LENGTH	NAME	CLASS
00000H	0003FH	0040H	STACKSG	STACK
00040H	00045H	0006H	DATASG	DATA
00050H	00063H	0014H	CODESG	CODE

Program entry point at 0005:0000

- The stack is the first segment and begins at offset zero bytes from the start of the program. Since it is defined as 32 words, it is 64 bytes long, as its length (40H) indicates.
- The data segment begins at the next paragraph boundary, offset 40H.
- The code segment begins at the next paragraph boundary, offset 50H. Some assemblers rearrange the segments into alphabetical order.
- Program entry point 0005:0000, which is in the form "relative (not absolute) segment:offset," refers to the address of the first executable instruction. In effect, the relative starting address is at segment 5[0], offset 0 bytes, which corresponds to the segment boundary at 50H. The program loader uses this value when it loads the program into memory for excution.

At this stage, the only error that you are likely to encounter is entering wrong filenames. The solution is to restart with the link command.

Link Map for the Second Program

The link map for the second program, which uses simplified segment directives, shows a somewhat different setup from that of the previous program. First, the assembler has physically rearranged the segments into alphabetical order, and second, succeeding segments are aligned on word (not paragraph) boundaries:

START	STOP	LENGTH	NAME	CLASS
00000H	00013H	0014H	_TEXT	CODE
00014H	00019H	0006H	_DATA	DATA
00020H	0005FH	0040H	STACK	STACK

Program entry point at 0000:0000

- The code segment is now the first segment and begins at offset zero bytes from the start of the program.
- The data segment begins at the next word boundary, offset 14H.
- The stack begins at the next word boundary, offset 20H.
- The program entry point is now 0000:0000, which means that the relative location of the code segment begins at segment 0, offset 0.

EXECUTING A PROGRAM

Having assembled and linked a program, you can now (at last!) execute it. If the .EXE file is in the default drive, you could cause DOS to load it for execution by entering

```
        P05ASM1.EXE or P05ASM1
```

If you omit typing the file extension, DOS assumes it is .EXE (or .COM). However, since this program produces no visible output, it is suggested that you run it under DEBUG instead and step through its execution with trace commands. Key in the following, including the extension .EXE:

```
        DEBUG D:P05ASM1.EXE
```

DEBUG loads the .EXE program module and displays its hyphen prompt. To view the stack segment, key in

```
            D SS:0
```

The stack contains all zeros because it was initialized that way. To view the data segment, key in

```
            D DS:0
```

The operation displays the three data items as FA 00 7D 00 00 00, with the bytes for each word in reverse sequence. To view the code segment, key in

```
            D CS:0
```

Compare the displayed machine code with that of code segment in the assembled listing:

```
        B8----8ED8A10000 ...
```

In this case, the assembled listing does not accurately show the machine code, since the assembler did not know the address for the operand of the first instruction. You can now determine this address by examining the displayed code.

Key in R to view the registers, and trace through program execution with successive T commands. As you step through the program, note the contents of the registers. When you reach the last instruction, you can use L to reload and rerun the program or Q to quit the DEBUG session.

CROSS-REFERENCE LISTING

The assembler generates an optional .CRF or .XRF file that you can use to produce a *cross-reference listing* of a program's identifiers, or symbols. However, you still have to convert this file to a properly sorted cross-reference file. A program on the assembler disk performs this function: CREF for Microsoft or TCREF for Borland. You can key in CREF or TCREF with a command line or by means of prompts. This section uses a command line; see Appendix D for using prompts. The command to convert the cross-reference file is

```
CREF/TCREF xreffile,reffile
```

- *xreffile* identifies the cross-reference file generated by the assembler. The program assumes the extension, so you need not enter it. You can also enter a disk drive number.
- *reffile* provides for generating a .REF file. The drive, subdirectory, and filename may be the same as or different from those in the source.

The Listing

Figure 5–4 contains the cross-reference listing produced by CREF for the program in Figure 5–2. The symbols in the first column are in alphabetic order. The numbers in the second column, shown as n#, indicate the lines in the .LST file where the symbols are defined. Numbers to the right of this column are line numbers showing where the symbol is referenced. For example, CODESG is defined in line 17 and is referenced in lines 19 and 29. FLDC is defined in line 14 and referenced in line 25+, where the "+" means its value is modified.

```
P04ASM1 (EXE)   Move and add operations

Symbol Cross-Reference   (# definition, + modification)

@CPU . . . . . . . . . . . . .   1#
@VERSION . . . . . . . . . . .   1#

BEGIN. . . . . . . . . . . . . 18#      28       30

CODE . . . . . . . . . . . . . 17
CODESG . . . . . . . . . . . . 17#      19       29

DATA . . . . . . . . . . . . . 11
DATASG . . . . . . . . . . . . 11#      15       19       20

FLDA . . . . . . . . . . . . . 12#      23
FLDB . . . . . . . . . . . . . 13#      24
FLDC . . . . . . . . . . . . . 14#      25+

STACK. . . . . . . . . . . . .  4
STACKSG. . . . . . . . . . . .  4#       9       19

 12 Symbols
```

Figure 5–4   Cross-Reference Table

Generated Files

Assembling a number of programs may use a lot of disk space. You can safely delete .OBJ, .CRF, and .LST files. Keep .ASM source programs in case of further changes and .EXE files for executing the programs.

ERROR DIAGNOSTICS

The assembler provides diagnostics for any programming errors that violate its rules. The program in Figure 5–5 is the same as the one in Figure 5–2, except that it has a number of intentional errors inserted for illustrative purposes. The program was run under MASM; TASM generates a similar error listing. Here are the errors, as coded:

LINE	EXPLANATION
14	FLDC requires an operand.
19	ASSUME does not relate the SS to STACKSG, although the assembler has not detected this omission.
20	DATSEG should be spelled DATASG.

```
 1                              page 60,132
 2                      TITLE   P05ASM3 (EXE)  Illustrate assembly errors
 3                      ; -------------------------------------------------
 4 0000                STACKSG SEGMENT PARA STACK 'Stack'
 5 0000    0020[       DW      32 DUP(0)
 6            0000
 7                 ]
 8
 9 0040                STACKSG ENDS
10                      ; -------------------------------------------------
11 0000                DATASG  SEGMENT PARA 'Data'
12 0000    00FA        FLDA    DW      250
13 0002    007D        FLDB    DW      125
14 0004                FLDC    DW
p05asm3.ASM(11): error A2027: Operand expected
15 0004                DATASG  ENDS
16                      ; -------------------------------------------------
17 0000                CODESG  SEGMENT PARA 'Code'
18 0000                BEGIN   PROC    FAR
19                              ASSUME  CS:CODESG,DS:DATASG
20 0000    A1 0000 U           MOV     AX,DATSEG       ;Address of DATASG
p05asm3.ASM(17): error A2009: Symbol not defined: DATSEG
21 0003    8B D0               MOV     DX,AX           ;  in DS register
22
23                              MOV     AS,FLDA         ;Move 0250 to AX
p05asm3.ASM(20): error A2009: Symbol not defined: AS
24 0005    03 06 0002 R        ADD     AX,FLDB         ;Add   0125 to AX
25 0009    A3 0000 U           MOV     FLDD,AX         ;Store sum in FLDC
p05asm3.ASM(22): error A2009: Symbol not defined: FLDD
26 000C    B8 4C00             MOV     AX,4C00H        ;Exit to DOS
27 000F    CD 21               INT     21H
28 0011                BEGIN   ENDP
p05asm3.ASM(25): error A2006: Phase error between passes
29 0011                CODESG  ENDS
30                              END     BEGIN
```

Figure 5–5   Assembly Diagnostics

21   DX should be coded as DS, although the assembler does not know that this is an error.
23   AS should be coded as AX.
25   FLDD should be coded as FLDC.
28   Correcting the other errors will cause this diagnostic to disappear.

The last error message, "Phase error between passes," occurs when addresses generated in pass 1 of a two-pass assembler differ from those of pass 2. To isolate an obscure error, use the /D option for MASM to list both the pass 1 and the pass 2 files, and compare the offset addresses.

KEY POINTS

- Both MASM and TASM provide a command line for assembling, including (at least) the name of the source program. MASM also provides prompts for entering options.
- The assembler converts a source program to an .OBJ file and generates optional listing and cross-reference files.
- The Segments and Groups table following an assembler listing shows any segments and groups defined in the program. The Symbols table shows all symbols (data names and instruction labels).
- The linker (LINK or TLINK) converts an .OBJ file to an executable .EXE file. You may link using a command line or by means of prompts (LINK only).
- The simplified segment directives generate the names _DATA for the data segment, STACK for the stack segment, and _TEXT for the code segment. They also generate a number of predefined equates.
- The CREF (or TCREF) program produces a useful cross-reference listing.

QUESTIONS

5–1. Code the command line to assemble a source program named DISCOUNT.ASM with files .LST, .OBJ, and .CRF. Assume that the source program and assembler are in drive C.

5–2. Code the LINK or TLINK command line to link DISCOUNT.OBJ from Question 5–1.

5–3. Code the commands for DISCOUNT.EXE from Question 5–2 for the following: (a) execution through DEBUG; (b) direct execution from DOS.

5–4. Give the purpose of each of the following files: (a) file.ASM; (b) file.CRF; (c) file.LST; (d) file.EXE; (e) file.OBJ; (f) file.MAP.

5–5. Code the two instructions to initialize the DS register. Assume that the name of the data segment is DATSEG.

5–6. Write an assembly program using conventional segment definitions for the following: (a) Move immediate value hex 40 to the AL register; (b) shift the AL contents one bit left (code SHL AL,1); (c) move immediate value hex 22 to the BL; (d) multiply AL by BL (code MUL BL). Remember the instructions required to end program execution. The program does not need to define or initialize the data segment. Be sure to COPY a skeleton program and use your editor to develop the program. Assemble and link. Use DEBUG to trace and to check the code segment and registers.

5–7. Revise the program in Question 5–6 for simplified segment directives. Assemble and link it, and compare the object code, symbol tables, and link map with those of the original program.

5–8. Add a data segment to the program in Question 5–6 for the following:

- Define a one-byte item (DB) named FIELDA containing hex 40 and another named FIELDB containing hex 22.
- Define a two-byte item (DW) named FIELDC with no constant.
- Move the contents of FIELDA to the AL register, and shift left one bit.
- Multiply the AL by FIELDB (code MUL FIELDB).
- Move the product in the AX to FIELDC.

Assemble, link, and use DEBUG to test the program.

5–9. Revise the program in Question 5–8 for simplified segment directives. Assemble and link it, and compare the object code, symbol tables, and link map with those of the original program.

CHAPTER 6 ───────────────────────

Processor Instructions and Addressing

┌───┐
│   │
│   Objective   │
│   │
│ To provide the basics of the assembly language instruc- │
│ tion set and the requirements for addressing data. │
│   │
└───┘

INTRODUCTION

This chapter introduces the processor instruction set, and then describes the basic addressing formats that are used throughout the rest of the book. The instructions formally covered in this chapter are MOV, MOVSX, MOVZX, XCHNG, LEA, INC, DEC, and INT. You can also define a constant in an instruction operand as an immediate value.

Finally, the chapter explains address alignment and the segment override prefix.

THE PROCESSOR INSTRUCTION SET

The following is a list of the instructions for the 8086 processor family, arranged by category. Although the list seems formidable, many of the instructions are rarely needed.

Arithmetic

- ADC: Add with Carry
- ADD: Add Binary Numbers

- DEC: Decrement by 1
- DIV: Unsigned Divide
- IDIV: Signed (Integer) Divide
- IMUL: Signed (Integer) Multiply
- INC: Increment by 1
- MUL: Unsigned Multiply
- NEG: Negate
- SBB: Subtract with Borrow
- SUB: Subtract Binary Values

ASCII-BCD Conversion

- AAA: ASCII Adjust After Addition
- AAD: ASCII Adjust Before Division
- AAM: ASCII Adjust After Multiplication
- AAS: ASCII Adjust After Subtraction
- DAA: Decimal Adjust After Addition
- DAS: Decimal Adjust After Subtraction

Bit Shifting

- RCL: Rotate Left Through Carry
- RCR: Rotate Right Through Carry
- ROL: Rotate Left
- ROR: Rotate Right
- SAL: Shift Algebraic Left
- SAR: Shift Algebraic Right
- SHL: Shift Logical Left
- SHR: Shift Logical Right
- SHLD/SHRD: Shift Double Precision (80386 and later)

Comparison

- BSF/BSR: Bit Scan (80386 and later)
- BT/BTC/BTR/BTS: Bit Test (80386 and later)
- CMP: Compare
- CMPS: Compare String
- TEST: Test Bits

Data Transfer

- LDS: Load Data Segment Register
- LEA: Load Effective Address

- LES: Load Extra Segment Register
- LODS: Load String
- LSS: Load Stack Segment Register
- MOV: Move Data
- MOVS: Move String
- MOVSX: Move With Sign-Extend
- MOVZX: Move With Zero-Extend
- STOS: Store String
- XCHG: Exchange
- XLAT: Translate

Flag Operations

- CLC: Clear Carry Flag
- CLD: Clear Direction Flag
- CLI: Clear Interrupt Flag
- CMC: Complement Carry Flag
- LAHF: Load AH from Flags
- POPF: Pop Flags off Stack
- PUSHF: Push Flags onto Stack
- SAHF: Store Contents of AH in Flags
- STC: Set Carry Flag
- STD: Set Direction Flag
- STI: Set Interrupt Flag

Input/Output

- IN: Input Byte or Word
- OUT: Output Byte or Word

Logical Operations

- AND: Logical AND
- NOT: Logical NOT
- OR: Logical OR
- XOR: Exclusive OR

Looping

- LOOP: Loop until Complete
- LOOPE/LOOPZ: Loop While Equal or Loop While Zero
- LOOPNE/LOOPNZ: Loop While Not Equal or Loop While Not Zero

Processor Control

- ESC: Escape
- HLT: Enter Halt State
- LOCK: Lock Bus
- NOP: No Operation
- WAIT: Put Processor in Wait State

Stack Operations

- POP: Pop Word off Stack
- POPA: Pop All General Registers (80286 and later)
- PUSH: Push onto Stack
- PUSHA: Push All General Registers (80286 and later)

String Operations

- CMPS: Compare String
- LODS: Load String
- MOVS: Move String
- REP: Repeat String
- REPE/REPZ: Repeat While Equal or Repeat While Zero
- REPNE/REPNZ: Repeat While Not Equal or Repeat While Not Zero
- SCAS: Scan String
- STOS: Store String

Transfer (Conditional)

- INTO: Interrupt on Overflow
- JA/JNBE: Jump If Above or Jump If Not Below or Equal
- JAE/JNB: Jump If Above or Equal or Jump If Not Below
- JB/JNAE: Jump If Below or Jump If Not Above or Equal
- JBE/JNA: Jump If Below or Equal or Jump If Not Above
- JC/JNC: Jump If Carry or Jump If No Carry
- JCXZ: Jump If CX is Zero
- JE/JZ: Jump If Equal or Jump If Zero
- JG/JNLE: Jump If Greater or Jump If Not Less or Equal
- JGE/JNL: Jump If Greater or Equal or Jump If Not Less
- JL/JNGE: Jump If Less or Jump If Not Greater or Equal
- JLE/JNG: Jump If Less or Equal or Jump If Not Greater
- JNE/JNZ: Jump If Not Equal or Jump If Not Zero

- JNP/JPO: Jump If No Parity or Jump If Parity Odd
- JO/JNO: Jump If Overflow or Jump If No Overflow
- JP/JPE: Jump If Parity or Jump If Parity Even
- JS/JNS: Jump If Sign or Jump If No Sign

Transfer (Unconditional)

- CALL: Call a Procedure
- INT: Interrupt
- IRET: Interrupt Return
- JMP: Unconditional Jump
- RET: Return
- RETN/RETF: Return Near or Return Far

Type Conversion

- CBW: Convert Byte to Word
- CDQ: Convert Doubleword to Quadword (80386 and later)
- CWD: Convert Word to Doubleword
- CWDE: Convert Word to Extended Doubleword (80386 and later)

OPERANDS

An operand provides a source of data for an instruction. Some instructions, such as CLC and RET, do not require an operand, whereas other instructions may have one or two operands. Where there are two operands, the second operand is the source, which contains either the data to be delivered (immediate) or the address (of a register or in memory) of the data. The source data is unchanged by the operation. The first operand is the destination, which contains data in a register or in memory and which is to be processed.

| operation | operand1,operand2 |

Let's now examine how the operand can affect the addressing of data.

Register Operands

For this type, the register provides the name of any one of the 8-, 16-, or 32-bit registers. Depending on the instruction, the register may be coded in the first operand, the second operand, or both:

```
        WORDX   DW   ?

          . . .

        MOV  CX,WORDX    ;Register in first operand

        MOV  WORDX,BX    ;Register in second operand

        MOV  CL,AH       ;Registers in both operands
```

Processing data between registers is the fastest type of operation, since there is no reference to memory.

Immediate Operands

In immediate format, the second operand contains a constant value or an expression. The destination field in the first operand defines the length of the data and may be a register or a memory location. Here are some examples:

```
SAVE    DB    ?

        . . .

ADD     CX,12    ;Add 12 to CX

MOV     SAVE,25  ;Move 25 to SAVE
```

A later section discusses immediate operands in more detail.

Direct Memory Operands

In this format, one of the operands references a memory location, and the other operand references a register. Note that there are no instructions that allow both operands to address memory. The DS register is the default register for addressing data in memory. Here are some examples:

```
WORD1   DW    0
BYTE1   DB    0

        . . .

MOV   AX,WORD1        Load WORD1 into AX

ADD   BYTE1,CL        ;Add CL to BYTE1

MOV   BX,DS:[38B0H]   ;Move word from memory at offset 38B0H

INC   BYTE PTR [2F0H] ;Increment byte at offset 2F0H
```

The last two examples use square brackets as *index specifiers* to indicate a reference to memory. (The offset is combined with the address in the DS.) The omission of square brackets, as in MOV BX,38B0H, indicates an immediate value—note the significant difference.

The last example increments the byte in memory at offset 2F0H (the offset combined with the DS address). Since the operand indicates only a starting memory location, we need the BYTE PTR modifier here to define the length.

In the following, a data item acts as an offset address in an instruction operand:

```
TABLEX   DB    25 DUP(?)

         . . .

MOV   AL,TABLEX[4]   ;Get byte 4 from TABLEX
MOV   AL,TABLEX+4    ;Same operation
```

The first MOV uses an index specifier to access the fourth byte from TABLEX. The second MOV uses a plus operator for exactly the same effect.

Indirect Memory Operands

Indirect addressing is a sophisticated technique that makes use of the computer's capability for segment:offset addressing. The registers used for this purpose are BX, DI, SI, and BP, coded within square brackets as an index operator. The BX, DI, and SI are associated with the DS register as DS:BX, DS:DI, and DS:SI, for processing data in the data segment. The BP is associated with the SS register as SS:BP, for handling data in the stack, which we'll do in Chapter 23 when calling subprograms and passing parameters.

When the first operand contains an indirect address, the second references a register or immediate value; when the second operand contains an indirect address, the first references a register. An indirect address such as [BX] tells the assembler that the memory address to use will be in the BX register when the program subsequently executes.

In the following example, the first MOV initializes the BX with the offset address of DATAFLD. The second MOV uses the address in the BX to store zero in the memory location to which it points, in this case, DATAFLD:

```
DATAFLD   DB    ?

    . . .

    MOV   BX,OFFSET DATAFLD     ;Load BX with offset

    MOV   [BX],0                ;Move 0 to DATAFLD
```

The effect of the two MOVs is the same as coding MOV DATAFLD,0, although the uses for indexed addressing are usually not so trivial. The following related instruction moves zero to a location two bytes immediately following DATAFLD:

```
    MOV   [BX+2],0         ;Move 0 to DATAFLD+2
```

You may also combine registers in an indirect address. Thus [BX+SI] means the address in BX plus the address in the SI.

Note that any reference in square brackets to the BX, DI, SI, or BP register implies an indirect operand, and the system treats the contents of the register as an offset address. Here are a few more examples:

```
    MOV   BL,[BX]            ;DS:BX

    SUB   BYTE PTR [DI],[SI] ;DS:DI and DS:SI

    MOV   [BP],AL            ;SS:BP
```

Address Displacement.   This method uses an address displacement for an operand. The following code moves the contents of the CL to TABLEX (a 26-byte table); exactly where in TABLEX is determined by the contents of the DI when the program is executing:

```
              TABLEX    DB     25 DUP(?)

                         ...

              MOV    TABLEX[DI],CL
```

Indexing on 80386 and Later Processors.   These processors allow an address to be generated from any combination of one or more general registers, an offset, and a scaling factor (1, 2, 4, or 8) associated with the contents of one of the registers. For example, the instruction

```
              MOV EBX,[ECX*2+ESP+4]
```

moves an address into the EBX that consists of the contents of (the ECX times 2) plus the contents of (the ESP plus 4).

THE MOV INSTRUCTION

The MOV instruction transfers (that is, copies) data referenced by the address of the second operand to the address of the first operand. The sending field is unchanged. The operands that reference memory or registers must agree in size (e.g., both must be bytes, both must be words, or both must be doublewords). The general format for MOV is

```
   [label:] | MOV | {register/memory},{register/memory/immediate}
```

Here are four examples of valid MOV operations by category, given the following data items:

```
              BYTEVAL   DB    ?

              WORDVAL   DW    ?
```

1. Immediate Moves

```
        MOV   AX,25            ;Immediate-to-register

        MOV   BYTEVAL,25       ;Immediate-to-memory, direct

        MOV   WORDVAL[BX],25   ;Immediate-to-memory, indirect
```

2. Register Moves

```
        MOV   EAX,ECX          ;Register-to-register

        MOV   DS,AX            ;Register-to-segment register

        MOV   BYTEVAL,BH       ;Register-to-memory, direct

        MOV   [SI],AX          ;Register-to-memory, indirect
```

3. Direct Memory Moves

```
MOV   BH,BYTEVAL            ;Memory-to-register, direct

MOV   AX,WORDVAL[BX]        ;Memory-to-register, indirect
```

4. Segment Register Moves

```
MOV   AX,DS                 ;Segment register-to-register

MOV   WORDVAL,DS            ;Segment register-to-memory
```

You can move to a register a byte (MOV AH,BYTEVAL), a word (MOV AX,WORDVAL), or a doubleword (MOV EAX,DWORDVAL). The operand affects only the portion of the referenced register; for example, moving a byte to the AH does not affect the AL.

MOV operations that are not allowed are memory-to-memory (keep that one in mind), immediate-to-segment register, and segment register-to-segment register. To handle these operations, you have to code more than one instruction.

MOVE-AND-FILL INSTRUCTIONS

A limitation of the MOV instruction is that the destination must be the same length as the source, such as byte to byte and word to word. On the 80386 and later processors, the MOVSX and MOVZX (move and fill) instructions facilitate transferring data from a byte or word source to a word or doubleword destination. Here is the general format for MOVSX and MOVZX:

```
[label]   MOVSX/MOVZX   {register/memory},{register/memory/immediate}
```

MOVSX, for use with signed arithmetic values, moves a byte or word to a word or doubleword destination and fills the sign bit (the leftmost bit of the source) into leftmost bits of the destination. MOVZX, for use with unsigned numeric values, moves a byte or word to a word or doubleword destination and fills zero bits into leftmost bits of the destination. As an example, consider moving a byte containing 1011 0000 to a word; the result in the destination word depends on the choice of instruction:

```
MOVSX:   1111 1111 1011 0000

MOVZX:   0000 0000 1011 0000
```

Here are some examples of using MOVSX and MOVZX:

```
BYTEVAL   DB    ?

WORDVAL   DW    ?

          ...

MOVSX AX,BYTEVAL      ;Byte to word
```

```
MOVSX EAX,WORDVAL     Word to doubleword

MOVZX WORDVAL,AH      ;Byte to word

MOVZX EAX,WORDVAL     ;Word to doubleword
```

Chapters 8 and 13 cover signed and unsigned data in detail.

IMMEDIATE OPERANDS

In the following example of an immediate operand, the instruction

```
MOV  AX,0123H
```

moves the immediate constant 0123H to the AX register. The three-byte object code for this instruction is B82301, where B8 means "move an immediate value to the AX register" and the following two bytes contain the value itself (2301H, in reverse-byte sequence). Many instructions provide for two operands; the first operand may be a register or memory location, and the second operand may be an immediate constant.

The use of an immediate operand provides more efficient processing than defining a numeric constant in the data segment and referencing it in the operand of the MOV, as, for example, in the following:

```
Data segment:   AMT1  DW   0123H      ;Define AMT1 as word

                      ...

Code segment    MOV AX,AMT1    ;Move AMT1 to AX
```

Length of Immediate Operands

The length of an immediate constant cannot exceed the length defined by the first operand. In the following invalid example, the immediate operand is two bytes, but the AL register is only one byte:

```
MOV  AL,0123H      ;Invalid length
```

However, if an immediate operand is shorter than a receiving operand, as in

```
ADD  AX,25H      ;Valid length
```

the assembler expands the immediate operand to two bytes, 0025H, and stores the object code as 2500H.

The 80386 and later processors permit four-byte (doubleword) immediate operands, such as in

```
MOV  EAX,12345678H      ;Move doubleword
```

Immediate Formats

An immediate constant may be any valid defined format. Here are some examples:

```
            PAGE   60,132
    TITLE   P06IMMED (EXE)   Example of immediate operands
    ;             (Coded for assembly only, NOT for execution)
            .MODEL SMALL
            .STACK 64                ;Define stack
            .DATA                    ;Define data
    FLDA    DB      ?
    FLDB    DW      ?
    .386
            .CODE
    BEGIN   PROC    FAR
            MOV     AX,275           ;Move immediate
            ADD     AX,125           ;Add immediate
            SUB     AX,200           ;Subtract immediate
            MOV     EBX,0            ;Move immediate (80386)
            ADD     BX,20H           ;Add immediate (hex)
    BEGIN   ENDP
            END
```

Figure 6–1   Immediate Operations

```
Hexadecimal:  0123H

Decimal:      291 (which the assembler converts to 0123H)

Binary:       100100011B (which converts to 0123H)
```

MOV, ADD, and SUB are three of many instructions that allow immediate operands. Figure 6–1 gives examples of these instructions. The .386 directive allows the assembler to recognize the reference to the EBX register. You don't need an 80386 or later processor to assemble this statement, but you do need one to execute it. Since the example is not intended for execution, it does not define a stack or initialize the DS register.

Processing items longer than the capacity of a register involves additional coding, covered in later chapters.

THE XCHG INSTRUCTION

The XCHG instruction performs another type of data transfer, but rather than copy the data from one location to another, XCHG swaps the two data items. The general format for XCHG is

```
[label:]  |  XCHG  |  {register/memory}, {register/immediate}
```

Valid XCHG operations involve exchanging data between two registers and between a register and memory. Here are examples:

```
WORDX   DW   ?

        ...

        XCHG AL,AH      ;Exchange the contents of two registers

        XCHG AX,WORDX   ;Exchange the contents of register and memory
```

THE LEA INSTRUCTION

The LEA instruction is useful for initializing a register with an offset address. In fact, a more descriptive name for this instruction would be "Load Offset Address." The general format for LEA is

```
[label:]   LEA   register,memory
```

A common use for LEA is to initialize an offset in the BX, DI, or SI register for indexing an address in memory. We'll be doing a lot of that throughout this book. Here's an example:

```
DATABLK DB   20  DUP  (?)

SAVBYTE DB   ?

        . . .

        LEA  BX,DATABLK       ;Load offset address

        MOV  SAVBYTE,[BX]     ;Move first byte of DATABLK
```

An equivalent operation to LEA is MOV with offset, coded like this:

```
        MOV BX,OFFSET DATABLK, ;Load offset address
```

THE INC AND DEC INSTRUCTIONS

INC and DEC are convenient instructions for incrementing and decrementing the contents of registers and memory locations by 1. The general format for INC and DEC is

```
[label:]   INC/DEC   {register/memory}
```

Note that these instructions require only one operand. Depending on the result, the operations clear or set the OF, SF, and ZF flags, which conditional jump instructions may test for minus, zero, or plus.

EXTENDED MOVE OPERATIONS

Previous programs moved immediate data into a register, moved data from defined memory to a register, moved register contents to memory, and moved the contents of one register to another. In all cases, the length of the data was limited to one or two bytes, and no operation moved data from one memory area directly to another memory area. This section explains how to move data that exceeds two bytes. Another method, the use of string instructions, is covered in Chapter 12.

In the program in Figure 6–2, the data segment contains two nine-byte fields defined as NAME1 and NAME2. The object of the program is to move the contents of NAME1 to NAME2:

```
        page    60,132
TITLE   P06MOVE (EXE)  Extended move operations
;------------------------------------------------------------
        .MODEL SMALL
        .STACK 64
;------------------------------------------------------------
        .DATA
NAME1   DB      'ABCDEFGHI'
NAME2   DB      'JKLMNOPQR'
;------------------------------------------------------------
        .CODE
BEGIN   PROC    FAR
        MOV     AX,@data        ;Initialize segment
        MOV     DS,AX           ;  registers
        MOV     ES,AX

        MOV     CX,09           ;Initialize to move 9 chars
        LEA     SI,NAME1        ;Initialize address of NAME1
        LEA     DI,NAME2        ;    and NAME2
B20:
        MOV     AL,[SI]         ;Get character from NAME1,
        MOV     [DI],AL         ;  move it to NAME2
        INC     SI              ;Increment next char in NAME1
        INC     DI              ;Increment next pos'n in NAME2
        DEC     CX              ;Decrement loop count
        JNZ     B20             ;Count not zero? Yes, loop

        MOV     AX,4C00H        ;Exit to DOS
        INT     21H
BEGIN   ENDP
        END     BEGIN
```

Figure 6–2   Extended Move Operations

```
NAME1:   A   B   C   D   E   F   G   H   I
         |   |   |   |   |   |   |   |   |
NAME2:   J   K   L   M   N   O   P   Q   R
```

Since these fields are each nine bytes long, more than a simple MOV instruction is required. The program contains a number of new features.

In order to step through NAME1 and NAME2, the routine initializes the CX register to 9 (the length of the two fields) and uses the SI and DI index registers. Two LEA instructions load the offset addresses of NAME1 and NAME2 into the SI and DI as follows:

```
LEA  SI,NAME1        ;Load offset addresses

LEA  DI,NAME2        ; of NAME1 and NAME2
```

The program uses the addresses in the SI and DI registers to move the first byte of NAME1 to the first byte of NAME2. The square brackets around SI and DI in the MOV operands mean that the instruction is to use the offset address in the given register for accessing the memory location. Thus

```
MOV AL,[SI]
```

means "Use the offset address in SI (NAME1+0) to move the referenced byte to the AL register." And the instruction

MOV [DI],AL

means "Move the contents of the AL to the offset address referenced by DI (NAME2+0)." The program has to repeat these two MOV instructions nine times, once for each character in the respective fields. To this end, it uses an instruction that we have not yet explained: JNE (Jump if Not Equal).

Two INC instructions increment the SI and DI registers by 1, and DEC decrements the CX by 1. DEC also sets or clears the Zero flag, depending on the result in the CX; if the contents are not zero, there are still more characters to move, and JNE jumps back to the label B20 to repeat the move instructions. And since the SI and DI have been incremented by 1, the next MOVs reference NAME1+1 and NAME2+1. The loop continues in this fashion until it has moved nine characters in all, up through moving NAME1+8 to NAME2+8.

(You might want to key in this program, assemble and link it, and use DEBUG to trace it. Note the effect on the registers, the instruction pointer, and the stack. Use D DS:0 to view the changes to NAME2.)

THE INT INSTRUCTION

On execution, an INT instruction interrupts processing and accesses the interrupt services table in low memory to determine the address of the required routine. The operation then transfers to DOS or to BIOS for specified action and returns to your program to resume processing. Most often, an interrupt has to perform the complex steps of an input or output operation. Interrupts require a trail that facilitates exiting a program and, on successful completion, returning to it. For this purpose, INT performs the following:

- Decrements the stack pointer by 2 and pushes the contents of the flags register onto the stack.
- Clears the interrupt and trap flags.
- Decrements the stack pointer by 2 and pushes the CS register onto the stack.
- Decrements the stack pointer by 2 and pushes the instruction pointer onto the stack.
- Causes the required operation to be performed.

To return from an interrupt, the routine issues an IRET (interrupt return), which pops the registers off the stack and returns to the instruction immediately following the INT in your program.

Since the preceding process is entirely automatic, your only concerns are to define a stack large enough for the necessary pushing and popping and to use the appropriate INT operations. Starting with Chapter 9, we'll be making considerable use of the INT instruction.

ALIGNMENT OF ADDRESSES

Since the 8086 and 80286 have a 16-bit (word) data bus, they execute faster if accessed words begin on an even-numbered (word) address. Consider a situation in which offsets 0012H and 0013H contain the word 63 A7H. The processor can access the full word at offset 0012H directly into a register. But the word could begin on an odd-numbered address, such as 0013H:

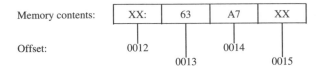

In this case, the processor has to perform *two* accesses. First, it accesses the bytes at 0012H and 0013H and delivers the byte from 0013H (63) to the AL register. Then, it accesses the bytes at 0014H and 0015H and delivers the byte from 0014H (A7) to the AH register. The AX now contains A763H.

You don't have to perform any special programming for even or odd locations, nor do you have to know whether an address is even or odd. The accessing operation automatically reverses a word from memory into a register so that it resumes its correct sequence.

The 80386 and later processors have a 32-bit data bus and, accordingly, prefer alignment of referenced items on addresses evenly divisible by four (a doubleword address). (Technically, the 486 and Pentium processors prefer alignment on a 16-byte (paragraph) boundary.)

Assembly language has an ALIGN directive that you can use to align items on boundaries. For example, ALIGN 2 aligns on a word boundary, and ALIGN 4 aligns on a doubleword boundary. Also, since the beginning of the data segment is always on a paragraph boundary, you could organize your data first with doubleword values, then with word values, and, finally, with byte values. However, the 80386 and later processors execute at such rapid speed that you'll probably never notice the effects of forcing alignment.

NEAR AND FAR ADDRESSES

An address in a program may be near or far. A *near* address consists of only the offset portion of an address. An instruction that references a near address assumes the current segment—namely, the DS for the data segment and the CS for the code segment.

A *far* address consists of both the segment and offset portions, in the form segment:offset. An instruction may reference a far address from any segment (including the current one).

Almost all assembly programming makes use of near addresses, which the assembler generates unless instructed otherwise. Larger programs in which segments occupy more than 64K of memory may require far addresses.

SEGMENT OVERRIDE PREFIX

For most purposes, a reference to a data area in a program is to locations in the data segment, handled via the DS register. There are occasions, however—especially for large programs—when you may have to handle data that is subject to another segment register, such as the ES or, on the 386 and later, the FS or GS. A good example would be a large table of data loaded from disk into memory.

You can use any instruction to process data in the other segment, but you must identify the appropriate segment register. Let's say that the address of the other segment is in the ES register, and the BX contains an offset address within that segment. Suppose the requirement is to move two bytes (a word) from that location to the CX register:

```
        MOV  CX,ES:[BX]   ;Move to CX from ES:[BX]
```

The coding of ES: indicates an override operator that means "Replace the normal use of the DS segment register with that of the ES."

The next example moves a byte value from the AL into this other segment, at an offset formed by the value in the DI plus 24:

```
        MOV  ES:[DI+24],AL  ;Move to ES:[DI+24] from AL
```

The assembler generates the machine language code with the override operator inserted as a one-byte prefix (26H) immediately preceding the instruction, just as if you had coded the instructions as

```
        ES: MOV  CX,[BX]     ;Move to CX from ES:[BX]

        ES: MOV  [DI+24]     ;Move to ES:[DI+24] from AL
```

KEY POINTS

- An operand provides a source of data for an instruction. Some instructions do not require an operand, whereas other instructions may have one or two operands.
- Where there are two operands, the second operand is the source, which contains either immediate data or the address (of a register or of memory) of the data. The first operand is the destination, which contains data in a register or in memory that is to be processed.
- In immediate format, the second operand contains a constant value or an expression. Immediate operands should match the size of a register: a one-byte constant with a one-byte register (AL, BH) and a one-word constant with a one-word register (AX, BX).
- In direct memory format, one of the operands references a memory location, and the other operand references a register.
- Indirect addressing makes use of the computer's capability for segment:offset addressing. The registers used are BX, DI, SI, and BP, coded within square brackets as an index operator. The BX, DI, and SI are associated with the DS as DS:BX, DS:DI, and DS:SI, respectively, for processing data in the data segment. The BP is associated with the SS as SS:BP, for handling data in the stack.
- You may combine registers in an indirect address as [BX+SI], which means the address in BX plus the address in the SI.

- The MOV instruction transfers (or copies) data referenced by the address in the second operand to the address in the first operand.
- The LEA instruction is useful for initializing a register with an offset address.
- INC and DEC are convenient instructions for incrementing and decrementing by 1 the contents of registers and memory locations.
- The INT instruction interrupts processing of your program, transfers to DOS or BIOS for specified action, and returns to your program to resume processing.

QUESTIONS

6–1. For an instruction with two operands, which is the source and which is the destination?

6–2. (a) In what significant way do the following instructions differ in execution?

```
MOV   AX,325AH

MOV   AX,[325AH]
```

(b) For the second MOV, one operand is in square brackets. What is the name of this feature?

6–3. (a) In what significant way do the following instructions differ in execution?

```
MOV   BX,0

MOV   [BX],0
```

(b) For the second MOV, what sort of addressing is involved with the first operand?

6–4. Explain the operation of the instruction

```
MOV CX,[BX+SI+4]
```

6–5. The following statement contains an error; that is, something is needed for the assembler to translate it:

```
MOV   [BX],[SI]
```

(a) What is the error?

(b) How would you correct the error?

6–6. Given the following data definitions, find the errors in the statements, and code the instructions necessary to correct them:

```
BYTE1   DB ?

BYTE2   DB ?

WORD1   DW ?

(a)      MOV BYTE1,BYTE2

(b)      MOV AL,WORD1        ;Operand 1 is correct

(c)      MOV BL,034AH        ;Operand 2 is correct
```

6–7. Code the following as instructions with immediate operands: (a) Store 320 in the AX; (b) compare FLDB to zero; (c) add hex 40 to BX; (d) subtract hex 40 from CX; (e) shift FLDB one bit left; (f) shift the CH one bit right.

6–8. Code one instruction that swaps the contents of a word named WORD1 with the CX.

6–9. Code the instruction to set the BX with the (offset) address of an item named TABLEX.

6–10. What, in general terms, is the purpose of the INT instruction?

6–11. (a) How does the INT instruction affect the stack? (b) How does the IRET instruction affect the stack?

6–12. Code, assemble, link, and use DEBUG to test the following program:

- Define byte items named BYTEA and BYTEB (containing any values) and a word item named WORDC (containing zero)
- Move the contents of BYTEA to the AL.
- Add the contents of BYTEB to the AL.
- Move the immediate value 25H to the BL.
- Exchange the contents of the AL and BL.
- Multiply the contents of the BL by the AL (MUL BL.)
- Store the product in the AX into WORDC.

CHAPTER 7 —————————

Writing .COM Programs

```
                    OBJECTIVE

    To explain the purpose and uses of .COM programs and how
    to prepare an assembly language program for that format.
```

INTRODUCTION

Up to now, we have written, assembled, and executed only .EXE programs. The linker automatically generates a particular format for an .EXE program and, when storing it on disk, precedes it with a special header block that is at least 512 bytes long. (Chapter 24 provides details of header blocks.)

You can also generate a .COM program for execution. One example of a commonly used .COM program is COMMAND.COM. The advantages of .COM programs are that they are smaller than comparable .EXE programs and are more easily adapted to act as resident programs. The .COM format has its roots in distant pre-DOS days, when program size was limited to 64K.

DIFFERENCES BETWEEN .EXE AND .COM PROGRAMS

Some significant differences between a program that is to execute as .EXE and one that is to execute as .COM involve the program's size, segmentation, and initialization.

Program Size

An .EXE program may be virtually any size, whereas a .COM program is restricted to one segment and a maximum of 64K, including the PSP. The PSP is a 256-byte (100H) block that DOS inserts immediately preceding a .COM and .EXE program when it loads them in memory. The 64K limit is a general rule; you may get around it by coding additional SEGMENT AT statements, a feature that is outside the scope of this chapter. A .COM program is always smaller than its counterpart .EXE program; one reason is that a 512-byte header block that precedes an .EXE program on disk does not precede a .COM program. (Don't confuse the header block with the PSP.) A .COM program is an absolute image of the executable program, but with no relocatable address information.

Segments

The use of segments for .COM programs is significantly different (and easier) than for .EXE programs.

Stack segment.   You define an .EXE program with a stack segment, whereas a .COM program automatically generates a stack. Thus, when you write an assembly language program that is to be converted to .COM format, you omit the defining stack. If the 64K program size is not large enough, the assembler establishes the stack outside of the program, in higher memory.

Data segment.   An .EXE program usually defines a data segment and initializes the DS register with the address of that segment. Since the data for a .COM program is defined within the code segment, you don't define the data segment either. As you'll see, there are simple ways to handle this situation.

Code segment.   An entire .COM program combines the PSP, stack, data segment, and code segment into one code segment, in a maximum of 64K bytes.

Initialization

When DOS loads a .COM program for execution, it automatically initializes all segment registers with the address of the PSP. Since the CS and DS registers will contain the correct initial segment address, your program does not have to load them.

Because addressing begins at an offset of 100H bytes from the beginning of the PSP, code an ORG directive as ORG 100H immediately following the code SEGMENT or .CODE statement. The ORG directive tells the assembler to begin generating the object code at an offset of 100H bytes past the start of the PSP, where the actual .COM program begins.

CONVERSION INTO .COM FORMAT

If your source program is already written in .EXE format, you can use an editor to convert the instructions into .COM format. MASM and TASM coding formats for .COM programs are identical, although their methods for conversion differ. When conversion to .COM format is complete, you can delete the generated .OBJ and .EXE files.

Microsoft Conversion

For both .EXE and .COM programs under Microsoft MASM, you assemble and produce an .OBJ file and then link the .OBJ file to produce an .EXE program. If you wrote the program to run as an .EXE program, you can now execute it. If you wrote the program to run as a .COM program, the linker produces a message:

```
Warning: No STACK Segment
```

You may ignore this message, since there is supposed to be no defined stack. A program named EXE2BIN converts Microsoft .EXE programs to .COM programs. (Actually, it converts .EXE programs to a .BIN (binary) file; the program name means "convert EXE-to-BIN," but you should name your output file extension .COM.) Assuming that EXE2BIN is in the default drive, and that a linked file named CALC.EXE is in drive D, type

```
EXE2BIN D:CALC D:CALC.COM [Enter]
```

Since the first operand of the command always references an .EXE file, do not code the .EXE extension. The second operand could be a name other than CALC.COM. If you omit the extension, EXE2BIN assumes BIN, which you would have to rename subsequently as .COM in order to execute the program. (Someone, somewhere, must have thought this was a good idea.)

Borland Conversion

As long as your source program is coded according to .COM requirements, you can convert your object program directly into a .COM program. Use the /T option for TLINK:

```
TLINK /T D:CALC
```

EXAMPLE OF A .COM PROGRAM

The program in Figure 7–1, named EXCOM1, is the same as the one in Figure 5–2, but now revised to conform to .COM requirements. Note the following changes from Figure 5–2:

- There is no defined stack or data segment.
- An ASSUME statement tells the assembler to begin offsets from the start of the code segment. The CS register also contains this address, which is that of the PSP. The ORG directive, however, causes the program to begin 100H bytes from this point, immediately following the PSP.
- ORG 100H sets an offset address for the start of execution. The program loader stores this address in the instruction pointer.
- A JMP instruction transfers control of execution around the defined data. Some programmers code data items following the instructions, so that no initial JMP instruction is required. Coding data items first may speed up the assembly process slightly, but provides no other advantage.

```
                page 60,132
TITLE           P07COM1    .COM program to move and add
CODESG  SEGMENT PARA 'Code'
        ASSUME  CS:CODESG,DS:CODESG,SS:CODESG,ES:CODESG
        ORG     100H           ;Start at end of PSP
BEGIN:  JMP     MAIN           ;Jump past data
; -----------------------------------------------------
FLDA    DW      250            ;Data definitions
FLDB    DW      125
FLDC    DW      ?
; -----------------------------------------------------
MAIN    PROC    NEAR
        MOV     AX,FLDA        ;Move 0250 to AX
        ADD     AX,FLDB        ;Add  0125 to AX
        MOV     FLDC,AX        ;Store sum in FLDC
        MOV     AX,4C00H       ;Exit to DOS
        INT     21H
MAIN    ENDP
CODESG  ENDS
        END     BEGIN
```

Figure 7–1   .COM Source Program with Conventional Segments

• INT 21H, function 4CH, ends processing and exits to DOS. You may also use the RET instruction for this purpose.

Here are the steps to convert the program for MASM and TASM:

MASM	**TASM**
MASM D:EXCOM1,D:	TASM D:EXCOM1,D:
LINK D:EXCOM1,D:	TLINK /T D:EXCOM1,D:
EXE2BIN D:EXCOM1 D:EXCOM1.COM	

The .EXE and .COM programs are 792 bytes and 24 bytes in size, respectively. The difference is largely caused by the 512-byte header block stored at the beginning of .EXE modules. Type DEBUG D:EXCOM1.COM to trace the execution of the .COM program up to (but not including) the last instruction.

You may also use simplified segment directives when coding a .COM program, as shown in Figure 7–2. Once again, define only a code segment, not a stack or data segment.

THE .COM STACK

For a .COM program, DOS automatically defines the stack and sets the same segment address in all four segment registers. If the 64K segment for the program is large enough, DOS sets the stack at the end of the segment and loads the SP register with FFFEH, the top of the stack.

If the 64K segment does not contain enough space for a stack, DOS sets the stack at the end of memory. In either case, DOS then pushes a zero word onto the stack, which acts as an offset for the IP if you use RET to terminate execution of the program.

If your program is large, or if memory is restricted, you may have to take care pushing words onto the stack. The DIR command indicates the size of a file and will give you

```
            page 60,132
  TITLE     P07COM2  COM program to move and add data
            .MODEL   SMALL
            .CODE
            ORG      100H           ;Start at end of PSP
  BEGIN:    JMP      MAIN           ;Jump past data
  ; -----------------------------------------------------
  FLDA      DW       250            ;Data definitions
  FLDB      DW       125
  FLDC      DW       ?
  ; -----------------------------------------------------
  MAIN      PROC     NEAR
            MOV      AX,FLDA        ;Move 0250 to AX
            ADD      AX,FLDB        ;Add  0125 to AX
            MOV      FLDC,AX        ;Store sum in FLDC
            MOV      AX,4C00H       ;Return to DOS
            INT      21H
  MAIN      ENDP
            END      BEGIN
```

Figure 7–2   .COM Source Program with Simplified Segment Directives

an idea as to the space available for a stack. Most of the smaller programs in this book are in .COM format, which should be easily distinguished from .EXE format.

DEBUGGING TIPS

The omission of only one .COM requirement may cause a program to fail. If EXE2BIN finds an error, it simply notifies you that it cannot convert the file, but does not provide a reason. Check the SEGMENT, ASSUME, and END statements. If you omit ORG 100H, the program incorrectly references data in the PSP, with unpredictable results.

If you run a .COM program under DEBUG, use D CS:100 to view the data and instructions. Do not follow the program through its termination; instead, use DEBUG's Q command.

An attempt to execute the .EXE module of a program written as .COM will fail.

KEY POINTS

- A .COM program is restricted to one 64K segment.
- A .COM program is smaller than its counterpart .EXE program.
- A program written to run as .COM does not define a stack or data segment, nor does it initialize the DS register.
- A program written to run as .COM uses ORG 100H immediately following the code SEGMENT statement. The statement sets the offset address to the beginning of execution following the PSP.
- For Microsoft MASM, the EXE2BIN program converts an .EXE file to .COM format. Borland's TLINK can convert an object program directly into .COM format.
- DOS defines a stack for a .COM program at the end of the program.

QUESTIONS

7–1. What is the maximum size of a .COM program?

7–2. For a source program to be converted to .COM format, what segments can you define?

7–3. Why do you code ORG 100H at the beginning of a program to be converted to .COM format?

7–4. How does the system handle the fact that you do not define a stack for a .COM program?

7–5. A source program is named SAMPLE.ASM. Provide the commands to convert it to .COM format under (a) MASM; (b) TASM.

7–6. Revise the program in Question 6–12 for .COM format. Assemble, link, and execute it under DEBUG.

CHAPTER 8 —————————————

Program Logic and Control

OBJECTIVES

To cover the requirements for program control (looping and jumping), for logical comparisons, for logical bit operations, and for program organization.

INTRODUCTION

Up to this chapter, the programs we have have examined have executed in a straight line, with one instruction sequentially following another. Seldom, however, is a programmable problem that simple. Most programs consist of a number of loops in which a series of steps repeats until reaching a specific requirement and various tests to determine which of several actions to take. A common practice is to test whether a program is to end execution.

Requirements such as these involve a transfer of control to the address of an instruction that does not immediately follow the one currently executing. A transfer of control may be *forward*, to execute a new series of steps, or *backward*, to reexecute the same steps.

Certain instructions can transfer control outside the normal sequential flow by adding an offset value to the IP. Following are the instructions introduced in this chapter, by category:

COMPARE OPERATIONS	TRANSFER OPERATIONS	LOGICAL OPERATIONS	SHIFT AND ROTATE
CMP	CALL	AND	SAR/SHR
TEST	JMP	NOT	SAL/SHL

Jnnn	OR	RCR/ROR
LOOP	XOR	RCL/ROL

SHORT, NEAR, AND FAR ADDRESSES

A jump operation reaches a *short* address by a one-byte offset, limited to a distance of −128 to 127 bytes. A jump operation reaches a *near* address by a one-word offset, limited to a distance of −32,768 to 32,767 bytes within the same segment. A *far* address may be in another segment and is reached by a segment address and offset; CALL is the normal instruction for this purpose.

The following table lists the rules on distances for JMP, LOOP, and CALL operations. There is little need to memorize these rules, because normal use of these instructions rarely causes problems.

Instructions	Short −128 to 127 Same segment	Near −32,768 to 32,767 Same segment	Far Another segment
JMP	yes	yes	yes
Jnnn	yes	yes: 80386 and on	no
LOOP	yes	no	no
CALL	N/A	yes	yes

INSTRUCTION LABELS

The JMP, Jnnn (conditional jump), and LOOP instructions require an operand that refers to the label of an instruction. The following example jumps to A90, which is the label given to a MOV instruction:

```
          JMP      A90

          . . .

A90:      MOV.     AII,00

          . . .
```

The label of an instruction, such as A90:, is terminated by a colon to give it the near attribute—that is, the label is inside a procedure in the same code segment. Watch out: Omission of the colon is a common error. Note that an address label in an instruction operand (such as JMP A90) does not have a colon.

You can also code a label on a separate line as

```
A90:

          MOV      AH,00
```

In both cases, the address of A90 references the first byte of the MOV instruction.

THE JMP INSTRUCTION

A commonly used instruction for transferring control is the JMP (Jump) instruction. A jump is unconditional, since the operation transfers control under all circumstances. JMP also flushes the processor's prefetch instruction queue; thus a program with many jump operations may lose some significant processing speed. The general format for JMP is

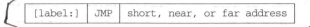

|`[label:]`|`JMP`|`short, near, or far address`|

A JMP operation within the same segment may be short or near (or, technically, far if the destination is a procedure with the FAR attribute). On its first pass through a source program, the assembler generates the length of each instruction. However, a JMP instruction may be either two or three bytes long. A JMP operation to a label within -128 to $+127$ bytes is a short jump. The assembler generates one byte for the operation (EB) and one byte for the operand. The operand acts as an offset value that the computer adds to the IP register when executing the program. The limits are 00H to FFH, or -128 to $+127$. The assembler may have already encountered the designated operand (a backward jump) within -128 bytes, as in

```
                              A50:

                               . . .

                              JMP   A50
```

In this case, the assembler generates a two-byte machine instruction. A JMP that exceeds -128 to $+127$ bytes becomes a near jump, for which the assembler generates different machine code (E9) and a two-byte operand (8086/80286) or four-byte operand (80386 and later). In a forward jump, the assembler has not yet encountered the designated operand:

```
                              JMP   A90

                               . . .

                              A90:
```

Since some assembler versions don't know at this point whether the jump is short or near, they automatically generate a three-byte instruction. However, provided that the jump really is short, you can use the SHORT operator to force a short jump and a two-byte instruction by coding

```
                              JMP   SHORT A90

                               . . .

                              A90:
```

Example of a Program Using JMP

The .COM program in Figure 8–1 illustrates the use of the JMP instruction. The program initializes the AX, BX, and CX registers to the value of 1, and a loop performs the following:

```
                              page 60,132
                      TITLE   P08JUMP (COM)    Use of JMP for looping
                              .MODEL SMALL
                              .CODE
0100                          ORG     100H
0100                  MAIN    PROC    NEAR
0100    B8 0001               MOV     AX,01      ;Initialize AX,
0103    BB 0001               MOV     BX,01      ;   BX, and
0106    B9 0001               MOV     CX,01      ;   CX to 01
0109                  A20:
0109    05 0001               ADD     AX,01      ;Add 01 to AX
010C    03 D8                 ADD     BX,AX      ;Add AX to BX
010E    D1 E1                 SHL     CX,1       ;Double CX
0110    EB F7                 JMP     A20        ;Jump to A20 instr'n
0112                  MAIN    ENDP
                              END     MAIN
```

Figure 8–1   Use of the JMP Instruction

• Add 1 to AX

• Add AX to BX

• Double the value in CX

At the end of the loop, the instruction JMP A20 transfers control to the instruction labeled A20. The effect of repeating the loop causes AX to increase as 1, 2, 3, 4, ...; BX to increase according to the sum of the digits 1, 3, 6, 10, . . . ; and CX to double as 1, 2, 4, 8, ... Since this loop has no exit, processing is endless—usually not a good idea.

In the program, A20 is −9 bytes from the JMP. You can confirm this distance by examining the object code for the JMP: EBF7. EB is the machine code for a near JMP and hex F7 is the two's complement notation for −9. The IP contains the offset (0112H) of the next instruction to execute. The JMP operation adds the F7 (technically, FFF7, since the IP is a word in size) to the IP, which contains the offset 0112H of the instruction following the JMP:

	DECIMAL	HEX	
Instruction pointer:	274	0112	
JMP operand:	−9	FFF7	(two's complement)
Jump address:	265	(1)0109	

The jump address is calculated to be 0109H, where the carry out of 1 is ignored (as a check of the program listing for the offset address of A20 shows). The operation changes the offset value in the IP and flushes the instruction queue. Since this is a backward jump, the operand FFF7 is negative, whereas the operand for a forward jump would be a positive value.

As a useful experience, key in the program, assemble it, link it, and convert it to .COM format. No data definitions are required, since immediate operands generate all the data. Use DEBUG to trace the .COM module for a number of iterations. Once the AX contains 08, the BX and CX will be incremented to 24H (decimal 36) and 80H (decimal 128), respectively. Key in Q to quit DEBUG.

THE LOOP INSTRUCTION

As used in Figure 8–1, the JMP instruction causes an endless loop. But a routine is more likely to loop a specified number of times or until it reaches a particular condition. The LOOP instruction, which serves this purpose, requires an initial value in the CX register. For each iteration, LOOP automatically deducts 1 from the CX. If the value in the CX is zero, control drops through to the following instruction; if the value in the CX is nonzero, control jumps to the operand address. The distance must be a short jump, within −128 to +127 bytes. For an operation that exceeds this limit, the assembler issues a message such as "relative jump out of range." The general format for LOOP is

The program in Figure 8–2 illustrates the use of LOOP and performs the same operation as the program in Figure 8–1, except that it terminates after 10 loops. A MOV instruction initializes the CX with the value 10. Since LOOP uses the CX, this program now uses the DX in place of CX for doubling the initial value 1. The LOOP instruction replaces JMP A20 and, for faster processing, INC AX (increment the AX by 1) replaces ADD AX,01.

Just as for JMP, the machine code operand contains the distance from the end of the LOOP instruction to the address of A20, which is added to the IP.

As a useful exercise, modify your copy of Figure 8–1 for these changes, and assemble, link, and convert the program to .COM. Use DEBUG to trace through the entire 10 loops. Once the CX is reduced to zero, the contents of AX, BX, and DX are, respectively, 000BH, 0042H, and 0400H. Press Q to quit DEBUG.

There are two variations on the LOOP instruction, both of which also decrement the CX by 1. LOOPE/LOOPZ (loop while equal or zero) continues looping as long as the value in the CX is zero or the zero condition is set. LOOPNE/LOOPNZ (loop while not equal or zero) continues looping as long as the value in the CX is not zero or the zero condition is not set.

```
                              page 60,132
                   TITLE   P08LOOP (COM)     Illustration of LOOP
                           .MODEL SMALL
                           .CODE
     0100                  ORG     100H
     0100          BEGIN   PROC    NEAR
     0100 B8 0001          MOV     AX,01        ;Initialize AX,
     0103 BB 0001          MOV     BX,01        ;  BX, and
     0106 BA 0001          MOV     DX,01        ;  DX to 01
     0109 B9 000A          MOV     CX,10        ;Initialize
     010C          A20:                         ;  number of loops
     010C 40               INC     AX           ;Add 01 to AX
     010D 03 D8            ADD     BX,AX        ;Add AX to BX
     010F D1 E2            SHL     DX,1         ;Double DX
     0111 E2 F9            LOOP    A20          ;Decrement CX,
                                                ;  loop if nonzero
     0113 B8 4C00          MOV     AX,4C00H     ;Exit to DOS
     0116 CD 21            INT     21H
     0118          BEGIN   ENDP
                           END     BEGIN
```

Fig. 8–2   Use of the LOOP Instruction

Neither LOOP nor its LOOPxx variations affects any flags in the flags register, which would be changed by other instructions within the loop routine. As a result, if the routine contains no instructions that affect the ZF (zero) flag, then using LOOPNE/LOOPNZ would be equivalent to using LOOP.

FLAGS REGISTER

The remaining material in this chapter requires a more detailed knowledge of the flags register. This register contains 16 bits, which various instructions set to indicate the status of an operation. In all cases, a flag remains set until another instruction changes it. The flags register for real mode contains the following commonly used bits:

```
Bit no.:   15  14  13  12  11  10  9  8  7  6  5  4  3  2  1  0
Flag:                          O   D  I  T  S  Z     A     P     C
```

CF (Carry flag).   Contains a carry (0 or 1) from the high-order (leftmost) bit following arithmetic operations and some shift and rotate operations.

PF (Parity flag).   Contains a check of the low-order eight bits of data operations. The parity flag is not to be confused with the parity bit and is seldom of concern in conventional programming. An odd number of 1-bits clears the flag to 0, and an even number of 1-bits sets it to 1.

AF (Auxiliary carry flag).   Is concerned with arithmetic on ASCII and BCD packed fields. An arithmetic operation that causes a carry out of bit 3 (the fourth bit from the right) of a register one-byte operation sets this flag.

ZF (Zero flag).   Cleared or set as a result of an arithmetic or compare operation. Unexpectedly, a nonzero result clears the flag to 0, and a zero result sets it to 1. However, the setting, if not apparently correct, is logically correct: 0 means no (the result is not equal to zero), and 1 means yes (the result equals zero). JE and JZ test this flag.

SF (Sign flag).   Set according to the sign (high-order or leftmost bit) after an arithmetic operation: Positive clears the flag to 0, and negative sets it to 1. JG and JL test this flag.

TF (Trap flag).   When set, causes the processor to execute in single-step mode, that is, one instruction at a time under user control. You already set this flag when you entered the T command in DEBUG, and that's about the only place where you'd expect to find its use.

IF (Interrupt flag).   Disables interrupts when 0, and enables interrupts when 1. This flag is rarely used in conventional programming.

DF (Direction flag).   Used by string operations to determine the direction of data transfer. When the flag is 0, the operation increments the SI and DI registers, causing left-to-right data transfer; when the flag is 1, the operation decrements the SI and DI causing right-to-left data transfer.

OF (Overflow flag).   Indicates a carry into and out of the high-order (leftmost) sign bit following a signed arithmetic operation.

THE CMP INSTRUCTION

The CMP instruction is commonly used to compare two data fields, one or both of which are contained in a register. The general format for CMP is

```
[label:]   CMP   {register/memory},{register/memory/immediate}
```

The result of a CMP operation affects the AF, CF, OF, PF, SF, and ZF flags, although you do not have to test these flags individually. The following code tests the BX register for a zero value:

```
        CMP   BX,00              ;Compare BX to zero
        JZ    B50                ;Jump if zero to B50
        .     (action if nonzero)

        .
B50:    ...                      ;Jump point if BX zero
```

If the BX contains zero, CMP sets the ZF to 1 and may or may not change the settings of other flags. The JZ (Jump if Zero) instruction tests only the ZF flag. Since ZF contains 1 (meaning a zero condition), JZ transfers control (jumps) to the address indicated by operand B50.

Note that the operation compares the first to the second operand; for example, is the value of the first operand higher than, equal to, or lower than the value of the second operand? The next section provides the various ways of transferring control based on tested conditions.

CONDITIONAL JUMP INSTRUCTIONS

The assembler supports a variety of conditional jump instructions that transfer control depending on settings in the flags register. For example, you can compare two fields and then jump according to flag values that the compare sets. The general format for the conditional jump is

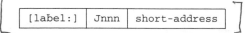

```
[label:]   Jnnn   short-address
```

As explained earlier, the LOOP instruction decrements the CX register; if it is nonzero, control transfers to the operand address. You could replace the LOOP A20 statement in Figure 8–2 with two statements—one that decrements the CX and another that performs a conditional jump:

```
DEC    CX           ;Equivalent to LOOP

JNZ    A20

...
```

DEC and JNZ perform exactly what LOOP does. DEC decrements the CX by 1 and sets or clears the zero flag in the flags register. JNZ then tests the setting of the zero flag; if the CX is nonzero, control jumps to A20, and if the CX is zero, control drops through to the next instruction. (The jump operation also flushes the processor's prefetch instruction queue.) Although LOOP has limited uses, in this example it is more efficient than using the DEC and JNZ instructions.

Just as for JMP and LOOP, the machine code operand contains the distance from the end of the JNZ instruction to the address of A20, which is added to the instruction pointer. For the 8086/286, the distance must be a short jump, within -128 to $+127$ bytes. If an operation exceeds this limit, the assembler issues a message "relative jump out of range." The 80386 and later processors provide for 8-bit (short) or 32-bit (near) offsets that allow reaching any address within a segment.

Signed and Unsigned Data

Distinguishing the purpose of conditional jumps should clarify their use. The type of data (unsigned or signed) on which you are performing comparisons or arithmetic can determine which instruction to use. An *unsigned* data item treats all bits as data bits; typical examples are character strings such as names and addresses and numeric values such as customer numbers. A *signed* data item treats the leftmost bit as a sign, where 0 is positive and 1 is negative. Many numeric values may be either positive or negative.

In the next example, the AX contains 11000110 and the BX contains 00010110. The instruction

```
CMP AX,BX
```

compares the contents of the AX to the contents of the BX. For unsigned data, the AX value is larger; for signed data, however, the AX value is smaller because of the negative sign.

Jumps Based on Unsigned Data

The following conditional jump instructions apply to unsigned data:

SYMBOL	DESCRIPTION	FLAGS TESTED
JE/JZ	Jump Equal or Jump Zero	ZF
JNE/JNZ	Jump Not Equal or Jump Not Zero	ZF
JA/JNBE	Jump Above or Jump Not Below or Equal	CF, ZF
JAE/JNB	Jump Above or Equal or Jump Not Below	CF
JB/JNAE	Jump Below or Jump Not Above or Equal	CF
JBE/JNA	Jump Below or Equal or Jump Not Above	CF, AF

You can express each of these tests in one of two symbolic operation codes. Choose the one that is clearest and most descriptive. For example, although JB and JNAE generate the same object code, the positive test JB is easier to understand than the negative test JNAE.

Jumps Based on Signed Data

The following conditional jump instructions apply to signed data:

SYMBOL	DESCRIPTION	FLAGS TESTED
JE/JZ	Jump Equal or Jump Zero	ZF
JNE/JNZ	Jump Not Equal or Jump Not Zero	ZF
JG/JNLE	Jump Greater or Jump Not Less or Equal	ZF, SF, OF
JGE/JNL	Jump Greater or Equal or Jump Not Less	SF, OF
JL/JNGE	Jump Less or Jump Not Greater or Equal	SF, OF
JLE/JNG	Jump Less or Equal or Jump Not Greater	ZF, SF, OF

The jumps for testing equal or zero (JE/JZ) and for testing not equal or zero (JNE/JNZ) are included in the lists for unsigned and signed data, since an equal or zero condition occurs regardless of the presence of a sign.

Special Arithmetic Tests

The following conditional jump instructions have special uses:

SYMBOL	DESCRIPTION	FLAGS TESTED
JS	Jump Sign (negative)	SF
JNS	Jump No Sign (positive)	SF
JC	Jump Carry (same as JB)	CF
JNC	Jump No Carry	CF
JO	Jump Overflow	OF
JNO	Jump No Overflow	OF
JP/JPE	Jump Parity or Jump Parity Even	PF
JNP/JPO	Jump No Parity or Jump Parity Odd	PF

JC and JNC are often used to test the success of disk operations. Another conditional jump, JCXZ, tests the contents of the CX register for zero. This instruction need not be placed immediately following an arithmetic or compare operation. One use for JCXZ could be at the start of a loop, to ensure that the CX actually contains a nonzero value.

Now, don't expect to memorize all of these instructions. As a reminder, however, note that a jump for *unsigned* data is equal, above, or below, whereas a jump for *signed* data is equal, greater, or less. The jumps for testing the carry, overflow, and parity flags have unique purposes. The assembler translates symbolic to object code, regardless of which instruction you use, but, for example, JAE and JGE, although apparently similar, do not test the same flags.

The 80386 and later processors permit far conditional jumps. You can indicate a short or far jump as, for example,

```
JNE  SHORT address

JAE  FAR address
```

CALLING PROCEDURES

Up to now, code segments have consisted of only one procedure, coded as

```
BEGIN  PROC  FAR
             .
             .
             .
BEGIN  ENDP
```

The FAR operand in this case informs the system that the indicated address is the entry point for program execution, whereas the ENDP directive defines the end of the procedure. A code segment, however, may contain any number of procedures, all distinguished by PROC and ENDP. A called procedure (or subroutine) is a section of code that performs a clearly defined task (such as set cursor or get keyboard input). Organizing a program into procedures provides the following benefits:

- Reduces the amount of code, since a common procedure can be called from anywhere in the code segment
- Encourages better program organization
- Facilitates debugging of the program, since bugs can be more clearly isolated
- Helps in the ongoing maintenance of programs because procedures are readily identified for modification.

CALL and RET Operations

The CALL instruction transfers control to a called procedure, and the RET instruction returns from the called procedure to the original calling procedure. RET should be the last instruction in a called procedure. The general formats for CALL and RET are:

[label:]	CALL	procedure
[label:]	RET	[immediate]

The particular object code that CALL and RET generate depends on whether the operation involves a NEAR or FAR procedure.

Near call and return.   A CALL to a procedure within the same segment is near and performs the following:

- Decrements the SP by 2 (one word).
- Pushes the IP (containing the offset of the instruction following the CALL) onto the stack.
- Inserts the offset address of the called procedure into the IP. (This operation also flushes the processor's prefetch instruction queue.)

A RET that returns from a near procedure performs the following:

- Pops the old IP value from the stack into the IP (which also flushes the processor's prefetch instruction queue).
- Increments the SP by 2.

The CS:IP now points to the instruction following the original CALL in the calling procedure, where execution resumes.

Far call and return.   A far CALL calls a procedure labeled FAR, possibly in a separate code segment. A far CALL pushes both the CS and IP onto the stack, and RET pops them from the stack. Far calls and returns are the subject of Chapter 23.

Example of a Near Call and Return

A typical organization of near calls and returns appears in Figure 8–3. Note the following features:

- The program is divided into a far procedure, BEGIN, and two near procedures, B10 and C10. Each procedure has a unique name and contains its own ENDP for ending its definition.

```
                        page 60,132
                TITLE   P08CALLP (EXE)   Calling procedures
                        .MODEL    SMALL
                        .STACK    64
                        .DATA
                ;---------------------------------------------------
                        .CODE
0000            BEGIN   PROC    FAR
0000 E8 0008 R          CALL    B10             ;Call B10
                ;        ...
0003 B8 4C00            MOV     AX,4C00H        ;Exit to DOS
0006 CD 21              INT     21H
0008            BEGIN   ENDP
                ;---------------------------------------------------
0008            B10     PROC    NEAR
0008 E8 000C R          CALL    C10             ;Call C10
                ;        ...
000B C3                 RET                     ;Return to
000C            B10     ENDP                    ;  caller
                ;---------------------------------------------------
000C            C10     PROC    NEAR
                ;        ...
000C C3                 RET                     ;Return to
000D            C10     ENDP                    ;  caller
                ;---------------------------------------------------
                        END     BEGIN
```

Figure 8–3   Called Procedures

- The PROC directives for B10 and C10 contain the attribute NEAR to indicate that these procedures are within the current code segment. Since omission of the attribute causes the assembler to default to NEAR, many subsequent examples omit it.
- In procedure BEGIN, the CALL instruction transfers program control to the procedure B10 and begins its execution.
- In procedure B10, the CALL instruction transfers control to the procedure C10 and begins its execution.
- In procedure C10, the RET instruction causes control to return to the instruction immediately following CALL C10.
- In procedure B10, the RET instruction causes control to return to the instruction immediately following CALL B10.
- Procedure BEGIN then resumes processing from that point.
- RET always returns to the calling routine. If B10 did not end with a RET instruction, instructions would execute through B10 and drop directly into C10. In fact, if C10 did not contain a RET, the program would execute past the end of C10 into whatever instructions (if any) happened to be there, with unpredictable results.

Technically, you can transfer control to a near procedure by means of a jump instruction or even by normal in-line code. But for clarity and consistency, use CALL to transfer control to a procedure, and use RET to end the execution of the procedure.

EFFECT OF PROGRAM EXECUTION ON THE STACK

Up to this point, our programs have had little need to push data onto the stack and, consequently, had to define only a very small stack. However, a called procedure can CALL another procedure, which in turn can CALL yet another procedure, so that the stack must be large enough to contain the pushed addresses. All this turns out to be easier than it first appears, and a stack definition of 32 words is ample for most of our purposes.

CALL and PUSH store a one-word address or value onto the stack. RET and POP pop the stack and access the previously pushed word. All of these operations change the offset address in the SP register for the next word. Because of this feature, RET and POP operations must match their original CALL and PUSH operations.

As a reminder, on loading an .EXE program for execution, the system loader sets the following register values:

- DS and ES: Address of the PSP, a 256-byte (100H) area that precedes an executable program module in memory.
- CS: Address of the code segment—the entry point to your program.
- IP: Zero, if the first executable instruction is at the beginning of the code segment.
- SS: Address of the stack segment.
- SP: Offset to the top of the stack. For example, for a stack defined as .STACK 64 (64 bytes or 32 words), the SP initially contains 64, or 40H.

Let's trace the simple program in Figure 8–3 through its execution. In practice, called procedures would contain any number of instructions.

The current available location for pushing or popping is the top of the stack. For this example, the system loader would have set the SP to the size of the stack, 64 bytes (40H). The program performs the following operations:

- CALL B10 decrements the SP by 2, from 40H to 3EH. It then pushes the IP (containing 0003) onto the top of the stack at offset 3EH. This is the offset of the instruction following the CALL. The processor uses the address formed by CS:IP to transfer control to B10. Words in memory contain bytes in reverse sequence; for example, 0003 becomes 0300.

CALL B10 (push 0003):	XXXX	XXXX	XXXX	XXXX	0300	SP = 3E00H
	|	|	|	|	|	
Stack offset:	0036	0038	003A	003C	003E	

- In procedure B10, CALL C10 decrements the SP by 2, to 3CH. It then pushes the IP (containing 000B) onto the top of the stack at offset 3CH. The processor uses the CS:IP addresses to transfer control to C10.

CALL B10 (push 000B):	XXXX	XXXX	XXXX	0B00	0300	SP = 3C00H
	|	|	|	|	|	
Stack offset:	0036	0038	003A	003C	003E	

- To return from C10, the RET instruction pops the offset (000B) from the top of the stack at 3CH, inserts it in the IP, and increments the SP by 2 to 3EH. This causes an automatic return to offset 000BH in procedure B10.

RET (pop 000B):	XXXX	XXXX	XXXX	0B00	0300	SP = 3E00H
	|	|	|	|	|	
Stack offset:	0036	0038	003A	003C	003E	

- The RET at the end of procedure B10 pops the address (0003) from the top of the stack at 3EH into the IP and increments the SP by 2 to 40H. This causes an automatic return to offset 0003H, where the program ends its execution.

RET (pop 0003):	XXXX	XXXX	XXXX	0B000	0300	SP = 4000H
	|	|	|	|	|	
Stack offset:	0036	0038	003A	003C	003E	

If you use DEBUG to view the stack, you may find harmless data left by a previously executed program.

BOOLEAN OPERATIONS

Boolean logic is important in circuitry design and has a parallel in programming logic. The instructions for Boolean logic are AND, OR, XOR, TEST, and NOT, which can be used to clear and set bits and to handle ASCII data for arithmetic purposes (Chapter 13). The general format for the Boolean operations is

[label:]	operation	{register/memory},{register/memory/immediate}

The first operand references one byte or word in a register or memory and is the only value that is changed. The second operand references a register or immediate value. The operation matches the bits of the two referenced operands and sets the CF, OF, PF, SF, and ZF flags accordingly (AF is undefined).

- AND. If matched bits are both 1, sets the result to 1. All other conditions result in 0.

- OR. If either (or both) of the matched bits is 1, sets the result to 1. If both bits are 0, the result is 0.

- XOR. If one matched bit is 0 and the other 1, sets the result to 1. If matched bits are the same (both 0 or both 1), the result is 0.

- TEST. Sets the flags as AND does, but does not change the bits.

The following AND, OR, and XOR operations illustrate the same bit values as operands:

```
               AND    OR    XOR

              0101   0101   0101

              0011   0011   0011
              ----   ----   ----
     Result:  0001   0111   0110
```

Here's a useful to rule to remember: ANDing bits with 0 clears them to 0, whereas ORing bits with 1 sets them to 1.

Examples of Boolean Operations

For the following unrelated examples, assume that the AL contains 1100 0101 and the BH contains 0101 1100:

```
          1. AND  AL,BH     ;Sets AL to 0100 0100

          2. AND  AL,00H     ;Sets AL to 0000 0000

          3. AND  AL,0FH     ;Sets AL to 0000 0101

          4. OR   BH,AL      ;Sets BH to 1101 1101

          5. OR   CL,CL      ;Sets SF and ZF

          6. XOR  AL,AL      ;Sets AL to 0000 0000
```

Examples 2 and 6 provide ways of clearing a register to zero. Example 3 zeros the left four bits of the AL. Although the use of CMP may be clearer, you can use OR for the following purposes:

```
1. OR   CX,CX     ;Test CX for zero
   JZ   ...        ;Jump if zero

2. OR   CX,CX     ;Test CX for sign
   JS   ...        ;Jump if negative
```

TEST acts like AND, but only sets flags. Here are some examples:

```
1. TEST  BL,11110000B   ;Any of leftmost bits
   JNZ   ...             ;  in BL nonzero?

2. TEST  AL,00000001B   ;Does the AL contain
   JNZ   ...             ;  an odd number?

3. TEST  DX,0FFH        ;Does the DX contain
   JZ    ...             ;  a zero value?
```

The NOT Instruction

The NOT instruction simply reverses the bits in a byte or word in a register or memory: 0s become 1s and 1s become 0s. The general format for NOT is

For example, if the AL contains 1100 0101, the instruction NOT AL changes the AL to 0011 1010. (The effect is exactly the same as that of XOR AL,0FFH in Example 7 earlier.) Flags are unaffected. NOT is not the same as NEG, which changes a binary value from positive to negative and vice versa by reversing the bits and adding 1.

CHANGING LOWERCASE TO UPPERCASE

There are various reasons for converting between uppercase and lowercase letters. For example, you may have received a data file from a system that processes only uppercase letters. Or a program has to allow users to enter a value as either uppercase or lowercase (such as 'YES' or 'yes') and converts it to uppercase to facilitate testing it. Uppercase letters A through Z are 41H through 5AH, and lowercase letters a through z are 61H through 7AH. The only difference is that bit 5 is 0 for uppercase and 1 for lowercase, as the following shows:

UPPERCASE		LOWERCASE	
Letter A:	01000001	Letter a:	01100001
Letter Z:	01011010	Letter z:	01111010
Bit:	76543210	Bit:	76543210

```
TITLE     P08CASE (COM)    Change lowercase to uppercase
          .MODEL SMALL
          .CODE
          ORG      100H
BEGIN:    JMP      MAIN
; ----------------------------------------------------------
TITLEX    DB       'Change to uppercase letters'
; ----------------------------------------------------------
MAIN      PROC     NEAR
          LEA      BX,TITLEX+1       ;1st char to change
          MOV      CX,26             ;No. of chars to change
B20:
          MOV      AH,[BX]           ;Character from TITLEX
          CMP      AH,61H            ;Is it
          JB       B30               ;  lower
          CMP      AH,7AH            ;  case
          JA       B30               ;  letter?
          AND      AH,11011111B      ;Yes - convert
          MOV      [BX],AH           ;Restore in TITLEX
B30:
          INC      BX                ;Set for next char
          LOOP     B20               ;Loop 26 times
          MOV      AX,4C00H          ;Done -- exit
          INT      21H
MAIN      ENDP
          END      BEGIN
```

Figure 8–4 Changing Lowercase to Uppercase

The .COM program in Figure 8–4 converts the contents of a data item, TITLEX, from lowercase to uppercase, beginning at TITLEX + 1. The program initializes the BX with the address of TITLEX + 1 and uses the address to move each character, starting at TITLEX + 1, to the AH. If the value is between 61H and 7AH, an AND instruction sets bit 5 to 0:

```
AND AH,11011111B
```

All characters other than a through z remain unchanged. The routine then moves the changed character back to TITLEX, increments the BX for the next character, and loops.

Used this way, the BX register acts as an index register for addressing memory locations. You may also use the SI and DI for the same purpose.

SHIFTING BITS

The shift instructions, which are part of the computer's logical capability, can perform the following actions:

- Reference a register or memory address
- Shift bits left or right
- Shift up to 8 bits in a byte, 16 bits in a word, and 32 bits in a doubleword (80386 and later)
- Shift logically (unsigned) or arithmetically (signed).

The second operand contains the shift value, which is a constant (an immediate value) or a reference to the CL register. For the 8088/8086 processors, the immediate constant may be only 1; a shift value greater than 1 must be contained in the CL register. Later processors allow immediate shift constants up to 31. The general format for shift is

| [label:] | shift | {register/memory},{CL/immediate} |

Shifting Bits Right

Right shifts (SHR and SAR) move bits in the designated register to the right. Each bit shifted off enters the carry flag. The right shift instructions provide for logical (unsigned) and arithmetic (signed) data:

SHR: Shift logical right

SAR: Shift arithmetic right

The following related instructions illustrate SHR and unsigned data:

INSTRUCTION	AL	COMMENT
MOV CL,03		
MOV AL,10110111B	; 10110111	
SHR AL,01	; 01011011	Shift right 1
SHR AL,CL	; 00001011	Shift right 3 more
SHR AX,03	; 80186 and later processors	

The first SHR shifts the contents of the AL one bit to the right. The shifted 1-bit now resides in the carry flag, and a 0-bit is filled to the left in the AL. The second SHR shifts the AL three more bits. The carry flag contains successively 1, 1, and 0, and three 0-bits are filled to the left in the AL.

SAR differs from SHR in one important way: SAR uses the *sign bit* to fill leftmost vacated bits. In this way, positive and negative values retain their signs. The following related instructions illustrate SAR and unsigned data in which the sign is a 1-bit:

INSTRUCTION	AL	COMMENT
MOV CL,03		
MOV AL,10110111B	; 10110111	
SAR AL,01	; 11011011	Shift right 1
SAR AL,CL	; 11111011	Shift right 3 more
SAR AX,03	; 80186 and later processors	

Right shifts are especially useful for *halving* values and are significantly faster than using a divide operation. In the examples of the shift right operation, the first right shift of one bit effectively divides by 2, and the second and third right shifts of three bits effectively divide by 8.

Halving odd numbers such as 5 and 7 generates 2 and 3, respectively, and sets the carry flag to 1. Also, if you have to shift two bits, coding two shift instructions is more efficient than storing 2 in the CL and coding one shift.

You can use the JC (Jump if Carry) instruction to test the bit shifted into the carry flag at the end of a shift operation.

Shifting Bits Left

Left shifts (SHL and SAL) move bits in the designated register to the left. SHL and SAL are identical in their operation. Each bit shifted off enters the carry flag. The left shift instructions provide for logical (unsigned) and arithmetic (signed) data:

SHL: Shift logical left   SAL: Shift arithmetic left

The following related instructions illustrate SHL for unsigned data:

INSTRUCTION	AL	COMMENT
MOV CL,03		
MOV AL,10110111B	; 10110111	
SHL AL,01	; 01101110	Shift left 1
SHL AL,CL	; 01110000	Shift left 3 more
SHL AX,03	; 80186 and later processors	

The first SHL shifts the contents of the AL one bit to the left. The shifted 1-bit now resides in the carry flag, and a 0-bit is filled to the right in the AL. The second SHL shifts the AL three more bits. The carry flag contains successively 0, 1, and 1, and three 0-bits are filled to the right in the AL.

Left shifts always fill 0-bits to the right. As a result, SHL and SAL are identical. Left shifts are especially useful for doubling values and are significantly faster than using a multiply operation. In the examples of the shift left operation, the first left shift of one bit effectively multiplies by 2, and the second and third left shifts of three bits effectively multiply by 8. Also, if you have to shift two bits, coding two shift instructions is more efficient than storing 2 in the CL and coding one shift.

You can use the JC (Jump if Carry) instruction to test the bit shifted into the carry flag at the end of a shift operation.

ROTATING BITS

The rotate instructions, which are part of the computer's logical capability, can perform the following actions:

- Reference a byte or a word.
- Reference a register or memory.
- Rotate right or left. The bit that is shifted off rotates to fill the vacated bit position in the memory or register location and is also copied into the carry flag.
- Rotate up to 8 bits in a byte, 16 bits in a word, and 32 bits in a doubleword (80386 and later).
- Rotate logically (unsigned) or arithmetically (signed).

The second operand contains the rotate value, which is a constant (an immediate value) or a reference to the CL register. For the 8088/8086 processors, the immediate constant may be only 1; a rotate value greater than 1 must be contained in the CL register. Later processors allow immediate constants up to 31. The general format for rotate is

```
[label:]   rotate   {register/memory},{CL/immediate}
```

Rotating Bits Right

Right rotates (ROR and RCR) rotate the bits in the designated register to the right. The right rotate instructions provide for logical (unsigned) and arithmetic (signed) data:

ROR: Rotate logical right

RCR: Rotate with carry right

The following related instructions illustrate ROR:

INSTRUCTION	BH	COMMENT
MOV CL,03		
MOV BH,10110111B	; 10110111	
ROR BH,01	; 11011011	Rotate right 1
ROR BH,CL	; 01111011	Rotate right 3 more
ROR BX,03	; 80186 and later processors	

The first ROR rotates the rightmost 1-bit of the BH to the leftmost vacated position. The second and third ROR operations rotate the three rightmost bits.

RCR causes the *carry flag* to participate in the rotation. Each shifted-off bit on the right moves into the CF, and the CF bit moves into the vacated bit position on the left.

Rotating Bits Left

Left rotates (ROL and RCL) rotate the bits in the designated register to the left. The left rotate instructions provide for logical (unsigned) and arithmetic (signed) data:

ROL: Rotate logical left

RCL: Rotate with cary left

The following related instructions illustrate ROL:

INSTRUCTION	BL	COMMENT
MOV CL,03		
MOV BL,10110111B	; 10110111	
ROL BL,01	; 01101111	Rotate left 1
ROL BL,CL	; 01111011	Rotate left 3 more
ROL BX,03	; 80186 and later processors	

The first ROL rotates the leftmost 1-bit of the BL to the rightmost vacated position. The second and third ROL operations rotate the three leftmost bits.

Similarly to RCR, RCL also causes the carry flag to participate in the rotation. Each shifted-off bit on the left moves into the CF, and the CF bit moves into the vacated bit position on the right.

You can use the JC (Jump if Carry) instruction to test the bit rotated into the CF at the end of a rotate operation.

Doubleword Shift and Rotate

You can also use shift and rotate instructions to multiply and divide doubleword values by multiples of 2. Consider a 32-bit value of which the leftmost 16 bits are in the DX and the rightmost 16 bits are in the AX, as DX:AX. Instructions to "multiply" the value by 2 could be:

```
SHL   AX,1    ;Use left shift to multiply
RCL   DX,1    ; DX:AX pair by 2
```

The SHL shifts all bits in the AX to the left, and the leftmost bit shifts into the carry flag. The RCL shifts the DX left and inserts the bit from the CF into the rightmost vacated bit. To multiply by 4, follow the SHL-RCL pair with an identical SHL-RCL pair.

For division, consider again a 32-bit value in the DX:AX. Instructions to "divide" the value by 2 would be

```
SAR   DX,1    ;Use right shift to divide
RCR   AX,1    ; DX:AX pair by 2
```

To divide by 4, follow the SAR-RCR pair with an identical SAR-RCR pair.
Double-precision shifts for the 80386 and later processors are SHRD and SHLD.

JUMP TABLES

A program may have a routine for testing a number of related conditions, each requiring a jump to another routine. Consider, for example, a system for a company that has established special codes for customers based on their credit rating and sales volume. The codes indicate the amount of discount to offer and other special processing that may be required for the customer. Customer codes are 0, 1, 2, 3, and 4.

A conventional way of handling codes is to compare for each customer code successively:

```
CMP     CUSCODE,0    ;Code = 0?

JE      D00DSCT

CMP     CUSCODE,1    ;Code = 1?

JE      D10DSCT

CMP     CUSCODE,2    ;Code = 2?

JE      D20DSCT

CMP     CUSCODE,3    ;Code = 3

JE      D30DSCT

CMP     CUSCODE,4    ;Code = 4?

JE      D40NSCT
```

With this approach, the opportunity for errors is great: Just consider matching the correct codes against their values and jumping to the correct routine. A more elegant solution involves a table of jump addresses. As shown in the partial program in Figure 8–5, CUSTTBL defines the five addresses successively in words (two bytes each). The routine at D10JUMP accesses the codes (as hex values 00–04) into the BX register. The value is doubled, so that 0 stays 0, 1 becomes 2, 2 becomes 4, and so forth. The doubled value provides an offset into the table: CUSTTBL+0 is the first address, CUSTTBL+2 is the second, CUSTTBL+4 is the third, and so forth. The operand of the JMP instruction, [CUSTTBL+BX], forms an address based on the start of the table plus an offset into the table. The operation then jumps directly to the appropriate routine.

An important constraint in the program is that the codes may be only the hex values 00–04; any other value would cause dire results! If you use DEBUG to run this program, enter valid hex values (00–04) into CUSCODE to check the effect of the logic.

For the 80386 and later processors, you could replace the two instructions at D10JUMP, that is,

```
MOV     BL,CUSCODE    ;Get discount code

XOR     BH,BH         ;Clear upper BX
```

with one instruction:

```
MOVZX   BX,CUSCODE    ;Get discount code
```

PROGRAM ORGANIZATION

The following are typical steps in writing an assembly language program:

1. Have a clear idea of the problem that the program is to solve.
2. Sketch your ideas in general terms, and plan the overall logic. For example, if a problem is to test multibyte move operations, start by defining the fields to be moved.

```
                              PAGE    60,132
                     TITLE    P08JMPTB (EXE)  Use of a jump table
                              .MODEL SMALL
                              .STACK 64
                   ; ----------------------------------------------
                              .DATA
   0000 001B R      CUSTTBL   DW      D00NODSC   ;Table of addresses
   0002 001E R                DW      D10DSCT
   0004 0021 R                DW      D20DSCT
   0006 0024 R                DW      D30DSCT
   0008 0027 R                DW      D40DSCT
   000A 04         CUSCODE    DB      04         ;Discount code
                   ; ----------------------------------------------
                              .CODE
   0000             BEGIN     PROC    FAR
   0000 B8 ---- R             MOV     AX,@data   ;Initialize
   0003 8E D8                 MOV     DS,AX      ;  segment
   0005 8E C0                 MOV     ES,AX      ;  registers
                   ;          ...
   0007 E8 000F R             CALL    D10JUMP    ;Invoke jump rtne
                   ;          ...
   000A B8 4C00               MOV     AX,4C00H   ;Exit to DOS
   000D CD 21                 INT     21H
   000F             BEGIN     ENDP

   000F             D10JUMP   PROC    NEAR
   000F 8A 1E 000A R          MOV     BL,CUSCODE ;Get discount code
   0013 32 FF                 XOR     BH,BH      ;Clear upper BX
   0015 D1 E3                 SHL     BX,01      ;Double value
   0017 FF A7 0000 R          JMP     [CUSTTBL+BX] ;To customer rtne
                   ;          ...
   001B             D00NODSC:                   ;Code 0 routine
                   ;          ...
   001B EB 0D 90              JMP     D90RET
   001E             D10DSCT:                    ;Code 1 routine
                   ;          ...
   001E EB 0A 90              JMP     D90RET
   0021             D20DSCT:                    ;Code 2 routine
                   ;          ...
   0021 EB 07 90              JMP     D90RET
   0024             D30DSCT:                    ;Code 3 routine
                   ;          ...
   0024 EB 04 90              JMP     D90RET
   0027             D40DSCT:                    ;Code 4 routine
                   ;          ...
   0027 EB 01 90              JMP     D90RET
   002A C3          D90RET:   RET
   002B             D10JUMP   ENDP
                              END     BEGIN
```

Figure 8-5 Jump Table

Then plan the strategy for the instructions: routines for initialization, for using a conditional jump, and for using a LOOP. The following, which shows the main logic, is pseudocode that many programmers use to plan a program:

- Initialize segment registers
- Call the Jump routine
- Call the Loop routine
- Return to DOS

The Jump routine could be planned as

- Initialize registers for count, addresses of names
- Jump1:
- Move one character of name
- Increment for next characters of names
- Decrement count: If nonzero, Jump1
- If zero, Return

The Loop routine could be sketched in a similar way.

3. Organize the program into logical units such that related routines follow one another. Procedures that are about 25 lines (the size of the screen) are easier to debug than procedures that are longer.

4. Use other programs as guides. Attempts to memorize all the technical material and code "off the top of the head" often result in even more program bugs.

5. Use comments to clarify what a procedure is supposed to accomplish, what arithmetic and comparison operations are performing, and what a seldom-used instruction is doing. (An example of the latter is LOOPNE: Does it loop *while* not equal or *until* not equal?)

6. For keying in the program, use a saved skeleton program that you can copy into a newly named file.

The remaining programs in this text make considerable use of JMP, LOOP, conditional jumps, CALL, and called procedures. Having covered the basics of assembly language, you are now in a position for more advanced and realistic programming.

KEY POINTS

- A short address is reached by an offset and is limited to a distance of -128 to 127 bytes. A near address is reached by an offset and is limited to a distance of $-32,768$ to $32,767$ bytes within the same segment. A far address in another segment is reached by a segment address and offset.
- A label such as "B20:" within a procedure requires a colon to indicate that it is a near label.
- Labels for conditional jump and LOOP instructions must be short. The operand generates one byte of object code: 01H to 7FH covers the range from decimal $+1$ to $+127$, and FFH to 80H covers the range from -1 to -128. Since machine instructions vary in length from one to four bytes, the range is not obvious, but about two screens full of source code is a practical guide.
- When using LOOP, initialize the CX with a positive number, since LOOP decrements the CX and checks for a zero value.
- When an instruction sets a flag, the flag remains set until another instruction changes it.
- Select the appropriate conditional jump instruction, depending on whether the operation processes signed or unsigned data.

- Use CALL to access a procedure, and include RET at the end of the procedure for returning. A called procedure may call other procedures, and if you follow the conventions, RET causes the correct address in the stack to pop. The only examples in this book that jump to a procedure are at the beginning of .COM programs.
- Use left shift to double a value and right shift to halve a value. Be sure to select the appropriate shift instruction for unsigned and for signed data.

QUESTIONS

8–1. Explain these terms: (a) short address; (b) near address; (c) far address.

8–2. **(a)** What is the maximum number of bytes that a near JMP, a LOOP, and a conditional jump instruction may jump? (b) What characteristic of the machine code operand causes this limit?

8–3. A JMP instruction begins at offset location 0624H. Determine the transfer address, based on the following object code for the JMP operand: (a) 27H; (b) 6BH; (c) C6H.

8–4. Code a routine using LOOP that calculates the Fibonacci series: 1, 1, 2, 3, 5, 8, 13, ... (Except for the first two numbers in the sequence, each number is the sum of the preceding two numbers.) Set the limit for 12 loops. Assemble, link, and use DEBUG to trace through the routine.

8–5. Assume that AX and BX contain signed data and that CX and DX contain unsigned data. Determine the CMP (where necessary) and conditional jump instructions for the following:

(a) Does the DX value exceed the CX? (b) Does the BX value exceed the AX? (c) Does the CX contain zero? (d) Is there an overflow? (e) Is the BX equal to or smaller than the AX? (f) Is the DX equal to or smaller than the CX?

8–6. In the following, what flags are affected, and what would they contain? (a) An overflow occurred; (b) a result is negative; (c) a result is zero; (d) processing is in single-step mode; (e) a string data transfer is to be right to left.

8–7. Refer to Figure 8–3. What would be the effect on program execution if the procedure B10 did not contain a RET?

8–8. What is the difference between coding a PROC operand with FAR and with NEAR?

8–9. What are the ways in which a program can begin executing a procedure?

8–10. In an .EXE program, A10 calls B10, B10 calls C10, and C10 calls D10. As a result of these calls, how many addresses does the stack contain?

8–11. Assume that the BL contains 1110 0011 and that a location named BOONO contains 0111 1001. Determine the effect on the BL for the following: (a) XOR BL,BOONO; (b) AND BL,BOONO; (c) OR BL,BOONO; (d) XOR BL,11111111B; (e) AND BL,00000000B.

8–12. Revise the program in Figure 8–4 as follows: Define the contents of TITLEX as uppercase letters, and code the instructions that convert uppercase to lowercase.

8–13. Assume that the DX contains binary 10111001 10111001 and the CL contains 03. Determine the hex contents of the DX after execution of the following unrelated instructions: (a) SHR DX,1; (b) SHR DX,CL; (c) SHL DX,CL; (d) SHL DL,1; (e) ROR DX,CL; (f) ROR DL,CL; (g) SAL DH,1.

8–14. Use shift, move, and add instructions to multiply the contents of the AX by 10.

8–15. A routine at the end of the section entitled "Rotating Bits" multiplies the DX:AX by 2. Revise the routine to (a) multiply by 4; (b) divide by 4; (c) multiply the 48 bits in the DX:AX:BX by 2.

CHAPTER 9 ——————————————

Introduction to Screen and Keyboard Processing

OBJECTIVE:

To introduce the requirements for displaying information on a screen and accepting input from a keyboard.

INTRODUCTION

Up to this point, our programs have defined data items either in the data area or as immediate data within an instruction operand. However, most programs require input from a keyboard, disk, mouse, or modem and provide output in a useful format on a screen, printer, or disk. This chapter covers the basic requirements for displaying information on a screen and for accepting input from a keyboard.

There are various requirements for specifying a device to the system and for requesting an input or output operation. The INT (Interrupt) instruction handles input and output for most purposes. The two types of interrupts covered in this chapter are BIOS INT 10H functions for screen handling and DOS INT 21H functions for displaying screen output and accepting keyboard input. These *functions* (or services) request an action; you insert a function value in the AH register to identify the type of operation the interrupt is to perform.

Low-level BIOS operations such as INT 10H transfer control directly to BIOS. However, to facilitate some of the more complex operations, DOS INT 21H provides an interrupt service that first transfers control to DOS. For example, input from a keyboard may involve a count of characters entered and a check against a maximum number. The DOS INT 21H operation handles much of this additional high-level processing and then transfers control automatically to BIOS, which handles the low-level part of the operation.

As a convention, this book refers to the value 0DH as the Enter character for the keyboard and as a Carriage Return for the screen and printer.

Operations introduced in this chapter are:

BIOS INT 10H FUNCTIONS		DOS INT 21H FUNCTIONS	
02H	Set cursor	02H	Screen display
06H	Scroll screen	09H	Screen display
		0AH	Keyboard input
		3FH	Keyboard input
		40H	Screen display

Chapters 10 and 11 cover advanced screen- and keyboard-handling features.

THE SCREEN

The screen is a grid of addressable locations at any one of which the cursor can be set. A typical video monitor, for example, has 25 rows (numbered 0 to 24) and 80 columns (numbered 0 to 79). Here are some examples of cursor locations:

	Decimal Format		Hex Format	
Screen Location	Row	Column	Row	Column
Upper left corner	00	00	00H	00H
Upper right corner	00	79	00H	4FH
Center of screen	12	39/40	0CH	27H/28H
Lower left corner	24	00	18H	00H
Lower right corner	24	79	18H	4FH

The system provides space in memory for a *video display area,* or buffer. The monochrome display area begins at BIOS location B000[0]H and supports 4K bytes of memory, 2K of which are available for characters and 2K for an attribute for each character, such as reverse video, blinking, high intensity, and underlining. The basic color graphics video display area supports 16K bytes, starting at BIOS location B800[0]H. You can process either in text mode for normal character display or in graphics mode. For text mode, the display area provides for screen "pages" numbered 0 through 3 for an 80-column screen, with bytes for each character and its attribute.

The interrupts that handle screen displays transfer your data directly to a video display area, depending on the type of video adapter installed, such as EGA or VGA. Although technically your programs may transfer data directly to a video display area, there is no assurance that the memory addresses will be the same on all models, so writing data directly to a display area, although fast, can be risky. The recommended practice is to use the appropriate interrupt instructions: INT 10H functions to display, to set the cursor at any location, and to clear the screen and INT 21H functions for various types of display.

SETTING THE CURSOR

Setting the cursor is a common requirement for text mode, since its position determines where the next character is to display. (Graphics mode does not support the cursor.) INT 10H is the BIOS operation for screen handling, and function 02H in the AH tells the operation to set the cursor. Load the page (or screen) number, normally 0, in the BH register and the required row and column in the DX. The contents of the other registers are not important.

The following instructions set the cursor to row 05, column 12:

```
MOV   AH,02H           ;Request set cursor

MOV   BH,00            ;Page number 0

MOV   DH,05            ;Row 05

MOV   DL,12            ;Column 12

INT   10H             ;Interrupt—call BIOS
```

To set the row and column in the DX, you could also use one MOV instruction with an immediate hex value, such as

```
MOV DX,050CH           ;Row 05, column 12
```

CLEARING THE SCREEN

BIOS INT 10H function 06H handles screen clearing or scrolling. You can clear all or part of a display beginning at any screen location and ending at any higher numbered location. For example, to clear the entire screen, specify the starting row:column as 00:00H and the ending row:column as 18:4FH. Load these registers:

- AH = function 06H
- AL = 00H for full screen
- BH = attribute value
- CX = starting row:column
- DX = ending row:column

Attribute 71H in the following example sets the entire screen to white background (7) with blue foreground (1):

```
MOV   AX,0600H         ;AH 06 (scroll), AL 00 (full screen)

MOV   BH,71H           ;Attribute: white (7) on blue (1)

MOV   CX,0000H         ;Upper left row:column

MOV   DX,184FH         ;Lower right row:column

INT   10H             ;Interrupt—call BIOS
```

If you mistakenly set the lower right screen location higher than 184FH, the operation wraps around the screen and clears some locations twice. This may cause an error on some systems. The next chapter describes scrolling in more detail.

A program often has to display messages to a user that request data or an action the user must take. We'll first examine the methods for original DOS versions, which are useful for exercises and small programs, and later examine the methods that involve file handles. The original DOS operations work under all versions and in some respects are simpler and easier to use, although use of the newer operations for software production is recommended.

DOS FUNCTION 09H FOR SCREEN DISPLAY

The simplicity of the original DOS function 09H for displaying still keeps it in common use. It requires definition of a display string in the data area. The string is immediately followed by a dollar sign ($, or 24H) delimiter, which the operation uses to end the display. The following example illustrates:

```
NAMPRMP DB 'Customer name?','$' ;Display string
```

You can code the dollar sign immediately following the display string as just shown, inside the string as 'Customer name?$', or on the next line as DB '$'. The effect, however, is that you can't use this function to display a $ character on the screen.

Set function 09H in the AH register, use LEA to load the address of the display string in the DX, and issue an INT 21H instruction. The operation displays the characters from left to right and recognizes the end of data on encountering the dollar sign ($) delimiter. The assembly language code is:

```
MOV    AH,09H         ;Request display
LEA    DX,NAMPRMP     ;Load address of prompt
INT    21H            ;Call DOS
```

The INT operation does not change the contents of the registers. A displayed string that exceeds the rightmost screen column automatically continues on the next row and scrolls the screen as necessary. If you omit the dollar sign at the end of the string, the operation displays characters from memory until it finds one—if there is any.

Using INT 21H Function 09H to Display ASCII Characters

Most of the 256 ASCII characters are represented by symbols that can be displayed on a video screen. Some values, such as 00H and FFH, may have no displayable symbol and appear as blank, although the true ASCII blank character is 20H.

The .COM program in Figure 9–1 displays the entire range of ASCII characters. The program calls three procedures:

- B10CLR uses INT 10H, function 06H, to clear the screen.
- C10SET uses INT 10H, function 02H, to initialize the cursor to 00,00H.

```
            page 60,132
TITLE       P09DOSAS (COM)  Display ASCII characters 00H-FFH
            .MODEL SMALL
            .CODE
            ORG     100H
BEGIN:      JMP     SHORT MAIN
CHAR        DB      00,'$'

;                   Main procedure:
;                   --------------
MAIN        PROC    NEAR
            CALL    B10CLR          ;Clear screen
            CALL    C10SET          ;Set cursor
            CALL    D10DISP         ;Display characters
            MOV     AX,4C00H        ;Exit to DOS
            INT     21H
MAIN        ENDP
;                   Clear screen:
;                   ------------
B10CLR      PROC    NEAR
            MOV     AX,0600H        ;Scroll full screen
            MOV     BH,07           ;Attribute: white on black
            MOV     CX,0000         ;Upper left location
            MOV     DX,184FH        ;Lower right location
            INT     10H
            RET
B10CLR      ENDP
;                   Set cursor to 00,00:
;                   -------------------
C10SET      PROC    NEAR
            MOV     AH,02H          ;Request set cursor
            MOV     BH,00           ;Page number 0
            MOV     DX,0000         ;Row 0, column 0
            INT     10H
            RET
C10SET      ENDP
;                   Display ASCII characters:
;                   ------------------------
D10DISP     PROC
            MOV     CX,256          ;Initialize 256 iterations
            LEA     DX,CHAR         ;Initialize address of char
D20:
            MOV     AH,09H          ;Display ASCII char
            INT     21H
            INC     CHAR            ;Increment for next character
            LOOP    D20             ;Decrement CX, loop nonzero
            RET                     ;Return
D10DISP     ENDP
            END     BEGIN
```

Figure 9–1   DOS Function to Display the ASCII Character Set

- D10DISP uses INT 21H, function 09H, to display the contents of CHAR, which is initialized to 00H and is successively incremented by 1 to display each character until reaching FFH.

The first displayed line begins with a blank (00H), two "happy faces" (01H and 02H), and then a heart (03H), diamond (04H), and club (05H). Character 06H would have displayed a spade, but is erased by later control characters. Character 07H causes the speaker to sound, 08H causes a backspace, 09H causes a tab, 0AH causes a line feed, and 0DH

(Enter) causes a "carriage return" to the start of the next line. And, of course, under this operation, the dollar symbol, 24H, is not displayed at all. (As you'll see in Chapter 10, BIOS services can display proper symbols for these special characters.) The musical note is 0EH, and 7FH through FFH are extended ASCII characters.

You can revise the program to bypass attempting to display the control characters. The following instructions bypass all characters between 08H and 0DH; you may want to experiment with bypassing, say, only 08H (Backspace) and 0DH (Carriage Return).

```
        CMP   CHAR,08H        ;Below 08H?

        JB    D30             ;Yes—accept

        CMP   CHAR,0DH        ;Below or equal 0DH?

        JBE   D40             ;Yes—bypass

D30:

        MOV   AH,09H          ;Display < 08H

        ...                   ; and > 0DH

        INT   21H             ;Call DOS

D40:

        INC   CHAR
```

Although this exercise bypasses them, displaying the Backspace, Tab, Line Feed, and Carriage Return characters is the normal way to perform these operations.

Suggestion: Reproduce the preceding program, assemble it, link it, and convert it to a .COM file.

DOS FUNCTION 0AH FOR KEYBOARD INPUT

INT 21H function 0AH for accepting data from the keyboard is particularly powerful. The input area for keyed-in characters requires a *parameter list* containing specified fields that the INT operation is to process. First, the interrupt needs to know the maximum length of the input data. The purpose is to warn users who key in too many characters; the operation sounds the speaker and does not accept additional characters. Second, the operation delivers to the parameter list the number of bytes actually entered.

The code that follows defines a parameter list for an input area. (If you've worked in a high-level language, you may be used to the term *record* or *structure*.) LABEL is a directive with the type attribute of BYTE, which simply causes alignment on a byte boundary. The first byte contains your limit for the maximum number of input characters. The minimum is 0 and, since this is a one-byte field, the maximum is FFH, or 255. You decide on the maximum, based on the kind of data you expect users to enter. The second byte is for the operation to store the actual number of characters entered as a binary value. The third byte begins a field that is to contain the typed characters, from left to right. The assembly language code is:

```
NAMEPAR   LABEL   BYTE                ;Start of parameter list

MAXLEN    DB      20                  ;Maximum number of input characters

ACTLEN    DB      ?                   ;Actual number of input characters

NAMEFLD   DB      20 DUP(' ')         ;Characters entered from keyboard
```

In the parameter list, the LABEL directive tells the assembler to align on a byte boundary and gives the location the name NAMEPAR. Since LABEL takes no space, NAMEPAR and MAXLEN refer to the same memory location.

To request input, set function 0AH in the AH, load the address of the parameter list (NAMEPAR in the example), into the DX, and issue INT 21H:

```
MOV   AH,0AH            ;Request input function

LEA   DX,NAMEPAR        ;Load address of parameter list

INT   21H              ;Call DOS
```

The INT operation waits for a user to enter characters and checks that they do not exceed the maximum (20 in MAXLEN in the parameter list). The operation echoes each entered character onto the screen and advances the cursor. The user presses the Enter key to signal the end of an entry. The operation also transfers this Enter character (0DH) to the input field (NAMEFLD in the example), but does not count its entry in the actual length. If you key in a name such as BROWN (Enter), the parameter list appears like this:

ASCII:	20	5	B	R	O	W	N	#					...
HWX:	14	05	42	52	4F	57	4E	OD	20	20	20	20	...

The operation delivers the length of the input name, 05H, into the second byte of the parameter list, named ACTLEN in the example. The Enter character (0DH) is at NAMEFLD+5. (The # symbol here indicates this character, because 0DH has no printable symbol.) Since the maximum length of 20 includes the 0DH, the actual entered name may be up to only 19 characters.

The operation accepts and acts on the Backspace character, but doesn't add it to the count. Other than Backspace, the operation does not accept more than the maximum number of characters. If in the preceding example a user keys in 20 characters without pressing Enter, the operation causes the speaker to beep; at this point, it accepts only the Enter character.

The operation bypasses extended function keys such as F1, Home, PgUp, and Arrows. If you expect a user to enter any of them, use BIOS INT 16H or DOS INT 21H, function 01H, both covered in Chapter 11.

ACCEPTING AND DISPLAYING NAMES

The program in Figure 9–2 requests a user to enter a name, and then displays the name at the center of the screen and sounds the speaker. If a user enters, for example, the name Pat Brown, the program performs the following:

1. Divides the length 09 by 2: 9/2 = 4, with the fraction ignored.
2. Subtracts this value from 40: 40 − 4 = 36.

In F10CENT, the SHR instruction shifts the length 09 one bit to the right, effectively dividing the length by 2: Bits 00001001 become 00000100, or 4. The NEG instruction reverses the sign, changing +4 to −4. ADD adds the value 40, giving the starting position for the column, 36, in the DL register. With the cursor set at row 12, column 36, the name appears on the screen as follows:

```
          page   60,132
TITLE     P09CTRNM (EXE)  Accept names, center on screen
;-----------------------------------------------------------
          .MODEL SMALL
          .STACK 64
;-----------------------------------------------------------
          .DATA
NAMEPAR   LABEL  BYTE                 ;Name parameter list:
MAXNLEN   DB     20                   ;  maximum length of name
NAMELEN   DB     ?                    ;  no. of characters entered
NAMEFLD   DB     21 DUP(' ')          ;  entered name
PROMPT    DB     'Name? ', '$'
;-----------------------------------------------------------
          .CODE
BEGIN     PROC   FAR
          MOV    AX,@data             ;Initialize segment
          MOV    DS,AX                ;  registers
          MOV    ES,AX
          CALL   Q10CLR               ;Clear screen
A20LOOP:
          MOV    DX,0000              ;Set cursor to 00,00
          CALL   Q20CURS
          CALL   B10PRMP              ;Display prompt
          CALL   D10INPT              ;Provide for input of name
          CALL   Q10CLR               ;Clear screen
          CMP    NAMELEN,00           ;Name entered?
          JE     A30                  ;  no, exit
          CALL   E10CODE              ;Set bell & '$'
          CALL   F10CENT              ;Center & display name
          JMP    A20LOOP
A30:
          MOV    AX,4C00H             ;Exit to DOS
          INT    21H
BEGIN     ENDP
;                Display prompt:
;                --------------
B10PRMP   PROC   NEAR
          MOV    AH,09H               ;Request display
          LEA    DX,PROMPT
          INT    21H
          RET
B10PRMP   ENDP
;                Accept input of name:
;                --------------------
D10INPT   PROC   NEAR
          MOV    AH,0AH               ;Request keyboard
          LEA    DX,NAMEPAR           ;  input
          INT    21H
          RET
D10INPT   ENDP
```

Figure 9–2   Accepting and Displaying Names

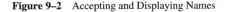

```
;                          Set bell and '$' delimiter:
;                          ---------------------------
E10CODE    PROC     NEAR
           MOV      BH,00                ;Replace Enter char (0D)
           MOV      BL,NAMELEN           ; with bell (07)
           MOV      NAMEFLD[BX],07
           MOV      NAMEFLD[BX+1],'$'  ;Set display delimiter
           RET
E10CODE    ENDP
;                          Center and display name:
;                          -----------------------
F10CENT    PROC     NEAR
           MOV      DL,NAMELEN           ;Locate center column:
           SHR      DL,1                 ;  divide length by 2,
           NEG      DL                   ;  reverse sign,
           ADD      DL,40                ;  add 40
           MOV      DH,12                ;Center row
           CALL     Q20CURS              ;Set cursor
           MOV      AH,09H
           LEA      DX,NAMEFLD           ;Display name
           INT      21H
           RET
F10CENT    ENDP
;                          Clear screen:
;                          ------------
Q10CLR     PROC     NEAR
           MOV      AX,0600H             ;Request scroll screen
           MOV      BH,30                ;Color (07 for BW)
           MOV      CX,0000              ;From 00,00
           MOV      DX,184FH             ;To 24,79
           INT      10H
           RET
Q10CLR     ENDP
;                          Set cursor row/column:
;                          ----------------------
Q20CURS    PROC     NEAR                 ;DX set on entry
           MOV      AH,02H               ;Request set cursor
           MOV      BH,00                ;Page #0
           INT      10H
           RET
Q20CURS    ENDP

           END      BEGIN
```

Figure 9–2   (continued)

```
Row 12:    Pat Brown
            |   |
Column:  36  40
```

Note the instructions in E10CODE that insert the Bell (07H) character in the input area immediately following the name:

```
MOV   BH,00                  ;Replace Enter character (0DH)

MOV   BL,NAMELEN             ; with Bell (07H)

MOV   NAMEFLD[BX],07H
```

The first two MOVs set the BX with the length. The third MOV references an index specifier in square brackets, which means that the BX is to act as a special index register to facilitate extended addressing. The MOV combines the length in the BX with the address of NAMEFLD and moves the 07H to the calculated address. Thus for a length of 05, the instruction inserts 07H at NAMEFLD+05 (replacing the Enter character) following the name. The last instruction in E10CODE inserts a '$' delimiter following the 07H so that DOS function 09H can display the name and sound the speaker.

Replying with Only the Enter Key

The program continues accepting and displaying names until the user presses only the Enter key as a reply to a prompt. DOS function 09H accepts it and inserts a length of 00H in the parameter list, like this:

```
Parameter list (hex): |14|00|0D| ...
```

If the length is zero, the program determines that input is ended, as shown by the instruction CMP NAMELEN,00 in A20LOOP.

Clearing the Enter Character

You can use input characters for various purposes, such as printing on a report, storing in a table, or writing on disk. For these purposes, you may have to replace the Enter character (0DH) wherever it is in NAMEFLD with a blank (20H). The field containing the actual length of the input data, NAMELEN, provides the relative position of the Enter character. For example, if NAMELEN contains 05, then the Enter character is at NAMEFLD+5. You can move this length into the BX register for indexing the address of NAMEFLD as follows:

```
MOV   BH,00            ;Set BX

MOV   BL,NAMELEN       ; to 00 05

MOV   NAMEFLD[BX],20H  ;Clear Enter character
```

The first two MOV instructions set the BX with the length 05. The third MOV moves a blank (20H) to the address specified in the first operand: the address of NAMEFLD plus the contents of BX—in effect, NAMEFLD+5.

Clearing the Input Area

Entered characters replace the previous contents in an input area and remain there until other characters replace them. Consider the following successive input:

INPUT	NAMEPAR (HEX)
1. PAINE	|14|05|50|41|49|4E|45|0D|20|20|20| ... |20|
2. HAMILTON	|14|08|48|41|4D|49|4C|54|4F|4E|0D| ... |20|
3. ADAMS	|14|05|41|44|41|4D|53|0D|45|5A|0D| ... |20|

The name HAMILTON replaces the shorter name PAINE. But because the name ADAMS is shorter than HAMILTON, it replaces HAMIL and the Enter character replaces the T. The remaining letters, ON, still follow ADAMS. You may want to clear NAMEFLD prior to prompting for a name, as follows:

```
         MOV  CX,20                 ;Initialize for 20 loops

         MOV  SI,0000               ;Start position for name

B30:

         MOV  NAMEFLD[SI],20H  ;One blank to name

         INC  SI                    ;Increment for next character

         LOOP B30                   ;20 times
```

Instead of the SI register, you could use DI or BX. A more efficient method that moves a word of two blanks requires only 10 loops. However, because NAMEFLD is defined as DB (byte), you would have to override its length with a WORD and PTR (pointer) operand, as the following indicates:

```
         MOV  CX,10                 ;Initialize for 10 loops

         LEA  SI,NAMEFLD            ;Initialize start of name

B30:

         MOV  WORD PTR[SI],2020H    ;Two blanks to name

         INC  SI                    ;Increment two positions

         INC  SI                    ; in name

         LOOP B30                   ;Loop 10 times
```

Interpret the MOV at B30 as "Move a blank word to the memory location where the address in the SI register points." This example uses LEA to initialize the clearing of NAMEFLD and uses a slightly different method for the MOV at B30 because you cannot code an instruction such as

```
    MOV WORD PTR[NAMEFLD],2020H ;Invalid
```

Clearing the input area solves the problem of short names being followed by previous data. A more efficient practice is to clear only positions to the right of the most recently entered name.

USE OF CONTROL CHARACTERS FOR DISPLAYING

One way to make more effective use of displays is to use the Carriage Return, Line Feed, and Tab control characters. you can code them as ASCII or hex values, like this:

CONTROL CHARACTER	ASCII	HEX	EFFECT ON CURSOR
Carriage return	13	0DH	Resets to leftmost position
Line feed	10	0AH	Advances to next line
Tab	09	09H	Advances to next tab stop

Use these control characters for handling the cursor whenever you display output or accept input. Here's an example that displays the contents of a character string named MESSAGE, followed by Carriage Return and Line Feed to set the cursor to the next line:

```
MESSAGE DB    09, 'PC Users Group Annual Report', 13, 10, '$'

        . . .

        MOV   AH,09H         ;Request display
        LEA   DX,MESSAGE     ;Load address of title
        INT   21H            ;Call DOS
```

Using EQU to redefine the control characters may make a program more readable:

```
CR        EQU   13     (or EQU 0DH)
LF        EQU   10     (or EQU 0AH)
TAB       EQU   09     (or EQU 09H)
MESSAGE DB    TAB, 'PC Users Group Annual Report', CR, LF, '$'
```

DOS FUNCTION 02H FOR SCREEN DISPLAY

You may find INT 21H, function 02H, useful for displaying single characters. Load in the DL the character that is to display at the current cursor position, and request INT 21H. The Tab, Carriage Return, and Line Feed characters act normally, and the operation automatically advances the cursor. The assembly language code is:

```
        MOV   AH,02H         ;Request display character
        MOV   DL,char        ;Character to display
        INT   21H            ;Call DOS
```

The following example shows how to use this service to display a string of characters. The string to display is defined in CONAME. The program loads the address of CONAME in the DI register and its length in the CX. The loop involves incrementing the DI (by INC) for each successive character and decrementing the CX (by LOOP) for the number of characters to display. The code is as follows:

```
CONAME  DB    'Software Services', 13, 10

        . . .

        MOV   AH,02H         ;Request display character
        MOV   CX,19          ;Length of character string
        LEA   DI,CONAME      ;Address of character string
A30:    MOV   DL,[DI]        ;Character to display
        INT   21H            ;Call DOS
```

```
INC   DI                ;Increment for next character

LOOP A30                ;Loop if not yet at end

   ...                  ;Finished
```

FILE HANDLES

We'll now examine the use of *file handles* for screen and keyboard operations, which is more in the UNIX and OS/2 style. A file handle is simply a number that refers to a specific device. Since the following standard file handles are preset, you do not have to define them:

HANDLE	DEVICE
00	Input, normally keyboard (CON), but may be redirected
01	Output, normally display (CON), but may be redirected
02	Error output, display (CON), may not be redirected
03	Auxiliary device (AUX)
04	Printer (LPT1 or PRN)

As can be seen, the normal file handles are 00 for keyboard input and 01 for screen display. Other file handles, such as those for disk devices, have to be set by your program. You can also use these services for redirecting input and output to other devices, although this feature doesn't concern us here.

FILE HANDLES FOR SCREEN DISPLAY

DOS INT 21H, function 40H, uses file handles to request display operations. Load the following registers:

- AH = Function 40H
- BX = File handle 01
- CX = Number of characters to display
- DX = Address of the display area

A successful INT operation returns to the AX the number of bytes written and clears the carry flag (which you may test).

An unsuccessful INT operation sets the carry flag and returns an error code in the AX: 05H = access denied (for an invalid or disconnected device) or 06H = invalid handle. Since the AX could contain either a length or an error code, the only way to determine an error condition is to test the carry flag, although display errors are rare:

```
JC error-routine ;Test for display error
```

The operation responds like DOS function 09H to control characters 07H (Beep), 08H (Backspace), 0AH (Line Feed), and 0DH (Carriage Return). The following instructions illustrate this operation:

```
DISAREA DB    'PC Users Society', 0DH, 0AH      ;Display area

    ...

        MOV   AH,40H                             ;Request display

        MOV   BX,01                              ;File handle for output

        MOV   CX,18                              ;Display 18 characters

        LEA   DX,DISAREA                         ;Display area

        INT   21H                                ;Call DOS
```

Exercise: Displaying on the Screen

Let's use DEBUG to examine the internal effects of using a file handle to display your name. Load DEBUG, and when its prompt appears, type A 100 to begin entering the following instructions (but not the leftmost numbers) at offset location 100H (remember that DEBUG assumes that entered numbers are in hexadecimal format):

```
100   MOV AH,40

102   MOV BX,01

105   MOV CX,xx   (Insert length of name)

108   MOV DX,10E

10B   INT 21

10D   NOP

10E   DB 'Your name'
```

The program sets the AH to request a display and sets offset 10EH in the DX—the location of the DB containing your name.

When you have keyed in the instructions, press Enter again. To unassemble the program, use the U command (U 100,10D), and to trace execution, press R and then repeated T commands. On reaching the INT instruction, use the P (Proceed) command to execute the interrupt through to the NOP instruction. Your name should be displayed on the screen. Use the Q command to quit DEBUG.

FILE HANDLES FOR KEYBOARD INPUT

DOS INT 21H, function 3FH, uses file handles to request keyboard input, although it's a somewhat clumsy operation. Load the following registers:

- AH = Function 3FH
- BX = File handle 00
- CX = Maximum number of characters to accept
- DX = Address of the data area for entering characters

A successful INT operation clears the carry flag (which you may test) and sets the AX with the number of characters entered.

An unsuccessful INT operation could occur because of an invalid handle; the operation sets the carry flag and inserts an error code in the AX: 05H = access denied (for an invalid or disconnected device) or 06H = invalid handle. Since the AX could contain either a length or an error code, the only way to determine an error condition is to test the carry flag, although keyboard errors presumably are rare.

Like DOS function 0AH, function 3FH also acts on the Backspace, but ignores extended function keys such as F1, Home, and PageUp.

The following instructions illustrate the use of DOS function 3FH:

```
INAREA DB   20 DUP(' ')   ;Input area

       ...

       MOV  AH,3FH         ;Request input

       MOV  BX,00          ;File handle for keyboard

       MOV  CX,20          ;Maximum 20 characters

       LEA  DX,INAREA      ;Input area

       INT  21H           ;Call DOS
```

The INT operation waits for you to enter characters, but unfortunately does not check whether the number of characters exceeds the maximum in the CX register (20 in the example). Pressing the Enter key (0DH) signals the end of an entry. For example, typing the characters "PC Users Group" enters the following in INAREA:

```
|PC Users Group|0DH|0AH|
```

The typed characters are immediately followed by Enter (0DH), which you typed, and Line Feed (0AH), which you did not type. Because of this feature, the maximum number and the length of the input area should provide for an additional two characters. If you type fewer characters than the maximum, the locations in memory following the entered characters still contain the previous contents.

A successful INT operation clears the carry flag and sets the AX with the number of characters delivered. In the preceding example, this number is 14, plus 2 for the Enter and Line Feed characters, or 16. Accordingly, a program can determine the actual number of characters entered. Although this feature is trivial for YES and NO type of replies, it is useful for replies with variable length, such as names.

If you key in a name that exceeds the maximum in the CX register, the operation actually accepts all the characters. Consider a situation in which the CX contains 08 and a user enters the characters "PC Exchange". The operation sets the first eight characters in the input area to "PC Excha" with no Enter and Line Feed following and sets the AX with a length of 08. Now, watch this—the next INT operation to execute does not accept a name directly from the keyboard, because it still has the rest of the previous string in its buffer. It delivers "nge" followed by the Enter and Line Feed characters to the input area and sets the AX to 05. Both operations are "normal" and clear the carry flag:

```
First INT:  PC Excha        AX = 08

Second INT: nge, 0DH, 0AH   AX = 05
```

A program can tell whether a user has keyed in a "valid" number of characters if (a) the number returned in the AX is less than the number in the CX or (b) the number returned in the AX is equal to that in the CX, and the last two characters in the input area are 0DH and 0AH. If neither condition is true, you'll have to issue additional INTs to accept the remaining characters. After all this, you may well wonder what is the point of specifying a maximum length in the CX at all!

Exercise: Entering Data

Here's a DEBUG exercise in which you can view the effect of using DOS function 3FH for entering data. The program allows you to key in up to 12 characters, including a character for Enter and one for Line Feed. Load DEBUG, and when the prompt appears, type A 100 to begin entering the following instructions (but not the numbers) at location 100H:

```
100   MOV AH,3F

102   MOV BX,00

105   MOV CX,0C

108   MOV DX,10F

10B   INT 21

10D   JMP 100

10F   DB 20 20 20 20 20 20 20 20 20 20 20 20
```

The program sets the AH and BX to request keyboard input and inserts the maximum length in the CX. It also sets offset 10FH in the DX—the location of the DB, where the entered characters are to begin.

When you have keyed in the instructions, press Enter again. Try the U command (U 100,10E) to unassemble the program. Use R and repeated T commands to trace the execution of the four MOV instructions. At location 10BH, use P (Proceed) to execute through the interrupt. The operation waits for you to key in characters followed by Enter. Check the contents of the AX register and the carry flag, and use D DS:10F to display the entered characters in memory. You can continue looping indefinitely. Key in Q to quit DEBUG.

KEY POINTS

- Monochrome display supports 4K bytes of memory, 2K of which are available for characters and 2K for an attribute for each character.
- The basic color display supports 16K bytes and can operate in color or monochrome. You can process either in text mode for normal character display or in graphics mode.
- Be consistent in using hex notation. For example, INT 21 is not the same as INT 21H.

- The INT 10H instruction transfers control to BIOS for display operations. Two common operations are function 02H (set cursor) and 06H (scroll screen).
- DOS INT 21H provides special functions to handle some of the complexity of input/output.
- When using INT 21H, function 09H, for displaying, define a delimiter ($) immediately following the display area. A missing delimiter can cause spectacular effects on the screen.
- INT 21H, function 0AH, for keyboard input expects the first byte to contain a maximum value and automatically inserts an actual value in the second byte.
- A file handle is a number that refers to a specific device. Some numbers for file handles are preset, while others can be set by your program.
- For DOS function 40H to display, use handle 01 in the BX.
- For DOS function 3FH for keyboard input, use handle 00 in the BX. The operation includes Enter and Line Feed characters following the typed characters in the input area. It does not check for entries that exceed your specified maximum.

QUESTIONS

9–1. What are the hex values for (a) the top leftmost location and (b) the bottom rightmost location on an 80-column screen?

9–2. Code the instructions to set the cursor to row 12, column 8.

9–3. Code the instructions to clear the screen, beginning at row 12, column 0, through row 22, column 79.

9–4. Code data items and DOS INT 21H, function 09H, to display the message "What is the date (mm/dd/yy)?" Follow the message with a beep.

9–5. Code data items and DOS INT 21H, function 0AH, to accept input from the keyboard according to the format in Question 9–4.

9–6. The section titled "Clearing the Input Area" shows how to clear to blank the entire keyboard input area, defined as NAMEFLD. Change the example so that it clears only the characters immediately to the right of the most recently entered name.

9–7. Key in the program in Figure 9–2 with the following changes: (a) Instead of row 12, set the center at row 15; (b) instead of clearing the entire screen, clear only rows 0 through 15. Assemble, link, and test the new program.

9–8. Identify the standard file handles for (a) keyboard input; (b) normal screen display; (c) the printer.

9–9. Code data items and DOS INT 21H, function 40H, to display the message "What is the date (mm/dd/yy)?" Follow the message with a beep.

9–10. Code data items and DOS INT 21H, function 3FH, to accept input from the keyboard according to the format in Question 9–4.

9–11. Revise Figure 9–2 for use with DOS INT 21H, functions 3FH and 40H, for input and display. Assemble, link, and test the new program.

CHAPTER 10

Advanced Screen Processing

OBJECTIVE:

To cover advanced features of screen handling, including scrolling, reverse video, blinking, and the use of color graphics.

INTRODUCTION

Chapter 9 introduced the basic features concerned with screen handling and keyboard input. This chapter provides advanced features related to video adapters, setting modes (text or graphics), and screen handling. The first section describes the common video adapters and their associated video display areas.

The sections on text mode explain the use of the attribute byte for color, blinking, and high intensity, as well as the instructions to set the cursor size and location, to scroll up or down the screen, and to display characters. The last few sections explain the use of graphics mode, together with the various instructions used for its display.

This chapter introduces the following services offered by BIOS INT 10H:

00H	Set video mode
01H	Set cursor size
02H	Set cursor position
03H	Read cursor position
04H	Read light pen position
05H	Select active page

06H   Scroll up screen
07H   Scroll down screen
08H   Read attribute or character at cursor position
09H   Display attribute or character at cursor position
0AH   Display character at cursor position
0BH   Set color palette
0CH   Write pixel dot
0DH   Read pixel dot
0EH   Write teletype
0FH   Get current video mode
11H   Character generator
12H   Select alternative screen routine
13H   Display character string
1BH   Return functionality or state information
1CH   Save or restore video state

VIDEO ADAPTERS

The common video adapters include:

MDA   Monochrome display adapter
HGC   Hercules graphics card
CGA   Color graphics adapter
EGA   Enhanced graphics adapter
MCGA   Multicolor graphics array (PS/2 models 25 and 30)
VGA   Video graphics array

The VGA and its superVGA clones replaced the CGA and EGA video adapters. Software written for a CGA or an EGA usually can run on a VGA system, although software written specifically for a VGA doesn't run on a CGA or an EGA.

A video adapter consists of three basic units: the video controller, video BIOS, and video display area.

1. The *video controller*, the workhorse unit, generates the monitor's scan signals for the selected text or graphics mode. The computer's processor sends instructions to the controller's registers and reads status information from them.
2. The *video BIOS*, which acts as an interface to the video adapter, contains such routines as setting the cursor and displaying characters.
3. The *video display area* in memory contains the information that the monitor is to display. The interrupts that handle screen displays transfer your data directly to this area. The locations of the video display area depend on the video modes in use. Following are the beginning video display segment addresses for major video adapters:
   • A000:[0] Used for font descriptors when in text mode and for high-resolution graphics for EGA, MCGA, and VGA
   • B000:[0] Monochrome text mode for MDA, EGA, and VGA

- B100:[0] For HGC
- B800:[0] Text modes for CGA, MCGA, EGA, and VGA and graphics modes for CGA, EGA, MCGA, and VGA.

The common RGB color graphics monitor accepts input signals that are sent to three separate electron guns—red, green, and blue, for each of the primary additive colors.

SETTING THE VIDEO MODE

BIOS INT 10H, function 00H, can set the *mode* for the currently executing program or can switch between text and graphics. Setting the mode also clears the screen. As an example, mode 03 represents text mode, color, and screen resolution, depending on the type of monitor.

To set a new mode, request INT 10H, with function 00H in the AH register and the mode in the AL. The following example sets the video mode for standard color text on any type of color monitor (if you try this operation, you'll notice that it is also a fast way to clear the screen):

```
MOV   AH,00H       ;Request set mode

MOV   AL,03H       ;80 X 25 standard color text

INT   10H          ;Call BIOS
```

If you write software for unknown video monitors, you can use INT 10H, function 0FH (covered later), which returns the current video mode in the AL. Another approach is to use BIOS INT 11H to determine the device attached to the system, although the information delivered is rather primitive. The operation returns a value to the AX, with bits 5 and 4 indicating video mode:

- 01: 40 X 25, using a color adapter
- 10: 80 X 25, using a color adapter
- 11: 80 X 25, using a monochrome adapter.

You can test the AX for the type of monitor and then set the mode accordingly.

TEXT MODE

Text mode is used for the normal display of ASCII characters on the screen. Processing is similar for both monochrome and color, except that color does not support the underline attribute. Text mode provides access to the full extended ASCII 256-character set. Figure 10–1 shows common text modes, with the mode number on the left.

Text modes 00 (mono) and 01 (color).   These modes provide 40-column format. Although originally designed for the CGA, they are upward compatible and also work on EGA and VGA systems.

Mode	Size	Type	Adapter	Resolution	Colors
00	(25 rows, 40 cols)	Mono	CGA	320 x 200	
			EGA	320 x 350	
			MCGA	320 x 400	
			VGA	360 x 400	
01	(25 rows, 40 cols)	Color	CGA	320 x 200	16
			EGA	320 x 350	16 of 64
			MCGA	320 x 400	16 of 262,144
			VGA	360 x 400	16 of 262,144
02	(25 rows, 80 cols)	Mono	CGA	640 x 200	
			EGA	640 x 350	
			MCGA	640 x 400	
			VGA	720 x 400	
03	(25 rows, 80 cols)	Color	CGA	640 x 200	16
			EGA	640 x 350	16 of 64
			MCGA	640 x 400	16 of 262,144
			VGA	720 x 400	16 of 262,144
07	(25 rows, 80 cols)	Mono	MDA	720 x 350	
			EGA	720 x 350	
			VGA	720 x 400	

Note: MDA: Monochrome display adapter
       CGA: Color graphics adapter
      MCGA: Multicolor graphics array
       VGA: Video graphics array

Figure 10–1 Text Modes for Video Displays

Text modes 02 (mono) and 03 (color).   These modes provide conventional 80-column format. Although originally designed for the CGA, they are upward compatible and also work on EGA and VGA systems.

Text mode 07 (mono).   This is the standard monochrome mode for MDA, EGA, and VGA and offers respectable screen resolutions.

Attribute Byte

An *attribute byte* in text (not graphics) mode determines the characteristics of each displayed character. When a program sets an attribute, it remains set; that is, all subsequent displayed characters have the same attribute until another operation changes it. You can use INT 10H functions to generate a screen attribute and perform such actions as scroll up, scroll down, read attribute or character, or display attribute or character. If you use DEBUG to view the video display area of your system, you'll see each one-byte character, immediately followed by its one-byte attribute.

The attribute byte has the following format, according to bit position:

		Background			Foreground		
Attribute:	BL	R	G	B	I	R	G	B
Bit number:	7	6	5	4	3	2	1	0

The letters R, G, and B indicate bit positions for red, green, and blue, respectively.

- Bit 7 (BL) sets blinking
- Bits 6–4 determine the screen *background*
- Bit 3 (I) sets high intensity
- Bits 2–0 determine the *foreground* (for the character being displayed)

The RGB bits define a color—on both color and monochrome, 000 is black and 111 is white. For example, an attribute set with the value 0000 0111 means black background with white foreground.

Monochrome Display

For a monochrome monitor, bit 0 sets the underline attribute. To specify attributes, you may set combinations of bits as follows:

Back-ground	Fore-ground	Feature	Background BL R G B	Foreground I R G B	Hex
Black	Black	Nondisplay	0 0 0 0	0 0 0 0	00H
Black	White	Normal	0 0 0 0	0 1 1 1	07H
Black	White	Blinking	1 0 0 0	0 1 1 1	87H
Black	White	Intense	0 0 0 0	1 1 1 1	0FH
White	Black	Reverse video	0 1 1 1	0 0 0 0	70H
White	Black	Reverse blinking	1 1 1 1	0 0 0 0	F0H
		Underline	0 0 0 0	0 0 0 1	01H

Color Display

For many color displays, the background can display 1 of 8 colors and the foreground characters can display 1 of 16 colors. Blinking and intensity apply only to the foreground. You can also select 1 of 16 colors for the border. Color monitors do not provide underlining; instead, setting bit 0 selects the blue color as foreground.

The attribute byte is used the same way as was shown for a monochrome monitor. The three basic colors are red, green, and blue. You can combine these in the attribute byte to form a total of 8 colors (including black and white) and can set high intensity, for a total of 16 colors:

Color	I R G B	Color	I R G B
Black	0 0 0 0	Gray	1 0 0 0
Blue	0 0 0 1	Light blue	1 0 0 1
Green	0 0 1 0	Light green	1 0 1 0
Cyan	0 0 1 1	Light cyan	1 0 1 1
Red	0 1 0 0	Light red	1 1 0 0
Magenta	0 1 0 1	Light magenta	1 1 0 1
Brown	0 1 1 0	Yellow	1 1 1 0
White	0 1 1 1	High-intensity white	1 1 1 1

If the background and foreground colors are the same, the displayed character is invisible. You can also use the attribute byte to cause a foreground character to blink. Here are some typical attributes:

Back-ground	Fore-ground	Background BL R G B	Foreground I R G B	Hex
Black	Black	0 0 0 0	0 0 0 0	00
Black	Blue	0 0 0 0	0 0 0 1	01
Blue	Red	0 0 0 1	0 1 0 0	14
Green	Cyan	0 0 1 0	0 0 1 1	23
White	Light magenta	0 1 1 1	1 1 0 1	7D
Green	Gray (blinking)	1 0 1 0	1 0 0 0	A8

You can use INT 11H to determine the type of monitor installed. Then, for monochrome, use 07H to set the normal attribute (black background, white foreground) and, for color, use any of the color combinations described. The color stays set until another operation changes it. Text mode also supports screen pages 0–3, where page 0 is the normal screen.

As an example, the following INT 10H operation (explained later) uses function 09H to display five light green, blinking asterisks on a magenta background:

```
MOV   AH,09H        ;Request display

MOV   AL,'*'        ;Asterisk

MOV   BH,00H        ;Page number 0

MOV   BL,0DAH       ;Color attribute

MOV   CX,05         ;Five times

INT   10H           ;Call BIOS
```

You can use DEBUG to check out this example, as well as trying other color combinations.

SCREEN PAGES

Text modes allow you to store data in video memory in *pages*. Page numbers are 0 through 3 for normal 80-column mode (and 0 through 7 for the rarely used 40-column screen). In 80-column mode, page number 0 is the default and begins in the video display area at B800[0], page 1 begins at B900[0], page 2 at BA00[0], and page 3 at BB00[0].

You may format any of the pages in memory, although you can display only one page at a time. Each character to be displayed on the screen requires two bytes of memory—one byte for the character and a second for its attribute. In this way, a full page of characters for 80 columns and 25 rows requires $80 \times 25 \times 2 = 4,000$ bytes. The amount of memory actually allocated for each page is 4K, or 4,096 bytes, so that 96 unused bytes immediately follow each page.

BIOS INTERRUPT 10H FOR TEXT MODE

Earlier, we used INT 10H, function 00H, for setting the display mode. INT 10H also has other services (available through function codes in the AH), to facilitate full screen handling. The interrupt preserves the contents of the BX, CX, DX, DI, SI, and BP registers, but not the AX—a point to remember if you use INT 10H in a loop. The following sections describe each function.

INT 10H, Function 00H: Set Video Mode

As described earlier, this sets the AL with the mode, commonly 03 for color or 07 for monochrome. (See Figure 10–1.)

INT 10H, Function 01H: Set Cursor Size

The cursor is not part of the ASCII character set and exists only in text mode. The computer maintains its own hardware for cursor control, with special INT operations for its use. The normal cursor symbol is similar to an underline or break character, but you can use INT 10H, function 01H, to adjust the cursor size vertically. Set these registers:

- CH (bits 4–0) = top of cursor ("start scan line")
- CL (bits 4–0) = bottom of cursor ("end scan line")

You can adjust the cursor size between the top and bottom—0:14 for VGA, 0:13 for monochrome and EGA, and 0:7 for CGA. The following code enlarges the cursor from top to bottom for a VGA:

```
MOV   AH,01H     ;Request set cursor size
MOV   CH,00      ;Start scan line
MOV   CL,14      ;End scan line
INT   10H        ;Call BIOS
```

The cursor now blinks as a solid rectangle. You can adjust its size anywhere between the stated bounds—for example, 04:08, 03:10, and so forth. The cursor retains these attributes until another operation changes them. Using 0:14 (VGA), 12:13 (monochrome or EGA), or 6:7 (CGA) resets the cursor to normal. If you are unsure of your monitor's bounds, first try executing function 03H under DEBUG.

INT 10H, Function 02H: Set Cursor Position

This useful operation sets the cursor anywhere on a screen, according to row:column coordinates. Set these registers:

- BH = Page number, can be 0 (default), 1, 2, or 3 for 80-column text mode.
- DH = Row
- DL = Column

The cursor location on each page is independent of its location on the other pages. This code sets row 5, column 20, for page 0:

```
MOV   AH,02H        ;Request set cursor
MOV   BH,00         ;Page number 0
MOV   DH,05         ;Row
MOV   DL,20         ;Column
INT   10H           ;Call BIOS
```

INT 10H, Function 03H: Read Cursor Position

A program can use function 03H to determine the present row, column, and size of the cursor, particularly in situations where a program has to use the screen temporarily and has to save and reset the original screen. Set the page number in the BH, just as for function 02H:

```
MOV   AH,03H        ;Request cursor location
MOV   BH,00         ;Page number 0 (normal)
INT   10H           ;Call BIOS
```

The operation returns these values:

- AX and BX = Unchanged
- CH = Starting scan line of the cursor
- CL = Ending scan line
- DH = Row
- DL = Column

The following example uses function 03H to read the cursor and determine its location and size and then uses function 02H to advance the cursor to the next column on the screen:

```
MOV   AH,03H        ;Request cursor position
MOV   BH,00         ;Page 0
INT   10H           ;Call BIOS
MOV   AH,02H        ;Set cursor
INC   DL           ; at next column
INT   10H           ;Call BIOS
```

INT 10H, Function 05H: Select Active Page

Function 05H lets you set the page that is to be displayed for text modes 0–3 and 13–16. You can create different pages and request shifting from one page to another. Pages in 80-column mode are 0–3. Here is the code for this function:

```
    MOV   AH,05H        ;Request active page

    MOV   AL,page#      ;Page number

    INT   10H           ;Call BIOS
```

INT 10H, Function 06H: Scroll Up Screen

When a program inadvertently displays text down the screen past the bottom, the next line wraps around to start at the top. But even if the interrupt operation specifies column 0, the new lines are indented, and succeeding lines may be badly skewed. The solution is to scroll the screen, so that displayed lines scroll off at the top and blank lines appear at the bottom.

You already used function 06H in Chapter 9 to clear the screen. Setting a zero value in the AL causes the entire screen to scroll up, effectively clearing it. Setting a nonzero value in the AL causes that number of lines to scroll up. Load the following registers:

- AL = Number of lines, or zero for full screen
- BH — Attribute
- CX = Starting row:column
- DX = Ending row:column

The following code scrolls the full screen one line and sets a color attribute:

```
    MOV   AX,0601H      ;Scroll up one line

    MOV   BH,30H        ;Cyan background, black foreground

    MOV   CX,0000       ;From 00,00

    MOV   DX,184FH      ; to 24,79 (full screen)

    INT   10H           ;Call BIOS
```

Here's a standard approach to scrolling one line:

1. Define an item named, for example, ROW, initialized to zero, for setting the row location of the cursor.
2. Display a line and advance the cursor to the next line.
3. Test to see whether ROW is near the bottom of the screen (CMP ROW,22).
4. If no, increment ROW (INC ROW) and exit.
5. If yes, scroll one line, use ROW to set the cursor, and clear ROW to 00.

The CX and DX registers permit scrolling any portion of the screen. But be especially careful to match the AL value with the distance in the CX:DX, especially when you reference a partial screen. The following instructions scroll five lines, in effect creating a window at the center of the screen with its own attributes:

```
    MOV   AX,0605H      ;Scroll five lines

    MOV   BH,61H        ;Brown background, blue foreground

    MOV   CX,0A1CH      ;From row 10, column 28
```

```
MOV  DX,0E34H    ; to row 14, column 52 (part screen)

INT  10H            ;Call BIOS
```

This example specifies scrolling five lines, which is the same value as the distance between rows 10 and 14. Since the attribute for a window remains set until another operation changes it, you may set various windows to different attributes at the same time.

INT 10H, Function 07H: Scroll Down Screen

For text mode, scrolling down the screen causes the bottom lines to scroll off and blank lines to appear at the top. Load the following registers just as for function 06H, scroll up:

- AL = Number of lines, or zero for full screen
- BH = Attribute
- CX = Starting row:column
- DX = Ending row:column

INT 10H, Function 08H: Read Attribute or Character at Cursor Position

Function 08H can read both a character and its attribute from the video display area in either text or graphics mode. Load the page number, normally 0, in the BH, as the following example shows:

```
MOV   AH,08H     ;Request read attribute or character

MOV   BH,00      ;Page number 0 (normal)

INT   10H        ;Call BIOS
```

The operation returns the character in the AL and its attribute in the AH. In graphics mode, the operation returns 00H for a non-ASCII character. Since only one character at a time is read, you have to code a loop to read successive characters.

INT 10H, Function 09H: Display Attribute or Character at Cursor Position

Here's a fun operation that displays characters in text or graphics mode with blinking, reverse video, and all that. Set these registers:

- AL = Single ASCII character to be displayed any number of times
- BH = Page number
- BL = Attribute
- CX = Number of times the operation is to repetitively display the character in the AL.

Here's an example that displays 80 dashes and sets a color attribute:

```
        MOV   AH,09H              ;Request display

        MOV   AL,'-'              ;Character to display

        MOV   BH,0                ;Page number 0

        MOV   BL,61H              ;Brown background, blue foreground

        MOV   CX,80               ;80 repeated characters

        INT   10H                 ;Call BIOS
```

The operation does not advance the cursor or respond to the Bell, Carriage Return, Line Feed, or Tab character; instead, it attempts to display them as ASCII characters. The following code displays five blinking hearts with reverse video:

```
        MOV   AH,09H              ;Request display

        MOV   AL,03H              ;Heart (to be displayed)

        MOV   BH,00               ;Page number 0 (normal)

        MOV   BL,0F0H             ;Blink reverse video

        MOV   CX,05               ;Five times

        INT   10H                 ;Call BIOS
```

Displaying different characters requires a loop. In text but not graphics mode, displayed characters automatically carry over from one line to the next. To display a prompt or message, code a routine that sets the CX to 01 and loops to move one character at a time from memory into the AL. (Since the CX is occupied, you can't easily use the LOOP instruction.) Also, after displaying each character, use INT 10H, function 02H, to advance the cursor to the next column.

You can use this operation to change any valid video page and then use function 05H to display the page.

INT 10H, Function 0AH: Display Character at Cursor Position

This operation displays a character in text or graphics mode. The only difference between functions 0AH and 09H in text mode is that function 0AH uses the current attribute, whereas function 09H sets the attribute. Here is the code for this function:

```
        MOV   AH,0AH              ;Request display

        MOV   AL,char             ;Character to display

        MOV   BH,page#            ;Page number

        MOV   CX,repetition       ;Number of repeated characters

        INT   10H                 ;Call BIOS
```

DOS INT 21H functions that can print a string of characters and respond to screen control characters are often more convenient than BIOS operations.

INT 10H, Function 0EH: Write Teletype

This operation lets you use a monitor as a terminal for simple displays. Set function 0EH in the AH, the character to display in the AL, page number in the BH, and foreground color (graphics mode) in the BL:

```
MOV   AH,0EH          ;Request display

MOV   AL,char         ;Character to display

MOV   BH,page#        ;Active page number (some systems)

MOV   BL,color        ;Foreground color (graphics mode)

INT   10H             ;Call BIOS
```

The Backspace (08H), Bell (07H), Carriage Return (0DH), and Line Feed (0AH) control characters act as commands for screen formatting. The operation automatically advances the cursor, wraps characters onto the next line, scrolls the screen, and maintains the present screen attributes.

INT 10H, Function 0FH: Get Current Video Mode

Use this function to determine the current video mode. (See also function 00H.) Here's an example:

```
MOV   AH,0FH          ;Request video mode

INT   10H             ;Call BIOS

CMP   AL,03           ;If mode 3,

JE  ...               ; jump
```

The operation returns these values:

- AL = Current video mode
- AH = Characters per line (20, 40, or 80, where 50H − 80)
- BH = Current page number.

INT 10H, Function 11H: Character Generator

This complex function for EGA, MCGA, and VGA systems initiates a mode set and resets the video environment. A discussion is outside the scope of the text.

INT 10H, Function 12H: Select Alternative Screen Routine

This function supports EGA and VGA monitors. To get information on either of these monitors, load 10H in the BL; the operation returns:

- BH = 00H for color and 01H for monochrome
- BL = 00H for 64K, 01H for 128K, 02H for 192K, and 03H for 256K
- CH = Adapter bits
- CL = Switch setting.

The operation supports a number of elaborate functions for PS/2-type computers, such as 30H (select scan lines), 31H (default palette loading), and 34H (cursor emulation).

INT 10H, Function 13H: Display Character String

For EGA and VGA monitors, this operation displays strings with options of setting attributes and moving the cursor and acts on the Backspace, Bell, Carriage Return, and Line Feed control characters. The ES:BP registers should contain the segment:offset address of the string to display. The code is as follows:

```
MOV   AH,13H            ;Request display
MOV   AL,subfunction    ;0, 1, 2, or 3
MOV   BH,page#          ;Page number
MOV   BL,attribute      ;Screen attribute
LEA   BP,address        ;Address of string in ES:BP
MOV   CX,length         ;Length of string
MOV   DX,screen         ;Relative starting location on screen
INT   10H               ;Call DIOS
```

The four subfunctions in the AL are:

00   Display attribute and string; do not advance cursor.
01   Display attribute and string; advance cursor.
02   Display character and then attribute; do not advance cursor.
03   Display character and then attribute; advance cursor.

USING BIOS TO DISPLAY THE ASCII CHARACTER SET

The program in Figure 9–1 used DOS INT 21H to display the ASCII character set, but the operation *acted on* the Backspace, Bell, Carriage Return, and Line Feed control characters, rather than *displaying* them. The revised program in Figure 10–2 illustrates the use of BIOS INT 10H with the following functions:

0FH   Get the current video mode and save it.
00H   Set video mode 03 for this program, and restore the original mode on exiting.
08H   Read the attribute at the current cursor position, for use by function 06H.
06H   Scroll up the screen to clear the entire screen, using the attribute just read. Also, create a 16-line window with brown foreground and blue background for the displayed characters.
02H   Set the cursor initially, and advance it for each displayed character.

0AH   Display each character, including control characters, at the current cursor position.

The characters are displayed in 16 columns and 16 rows. This program, like others in this book, are written for clarity rather than processing efficiency. You could revise the program to make it more efficient—for example, by using registers for the row, column, and ASCII character generator. Also, since INT 10H destroys only the contents of the AX register, the values in the other registers don't have to be reloaded. However, the program won't run noticeably faster and it would lose some clarity.

EXTENDED ASCII CHARACTERS

Among the extended ASCII characters 128–255 (80H–FFH) are a number of special characters that are useful for displaying prompts, menus, and logos. For example, these characters are used to draw a rectangle with solid single or double lines:

```
TITLE       P10BIOAS (COM)  INT 10H to display ASCII character set
            .MODEL SMALL
            .CODE
            ORG     100H
BEGIN:      JMP     SHORT MAIN
CTR         DB      00              ;Counter for ASCII characters
COL         DB      24              ;Column of screen
ROW         DB      04              ;Row of screen
MODE        DB      ?               ;Video mode
;                   Main procedure:
;                   --------------
MAIN        PROC    NEAR
            CALL    B10MODE         ;Get/set video mode
            CALL    C10CLR          ;Clear screen
A20:
            CALL    D10SET          ;Set cursor
            CALL    E10DISP         ;Display characters
            CMP     CTR,0FFH        ;Last character displayed?
            JE      A30             ;  yes, exit
            INC     CTR             ;Increment ASCII counter
            ADD     COL,02          ;Increment column
            CMP     COL,56          ;At end of column?
            JNE     A20             ;  no, bypass
            INC     ROW             ;  yes, increment row
            MOV     COL,24          ;  and reset column
            JMP     A20
A30:
            CALL    F10READ         ;Get keyboard character
            CALL    G10MODE         ;Restore video mode
            MOV     AX,4C00H        ;Exit to DOS
            INT     21H
MAIN        ENDP
;                   Get and set video mode
;                   ----------------------
B10MODE     PROC    NEAR
            MOV     AH,0FH          ;Request get mode
            INT     10H
            MOV     MODE,AL         ;Save mode
            MOV     AH,00H          ;Request set new mode
            MOV     AL,03           ;Standard color
            INT     10H
            RET
B10MODE     ENDP
```

Figure 10–2   INT 10H to Display the ASCII Character Set

```
;                          Clear screen and create window:
;                          ------------------------------
C10CLR     PROC     NEAR
           MOV      AH,08H         ;Request get current
           INT      10H            ;  attribute in AH
           MOV      BH,AH          ;Move it to BH
           MOV      AX,0600H       ;Scroll whole screen
           MOV      CX,0000        ;Upper left location
           MOV      DX,184FH       ;Lower right location
           INT      10H
           MOV      AX,0610H       ;Create 16-line window
           MOV      BH,16H         ;Brown on blue
           MOV      CX,0418H       ;Upper left corner 04:24
           MOV      DX,1336H       ;Lower right corner 19:54
           INT      10H
           RET
C10CLR     ENDP
;                          Set cursor to row and column:
;                          -----------------------------
D10SET     PROC     NEAR
           MOV      AH,02H         ;Request set cursor
           MOV      BH,00          ;Page 0 (normal)
           MOV      DH,ROW         ;New row
           MOV      DL,COL         ;New column
           INT      10H
           RET
D10SET     ENDP
;                          Display ASCII characters:
;                          -------------------------
E10DISP    PROC     NEAR
           MOV      AH,0AH         ;Display
           MOV      AL,CTR         ;ASCII char
           MOV      BH,00          ;Page 0
           MOV      CX,01          ;One character
           INT      10H
           RET
E10DISP    ENDP
;                          Force pause, get keyboard character
;                          -----------------------------------
F10READ    PROC     NEAR
           MOV      AH,10H         ;Request get character
           INT      16H
           RET
F10READ    ENDP
;                          Restore original video mode
;                          ---------------------------
G10MODE    PROC     NEAR
           MOV      AH,00H         ;Request set mode
           MOV      AL,MODE        ;Original value
           INT      10H
           RET
G10MODE    ENDP
           END      BEGIN
```

Figure 10–2 (continued)

Character	Single Line	Double Line
Top left corner angle	DAH	C9H
Top right corner angle	BFH	BBH
Bottom left corner angle	C0H	C8H
Bottom right corner angle	D9H	BCH
Solid horizontal line	C4H	CDH
Solid vertical line	B3H	BAH

The following code uses INT 10H, function 09H, to draw a solid horizontal line 25 positions long:

```
MOV   AH,09H        ;Request display
MOV   AL,0C4H       ;Solid single line
MOV   BH,00         ;Page number 0
MOV   BL,0FH        ;Black fore, white back, intense
MOV   CX,25         ;25 repetitions
INT   10H           ;Call BIOS
```

Remember that function 09H does not advance the cursor.

The simplest way to display a box is to define it in the data segment and display the whole area. This next example defines and displays a menu in a single-line box:

```
MENU      DB   0DAH,  17 DUP(0C4H),    0BFH
          DB   0B3H,  ' Add records        ', 0B3H
          DB   0B3H,  ' Delete records   ', 0B3H
          DB   0B3H,  ' Enter orders       ', 0B3H
          DB   0B3H,  ' Print report       ', 0B3H
          DB   0B3H,  ' Update accounts ', 0B3H
          DB   0B3H,  ' View records      ', 0B3H
          DB   0C0H,  17 DUP(0C4H),    0D9H
          ...
          MOV   AH,40H            ;Request display
          MOV   BX,01             ;File handle for screen
          MOV   CX,152            ;Number of characters
          LEA   DX,MENU           ;Prompt
          INT   21H
```

In the next chapter, Figure 11–1 displays a similar menu in a double-line box. The "dots on" characters for drop shadows are often used to the right or bottom of a box:

Value	Character
B0	One-quarter dots on (light)
B1	One-half dots on (medium)
B2	Three-quarter dots on (dark)
DBH	Full shadow (black)

BLINKING, REVERSE VIDEO, AND SCROLLING

The program in Figure 10–3 accepts names from the keyboard and displays them on the screen. To make things more interesting, it displays the prompt with reverse video (blue on white), accepts the name normally (white on blue), and displays the name at column 40 in the same row with blinking and reverse video. Here is the format:

```
        Name? Benjamin Franklin    Benjamin Franklin [blinking]
         |                          |
     Column 0                    Column 40
```

To control the placement of the cursor, the program defines ROW for incrementing the screen row and COL for advancing the cursor when displaying the prompt and name. (INT 10H, function 09H, does not automatically advance the cursor.) The program displays down the screen until it reaches row 20 and then begins scrolling up one line for each additional prompt.

For keyboard input, the procedure D10INPT uses INT 21H, function 0AH.

```
              page      60,132
     TITLE    P10NMSCR (EXE) Reverse video, blinking, scrolling
              .MODEL   SMALL
              .STACK   64
;    --------------------------------------------------------
              .DATA
     NAMEPAR  LABEL    BYTE                ;Name parameter list:
     MAXNLEN  DB       20                  ;  maximum length of name
     ACTNLEN  DB       ?                   ;  no. of chars entered
     NAMEFLD  DB       20 DUP(' ')         ;  name

     COL      DB       00
     COUNT    DB       ?
     PROMPT   DB       'Name? '
     ROW      DB       00
;    --------------------------------------------------------
              .CODE
     BEGIN    PROC     FAR
              MOV      AX,@data            ;Initialize segment
              MOV      DS,AX               ;  registers
              MOV      ES,AX
              MOV      AX,0600H
              CALL     Q10SCR              ;Clear screen
     A20LOOP:
              MOV      COL,00              ;Set column to 0
              CALL     Q20CURS
              CALL     B10PRMP             ;Display prompt
              CALL     D10INPT             ;Provide for input of name
              CMP      ACTNLEN,00          ;No name? (indicates end)
              JNE      A30
              MOV      AX,0600H
              CALL     Q10SCR              ;If so, clear screen,
              MOV      AX,4C00H            ;Exit to DOS
              INT      21H
     A30:
              CALL     E10NAME             ;Display name
              JMP      A20LOOP
     BEGIN    ENDP
```

Figure 10–3 Blinking, Reverse Video, and Scrolling

```
;                          Display prompt:
;                          --------------
B10PRMP     PROC    NEAR
            LEA     SI,PROMPT          ;Set address of prompt
            MOV     COUNT,05
B20:
            MOV     BL,71H             ;Reverse video
            CALL    F10DISP            ;Display routine
            INC     SI                 ;Next character in name
            INC     COL                ;Next column
            CALL    Q20CURS            ;Set cursor
            DEC     COUNT              ;Countdown
            JNZ     B20                ;Loop n times
            RET
B10PRMP     ENDP
;                          Accept input of name:
;                          --------------------
D10INPT     PROC    NEAR
            MOV     AH,0AH             ;Request keyboard
            LEA     DX,NAMEPAR         ;  input
            INT     21H
            RET
D10INPT     ENDP
;                          Display name with blinking reverse video:
;                          ----------------------------------------
E10NAME     PROC    NEAR
            LEA     SI,NAMEFLD         ;Initialize name
            MOV     COL,40             ;Set screen column
    E20:
            CALL    Q20CURS            ;Set cursor
            MOV     BL,0F1H            ;Blink reverse video
            CALL    F10DISP            ;Display routine
            INC     SI                 ;Next character in name
            INC     COL                ;Next screen column
            DEC     ACTNLEN            ;Countdown name length
            JNZ     E20                ;Loop n times

            CMP     ROW,20             ;Near bottom of screen?
            JAE     E30
            INC     ROW                ;  no, increment row
            RET
    E30:
            MOV     AX,0601H           ;  yes,
            CALL    Q10SCR             ;  scroll screen
            RET
E10NAME     ENDP

;                          Display character:
;                          -----------------
F10DISP     PROC    NEAR               ;BL (attribute) set on en
            MOV     AH,09H             ;Request display
            MOV     AL,[SI]            ;Get name character
            MOV     BH,00              ;Page number
            MOV     CX,01              ;One character
            INT     10H
            RET
F10DISP     ENDP
;                          Scroll screen:
;                          -------------
Q10SCR      PROC    NEAR               ;AX set on entry
            MOV     BH,17H             ;White on blue
            MOV     CX,0000
            MOV     DX,184FH           ;Full screen
            INT     10H
            RET
Q10SCR      ENDP
;                          Set cursor row/col:
;                          -----------------
```

Figure 10–3   (continued)

```
Q20CURS    PROC    NEAR
           MOV     AH,02H
           MOV     BH,00              ;Page
           MOV     DH,ROW             ;Row
           MOV     DL,COL             ;Column
           INT     10H
           RET
Q20CURS    ENDP
           END     BEGIN
```

Figure 10–3   (continued)

DIRECT VIDEO DISPLAY

For some applications, the video display as routed through DOS and BIOS may be noticeably slow. The fastest way to display screen characters (text or graphics) is to transfer them directly to the appropriate video display area. For example, the address of page 0 in the video area for mode 03 (color, text) is B800[0]H. Each screen character requires two bytes of memory—one for the character and one immediately following for its attribute. With a screen size of 80 columns and 25 rows, a page in the video area requires $80 \times 25 \times 2 = 4,000$ bytes.

The first two bytes in the video display area represent one screen location, for row 00, column 00, and the last bytes at F9EH and F9FH represent the screen location for row 24, column 79. Simply moving a character:attribute into the video area of the active page causes the character to appear immediately on the screen. You can check this with DEBUG commands. First, display the video area at B800[0]H:

```
                                 D B800:00
```

The display shows what was on the screen at the time you typed the command, which is usually a set of bytes containing 20 07H (for blank character, black background, and white foreground). Note that DEBUG and you are both competing for the same display area and screen. Try changing the screen with these commands to display happy faces on the top and bottom rows:

```
                  E B800:000 01 25 02 36 03 47

                  E B800:F90 01 25 02 36 03 47
```

The program in Figure 10–4 gives an example of transferring data directly to the video display area at B900[0]H—that is, page 1, rather than the default page 0. The program uses the SEGMENT AT feature to define the BIOS video display area, in effect as a dummy segment. (This is not a violation of the rule that a .COM program may have only one segment.) VIDAREA identifies the location of page 01, at the start of the segment.

The program displays characters in rows 5 through 20 and columns 10 through 70. The first row displays a string of the character A (41H) with an attribute of 01H, the second row displays a string of the character B (42H) with an attribute of 02H, and so forth, with the character:attribute incremented for each row.

```
                        TITLE      P10DRVID (EXE) Direct video display
                                   .MODEL   SMALL
0000                    VIDSEG     SEGMENT AT 0B900H   ;Page 1 of video area
0000 1000[?]           VIDAREA    DB       1000H DUP(?)
1000                    VIDSEG     ENDS
              ; --------------------------------------------------
                                   .STACK 64
              ; --------------------------------------------------
                                   .CODE
0000                    BEGIN      PROC     FAR
0000 B8 ---- R                     MOV      AX,VIDSEG      ;Addressability for
0003 8E C0                         MOV      ES,AX          ;  video area
                                   ASSUME ES:VIDSEG
0005 B4 0F                         MOV      AH,0FH         ;Request get
0007 CD 10                         INT      10H            ;  and save
0009 50                            PUSH     AX             ;  current mode
000A 53                            PUSH     BX             ;  and page
000B B4 00                         MOV      AH,00H         ;Request set
000D B0 03                         MOV      AL,03          ;  mode 03, clear screen
000F CD 10                         INT      10H;
0011 B4 05                         MOV      AH,05H         ;Request set
0013 B0 01                         MOV      AL,01H         ;  page #01
0015 CD 10                         INT      10H
0017 E8 002E R                     CALL     C10PROC        ;Process display area
001A E8 004D R                     CALL     E10INPT        ;Provide for input
001D B4 05                         MOV      AH,05H         ;Restore
001F 5B                            POP      BX             ;  original
0020 8A C7                         MOV      AL,BH          ;  page number
0022 CD 10                         INT      10H
0024 58                            POP      AX             ;Restore video
0025 B4 00                         MOV      AH,00H         ;  mode (in AL)
0027 CD 10                         INT      10H
0029 B8 4C00                       MOV      AX,4C00H       ;Exit to DOS
002C CD 21                         INT      21H
002E                    BEGIN      ENDP

002E                    C10PROC    PROC     NEAR
002E B0 41                         MOV      AL,41H         ;Character to display
0030 B4 01                         MOV      AH,01H         ;Attribute
0032 BF 0294                       MOV      DI,660         ;Start of display area
0035 B9 003C           C30:        MOV      CX,60          ;Characters per row
                       C40:        MOV      WORD PTR[VIDAREA+DI],AX
0038 26: 89 85 0000 R                                      ;AX in display area
003D 47                            INC      DI             ;Next video
003E 47                            INC      DI             ;  locations
003F E2 F7                         LOOP     C40            ;Repeat 60 times
0041 FE C4                         INC      AH             ;Next atribute
0043 FE C0                         INC      AL             ;Next character
0045 83 C7 28                      ADD      DI,40          ;Indent for next row
0048 3C 51                         CMP      AL,51H         ;Last character to display?
004A 75 E9                         JNE      C30            ;  no, repeat
004C C3                            RET                     ;  yes, return
004D                    C10PROC    ENDP

004D                    E10INPT    PROC     NEAR
004D B4 10                         MOV      AH,10H         ;Request input
004F CD 16                         INT      16H
0051 C3                            RET
0052                    E10INPT    ENDP
                                   END      BEGIN
```

Figure 10–4   Direct Video Display

The program establishes the starting position of a page in the video display area based on the fact that there are $80 \times 2 = 160$ columns in a row. The starting position, then, for row 10, column 10, is $(160 \times 10 \text{ rows}) + (10 \text{ columns} \times 2) = 660$. After displaying one row, the program advances 40 positions in the display area for the start of the next line and ends on reaching the letter Q (51H).

The video display segment for page 1 is defined as VIDSEG and the page as VIDAREA. The program establishes the ES register as the segment register for VIDSEG. At the start, the program saves the current mode and page and then sets mode 03 and page 01.

In the procedure C10PROC, the starting character and attribute are initialized in the AX and the starting video area offset in the DI. The instruction MOV WORD PTR [VIDAREA+DI],AX moves the contents of the AL (the character) to the first byte of the display area and the AH (the attribute) to the second byte. The LOOP routine executes this instruction 60 times, displaying the character:attribute across the screen. It then increments the character:attribute and adds 40 to the DI—20 for the end of the current row and 20 for indenting the start of the next row (on the screen, 10 columns each). The routine then repeats the display of the next row of characters.

On completion of the display, the procedure E10INPT waits for the user to press a key and then the program restores the original mode and page.

GRAPHICS MODE

Graphics adapters have two basic modes of operation: text (the default) and graphics. Use BIOS INT 10H, function 00H, to set graphics or text mode, as the following two examples show.

1. Set graphics mode for VGA:

```
MOV    AH,00H        ;Request set mode

MOV    AL,0CH        ;Color graphics

INT    10H           ;Call BIOS
```

2. Set text mode:

```
MOV    AH,00H        ;Request set mode

MOV    AL,03H        ;Color text

INT    10H           ;Call BIOS
```

The EGA and the VGA provide significantly better resolution than the original CGA and are compatible with it in many ways. Resolutions and modes for graphics adapters are shown in Figure 10–5 and are as follows:

- *Graphics modes 04H, 05H, and 06H.* The address of the video display area for these modes is B800[0]. These are the original CGA modes, which are also used by the EGA and VGA for upward compatibility, so that programs written for the CGA can often run on an EGA or VGA.

Mode	Type	Adapter	Resolution	Colors
04H	Color	CGA,EGA,MCGA,VGA	320 x 200	4
05H	Mono	CGA,EGA,MCGA,VGA	320 x 200	
06H	Mono	CGA,EGA,MCGA,VGA	640 x 200	
0DH	Color	EGA,VGA	320 x 200	16
0EH	Color	EGA,VGA	640 x 200	16
0FH	Mono	EGA,VGA	640 x 350	
10H	Color	EGA,VGA	640 x 350	16
11H	Color	MCGA,VGA	640 x 480	2 of 262,144
12H	Color	VGA	640 x 480	16 of 262,144
13H	Color	MCGA,VGA	320 x 200	256 of 262,144

Figure 10–5 Graphics Modes for Video Displays

- *Graphics modes 0DH, 0EH, 0FH, and 10H.* The address of the video display area for these modes is A000[0]. These are the original EGA modes, which are also used by the VGA for upward compatibility, so that programs written for the EGA can usually run on a VGA. These modes also support 8, 4, 2, and 2 pages of video display area, respectively, with page 0 the default.

- *Graphics modes 11H, 12H, and 13H.* The address of the video display area for these modes is A000[0]. These modes are specifically designed for the VGA (and the now rare MCGA) and are not usable by other video adapters.

In graphics mode, ROM contains dot patterns for only the first (bottom) 128 characters. INT 1FH provides access to a 1K area in memory that defines the top 128 characters, eight bytes per character.

Pixels

Graphics mode uses *pixels* (also, picture elements or pels) to generate color patterns. For example, mode 04H for standard color graphics provides 200 rows of 320 pixels. Each byte represents four pixels (that is, two bits per pixel), numbered 0 through 3, as follows:

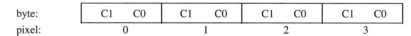

At any given time, there are four available colors, numbered 0 through 3. The limitation of four colors is because a two-bit pixel provides four bit combinations: 00, 01, 10, and 11. You can choose pixel 00 for any one of the 16 available colors for the background:

Color		Color	
Black	0000	Gray	1000
Blue	0001	Light blue	1001
Green	0010	Light green	1010
Cyan	0011	Light cyan	1011
Red	0100	Light red	1100
Magenta	0101	Light magenta	1101
Brown	0110	Yellow	1110
Light gray	0111	White	1111

And you can choose pixels 01, 10, and 11 for any one of two three-color palettes:

C1	C0	Palette 0	Palette 1
0	0	background	background
0	1	green	cyan
1	0	red	magenta
1	1	brown	white

Use INT 10H, function 0BH, to select a color palette and the background. Thus if you choose background color yellow and palette 0, the available colors are yellow, green, red, and brown. A byte consisting of the pixel value 10101010 would display as all red. If you choose background color blue and palette 1, the available colors are blue, cyan, magenta, and white. A byte consisting of pixel value 00011011 would display blue, cyan, magenta, and white.

BIOS INTERRUPT 10H FOR GRAPHICS

INT 10H facilitates full screen handling for both graphics and text mode, as described earlier. The operation preserves the contents of the BX, CX, DX, DI, SI, and BP registers, but not the AX. The following sections describe each of the functions of INT 10H.

INT 10H, Function 00H: Set Video Mode

Function 00H in the AH and mode 12H in the AL set standard VGA color graphics mode:

```
MOV   AH,00H     ;Request set mode for
MOV   AL,12H     ; 640 × 480 VGA resolution
INT   10H        ;Call BIOS
```

Setting graphics mode causes the cursor to disappear.

INT 10H, Function 04H: Read Light Pen Position

Use this function with graphics to determine the status of a light pen. The operation returns the following information:

AH   0 if status is not triggered and 1 if triggered.

DX   Row in the DH and column in the DL.

CH/BX   Pixel location, with raster (horizontal) line in the BH and column or dot in the BX.

INT 10H, Function 08H: Read Attribute or Character at Cursor Position

This function can read both characters and attributes from the display area in either text or graphics mode. See the earlier section, "BIOS Interrupt 10H for Text Mode."

INT 10H, Function 09H: Display Attribute or Character at Current Cursor Position

For graphics mode, use the BL for defining the foreground color. If bit 7 is 0, the defined color replaces present pixel colors; if bit 7 is 1, the defined color is combined (XORed) with them. For details, see the earlier section, "BIOS Interrupt 10H for Text Mode."

INT 10H, Function 0AH: Display a Character at Cursor Position

See the earlier section, "BIOS Interrupt 10H for Text Mode."

INT 10H, Function 0BH: Set Color Palette

Use this function to set the color palette and display a graphics character. The value in the BH (00 or 01) determines the purpose of the BL register:

1. BH = 00. Select the background color, where the BL contains the color value in bits 0-3 (any of 16 colors):

```
        MOV   AH,0BH        ;Request
        MOV   BH,00         ; background
        MOV   BL,04         ; color red
        INT   10H           ;Call BIOS
```

2. BH = 01. Select the palette for graphics, where the BL contains the palette (0 or 1):

```
        MOV   AH,0BH        ;Request color
        MOV   BH,01         ;Select palette
        MOV   BL,00         ; number 0 (green, red, brown)
        INT   10H           ;Call BIOS
```

Once you set a palette, it remains set. But once you change the palette, the whole screen changes to that color combination. If you use function 0BH while in text mode, the value set for color 0 for the palette determines the color of the border.

INT 10H, Function 0CH: Write Pixel Dot

Use function 0CH to display a selected color (background and palette). Set these registers:

- AL = Color of the pixel
- BH = Page number (EGA or VGA)
- CX = Column
- DX = Row.

The minimum value for the column or row is 0, and the maximum value depends on the video mode. The following example sets a pixel at column 50, row 70, on the screen:

```
MOV   AH,0CH          ;Request write dot

MOV   AL,03           ;Color of pixel

MOV   BH,0            ;Page number 0

MOV   CX,50           ;Horizontal position (column)

MOV   DX,70           ;Vertical position (row)

INT   10H            ;Call BIOS
```

EGA/VGA modes 0DH, 0EH, 0FH, and 10H provide 8, 4, 2, and 2 pages of video display area, respectively. The default page is number 0.

INT 10H, Function 0DH: Read Pixel Dot

This operation, the opposite of function 0CH, reads a dot to determine its color value. Set the BH for page number (EGA or VGA), the CX for column, and the DX for row. The minimum value for the column or row is 0, and the maximum value depends on the video mode. The operation returns the pixel color in the AL.

INT 10H, Function 0EH: Write Teletype

See the earlier section, "BIOS Interrupt 10H for Text Mode."

INT 10H, Function 10H: Set Palette Registers

This function handles EGA and VGA systems. A subfunction code in the AL determines the operation:

00   Set a palette register, where the BH contains the value to set and the BL contains the register to set.

01   Set the overscan register, where the BH contains the value to set.

02   Set all palette registers and overscan. ES:DX points to a 17-byte table, where bytes 0–15 are palette values and byte 16 is the overscan value.

03   Toggle the intensify/blinking bit, where 00 in the BL enables intensify and 01 enables blinking.

Other AL subfunction codes for the VGA under function 10H are 07H (read individual palette register), 08H (read overscan register), 09H (read all palette registers and overscan), 10H (set individual color register), 12H (set block of color registers), 13H (select color page), 15H (read individual color register), 17H (read block of color registers), and 1AH (read color page state).

INT 10H, Function 1AH: Read/Write Display Combination Code

This operation returns codes that identify the type of display that is in use.

INT 10H, Function 1BH: Return Functionality/State Information

This complex operation returns information to a 64-byte buffer identifying the video mode, cursor size, page supported, and so forth.

INT 10H, Function 1CH: Save or Restore Video State

This function saves and restores the video state, including the status of color registers, BIOS data area, and video hardware.

SETTING AND DISPLAYING GRAPHICS MODE

The program in Figure 10–6 uses a number of INT 10H functions, including the following, for a display of graphics:

- 0FH: Preserves the original mode
- 00H: Sets graphics mode
- 0BH: Selects background color green
- 0CH: Writes pixel dots for 640 columns and 350 rows.

The actual screen displayed is 210 rows and 512 columns. Note that rows and columns are in terms of dots, not characters.

The program increments the color for each row (so that bits 0000 become 0001, etc.) and, since only the rightmost four bits are used, the colors repeat after every 16 rows. The display begins 64 columns from the left of the screen and ends 64 columns from the right.

At the end, the program waits for the user to press a key, and then it resets the display to the original mode. For a VGA system, you could experiment by trying various graphics modes.

DETERMINING THE TYPE OF VIDEO ADAPTER

Since video graphics adapters support various services, there may be times when you want to know what type of adapter is installed in a system. A recommended way is to check first for VGA, then for EGA, and last for CGA or MDA. Here are the steps:

1. To determine whether a VGA is installed:

```
MOV    AH,1AH       ;Request VGA function
MOV    AL,0         ; and subfunction 0
INT    10H          ;Call BIOS
CMP    AL,1AH       ;If AL contains 1AH on return,
JE     VGAFOUND     ; system contains a VGA
```

2. To determine whether an EGA is installed:

```
MOV    AH,12H       ;Request EGA function
MOV    BL,10H       ;Amount of EGA memory
INT    10H          ;Call BIOS
```

```
TITLE       P10GRAFX (COM)  Graphics display
            .MODEL SMALL
            .CODE
            ORG     100H
BEGIN       PROC    NEAR
            MOV     AH,0FH          ;Preserve
            INT     10H             ;  original
            PUSH    AX              ;   video mode
            CALL    B10MODE         ;Set graphics mode
            CALL    C10DISP         ;Display color graphics
            CALL    D10KEY          ;Get keyboard response
            POP     AX              ;Restore
            MOV     AH,00H          ;  original mode
            INT     10H             ;   (in AL)
            MOV     AX,4C00H        ;Exit to DOS
            INT     21H
BEGIN       ENDP

B10MODE     PROC    NEAR
            MOV     AH,00H          ;Set EGA/VGA graphics mode
            MOV     AL,10H          ;640 cols x 350 rows
            INT     10H
            MOV     AH,0BH          ;Set background palette
            MOV     BH,00           ;Background
            MOV     BL,07H          ;Gray
            INT     10H
            RET
B10MODE     ENDP

C10DISP     PROC    NEAR
            MOV     BX,00           ;Set initial page,
            MOV     CX,64           ;  color, column,
            MOV     DX,70           ;  and row
C20:
            MOV     AH,0CH          ;Write pixel dot
            MOV     AL,BL           ;Set color
            INT     10H             ;BX, CX, & DX are preserved
            INC     CX              ;Increment column
            CMP     CX,576          ;Column at 576?
            JNE     C20             ;  no, loop
            MOV     CX,64           ;  yes, reset column
            INC     BL              ;Change color
            INC     DX              ;Increment row
            CMP     DX,280          ;Row at 280?
            JNE     C20             ;  no, loop
            RET                     ;  yes, terminate
C10DISP     ENDP

D10KEY      PROC    NEAR
            MOV     AH,10H          ;Request keyboard
            INT     16H             ;  input
            RET
D10KEY      ENDP
            END     BEGIN
```

Figure 10–6   Color Graphics Display

```
CMP     BL,10H          ;If BL no longer contains 10H,

JNE     EGAFOUND        ; system contains an EGA
```

Since an EGA may be installed along with an MDA or CGA, you may want to determine whether the EGA is active. The BIOS data area at 40:0087 contains an EGA instruction byte. Check bit 3, where 0 means that the EGA is active and 1 means that it is inactive.

3. To determine whether a CGA or MDA is installed, examine the word at location 40:0063, which contains the base address of the memory controller. Note that 3BxH means MDA and 3DxH means CGA.

KEY POINTS

- The attribute byte for text mode provides for blinking, reverse video, and high intensity. For color text, the RGB bits enable you to select colors, but not underlining.
- BIOS INT 10H provides functions for full screen processing, such as setting the video mode, setting the cursor location, scrolling the screen, reading from the keyboard, and writing characters.
- If your program displays lines down the screen, use BIOS INT 10H, function 06H, to scroll up before the display reaches the bottom.
- For INT 10H services that display a character, you have to advance the cursor and possibly echo the character to the screen.
- The 16K memory for color display permits storing additional "pages" or "screens." There are four pages per 80-column screen.
- The fastest way to display screen characters (text or graphics) is to transfer them directly to the appropriate video display area.
- A pixel (picture element) consists of a specified number of bits, depending on the graphics adapter and resolution (low, medium, or high).
- For graphics modes 04 and 05, you can select 4 colors, of which 1 is any of the 16 available colors and the other 3 are from a color palette.

QUESTIONS

10–1. Provide the attribute bytes, in binary, for monochrome screens for the following: (a) underline only; (b) white on black, normal intensity; (c) reverse video, intense.

10–2. Provide the attribute bytes, in binary, for the following: (a) magenta on light cyan; (b) brown on yellow; (c) red on gray, blinking.

10–3. Code the following routines: (a) Set the mode for 80-column monochrome; (b) set the cursor size to start at line 5 and end at line 12; (c) scroll up the screen 10 lines; (d) display 10 blinking "dots" with one-half dots (hex B1) on.

10–4. Under text mode 03, how many colors are available for background and for foreground?

10–5. Code the instructions for displaying five diamond characters in text mode with light green on magenta.

10–6. What mode permits the use of screen pages?

10–7. Write a program that uses INT 21H, function 0AH, to accept data from the keyboard and function 09H to display the characters. The program will clear the screen, set screen colors (your choice), and accept a set of data from the keyboard beginning at the current position of the cursor. The set of data could be four or five lines (say, any length up to 25 characters) entered from the keyboard, each followed by Enter. You could use a variety of colors, reverse video, or beeping as an experiment. Then set the cursor to a different row and column (you decide), and display the entered data at that location. The program is to accept any number of sets of data. It could terminate when the user presses Enter with no data. Write the program with a short main logic routine and a series of called subroutines. Include some concise comments.

10–8. Revise the program in Question 10–7 so that it uses INT 16H for keyboard input and INT 10H, function 09H, for display.

10–9. Explain how the common attribute byte limits the number of available colors.

10–10. Code the instructions to set graphics mode for these resolutions: (a) 320 × 200; (b) 640 × 200; (c) 640 × 480.

10–11. Code the instructions for selecting the background color blue in graphics mode.

10–12. Code the instructions to read a dot from row 12, column 13, in graphics mode.

10–13. Revise the program in Figure 10–6 so that it provides for the following: (a) a suitable graphics mode for your own monitor; (b) background color red; (c) row beginning at 10 and ending at 30; (d) column beginning at 20 and ending at 300.

10–14. Based on the changes you made in Question 10–13, revise the program to display graphics dots one column (instead of row) at a time. That is, display dots down the screen, then advance to the next column, and so forth.

CHAPTER 11 ————————————

Advanced Keyboard Processing

OBJECTIVES:

To cover all the keyboard operations and advanced features of keyboard input, including the shift status, keyboard buffer, and scan codes.

INTRODUCTION

This chapter describes the many different operations for handling keyboard input, some of which have specialized uses. Of these operations, INT 21H function 0AH (covered in Chapter 9), and INT 16H (covered in this chapter) should provide almost all the keyboard operations you'll require.

Other topics in the chapter include the keyboard shift status bytes, scan codes, and the keyboard buffer area. The shift status bytes in the BIOS data area enables a program to determine, for example, whether the Ctrl, Shift, or Alt keys have been pressed. The scan code is a unique number assigned to each key on the keyboard that enables the system to identify the source of a pressed key and enables a program to check for extended function keys such as Home, PgUp, and Arrows. And the keyboard buffer area provides space in memory for you to type ahead before a program actually requests input.

Operations introduced in this chapter are as follows:

DOS INT 21H FUNCTIONS

01H   Keyboard input with echo

06H	Direct console I/O
07H	Direct keyboard input without echo
08H	Keyboard input without echo
0AH	Buffered keyboard input
0BH	Check keyboard status
0CH	Clear keyboard buffer and invoke function

BIOS INT 16H FUNCTIONS

00H	Read a character
01H	Determine whether a character is present
02H	Return the current shift status
05H	Keyboard write
10H	Read a keyboard character
11H	Determine whether a character is present
12H	Return the current keyboard shift status

THE KEYBOARD

The keyboard provides three basic types of keys:

1. The letters A through Z, the numbers 0 through 9, and such characters as %, $, and #.
2. Extended function keys, which consist of:
   - Program function keys (F1, etc., Shift+F1, etc.)
   - Numeric keypad keys with NumLock toggled off (Home, End, Arrows, Del, Ins, PgUp, and PgDn) and the duplicate keys for them on the 101-key keyboard
   - Alt+alphabetics and Alt+program function keys.
3. Control keys for Alt, Ctrl, and Shift, which work in association with other keys. BIOS treats these differently from other keys by updating their current state in the shift status bytes in the BIOS data area. BIOS does not deliver them as ASCII characters to your program.

The original PC with its 83 keys suffered from a short-sighted design decision that caused keys on the so-called numeric keypad to perform two actions. Thus numbers shared keys with the Home, End, Arrows, Del, Ins, PgUp, and PgDn keys, with the NumLock key toggling between them. To overcome problems caused by this layout, designers produced an enhanced keyboard with 101 keys. Of the 18 new keys, only two, F11 and F12, provide a new function; the rest duplicate the function of keys on the original keyboard. If your programs allow users to press F11, F12, or any of the fancy new key combinations, the users must have an enhanced keyboard and a computer with a BIOS that can process them. For most other keyboard operations, your programs need not be concerned with the type of keyboard that is installed.

KEYBOARD SHIFT STATUS

The BIOS data area at segment 40[0]H contains a number of useful data items. These include the first byte of the current keyboard shift status at 40:17H, where, when set to 1, the bits indicate the following:

Bit	Action	Bit	Action
7	Insert active	3	Alt pressed
6	CapsLock state active	2	Ctrl pressed
5	NumLock state active	1	Left Shift pressed
4	Scroll Lock state active	0	Right Shift pressed

You may use INT 16H, function 02H (covered later), to check these values. Note that "active" means that the user is currently holding down the key; releasing the key clears the bit value. The 83-key keyboard requires only this shift status byte.

The enhanced 101-key keyboard has duplicate (left and right) Ctrl and Alt keys, so that additional information is needed to test for them. The second byte of the keyboard status needed for the 101-key keyboard is at 40:18H, where a 1-bit indicates the following:

Bit	Action	Bit	Action
7	Insert pressed	3	Ctrl/NumLock (pause) active
6	CapsLock pressed	2	SysReq pressed
5	NumLock pressed	1	Left Alt pressed
4	ScZroll Lock pressed	0	Left Ctrl pressed

Bits 0, 1, and 2 are associated with the enhanced (101-key) keyboard. You can now test, for example, whether either Ctrl or Alt is pressed, or both.

Another keyboard status byte resides at 40:96H. The item of interest to us here is bit 4; when on, it indicates that a 101-key keyboard is installed.

Shift Status Exercise

To see the effect of the Ctrl, Alt, and Shift keys on the shift status bytes, load DEBUG for execution. Enter D 40:17 to view the contents of the status bytes. Press the Caps-Lock, NumLock, and ScrollLock keys, and enter D 40:17 again to see the result on both status bytes. The byte at 40:17H should show 70H (0111 0000B), and the byte at 40:18H is probably 00H. The byte at 40:96H should show the presence (or absence) of a 101-key keyboard.

Try changing the contents of the status byte at 40:17H—enter E 40:17 00. If your keyboard Lock keys have indicator lights, they should turn off. Now try entering E 40:17 70 to turn them on again.

You could try various combinations, although it's difficult to type a valid DEBUG command while holding down the Ctrl and Alt keys. Enter Q to quit DEBUG.

KEYBOARD BUFFER

An item of interest in the BIOS data area at 40:1EH is the *keyboard buffer*. This feature allows you to type up to 15 characters before a program requests input. When you press a key, the keyboard's processor generates the key's scan code (its unique assigned number) and automatically requests INT 09H.

In simple terms, the BIOS INT 09H routine gets the scan code from the keyboard, converts it to an ASCII character, and delivers it to the keyboard buffer area. Subsequently, BIOS INT 16H (the lowest level keyboard operation) reads the character from the buffer and delivers it to your program. Your program need never request INT 09H, because BIOS performs it automatically when you press a key. A later section covers INT 09H and the keyboard buffer in detail.

DOS INTERRUPT 21H FOR KEYBOARD INPUT

This section covers the DOS services that handle keyboard input. All of these operations except function 0AH accept only one character. (To handle a string of characters, you would have to code a loop that accepts a character, checks for the Backspace and Enter keys, echoes the character to the screen if necessary, and advances the cursor.) For DOS keyboard input, insert a function in the AH and request INT 21H. In the discussion of the operations that follow, the term "respond to a Ctrl+Break request" means that DOS will terminate the program if the user presses the Ctrl+Break or Ctrl+C keys together. These operations have been superseded by function 3FH (covered in Chapter 10), but are included here for completeness.

INT 21H, Function 01H: Keyboard Input with Echo

This operation accepts a character from the keyboard buffer or, if none is present, waits for keyboard entry. The operation returns one of two status codes:

- AL = a nonzero value means that a standard ASCII character is present, such as a letter or number, which the operation echoes on the screen
- AL = zero means that the user has pressed an extended function key such as Home, F1, or PgUp, and the AH still contains the original function. The operation handles extended functions clumsily, attempting to echo them on the screen. And to get the scan code for the function key in the AL, you immediately have to repeat the INT 21H operation. The operation also responds to a Ctrl+Break request.

The following code illustrates this function:

```
MOV   AH,01H    ;Request keyboard input

INT   21H       ;Call DOS

CMP   AL,00     ;Extended function key pressed?

JNZ   ...       ;  no-ASCII character
```

```
         INT   21H         ;  yes—repeat operation

         ...               ;  for scan code
```

INT 21H, Function 06H: Direct Console I/O

This rather obscure, if not bizarre, operation can transfer any character or control code with no interference from DOS. There are two versions, for input and for output. For input, load 0FFH into the DL. If no character is in the keyboard buffer, the operation sets the zero flag and does not wait for input. If a character is waiting in the buffer, the operation stores the character in the AL and clears the zero flag. The operation does not echo the character on the screen and does not check for Ctrl+Break or Ctrl+PrtSc. A nonzero value in the AL represents a standard ASCII character, such as a letter or number. Zero in the AL means that the user has pressed an extended function key such as Home, F1, or PgUp. To get its scan code in the AL, immediately repeat the INT 21H operation:

```
         K10:   MOV   AH,06H       ;Request direct console

                MOV   DL,0FFH      ;Keyboard input

                INT   21H          ;Call DOS

                JZ    K10          ;Buffer empty—repeat

                CMP   AL,00        ;Extended function key pressed?

                JNZ   K30          ; no—ASCII character

                INT   21H          ; yes—repeat operation

                ...                ; for scan code
```

For screen output, load the ASCII character (not 0FFH) into the DL.

INT 21H, Function 07H: Direct Keyboard Input without Echo

This operation works like function 01H, except that the entered character does not echo on the screen and the operation does not respond to a Ctrl+Break request. You could use the operation to enter a password that is to be invisible or where you don't want to disturb the screen.

INT 21H, Function 08H: Keyboard Input without Echo

This operation works like function 01H, except that the entered character does not echo on the screen.

INT 21H, Function 0AH: Buffered Keyboard Input

This useful keyboard operation is covered in detail in Chapter 9. However, its inability to accept extended function keys limits its capability.

INT 21H, Function 0BH: Check Keyboard Status

This operation returns FFH in the AL if an input character is available and 00H if no character is available. The function is related to those others that do not wait for keyboard input.

INT 21H, Function 0CH: Clear Keyboard Buffer and Invoke Function

You may use this operation in association with function 01H, 06H, 07H, 08H, or 0AH. Load the required function into the AL:

```
        MOV   AH,0CH       ;Request keyboard input

        MOV   AL,function  ;Required function

        MOV   DX,KBAREA     ;Keyboard input area

        INT   21H          ;Call DOS
```

The operation clears the keyboard buffer, executes the function in the AL, and accepts (or waits for) a character, according to the function request in the AL. You could use this operation for a program that does not allow a user to type ahead.

BIOS INTERRUPT 16H FOR KEYBOARD INPUT

BIOS INT 16H, the basic BIOS keyboard operation used extensively by software developers, provides the following services according to a function in the AH.

INT 16H, Function 00H: Read a Character

This operation handles the keys on the 83-key keyboard, but does not accept input from the additional keys on the enhanced 101-key keyboard. (For full keyboard input, see function 10H.)

The operation checks the keyboard buffer for an entered character. If none is present, the operation waits for the user to press a key. If a character is present, the operation returns it in the AL and its scan code in the AH. (A later section covers scan codes.) If the pressed key is an extended function such as Home or F1, the character in the AL is 00H. Here are the two possibilities:

Key Pressed	AH	AL
Regular ASCII character:	Scan code	ASCII character
Extended function key:	Scan code	00H

The following code tests the AL for 00H to determine whether the user has pressed an extended function key:

```
        MOV   AH,00H       ;Request BIOS keyboard input

        INT   16H          ;Call BIOS

        CMP   AL,00H       ;Extended function key?

        JE    G40          ; —yes
```

Since the operation does not echo the character to the screen, you have to issue a screen display interrupt for that purpose.

INT 16H, Function 01H: Determine Whether a Character Is Present

This operation is similar to function 00H, but with a significant difference. If an entered character is present in the keyboard buffer, the operation clears the zero flag (ZF = 0) and delivers the character to the AL and its scan code to the AH; the entered character remains in the buffer. If no character is present, the operation sets the zero flag and does not wait. Note that the operation provides a look-ahead feature, since the character remains in the keyboard buffer until function 00H reads it.

INT 16H, Function 02H: Return the Current Shift Status

This operation returns to the AL the status of keyboard shift from the BIOS data area at location 417H (40:17H). (An earlier section described the status byte.) The following code tests whether the Left (bit 1) or Right (bit 0) Shift keys are pressed:

```
MOV   AH,02H          ;Request shift status

INT   16H             ;Call BIOS

OR    AL,00000011B    ;Left or right shift pressed?

JE    xxxx            ; —yes
```

See function 11H for handling the shift status at location 418H for extended functions on the enhanced keyboard.

INT 16H, Function 05H: Keyboard Write

This operation allows your program to insert characters in the keyboard buffer as if a user had pressed a key. Load the ASCII character into the CH and its scan code into the CL. The operation allows you to enter characters into the buffer until it is full.

INT 16H, Function 10H: Read a Keyboard Character

This operation is the same as function 00H, except that it also accepts the additional extended functions (such as F11 and F12) from the enhanced keyboard, whereas function 00H does not.

The operation checks the keyboard buffer for an entered character. If none is present, the operation waits for the user to press a key. If a character is present, the operation returns it in the AL and its scan code in the AH. If the pressed key is an extended function such as Home or F1, the character in the AL is 00H. On the enhanced keyboard, F11 and F12 also return 00H to the AL, but the other new (duplicate) control keys, such as Home and PgUp, return E0H. Here are the two possibilities:

Key Pressed	AH	AL
Regular ASCII character:	Scan code	ASCII character
Extended function key:	Scan code	00H or E0H

You can test the AL for 00H or E0H to determine whether the user has pressed an extended function key:

```
MOV   AH,10H     ;Request BIOS keyboard input

INT   16H        ;Call BIOS

CMP   AL,00H     ;Extended function key?

JE    G40        ; —yes

CMP   AL,0E0H    ;Extended function key?

JE    G40        ; —yes
```

Since the operation does not echo the character to the screen, you have to issue a screen display interrupt for that purpose.

INT 16H, Function 11H: Determine Whether a Character Is Present

This operation is the same as function 01H, except that it recognizes the additional extended functions from the enhanced keyboard, whereas 01H does not.

INT 16H, Function 12H: Return the Current Keyboard Shift Status

This operation is similar to function 02H, which returns to the AL the status of the keyboard shift from the BIOS data area at location 417H (40:17H). The operation also delivers the extended shift status to the AH:

Bit	Key	Bit	Key
7	SysReq pressed	3	Right Alt pressed
6	Caps Lock pressed	2	Right Ctrl pressed
5	Num Lock pressed	1	Left Alt pressed
4	Scroll Lock pressed	0	Left Ctrl pressed

EXTENDED FUNCTION KEYS AND SCAN CODES

An extended function key such as F1 or Home requests an action rather than delivers a character. There is nothing in the system design that compels these keys to perform a specific action: As the programmer, you determine, for example, that pressing the Home key is to set the cursor at the top left corner of the screen or that pressing the End key sets the cursor at the end of text on the screen. You could as easily program these keys to perform wholly unrelated operations.

Each key has a designated *scan code*, beginning with 01 for Esc. (See Appendix F for a complete list of these codes.) By means of the scan codes, a program may determine the source of any keystroke. For example, a program could issue INT 16H, function 10H, to request input of one character. The operation responds in one of two ways, depending on whether you press a character key or an extended function key. For a character, such as the letter A, the operation delivers these two items:

1. In the AL register, the ASCII character A (41H).
2. In the AH register, the scan code for the letter A, 1EH.

AH	AL
1E	41

The keyboard contains two keys each for such characters as −, +, and *. Pressing the asterisk key, for example, sets the character code 2AH in the AL and one of two scan codes in the AH, depending on which key was pressed: 09H for the asterisk above the number 8, or 29H for the asterisk by the numeric keypad.

The following logic tests the scan code to determine which asterisk was pressed:

```
CMP  AL,2AH     ;Asterisk?

JNE  EXIT1      ; no—exit

CMP  AH,09H     ;Which scan code?

JE   EXIT2
```

If you press an extended function key, such as Ins, the operation delivers these two items:

1. In the AL register: Zero, or E0H for a new control key on the enhanced keyboard.
2. In the AH register: The scan code for Ins, 52H.

AH	AL
52	00

Thus after an INT 16H operation (and some INT 21H operations), you can test the AL. If it contains 00H or E0H, the request is for an extended function; otherwise, the operation has delivered a character. The following tests for an extended function key:

```
MOV  AH,10H     ;Request keyboard input

INT  16H        ;Call BIOS

CMP  AL,00H     ;Extended function?

JZ   exit       ; yes—exit

CMP  AL,0E0H    ;Extended function?

JZ   exit       ; yes—exit
```

In the following code, if a user presses the Home key (scan code 47H), the cursor is set to row 0, column 0:

```
           MOV   AH,10H      ;Request input

           INT   16H         ;Call BIOS

           CMP   AL,00H      ;Extended function?

           JE    G30         ; yes—bypass

           CMP   AL,0E0H     ;Extended function?

           JNE   G90         ; no—exit

     G30:  CMP   AH,47H      ;Scan code for Home?

           JNE   G90         ; no—exit

           MOV   AH,02H      ;Request

           MOV   BH,00       ; set cursor

           MOV   DX,00       ; to 0,0

           INT   10H         ;Call BIOS
```

Program function keys F1–F10 generate scan codes 3BH–44H, respectively, and F11 and F12 generate 85H and 86H. The following code tests for program function key F10:

```
     CMP   AH,44H    ;Program function key F10?

     JE    EXIT1     ; yes—exit
```

At EXIT1, the program could perform any required action.

Keyboard Exercise

The following DEBUG exercise examines the effects of entering various keyboard characters. For an 83-key keyboard, use function 00H, and for a 101-key keyboard, use function 10H. Use the command A 100 to enter these instructions:

```
     MOV   AH,00 or MOV AH,10

     INT   16

     JMP   100
```

Use the P (Proceed) command to execute the INT operation. Key in various characters, and compare the results in the AX with the listing in Appendix F.

SELECTING FROM A MENU

The partial program in Figure 11–1 illustrates displaying a menu and letting a user press the Up and Down Arrow keys to select an item from it. The menu itself is defined in the data segment within a double-lined box (as explained in Chapter 10). The procedures and what actions they perform are follows:

```
                    page    60,132
          TITLE     P11SELMU (EXE) Select item from menu
          ; -------------------------------------------------------
                    .MODEL SMALL
                    .STACK 64
          ; -------------------------------------------------------
                    .DATA
          TOPROW    EQU     00                  ;Top row of menu
          BOTROW    EQU     07                  ;Bottom row of menu
          LEFCOL    EQU     16                  ;Left column of menu
          COL       DB      00                  ;Screen column
          ROW       DB      00                  ;Screen row
          COUNT     DB      ?                   ;Characters per line
          LINES     DB      ?                   ;Lines displayed
          ATTRIB    DB      ?                   ;Screen attribute
          NINTEEN   DB      1                   ;Width of menu
          MENU      DB      0C9H, 17 DUP(0CDH), 0BBH
                    DB      0BAH, ' Add records      ', 0BAH
                    DB      0BAH, ' Delete records   ', 0BAH
                    DB      0BAH, ' Enter orders     ', 0BAH
                    DB      0BAH, ' Print report     ', 0BAH
                    DB      0BAH, ' Update accounts  ', 0BAH
                    DB      0BAH, ' View records     ', 0BAH
                    DB      0C8H, 17 DUP(0CDH), 0BCH

          PROMPT    DB      09, 'To select an item, use up/down arrow'
                    DB      ' and press Enter.'
                    DB      13, 10, 09, 'Press Esc to exit.'
          ; -------------------------------------------------------
                    .CODE
          BEGIN     PROC    FAR
                    MOV     AX,@data            ;Initialize segment
                    MOV     DS,AX               ;  registers
                    MOV     ES,AX
                    CALL    Q10CLR              ;Clear screen
                    MOV     ROW,BOTROW+2
                    MOV     COL,00
                    CALL    Q20CURS             ;Set cursor
                    MOV     AH,40H              ;Request display
                    MOV     BX,01               ;Handle for screen
                    MOV     CX,75               ;Number of characters
                    LEA     DX,PROMPT           ;Prompt
                    INT     21H

          A10LOOP:
                    CALL    B10MENU             ;Display menu
                    MOV     COL,LEFCOL+1
                    CALL    Q20CURS             ;Set cursor
                    MOV     ROW,TOPROW+1        ;Set row to top item
                    MOV     ATTRIB,16H          ;Set reverse video
                    CALL    H10DISP             ;Highlight current menu line
                    CALL    D10INPT             ;Provide for menu selection
                    CMP     AL,0DH              ;Enter pressed?
                    JE      A10LOOP             ;  yes, continue
                    MOV     AX,0600H            ;Esc pressed (indicates end)
                    CALL    Q10CLR              ;Clear screen
                    MOV     AX,4C00H            ;Exit to DOS
                    INT     21H
          BEGIN     ENDP
          ;                 Display full menu:
          ;                 -----------------
          B10MENU   PROC    NEAR
                    MOV     ROW,TOPROW          ;Set top row
                    MOV     LINES,08            ;Number of lines
```

Figure 11–1   Select Item from Menu

```
                LEA     SI,MENU
                MOV     ATTRIB,71H              ;Blue on white
        B20:
                MOV     COL,LEFCOL             ;Set left column of menu
                MOV     COUNT,19
        B30:
                CALL    Q20CURS                ;Set cursor next column
                MOV     AH,09H                 ;Request display
                MOV     AL,[SI]                ;Get character from menu
                MOV     BH,00                  ;Page 0
                MOV     BL,71H                 ;New attribute
                MOV     CX,01                  ;One character
                INT     10H
                INC     COL                    ;Next column
                INC     SI                     ;Set for next character
                DEC     COUNT                  ;Last character?
                JNZ     B30                    ;No, repeat
                INC     ROW                    ;Next row
                DEC     LINES
                JNZ     B20                    ;All lines printed?
                RET                            ;If so, return
        B10MENU ENDP
        ;                       Accept input for request:
        ;                       -------------------------
        D10INPT PROC    NEAR
                MOV     AH,10H                 ;Request keyboard
                INT     16H                    ;  input
                CMP     AH,50H                 ;Down arrow?
                JE      D20
                CMP     AH,48H                 ;Up arrow?
                JE      D30
                CMP     AL,0DH                 ;Enter key?
                JE      D90
                CMP     AL,1BH                 ;Escape key?
                JE      D90
                JMP     D10INPT                ;None, retry
        D20:    MOV     ATTRIB,71H             ;Blue on white
                CALL    H10DISP                ;Set old line to normal video
                INC     ROW
                CMP     ROW,BOTROW-1           ;Past bottom row?
                JBE     D40                    ;  no, ok
                MOV     ROW,TOPROW+1           ;  yes, reset
                JMP     D40
        D30:    MOV     ATTRIB,71H             ;Normal video
                CALL    H10DISP                ;Set old line to normal video
                DEC     ROW
                CMP     ROW,TOPROW+1           ;Below top row?
                JAE     D40                    ;  no, ok
                MOV     ROW,BOTROW-1           ;  yes, reset
        D40:    CALL    Q20CURS                ;Set cursor
                MOV     ATTRIB,16H             ;Reverse video
                CALL    H10DISP                ;Set new line to reverse video
                JMP     D10INPT
        D90:    RET
        D10INPT ENDP
        ;                       Set menu line to normal/highlight:
        ;                       ----------------------------------
        H10DISP PROC    NEAR
                MOV     AH,00
                MOV     AL,ROW                 ;Row tells which line to set
                MUL     NINTEEN                ;Multiply by length of line
                LEA     SI,MENU+1              ;  for selected menu line
                ADD     SI,AX
                MOV     COUNT,17               ;Characters to display
```

Figure 11-1   (continued)

```
H20:
                  CALL    Q20CURS            ;Set cursor next column
                  MOV     AH,09H             ;Request display
                  MOV     AL,[SI]            ;Get character from menu
                  MOV     BH,00              ;Page 0
                  MOV     BL,ATTRIB          ;New attribute
                  MOV     CX,01              ;One character
                  INT     10H
                  INC     COL                ;Next column
                  INC     SI                 ;Set for next character
                  DEC     COUNT              ;Last character?
                  JNZ     H20                ;No, repeat
                  MOV     COL,LEFCOL+1       ;Reset column to left
                  CALL    Q20CURS            ;Set cursor
                  RET
H10DISP           ENDP
;                         Clear screen:
;                         -----------
Q10CLR            PROC    NEAR
                  MOV     AX,0600H
                  MOV     BH,61H             ;Blue on brown
                  MOV     CX,0000
                  MOV     DX,184FH
                  INT     10H                ;Call BIOS
                  RET
Q10CLR            ENDP


;                         Set cursor row:column:
;                         ---------------------
Q20CURS           PROC    NEAR
                  MOV     AH,02H
                  MOV     BH,00              ;Page 0
                  MOV     DH,ROW             ;Row
                  MOV     DL,COL             ;Column
                  INT     10H
                  RET
Q20CURS           ENDP
                  END     BEGIN
```

Figure 11–1   (continued)

- BEGIN calls Q10CLR to clear the screen, calls B10MENU to display the menu items and to set the first item to reverse video, and calls D10INPT to accept keyboard input.
- B10MENU displays the full set of menu selections.
- D10INPT uses INT 16H for input: the Down Arrow to move down the menu, the Up Arrow to move up the menu, Enter to accept a menu item, and Esc to quit. All other keyboard entries are ignored. The routine wraps the cursor around, so that trying to move the cursor above the first menu line sets it to the last line, and vice versa. The routine also calls H10DISP to reset the previous menu line to normal video and the new (selected) menu line to reverse video.
- H10DISP displays the currently selected line according to an attribute (normal or reverse video) that has been provided.
- Q10CLR clears the entire screen and sets it to blue foreground and brown background.

The program illustrates menu selection in a simple manner; a full program would execute a routine for each selected item. You'll get a better understanding of this program by typing it in and testing it.

INTERRUPT 09H AND THE KEYBOARD BUFFER

When you press a key, the keyboard's processor generates the key's scan code and requests INT 09H. This interrupt (at location 36 of the interrupt services table) points to an interrupt-handling routine in ROM BIOS. The routine issues a request for input from port 96 (60H):

```
IN AL,60H
```

The BIOS routine reads the scan code and compares it with entries in a scan code table for the associated ASCII character (if any). The routine combines the scan code with its associated ASCII character and delivers the two bytes to the keyboard buffer. Figure 11–2 illustrates this procedure.

Note that INT 09H handles the keyboard status bytes at 40:17H, 40:18H and 40:96H for Shift, Alt, and Ctrl, respectively. However, although pressing these keys generates INT 09H, the interrupt routine sets the appropriate bits in the status bytes, but doesn't deliver any characters to the keyboard buffer. Also, INT 09H ignores undefined keystroke combinations.

When you *press* a key, the keyboard processor automatically generates a scan code and INT 09H. When you *release* the key within one-half second, it generates a second scan code [the value of the first code plus 128 (1000 0000B), which sets the leftmost bit] and issues another INT 09H. The second scan code tells the interrupt routine that you have released the key. If you hold the key for more than one-half second, the keyboard process becomes typematic and automatically repeats the key operation.

The Keyboard Buffer

The keyboard buffer requires one address to tell INT 09H where to insert the next character and another address to tell INT 16H where to extract the next character. The two addresses are offsets within segment 40[0]H. The following describes the contents of the buffer:

ADDRESS	EXPLANATION
41AH	Address of current head of the buffer, the next position for INT 16H to read.
41CH	Address of current tail of the buffer, the next position for INT 09H to store an entered character.
41EH	Address of the beginning of the keyboard buffer itself: 16 words (32 bytes), although it can be longer. The buffer holds keyboard characters and scan codes as entered for later reading via INT 16H. Two bytes are required for each character and its associated scan code:

Address of head	Address of tail	Address of buffer
41A	41C	41E ...

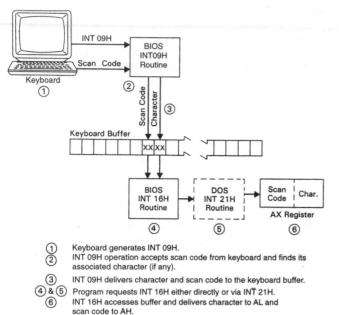

① Keyboard generates INT 09H.
② INT 09H operation accepts scan code from keyboard and finds its
　　associated character (if any).
③ INT 09H delivers character and scan code to the keyboard buffer.
④ & ⑤ Program requests INT 16H either directly or via INT 21H.
⑥ INT 16H accesses buffer and delivers character to AL and
　　scan code to AH.

Figure 11–2　Keyboard Buffer

When you type a character, INT 09H advances the tail. When INT 16H reads a character, it advances the head. In this way, the process is circular, with the head continually chasing the tail.

When the buffer is *empty*, the head and tail are at the same address. In the following example, a user has keyed 'abcd<Enter>'. INT 09H has stored the characters in the buffer and has advanced the tail to 428H. (For simplicity, the example does not show the associated scan codes.) The program has issued INT 16H five times to read all the characters and has advanced the tail to 428H, so that the buffer is now empty:

```
     a     b     c     d    <0DH>    .    .    .
     |     |     |     |      |           |
    41E   420   422   424    426         428
```

When the buffer is *full*, the tail is immediately behind the head. To see this, suppose the user now types 'fghijklmnopqrs'. Then INT 09H stores the characters beginning with the tail at 428H and circles around to store the 's' at 424H, immediately before the head at 426H.

```
p    q    r    s   <0DH>   e    f    g    h    i    j    k    l    m    n    o
|    |    |    |     |      |    |    |    |    |    |    |    |    |    |    |
41E  420  422  424   426    428  42A  42C  42E  430  432  434  436  438  43A  43C
```

At this point, INT 09H does not accept any more characters typed ahead and, indeed, accepts only 15 at most, although the buffer holds 16. (Can you tell why?) If INT 09H were

to accept another character, it would advance the tail to the same address as the head, and
INT 16H would suppose that the buffer is empty.

The Ctrl, Shift, and Alt Keys

INT 09H also handles the keyboard status byte at 40:17H in the BIOS data area [Right Shift
(bit 0), Left Shift (bit 1), Ctrl (bit 2), and Alt (bit 3)], as well as 40:18H and 40:96H for the
enhanced keyboard. When you press one of these keys, the BIOS routine sets the appropriate bit to 1, and when you release the key, it clears the bit to 0.

Your program may test whether any of the preceding keys are pressed either by means
of INT 16H (function 02H) or by direct reference to the status byte. The following partial
.COM program illustrates the use of direct reference to the status byte:

```
        BIODATA SEGMENT AT 40H         ;Locate BIOS data area

                ORG 17H                ; and

        KBSTATE DB ?                   ; status byte

        BIODATA ENDS

        CODESG  SEGMENT PARA

                ASSUME  CS:CODESG,DS:BIODATA

                ORG  100H

        BEGIN:

                MOV  AX,BIODATA        ;Initialize address of

                MOV  DS,AX             ; BIODATA in DS

                MOV  AL,KBSTATE        ;Get keyboard status byte

                TEST AL,00000011B      ;Test either shift pressed

                JNZ  xxx               ; yes—jump

                ...
```

The program uses the SEGMENT AT feature to define the BIOS data area as, in effect, a dummy segment. KBSTATE identifies the location of the keyboard status byte at
40:17H. The code segment initializes the address of BIODATA in the DS and stores the
keyboard status byte in the AL. An OR operation tests the byte for either Shift key pressed.

You could modify this code to test as well for the enhanced keyboard status bytes at
40:18H and 40:96H.

ENTERING THE FULL ASCII CHARACTER SET

The entire ASCII set consists of 256 characters numbered 0 through 255 (FFH). Many of
these are standard displayable characters, from ASCII 20H (space) through ASCII 7EH (the
tilde character, ~). Since the keyboard is limited to 83 or 101 keys, most of the 256 ASCII

characters are not represented on it. You can, however, enter any of the codes 01 through 255 by holding down the Alt key and entering the appropriate code as a decimal value on the numeric keypad. The system stores your entered value as two bytes in the keyboard buffer, the first of which is the generated ASCII character and the second of which is zero. For example, Alt+001 delivers 01H, and Alt+255 delivers FFH. You could use DEBUG to examine the effect of entering various values:

```
100   MOV   AH,10
102   INT   16
104   JMP   100
```

KEY POINTS

- The shift status bytes in the BIOS data area indicate the current status of Ctrl, Alt, Shift, CapsLock, NumLock, and ScrollLock.
- DOS INT 21H keyboard operations provide a variety of services to echo or not echo on the screen, to recognize or ignore Ctrl+Break, and to accept scan codes.
- BIOS INT 16H provides the basic BIOS keyboard operation for accepting characters from the keyboard buffer. For a character key, the operation delivers the character to the AL and the key's scan code to the AH. For an extended function key, the operation delivers zero to the AL and the key's scan code to the AH.
- The scan code is a unique number assigned to each key that enables the system to identify the source of a pressed key and enables a program to check for extended function keys such as Home, PgUp, and Arrow.
- The BIOS data area at 40:1EH contains the keyboard buffer. This area allows you to type up to 15 characters before a program requests input.
- When you press a key, the keyboard's processor generates the key's scan code (its unique assigned number) and requests INT 09H. When you release the key, it generates a second scan code (the first code plus 128—the leftmost bit is set) to tell INT 09H that the key is released.
- BIOS INT 09H gets a scan code from the keyboard, and either it generates an associated ASCII character and delivers the scan code and character to the keyboard buffer area or it sets the Ctrl, Alt, Shift status.

QUESTIONS

11–1. (a) What is the location of the first byte of the keyboard shift status in the BIOS data area? (b) What do the contents 00001100 mean? (c) What do the contents 00000010 mean?

11–2. Explain the features of the following functions for INT 21H keyboard input: (a) 01H; (b) 07H; (c) 08H; (d) 0AH.

11–3. Explain the differences among INT 16H functions 00H, 01H, and 10H.

11–4. Provide the scan codes for the following extended functions: (a) Up Arrow; (b) program function key F3; (c) Home; (d) PgUp.

11–5. Use DEBUG to examine the effects of entered keystrokes. To request entry of assembly language statements, type A 100 and enter the following instructions:

```
MOV     AH,00 (or AH,10)

INT     16

JMP     100
```

Use U 100,104 to unassemble the program, and use the P command to get DEBUG to execute through the INT. Execution stops, waiting for your input. Press any key and examine the AH and AL registers. Continue entering a variety of keys. Press Q to quit DEBUG.

11–6. Code the instructions to enter a keystroke; if the key is PgDn, set the cursor to row 24, column 0.

11–7. Revise Figure 11–1 to provide for the following features: (a) After the initial clearing of the screen, display a prompt that asks users to press F1 for a menu screen. (b) When F1 is pressed, display the menu. (c) Allow users to select menu items also by pressing the first character (upper- or lowercase) of each item. (d) On request of an item, display a message for that particular selection, such as "Procedure to Delete Records." (e) Allow users to press Esc to return to the main menu for the selected routine.

11–8. Under what circumstances does an INT 09H occur?

11–9. Explain in simple terms how INT 09H handles Ctrl and Shift keys differently from the way it handles the standard keyboard keys.

11–10. (a) Where is the BIOS memory location of the keyboard buffer? (b) What is the buffer's size, in bytes? (c) How many keyboard characters can it contain?

11–11. (a) What does it mean when the address of the head and tail in the keyboard buffer are the same? (b) What does it mean when the address of the tail immediately follows the head?

PART D — Data Manipulation

CHAPTER 12 ————————————

String Operations

OBJECTIVE:

To explain the special instructions used to process string data.

INTRODUCTION

To this point, the instructions presented have handled data defined as only one byte, word, or doubleword. It is often necessary, however, to move or compare data fields that exceed these lengths. For example, you may want to compare descriptions or names in order to sort them into ascending sequence. Items in this format are known as *string data* and may be either character or numeric. For processing string data, assembly language provides five string instructions:

MOVS   Moves one byte, word, or doubleword from one location to another in memory.

LODS   Loads from memory a byte into the AL, a word into the AX, or a doubleword into the EAX.

STOS   Stores the contents of the AL, AX, or EAX registers into memory.

CMPS   Compares byte, word, or doubleword memory locations.

SCAS   Compares the contents of the AL, AX, or EAX with the contents of a memory location.

200

An associated instruction, the REP prefix, causes a string instruction to perform repetitively a specified number of times.

FEATURES OF STRING OPERATIONS

A string instruction can specify the repetitive processing of one byte, word, or (80386 and later) doubleword at a time. Thus you could select a byte operation for a string with an odd number of bytes and a word operation for a string with an even number of bytes. Each string instruction has a byte, word, and doubleword version and assumes use of the ES:DI or DS:SI registers. The DI and SI should contain valid offset addresses.

There are basically two ways to code string instructions. In the following table, the second column shows the basic format for each operation, which uses the implied operands listed in the third column (if you code an instruction as MOVS, you include the operands—for example, as MOVS BYTE1,BYTE2, where the definition of the operands indicates the length of the move):

Operation	Basic Instruction	Implied Operands	Byte Operation	Word Operation	Doubleword Operation
Move	MOVS	ES:DI,DS:SI	MOVSB	MOVSW	MOVSD
Load	LODS	AX,DS:SI	LODSB	LODSW	LODSD
Store	STOS	ES:DI,AX	STOSB	STOSW	STOSD
Compare	CMPS	DS:SI,ES:DI	CMPSB	CMPSW	CMPSD
Scan	SCAS	ES:DI,AX	SCASB	SCASW	SCASD

The second way to code string instructions is the standard practice, as shown in the fourth, fifth, and sixth columns. You load the addresses of the operands in the DI and SI registers and code, for example, MOVSB, MOVSW, and MOVSD without operands.

The string instructions assume that the DI and SI contain valid offset addresses that reference bytes in memory. The SI register is normally associated with the DS (data segment) register as DS:SI. The DI register is always associated with the ES (extra segment) register as ES:DI. Consequently, MOVS, STOS, CMPS, and SCAS require that an .EXE program initialize the ES register, usually, but not necessarily, with the same address as that in the DS register:

```
MOV  AX,@data    ;Get address of data segment

MOV  DS,AX       ;Store it in DS

MOV  ES,AX       ; and in ES
```

REP: REPEAT STRING PREFIX

The REP prefix immediately before a string instruction, such as REP MOVSB, provides for repeated execution based on an initial count that you set in the CX register. REP executes the string instruction, decrements the CX, and repeats this operation until the count in the CX is zero. In this way, you can handle strings of virtually any length.

The direction flag (DF) determines the direction of a repeated operation:

- For processing from left to right (the normal way of processing), use CLD to clear the DF to zero.
- For processing from right to left, use STD to set the DF to 1.

The following example moves (or rather, copies) the 20 bytes of STRING1 to STRING2 (assume that the DS and ES are both initialized with the address of the data segment, as shown earlier):

```
STRING1 DB  20 DUP('*')

STRING2 DB  20 DUP(' ')

        ...

        CLD                 ;Clear direction flag

        MOV  CX,20          ;Initialize for 20 bytes

        LEA  DI,STRING2     ;Initialize receiving name

        LEA  SI,STRING1     ;Initialize sending address

        REP MOVSB           ;Copy STRING1 to STRING2
```

During execution, the CMPS and SCAS instructions also set status flags, so that the operation can terminate immediately on finding a specified condition. The variations of REP for this purpose are the following:

- REP   Repeat the operation until the CX is decremented to zero.
- REPE or REPZ   Repeat the operation while the zero flag (ZF) indicates equal or zero. Stop when the ZF indicates not equal or zero or when the CX is decremented to zero.
- REPNE or REPNZ   Repeat the operation while the ZF indicates not equal or zero. Stop when the ZF indicates equal or zero or when the CX is decremented to zero.

For the 80286 and more advanced processors, the use of word and doubleword operations can provide faster processing. We'll now examine each string operation in detail.

MOVS: MOVE STRING

MOVS combined with a REP prefix and a length in the CX can move any number of characters. Although you don't code the operands, the instruction looks like this:

```
[label:] REP MOVSn [ES:DI,DS:SI]
```

For the receiving string, the segment:offset registers are the ES:DI; for the sending string, the segment:offset registers are the DS:SI. As a result, at the start of an .EXE program, initialize the ES register along with the DS register, and prior to executing the MOVS, use LEA to initialize the DI and SI registers. Depending on the direction flag, MOVS increments or decrements the DI and SI registers by 1 for byte, 2 for word, and 4 for doubleword. The following code is illustrative:

```
          MOV    CX,number        ;Number of bytes/words

          LEA    DI,STRING2       ;Address of STRING2

          LEA    SI,STRING1       ;Address of STRING1

          REP MOVSn               ;Move n bytes/words
```

The instructions equivalent to REP MOVSB are:

```
          JCXZ   LABEL2           ;Jump if CX zero

LABEL1:   MOV    AL,[SI]          ;Get character from STRING1

          MOV    [DI],AL          ;Store character in STRING2

          INC    DI               ;Or DEC DI

          INC    SI               ;Or DEC SI

          LOOP   LABEL1

LABEL2:   ...
```

Earlier, Figure 6–2 illustrated moving a 9-byte field. The program could also have used MOVSB for this purpose. In Figure 12–1, the procedure C10MVSB uses MOVSB to move a 10-byte field, NAME1, 1 byte at a time to NAME2. The first instruction, CLD, clears the direction flag to zero so that the MOVSB processes data from left to right. The direction flag is normally zero at the start of execution, but CLD is coded here as a precaution.

The two LEA instructions load the SI and DI registers with the offset addresses of NAME1 and NAME2, respectively. Since the DOS loader for a .COM program automatically initializes the DS and ES registers, the segment:offset addresses are correct for ES:DI and DS:SI. A MOV instruction initializes the CX with 10 (the length of NAME1 and of NAME2). The instruction REP MOVSB now performs the following:

- Moves the leftmost byte of NAME1 (addressed by DS:SI) to the leftmost byte of NAME2 (addressed by ES:DI).
- Increments the DI and SI by 1 for the next bytes to the right.
- Decrements the CX by 1.
- Repeats this operation, 10 loops in all, until the CX becomes zero.

Because the direction flag is zero and MOVSB increments DI and SI, each iteration processes one byte farther to the right, as NAME1+1 to NAME2+1, and so on. At the end of execution, the CX contains 00, the DI contains the address of NAME2+10, and the SI contains the address of NAME1+10—both 1 byte past the end of the name.

If the direction flag is 1, MOVSB would decrement DI and SI, causing processing to occur from right to left. But in that case, to move the contents correctly, you would have to initialize the SI with NAME1+9 and the DI with NAME2+9.

The next procedure in Figure 12–1, D10MVSW, uses MOVSW to move five words from NAME2 to NAME3. At the end of execution, the CX contains 00, the DI contains the address of NAME3+10, and the SI contains the address of NAME2+10.

```
TITLE     P12MOVST (COM)   MOVS string operations
          .MODEL SMALL
          .CODE
          ORG      100H
BEGIN:    JMP      SHORT MAIN
; ----------------------------------------------
NAME1     DB       'Assemblers'       ;Data items
NAME2     DB       10 DUP(' ')
NAME3     DB       10 DUP(' ')
; ----------------------------------------------
MAIN      PROC     NEAR               ;Main procedure
          CALL     C10MVSB            ;MVSB subroutine
          CALL     D10MVSW            ;MVSW subroutine
          MOV      AX,4C00H           ;Exit to DOS
          INT      21H
MAIN      ENDP
;         Use of MOVSB:
;         -----------
C10MVSB   PROC     NEAR
          CLD                         ;Left to right
          MOV      CX,10              ;Move 10 bytes,
          LEA      DI,NAME2           ;  NAME1 to NAME2
          LEA      SI,NAME1
          REP MOVSB
          RET
C10MVSB   ENDP
;             Use of MOVSW:
;             -----------
D10MVSW   PROC     NEAR
          CLD                         ;Left to right
          MOV      CX,05              ;Move 5 words,
          LEA      DI,NAME3           ;  NAME2 to NAME3
          LEA      SI,NAME2
          REP MOVSW
          RET
D10MVSW   ENDP
          END      BEGIN
```

Figure 12–1   Use of MOVS String Operations

Since MOVSW increments the DI and SI registers by 2, the operation requires only five loops. For processing right to left, initialize the SI with NAME1+8 and the DI with NAME2+8.

LODS: LOAD STRING

LODS loads the AL with a byte, the AX with a word, or the EAX with a doubleword from memory. The memory address is subject to the DS:SI registers, although you can override the SI. Depending on the direction flag, the operation also increments or decrements the SI by 1 for byte, 2 for word, and 4 for doubleword.

Since one LODS operation fills the register, there is no practical reason to use the REP prefix with it. For most purposes, a simple MOV instruction is adequate. But MOV generates 3 bytes of machine code, whereas LODS generates only 1, although it requires that you initialize the SI register. You could use LODS to step through a string 1 byte, word, or doubleword at a time, examining successively for a particular value.

The instructions equivalent to LODSB are

```
TITLE     P12LODST (COM)   Use of LODSB string operation
          .MODEL   SMALL
          .CODE
          ORG      100H
BEGIN:    JMP      SHORT MAIN
;  -------------------------------------------------------------
FIELDA    DB       'Assemblers'       ;Data item
FIELDB    DB       10 DUP(20H)
;  -------------------------------------------------------------
MAIN      PROC     NEAR               ;Main procedure
          CLD                         ;Left to right
          MOV      CX,10
          LEA      SI,FIELDA          ;Load address of FIELDA
          LEA      DI,FIELDB+9        ;Load address of FIELDB+9
A20:      LODSB                       ;Get character in AL,
          MOV      [DI],AL            ;  store in FIELDB,
          DEC      DI                 ;  left to right
          LOOP     A20                ;Ten characters?
          MOV      AX,4C00H           ;  yes, exit
          INT      21H
MAIN      ENDP
          END      BEGIN
```

Figure 12–2   Use of LODSW String Operation

```
MOV      AL,[SI]        ;Load byte in AL

INC      SI             ;Increment SI for next byte
```

In Figure 12–2, the data area defines a 10-byte field named FIELDA containing the value "Assemblers" and another 10-byte field named FIELDB. The objective is to transfer the bytes from FIELDA to FIELDB in reverse sequence, so that FIELDB contains "srelbmessA." LODSB is used to access 1 byte at a time from FIELDA into the AL, and the instruction MOV [DI],AL transfers the bytes to FIELDB, from right to left.

STOS: STORE STRING

STOS stores the contents of the AL, AX, or EAX register into a byte, word, or doubleword in memory. The memory address is always subject to the ES:DI registers. Depending on the direction flag, STOS also increments or decrements the DI register by 1 for byte, 2 for word, and 4 for doubleword.

A practical use of STOS with a REP prefix is to initialize a data area to any specified value, such as clearing a display area to blanks. You set the number of bytes, words, or doublewords in the CX. The instructions equivalent to REP STOSB are:

```
          JCXZ     LABEL2         ;Jump if CX zero

LABEL1:   MOV      [DI],AL        ;Store AL in memory

          INC/DEC  DI             ;Increment or decrement

          LOOP     LABEL1

LABEL2:   ...
```

```
TITLE     P12STOST (COM)   STOSW string operation
          .MODEL   SMALL
          .CODE
          ORG      100H
BEGIN:    JMP      SHORT MAIN
; --------------------------------------------
NAME1     DB       'Assemblers'        ;Data item
; --------------------------------------------
MAIN      PROC  NEAR                   ;Main procedure
          CLD                          ;Left to right
          MOV      AX,2020H            ;Move
          MOV      CX,05               ;  5 blanks
          LEA      DI,NAME1            ;  to NAME1
          REP STOSW
          MOV      AX,4C00H            ;Exit to DOS
          INT      21H
MAIN      ENDP
          END      BEGIN
```

Figure 12–3   Use of STOSW String Operation

The STOSW instruction in Figure 12–3 repeatedly stores a word containing 2020H (blanks) five times through NAME1. The operation stores the AL in the first byte and the AH in the next byte (that is, reversed). At the end, all of NAME1 is blank, the CX contains 00, and the DI contains the address of NAME1+10.

TRANSFERRING DATA WITH LODS AND STOS

The program in Figure 12–4 illustrates the use of both the LODS and STOS instructions. The example is similar to the program in Figure 10–4, which transfers characters and attributes directly to the video display area, except that Figure 12–4 contains these differences:

- For the video area, it uses page number 02 rather than page 01.
- In C10PROC, it uses STOSW to store characters and associated attributes in the video area, instead of this instruction and its accompanying two DEC instructions that decrement the DI:

  ```
  MOV WORD PTR [VIDAREA+DI],AX
  ```

- It defines an item named PROMPT in the data segment, prompting the user to "Press any key . . .", to be used at the end of processing.
- On completion of processing, the procedure D10PROMPT transfers the defined prompt to the video display area. To this end, it uses LODSB to access characters one at a time from PROMPT into the AL and uses STOSW to transfer each character and its associated attribute from the AX into the video area.

CMPS: COMPARE STRING

CMPS compares the contents of one memory location (addressed by DS:SI) with that of another memory location (addressed by ES:DI). Depending on the direction flag, CMPS also increments or decrements the SI and DI registers, by 1 for byte, 2 for word, and 4 for

```
          TITLE     P12DRVID (EXE)  Direct video display
                    .MODEL SMALL
;   -------------------------------------------------------
VIDSEG    SEGMENT AT 0BA00H    ;Page 2 of video area
VIDAREA   DB      1000H DUP(?)
VIDSEG    ENDS
;   -------------------------------------------------------
          .DATA
PROMPT    DB      'Press any key...'
;   -------------------------------------------------------
          .STACK 64
;   -------------------------------------------------------
          .CODE
BEGIN     PROC    FAR
          MOV     AX,@data       ;Addressability for
          MOV     DS,AX          ;   data segment
          MOV     AX,VIDSEG      ;   and for
          MOV     ES,AX          ;   video area
          ASSUME  ES:VIDSEG
          MOV     AH,0FH         ;Request get
          INT     10H            ;   and save
          PUSH    AX             ;   current mode
          PUSH    BX             ;   and page
          MOV     AH,00H         ;Request set
          MOV     AL,03          ;   mode 03, clear screen
          INT     10H
          MOV     AH,05H         ;Request set
          MOV     AL,02H         ;   page #02
          INT     10H
          CALL    C10PROC        ;Process display area
          CALL    D10PROMPT      ;Display user prompt
          CALL    E10INPT        ;Provide for input
          MOV     AH,05H         ;Restore
          POP     BX             ;   original
          MOV     AL,BH          ;   page number
          INT     10H
          POP     AX             ;Restore video
          MOV     AH,00H         ;   mode (in AL)
          INT     10H
          MOV     AX,4C00H       ;Exit to DOS
          INT     21H
BEGIN     ENDP
;                   Store character and attribute in video area
;                   ----------------------------------------
C10PROC   PROC    NEAR
          MOV     AL,41H         ;Character to display
          MOV     AH,01H         ;Attribute
          MOV     DI,660         ;Start of display area
C30:      MOV     CX,60          ;Characters per row
C40:      STOSW                  ;AX in display area
          LOOP    C40            ;Repeat 60 times
          INC     AH             ;Next atribute
          INC     AL             ;Next character
          ADD     DI,40          ;Indent for next row
          CMP     AL,51H         ;Last character to display?
          JNE     C30            ;   no, repeat
          RET                    ;   yes, return
C10PROC   ENDP
;                   Prompt user to press key
;                   ------------------------
D10PROMPT PROC    NEAR
          MOV     CX,16          ;Characters to display
          LEA     SI,PROMPT      ;Address of prompt
```

Figure 12–4   Direct Video Display

```
                    MOV      DI,3840        ;Location in display area
                    MOV      AH,03H         ;New attribute in AH
          D20:      LODSB                   ;Character into AL
                    STOSW                   ;Store in display area
                    LOOP     D20            ;16 times
                    RET                     ;Return
          D10PROMPT ENDP
          ;                   Accept input:
          ;                   ------------
          E10INPT   PROC     NEAR
                    MOV      AH,10H         ;Request keyboard
                    INT      16H            ;  input
                    RET
          E10INPT   ENDP
                    END      BEGIN
```

Figure 12–4B   (continued)

doubleword. The operation sets the AF, CF, OF, PF, SF, and ZF flags. When combined with a REP prefix and a length in the CX, CMPS can successively compare strings of any length.

But note that CMPS provides an *alphanumeric* comparison, that is, a comparison according to ASCII values. The operation is not suited to algebraic comparisons, which consist of signed numeric values. Consider the comparison of two strings containing JEAN and JOAN. A comparison from left to right, one byte at a time, results in the following:

J:J   Equal
E:O   Unequal (E is low)
A:A   Equal
N:N   Equal

A comparison of the entire four bytes ends with a comparison of N with N (equal). Now since the two names are not identical, the operation should terminate as soon as the comparison is between two different characters. For this purpose, REP has a variation, REPE (Repeat on Equal), which repeats the operation as long as the comparison is between equal characters, or until the CX register equals zero. The coding for repeated one-byte comparisons is REPE CMPSB.

Figure 12–5 consists of two examples that use CMPSB. The first example compares NAME1 with NAME2, which contain the same values. The CMPSB operation therefore continues for the entire 10 bytes. At the end of execution, the CX contains 00, the DI contains the address of NAME2+10, the SI contains the address of NAME1+10, the sign flag is positive, and the zero flag indicates equal or zero.

The second example compares NAME2 with NAME3, which contain different values. The CMPSB operation terminates after comparing the first byte and results in a high or unequal condition: The CX contains 09, the DI contains the address of NAME3+1, the SI contains the address of NAME2+1, the sign flag is positive, and the zero flag indicates unequal.

The first example results in equal or zero and (for illustrative reasons only) moves 01 to the BH register. The second example results in unequal and moves 02 to the BL register. If you use DEBUG to trace the instructions, you'll see 0102 in the BX at the end of execution.

Warning!: These examples use CMPSB to compare data one byte at a time. If you use CMPSW to compare data a word at a time, initialize CX to 5. But that's not the prob-

```
TITLE      P12CMPST (COM)   Use of CMPS string operations
           .MODEL   SMALL
           .CODE
           ORG      100H
BEGIN:     JMP      SHORT MAIN
; -------------------------------------------------------------
NAME1      DB       'Assemblers'       ;Data items
NAME2      DB       'Assemblers'
NAME3      DB       10 DUP(' ')
; -------------------------------------------------------------
MAIN       PROC     NEAR               ;Main procedure
           CLD                         ;Left to right
           MOV      CX,10              ;Initialize for 10 bytes
           LEA      DI,NAME2
           LEA      SI,NAME1
           REPE CMPSB                  ;Compare NAME1 : NAME2
           JNE      G20                ;  not equal, bypass
           MOV      BH,01              ;  equal, set BH
G20:
           MOV      CX,10              ;Initialize for 10 bytes
           LEA      DI,NAME3
           LEA      SI,NAME2
           REPE CMPSB                  ;Compare NAME2 : NAME3
           JE       G30                ;  equal, exit
           MOV      BL,02              ;  not equal, set BL
G30:
           MOV      AX,4C00H           ;Exit to DOS
           INT      21H
MAIN       ENDP
           END      BEGIN
```

Figure 12–5 Use of CMPS String Operations

lem. When comparing words, CMPSW reverses the bytes. For example, let's compare the names SAMUEL and ARNOLD. For the initial comparison of words, instead of comparing SA with AR, the operation compares AS with RA. So, instead of the name SAMUEL indicating a higher value, it will be lower—and incorrect. CMPSW works correctly only if the compared strings contain unsigned numeric data defined as DW, DD, or DQ.

SCAS: SCAN STRING

SCAS differs slightly from CMPS in that SCAS scans a string for a specified byte, word, or doubleword value. SCAS compares the contents of a memory location (addressed by ES:DI) with the contents of the AL, AX, or EAX register. Depending on the direction flag, SCAS also increments or decrements the DI register by 1 for byte, 2 for word, and 4 for doubleword. At the end of execution, SCAS sets the AF, CF, OF, PF, SF, and ZF flags. When combined with the REP prefix and a length in the CX, SCAS can scan any string length.

SCAS would be particularly useful for a text-editing application in which the program has to scan for punctuation, such as periods, commas, and blanks.

The code in Figure 12–6 scans NAME1 for the lowercase letter 'm'. Since the SCASB operation is to continue scanning while the comparison is not equal or until the CX is zero, the operation in this case is REPNE SCASB.

Since NAME1 contains "Assemblers", SCASB finds a match on the fifth comparison. If you use DEBUG to trace the instructions, at the end of execution of the REP SCASB op-

```
TITLE      P12SCAST (COM)   SCAS string operation
           .MODEL    SMALL
           .CODE
           ORG       100H
BEGIN:     JMP       SHORT MAIN
; -------------------------------------------------
NAME1      DB        'Assemblers'          ;Data item
; -------------------------------------------------
MAIN       PROC      NEAR                  ;Main procedure
           CLD                             ;Left to right
           MOV       AL,'m'
           MOV       CX,10                 ;Scan NAME1
           LEA       DI,NAME1              ;  for 'm'
           REPNE     SCASB
           JNE       H20                   ;If found,
           MOV       AL,03                 ;  store 03 in AL
H20:
           MOV       AH,4CH
           INT       21H                   ;Exit to DOS
MAIN       ENDP
           END       BEGIN
```

Figure 12–6   Use of SCASB String Operation

eration you will see that the zero flag shows zero, the CX is decremented to 05, and the DI is incremented by 05. (The DI is incremented one byte past the actual location of the 'm'.)

The program stores 03 in the AL register (for illustrative reasons) to indicate that an "m" was found.

SCASW scans for a word in memory that matches the word in the AX register. If you used LODSW or MOV to transfer a word into the AX register, the first byte would be in the AL and the second byte in the AH. Since SCASW compares the bytes in reversed sequence, the operation works correctly.

SCAN AND REPLACE

You may also want to replace a specific character with another character, for example, to clear editing characters such as paragraph and end-of-page symbols from a document. The following partial program scans STRING for an ampersand (&) and replaces it with a blank. If SCASB locates an ampersand, it ends the operation. In this example, there is an ampersand at STRING+8, where the blank is to be inserted, although at the end, SCASB will have incremented the DI register to STRING+9. Decrementing DI by 1 provides the correct address to insert the blank replacement character. The code is as follows:

```
STRLEN   EQU 15                    ;Length of STRING

STRING   DB   'The time&is now'

         ...

         CLD                       ;Left to right

         MOV   AL,'&'              ;Search character
```

```
MOV   CX,STRLEN              ;Length of STRING

LEA   DI,STRING              ;Address of STRING

REPNE SCASB                 ;Scan

JNZ   K20                   ;Character found?

DEC   DI                    ; yes—adjust address

MOV   BYTE PTR[DI],20H      ;Replace with blank

K20:   ...
```

ALTERNATIVE CODING FOR STRING INSTRUCTIONS

As discussed earlier, if you code explicitly with a byte, word, or doubleword instruction such as MOVSB, MOVSW, or MOVSD, the assembler assumes the correct length and does not require operands. You can also use the basic instruction formats for the string operations. For instructions such as MOVS, which have no suffix to indicate byte, word, or doubleword, you must indicate the length in the operands. For example, if FLDA and FLDB are defined as byte (DB), the instruction

```
                REP MOVS FLDA,FLDB
```

implies a repeated move of the byte beginning at FLDB to the byte beginning at FLDA. If you load the DI and SI registers with the addresses of FLDA and FLDB, you can also code the MOVS instruction as

```
        REP MOVS ES:BYTE PTR[DI],DS:[SI]
```

Few programs are coded this way, and the format is covered here just for the record.

DUPLICATING A PATTERN

The STOS instruction is useful for setting an area according to a specific byte, word, or doubleword value. However, for repeating a pattern that exceeds these lengths, you can use MOVS with a minor modification. Let's say that you want to set a display line to the following pattern:

```
        ***##***####***####***####***###  ...
```

Rather than define the entire pattern repetitively, you need only define the first six bytes that immediately precede the display line. Here is the required coding:

```
        PATTERN DB    '***###'

        DISAREA DB    42 DUP(?)
```

```
        ...
        CLD                         ;Left to right

        MOV  CX,21                  ;21 words

        LEA  DI,DISAREA             ;Destination

        LEA  SI,PATTERN             ;Source

        REP MOVSW                   ;Move characters
```

On execution, MOVSW moves the first word of PATTERN (**) to the first word of DIS-
AREA and then moves the second (*#) and third (##) words:

```
                        ***########***###
                          |       |
                       PATTERN   DISAREA
```

At this point, the DI contains the address of DISAREA+6, and the SI contains the address
of PATTERN+6, which is also the address of DISAREA. The operation now automatically
duplicates the pattern by moving the first word of DISAREA to DISAREA+6, DIS-
AREA+2 to DISAREA+8, DISAREA+4 to DISAREA+10, and so forth. Eventually the
pattern is duplicated through the end of DISAREA:

```
          ***########***######***###***######***###    ...    ***###
            |               |             |                     |
         PATTERN        DISAREA+6    DISAREA+12            DISAREA+42
```

You can use this technique to duplicate a pattern any number of times. The pattern itself may be any length, but must immediately precede the target field.

RIGHT ADJUSTING ON THE SCREEN

The program in Figure 12–7 illustrates most of the material described in this chapter. The
procedures perform the following:

- B10INPT accepts a name up to 30 characters in length at the top of the screen.
- D10SCAS uses SCASB to scan the name and bypasses any input containing an asterisk.
- E10RGHT uses MOVSB to right adjust each entered name to the right of the screen,
  one under the other. The length in ACTNLEN in the input parameter list is used to
  calculate the rightmost character of a name, as follows:

```
                        Babe Ruth

                      Mickey Mantle

                      Reggie Jackson
```

- F10CLNM Uses STOSW to clear the keyboard input field.

```
TITLE       P12RIGHT (EXE)  Right-adjust displayed names
            .MODEL SMALL
            .STACK 64
;  --------------------------------------------------------
            .DATA
NAMEPAR     LABEL  BYTE                    ;Name parameter list
MAXNLEN     DB     31                      ;Maximum length
ACTNLEN     DB     ?                       ;No. of chars entered
NAMEFLD     DB     31 DUP(' ')             ;Name

PROMPT      DB     'Name?', '$'
NAMEDSP     DB     31 DUP(' '), 13, 10, '$'
ROW         DB     00
;  --------------------------------------------------------
            .CODE
BEGIN       PROC   FAR                     ;Main procedure
            MOV    AX,@data                ;Initialize
            MOV    DS,AX                   ;  data segment
            MOV    ES,AX
            MOV    AX,0600H
            CALL   Q10SCR                  ;Clear screen
            SUB    DX,DX                   ;Set cursor 00,00
            CALL   Q20CURS
A10LOOP:
            CALL   B10INPT                 ;Request input of name
            TEST   ACTNLEN,0FFH            ;No name? (indicates end)
            JZ     A90                     ;  yes, exit
            CALL   D10SCAS                 ;Scan for asterisk
            CMP    AL,'*'                  ;Found?
            JE     A10LOOP                 ;  yes, bypass
            CALL   E10RGHT                 ;Right adjust name
            CALL   F10CLNM                 ;Clear name
            JMP    A10LOOP
A90:        MOV    AX,4C00H                ;Exit to DOS
            INT    21H
BEGIN       ENDP
;                  Prompt for input:
;                  ----------------
B10INPT     PROC
            MOV    AH,09H
            LEA    DX,PROMPT               ;Display prompt
            INT    21H
            MOV    AH,0AH
            LEA    DX,NAMEPAR              ;Accept input
            INT    21H
            RET
B10INPT     ENDP
;                  Scan name for asterisk:
;                  ----------------------
D10SCAS     PROC
            CLD                            ;Left to right
            MOV    AL,'*'                  ;Character for scan
            MOV    CX,30                   ;Set 30-byte scan
            LEA    DI,NAMEFLD
            REPNE SCASB                    ;Asterisk found?
            JE     D20                     ;  no, exit
            MOV    AL,20H                  ;  yes, clear * in AL
D20:        RET
D10SCAS     ENDP

;                  Right adjust and display name:
;                  ----------------------------
E10RGHT     PROC
```

Figure 12–7   Right Adjusting on the Screen

```
                STD                         ;Right to left
                MOV     CH,00
                MOV     CL,ACTNLEN          ;Length in CX for REP
                LEA     SI,NAMEFLD          ;Calculate rightmost
                ADD     SI,CX               ;  position
                DEC     SI                  ;  of input name
                LEA     DI,NAMEDSP+30       ;Right pos'n of display
name
                REP MOVSB                   ;Move string right to
left
                MOV     DH,ROW
                MOV     DL,48
                CALL    Q20CURS             ;Set cursor
                MOV     AH,09H
                LEA     DX,NAMEDSP          ;Display name
                INT     21H

                CMP     ROW,20              ;Bottom of screen?
                JAE     E20                 ;  no,
                INC     ROW                 ;    increment row
                JMP     E90
E20:
                MOV     AX,0601H            ;  yes,
                CALL    Q10SCR              ;  scroll and
                MOV     DH,ROW              ;  set cursor
                MOV     DL,00
                CALL    Q20CURS
E90:            RET
E10RGHT         ENDP
;                       Clear name:
;                       ----------
F10CLNM         PROC
                CLD                         ;Left to right
                MOV     AX,2020H
                MOV     CX,15               ;Clear 15 words
                LEA     DI,NAMEDSP
                REP STOSW
                RET
F10CLNM         ENDP
;                       Scroll screen:
;                       -------------
Q10SCR          PROC                        ;AX set on entry
                MOV     BH,30               ;Color attribute
                MOV     CX,00
                MOV     DX,184FH
                INT     10H
                RET
Q10SCR          ENDP
;                       Set cursor row/col:
;                       ------------------
Q20CURS         PROC                        ;DX set on entry
                MOV     AH,02H
                SUB     BH,BH
                INT     10H
                RET
Q20CURS         ENDP
                END     BEGIN
```

Figure 12–7   (continued)

KEY POINTS

- For the string instructions MOVS, STOS, CMPS, and SCAS, be sure that your .EXE programs initialize the ES register.
- For string instructions, use the suffixes B, W, or D for handling byte, word, or doubleword strings.
- Clear (CLD) or set (STD) the direction flag for the required direction of processing.
- Double check the initialization of the DI and SI registers. For example, MOVS implies operands DI,SI, whereas CMPS implies operands SI,DI.
- Initialize the CX register for REP to process the required number of bytes, words, or doublewords.
- For normal processing, use REP with MOVS and STOS, and use a conditional REP (REPE or REPNE) with CMPS and SCAS.
- CMPSW and SCASW reverse the bytes in words that are compared.
- Where you want to process right to left, watch out for addressing beginning at the rightmost byte of a field. For example, if the field is NAME1 and is 10 bytes long, then for processing bytes, the load address for LEA is NAME+9. For processing words, however, the load address for LEA is NAME+8 because the string operation initially accesses NAME+8 and NAME+9.

QUESTIONS

12–1. The string operations assume that the operands relate to the DI or SI registers. Identify these registers for the following: (a) MOVS (operands 1 and 2); (b) CMPS (operands 1 and 2); (c) SCAS (operand 1).

12–2. For string operations using REP, how do you define the number of repetitions that are to occur?

12–3. For string operations using REP, how do you set processing right to left?

12–4. The chapter gives the instructions equivalent to (a) MOVSB, (b) LODSB, and (c) STOSB, each with a REP prefix. For each case, provide equivalent code for processing words.

12–5. Revise the program in Figure 12–1. Convert the program from .COM to .EXE format, and be sure to initialize the ES register. Change the MOVSB and MOVSW operations to move data from right to left. Use DEBUG to trace through the procedures, and note the contents of the data segment and registers.

12–6. Use the following data definitions and code string operations for parts (a)-(f):

```
DATASG   SEGMENT PARA

CONAME   DB 'SPACE LAUNCHES, INC.'

PRLINE   DB 20 DUP(' ')
```

(a) Move CONAME to PRLINE, from left to right.
(b) Move CONAME to PRLINE, from right to left.
(c) Load the third and fourth bytes of CONAME into the AX.
(d) Store the AX beginning at PRLINE+5.

(e) Compare CONAME with PRLINE (they will be unequal).

(f) Scan CONAME for a blank character and, if one is found, move it to the BH.

12–7. Revise Figure 12–6 so that the operation scans NAME1 for "er." A check of NAME1 discloses that the characters "er" do not appear as a word, as shown by the following: /As/se/mb/le/rs/. Two possible solutions are:

(a) Use SCASW twice. The first SCASW begins at NAME1 and the second SCASW begins at NAME1+1.

(b) Use SCASB and on finding an "e", compare the byte that follows the 'e' for an r.

12–8. Define a 4-byte field containing the hex value 030405B4. Use MOVSW to duplicate this field 20 times into an 80-byte area, and display the result.

CHAPTER 13 ——————————

Arithmetic:
I—Processing Binary Data

OBJECTIVE:

To cover the requirements for addition, subtraction, multiplication, and division of binary data.

INTRODUCTION

This chapter covers addition, subtraction, multiplication, and division and the use of unsigned and signed data. The chapter also provides many examples and warnings of various pitfalls for the unwary traveler in the realm of the microprocessor. Chapter 14 covers special requirements involved with conversion between binary and ASCII data formats.

Although we are accustomed to performing arithmetic in decimal (base 10) format, a microcomputer performs its arithmetic only in binary (base 2). Further, the limitation of 16-bit registers on pre-80386 processors involves special treatment for large values.

Instructions introduced in this chapter are:

ADD	Add	SUB	Subtract
MUL	Multiply unsigned	IMUL	Multiply signed
DIV	Divide unsigned	IDIV	Divide signed
CBW	Convert byte to word	NEG	Negate

ADDITION AND SUBTRACTION

The ADD and SUB instructions perform simple addition and subtraction of binary data. As described in earlier chapters, negative binary numbers are represented in two's complement form: Reverse the bits of the positive number and add 1. The general formats for the ADD and SUB instructions are:

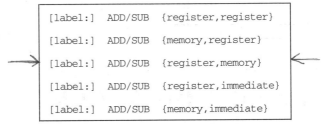

```
[label:]   ADD/SUB   {register,register}

[label:]   ADD/SUB   {memory,register}

[label:]   ADD/SUB   {register,memory}

[label:]   ADD/SUB   {register,immediate}

[label:]   ADD/SUB   {memory,immediate}
```

As with other instructions, there are no direct memory-to-memory operations. The following example uses the AX register to add WORDA to WORDB:

```
WORDA  DW    123          ;Define WORDA

WORDB  DW    25           ;Define WORDB

       . . .

       MOV  AX,WORDA      ;Move WORDA to AX

       ADD  AX,WORDB      ;Add WORDB to AX

       MOV  WORDB,AX      ;Move AX to WORDB
```

Figure 13–1 provides examples of ADD and SUB for processing byte and word values. The procedure B10ADD uses ADD to process bytes, and the procedure C10SUB uses SUB to process words.

Overflows

Be alert for overflows in arithmetic operations. Since a byte provides for only a sign bit and seven data bits (from −128 to +127), an arithmetic operation can easily exceed the capacity of a one-byte register. And a sum in the AL register that exceeds its capacity may cause unexpected results. Suppose, for example, that the AL contains 60H. Then the instruction

```
ADD AL,20H
```

generates a sum of 80H in the AL. Having added two positive values, we expect the sum to be positive, but the operation sets the overflow flag to overflow and the sign flag to negative. The reason? The value 80H, or binary 10000000, is a negative number; instead of +128, the sum is −128. The problem is that the AL register is too small for the sum, which should be in the full AX register, as shown in the next section.

```
TITLE      P13ADD (COM)   ADD and SUB operations
           .MODEL SMALL
           .CODE
           ORG      100H
BEGIN:     JMP      SHORT MAIN
; -----------------------------------------------------
BYTEA      DB       64H                   ;Data items
BYTEB      DB       40H
BYTEC      DB       16H
WORDA      DW       4000H
WORDB      DW       2000H
WORDC      DW       1000H
; -----------------------------------------------------
MAIN       PROC     NEAR                  ;Main procedure:
           CALL     B10ADD                ;Call ADD routine
           CALL     C10SUB                ;Call SUB routine
           MOV      AX,4C00H              ;Exit to DOS
           INT      21H
MAIN       ENDP

;          Examples of ADD bytes:
;          ----------------------
B10ADD     PROC
           MOV      AL,BYTEA
           MOV      BL,BYTEB
           ADD      AL,BL                 ;Register to register
           ADD      AL,BYTEC              ;Memory to register
           ADD      BYTEA,BL              ;Register to memory
           ADD      BL,10H                ;Immediate to register
           ADD      BYTEA,25H             ;Immediate to memory
           RET
B10ADD     ENDP

;          Examples of SUB words:
;          ----------------------
C10SUB     PROC
           MOV      AX,WORDA
           MOV      BX,WORDB
           SUB      AX,BX                 ;Register from register
           SUB      AX,WORDC              ;Memory from register
           SUB      WORDA,BX              ;Register from memory
           SUB      BX,1000H              ;Immediate from register
           SUB      WORDA,256H            ;Immediate from memory
           RET
C10SUB     ENDP
           END      BEGIN
```

Figure 13–1   Examples of ADD and SUB

Extending a Value in a Register

In the previous section, we saw how adding 20H to the value 60H in the AL caused an incorrect sum. A better solution would be for the AX to represent the sum properly. The instruction for this purpose is CBW (Convert Byte to Word), which automatically propagates the sign bit of the AL (0 or 1) through the AH. Note that CBW is restricted to the use of the AX.

In the next example, CBW extends the sign (0) in the AL through the AH, which generates 0060H in the AX. The code then adds 20H to the AX (rather than to the AL) and generates the correct result in the AX· 0080H, or +128:

```
                                                    AH    AL

      ...                                           xx    60H

      CBW              ;Extend AL sign into AH      00    60

      ADD    AX,20H    ;Add to AX                   00    80
```

The numeric result in the second example is the same, but the operation on the AX does not treat it as overflow or negative. Still, <u>although a full word in the AX allows for a sign bit and 15 data bits, the AX is limited to values from −32,768 to +32,767.</u> The next section examines how to handle numbers that exceed these limits.

MULTIWORD ARITHMETIC

As we have seen, large numeric values may exceed the capacity of a word, in effect requiring multiword capacity. A major requirement in multiword arithmetic is reverse-byte and reverse-word sequence. Recall that the assembler automatically converts the contents of defined numeric words into reverse-byte sequence, so that, for example, a definition of 0134H becomes 3401H. But <u>for doubleword values, it is *your* responsibility to define the related pair of words in reverse-word sequence.</u> Let's say that a doubleword pair looks like this:

```
              Hex | 01 23 | BC 62 |
```

Then you have to define the *words* in reverse order:

```
                  DW    0BC62H

                  DW    0123H
```

The assembler then converts these definitions into reverse-byte sequence, suitable for doubleword arithmetic:

```
              Hex | 62 BC | 23 01 |
```

Let's examine two ways to perform multiword arithmetic. The first is simple and specific, whereas the second is more sophisticated and general.

In Figure 13–2, the procedure D10DWD illustrates adding one pair of words (WORD1A and WORD1B) to a second pair (WORD2A and WORD2B) and storing the sum in a third pair (WORD3A and WORD3B). In effect, the operation is to add values, such as the following:

```
          Initial value:     0123   BC62H

          Add:               0012   553AH

          Total:             0136   119CH
```

Because of the reverse-byte sequence in memory, the program defines the values with the words reversed: BC62 0123 and 553A 0012, respectively. The assembler then stores these doubleword values in memory in proper reverse-byte sequence:

```
TITLE     P13DBADD (COM)   Adding doublewords
          .MODEL   SMALL
          .CODE
          ORG      100H
BEGIN:    JMP      SHORT MAIN
; ---------------------------------------------------
WORD1A    DW       0BC62H              ;Data items
WORD1B    DW       0123H
WORD2A    DW       553AH
WORD2B    DW       0012H
WORD3A    DW       ?
WORD3B    DW       ?
; ---------------------------------------------------
MAIN      PROC     NEAR                ;Main procedure
          CALL     D10DWD              ;Call 1st ADD
          CALL     E10DWD              ;Call 2nd ADD
          MOV      AX,4C00H            ;Exit to DOS
          INT      21H
MAIN      ENDP
;                  Example of ADD doublewords:
;                  --------------------------
D10DWD    PROC
          MOV      AX,WORD1A           ;Add leftmost word
          ADD      AX,WORD2A
          MOV      WORD3A,AX
          MOV      AX,WORD1B           ;Add rightmost word
          ADC      AX,WORD2B           ;  with carry
          MOV      WORD3B,AX
          RET
D10DWD    ENDP
;                  Generalized add operation:
;                  --------------------------
E10DWD    PROC
          CLC                          ;Clear carry flag
          MOV      CX,02               ;Set loop count
          LEA      SI,WORD1A           ;Leftmost word
          LEA      DI,WORD2A           ;Leftmost word
          LEA      BX,WORD3A           ;Leftmost word of sum
E20:
          MOV      AX,[SI]             ;Move word to AX
          ADC      AX,[DI]             ;Add with carry to AX
          MOV      [BX],AX             ;Store word
          INC      SI                  ;Adjust addresses for
          INC      SI                  ;  next word to right
          INC      DI
          INC      DI
          INC      BX
          INC      BX
          LOOP     E20                 ;Repeat for next word
          RET
E10DWD    ENDP
          END      BEGIN
```

Figure 13–2   Multiword Addition

```
WORD1A and WORD1B:     62BC   2301

WORD2A and WORD2B:     3A55   1200
```

The procedure first adds WORD2A to WORD1A in the AX (they are really the low-order portions) and stores the sum in WORD3A. It next adds WORD2B to WORD1B (the high-order portions) in the AX, along with the carry from the previous addition. It then stores the sum in WORD3B. Let's examine the operations in detail. The first MOV and ADD operations reverse the bytes in the AX and add the leftmost words:

```
WORD1A:     BC62H

WORD2A:     +553AH
            ───────
Total:      (1)119CH (9C11H is stored in WORD3A)
```

Since the sum of WORD1A plus WORD2A exceeds the capacity of the AX, a carry occurs, and the carry flag is set to 1. Next, the example adds the words at the right, but this time using ADC (Add With Carry) instead of ADD. ADC adds the two values and, since the carry flag is set, adds 1 to the sum:

```
WORD1B        0123H

WORD2B        +0012H

Plus carry    +   1H
              ───────
Total         0136H (3601H is stored in WORD3B)
```

By using DEBUG to trace the arithmetic, you can see the sum 0136H in the AX and the reversed values 9C11H in WORD3A and 3601H in WORD3B.

    Also in Figure 13–2, the more sophisticated procedure E10DWD provides an approach to adding values of any length, although here it adds the same pairs of words as before, WORD1A:WORD1B and WORD2A:WORD2B. The procedure uses the SI, DI, and BX as base registers for the addresses of WORD1A, WORD2A, and WORD3A, respectively. It loops once through the instructions for each pair of words to be added—in this case, two times. The first loop adds the leftmost words, and the second loop adds the rightmost words. Since the second loop is to process the words to the right, the addresses in the SI, DI, and BX registers are incremented by 2. Two INC instructions perform this operation for each register. INC (rather than ADD) is used for a good reason: The instruction ADD reg,02 would clear the carry flag and would cause an incorrect answer, whereas INC does not affect the carry flag.

    Because of the loop, there is only one add instruction, ADC. At the start, a CLC (Clear Carry) instruction ensures that the carry flag is initially clear. To make this method work, be sure to (1) define the words adjacent to each other, (2) process words from left to right, and (3) initialize the CX to the number of words to be added.

    For multiword subtraction, the instruction equivalent to ADC is SBB (Subtract With Borrow). Simply replace ADC with SBB in the procedure E10DWD.

Arithmetic in 32-Bit Registers

The 80386 and later processors provide 32-bit registers for doubleword arithmetic. For example, to add the EBX to the EAX, simply code

```
ADD EAX,EBX ;32-bit registers
```

You could add quadwords using the technique covered earlier for adding multiwords.

UNSIGNED AND SIGNED DATA

Some numeric fields—for example, a customer number and a memory address—are unsigned. Some signed numeric fields—for example, customer's balance owing and an algebraic number—may contain positive or negative values. Other signed numeric fields—for example, and employee rate of pay, the day of the month, and the value of pi—are supposed to be always positive.

For unsigned data, all bits are intended to be data bits. Hence, instead of a maximum of 32,767, a 16-bit register can contain 65,535. For signed data, the leftmost bit is a sign bit. But note that the ADD and SUB instructions do not distinguish between unsigned and signed data and, indeed, simply add and subtract bits. The following example illustrates the addition of two binary numbers, with the values taken to be unsigned and then signed. The top number contains a 1-bit to the left; for unsigned data, the bits represent 249, whereas for signed data, the bits represent -7. The addition does not set the overflow or carry flags:

BINARY	UNSIGNED DECIMAL	SIGNED DECIMAL	OF	CF
11111001	249	-7		
+00000010	+ 2	+2		
11111011	251	-5	0	0

The binary result of the addition in this example is the same for both unsigned and signed data. However, the bits in the unsigned field represent decimal 251, whereas the bits in the signed field represent decimal -5. In effect, the contents of a field mean whatever you intend them to mean.

Arithmetic Carry

An arithmetic operation that causes a carry out of the sign bit also sets the carry flag. Where a carry occurs on unsigned data, the result is invalid. The following example of addition causes a carry:

BINARY	UNSIGNED DECIMAL	SIGNED DECIMAL	OF	CF
11111100	252	-4		
+00000101	+ 5	+5		
(1)00000001	1 (invalid)	1 (valid)	0	1

The operation on the unsigned data is invalid because of the carry out of a data bit, whereas the operation on the signed data is valid.

Arithmetic Overflow

An arithmetic operation sets the overflow flag when a carry *into* the sign bit does not carry out, or a carry *out* occurs with no carry in. Where an overflow occurs on signed data, the result is invalid (because of an overflow into the sign bit), as this example shows:

BINARY	UNSIGNED DECIMAL	SIGNED DECIMAL	OF	CF
01111001	121	+121		
+00001011	+ 11	+11		
10000100	132	−124	1	0
	(valid)	(invalid)		

An add operation may set both the carry and the overflow flag. In the next example, the carry makes the unsigned operation invalid, and the overflow makes the signed operation invalid:

BINARY	UNSIGNED DECIMAL	SIGNED DECIMAL	OF	CF
11110110	246	−10		
+10001001	+137	−119		
(1)01111111	127	+127	1	1
	(invalid)	(invalid)		

The upshot of all this is that you must have a good idea as to the magnitude of the numbers that your program will process, and you must define field sizes accordingly.

MULTIPLICATION

For multiplication, the MUL instruction handles unsigned data, and the IMUL (Integer Multiplication) instruction handles signed data. Both instructions affect the carry and overflow flags. As programmer, you have control over the format of the data you process, and you have the responsibility of selecting the appropriate multiply instruction. The general format for MUL and IMUL is

| [label:] | MUL/IMUL | {register/memory} |

The basic multiplication operations are byte times byte, word times word, and (80386 and later processors) doubleword times doubleword.

Byte Times Byte

For multiplying two one-byte values, the multiplicand is in the AL register, and the multiplier is a byte in memory or another register. For the instruction MUL DL, the operation multiplies the contents of the AL by the contents of the DL. The generated product is in the AX register. The operation ignores and erases any data that may already be in the AH.

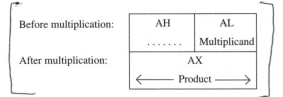

Word Times Word

For multiplying two one-word values, the multiplicand is in the AX register and the multiplier is a word in memory or another register. For the instruction MUL DX, the operation multiplies the contents of the AX by the contents of the DX. The generated product is a doubleword that requires two registers: the high-order (leftmost) portion in the DX and the low-order (rightmost) portion in the AX. The operation ignores and erases any data that may already be in the DX.

	DX	AX
Before multiplication:	Ignored	Multiplicand
After multiplication:	High product	Low product

Doubleword Times Doubleword

For multiplying two doubleword values, the multiplicand is in the EAX register and the multiplier is a doubleword in memory or another register. The product is generated in the EDX:EAX pair. The operation ignores and erases any data already in the EDX.

	EDX	EAX
Before multiplication:	Ignored	Multiplicand
After multiplication:	High product	Low product

Field Sizes

The operand of MUL or IMUL references only the multiplier, which determines the field sizes. In the following examples, the multiplier is in a register, which specifies the type of operation:

INSTRUCTION	MULTIPLIER	MULTIPLICAND	PRODUCT
MUL CL	byte	AL	AX
MUL BX	word	AX	DX:AX
MUL EBX	doubleword	EAX	EDX:EAX

In the next few examples, the multipliers are defined in memory:

```
BYTE1    DB    ?

WORD1    DW    ?

DWORD1   DD    ?
```

OPERATION	MULTIPLIER	MULTIPLICAND	PRODUCT
MUL BYTE1	BYTE1	AL	AX
MUL WORD1	WORD1	AX	DX·AX
MUL DWORD1	DWORD1	EAX	EDX:EAX

Unsigned Multiplication: MUL

The purpose of the MUL instruction is to multiply unsigned data. In Figure 13–3, C10MUL gives three examples of the use of MUL: byte times byte, word times word, and word times byte. The first example multiplies 80H (128) by 40H (64). The product in the AX is 2000H (8,192). The second example generates 1000 0000H in the DX:AX registers.

The third example involves word times byte and requires extending BYTE1 to a word. Since the values are supposed to be unsigned, the example assumes that bits in the AH register are to be zero. (The problem with using CBW here is that the leftmost bit of the AL could be 1, and propagating 1-bits in the AH would result in a larger unsigned value.) The product in the DX:AX is 0040 0000H.

Signed Multiplication: IMUL

The purpose of the IMUL (Integer Multiplication) instruction is to multiply signed data. In Figure 13–3, D10IMUL gives the same three examples as C10MUL, but replacing MUL with IMUL.

The first example multiplies 80H (a negative number) by 40H (a positive number). The product in the AX register is E000H. Using the same data, MUL generated a product of 2000H, so you can see the difference between using MUL and using IMUL. MUL treats 80H as $+128$, whereas IMUL treats 80H as -128. The product of -128 times $+64$ is -8192H, which equals E000H. (Try converting E000H to bits, reverse the bits, add 1, and add up the bit values.)

The second example multiplies 8000H (a negative value) by 2000H (a positive value). The product in the DX:AX is F000 0000H, which is the negative of the product that MUL generated.

The third example extends BYTE1 to a word in the AX. Since the values are supposed to be signed, the example uses CBW to extend the leftmost sign bit into the AH register: 80H in the AL becomes FF80H in the AX. Since the multiplier, WORD1, is also negative, the product should be positive. And indeed it is: 0040 0000H in the DX:AX—the same result as MUL, which multiplied two unsigned numbers.

In effect, if the multiplicand and multiplier have the same sign bit, MUL and IMUL generate the same product. But if the multiplicand and multiplier have different sign bits, MUL produces a positive product and IMUL produces a negative product. The upshot is that your program must know the format of the data and use the appropriate instructions.

You may find it worthwhile to use DEBUG to trace through these examples.

MULTIWORD MULTIPLICATION

Conventional multiplication involves multiplying byte by byte, word by word, or doubleword by doubleword. As we have already seen, the maximum signed value in a word is $+32,767$. Multiplying larger values on pre-80386 processors involves additional steps. The approach on these processors is to multiply each word separately and then add each product together. The following example multiplies a four-digit decimal number by a two-digit number:

```
TITLE     P13MULT (COM)   MUL and IMUL operations
          .MODEL SMALL
          .CODE
          ORG     100H
BEGIN:  JMP     SHORT MAIN
; ----------------------------------------------------------
BYTE1   DB      80H
BYTE2   DB      40H
WORD1   DW      8000H
WORD2   DW      2000H
; ----------------------------------------------------------
MAIN    PROC    NEAR               ;Main procedure
        CALL    C10MUL             ;Call MUL   routine
        CALL    D10IMUL            ;Call IMUL routine
        MOV     AX,4C00H           ;Exit to DOS
        INT     21H
MAIN    ENDP
;               Examples of MUL:
;               ---------------
C10MUL  PROC
        MOV     AL,BYTE1           ;Byte x byte
        MUL     BYTE2              ;  product in AX

        MOV     AX,WORD1           ;Word x word
        MUL     WORD2              ;  product in DX:AX

        MOV     AL,BYTE1           ;Byte x word
        SUB     AH,AH              ;  extend multiplicand in AH
        MUL     WORD1              ;  product in DX:AX
        RET
C10MUL  ENDP
;               Examples of IMUL:
;               ----------------
D10IMUL PROC
        MOV     AL,BYTE1           ;Byte x byte
        IMUL    BYTE2              ,  product in AX

        MOV     AX,WORD1           ;Word x word
        IMUL    WORD2              ;  product in DX:AX

        MOV     AL,BYTE1           ;Byte x word
        CBW                        ;  extend multiplicand in AH
        IMUL    WORD1              ;  product in DX:AX
        RET
D10IMUL ENDP
        END     BEGIN
```

Figure 13–3   Unsigned and Signed Multiplication

$$
\begin{array}{r}
1,365 \\
\times \quad 12 \\
\hline
16,380
\end{array}
$$

What if you could multiply only two-digit numbers? Then you could multiply the 13 and the 65 by 12 separately, like this:

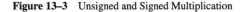

$$
\begin{array}{r}
13 \\
\times \ 12 \\
\hline
156
\end{array}
\qquad
\begin{array}{r}
65 \\
\times \ 12 \\
\hline
780
\end{array}
$$

Next, add the two products; but remember, since the 13 is in the hundreds position, its product is actually 15,600:

$$
\begin{array}{rl}
15,600 & (13 \times 12 \times 100) \\
+ \quad 780 & (65 \times 12) \\
\hline
16,380 &
\end{array}
$$

An assembly program can use this same technique, except that the data consists of words (four digits) in hexadecimal format. Let's now examine the requirements for multiplying doubleword by word and doubleword by doubleword.

Doubleword by Word

In Figure 13–4, E10XMUL multiplies a doubleword by a word. The multiplicand, MULTCND, consists of two words containing 3206H and 2521H, respectively. The reason for defining two DWs instead of a DD is to facilitate addressing for MOV instructions that move words to the AX register. The values are defined in reverse-word sequence, and the assembler stores each word in reverse-byte sequence. Thus MULTCND, which has a defined value of 32062521H, is stored as 21250632H.

```
TITLE       P13DWMUL (COM)   Multiplication of doublewords
            .MODEL SMALL
            .CODE
            ORG     100H
BEGIN:      JMP     SHORT MAIN
; -------------------------------------------------
MULTCND     DW      2521H                   ;Data items
            DW      3206H
MULTPLR     DW      0A26H
            DW      6400H
PRODUCT     DW      0
            DW      0
            DW      0
            DW      0
; -------------------------------------------------
MAIN        PROC    NEAR                    ;Main procedure
            CALL    E10XMUL                 ;Call 1st multiply
            CALL    Z10ZERO                 ;Clear product
            CALL    F10XMUL                 ;Call 2nd multiply
            MOV     AX,4C00H                ;Exit to DOS
            INT     21H
MAIN        ENDP
;                   Doubleword x word:
;                   ----------------
E10XMUL     PROC
            MOV     AX,MULTCND              ;Multiply left word
            MUL     MULTPLR+2               ;  of multiplicand
            MOV     PRODUCT,AX              ;Store product
            MOV     PRODUCT+2,DX

            MOV     AX,MULTCND+2            ;Multiply right word
            MUL     MULTPLR+2               ;  of multiplicand
            ADD     PRODUCT+2,AX            ;Add to stored product
            ADC     PRODUCT+4,DX
            RET
E10XMUL     ENDP
```

Figure 13–4 Multiword Multiplication

```
;                     Doubleword x doubleword:
;                     ------------------------
F10XMUL   PROC
          MOV    AX,MULTCND        ;Multiplicand word 1
          MUL    MULTPLR           ;  x multiplier word 1
          MOV    PRODUCT+0,AX      ;Store product
          MOV    PRODUCT+2,DX

          MOV    AX,MULTCND        ;Multiplicand word 1
          MUL    MULTPLR+2         ;  x multiplier word 2
          ADD    PRODUCT+2,AX      ;Add to stored product
          ADC    PRODUCT+4,DX
          ADC    PRODUCT+6,00      ;Add any carry

          MOV    AX,MULTCND+2      ;Multiplicand word 2
          MUL    MULTPLR           ;  x multiplier word 1
          ADD    PRODUCT+2,AX      ;Add to stored product
          ADC    PRODUCT+4,DX
          ADC    PRODUCT+6,00      ;Add any carry

          MOV    AX,MULTCND+2      ;Multiplicand word 2
          MUL    MULTPLR+2         ;  x multiplier word 2
          ADD    PRODUCT+4,AX      ;Add to product
          ADC    PRODUCT+6,DX
          RET
F10XMUL   ENDP
;                     Clear product area:
;                     ------------------
Z10ZERO   PROC
          MOV    PRODUCT,0000      ;Clear words
          MOV    PRODUCT+2,0000    ;  left to right
          MOV    PRODUCT+4,0000
          MOV    PRODUCT+6,0000
          RET
Z10ZERO   ENDP
          END    BEGIN
```

Figure 13–4B   (continued)

The multiplier, MULTPLR+2, contains 6400H. The field for the generated product, PRODUCT, provides for three words. The first MUL operation multiplies MULTPLR+2 and the left word of MULTCND; the product is hex 0E80 E400H, stored in PRODUCT+2 and PRODUCT+4. The second MUL multiplies MULTPLR+2 and the right word of MULTCND; the product is 138A 5800H. The routine then adds the two products, like this:

```
Product 1:    0000 0E80 E400

Product 2:   +138A 5800
             _____

Total:        138A 6680 E400
```

Since the first ADD may cause a carry, the second add is ADC (Add with Carry). Because numeric data is stored in reversed byte format, PRODUCT will actually contain 00E4 8066 8A13. The routine requires that the first word of PRODUCT initially contain zero.

Doubleword by Doubleword

Multiplying two doublewords on pre-80386 processors involves four multiplications:

MULTIPLICAND		MULTIPLIER
word 2	×	word 2
word 2	×	word 1
word 1	×	word 2
word 1	×	word 1

You add each product in the DX and AX to the appropriate word in the final product. In Figure 13–4, F10XMUL gives an example. MULTCND contains 3206 2521H, MULTPLR contains 6400 0A26H, and PRODUCT provides for four words.

Although the logic is similar to multiplying doubleword by word, this problem requires an additional feature. Following the ADD/ADC pair is another ADC that adds 0 to PRODUCT. The first ADC itself could cause a carry, which subsequent instructions would clear. The second ADC, therefore, adds 0 if there is no carry and adds 1 if there is a carry. The final ADD/ADC pair does not require an additional ADC: Since PRODUCT is large enough for the final generated answer, there is no carry.

The final product is 138A 687C 8E5C CCE6, stored in PRODUCT with the bytes reversed. Try using DEBUG to trace through this example.

SPECIAL MULTIPLICATION INSTRUCTIONS

The 80286 and later processors have additional IMUL formats that provide for immediate operands and allow for generating products in registers other than the AX. You can use these instructions for either signed or unsigned multiplication, since the results are the same. The values must be all the same length: 16 or (for the 80386 and later) 32 bits.

16-Bit IMUL operation

For the 16-bit IMUL, the first operand (a register) contains the multiplicand, and the second operand (an immediate value) is the multiplier. The product is generated in the first operand. A product that exceeds the register causes the carry and overflow flags to be set. The general format for this 16-bit IMUL operation is

| [label:] | IMUL | register,immediate |

32-Bit IMUL operation

The 32-bit IMUL has three operands: The second operand (memory) contains the multiplicand, and the third operand (an immediate value) contains the multiplier. The product is generated in the first operand (a register). The general format for the 32-bit IMUL is

| [label:] | IMUL | register,memory,immediate |

16/32-Bit IMUL operation

The 80386 and later processors provide yet another IMUL format for 16- or 32-bit operations. The first operand (a register) contains the multiplicand, and the second operand (register/memory) contains the multiplier. The product is generated in the first operand.

```
┌──────────┬──────┬─────────────────────────┐
│ [label:] │ IMUL │ register,{register/memory} │
└──────────┴──────┴─────────────────────────┘
```

Here are examples of these three IMUL instructions:

		Multiplicand	Multiplier	Product
16-bit IMUL:	IMUL DX,25	DX	25	DX
32-bit IMUL:	IMUL ECX,MULTCAND,25	MULTCAND	25	ECX
16/32-bit IMUL:	IMUL BX,CX	BX	CX	BX

MULTIPLICATION BY SHIFTING

For multiplying by a power of 2 (2, 4, 8, etc.), it is more efficient simply to shift left the necessary number of bits. For the 8088/8086, a shift greater than 1 requires that you load the shift value in the CL register. In the following examples, the multiplicand is in the AX:

Multiply by 2 (shift left 1): SHL AX,01
Multiply by 8 (shift left 3): MOV CL,03   ;8088/8086
                              SHL AX,CL
Multiply by 8 (shift left 3): SHL AX,03   ;80286 and later

Shifting in the DX:AX Registers

The following routine could be useful for left shifting a product in the DX:AX registers. You could contrive a more efficient method, but this example is generalized for any number of loops (and shifts) in the CX. Note that a shifted-off 1-bit enters the carry flag, which is used by RCL:

```
        MOV  CX,04        ;Initialize 4 loops

C20:    SHL  AX,01        ;Shift AX

        RCL  DX,01        ;Rotate DX left

        LOOP C20          ;Repeat
```

The next method for left shifting requires an 80286 or later processor and does not require looping. Although specific to a four-bit shift, it could be adapted to other values:

```
        SHL  DX,04        ;Shift DX left 4 bits

        MOV  BL,AH        ;Store AH in BL

        SHL  AX,04        ;Shift AX left 4 bits

        SHR  BL,04        ;Shift BL right 4 bits

        OR   DL,BL        ;Insert BL 4 bits in DL
```

DIVISION

For division, the DIV (Divide) instruction handles unsigned data, and IDIV (Integer Divide) handles signed data. You are responsible for selecting the appropriate instruction. The general format for DIV/IDIV is

| [label:] | DIV/IDIV | {register/memory} |

The basic divide operations are byte into word, word into doubleword, and (80386 and later) doubleword into quadword.

Byte into Word

Here, the dividend is in the AX and the divisor is a byte in memory or another register. After division, the remainder is in the AH and the quotient is in the AL. Since a one-byte quotient is very small—a maximum of +255 (FFH) if unsigned and +127 (7FH) if signed—this operation has limited use.

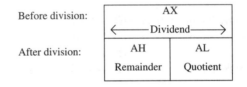

Before division:
AX — Dividend —

After division:
AH Remainder | AL Quotient

Word into Doubleword

For this operation, the dividend is in the DX:AX pair and the divisor is a word in memory or another register. After division, the remainder is in the DX and the quotient is in the AX. The quotient of one word allows a maximum of +32,767 (FFFFH) if unsigned and +16,383 (7FFFH) if signed. We have:

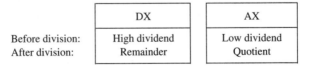

	DX	AX
Before division:	High dividend	Low dividend
After division:	Remainder	Quotient

Doubleword into Quadword

In dividing a doubleword into a quadword, the dividend is in the EDX:EAX pair and the divisor is a doubleword in memory or another register. After division, the remainder is in the EDX and the quotient is in the EAX.

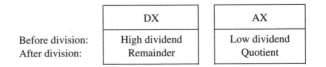

	DX	AX
Before division:	High dividend	Low dividend
After division:	Remainder	Quotient

Field Sizes

The operand of DIV or IDIV references the divisor, which specifies the field sizes. In the following DIV examples, the divisors are in a register, which determines the type of operation:

OPERATION	DIVISOR	DIVIDEND	QUOTIENT	REMAINDER
DIV CL	byte	AX	AL	AH
DIV CX	word	DX:AX	AX	DX
DIV EBX	doubleword	EDX:EAX	EAX	EDX

In the following DIV examples, the divisors are defined in memory:

```
BYTE1    DB    ?

WORD1    DW    ?

DWORD1   DD    ?
```

...		DIVISOR	DIVIDEND	QUOTIENT	REMAINDER
DIV	BYTE1	BYTE1	AX	AL	AH
DIV	WORD1	WORD1	DX:AX	AX	DX
DIV	DWORD1	DWORD1	EDX:EAX	EAX	EDX

Remainder.   If you divide 13 by 3, the result is $4\frac{1}{3}$, where the quotient is 4 and the true remainder is 1. Note that a calculator (and a high-level programming language) would deliver a quotient of 4.333. . . , which consists of an integer portion (4) and a fraction portion (.333 . . .). The values $\frac{1}{3}$ and .333 are fractions, whereas the 1 is a remainder.

Unsigned Division: DIV

The purpose of the DIV instruction is to divide unsigned data. Figure 13–5 gives four examples of DIV in the procedure D10DIV: byte into word, byte into byte, word into doubleword, and word into word. The first example divides 2000H (8092) by 80H (128). The remainder in the AH is 00H, and the quotient in the AL is 40H (64).

The second example requires extending BYTE1 to a word. Since the value is supposed to be unsigned, the example assumes that bits in the AH register are to be zero. The remainder in the AH is 12H, and the quotient in the AL is 05H.

In the third example, the remainder in the DX is 1000H, and the quotient in the AX is 0080H.

The fourth example requires extending WORD1 to a doubleword in the DX register. After the division, the remainder in the DX is 0000H, and the quotient in the AX is 0002H.

Signed Division: IDIV

The purpose of the IDIV instruction is to divide signed data. In Figure 13–5, E10IDIV gives the same four examples as D10DIV, but replacing DIV with IDIV. The first example divides 2000H (positive) by 80H (negative). The remainder in the AH is 00H, and the quotient in the AL is C0H (−64). (Using the same data, DIV resulted in a quotient of +64.)

```
TITLE     P13DIV (COM)  DIV and IDIV operations
          .MODEL   SMALL
          .CODE
          ORG      100H
BEGIN:    JMP      SHORT MAIN
; --------------------------------------------------------
BYTE1     DB       80H                    ;Data items
BYTE3     DB       16H
WORD1     DW       2000H
WORD2     DW       0010H
WORD3     DW       1000H
; --------------------------------------------------------
MAIN      PROC     NEAR                   ;Main procedure
          CALL     D10DIV                 ;Call DIV  routine
          CALL     E10IDIV                ;Call IDIV routine
          MOV      AX,4C00H               ;Exit to DOS
          INT      21H
MAIN      ENDP
;                  Examples of DIV:
;                  ---------------
D10DIV    PROC
          MOV      AX,WORD1               ;Word / byte
          DIV      BYTE1                  ;  rmdr:quot in AH:AL
          MOV      AL,BYTE1               ;Byte / byte
          SUB      AH,AH                  ;  extend dividend in AH
          DIV      BYTE3                  ;  rmdr:quot in AH:AL

          MOV      DX,WORD2               ;Doubleword / word
          MOV      AX,WORD3               ;  dividend in DX:AX
          DIV      WORD1                  ;  rmdr:quot in DX:AX
          MOV      AX,WORD1               ;Word / word
          SUB      DX,DX                  ;  extend dividend in DX
          DIV      WORD3                  ;  rmdr:quot in DX:AX
          RET
D10DIV    ENDP
;                  Examples of IDIV:
;                  ----------------
E10IDIV   PROC
          MOV      AX,WORD1               ;Word / byte
          IDIV     BYTE1                  ;  rmdr:quot in AH:AL
          MOV      AL,BYTE1               ;Byte / byte
          CBW                             ;  extend dividend in AH
          IDIV     BYTE3                  ;  rmdr:quot in AH:AL

          MOV      DX,WORD2               ;Doubleword / word
          MOV      AX,WORD3               ;  dividend in DX:AX
          IDIV     WORD1                  ;  rmdr:quot in DX:AX
          MOV      AX,WORD1               ;Word / word
          CWD                             ;  extend dividend in DX
          IDIV     WORD3                  ;  rmdr:quot in DX:AX
          RET
E10IDIV   ENDP
          END      BEGIN
```

Figure 13–5 Unsigned and Signed Division

The results, in hex, of the remaining three examples of IDIV are:

IDIV EXAMPLE	REMAINDER	QUOTIENT
2	EE (−18)	FB (−5)
3	1000 (4096)	0080 (128)
4	0000	0002

Only Example 4 produces the same answer as did DIV. In effect, <u>if the dividend and divisor have the same sign bit, DIV and IDIV generate the same result. But if the dividend and divisor have different sign bits, DIV generates a positive quotient, and IDIV generates a negative quotient.</u>

You may find it worthwhile to use DEBUG to trace through these examples.

Overflows and Interrupts

DIV and IDIV operations assume that the quotient is significantly smaller than the original dividend. As a consequence, the operation can easily cause an overflow; when it does, an interrupt occurs, with unpredictable results. Dividing by zero always causes an interrupt. But dividing by 1 generates a quotient that is the same as the dividend and could also cause an interrupt.

Here's a useful rule: <u>If the divisor is a byte, its contents must be greater than the left byte (AH) of the dividend; if the divisor is a word, its contents must be greater than the left word (DX) of the dividend; if the divisor is a doubleword, its contents must be greater than the left doubleword (EDX) of the dividend.</u> Here's an illustration using a divisor of 1, although other values could also serve:

DIVIDE OPERATION	DIVIDEND	DIVISOR	QUOTIENT
Word by byte:	0123	01	(1)23
Doubleword by word:	0001 4026	0001	(1)4026

In both cases, the generated quotient would exceed its available space. You may be wise to include a test prior to a DIV or IDIV operation, as shown in the next two examples. In the first, DIVBYTE is a one-byte divisor, and the dividend is already in the AX:

```
CMP   AH,DIVBYTE        ;Compare AH to divisor

JNB   overflow-rtne     ;Jump if not smaller

DIV   DIVBYTE           ;Divide word by byte
```

In the second example, DIVWORD is a one-word divisor, and the dividend is in the DX:AX:

```
CMP   DX,DIVWORD        ;Compare DX to divisor

JNB   overflow-rtne     ;Jump if not smaller

DIV   DIVWORD           ;Divide doubleword by word
```

For IDIV, the logic should account for the fact that either the dividend or the divisor could be negative. Since the absolute value of the divisor must be the smaller of the two, you could use the NEG instruction to set a negative value temporarily to positive and restore the sign after the division.

Division by Subtraction

<u>If a quotient is too large for the divisor, you could perform division by means of successive subtraction. That is, subtract the divisor from the dividend, increment a quotient value by</u>

1, and continue subtracting until the dividend is less than the divisor. In the following example, the dividend is in the AX, the divisor is in the BX, and the quotient is developed in the CX:

```
          SUB   CX,CX      ;Clear quotient
  C20:    CMP   AX,BX      ;If dividend < divisor,
          JB    C30        ; exit
          SUB   AX,BX      ;Subtract divisor from dividend
          INC   CX         ;Add 1 to quotient
          JMP   C20        ;Repeat
  C30:    RET              ;Quotient in CX, remainder in AX
```

At the end of the routine, the CX contains the quotient and the AX contains the remainder. The example is intentionally primitive to demonstrate the technique. If the quotient is in the DX:AX pair, include these two operations:

1. At C20, compare AX to BX only if DX is zero.
2. After the SUB instruction, insert SBB DX,00.

Note that a very large quotient and a small divisor may cause thousands of loops at a cost of processing time.

DIVISION BY SHIFTING

For division by a power of 2 (2, 4, 8, and so on), it is more efficient simply to shift right the required number of bits. For the 8088/8086, a shift greater than 1 requires a shift value in the CL register. The following examples assume that the dividend is in the AX:

```
Divide by 2 (shift right 1): SHR  AX,01
Divide by 8 (shift right 3): MOV  CL,03         ;8088/8086
                             SHR  AX,CL
Divide by 8 (shift right 3): SHR  CL,03         ;80286 and later
```

Shifting in the DX:AX Registers

The following routine could be useful for right shifting a product in the DX:AX pair. You could contrive a more efficient method, but this example is generalized for any number of loops (and shifts) in the CX. Note that a shifted off 1-bit enters the carry flag, which is used by RCR:

```
          MOV   CX,04      ;Initialize 4 loops
  D20:    SAR   DX,01      ;Shift DX
          RCR   AX,01      ;Rotate AX right
          LOOP  D20        ;Repeat
```

REVERSING THE SIGN

The NEG (negate) instruction reverses the sign of a binary value, from positive to negative and vice versa. In effect, NEG reverses the bits, just like NOT, and then adds 1 for proper two's complement notation. The general format for NEG is

```
[label:]   NEG   {register/memory}
```

Here are some examples:

```
NEG   AX        ;16 bits

NEG   BL        ;8 bits

NEG   BINAMT    ;Byte or word in memory

NEG   ECX       ;32 bits
```

Reversing the sign of a 32-bit (or larger) value involves more steps. Assume that the DX:AX pair contains a 32-bit binary number. NEG cannot act on the DX:AX pair concurrently, and using it on both registers would mean adding 1 to both. Instead, use NOT to flip the bits, and use ADD and ADC to add the 1 for two's complement:

```
NOT   DX        ;Flip bits

NOT   AX        ;Flip bits

ADD   AX,1      ;Add 1 to AX

ADC   DX,0      ;Add carry to DX
```

One minor problem remains: It is all very well to perform arithmetic on binary data that the program itself defines or on data already in binary form on a disk file. However, data that enters a program from a terminal is in ASCII format. Although ASCII data is suitable for displaying and printing, it requires special adjusting for arithmetic—a topic discussed in the next chapter.

NUMERIC DATA PROCESSORS

This section provides a general introduction to the numeric data processor; a full discussion is outside the scope of the book. The system board contains a socket for an Intel Numeric Data Processor, known as a coprocessor. The 8087 coprocessor operates in conjunction with an 8088/86, the 80287 with an 80286, the 80387 with an 80386, and so forth.

The coprocessor has its own instruction set and floating-point hardware for performing such operations as exponentiation and logarithmic and trigonometric operations. The eight 80-bit floating-point registers can represent numeric values up to 10 to the 400th power. The coprocessor's mathematical processing is rated about 100 times faster than a regular processor.

The 8087 consists of eight 80-bit registers, R1–R8, in the following format:

S	exponent	significand
79	78 64	63 0

Each register has an associated 2-bit tag that indicates its status:

00   Contains a valid number
01   Contains a zero value
10   Contains an invalid number
11   Is empty

The coprocessor recognizes seven types of numeric data:

1. *Word integer*: 16 bits of binary data.

S	number
15	14 0

2. *Short integer*: 32 bits of binary data.

S	number
31	30 0

3. *Long integer*: 64 bits of binary data.

S	number
63	62 0

4. *Short real*: 32 bits of floating-point data.

S	exponent	significand
31	30 23	22 0

5. *Long real*: 64 bits of floating-point data.

S	exponent	significand
63	62 52	51 0

6. *Temporary real*: 80 bits of floating-point data.

S	exponent	significand
79	78 64	63 0

7. *Packed decimal*: 18 significant decimal digits.

S	zeros		significand	
79	78	72	71	0

Types 1, 2, and 3 are common binary two's-complement formats. Types 4, 5, and 6 represent floating-point numbers. Type 7 contains 18 4-bit decimal digits. You can load any of these formats from memory into a coprocessor register and can store the register contents into memory. However, for its calculations, the coprocessor converts all formats in its registers into temporary real. Data is stored in memory in reverse-byte sequence.

The processor requests a specific operation and delivers numeric data to the coprocessor, which performs the operation and returns the result. For assembling, use the appropriate .80x86 directive.

The INT 11H instruction can help determine the presence of a coprocessor. The operation delivers the equipment status to the AX, where bit 1 on means that a coprocessor is present.

KEY POINTS

- The maximum signed values for one-byte accumulators are $+127$ and -128.
- For multiword addition, use ADC to account for any carry from a previous ADD. If the operation is performed in a loop, use CLC to initialize the carry flag to zero.
- Use MUL for unsigned data and IMUL for signed data.
- With MUL, if a multiplier is defined as a byte, the multiplicand is AL; if the multiplier is a word, the multiplicand is AX; if the multiplier is a doubleword, the multiplicand is EAX.
- Shift left (SHL or SAL) for multiplying by powers of 2.
- Use DIV for unsigned data and IDIV for signed data.
- For division, be especially careful of overflows. The divisor must be greater than the contents of the AH if the divisor is a byte, DX if the divisor is a word, or EDX if the divisor is a doubleword.
- With DIV, if a divisor is defined as a byte, the dividend is AX; if the divisor is a word, the dividend is DX:AX; if the divisor is a doubleword, the dividend is EDX:EAX.
- Shift right for dividing by powers of 2—SHR for unsigned fields and SAR for signed fields.

QUESTIONS

13–1. (a) What are the maximum values in a byte for signed data and for unsigned data? (b) What is the maximum value in a word for signed data and for unsigned data?

13–2. Distinguish between a carry and an overflow.

Questions 13–3 through 13–7 refer to the following data, with words defined in reverse sequence:

```
DATAX   DW  0148H

        DW  2316H

DATAY   DW  0237H

        DW  4052H

DATAZ   DW  0

        DW  0

        DW  0
```

13–3. Code the instructions to add the following: (a) the word DATAX to the word DATAY; (b) the doubleword beginning at DATAX to the doubleword at DATAY.

13–4. Explain the effect of the following related instructions:

```
STC

MOV     BX,DATAX

ADC     BX,DATAY
```

13–5. Code the instructions to multiply (MUL) the following: (a) the the word DATAX by the word DATAY; (b) the doubleword beginning at DATAX by the word DATAY. Store the product in DATAZ.

13–6. Other than zero, what divisors cause an overflow error?

13–7. Code the instructions to divide (DIV) the following: (a) the word DATAX by 23; (b) the doubleword beginning at DATAX by the word DATAY.

13–8. Revise Figure 13–2 so that the routine adds three pairs of words instead of two. Name the additional words on the right WORD3A and WORD3B.

13–9. Refer to the section "Multiplication by Shifting." The second part contains a more efficient method of shifting left four bits. Revise the example for a right shift of four bits.

CHAPTER 14

Arithmetic: II—Processing ASCII and BCD Data

OBJECTIVE:

To examine ASCII and BCD data formats, to perform arithmetic in these formats, and to cover conversions between these formats and binary.

INTRODUCTION

The natural data format for arithmetic on a computer is binary. As seen in Chapter 13, binary format causes no major problems, as long as the program itself defines the data. For many purposes, however, numeric data enters a program from a keyboard as ASCII characters, in base 10 format. Similarly, the display of numeric values on a screen is in ASCII format.

A related format, *binary-coded decimal (BCD)*, has occasional uses and appears as unpacked and as packed. The PC provides a number of instructions that facilitate simple arithmetic and conversion between formats. This chapter also covers techniques for converting ASCII data into binary format to perform arithmetic, as well as techniques for converting the binary results back into ASCII format for viewing. The program at the end of the chapter combines much of the material covered in Chapters 1 through 13.

If you have programmed in a high-level language such as C, you are used to the compiler accounting for the radix (decimal or binary) point. However, the computer does not recognize a radix point in an arithmetic field, so that you as the programmer have to account for its position.

Instructions introduced in this chapter are:

AAA   ASCII Adjust After Addition
AAS   ASCII Adjust After Subtraction
AAM   ASCII Adjust After Multiplication
AAD   ASCII Adjust For Division
DAA   Decimal Adjustment After Addition
DAS   Decimal Adjustment After Subtraction

DATA IN DECIMAL FORMAT

To this point, we have handled numeric values in binary and ASCII formats. The PC system also supports *binary-coded decimal* (*BCD*) format, which allows for some limited arithmetic operations. Two uses for BCD format are:

1. BCD permits proper rounding of numbers with no loss of precision, a feature that is particularly useful for handling dollars and cents. (Rounding of binary numbers that represent dollars and cents may well cause a loss of precision.)
2. It is often simpler to perform arithmetic on small values entered from a keyboard or to be written on the screen or printer.

A BCD digit consists of four bits that can represent the decimal digits 0 through 9:

Binary	BCD digit	Binary	BCD digit
0000	0	0101	5
0001	1	0110	6
0010	2	0111	7
0011	3	1000	8
0100	4	1001	9

You can store BCD digits as unpacked or as packed:

1. *Unpacked BCD* contains a single BCD digit in the lower four bits of each byte, with zeros in the upper four bits. Note that although ASCII format is also "unpacked," it isn't called that.
2. *Packed BCD* contains two BCD digits, one in the upper four bits and one in the lower four bits. This format is commonly used for arithmetic using the numeric coprocessor, defined as 10 bytes with the DT directive.

Let's examine the representation of the decimal number 1,527 in the three decimal formats:

- ASCII   31 35 32 37 (four bytes)
- Unpacked BCD 01 05 02 07 (four bytes)
- Packed BCD   15 27   (two bytes)

The processor performs arithmetic on ASCII and BCD values one digit at a time. You have to use special instructions for converting from one format to another.

PROCESSING ASCII DATA

Since data that you enter from a keyboard is in ASCII format, the representation in memory of an entered decimal value such as 1234 is 31323334H. But performing arithmetic on such a value involves special treatment. The AAA and AAS instructions perform arithmetic directly on ASCII numbers:

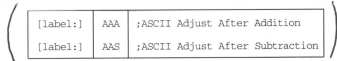

```
[label:]    AAA    ;ASCII Adjust After Addition

[label:]    AAS    ;ASCII Adjust After Subtraction
```

These instructions are coded without operands and automatically adjust an ASCII value in the AX register. The adjustment occurs because an ASCII value represents an unpacked base-10 number, whereas the processor performs base-2 arithmetic.

ASCII Addition

Consider the effect of adding the ASCII numbers 8 (38H) and 4 (34H):

hex   38

hex   34

———

hex   6C

The sum 6CH is neither a correct ASCII nor a correct binary value. However, ignore the leftmost 6, and add 6 to the rightmost hex C: Hex C plus 6 = hex 12, the correct answer in terms of decimal numbers. Why add 6? Because that's the difference between hexadecimal (16) and decimal (10). This is a little oversimplified, but it does indicate the way in which AAA performs its adjustment.

The AAA operation checks the rightmost hex digit (four bits) of the AL register. If the digit is between A and F or the auxiliary carry flag is 1, the operation adds 6 to the AL register, adds 1 to the AH register, and sets the carry and auxiliary carry flags to 1. In all cases, AAA clears the leftmost hex digit of the AL to zero.

As an example, assume that the AX contains 0038H and the BX contains 0034H. The 38 in the AL and the 34 in the BL represent two ASCII bytes that are to be added. Addition and adjustment are as follows:

```
ADD   AL,BL    ;Add 34H to 38H, equals 006CH

AAA            ;Adjust for ASCII add, equals 0102H
```

Since the rightmost hex digit of the AL is C, AAA adds 6 to the AL, adds 1 to the AH, sets the carry and auxiliary carry flags, and clears to zero the leftmost hex digit of the AL. The result in the AX is now 0102H.

To restore the ASCII representation, simply insert 3s in the leftmost hex digits of the AH and AL to get 3132H, or decimal 12:

```
OR    AX,3030H  ;Result is now 3132H
```

All that is very well for adding one-byte ASCII numbers. Adding multibyte ASCII numbers, however, requires a loop that processes from right to left (low order to high

```
TITLE     P14ASCAD (COM)   Adding ASCII numbers
          .MODEL SMALL
          .CODE
          ORG       100H
BEGIN:    JMP       SHORT MAIN
; ------------------------------------------------
ASC1      DB        '578'                 ;Data items
ASC2      DB        '694'
ASCSUM    DB        '0000'
; ------------------------------------------------
MAIN      PROC      NEAR
          CLC                             ;Clear carry flag
          LEA       SI,ASC1+2             ;Initialize ASCII
          LEA       DI,ASC2+2             ;  numbers
          LEA       BX,ASCSUM+3
          MOV       CX,03                 ;Initialize 3 loops
A20:
          MOV       AH,00                 ;Clear AH
          MOV       AL,[SI]               ;Load ASCII byte
          ADC       AL,[DI]               ;Add (with carry)
          AAA                             ;Adjust for ASCII
          MOV       [BX],AL               ;Store sum
          DEC       SI
          DEC       DI
          DEC       BX
          LOOP      A20                   ;Loop 3 times
          MOV       [BX],AH               ;At end, store carry

          LEA       BX,ASCSUM+3           ;Convert ASCSUM
          MOV       CX,04                 ;  to ASCII
A30:
          OR        BYTE PTR[BX],30H
          DEC       BX
          LOOP      A30                   ;Loop 4 times
          MOV       AX,4C00H              ;Exit to DOS
          INT       21H
MAIN      ENDP
          END       BEGIN
```

Figure 14–1 ASCII Addition

order) and accounts for carries. The code in Figure 14–1 adds two three-byte ASCII numbers, ASC1 and ASC2, and produces a four-byte sum, ASCSUM. Note the following points:

- A CLC instruction at the start initializes the carry flag to zero.
- Following A20, ADC is used for addition because an ADD may cause a carry that should be added to the next (left) byte.
- A MOV instruction clears the AH on each loop because each AAA may add 1 to the AH. ADC, however, accounts for any carry. Note that the use of XOR or SUB to clear the AH would change the carry flag.
- When looping is complete, the routine moves the AH (containing either a final 00 or 01) to the leftmost byte of ASCSUM.
- At the end, ASCSUM contains 01020702H. To insert ASCII 3 in each byte, the program loops through ASCSUM in memory and ORs each byte with 30H. The result is 31323732H, or decimal 1272.

The routine did not use OR after AAA to insert leftmost 3s, because OR sets the carry flag and changes the effect for the ADC instructions. A solution that saves the flag settings is to push (PUSHF) the flags register, execute the OR, and then pop (POPF) the flags to restore them:

```
ADC     AL,[DI]     ;Add with carry

AAA                 ;Adjust for ASCII

PUSHF               ;Save flags

OR      AL,30H      ;Insert ASCII 3

POPF                ;Restore flags

MOV     [BX],AL     ;Store sum
```

ASCII Subtraction

The AAS instruction works like AAA. AAS checks the rightmost hex digit (four bits) of the AL. If the digit is between A and F or the auxiliary carry is 1, the operation subtracts 6 from the AL, subtracts 1 from the AH, and sets the auxiliary (AF) and carry (CF) flags. In all cases, AAS clears the leftmost hex digit of the AL to zero.

The next two examples assume that ASC1 contains 38H and ASC2 contains 34H. The first example subtracts ASC2 (34H) from ASC1 (38H). AAS does not need to make an adjustment, because the rightmost hex digit is less than hex A:

```
                        AX      AF

MOV   AL,ASC1       ;0038

SUB   AL,ASC2       ;0004    0

AAS                 ;0004    0

OR    AL,30H        ;0034
```

The second example subtracts ASC1 (38H) from ASC2 (34H). Since the rightmost digit is hex C, AAS subtracts 6 from the AL, subtracts 1 from the AH, and sets the AF and CF flags. The answer, which should be −4, is FF06H, its 10's complement, which has little value:

```
                        AX      AF

MOV   AL,ASC2       ;0034

SUB   AL,ASC1       ;00FC    1

AAS                 ;FF06    1
```

PROCESSING UNPACKED BCD DATA

Multiplication and division of ASCII numbers require that the numbers first be converted into unpacked BCD format. The AAM and AAD instructions perform arithmetic directly on unpacked BCD numbers.

| [label:] | AAM | ;ASCII Adjust After Multiplication |
| [label:] | AAD | ;ASCII Adjust Before Division |

ASCII Multiplication

The AAM instruction corrects the result of multiplying ASCII data in the AX register. However, you must first clear the 3 in the leftmost hex digit of each byte, thus converting the value to unpacked BCD. For example, the ASCII number 31323334 becomes 01020304 as unpacked BCD. Also, because the adjustment is only one byte at a time, you can multiply only one-byte fields and have to perform the operation repetitively in a loop. Use only the MUL, not the IMUL, operation.

AAM divides the AL by 10 (0AH) and stores the quotient in the AH and the remainder in the AL. For example, suppose that the AL contains 35H and the CL contains 39H. The following code multiplies the contents of the AL by the CL and converts the result to ASCII format:

INSTRUCTION	COMMENT	AX	CL
AND CL,0FH	;Convert CL to 09	0035	09
AND AL,0FH	;Convert AL to 05	0005	
MUL CL	;Multiply AL by CL	002D	
AAM	;Convert to unpacked BCD	0405	
OR AX,3030H	;Convert to ASCII	3435	

The MUL operation generates 45 (002DH) in the AX. AAM divides this value by 10, generating a quotient of 04 in the AH and a remainder of 05 in the AL. The OR instruction then converts the unpacked BCD value to ASCII format.

Figure 14–2 depicts multiplying a four-byte multiplicand by a one-byte multiplier. Since AAM can accommodate only one-byte operations, the routine steps through the multiplicand one byte at a time, from right to left. At the end, the unpacked BCD product is 0108090105, which a loop routine converts to true ASCII format as 3138393135, or decimal 18,915.

If a multiplier is greater than one byte, you have to provide yet another loop that steps through the multiplier. It may be simpler to convert the ASCII data to binary format, as covered in a later section.

ASCII Division

The AAD instruction provides a correction of an ASCII dividend prior to dividing. Just as with AAM, you first clear the leftmost 3s from the ASCII bytes to create unpacked BCD format. AAD allows for a two-byte dividend in the AX. The divisor can be only a single byte containing 01 to 09.

Assume that the AX contains the ASCII value 28 (3238H) and the CL contains the divisor, ASCII 7 (37H). The following instructions perform the adjustment and division:

```
TITLE     P14ASCMU (COM)  Multiplying ASCII numbers
          .MODEL SMALL
          .CODE
          ORG     100H
BEGIN:    JMP     MAIN
;----------------------------------------------------------
MULTCND   DB      '3783'                ;Data items
MULTPLR   DB      '5'
PRODUCT   DB      5 DUP(0)
;----------------------------------------------------------
MAIN      PROC    NEAR
          MOV     CX,04                 ;Initialize 4 loops
          LEA     SI,MULTCND+3
          LEA     DI,PRODUCT+4
          AND     MULTPLR,0FH           ;Clear ASCII 3
A20:
          MOV     AL,[SI]               ;Load ASCII character
          AND     AL,0FH                ;Clear ASCII 3
          MUL     MULTPLR               ;Multiply
          AAM                           ;Adjust for ASCII
          ADD     AL,[DI]               ;Add to
          AAA                           ;   stored
          MOV     [DI],AL               ;   product
          DEC     DI
          MOV     [DI],AH               ;Store product carry
          DEC     SI
          LOOP    A20                   ;Loop 4 times

          LEA     BX,PRODUCT+4          ;Convert PRODUCT
          MOV     CX,05                 ;   to ASCII
A30:
          OR      BYTE PTR[BX],30H
          DEC     BX
          LOOP    A30                   ;Loop 4 times
          MOV     AX,4C00H              ;Exit to DOS
          INT     21H
MAIN      ENDP
          END     BEGIN
```

Figure 14–2 ASCII Multiplication

INSTRUCTION		COMMENT	AX	CL
AND	CL,0FH	;Convert to unpacked BCD	3238	07
AND	AX,0F0FH	;Convert to unpacked BCD	0208	
AAD		;Convert to binary	001C	
DIV	CL	;Divide by 7	0004	

AAD multiplies the AH by 10 (0AH), adds the product 20 (14H) to the AL, and clears the AH. The result, 001CH, is the hex representation of decimal 28.

Figure 14–3 allows for dividing a one-byte divisor into a four-byte dividend. The routine steps through the dividend from left to right. LODSB gets a byte from DIVDND into the AL (via the SI), and STOSB stores bytes from the AL into QUOTNT (via the DI). The remainder stays in the AH register so that AAD will adjust it in the AL. At the end, the quotient, in unpacked BCD format, is 00090204, and the remainder in the AH is 02. Another loop (not coded) could convert the quotient to ASCII format as 30393234.

If the divisor is greater than one byte, you have to provide yet another loop to step through the divisor. Better yet, see the later section, "Conversion of ASCII to Binary Format."

```
TITLE       P14ASCDV (COM)   Dividing ASCII numbers
            .MODEL SMALL
            .CODE
            ORG     100H
BEGIN:      JMP     SHORT MAIN
;--------------------------------------------------------------
DIVDND  DB      '3698'              ;Data items
DIVSOR  DB      '4'
QUOTNT  DB      4 DUP(0)
;-------------------------------------- --------------------
MAIN    PROC    NEAR
        MOV     CX,04               ;Initialize 4 loops
        SUB     AH,AH               ;Clear left byte of dividend
        AND     DIVSOR,0FH          ;Clear divisor of ASCII 3
        LEA     SI,DIVDND
        LEA     DI,QUOTNT
A20:
        LODSB                       ;Load ASCII byte
        AND     AL,0FH              ;Clear ASCII 3
        AAD                         ;Adjust for divide
        DIV     DIVSOR              ;Divide
        STOSB                       ;Store quotient
        LOOP    A20                 ;Four times?
        INT     21H                 ;  yes, exit to DOS
MAIN    ENDP
        END     BEGIN
```

Figure 14–3   ASCII Division

PROCESSING PACKED BCD DATA

In the preceding example of ASCII division, the quotient was 00090204. If you were to
compress this value, keeping only the right digit of each byte, the result would be 0924, now
in packed BCD format. You can also perform addition and subtraction on packed BCD data.
For this purpose, there are two adjustment instructions:

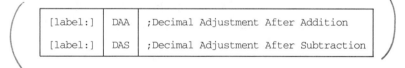

```
[label:]   DAA   ;Decimal Adjustment After Addition

[label:]   DAS   ;Decimal Adjustment After Subtraction
```

DAA corrects the result of adding two packed BCD values in the AL, and DAS corrects the result of subtracting them. Once again, you have to process the fields one byte at
a time.

The program in Figure 14–4 illustrates BCD addition. The procedure B10CONV converts the ASCII values ASC1 and ASC2 to packed BCD values BCD1 and BCD2, respectively. Processing, which is from right to left, could just as easily be from left to right. Also,
processing words is easier than processing bytes because you need two ASCII bytes to generate one packed BCD byte. However, the use of words does require an even number of
bytes in the ASCII field.

The procedure C10ADD performs a loop three times to add the packed BCD numbers to BCDSUM. The final total is 00127263.

```
          TITLE     P14BCDAD (COM)  Convert ASCII to BCD and add
                    .MODEL   SMALL
                    .CODE
                    ORG      100H
          BEGIN:    JMP      SHORT MAIN
          ;-------------------------------------------------
          ASC1      DB       '057836'          ;Data items
          ASC2      DB       '069427'
          BCD1      DB       '000'
          BCD2      DB       '000'
          BCDSUM    DB       4 DUP(0)
          ;-------------------------------------------------
          MAIN      PROC     NEAR
                    LEA      SI,ASC1+4         ;Initialize for ASC1
                    LEA      DI,BCD1+2
                    CALL     B10CONV           ;Call convert routine
                    LEA      SI,ASC2+4         ;Initialize for ASC2
                    LEA      DI,BCD2+2
                    CALL     B10CONV           ;Call convert routine
                    CALL     C10ADD            ;Call add routine
                    MOV      AX,4C00H          ;Exit to DOS
                    INT      21H
          MAIN      ENDP
          ;                  Convert ASCII to BCD:
          ;                  --------------------
          B10CONV   PROC
                    MOV      CL,04             ;Shift factor
                    MOV      DX,03             ;No. of words to convert
          B20:
                    MOV      AX,[SI]           ;Get ASCII pair
                    XCHG     AH,AL
                    SHL      AL,CL             ;Shift off
                    SHL      AX,CL             ;  ASCII 3s
                    MOV      [DI],AH           ;Store BCD digits
                    DEC      SI
                    DEC      SI
                    DEC      DI
                    DEC      DX
                    JNZ      B20               ;Three times?
                    RET                        ;  yes, return
          B10CONV   ENDP
          ;                  Add BCD numbers:
          ;                  ---------------
          C10ADD    PROC
                    XOR      AH,AH             ;Clear AH
                    LEA      SI,BCD1+2         ;Initialize
                    LEA      DI,BCD2+2         ;  BCD
                    LEA      BX,BCDSUM+3       ;  addresses
                    MOV      CX,03             ;3-byte fields
                    CLC
          C20:
                    MOV      AL,[SI]           ;Get BCD1 (or LODSB)
                    ADC      AL,[DI]           ;Add BCD2
                    DAA                        ;Decimal adjust
                    MOV      [BX],AL           ;Store in BCDSUM
                    DEC      SI
                    DEC      DI
                    DEC      BX
                    LOOP     C20               ;Loop 3 times
                    RET
          C10ADD    ENDP
                    END      MAIN
```

Figure 14–4   BCD Conversion and Arithmetic

CONVERSION OF ASCII TO BINARY FORMAT

Performing arithmetic in ASCII or BCD format is suitable only for short fields. For most arithmetic purposes, it is more practical to convert such numbers into binary format. In fact, it is easier to convert from ASCII directly to binary than to convert from ASCII to BCD to binary.

The conversion method is based on the fact that an ASCII number is in base 10 and the computer performs arithmetic in base 2. Here is the procedure:

1. Start with the rightmost byte of the ASCII number and process from right to left.
2. Strip the 3 from the left hex digit of each ASCII byte, thus forming a packed BCD number.
3. Multiply the first BCD digit by 1, the second by 10 (0AH), the third by 100 (64H), and so forth, and sum the products.

The following example converts ASCII number 1234 to binary:

Decimal		Hexadecimal	
Step	Product	Step	Product
$4 \times 1 =$	4	$4 \times 01H =$	4H
$3 \times 10 =$	30	$3 \times 0AH =$	1EH
$2 \times 100 =$	200	$2 \times 64H =$	C8H
$1 \times 1000 =$	1000	$1 \times 3E8H =$	3E8H
Total:	1234		04D2H

Try checking that the sum 04D2H really equals decimal 1234. In Figure 14–5, the program converts ASCII number 1234 to its binary equivalent. An LEA instruction initializes the address of the rightmost byte of the ASCII field, ASCVAL+3, in the SI register. The instruction at B20 that moves the ASCII byte to the AL is

```
MOV AL, [SI]
```

The operation uses the address of ASCVAL+3 to copy the rightmost byte of ASCVAL into the AL. Each iteration of the loop decrements the SI by 1 and references the next byte to the left. The loop repeats for each of the four bytes of ASCVAL. Also, each iteration multiplies MULT10 by 10 (0AH), giving multipliers of 1, 10 (0AH), 100 (64H), and so forth. At the end, BINVAL contains the correct binary value, D204H, in reverse-byte sequence.

The routine is coded for clarity; for faster processing, the multiplier could be stored in the DI register.

CONVERSION OF BINARY TO ASCII FORMAT

To print or display the result of binary arithmetic, you have to convert it into ASCII format. The operation involves reversing the previous step: Instead of multiplying, continue dividing the binary number by 10 (0AH) until the quotient is less than 10. The remainders, which

```
TITLE    P14ASCBI (COM)   Convert ASCII to binary format
         .MODEL SMALL
         .CODE
         ORG    100H
BEGIN:   JMP    SHORT MAIN
; -----------------------------------------------------
ASCVAL   DB     '1234'              ;Data items
BINVAL   DW     0
ASCLEN   DW     4
MULT10   DW     1
; -----------------------------------------------------
MAIN     PROC   NEAR                ;Main procedure
         MOV    BX,10               ;Mult factor
         MOV    CX,04               ;Count for loop
         LEA    SI,ASCVAL+3         ;Address of ASCVAL
B20:
         MOV    AL,[SI]             ;Select ASCII character
         AND    AX,000FH            ;Remove 3-zone
         MUL    MULT10              ;Multiply by 10 factor
         ADD    BINVAL,AX           ;Add to binary
         MOV    AX,MULT10           ;Calculate next
         MUL    BX                  ;  10 factor
         MOV    MULT10,AX
         DEC    SI                  ;Last ASCII character?
         LOOP   B20                 ;  no, continue
         MOV    AX,4C00H
         INT    21H                 ;Exit to DOS
MAIN     ENDP
         END    BEGIN
```

Figure 14–5 Conversion of ASCII to Binary Format

can be only 0 through 9, successively generate the ASCII number. As an example, let's convert 4D2H back into decimal format:

DIVIDE BY 10	QUOTIENT	REMAINDER
A ⟌ 4D2	7B	4
A ⟌ 7B	C	3
A ⟌ C	1	2

Since the quotient (1) is now less than the divisor (0AH), the operation is complete. The remainders, along with the last quotient, form the BCD result, from right to left: 1234. All that remains is to store these digits in memory with ASCII 3s, as 31323334.

The program in Figure 14–6 converts binary number 04D2H to ASCII format. The routine divides the binary number successively by 10, until the remaining quotient is less than 10 (0AH), and stores the generated hex digits in ASCII format as 31323334. You may find it useful, if not downright entertaining, to reproduce this program and trace its execution step by step.

SHIFTING AND ROUNDING

Suppose you are to round a product that contains three decimal places to two decimal places. If the product is 12.345, add 5 to the rightmost (unwanted) decimal position, and shift right one digit.

```
TITLE    P14BINAS (COM)   Convert binary format to ASCII
         .MODEL   SMALL
         .CODE
         ORG      100H
BEGIN:   JMP      SHORT MAIN
; --------------------------------------------------
ASCVAL   DB       4 DUP(' ')        ;Data items
BINVAL   DW       04D2H
; --------------------------------------------------
MAIN     PROC     NEAR              ;Main procedure
         MOV      CX,0010           ;Division factor
         LEA      SI,ASCVAL+3       ;Address of ASCVAL
         MOV      AX,BINVAL         ;Get binary field
C20:
         CMP      AX,CX             ;Value < 10?
         JB       C30               ;   yes, exit
         XOR      DX,DX             ;Clear upper quotient
         DIV      CX                ;Divide by 10
         OR       DL,30H
         MOV      [SI],DL           ;Store ASCII character
         DEC      SI
         JMP      C20
C30:
         OR       AL,30H            ;Store last quotient
         MOV      [SI],AL           ;   as ASCII character
         MOV      AX,4C00H          ;Exit to DOS
         INT      21H
MAIN     ENDP
         END      BEGIN
```

AX = Quotient
DX = Remainder

remainder

Figure 14–6   Conversion of Binary to ASCII Format

Product: 12.345
Add 5:   +   5
                ─────────────
Rounded product: 12.350 = 12.35

If the product is 12.3455, add 50 and shift two digits, and if the product is 12.34555, add 500 and shift three digits:

        12.3455   12.34555
    +   50   +   500
    ─────────────   ─────────────
    12.3505 = 12.35   12.35055 = 12.35

Further, a number with six decimal places requires adding 5,000 and shifting four digits, and so forth. Now, since a computer normally processes binary data, 12.345 appears as 3039H. Adding 5 to 3039H gives 303EH, or 12350 in decimal format. So far, so good. But shifting one binary digit results in 181FH, or 6175—indeed, the shift simply halves the value. We require a shift that is equivalent to shifting right one decimal digit. You can accomplish this shift by dividing the rounded value by 10, or hex A: Hex 303E divided by hex A = 4D3H, or decimal 1235. Conversion of 4D3H to a decimal number gives 1235. Now just insert a decimal point in the correct position, and you can display a rounded, shifted value as 12.35.

In this fashion, you can round and shift any binary number. For three decimal places, add 5 and divide by 10; for four decimal places, add 50 and divide by 100. Perhaps you have noticed a pattern: The rounding factor (5, 50, 500, etc.) is always one-half of the value of the shift factor (10, 100, 1,000, etc.).

Of course, the radix point in a binary number is implied and is not actually present.

PROGRAM TO CONVERT ASCII DATA

The program in Figure 14–7 allows users to enter the number of hours worked and the rate of pay for employees and displays the calculated wage. For brevity, the program omits some error checking that would otherwise be included. The procedures are as follows:

B10INPT	Accepts hours and rate of pay in ASCII format from the keyboard. These values may contain a decimal point.
D10HOUR	Initializes conversion of ASCII hours to binary.

```
                page 60,132
       TITLE    P14SCREMP (EXE) Enter hours and rate, display wage
                .MODEL SMALL
                .STACK 64
;  -----------------------------------------------------
                .DATA
LEFCOL          EQU    28                      ;Equates for screen
RITCOL          EQU    52
TOPROW          EQU    10
BOTROW          EQU    14

HRSPAR          LABEL  BYTE                    ;Hours parameter list:
MAXHLEN         DB     6                       ;----- --------- ----
ACTHLEN         DB     ?
HRSFLD          DB     6 DUP(?)

RATEPAR         LABEL  BYTE                    ;Rate parameter list:
MAXRLEN         DB     6                       ;---- --------- ----
ACTRLEN         DB     ?                       ;
RATEFLD         DB     6 DUP(?)                ;

MESSG1          DB     'Hours worked? ','$'
MESSG2          DB     'Rate of pay?  ','$'
MESSG3          DB     'Wage =  '
ASCWAGE         DB     10 DUP(30H), 13, 10,'$'
MESSG4          DB     'Press any key to continue or Esc to quit','$'

ADJUST          DW     ?                       ;Data items
BINVAL          DW     00
BINHRS          DW     00
BINRATE         DW     00
COL             DB     00
DECIND          DB     00
MULT10          DW     01
NODEC           DW     00
ROW             DB     00
SHIFT           DW     ?
TENWD           DW     10
;  -----------------------------------------------------
                .CODE
BEGIN           PROC   FAR
                MOV    AX,@data                ;Initialize DS
                MOV    DS,AX                   ;  and ES registers
                MOV    ES,AX
                CALL   Q10SCR                  ;Clear screen
```

Figure 14–7 Displaying Employee Wages

```
A20LOOP:
            CALL    Q15WIN          ;Clear window
            CALL    Q20CURS         ;Set cursor
            CALL    B10INPT         ;Accept hours & rate
            CALL    D10HOUR         ;Convert hours to binary
            CALL    E10RATE         ;Convert rate to binary
            CALL    F10MULT         ;Calculate wage, round
            CALL    G10WAGE         ;Convert wage to ASCII
            CALL    K10DISP         ;Display wage
            CALL    L10PAUS         ;Pause for user
            CMP     AL,1BH          ;Esc pressed?
            JNE     A20LOOP         ;  no, continue
;                                   ;  yes, end of input
            CALL    Q10SCR          ;Clear screen
            MOV     AX,4C00H        ;Exit to DOS
            INT     21H
BEGIN       ENDP
;                   Input hours and rate:
;                   ---------------------
  B10INPT   PROC    NEAR
            MOV     ROW,TOPROW+1        ;Set cursor
            MOV     COL,LEFCOL+3
            CALL    Q20CURS
            INC     ROW
            MOV     AH,09H
            LEA     DX,MESSG1           ;Prompt for hours
            INT     21H
            MOV     AH,0AH
            LEA     DX,HRSPAR           ;Accept hours
            INT     21H
            MOV     COL,LEFCOL+3        ;Set column
            CALL    Q20CURS
            INC     ROW
            MOV     AH,09H
            LEA     DX,MESSG2           ;Prompt for rate
            INT     21H
            MOV     AH,0AH
            LEA     DX,RATEPAR          ;Accept rate
            INT     21H
            RET
  B10INPT   ENDP
;                   Process hours:
;                   --------------
D10HOUR     PROC    NEAR
            MOV     NODEC,00
            MOV     CL,ACTHLEN
            SUB     CH,CH
            LEA     SI,HRSFLD-1         ;Set right position
            ADD     SI,CX               ;  of hours
            CALL    M10ASBI             ;Convert to binary
            MOV     AX,BINVAL
            MOV     BINHRS,AX
            RET
D10HOUR     ENDP
;                   Process rate:
;                   ------------
E10RATE     PROC    NEAR
            MOV     CL,ACTRLEN
            SUB     CH,CH
            LEA     SI,RATEFLD-1        ;Set right position
            ADD     SI,CX               ;  of rate
            CALL    M10ASBI             ;Convert to binary
            MOV     AX,BINVAL
            MOV     BINRATE,AX
            RET
```

Figure 14–7   (continued)

```
E10RATE    ENDP
;                     Multiply, round, and shift:
;                     ---------------------------
F10MULT    PROC    NEAR
           MOV     CX,05
           LEA     DI,ASCWAGE      ;Set ASCII wage
           MOV     AX,3030H        ;  to 30s
           CLD
           REP STOSW

           MOV     SHIFT,10
           MOV     ADJUST,00
           MOV     CX,NODEC
           CMP     CL,06           ;If more than 6
           JA      F40             ;  decimals, error
           DEC     CX
           DEC     CX
           JLE     F30             ;Bypass if 0, 1, 2 decs
           MOV     NODEC,02
           MOV     AX,01
F20:
           MUL     TENWD           ;Calculate shift factor
           LOOP    F20
           MOV     SHIFT,AX
           SHR     AX,1            ;Calculate round value
           MOV     ADJUST,AX
F30:
           MOV     AX,BINHRS
           MUL     BINRATE         ;Calculate wage
           ADD     AX,ADJUST       ;Round wage
           ADC     DX,00
           CMP     DX,SHIFT        ;Product too large
           JB      F50             ;   for DIV?
F40:
           SUB     AX,AX
           JMP     F70
F50:
           CMP     ADJUST,00       ;Shift required?
           JZ      F80             ;  no, bypass
           DIV     SHIFT           ;Shift wage
F70:       SUB     DX,DX           ;Clear remainder
F80:       RET
F10MULT    ENDP
;                     Convert to ASCII:
;                     -----------------
G10WAGE    PROC    NEAR
           LEA     SI,ASCWAGE+7    ;Set decimal point
           MOV     BYTE PTR[SI],'.'
           ADD     SI,NODEC        ;Set right start pos'n
G30:
           CMP     BYTE PTR[SI],'.'
           JNE     G40             ;Bypass if at dec pos'n
           DEC     SI
G40:
           CMP     DX,00           ;If DX:AX < 10,
           JNZ     G50
           CMP     AX,0010         ;  operation finished
           JB      G60
G50:
           DIV     TENWD           ;Remainder is ASCII digit
           OR      DL,30H
           MOV     [SI],DL         ;Store ASCII character
           DEC     SI
           SUB     DX,DX           ;Clear remainder
           JMP     G30
```

Figure 14–7   (continued)

```
G60:
               OR      AL,30H              ;Store last ASCII
               MOV     [SI],AL             ;  character
               RET
G10WAGE        ENDP
;                      Display wage:
;                      ------------
K10DISP        PROC    NEAR
               MOV     COL,LEFCOL+3        ;Set column
               CALL    Q20CURS
               MOV     CX,09
               LEA     SI,ASCWAGE
K20:                                       ;Clear leading zeros
               CMP     BYTE PTR[SI],30H
               JNE     K30                 ;  to blanks

               MOV     BYTE PTR[SI],20H
               INC     SI
               LOOP    K20
K30:
               MOV     AH,09H              ;Request display
               LEA     DX,MESSG3           ;Wage
               INT     21H
               RET
K10DISP        ENDP
;                      Pause for user:
;                      --------------
L10PAUS        PROC    NEAR
               MOV     COL,20              ;Set cursor
               MOV     ROW,22
               CALL    Q20CURS
               MOV     AH,09H
               LEA     DX,MESSG4           ;Display pause
               INT     21H
               MOV     AH,10H              ;Request reply
               INT     16H
               RET
L10PAUS        ENDP
;                      Convert ASCII to binary:
;                      -----------------------
M10ASBI        PROC    NEAR
               MOV     MULT10,0001
               MOV     BINVAL,00
               MOV     DECIND,00
               SUB     BX,BX
M20:
               MOV     AL,[SI]             ;Get ASCII character
               CMP     AL,'.'              ;Bypass if dec point
               JNE     M40
               MOV     DECIND,01
               JMP     M90
M40:
               AND     AX,000FH
               MUL     MULT10              ;Multiply by factor
               ADD     BINVAL,AX           ;Add to binary
               MOV     AX,MULT10           ;Calculate next
               MUL     TENWD               ;  factor x 10
               MOV     MULT10,AX
               CMP     DECIND,00           ;Reached decimal point?
               JNZ     M90
               INC     BX                  ;  yes, add to count
M90:
               DEC     SI
               LOOP    M20
               CMP     DECIND,00           ;End of loop
               JZ      M100                ;Any decimal point?
               ADD     NODEC,BX            ;  yes, add to total
```

Figure 14–7F   (continued)

```
M100:       RET
M10ASBI     ENDP
;                       Scroll whole screen:
;                       --------------------
Q10SCR      PROC    NEAR
            MOV     AX,0600H
            MOV     BH,30H              ;Attribute
            SUB     CX,CX
            MOV     DX,184FH
            INT     10H
            RET
Q10SCR      ENDP
;                       Scroll display window:
;                       ---------------------
Q15WIN      PROC    NEAR
            MOV     AX,0605H            ;Five rows
            MOV     BH,16H              ;Attribute
            MOV     CH,TOPROW
            MOV     CL,LEFCOL
            MOV     DH,BOTROW
            MOV     DL,RITCOL
            INT     10H
            RET
Q15WIN      ENDP
;                       Set cursor:
;                       ----------
Q20CURS     PROC    NEAR
            MOV     AH,02H
            SUB     BH,BH
            MOV     DH,ROW              ;Set row
            MOV     DL,COL              ;Set column
            INT     10H
            RET
Q20CURS     ENDP
            END     BEGIN
```

Figure 14–7   (continued)

E10RATE   Initializes conversion of ASCII rate to binary.

F10MULT   Performs the multiplication, rounding, and shifting. A wage with zero, one, or two decimal places does not require rounding or shifting.

G10WAGE   Inserts the decimal point, determines the rightmost position to begin storing ASCII characters, and converts the binary wage to ASCII.

K10DISP   Clears leading zeros of wage to blanks and displays the wage.

L10PAUS   Displays the calculated wage until the user presses a key. Pressing Esc tells the program to discontinue processing.

M10ASBI   Converts ASCII to binary (a common routine for hours and for rate) and determines the number of decimal places in the entered value.

Q10SCR   Scrolls the whole screen and sets it to black on cyan.

Q15WIN   Scrolls a window in the middle of the screen where hours, rate, and wage are displayed as brown on blue.

Limitations.   A limitation of this program is that it allows only a total of six decimal places in the calculated wage. Another limitation is the magnitude of the wage itself and the fact that shifting involves dividing by a multiple of 10 and converting to ASCII involves dividing by 10. If hours and rate of pay contain a total that exceeds six decimal places, or if the wage exceeds about 655,350, the program clears the wage to zero. In practice, a program would print a warning message or would contain subroutines to overcome these limitations.

Error checking.   A program designed for users other than the programmer not only should produce warning messages, but also should validate hours and rate of pay. The only valid characters are the numbers 0 through 9 and one decimal point. For any other character, the program should display a message and return to the input prompt. A useful instruction for validating is XLAT, which Chapter 15 covers.

In practice, test your program thoroughly for all possible conditions, such as zero values, extremely high and low values, and negative values.

Negative values.   Some applications involve negative amounts, especially for reversing and correcting entries. You could allow a minus sign following a value, such as 12.34−, or preceding the value, such as −12.34. The program could then check for a minus sign during conversion to binary. On the other hand, you may want to leave the binary number positive and simply set an indicator to record the fact that the amount is negative. When the arithmetic is complete, the program, if required, can insert a minus sign in the ASCII field.

If you want the binary number to be negative, convert the ASCII input to binary as usual. (See the section, "Reversing the Sign," in Chapter 13 for changing the sign of a binary field.) And watch out for using IMUL and IDIV to handle signed data. For rounding a negative amount, subtract 5 instead of adding 5.

KEY POINTS

- An ASCII field requires one byte for each character. For a numeric field, the rightmost half-byte contains the digit, and the leftmost half-byte contains 3.
- Clearing the leftmost ASCII 3s to 0s converts the field to unpacked binary-coded decimal (BCD) format.
- Compressing ASCII characters to two digits per byte converts the field to packed binary-coded decimal (BCD) data.
- After an ASCII add, use AAA to adjust the answer; after an ASCII subtract, use AAS to adjust the answer.
- Before an ASCII multiplication, convert the multiplicand and multiplier to unpacked BCD by clearing the leftmost hex 3s to 0s. After the multiplication, use AAM to adjust the product.
- Before an ASCII division, convert the dividend and divisor to unpacked BCD by clearing the leftmost hex 3s, and use AAD to adjust the dividend.
- For most arithmetic purposes, convert ASCII numbers to binary. When converting from ASCII to binary format, check that the ASCII characters are valid: 30 though 39, a decimal point, and possibly a minus sign.

QUESTIONS

14–1. Suppose that the AX contains ASCII 9 (0039H) and the BX contains ASCII 7 (0037H). Explain the exact results of the following unrelated operations:

    (a)   ADD   AX,33H   (b)   ADD   AX,BX

           AAA   AAA

    (c)   SUB   AX,BX   (d)   SUB AX,0DH

           AAS   AAS

14–2. An unpacked BCD field named UNPAK contains 01040705H. Code a loop that causes its contents to be proper ASCII 31343735H.

14–3. A field named ASCA contains the ASCII decimal value 173, and another field named ASCB contains ASCII 5. Code the instructions to multiply the ASCII numbers together and to store the product in ASCPRO.

14–4. Use the same fields as in Question 14–3 to divide ASCA by ASCB and store the quotient in ASCQUO.

14–5. Provide the manual calculations for the following: (a) Convert ASCII decimal value 46328 to binary, and show the result in hex format; (b) convert the hex value back to ASCII.

14–6. Code and run a program that determines a computer's memory size (see INT 12H in Chapter 3), converts the size to ASCII format, and displays it on the screen as follows:

        Memory size is nnn bytes

CHAPTER 15 ⎯⎯⎯⎯⎯⎯⎯⎯⎯

Table Processing

OBJECTIVE:

To cover the requirements for defining tables, performing searches of tables, and sorting table entries.

INTRODUCTION

Many program applications require *tables* containing such data as names, descriptions, quantities, and prices. The definition and use of tables largely involves applying what you have already learned. This chapter begins by defining some conventional tables and then covers methods for searching through them. Techniques for searching tables are subject to the way in which the tables are defined, and many methods of defining and searching other than those given here are possible. Other commonly used features are the use of sorting, which rearranges the sequence of data in a table, and the use of linked lists, which use pointers to locate items in a table.

The only instruction introduced in this chapter is XLAT (Translate).

DEFINING TABLES

To facilitate searching through them, most tables are arranged in a consistent manner, with each entry defined with the same format (character or numeric), with the same length, and in either ascending or descending order.

A table that you have been using throughout this book is the definition of the stack, which in the following is a table of 64 uninitialized words (the name STACK refers to the first word of the table):

```
STACK DW 64 DUP(?)
```

The following two tables, MONTAB and EMPTAB, initialize character and numeric values, respectively. MONTAB defines alphabetic abbreviations of the months, whereas EMPTAB defines a table of employee numbers:

```
MONTAB   DB   'Jan', 'Feb', 'Mar', ..., 'Dec'

EMPTAB   DB   205, 208, 209, 212, 215, 224, ...
```

All entries in MONTAB are three characters, and all entries in EMPTAB are three digits. But note that the assembler converts the decimal numbers to binary format and, provided that they don't exceed the value 255, stores them each in a byte.

A table may also contain a mixture of numeric and character values, provided that they are defined consistently. In the following table of stock items, each numeric entry (stock number) is two digits (one byte), and each character entry (stock description) is nine bytes. The four dots following the description "Paper" are to show that spaces should be present; that is, spaces, not dots, are to be keyed in the description:

```
STOKTBL DB   12,'Computers',14, 'Paper....',17, 'Diskettes', ...
```

For clarity, you may also code table entries on separate lines:

```
STOKTBL DB   12, 'Computers'
        DB   14, 'Paper....'
        DB   17, 'Diskettes'

             ...
```

The next example defines a table with 50 entries, each initialized to 20 blanks:

```
STORETAB DB 50 DUP(20 DUP(' '))
```

A program could use this table to store up to 50 values that it has generated internally, or it could use it to store the contents of up to 50 entries that it reads from a disk file.

Tables on Disk

In real-world situations, many programs are table driven. Tables are stored as disk files, which any number of programs may read into their data segment for processing. The reason for this practice is because the contents of tables change over time. If each program defined it own tables, any changes would require all the programs to redefine the tables and be reassembled. With table files on disk, you just need to change the contents of the file. Chapter 17 gives an example of a table file.

Now let's examine different ways to use tables in programs.

DIRECT TABLE ADDRESSING

Suppose that a user enters a numeric month such as 03 and that a program is to convert it to alphabetic format—in this case, March. The routine to perform this conversion involves defining a table of alphabetic months, all of equal length. The length of each entry should be that of the longest name, September:

```
MONTAB  DB    'January..'

        DB    'February.'

        DB    'March....'

        ...

        DB    'December.'
```

The entry 'January' is at MONTAB+00, 'February' is at MONTAB+09, 'March' is at MONTAB+18, and so forth. To locate month 03, the program has to perform the following actions:

1. Convert the entered month from ASCII 33 to binary 3.
2. Deduct 1 from this number: $3 - 1 = 2$ (because month 01 is at MONTAB+00)
3. Multiply the new number by 9 (the length of each entry): $2 \times 9 = 18$.
4. Add this product to the address of MONTAB; the result is the address of the required description: MONTAB+18, where "March" begins.

This technique is known as known as *direct table addressing*. Since the algorithm calculates the required table address directly, the program does not have to search successively through each entry in the table.

Direct Addressing, Example 1: Table of Months

The program in Figure 15–1 provides an example of a direct access of a table with the names of the months. The procedure C10CONV uses 12 (December) as input and converts the month like this (values are in hex):

Load ASCII month in AX:	3132
Use 3030 for XOR:	3030
Unpacked month:	0102
If leftmost byte nonzero, clear	0002
and add 0AH (decimal 10)	000C (decimal 12)

The procedure D10LOC determines the actual location of entries in the table:

Deduct 1 from month in the AX	000B (decimal 11)
Multiply by 9 (length of entries)	0063 (decimal 99)
Add address of table (MONTAB)	MONTAB+63H

One way to improve this program is to accept numeric months from the keyboard and to verify that their values are between 01 and 12, inclusive.

```
          TITLE      P15DIREC (COM)   Direct table addressing
                     .MODEL SMALL
                     .CODE
                     ORG     100H
          BEGIN:  JMP     SHORT MAIN
          ; --------------------------------------------------------
          NINE    DB      9
          MONIN   DB      '12'
          ALFMON  DB      9 DUP (20H), '$'
          MONTAB  DB      'January  ', 'February ', 'March    '
                  DB      'April    ', 'May      ', 'June     '
                  DB      'July     ', 'August   ', 'September'
                  DB      'October  ', 'November ', 'December '
          ; --------------------------------------------------------
          .386
          MAIN    PROC    NEAR                 ;Main procedure
                  CALL    C10CONV              ;Convert to binary
                  CALL    D10LOC               ;Locate month
                  CALL    F10DISP              ;Display alpha month
                  MOV     AX,4C00H             ;Exit to DOS
                  INT     21H
          MAIN    ENDP
          ;               Convert ASCII to binary:
          ;               -----------------------
          C10CONV PROC
                  MOV     AH,MONIN             ;Set up month
                  MOV     AL,MONIN+1
                  XOR     AX,3030H             ;Clear ASCII 3s
                  CMP     AH,00                ;Month 01-09?
                  JZ      C20                  ;  yes, bypass
                  SUB     AH,AH                ;  no, clear AH,
                  ADD     AL,10                ;   correct for binary
          C20:    RET
          C10CONV ENDP
          ;               Locate month in table:
          ;               ---------------------
          D10LOC  PROC
                  LEA     SI,MONTAB
                  DEC     AL                   ;Correct for table
                  MUL     NINE                 ;Multiply AL by 9
                  ADD     SI,AX
                  MOVZX   CX,NINE              ;Initialize 9-char move
                  CLD
                  LEA     DI,ALFMON
                  REP MOVSB                    ;Move 9 characters
                  RET
          D10LOC  ENDP
          ;               Display alpha month:
          ;               -------------------
          F10DISP PROC
                  MOV     AH,09H               ;Request display
                  LEA     DX,ALFMON
                  INT     21H
                  RET
          F10DISP ENDP
                  END     BEGIN
```

Figure 15–1   Direct table Addressing: Example 1

Direct Addressing, Example 2: Tables of Months and Days

The program in Figure 15–2 retrieves today's date from DOS and displays it. DOS 21H, function 2AH, delivers the following binary values:

```
TITLE        P15DISDA (EXE) Display day of week and month
             .MODEL  SMALL
             .STACK  64
; ------------------------------------------------------------
             .DATA
SAVEDAY   DB    ?
SAVEMON   DB    ?
TEN       DB    10
ELEVEN    DB    11
TWELVE    DB    12
DAYSTAB   DB    'Sunday, $   ', 'Monday, $   '
          DB    'Tuesday, $  ', 'Wednesday, $'
          DB    'Thursday, $ ', 'Friday, $   '
          DB    'Saturday, $ '
MONTAB    DB    'January $  ', 'February $ ', 'March $    '
          DB    'April $    ', 'May $      ', 'June $     '
          DB    'July $     ', 'August $   ', 'September $'
          DB    'October $  ', 'November $ ', 'December $ '
; ------------------------------------------------------------
             .CODE
BEGIN     PROC  FAR
          MOV   AX,@data       ;Initialize
          MOV   DS,AX          ;  segment registers
          MOV   ES,AX
          MOV   AX,0600H
          CALL  Q10SCR         ;Clear screen
          CALL  Q20CURS        ;Set cursor
          MOV   AH,2AH         ;Get today's date
          INT   21H
          MOV   SAVEMON,DH     ;Save month
          MOV   SAVEDAY,DL     ;Save day of month
          CALL  B10DAYWK       ;Display day of week
          CALL  C10MONTH       ;Display month
          CALL  D10DAYMO       ;Display day
          CALL  E10INPT        ;Wait for input
          CALL  Q10SCR         ;Clear screen
          MOV   AX,4C00H       ;Exit to DOS
          INT   21H
BEGIN     ENDP

B10DAYWK  PROC  NEAR           ;Display day of week
          MUL   TWELVE         ;Day (in AL) x 12
          LEA   DX,DAYSTAB     ;Address of table
          ADD   DX,AX          ;  plus offset
          MOV   AH,09H         ;Display
          INT   21H
          RET
B10DAYWK  ENDP
C10MONTH  PROC  NEAR           ;Display month
          MOV   AL,SAVEMON     ;Get month
          DEC   AL             ;Decrement by 1
          MUL   ELEVEN         ;Multiply by entry length
          LEA   DX,MONTAB      ;Address of table
          ADD   DX,AX          ;  plus offset
          MOV   AH,09H         ;Display
          INT   21H
          RET
C10MONTH  ENDP
.386
D10DAYMO  PROC  NEAR           ;Display day of month
          MOVZX AX,SAVEDAY     ;Get day
          DIV   TEN            ;Convert from binary
          OR    AX,3030H       ;  to ASCII
          MOV   BX,AX          ;Save ASCII day
```

Figure 15–2   Direct Table Addressing: Example 2

```
              MOV      AH,02H         ;Display
              MOV      DL,BL          ;  first digit
              INT      21H
              MOV      AH,02H         ;Display
              MOV      DL,BH          ;  second digit
              INT      21H
              RET
D10DAYMO      ENDP

E10INPT       PROC     NEAR           ;Wait for keyboard input
              MOV      AH,10H         ;Request input
              INT      16H            ;Call BIOS
              RET
E10INPT       ENDP

Q10SCR        PROC     NEAR           ;Scroll screen
              MOV      AX,0600H
              MOV      BH,17H         ;White on blue
              MOV      CX,0000
              MOV      DX,184FH
              INT      10H            ;Call BIOS
              RET
Q10SCR        ENDP

Q20CURS       PROC     NEAR
              MOV      AH,02H         ;Request set cursor
              MOV      BH,00          ;Page
              MOV      DH,10          ;Row
              MOV      DL,24          ;Column
              INT      10H
              RET
Q20CURS       ENDP
              END      BEGIN
```

Figure 15–2   (continued)

AL	Day of the week (where Sunday = 0)
CX	Year (not used by this program)
DH	Month (01–12)
DL	Day of the month (01–31)

The program uses these values to display the alphabetic day of the week and the month in the form "Wednesday, September 12." To this end, the program defines a table of days of the week named DAYSTAB, beginning with Sunday, and a table of months named MONTAB, beginning with January.

Entries in DAYSTAB are 12 bytes long, with each description followed by a comma, blank, and $ sign and padded with blanks to the right. DOS INT 21H, function 09H, displays all characters up to the $ sign; the comma and blank are followed on the screen by the month. The procedure B10DAYWK multiplies the day of the week by 12 (the length of each entry in DAYSTAB). The product is an offset into the table, where, for example, Sunday is at DAYSTAB+0, Monday is at DAYSTAB+12, and so forth. The day is displayed directly from the table.

Entries in MONTAB are 11 bytes long, with each description followed by a blank, and $ sign and padded with blanks to the right. The procedure C10MONTH first decrements the month by 1 so that, for example, month 01 becomes entry zero in MONTAB. It then multiplies the month by 11 (the length of each entry in MONTAB). The product is an offset into the table, where, for example, January is at MONTAB+0, February at MONTAB+11, and so forth. The month is displayed directly from the table.

The procedure D10DAYMO divides the day of the month by 10 to convert it from binary to ASCII format. Since the maximum value for day is 31, both the quotient and the remainder can be only one digit. (For example, 31 divided by 10 gives a quotient of 3 and a remainder of 1.) DOS function 02H displays each of the two characters, including the leading zero for days less than 10; suppressing the leading zero involves some minor program changes.

At the end, the program waits for the user to press a key before exiting to DOS.

Although direct table addressing is very efficient, it works best when entries are sequential and in a predictable order. Thus it would work well for entries that are in the order 1, 2, 3, . . . , or 106, 107, 108, . . . , or even 5, 10, 15, ... Unfortunately, few applications provide such a neat arrangement of table values. A later section examines tables with values that are sequential, but not in any particular order.

SEARCHING A TABLE

Some tables consist of unique numbers with no apparent pattern. A typical example is a table of stock items with nonconsecutive numbers such as 134, 138, 141, 239, and 245. Another type of table—such as an income tax table—contains ranges of values. The following sections examine both of these types of tables and the requirements for searching them.

Tables with Unique Entries

The stock item numbers for most firms are usually not in consecutive order. Rather, they tend to be grouped by category, with a leading number to indicate furniture or appliance or to indicate that it is located in a certain department. Also, over time, some items are deleted from stock and other items are added. As an example, let's define a table with stock numbers and their related descriptions. These could be defined in separate tables, such as

```
STOKNOS  DB  '05','10','12', ...

STOKDESC DB  'Excavators', 'Lifters...', 'Presses...' , ...
```

Each step in a search could increment the address of the first table by 2 (the length of each entry in STOKNOS) and the address of the second table by 10 (the length of each entry in STOKDESC). Or, a procedure could keep a count of the number of loops executed and, on finding a match with a certain key stock number, multiply the count by 10 and use the product as an offset to the address of STOKDESC.

On the other hand, it may be clearer to define stock numbers and descriptions in the same table, with one line for each pair:

```
STOKTAB  DB   '05','Excavators'
         DB   '10','Lifters...'
```

```
DB    '12','Presses...'

      . . .
```

The program in Figure 15–3 defines this table with six pairs of stock numbers and descriptions. The search loop at A20 begins comparing the first byte of the input stock number, STOKNIN, with the first byte of stock numbers in the table. If the comparison is equal, the routine compares the second bytes. If these are *equal*, the stock number is found and, at A50, the program copies the description from the table into DESCRN, where it is displayed.

If the comparison of the first or second bytes is *low*, the stock number is known to be not in the table and, at A40, the program could display an error message (not coded).

If the comparison of the first or second bytes is *high*, the program has to continue the search; to compare the input stock number with the next stock number in the table, it increments the SI, which contains the table address. The search loop performs a maximum of six comparisons. If the loops exceed six, the stock number is known to be not in the table.

Let's verify this logic by comparing entered stock numbers 01, 06, and 10 successively with items in the table:

- *Stock number 01 with table item 05.* The first byte is equal, but the second is low, so the item is not in the table.
- *Stock number 06 with table item 05.* The first byte is equal, but the second is high, so we compare the input with the next item in the table: stock number 06 with table item 10. The first byte is low, so the item is not in the table.
- *Stock number 10 with table item 05.* The first byte is high, so we compare the input with the next item in the table: stock number 10 with table item 10. The first byte is equal and the second is equal, so the item is found.

The table could also define unit prices. The user enters stock number and quantity sold. The program could locate the stock item in the table, calculate amount of sale (quantity sold times unit price), and display description and amount of sale.

In Figure 15–3, the item number is 2 characters and the description is 10. Programming details would vary for different numbers of entries and different lengths of entries. For example, to compare three-byte fields, you could use REPE CMPSB, although the instruction involves the CX register, which LOOP already uses.

Tables with Ranges

Income tax provides a typical example of a table with ranges of values. Consider the following hypothetical table of taxable income, tax rates, and adjustment factors:

TAXABLE INCOME($)	RATE	ADJUSTMENT FACTOR
0–1,000.00	.10	0.00
1,000.01–2,500.00	.15	050.00
2,501.01–4,250.00	.18	125.00
4,250.01–6,000.00	.20	260.00
6,000.01 and over	.23	390.00

```
TITLE     P15TABSR (COM)   Table search Using CMP
          .MODEL  SMALL
          .CODE
          ORG     100H
BEGIN:    JMP     SHORT MAIN
; -------------------------------------------------------
STOKNIN DB      '12'                    ;Input stock no.
STOKTAB DB      '05','Excavators'       ;Start of table
        DB      '10','Lifters    '      ;
        DB      '12','Presses    '      ;
        DB      '15','Valves     '      ;
        DB      '23','Processors'       ;
        DB      '27','Pumps      '      ;End of table
DESCRN  DB      10 DUP(?),'$'           ;Save area
; -------------------------------------------------------
MAIN      PROC    NEAR
          MOV     CX,06                 ;Initialize compares
          LEA     SI,STOKTAB
A20:
          MOV     AL,STOKNIN
          CMP     AL,[SI]               ;Stock#(1) : table
          JNE     A30                   ;Not equal, exit
          MOV     AL,STOKNIN+1          ;Equal:
          CMP     AL,[SI+1]             ;   stock#(2) : table
          JE      A50                   ;   equal, found
A30:
          JB      A40                   ;Low, not in table
          ADD     SI,12                 ;High, get next entry
          LOOP    A20
A40:                                    ;Not in table
;         ...                           ;Display error message
          JMP     A90
A50:
          MOV     CX,05                 ;Length of description
          LEA     DI,DESCRN             ;Address of description
          INC     SI
          INC     SI                    ;Extract description
          REP MOVSW                     ;  from table
          MOV     AH,09H                ;Request display
          LEA     DX,DESCRN             ;  stock description
          INT     21H
;         ...
A90:      MOV     AX,4C00H              ;Exit to DOS
          INT     21H
MAIN      ENDP
          END     BEGIN
```

Figure 15–3   Table Search Using CMP

In the tax table, rates increase as taxable income increases. The adjustment factor compensates for our calculating tax at the high rate, whereas lower rates apply to lower levels of income. Entries for taxable income contain the maximum income for each step:

```
TAXTAB  DD   100000, 10, 00000

        DD   250000, 15, 05000

        DD   425000, 18, 12500

        DD   600000, 20, 26000

        DD   999999, 23, 39000
```

To perform a search of the table, the program compares the taxpayer's actual taxable income with entries in the table and does the following, according to results of the comparison:

- High: Increment for the next entry in the table.
- Low or equal: Use the associated rate and adjustment factor.
- Calculate the tax deduction as (taxable income × table rate) − adjustment factor. Note that the last entry in the table contains the maximum value (999999), which would always correctly end the search.

Searching a Table Using String Comparisons

REPE CMPS is useful for comparing item numbers that are two or more bytes long. The program in Figure 15–4 defines STOKTAB, but this time revised as a three-byte stock number. Since STOKNIN is the first field in the data area and STOKTAB is next, they appear in the data segment as follows:

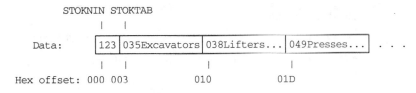

The last entry in the table contains '999' to force the search to end, since REPE makes the CX unavailable for the LOOP instruction. The search routine compares STOKNIN (arbitrarily defined to contain 123) with each table entry, as follows:

STOKNIN	TABLE ENTRY	RESULT OF COMPARISON
123	035	High: check next entry
123	038	High: check next entry
123	049	High: check next entry
123	102	High: check next entry
123	123	Equal: entry found

The program initializes the DI to the offset address of STOKTAB (003), the CX to the length (03) of each stock number, and the SI to the offset of STOKNIN (000). The CMPSB operation compares byte for byte, as long as the bytes contain equal values, and automatically increments the DI and SI registers. A comparison with the first table entry (123:035) causes termination after one byte; the DI contains 004, the SI contains 001, and the CX contains 02. For the next comparison, the DI should contain 010 and the SI should contain 000. Correcting the SI simply involves reloading the address of STOKNIN. For the address of the table entry that should be in the DI, however, the increment depends on whether the comparison ends after one, two, or three bytes. The CX contains the number of the remaining uncompared bytes, in this case, 02. Adding the CX value plus the length of the stock description gives the offset of the next table item, as follows:

```
                                      page  60,132
                             TITLE    P15STRSR (EXE)  Search using CMPSB
                                      .MODEL  SMALL
                                      .STACK  64
                             ; ----------------------------------------------
                                      .DATA
0000 31 32 33                STOKNIN  DB   '123'
0003 30 33 35 45 78 63       STOKTAB  DB   '035','Excavators'   ;Start table
     61 76 61 74 6F 72
     73
0010 30 33 38 4C 69 66                DB   '038','Lifters   '
     74 65 72 73 20 20
     20
001D 30 34 39 50 72 65                DB   '049','Presses   '
     73 73 65 73 20 20
     20
002A 31 30 32 56 61 6C                DB   '102','Valves    '
     76 65 73 20 20 20
     20
0037 31 32 33 50 72 6F                DB   '123','Processors'
     63 65 73 73 6F 72
     73
0044 31 32 37 50 75 6D                DB   '127','Pumps     '
     70 73 20 20 20 20
     20
0051 39 39 39                         DB   '999', 10 DUP(' ')  ;End table
     000A[ 20 ]
005E 000A[ ?? ]             DESCRN    DB   10 DUP(?),'$'        ;Save area
     24

                             ; ----------------------------------------------
                                      .CODE
0000                         BEGIN    PROC   FAR
0000 B8 ---- R                        MOV    AX,@data        ;Initialize
0003 8E D8                            MOV    DS,AX           ;  segment
0005 8E C0                            MOV    ES,AX           ;  registers
0007 FC                               CLD
0008 8D 3E 0003 R                     LEA    DI,STOKTAB      ;Initialize table
000C                         A20:                            ;  address
000C B9 0003                          MOV    CX,03           ;Compare 3 bytes
000F 8D 36 0000 R                     LEA    SI,STOKNIN      ;Init stock# addr
0013 F3/ A6                           REPE CMPSB             ;Stock# : table
0015 74 09                            JE     A30             ;  equal, exit
0017 72 1D                            JB     A40             ;  low, not entry
0019 03 F9                            ADD    DI,CX           ;Add CX to offset
001B 83 C7 0A                         ADD    DI,10           ;Next table item
001E EB EC                            JMP    A20
0020                         A30:
0020 B9 0005                          MOV    CX,05           ;Set for 5 words
0023 8B F7                            MOV    SI,DI
0025 8D 3E 005E R                     LEA    DI,DESCRN       ;Addr of descr'n
0029 F3/ A5                           REP MOVSW              ;Get description
                                                             ;  from table
002B B4 09                            MOV    AH,09H          ;Request display
002D 8D 16 005E R                     LEA    DX,DESCRN       ;  stock descrip'n
0031 CD 21                            INT    21H
0033 EB 01 90                         JMP    A90             ;Go to exit
0036                         A40:
                             ;               <Display error message>
0036                         A90:
0036 B8 4C00                          MOV    AX,4C00H        ;Exit to DOS
0039 CD 21                            INT    21H
003B CB                               RET
003C                         BEGIN    ENDP
                                      END    BEGIN
```

Figure 15–4   Table Search Using CMPSB

Address in DI after CMPSB:	004H
Add remaining length in CX:	+ 02H
Add length of description:	+ 0AH
Next table offset address:	010H

Since the CX contains the number of the remaining uncompared bytes (if any), the arithmetic works for all cases and terminates after one, two, or three comparisons. On an equal comparison, the CX contains 00, and the DI is already incremented to the address of the required description. A REP MOVSW operation then copies the description into DESCRN, where it is displayed.

Tables with Variable-Length Entries

It is possible to define a table with variable-length entries. A special delimiter character such as 00H could follow each entry, and FFH could distinguish the end of the table. However, you must be sure that no byte within an entry contains the bit configuration of a delimiter; for example, an arithmetic binary amount can contain any possible bit configuration. Use the SCAS instruction to scan for the delimiters.

THE XLAT (TRANSLATE) INSTRUCTION

The XLAT instruction translates the contents of a byte into another predefined value. You could use XLAT, for example, to validate the contents of data items or, if you transfer data between a PC and an IBM mainframe computer, to translate data between ASCII and EBCDIC formats. The general format for XLAT is

```
[label:]   XLAT   ;No operands
```

The following example converts ASCII numbers 0–9 into EBCDIC. Since the representation in ASCII is 30–39 and in EBCDIC is F0–F9, you could use an OR operation to make the change. However, let's also convert all other characters to a blank, EBCDIC 40H. For XLAT, you define a translation table that accounts for all 256 possible characters, with EBCDIC codes inserted in the ASCII positions:

```
XLTBL   DB   48 DUP(40H)                    ;EBCDIC blanks

        DB   0F0H,0F1H,0F2H,0F3H, ...,0F9H  ;EBCDIC 0-9

        DB   198 DUP(40H)                    ;EBCDIC blanks
```

XLAT expects that the address of the table is in the BX register and the byte to be translated (let's name it ASCNO) is in the AL. The following performs the initialization and translation:

```
LEA  BX,XLTBL    ;Load address of table

MOV  AL,ASCNO    ;Load character to translate

XLAT             ;Translate to EBCDIC
```

```
TITLE     P15XLATE   (COM)   Translate ASCII to EBCDIC
          .MODEL   SMALL
          .CODE
          ORG      100H
BEGIN:    JMP      MAIN
;-------------------------------------------------------------
ASCNO     DB       '-31.5 '            ;ASCII item to convert
EBCNO     DB       6 DUP(' ')          ;Converted EBCDIC item
XLTAB     DB       45 DUP(40H)         ;Translate table
          DB       60H, 4BH
          DB       40H
          DB       0F0H,0F1H,0F2H,0F3H,0F4H
          DB       0F5H,0F6H,0F7H,0F8H,0F9H
          DB       198 DUP(40H)
;-------------------------------------------------------------
MAIN      PROC     NEAR
          LEA      SI,ASCNO            ;Address of ASCNO
          LEA      DI,EBCNO            ;Address of EBCNO
          MOV      CX,06               ;Length of items
          LEA      BX,XLTAB            ;Address of table
A20:
          LODSB                        ;Get ASCII char in AL
          XLAT                         ;Translate character
          STOSB                        ;Store AL in EBCNO
          LOOP     A20                 ;Repeat 6 times
;         ...
          MOV      AX,4C00H            ;Exit to DOS
          INT      21H
MAIN      ENDP
          END      BEGIN
```

Figure 15–5   Conversion of ASCII to EBCDID

XLAT uses the AL value as an offset address; in effect, the BX contains the starting address of the table, and the AL contains an offset value within the table. If the AL value is 00, for example, the table address would be XLTBL+0 (the first byte of XLTBL containing 40H). XLAT would replace the 00 in the AL with 40H from the table.

Note that the first DB in XLTBL defines 48 bytes, addressed as XLTBL+00 through XLTBL+47. The second DB in XLTBL defines data beginning at XLTBL+48. If the AL value is 32H (decimal 50), the table address is XLTBL+50; this location contains F2 (EBCDIC 2), which XLAT would insert in the AL register.

The program in Figure 15–5 expands this example to convert ASCII minus sign (2D) and decimal point (2E) to EBCDIC (60 and 4B, respectively) and to loop through a six-byte field. Initially, ASCNO contains −31.5 followed by a blank, or hex 2D33312E3520. At the end of the loop, EBCNO should contain hex 60F3F14BF540.

DISPLAYING HEX AND ASCII CHARACTERS

The program in Figure 15–6 displays all 256 hex values (00–FF), including most of their related ASCII symbols. For example, the program displays both the ASCII symbol S and its hex representation, 53. The full display appears on the screen as a 16-by-16 matrix:

```
                    page 60,132
     TITLE          P15ASCHX (COM)  Display ASCII and hex characters
                    .MODEL SMALL
                    .CODE
                    ORG    100H
     BEGIN:         JMP    SHORT MAIN
     ; --------------------------------------------------------------
     DISPROW        DB     16 DUP(5 DUP(' ')), 13
     HEXCTR         DB     00
     XLATAB         DB     30H,31H,32H,33H,34H,35H,36H,37H,38H,39H
                    DB     41H,42H,43H,44H,45H,46H
     ; --------------------------------------------------------------
     MAIN           PROC   NEAR                    ;Main procedure
                    CALL   Q10CLR                  ;Clear screen
                    LEA    SI,DISPROW
     A20LOOP:
                    CALL   C10HEX                  ;Translate
                    CALL   D10DISP                 ;  and display
                    CMP    HEXCTR,0FFH             ;Last hex value (FF)?
                    JE     A50                     ;  yes, terminate
                    INC    HEXCTR                  ;  no, get next hex
                    JMP    A20LOOP
     A50:           MOV    AX,4C00H                ;Exit to DOS
                    INT    21H
     MAIN           ENDP

     C10HEX         PROC   NEAR                    ;Convert to hex
                    MOV    AH,00
                    MOV    AL,HEXCTR               ;Get hex pair
                    MOV    CL,04                   ;Set shift value
                    SHR    AX,CL                   ;Shift off right hex digit
                    LEA    BX,XLATAB               ;Set table address
                    XLAT                           ;Translate hex
                    MOV    [SI],AL                 ;Store left character

                    MOV    AL,HEXCTR
                    AND    AL,0FH                  ;Clear left hex digit
                    XLAT                           ;Translate hex
                    MOV    [SI]+1,AL               ;Store right character
                    RET
     C10HEX         ENDP
     D10DISP        PROC   NEAR                    ;Display
                    MOV    AL,HEXCTR
                    MOV    [SI]+3,AL
                    CMP    AL,1AH                  ;EOF character?
                    JE     D20                     ;  yes, bypass
                    CMP    AL,07H                  ;Lower than 7?
                    JB     D30                     ;  yes, ok
                    CMP    AL,10H                  ;Higher/equal 16?
                    JAE    D30                     ;  yes, ok
     D20:                                          ;Else force blank
                    MOV    BYTE PTR [SI]+3,20H
     D30:
                    ADD    SI,05                   ;Next location in row
                    LEA    DI,DISPROW+80
                    CMP    DI,SI                   ;Filled up row?
                    JNE    D40                     ;  no, bypass

                    MOV    AH,40H                  ;Yes, request display
                    MOV    BX,01                   ;  file handle
                    MOV    CX,81                   ;  entire row
                    LEA    DX,DISPROW
                    INT    21H
                    LEA    SI,DISPROW              ;Reset display row
```

Figure 15–6   Displaying ASCII and Hex

```
D40:        RET
D10DISP     ENDP

Q10CLR      PROC    NEAR                    ;Clear screen
            MOV     AX,0600H
            MOV     BH,61H                  ;Attribute
            MOV     CX,0000
            MOV     DX,184FH
            INT     10H
            RET
Q10CLR      ENDP
            END     BEGIN
```

Figure 15–6 (continued)

```
00 01 02 03 04 05 06 07 08 09 0A 0B 0C 0D 0E 0F
 .  .  .  .  .  .  .  .  .  .  .  .  .  .  .  .
 .  .  .  .  .  .  .  .  .  .  .  .  .  .  .  .
 .  .  .  .  .  .  .  .  .  .  .  .  .  .  .  .
F0 F1 F2 F3 F4 F5 F6 F7 F8 F9 FA FB FC FD FE FF
```

As we saw in Figure 8–1, displaying ASCII symbols causes no serious problem. However, displaying the hex representation of an ASCII value is more involved. For example, to display hex as ASCII, you have to convert 00H to 3030H, 01H to 3031H, and so forth.

The program initializes HEXCTR to 00 and subsequently increments it by 1 for each loop. The procedure C10HEX splits HEXCTR into its two hex digits. For example, suppose HEXCTR contains 4FH. The routine extracts the hex 4 and uses it and a table for a translation. The value returned to the AL is 34H. The routine then extracts the F and translates it to 46H. The result, 3446H, displays as 4F.

The procedure D10DISP converts non-ASCII characters to blanks. Since DOS INT 21H, function 40H, treats 1AH as an end-of-file character, the program also changes it to blank. When a row is full with 16 characters, the procedure displays it; the procedure ends after displaying the 16th row.

There are many other ways of converting hex digits to ASCII characters; for example, you could experiment with shifting and comparing.

SORTING TABLE ENTRIES

Often, an application requires *sorting* data in a table into ascending or descending sequence. For example, a user may want a list of stock descriptions in ascending sequence, or a list of sales agents' total sales in descending sequence. There are a number of table sort routines, varying from not efficient but clear to efficient but obscure. The routine presented in this section is fairly efficient and could serve for most table sorting.

A general approach to sorting a table is to compare a table entry with the entry immediately following it. If the comparison is high, exchange the entries. Continue in this fashion, comparing entry 1 with entry 2, entry 2 with entry 3, and so on to the end of the table, exchanging where necessary. If you made any exchanges, repeat the entire process from the start of the table, comparing entry 1 with entry 2 again. If you didn't make any exchanges, the table is in sequence and you can end the sort.

In the following pseudocode, SWAP is an item that indicates whether an exchange was made (YES) or not made (NO).

```
G10:    Initialize address of last entry in table

G20:    Set SWAP to NO

        Initialize address of start of table

G30:    Table entry > next entry?

            Yes: Exchange entries

                    Set SWAP to YES

        Increment for next entry in table

        At end of table?

            No:  Jump to G30

            Yes: Does SWAP = YES?

                    Yes: Jump to G20 (repeat sort)

                    No:  End of sort
```

The program in Figure 15–7 allows a user to enter up to 30 names from the keyboard, which the program stores successively in a table named NAMETAB. When all the names are entered, the user just presses the Enter key, with no name. The program then sorts the table of names into ascending sequence and displays them on the screen. Note that the table entries are all fixed-length 20 bytes; a routine for sorting variable-length data would be more complicated.

LINKED LISTS

A *linked list* contains data in what are called cells, like entries in a table, but in no specified sequence. Each cell contains a *pointer* to the next cell in the list to facilitate forward searches. (A cell may also contain a pointer to the preceding cell so that searching may proceed in either direction.) The method facilitates additions and deletions to a list without the need for expanding and contracting it.

For our purposes, the linked list contains cells with part number (four-byte ASCII value), unit price (binary word), and a pointer (binary word) to the next cell in the list, which contains the next part number in the sequence. Thus each entry is eight bytes in length. The pointer is an offset from the start of the list. The linked list begins at offset 0000, the second item in the series is at 0024, the third is at 0032, and so forth:

```
                page 60,132
TITLE           P15NMSRT (EXE)   Sort names entered from terminal
                .MODEL SMALL
                .STACK 64
; ----------------------------------------------------------
                .DATA
NAMEPAR    LABEL   BYTE                    ;Name parameter list:
MAXNLEN    DB      21                      ;   maximum length
NAMELEN    DB      ?                       ;   no. of chars entered
NAMEFLD    DB      21 DUP(' ')             ;   name

CRLF       DB      13, 10, '$'
ENDADDR    DW      ?
MESSG1     DB      'Name? ', '$'
NAMECTR    DB      00
NAMETAB    DB      30 DUP(20 DUP(' '))  ;Name table
NAMESAV    DB      20 DUP(?), 13, 10, '$'
SWAPPED    DB      00
; ----------------------------------------------------------
                .CODE
BEGIN      PROC    FAR
           MOV     AX,@data                ;Initialize DS and
           MOV     DS,AX                   ;   ES registers
           MOV     ES,AX
           CLD
           CALL    Q10CLR                  ;Clear screen
           CALL    Q20CURS                 ;Set cursor
           LEA     DI,NAMETAB
A20LOOP:
           CALL    B10READ                 ;Accept name
           CMP     NAMELEN,00              ;Any more names?
           JZ      A30                     ;   no, go to sort
           CMP     NAMECTR,30              ;30 names entered?
           JE      A30                     ;   yes, go to sort
           CALL    D10STOR                 ;Store entered name in table
           JMP     A20LOOP
A30:                                       ;End of input
           CALL    Q10CLR                  ;Clear screen
           CALL    Q20CURS                 ;   and set cursor
           CMP     NAMECTR,01              ;One or no name entered?
           JBE     A40                     ;   yes, exit
           CALL    G10SORT                 ;Sort stored names
           CALL    K10DISP                 ;Display sorted names
A40:       MOV     AX,4C00H                ;Exit to DOS
           INT     21H
BEGIN      ENDP
;                    Accept name as input:
;                    --------------------
B10READ    PROC
           MOV     AH,09H
           LEA     DX,MESSG1               ;Display prompt
           INT     21H
           MOV     AH,0AH
           LEA     DX,NAMEPAR              ;Accept name
           INT     21H
           MOV     AH,09H
           LEA     DX,CRLF                 ;Return/line feed
           INT     21H

           MOV     BH,00                   ;Clear characters after name
           MOV     BL,NAMELEN              ;Get count of chars
           MOV     CX,21
           SUB     CX,BX                   ;Calc remaining length
```

Figure 15–7   Sorting a Table of Names

```
B20:
            MOV     NAMEFLD[BX],20H    ;Set name to blank
            INC     BX
            LOOP    B20
            RET
B10READ     ENDP
;                   Store name in table:
;                   ------------------
D10STOR     PROC
            INC     NAMECTR            ;Add to number of names
            CLD
            LEA     SI,NAMEFLD
            MOV     CX,10              ;Ten words
            REP MOVSW                  ;Name (SI) to table (DI)
            RET
D10STOR     ENDP
;                   Sort names in table:
;                   ------------------
G10SORT     PROC
            SUB     DI,40              ;Set up stop address
            MOV     ENDADDR,DI
G20:
            MOV     SWAPPED,00         ;Set up start
            LEA     SI,NAMETAB         ; of table
G30:
            MOV     CX,20              ;Length of compare
            MOV     DI,SI
            ADD     DI,20              ;Next name for compare
            MOV     AX,DI
            MOV     BX,SI
            REPE CMPSB                 ;Compare name to next
            JBE     G40                ; no exchange
            CALL    H10XCHG            ; exchange
G40:
            MOV     SI,AX
            CMP     SI,ENDADDR         ;End of table?
            JBE     G30                ; no, continue
            CMP     SWAPPED,00         ;Any swaps?
            JNZ     G20                ; yes, continue
            RET                        ; no, end of sort
G10SORT     ENDP

;                   Exchange table entries:
;                   ---------------------
H10XCHG     PROC
            MOV     CX,10              ;Number of characters
            LEA     DI,NAMESAV
            MOV     SI,BX
            REP MOVSW                  ;Move lower item to save

            MOV     CX,10              ;Number of characters
            MOV     DI,BX
            REP MOVSW                  ;Move higher item to lower

            MOV     CX,10
            LEA     SI,NAMESAV
            REP MOVSW                  ;Move save to higher item
            MOV     SWAPPED,01         ;Signal exchange made
            RET
H10XCHG     ENDP
;                   Display sorted names:
;                   ------------------
K10DISP     PROC
            LEA     SI,NAMETAB
```

Figure 15–7   (continued)

```
K20:
            LEA     DI,NAMESAV          ;Init'ze start of table
            MOV     CX,10               ;Count for loop
            REP MOVSW
            MOV     AH,09H              ;Request display
            LEA     DX,NAMESAV
            INT     21H
            DEC     NAMECTR             ;Is this last one?
            JNZ     K20                 ;  no, loop
            RET                         ;  yes, exit
K10DISP     ENDP
;                   Clear screen:
;                   ------------
Q10CLR      PROC
            MOV     AX,0600H
            MOV     BH,61H              ;Attribute
            MOV     CX,00               ;Full screen
            MOV     DX,184FH
            INT     10H
            RET
Q10CLR      ENDP
;                   Set cursor:
;                   ----------
Q20CURS     PROC
            MOV     AH,02H              ;Request set cursor
            MOV     BH,00               ;Page 0
            MOV     DX,00               ;Location 00:00
            INT     10H
            RET
Q20CURS     ENDP
            END     BEGIN
```

Figure 15–7C   (continued)

OFFSET	PART NO.	PRICE	NEXT ADDRESS
0000	0103	12.50	0024
0008	1720	08.95	0016
0016	1827	03.75	0000
0024	0120	13.80	0032
0032	0205	25.00	0008

The item at offset 0016 contains zero as the next address, either to indicate the end of the list or to make the list circular.

The program in Figure 15–8 uses the contents of the defined linked list, LINKLST, to locate a specified part number, in this case, 1720. The search begins with the first item in the table. The logic for using CMPSB is similar to that in Figure 15–4. The program compares the part number (1720) with each item in the table and does the following, according to the results of the comparison:

- Equal: The search is finished.
- Low: The item is not in the table.
- High: The program gets the offset from the table for the next item to be compared. If the offset is not zero, the comparison is repeated for the next item; if the offset is zero, the search ends without finding a match.

A more complete program could allow a user at a keyboard to enter any part number and could display the price as an ASCII value.

TYPE, LENGTH, AND SIZE OPERATORS

The assembler supplies a number of special operators that you may find useful. For example, the length of a table may change from time to time, and you may have to modify a program to account for the new definition and add routines that check for the end of the table. The use of the TYPE, LENGTH, and SIZE operators can help reduce the number of instructions that have to be changed.

Consider this definition of a table with 10 words:

```
TABLEX DW  10 DUP(?)    ;Table with 10 words
```

The program can use the TYPE operator to determine the definition (DW in this case), the LENGTH operator to determine the DUP factor (10), and the SIZE operator to determine the number of bytes (10 × 2, or 20). The following examples illustrate the three operators:

```
MOV   AX,TYPE TABLEX      ;AX = 0002   (2 bytes)

MOV   BX,LENGTH TABLEX    ;BX = 000A   (10 bytes)

MOV   CX,SIZE TABLEX      ;CX = 0014   (20 bytes)
```

You may use the values that LENGTH and SIZE return to end a search or a sort of a table. For example, if the SI register contains the incremented offset address of a search, you may test this offset using

```
CMP   SI,SIZE TABLEX
```

Chapter 27 describes the TYPE, LENGTH, and SIZE operators in detail.

KEY POINTS

- For most purposes, define tables so that their entries are related and have the same length and data format.
- Design tables based on their data format. For example, table entries may be character or numeric and one, two, or more bytes each in length.
- Remember that the maximum numeric value for a DB is 256 and that numeric DW and DD reverse the bytes. Also, CMP and CMPSW assume that words contain bytes in reverse sequence.
- If a table is subject to frequent changes, or if several programs reference the table, store it on disk. An updating program can handle changes to the table. Any program can then load the table from disk, and the programs need not be changed.
- Under direct table addressing, the program calculates the address of a table entry and accesses that entry directly.

```
TITLE     P15LNKLS (EXE)   Use of a Linked List
          .MODEL   SMALL
          .STACK   64                ;Define stack

          .DATA
PARTNO DB       '1720'              ;Part number
LINKLST DB      '0103'              ;Linked list table
        DW      1250, 24
        DB      '1720'
        DW      0895, 16
        DB      '1827'
        DW      0375, 00
        DB      '0120'
        DW      1380, 32
        DB      '0205'
        DW      2500, 08

        .CODE                       ;Define code segment
BEGIN   PROC    FAR
        MOV     AX,@data            ;Set address of DATASG
        MOV     DS,AX               ;   in DS and
        MOV     ES,AX               ;   ES register
        CLD
        LEA     DI,LINKLST          ;Initialize table address
A20:
        MOV     CX,04               ;Set to compare 4 bytes
        LEA     SI,PARTNO           ;Init'ze part# address
        REPE CMPSB                  ;Part# : table
        JE      A30                 ;   equal, exit
        JB      A40                 ;   low, not in table
        ADD     DI,CX               ;Add CX value to offset
        ADD     DI,02               ;Get offset of next item
        MOV     DX,[DI]
        LEA     DI,LINKLST
        ADD     DI,DX
        CMP     DX,00               ;Last table entry?
        JNE     A20
        JMP     A40
A30:
;                   <Item Found>
        JMP     A90
A40:
;                   <Display error message>

A90:
        MOV     AX,4C00H            ;Exit to DOS
        INT     21H
BEGIN   ENDP

        END     BEGIN
```

Figure 15–8 Linked List

- When searching a table, a program successively compares a data item against each entry in the table until it finds a match.
- The XLAT instruction facilitates translating data from one format to another.

QUESTIONS

15–1. Distinguish between processing a table by direct addressing and by searching.

15–2. Define a table named TABLEX with 50 words, initialized to blanks.

15-3. Define three separate related tables that contain the following data: (a) item numbers 06, 10, 14, 21, and 24; (b) item descriptions of videotape, receivers, modems, keyboards, and diskettes; (c) item prices 93.95, 82.25, 90.67, 85.80, and 13.85.

15-4. Code a program that allows a user to enter item numbers (ITEMIN) and quantities (QTYIN) from the keyboard. Use the tables defined in Question 15–3, and include a search routine that uses ITEMIN to locate an item number in the table. Extract the descriptions and prices from the table. Calculate the value (quantity × price) of each sale, and display description and value on the screen.

15-5. Using the description table defined in Question 15–3, code the following: (a) a routine that moves the contents of the table to another (empty) table; (b) a routine that sorts the contents of this new table into ascending sequence by description.

15-6. A program is required to provide simple encryption of data. Define an 80-byte data area named CRYPTEXT containing any ASCII data. Arrange a translation table to convert the data somewhat randomly, for example, A to X, B to E, C to R, and so forth. Provide for all possible byte values. Arrange a second translation table that reverses (decrypts) the data. The program should perform the following actions:

- Display the original contents of CRYPTEXT on a line.
- Encrypt CRYPTEXT and display the encrypted data on a second line.
- Decrypt CRYPTEXT and display the decrypted data on a third line. (This line should display the same data as the first line.)

CHAPTER 16 ———————————

Disk Storage Organization

> ### OBJECTIVE:
>
> To examine the basic formats for hard disk and diskette storage, the boot record, directory, and file allocation table.

INTRODUCTION

At some point, a serious programmer has to be familiar with the technical details of disk organization, particularly for developing utility programs that examine the contents of diskettes and hard disks. Where a reference to a disk or diskette is required, this text uses the general term *disk*.

This chapter explains the concepts of tracks, sectors, and cylinders and gives the capacities of some commonly used devices.

Also covered is the organization of important data recorded at the beginning of a disk, including the boot record (which helps the system load the DOS programs from disk into memory), the directory (which contains the name, location, and status of each file on the disk), and the file allocation table (or FAT, which allocates disk space for files).

DISK CHARACTERISTICS

For processing records on disks, it is useful to be familiar with the terms and characteristics of their organization. A diskette has two sides (or surfaces), whereas a hard disk contains a number of two-sided disks.

Tracks and Sectors

Each side of a diskette or hard disk contains a number of concentric *tracks*, numbered beginning with 00, the outermost track. Each track is formatted into *sectors* of 512 bytes, where the data is stored.

Both diskettes and hard disk devices are run by a *controller* that handles the placement of the read-write heads on the disk surface and the transfer of data between disk and memory. There is a read-write head for each disk surface. For both diskette and hard disk, a request for a read or a write causes the disk drive controller to move the read-write heads (if necessary) to the required track. The controller then waits for the required sector on the spinning surface to reach the head, at which point the read or write operation takes place. Figure 16–1 illustrates these features.

There are two main differences between a hard disk and a diskette drive. For hard disk, the read-write head rides just above the disk surface without ever touching it, whereas for diskette, the read-write head actually touches the surface. Also, a hard disk device is constantly spinning, whereas a diskette device starts and stops for each read/write operation.

Cylinders

A *cylinder* is a vertical set of all of the tracks with the same number on each surface of a diskette or hard disk. Thus cylinder 0 is the set of tracks numbered 0, cylinder 1 is the set of tracks numbered 1, and so forth. For a diskette, then, cylinder 0 consists of track 0 on side 1 and track 0 on side 2; cylinder 1 consists of track 1 on side 1 and track 1 on side 2; and so forth. When writing a file, the system fills all the tracks on a cylinder and then advances the read-write heads to the next cylinder.

A reference to disk sides (heads), tracks, and sectors is by number. Side and track numbers begin with 0, but sectors may be numbered one of two ways:

1. *Cylinder-track address*: Sector numbers on each track begin with 1, so that the first sector on the disk is addressed as cylinder 0, track 0, sector 1.

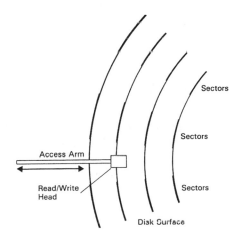

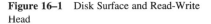

Figure 16–1   Disk Surface and Read-Write Head

2. *Relative sector number*: Sectors may be numbered relative to the start of the disk, so that the first sector on the disk, on cylinder 0, track 0, is addressed as relative sector 0.

Disk Controller

The disk controller is located between the processor and the disk drive and handles all communication between them. The controller accepts data from the processor and converts the data into a form that is usable by the device. For example, the processor may send a request for data from a specific cylinder, disk head, and sector. The role of the controller is to provide the appropriate commands to move the access arm to the required cylinder, select the read/write head, and accept the data from the sector when the data reaches the read-write head.

The processor is freed for other tasks while the controller is performing its work. Under this approach, the controller handles only one byte at a time. However, the controller can also perform faster I/O by bypassing the processor entirely and transferring data directly to and from memory. The method of transferring a large block of data in this manner is known as *direct memory access (DMA)*. To this end, the processor provides the controller with the read or write command, the address of the I/O buffer in memory, the number of sectors to transfer, and the numbers of the cylinder, head, and starting sector. With this method, the processor has to wait until the DMA is complete, since only one component at a time can use the memory path.

Clusters

A *cluster* is a group of sectors that DOS treats as a unit of storage space. A cluster size is always a power of 2, such as 1, 2, 4, or 8 sectors. A hard disk typically has four sectors per cluster. On a disk device that uses one sector per cluster, sector and cluster are the same. A file begins on a cluster boundary and requires a minimum of one cluster even if the file occupies only one of four sectors. A cluster may also overlap from one track to another.

A disk with two sectors per cluster would look like this:

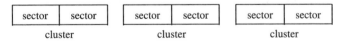

And a disk with four sectors per cluster would look like this:

A 100-byte file (small enough to occupy one sector) stored on disk with four sectors per cluster uses $4 \times 512 = 2,048$ bytes of storage, although only one sector would contain data. DOS stores clusters for files in ascending sequence, although a file may be fragmented so that it resides, for example, in clusters 8, 9, 10, 14, 17, and 18.

Disk Capacity

Here are common diskette storage capacities:

Capacity	Tracks per Side (Cylinders)	Sectors per Track	Bytes per Sector	Total, Two Sides	Sectors per Cluster
5.25" 360KB	40	9	512	368,640	2
5.25" 1.2MB	80	15	512	1,228,800	1
3.5" 720KB	80	9	512	737,280	2
3.5" 1.44MB	80	18	512	1,474,560	1
3.5" 2.88MB	80	36	512	2,949,120	—

For hard disks, capacities vary considerably by device and by partition. Useful operations for determining the number of cylinders, sectors per track, or read-write heads include INT 21H, functions 1FH and 440DH with minor code 60H, both covered in Chapter 18.

DISK SYSTEM AREA AND DATA AREA

To account for the information stored on disk, DOS reserves certain sectors for its own purposes. The organization of diskettes and hard disks varies according to their capacity. A hard disk and some diskettes are formatted to be self-booting—that is, they enable processing to start when the power is turned on or when a user presses the Ctrl+Alt+Del keys. The general organization of disk is a system area, followed by a data area that comprises the rest of the disk.

System Area

The *system area* is the first area of a disk, on the outermost track(s) beginning with side 0, track 0, sector 1. The information that DOS stores and maintains in its system area is used to determine, for example, the location of each file that is to be accessed. The three components of the system area are:

1. Boot record
2. File allocation table (FAT)
3. Directory

The system area and the data area are arranged like this:

Boot record	FAT	Directory	System files	User files

       System area   Data area

Assigned Sectors for the System Area

The following list gives the organization of several types of devices, showing the starting and ending sector numbers for the boot record, FAT, and directory (sectors are in terms of relative sector number, where relative sector 0 is cylinder 0, track 0, sector 1, the first sector on the device):

Device	Boot	FAT	Directory	Sectors/Cluster
5.25″ 360KB	0	1–4	5–11	2
5.25″ 1.2MB	0	1–14	15–28	1
3.5″ 720KB	0	1–6	7–13	2
3.5″ 1.44MB	0	1–18	19–32	1

For hard disk, the locations of the boot record and the FAT are usually the same as for diskette; the size of the FAT and the location of the directory vary by device.

Data Area

The *data area* for a bootable disk or diskette begins with two DOS system files named IO.SYS and MSDOS.SYS (for MS-DOS) or IBMBIO.COM and IBMDOS.COM (for IBM PC DOS). When you use FORMAT /S to format a disk, DOS copies its system files onto the first sectors of the data area. User files either immediately follow the system files or, if there are no system files, begin at the start of the data area.

A formatted two-sided diskette with nine sectors per track contains the following information:

Side 0, track 0, sector 1	Boot record
Side 0, track 0, sectors 2–3	File allocation table (FAT)
Side 0, track 0, sectors 4–7	Directory
Side 1, track 0, sectors 1–3	Directory
Side 1, track 0, sectors 4 and so on	Data area

Records for data files begin on side 1, track 0, sectors 3 through 9. The system stores records next on side 0, track 1, then side 1, track 1, then side 0, track 2, and so forth. This feature of filling data on opposite tracks (in the same cylinder) before proceeding to the next cylinder reduces the motion of the disk head and is the method used on both diskettes and hard disks.

For other devices, the FAT and directory may be different lengths. The next sections cover the boot record, directory, and FAT in detail.

BOOT RECORD

The boot record contains the instructions that load (or "boot") the system files IO.SYS, MS-DOS.SYS, and COMMAND.COM (if present) from disk into memory. All formatted disks contain this record even if the system files are not stored on it. The boot record contains the following information, in order of offset address:

00H	Short or far jump to the bootstrap routine at offset 1EH or 3EH in the boot record
03H	Manufacturer's name and DOS version number when boot was created
0BH	Bytes per sector, usually 200H (512)
0DH	Sectors per cluster (1, 2, 4, or 8)
0EH	Reserved sectors

10H	Number of copies of the FAT (1 or 2)
11H	Number of root directory entries
13H	Total number of sectors if volume is less than 32 MB
15H	Media descriptor byte (same as first byte of the FAT, described later)
16H	Number of sectors for the FAT
18H	Number of sectors per track
1AH	Number of read-write heads (sides or surfaces)
1CH	Number of hidden sectors
1EH	Bootstrap loader routine for DOS versions up through 3.3
20H	Total number of sectors if volume is greater than 32 MB
24H	Physical drive number (for diskette, A = 0; for hard disk, 80H = drive C, etc.)
25H	Reserved for DOS
26H	Extended boot sector signature (contains 29H)
27H	Volume ID
2BH	Volume label
36H	Reserved for DOS
3EH–1FFH	As of DOS 4.0, the bootstrap loader begins here.

DOS 4.0 extended the boot record with additional fields from 20H through 1FFH. Thus the original boot record is 20H (32) bytes, whereas the extended version is 200H (512) bytes.

DIRECTORY

All files on a disk begin on a cluster boundary, which is the first sector of the cluster. For each file, DOS creates a 32-byte (20H) directory entry that describes the name of the file, the date it was created, its size, and the location of its starting cluster. Directory entries have the following format:

BYTE	PURPOSE
00H–07H	Filename, as defined in the program that created the file. The first byte of the filename can also indicate the file status:
	00H File has never been used
	05H First character of filename is actually E5H
	2EH Entry is for a subdirectory
	E5H File has been deleted
08H–0AH	Filename extension
0BH	File attribute, defining the type of file (note that a file may have more than one attribute:
	00H Normal file
	01H File that can only be read (read only)
	02H Hidden file, not displayed by a directory search
	04H DOS system file, not displayed by a directory search

08H	Volume label (if this is a volume label record, the label itself is in the filename and extension fields)
10H	Subdirectory
20H	Archive file, which indicates whether the file was rewritten since the last update.

(As an example, code 07H would mean a system file (04H) that is read only (01H) and hidden (02H).)

0CH–15H	Reserved for DOS.
16H–17H	Time of day when the file was created or last updated; stored as 16 bits in binary format as |hhhhhmmmmmmssssss|.
18H–19H	Date when the file was created or last updated, stored as 16 bits in binary format as |yyyyyyym|mmmddddd|. The year can be 0–119 (assuming 1980 as the starting point), the month can be 01–12, and the day can be 01–31.
1AH–1BH	Starting cluster of the file. The number is relative to the last two sectors of the directory. Where there are no DOS system files, the first data file begins at relative cluster 002. The actual side, track, and cluster depend on disk capacity. A zero entry means that the file has no space allocated to it.
1CH–1FH	Size of the file in bytes. When you create a file, DOS calculates and stores its size in this field.

For numeric fields that exceed one byte in the directory, the bytes are stored in reverse sequence.

FILE ALLOCATION TABLE

The purpose of the FAT is to allocate disk space for files. The FAT contains an entry for every cluster on the disk. When you create a new file or revise an existing file, DOS revises the associated FAT entries according to the location of the file on disk. The FAT begins at sector 2, immediately following the boot record. On a disk where a cluster consists of four sectors, the same number of FAT entries can reference four times the data than disks where a cluster consists of one sector. Consequently, the use of clusters with multiple sectors reduces the number of entries in the FAT and enables DOS to address a larger disk storage space.

Too Much FAT

The original designers provided for two copies of the FAT (FAT1 and FAT2), presumably because FAT2 could be used if FAT1 became corrupted. However, although FAT2 is still maintained, its use has never been implemented. All discussions in this book concern FAT1.

First Entry in the FAT

The first byte of the FAT, the media descriptor, indicates the type of device (see also byte 15H in the boot record):

FOH	3.5", two sided, 18 sectors/track (1.44MB)
FOH	3.5", two sided, 36 sectors/track (2.88MB)
F8H	Hard disk (including RAM disk)
F9H	3.5", two sided, 9 sectors/track (720KB)
F9H	5.25", two sided, 15 sectors/track (1.2MB)
FCH	5.25", one sided, 9 sectors/track (180KB)
FDH	5.25", two sided, 9 sectors/track (360KB)
FFH	5.25", two sided, 8 sectors/track (320KB)

Note that F0H and F9H each identify two different disk formats.

Second Entry in the FAT

The second FAT entry contains FFFFH for diskette FATs that support 12-bit FAT entries and FFFFFFH for hard disks that support 16-bit FAT entries. The first two FAT entries look like this:

1.44MB diskette	FO	FF	FF	..	..	..	..	..	. . .	..

Hard disk	F8	FF	FF	FF	..	..	..	..	. . .	..

As already described, the first field on a disk is the boot record, followed by the FAT and then the directory. The data area is next. The entire picture is as follows:

cluster 0	cluster 1	cluster 2	cluster 3	. . .	cluster n

← directory area → ← ——————— data area ——————— →

You would expect that the data area would be the starting point for clusters, but instead, the first two cluster numbers (0 and 1) point to the directory, so that the data area for stored data files begins with cluster number 2. The reason for this odd state of affairs will soon be made clear.

Pointer Entries in the FAT

Following the first two FAT entries are *pointer entries* that relate to every cluster in the data area. The directory (at 1AH 1BH) contains the location of the first cluster for a file, and the FAT contains a chain of pointer entries for each succeeding cluster.

Since DOS 3.0, the entry length for diskettes is still three hex digits (1½ bytes, or 12 bits), but for hard disk it is four hex digits (2 bytes, or 16 bits). Each FAT pointer entry indicates the use of a particular cluster according to the following format:

12 Bits	16 Bits	Explanation
000	0000	Referenced cluster is currently unused
nnn	nnnn	Relative number of next cluster for a file
FF0–FF6	FFF0–FFF6	Reserved cluster
FF7	FFF7	Unusable (bad track)
FFF	FFFF	Last cluster of a file

The first two entries for a 1.44MB diskette (a 12-bit FAT) look like this:

```
FAT entry:              | FOF | FF. | . . . | . . . | . . . | . . . | . . . |   . . .   | . . . |

Relative cluster:          0     1     2       3       4       5       6       . . .      end
```

The term "relative cluster" means the cluster to which the FAT entry points. In a sense, the first two FAT entries (0 and 1) point to the last two clusters in the directory, which have been assigned as the start of clusters; the directory indicates the size and starting cluster for files.

The directory contains the starting cluster number for each file and a chain of FAT pointer entries that indicate the location of the next cluster, if any, at which the file continues. A pointer entry containing (F)FFFH indicates the last cluster for the file.

Sample FAT Entries

Let's now examine an example of FAT entries that should help clarify the FAT structure. Suppose a diskette contains only one file, named CUSTOMER.FIL, that is fully stored on clusters 2, 3, and 4. The directory entry for this file contains the filename CUSTOMER, the extension FIL, 00H to indicate a normal file, the creation date, 0002H for the location of the first relative cluster of the file, and an entry for the size of the file in bytes. The 12-bit FAT entry would appear as follows, except that pairs of bytes would be reversed:

```
FAT entry:              | FOF | FFF | 003 | 004 | FFF | . . . | . . . |   . . .   | . . . |

Relative cluster:          0     1     2     3     4     5       6       . . .      end
```

For the first two FAT entries, F0 indicates a two-sided nine-sectored (1.44MB) diskette, followed by FFFFH. To read CUSTOMER.FIL from disk into memory, the system takes the following steps:

- Searches the disk directory for the filename CUSTOMER and the extension FIL. DOS extracts from the directory the location of the first relative cluster (2) of the file and delivers its contents (data from the sectors) to the program in main memory.

- Accesses the FAT pointer entry that represents relative cluster 2. From the diagram, this entry contains 003, meaning that the file continues on relative cluster 3. DOS delivers the contents of this cluster to the program.

- Accesses the FAT pointer entry that represents relative cluster 3. This entry contains 004, meaning that the file continues on relative cluster 4. DOS delivers the contents of this cluster to the program.

The FAT entry for relative cluster 4 contains FFFH, to indicate that no more clusters are allocated for the file. DOS has now delivered all the file's data, from clusters 2, 3, and 4.

We've just seen how FAT entries work in principle; now let's see how they work in terms of reversed-byte sequence, where a little more ingenuity is required.

Handling 12-Bit FAT Entries in Reversed-byte Sequence

Following is the same example of FAT entries for CUSTOMER.FIL just covered, but now with pointer entries in reversed-byte sequence. The 12-bit FAT for this file looks like this:

FAT entry:	FOF	FFF	034	000	FFO	Fxx	. . .
Relative cluster:	0	1	2	3	4	5	

But what's needed now to decipher the entries is to represent them according to *relative byte* rather than cluster:

FAT entry:	FO	FF	FF	03	40	00	FF	OF	. . .
Relative byte:	0	1	2	3	4	5	6	7	

To process the first FAT entry:

- Multiply 2 (the file's first cluster) by 1.5 (the length of FAT entries) to get 3. (For programming, multiply by 3 and shift right one bit.) Access the word at bytes 3 and 4 in the FAT. These contain 03 40, which become, in reverse, 4003. Since cluster 2 was an even number, use the last three digits, so that 003 is the second cluster for the file.
- For the third cluster, multiply cluster number 3 by 1.5 to get 4. Access FAT bytes 4 and 5. These contain 40 00, which become, in reverse, 0040. Since cluster 3 was an odd number, use the first three digits, so that 004 is the third cluster for the file.
- For the fourth cluster, multiply 4 by 1.5 to get 6. Access FAT bytes 6 and 7. These contain FF 0F, which become, in reverse, 0FFF. Since cluster 4 was an even number, use the last three digits, FFF, which mean that this is the last entry. (Whew!)

Handling 16-Bit FAT Entries

As mentioned earlier, following the media descriptor for hard disk is FFFFFFH. FAT pointer entries are 16 bits long and begin with bytes 3 and 4, which represent cluster 2. The directory entry provides the starting clusters for files, and pointer entry FFFFH indicates end-of-file. Determining the cluster number from each FAT entry is simple, although the bytes in each entry are in reverse sequence.

As an example of 16-bit FAT entries, suppose the only file on a particular hard disk occupies four clusters (at 4 sectors per cluster, or 16 sectors in all). According to the directory, the file starts at cluster 2. Each FAT pointer entry is a full word, so that reversing the bytes involves only the one entry. Here is the FAT, with pointer entries in reversed-byte sequence:

FAT entry:	F8FF	FFFF	0300	0400	0500	FFFF	. . . .
Relative cluster:	0	1	2	3	4	5	

The FAT entry for relative cluster 2, 0300, reverses as 0003 for the next cluster. The FAT entry for relative cluster 3, 0400, reverses as 0004 for the next cluster. Continue with the chain of remaining entries in this fashion through to the entry for cluster number 5.

If your program has to determine the type of disk that is installed, it can check the media descriptor in the boot sector directly or, preferably, could use DOS INT 21H, function 1BH or 1CH.

EXERCISE INVOLVING THE FAT

Let's use DEBUG to examine the FAT for a disk. For this exercise, you'll need two formatted blank 3.5" diskettes with 720K and 1.44MB capacities. Copy two files onto each disk. The first file should be larger than 512 bytes and smaller than 1,024 bytes, to fit onto two sectors; P04ASM1.ASM is suggested. The second file should be larger than 1,536 bytes and smaller than 2,048 bytes, to fit onto four sectors; P10DRVID.ASM is suggested. You'll see that the FATs for the two diskettes are similar, but not identical.

720K Disk. First insert the 720K diskette in drive A (or B if necessary). Load DEBUG and enter the L (load) command (explained more fully in Appendix E):

```
L 100 0 0 20 (for drive B, use L 100 1 0 20 )
```

The L command entries are:

- 100H is the starting offset in DEBUG's segment
- The first 0 means use drive A (or 1 for drive B)
- The second 0 means read data beginning with relative sector 0
- 20 means read 20H (32) sectors.

You can now examine the boot record, directory, and FAT for this diskette. To display the boot record, enter the command D 100. Note some of the fields:

- Segment offset 103H shows the manufacturer's name and DOS version when the FAT was created
- 10BH shows the number of bytes per sector (where 0002H reverses as 0200H, or 512 bytes)
- 115H is the media descriptor, F9H for this diskette.
- Check out the other fields.

You'll find the directory at F00H:

- F00H shows the filename for the first file, P04ASM1.ASM.
- F1AH gives the starting cluster number (0200, or 0002) for this file.
- F1CH–F1FH gives the size of the file in bytes.
- F20H begins the entry for the second file, P10DRVID.ASM. Note that F3AH shows its starting cluster as 0300, or 0003.

You'll find the FAT at 300H looking like this:

FAT entry:	F9	FF	FF	FF	4F	00	FF	OF	. . . .
Relative byte:	0	1	2	3	4	5	6	7	

- F9 is the media descriptor.
- FF FF at bytes 1 and 2 is the content of the second field.

The pointer entries beginning at byte 3 can be calculated like this:

- For the first file, multiply 2 (its first cluster) by 1.5 to get 3. Access offset bytes 3 and 4 in the FAT, which contain FF 4F, and reverse the bytes to get 4FFF. Because cluster 2 was an even number, use the last three digits, FFF, which tell you that there are no more clusters for this file.
- For the second file, multiply 3 (its first cluster) by 1.5 to get 4. Access offset bytes 4 and 5 in the FAT, which contain 4F 00, and reverse the bytes to get 004F. Because cluster 3 was an odd number, use the first three digits, 004, which identify the next cluster in the series. Multiply cluster 4 by 1.5 to get 6. Access offset bytes 6 and 7 in the FAT, which contain FF 0F, and reverse the bytes to get 0FFF. Because cluster 4 was an even number, use the first three digits, FFF, which indicate the end of the data.

1.44MB Disk.   Now insert the 1.44MB diskette in drive A, and enter the DEBUG command L 100 0 0 30. (Load 30H sectors because there's more FAT on 1.44MB diskettes.) Display the boot record for this disk, and note that the media descriptor byte at 115H is F0 and the number of sectors per cluster (at 10DH) is 1. The directories at 2700H and 2720H should show that the starting cluster for the first file is 2 and for the second file is 4. (The starting cluster for the second file on the 720K diskette was 3 because that format has two sectors per cluster.)

Display the FAT at 300H, which appears as

FAT entry	FO	FF	FF	03	FO	FF	05	60	00	07	FO	FF
Relative byte:	0	1	2	3	4	5	6	7	8	9	10	11

Since the first file starts at cluster 2, multiply 2 by 1.5 to get relative byte 3. Bytes 3 and 4 contain 03 F0, which reverse as F003. Because cluster 2 was an even number, use the last three digits, 003. Cluster 3 × 1.5 is 4; relative bytes 4 and 5 contain F0 FF, which reverse as FFF0. Because cluster 3 was an odd number, use the first three digits, FFF, which indicate that the file does not continue. We now know that the file resides on clusters 2 and 3.

Use the same technique to trace through the chain for the second file, which begins with cluster 4, or relative byte 6.

DOS provides some supporting services for programs to access information about the directory and the FAT. Functions 47H (Get Current Directory) and 1BH and 1CH (Get FAT Information) are described in Chapter 18.

PROCESSING FILES ON DISK

Data on disk is stored in the form of a *file*, just as you have stored your programs. Although there is no restriction on the kind of data that you may keep in a file, a typical user file would consist of *records* for customers, inventory supplies, or name-and-address lists. Each record contains information about a particular customer or inventory item. Within a file, all records are usually the same length and format. A record contains one or more fields that provide information about the record. Records for a customer file, for example, could contain such fields as customer number, customer name, and amount owing. The records could be in ascending sequence by customer number, as follows:

$$\left[\begin{array}{c}\#1\end{array}\middle| \text{name} \middle| \text{amt}\right] \quad \left[\begin{array}{c}\#2\end{array}\middle| \text{name} \middle| \text{amt}\right] \quad \left[\begin{array}{c}\#3\end{array}\middle| \text{name} \middle| \text{amt}\right] \quad \ldots \quad \left[\begin{array}{c}\#n\end{array}\middle| \text{name} \middle| \text{amt}\right]$$

Processing for files on hard disk is similar to that for diskette, and for both, you have to supply a path name to access files in subdirectories.

Interrupt Services for Disk Input/Output

A number of special interrupt services support disk input/output. A program that writes a file first *creates* the file so that DOS can generate an entry for it in the directory. When all the file's records have been written, the program *closes* the file so that DOS can complete the directory entry for the size of the file.

A program that is to read a file first *opens* the file to ensure that it exists. Once all files have been read, the practice is to close the file, making it available to other programs. Because of the directory's design, you may process records in a disk file either sequentially (one record after another, successively) or randomly (records retrieved as required, throughout the file).

The *highest level* of disk processing is via DOS interrupt 21H, which supports disk accessing by means of a directory and "blocking" and "unblocking" of records. The DOS method performs some preliminary processing before linking to BIOS. Chapter 17 covers the use of DOS operations to write and read disk files, and Chapter 18 discusses various DOS operations that support directories and disk files.

The *lowest level* of disk processing is via BIOS interrupt 13H, which involves direct addressing of track and sector numbers. This operation is covered in Chapter 19.

KEY POINTS

- Each side of a diskette or hard disk contains a number of concentric tracks, starting with track number 00. Each track is formatted into sectors of 512 bytes, starting with sector number 1.
- A cylinder is the set of all tracks with the same number on each side.
- A cluster is a group of sectors that DOS treats as a unit of storage space. A cluster size is always a power of 2, such as 1, 2, 4, or 8 sectors. A file begins on a cluster boundary and requires a minimum of one cluster.

- Regardless of size, all files begin on a cluster boundary.
- The boot record contains the instructions that load (or "boot") the system files IOSYS.SYS, MSDOS.COM, and COMMAND.COM from disk into memory.
- The directory contains an entry for each file on a disk and indicates the filename, extension, file attribute, time, date, starting sector, and file size.
- The purpose of the file allocation table (FAT) is to allocate disk space for files. The FAT begins at sector 2 immediately following the boot record and contains one entry for each cluster for each file in the directory.

QUESTIONS

16–1. What is the length in bytes of a standard sector?

16–2. What is a cylinder?

16–3. What is the purpose of a disk controller?

16–4. (a) What is a cluster? (b) What is its purpose? (c) A file is 48 bytes long. What is the disk space used for cluster sizes 1, 2, 4, and 8?

16–5. Show how to calculate the capacity of a diskette, based on the number of cylinders, sectors per track, and bytes per sector, for (a) a 5.25″, 360KB diskette and (b) a 3.5″, 1.44MB diskette.

16–6. What does the disk system area contain?

16–7. (a) Where is the boot record located? (b) What is its purpose?

16–8. What is the indication in the directory for a deleted file?

16–9. What is the indication in the directory for (a) a normal file; (b) a hidden file?

16–10. What is the additional effect on a diskette or hard disk when you use FORMAT /S to format?

16–11. Consider a file with a size of 2,890 (decimal) bytes. (a) Where does the system store the size? (b) What is the size in hexadecimal format? Show the value as the system stores it.

16–12. Where and how does the FAT indicate that the device on which it resides is on (a) hard disk; (b) a 5.25″, 360KB diskette; (c) a 3.5″, 1.44MB diskette?

CHAPTER 17 —————————

Disk Processing:
I—Writing and Reading Files

OBJECTIVE:

To cover the use of file handles and the DOS functions for writing and reading disk files sequentially and randomly.

INTRODUCTION

The original DOS services for processing disk files used a method called file control blocks (FCBs). This method, although still supported by DOS, can address drives and filenames, but not subdirectories. Succeeding DOS versions introduced a number of extended services that are simpler than their original counterparts and are generally recommended. Some of these operations involve the use of an ASCIIZ string to initially identify a drive, path, and filename; a file handle for subsequent accessing of the file; and special return codes to identify errors. As a reminder, the term *cluster* denotes a group of one or more sectors of data, depending on the device.

Although no new assembly language instructions are required, this chapter introduces a number of DOS 21H services for processing disk files. Here they are, arranged by category:

OPERATIONS USING FILE HANDLES		OPERATIONS USING FCBS	
3CH	Create file	0FH	Open file
3DH	Open file	10H	Close file
3EH	Close file	14H	Read record
3FH	Read record	15H	Write record

296

40H	Write record	16H	Create file
42H	Move file pointer	21H	Read record randomly

OTHER DOS SERVICES   **22H WRITE RECORD RANDOMLY**

INT 25H	Absolute read	27H	Read block randomly
INT 26H	Absolute write	28H	Write block randomly

The chapter covers DOS services for writing and reading disk files. Chapter 18 covers the various support services required for handling disk drives, directories, and files.

ASCIIZ STRINGS

When using many of the extended services for disk processing, you first tell DOS the address of an *ASCIIZ string* containing the location of the file: disk drive, directory path, and filename (all optional and within apostrophes), followed by a byte of hex zeros; thus the name ASCIIZ string. The maximum length of the string is 128 bytes.

The following code defines a drive and filename:

```
PATHNM1 DB  'D:\TEST.ASM',00H
```

This code defines a drive, subdirectory, and filename:

```
PATHNM2 DB  'D:\UTILITY\NU.EXE',00H
```

The backslash, which may also be a forward slash, acts as a path separator. A byte of zeros terminates the string. For interrupts that require an ASCIIZ string, load its offset address in the DX register—for example, as

```
LEA DX,PATHNAME.
```

FILE HANDLES

As discussed in Chapter 9, you may use file handles directly for certain standard devices: 00 = input, 01 = output, 02 = error output, 03 = auxiliary device, and 04 = printer. Many DOS services also involve the use of a file handle for operations that access files, and you have to request the file handle number from DOS. A disk file must first be opened; unlike transferring data from the keyboard or to the screen, DOS has to address disk files through its directory and FAT entries and must update these entries. During program execution, each file referenced must be assigned its own unique file handle.

DOS delivers a file handle when you open a file for input or create a file for output. The operations involve the use of an ASCIIZ string and DOS function 3CH or 3DH. The file handle is a unique one-word number returned in the AX that you save in a word data item and use for all subsequent requests to access the file. Typically, the first file handle returned is 05, the second is 06, and so forth.

The PSP contains a default file handle table that provides for 20 handles (thus the nominal limit for opened files), but INT 21H, function 67H, can be used to increase the limit, as explained in Chapter 24.

ERROR RETURN CODES

The disk file handle operations return a *completion status* via the carry flag and the AX register. A *successful* operation clears the carry flag to zero and performs other appropriate functions. An *unsuccessful* operation sets the carry flag to 1 and returns an error code in the AX, depending on the operation. Figure 17–1 lists error codes 01–36; other codes are concerned with networking.

If these errors aren't enough, you can also use INT 59H for additional information about errors. (See Chapter 18.)

The following sections cover the requirements for creating, writing, and closing disk files for extended DOS.

```
01  Invalid function number       20  Unknown unit
02  File not found                21  Drive not ready
03  Path not found                22  Unknown command
04  Too many files open           23  CRC data error
05  Access denied                 24  Bad request structure length
06  Invalid handle                25  Seek error
07  Memory control block destroyed 26  Unknown media type
08  Insufficient memory           27  Sector not found
09  Invalid memory block address  28  Printer out of paper
10  Invalid environment           29  Write fault
11  Invalid format                30  Read fault
12  Invalid access code           31  General failure
13  Invalid data                  32  Sharing violation
15  Invalid drive specified       33  Lock violation
16  Attempt to remove directory   34  Invalid disk change
17  Not same device               35  FCB unavailable
18  No more files                 36  Sharing buffer overflow
19  Write-protected disk
```

Figure 17–1   Major Disk Error Return Codes

FILE POINTERS

DOS maintains a separate *file pointer* for each file that a program is processing. The create and open operations set the value of the file pointer to zero, the file's starting location. The file pointer subsequently accounts for the current offset location within the file.

Each read/write operation causes DOS to increment the file pointer by the number of bytes transferred. The file pointer then points to the location of the next record to be accessed. File pointers facilitate both sequential and random processing. For random processing, you can use DOS function 42H (covered in a later section) to set the file pointer to any location in a file.

USING FILE HANDLES TO CREATE DISK FILES

The procedure for writing a disk file is the following:

1. Use an ASCIIZ string to get a file handle from DOS.
2. Use DOS function 3CH to create the file.

3. Use DOS function 40H to write records in the file.

4. At the end, use DOS function 3EH to close the file.

INT 21H, Function 3CH: Create File

For *creating* a new file or overwriting an old file with the same name, first use DOS function 3CH. Load the CX with the required file attribute (covered in Chapter 16) and the DX with the address of the ASCIIZ string (where DOS is to deliver the new file). Here's an example that creates a normal file on drive D with attribute 0:

```
PATHNM1 DB   'D:\ACCOUNTS.FIL',00H
HANDLE1 DW   ?
        . . .
        MOV  AH,3CH        ;Request create file
        MOV  CX,00         ;Normal attribute
        LEA  DX,PATHNM1    ;ASCIIZ string
        INT  21H           ;Call DOS
        JC   error         ;Exit if error
        MOV  HANDLE1,AX    ;Save handle in word
```

For a valid operation, DOS creates a directory entry with the given attribute, clears the carry flag, and sets the handle for the file in the AX. Use this file handle for all subsequent disk operations. The named file is opened with its file pointer set to zero and is now available for writing. If a file with the given name already exists in the path, the operation sets up a zero length for overwriting the new file on the old one.

For error conditions, the operation sets the carry flag and returns a code in the AX: 03, 04, or 05 (see Figure 17–1). Code 05 means that either the directory is full or the referenced filename has the read-only attribute. Be sure to check the carry flag first. For example, creating a file probably delivers handle 05 to the AX, which could easily be confused with error code 05, access denied. Related services for creating a file are 5AH and 5BH, covered in Chapter 18.

INT 21H, Function 40H: Write Record

For *writing* records on disk, use DOS function 40H. Load the BX with the stored file handle, the CX with the number of bytes to write, and the DX with the address of the output area. The following example uses the file handle from the preceding create operation to write a 256-byte record from OUTREC:

```
HANDLE1 DW   ?
OUTREC  DB   256 DUP(' ')  ;Output area
        . . .
        MOV  AH,40H        ;Request write record
        MOV  BX,HANDLE1    ;File handle
        MOV  CX,256        ;Record length
        LEA  DX,OUTREC     ;Address of output area
        INT  21H           ;Call DOS
        JC   error2        ;Test for error
```

```
CMP   AX,256        ;All bytes written?
JNE   error3
```

A valid operation writes the record onto disk, increments the file pointer, clears the carry flag, and sets the AX to the number of bytes actually written. A full disk may cause the number written to differ from the number requested, although DOS does not report this condition as an error. An invalid operation sets the carry flag and returns to the AX error code 05 (access denied) or 06 (invalid handle).

INT 21H, Function 3EH: Close File

When you have finished writing a file, you have to close it. Load the file handle in the BX, and use DOS function 3EH:

```
MOV   AH,3EH        ;Request close
MOV   BX,HANDLE1    ;File handle
INT   21H          ;Call DOS
```

A successful close operation writes any remaining records still in the memory buffer and updates the FAT and the directory with the date and file size. An unsuccessful operation sets the carry flag and returns the only possible error code in the AX, 06 (invalid handle).

Program: Using a File Handle to Create a File

The program in Figure 17–2 creates a file from names that a user enters from a keyboard. Its major procedures are the following:

- C10CREA   Uses function 3CH to create the file and saves the handle in a data item named HANDLE.
- D10PROC   Accepts input from the keyboard and clears positions from the end of the name to the end of the input area.
- F10WRIT   Uses function 40H to write records.
- G10CLSE   At the end of processing, uses function 3EH to close the file in order to create a proper directory entry.

The input area is 30 bytes, followed by 2 bytes for the Enter (0DH) and Line Feed (0AH) characters, for 32 bytes in all. The program writes the 32 bytes as a fixed-length record. You could omit the Enter/Line Feed characters, but you should include them if you want to sort the records in the file, since the DOS SORT program requires these characters to indicate the end of records. For this example, the SORT command to sort the records from NAMEFILE.DAT into ascending sequence in NAMEFILE.SRT could be

```
SORT D:<NAMEFILE.DAT >NAMEFILE.SRT
```

The program in Figure 17–3 reads and displays the contents of NAMEFILE.SRT. Note two points: (1) The Enter/Line Feed characters are included after each record only to facilitate the sort and could otherwise be omitted. (2) The records could be of variable length,

```
        TITLE     P17HANCR (EXE)  Create disk file of names
                  .MODEL  SMALL
                  .STACK  64
        ; -------------------------------------------------
                  .DATA
        NAMEPAR   LABEL   BYTE                  ;Parameter list:
        MAXLEN    DB      30                    ;Maximum length
        NAMELEN   DB      ?                     ;Actual length
        NAMEREC   DB      30 DUP(' '), 0DH, 0AH ;Entered name,
                                                ;  CR/LF for writing
        ERRCDE    DB      00                    ;Error indicator
        HANDLE    DW      ?                     ;File handle
        PATHNAM   DB      'D:\NAMEFILE.DAT', 0
        PROMPT    DB      'Name? '
        ROW       DB      01
        OPNMSG    DB      '*** Open error  ***', 0DH, 0AH
        WRTMSG    DB      '*** Write error ***', 0DH, 0AH
        ; -------------------------------------------------
                  .CODE
        BEGIN     PROC    FAR
                  MOV     AX,@data              ;Initialize data
                  MOV     DS,AX                 ;  segment
                  MOV     ES,AX
                  MOV     AX,0600H
                  CALL    Q10SCR                ;Clear screen
                  CALL    Q20CURS               ;Set cursor
                  CALL    C10CREA               ;Create file, set DTA
                  CMP     ERRCDE,00             ;Create error?
                  JZ      A20LOOP               ;  yes, continue
                  JMP     A90                   ;  no, exit
        A20LOOP:
                  CALL    D10PROC
                  CMP     NAMELEN,00            ;End of input?
                  JNE     A20LOOP               ;  no, continue
                  CALL    G10CLSE               ;  yes, close,
        A90:      MOV     AX,4C00H              ;Exit to DOS
                  INT     21H
        BEGIN     ENDP
        ;                 Create disk file:
        ;                 -----------------
        C10CREA   PROC    NEAR
                  MOV     AH,3CH                ;Request create
                  MOV     CX,00                 ;Normal
                  LEA     DX,PATHNAM
                  INT     21H
                  JC      C20                   ;Error?
                  MOV     HANDLE,AX             ;  no, save handle
                  RET
        C20:                                    ;  yes, display
                  LEA     DX,OPNMSG             ;  error message
                  CALL    X10ERR
                  RET
        C10CREA   ENDP
        ;                 Accept input:
        ;                 ------------
        D10PROC   PROC    NEAR
                  MOV     AH,40H                ;Request display
                  MOV     BX,01                 ;Handle
                  MOV     CX,06                 ;Length of prompt
                  LEA     DX,PROMPT             ;Display prompt
                  INT     21H

                  MOV     AH,0AH                ;Request input
                  LEA     DX,NAMEPAR            ;Accept name
```

Figure 17–2   Using a Handle to Create a File

```
              INT      21H
              CMP      NAMELEN,00       ;Is there a name?
              JZ       D90              ;  no, exit
              MOV      AL,20H           ;Blank for storing
              SUB      CH,CH
              MOV      CL,NAMELEN       ;Length
              LEA      DI,NAMEREC
              ADD      DI,CX            ;Address + length
              NEG      CX               ;Calculate remaining
              ADD      CX,30            ;  length
              REP STOSB                 ;Set to blank
              CALL     F10WRIT          ;Write disk record
              CALL     E10SCRL          ;Check for scroll
D90:
              RET
D10PROC       ENDP
;                       Check for scroll:
;                       ----------------
E10SCRL       PROC     NEAR
              CMP      ROW,18           ;Bottom of screen?
              JAE      E10              ;  yes, bypass
              INC      ROW              ;  no, add to row
              JMP      E90
E10:
              MOV      AX,0601H         ;Scroll one row
              CALL     Q10SCR
E90:          CALL     Q20CURS          ;Reset cursor
              RET
E10SCRL       ENDP
;                       Write disk record:
;                       ----------------
F10WRIT       PROC     NEAR
              MOV      AH,40H           ;Request write
              MOV      BX,HANDLE
              MOV      CX,32            ;30 for name + 2 for CR/LF
              LEA      DX,NAMEREC
              INT      21H
              JNC      F20              ;Valid write?
              LEA      DX,WRTMSG        ;  no,
              CALL     X10ERR           ;  call error routine
              MOV      NAMELEN,00
F20:
              RET
F10WRIT       ENDP
;                       Close disk file:
;                       --------------
G10CLSE       PROC     NEAR
              MOV      NAMEREC,1AH      ;Set EOF mark
              CALL     F10WRIT
              MOV      AH,3EH           ;Request close
              MOV      BX,HANDLE
              INT      21H
              RET
G10CLSE  ENDP
;                       Scroll screen:
;                       ------------
Q10SCR        PROC     NEAR             ;AX set on entry
              MOV      BH,1EH           ;Set yellow on blue
              MOV      CX,0000
              MOV      DX,184FH
              INT      10H              ;Scroll
              RET
Q10SCR        ENDP
```

Figure 17–2   (continued)

```
;                       Set cursor:
;                       ----------
Q20CURS    PROC         NEAR
           MOV          AH,02H               ;Request
           MOV          BH,00                ;  set cursor
           MOV          DH,ROW               ;Row
           MOV          DL,00                ;Column
           INT          10H
           RET
Q20CURS    ENDP
;                       Display disk error message:
;                       --------------------------
X10ERR     PROC         NEAR                 ;DX contains
           MOV          AH,40H               ;  address of message
           MOV          BX,01
           MOV          CX,21                ;Length
           INT          21H
           MOV          ERRCDE,01            ;Set error code
           RET
X10ERR     ENDP
           END          BEGIN
```

Figure 17–2   (continued)

only up to the end of the names; this would involve some extra programming, as you'll see later.

USING FILE HANDLES TO READ DISK FILES

In this section, we cover the requirements for opening and reading disk files using file handles. The procedure for reading a disk file is the following:

1. Use an ASCIIZ string to get a file handle from DOS.
2. Use DOS function 3DII to open the file.
3. Use DOS function 3FH to read records from the file.
4. At the end, use DOS function 3EH to close the file.

INT 21H, Function 3DH: Open File

If your program is to read a file, first use DOS function 3DH to open it. This operation checks that the file actually exists. Load the DX with the address of the required ASCIIZ string, and set the AL with an access code:

BITS	REQUEST
0–2	000 = read only
	001 = write only
	010 = read/write
3	Reserved
4–6	Sharing mode
7	Inheritance flag

In writing a file, be sure to use function 3CH to create the file, not function 3DH to open it. The following example opens a file for reading:

```
MOV   AH,3DH          ;Request open file
MOV   AL,00           ;Read only
LEA   DX,PATHNM1      ;ASCIIZ string
INT   21H             ;Call DOS
JC    error4          ;Exit if error
MOV   HANDLE2,AX      ;Save handle in word
```

If a file with the given name exists, the operation sets the record length to 1 (which you can override), assumes the file's current attribute, sets the file pointer to 0 (the start of the file), clears the carry flag, and sets a handle for the file in the AX. Use this file handle for all subsequent operations.

If the file does not exist, the operation sets the carry flag and returns an error code in the AX: 02, 03, 04, 05, or 12 (see Figure 17–1). Be sure to check the carry flag first. For example, creating a file probably delivers handle 05 to the AX, which could easily be confused with error code 05, access denied.

INT 21H, Function 3FH: Read Record

To read records, use DOS function 3FH. Load the file handle in the BX, the number of bytes to read in the CX, and the address of the input area in the DX. The following code reads a 512-byte record:

```
HANDLE2 DW   ?
INPREC  DB   512 DUP(' ')
        ...
        MOV   AH,3FH          ;Request read record
        MOV   BX,HANDLE2      ;File handle
        MOV   CX,512          ;Record length
        LEA   DX,INPREC       ;address of input area
        INT   21H             ;Call DOS
        JC    error5          ;Test for error
        CMP   AX,00           ;Zero bytes read?
        JE    endfile
```

A valid operation delivers the record to the program, clears the carry flag, and sets the AX to the number of bytes actually read. Zero in the AX means an attempt to read from the end of the file; this is a warning, not an error. An invalid read sets the carry flag and returns to the AX error code 05 (access denied) or 06 (invalid handle).

Since DOS limits the number of files open at one time, a program that successively reads a number of files should close them as soon as possible.

Program: Using a File Handle to Read a File

The program in Figure 17–3 reads the file created by the program in Figure 17–2 and sorted by the DOS SORT command. Here are the main procedures:

- E10OPEN   Uses DOS function 3DH to open the file and saves the handle in a data item named HANDLE,

```
TITLE      P17HANRD (EXE)  Read disk records sequentially
           .MODEL  SMALL
           .STACK  64
;  -------------------------------------------------------
           .DATA
ENDCDE     DB      00                   ;End process indicator
HANDLE     DW      ?
IOAREA     DB      32 DUP(' ')
OPENMSG    DB      '*** Open error ***', 0DH, 0AH
PATHNAM    DB      'D:\NAMEFILE.SRT',0
READMSG    DB      '*** Read error ***', 0DH, 0AH
ROW        DB      00
; -------------------------------------------------------
           .CODE
BEGIN      PROC    FAR
           MOV     AX,@data             ;Initialize
           MOV     DS,AX                ;  segment
           MOV     ES,AX                ;  registers
           MOV     AX,0600H
           CALL    Q10SCR               ;Clear screen
           CALL    Q20CURS              ;Set cursor
           CALL    E10OPEN              ;Open file, set DTA
           CMP     ENDCDE,00            ;Valid open?
           JNZ     A90                  ;  no, exit
A20LOOP:
           CALL    F10READ              ;Read disk record
           CMP     ENDCDE,00            ;Normal read?
           JNZ     A90                  ;  no, exit
           CALL    G10DISP              ;  yes, display name,
           JMP     A20LOOP              ;  continue
A90:                                    ;End processing,
           MOV     AX,4C00H             ;  exit to DOS
           INT     21H
BEGIN      ENDP
;                  Open file:
;                  .......
E10OPEN    PROC    NEAR
           MOV     AH,3DH               ;Request open
           MOV     AL,00                ;Normal file
           LEA     DX,PATHNAM
           INT     21H
           JC      E20                  ;Error?
           MOV     HANDLE,AX            ;  no, save handle
           RET
E20:
           MOV     ENDCDE,01            ;  yes,
           LEA     DX,OPENMSG           ;  display
           CALL    X10ERR               ;  error message
           RET
E10OPEN    ENDP
;                  Read disk record:
;                  ----------------
F10READ    PROC    NEAR
           MOV     AH,3FH               ;Request read
           MOV     BX,HANDLE
           MOV     CX,32                ;30 for name, 2 for CR/LF
           LEA     DX,IOAREA
           INT     21H
           JC      F20                  ;Error on read?
           CMP     AX,00                ;End of file?
           JE      F30
           CMP     IOAREA,1AH           ;EOF marker?
           JE      F30                  ;  yes, exit
           JMP     F90
```

Figure 17–3　Using a Handle to Read a File

```
F20:                                         ;  no,
            LEA     DX,READMSG               ;  invalid read
            CALL    X10ERR
F30:
            MOV     ENDCDE,01                ;Force end
F90:        RET
F10READ     ENDP
;                   Display name:
;                   ------------
G10DISP     PROC    NEAR
            MOV     AH,40H                   ;Request display
            MOV     BX,01                    ;Set handle
            MOV     CX,32                    ;  and length
            LEA     DX,IOAREA
            INT     21H
            CMP     ROW,20                   ;Bottom of screen?
            JAE     G80                      ;  yes, bypass
            INC     ROW                      ;  no, increment row
            JMP     G90
G80:
            MOV     AX,0601H
            CALL    Q10SCR                   ;Scroll
            CALL    Q20CURS                  ;Set cursor
G90:        RET
G10DISP     ENDP
;                   Scroll screen:
;                   -------------
Q10SCR      PROC    NEAR                     ;AX set on entry
            MOV     BH,1EH                   ;Set color
            MOV     CX,0000
            MOV     DX,184FH                 ;Request scroll
            INT     10H
            RET
Q10SCR      ENDP
;                   Set cursor:
;                   ----------
Q20CURS     PROC    NEAR
            MOV     AH,02H                   ;Request set
            MOV     BH,00                    ;  cursor
            MOV     DH,ROW                   ;  row
            MOV     DL,00                    ;  column
            INT     10H
            RET
Q20CURS     ENDP
;                   Display disk error message:
;                   --------------------------
X10ERR      PROC    NEAR
            MOV     AH,40H                   ;DX contains address
            MOV     BX,01                    ;Handle
            MOV     CX,20                    ;Length
            INT     21H                      ;  of message
            RET
X10ERR      ENDP
            END     BEGIN
```

Figure 17–3   (continued)

- **F10READ**   Issues DOS function 3FH, which uses the handle to read the records.
- **G10DISP**   Displays the records and scrolls the screen. Since Enter and Line Feed characters already follow each record, the program does not have to advance the cursor when displaying records.

PROCESSING ASCII FILES

The preceding examples created files and read them, but you may also want to process ASCII files created by DOS or an editor. All you need to know are the organization of the directory and FAT and the way in which the system stores data in a sector. DOS stores your data in an .ASM file, for example, exactly the way you key it in, including the characters for Tab (09H), Enter (0DH), and Line Feed (0AH). To conserve disk space, DOS does not store spaces that appear on the screen immediately preceding a Tab character or spaces on a line to the right of an Enter character. The following illustrates an assembly language instruction as it would be entered on a keyboard:

```
<Tab>MOV<Tab>AH,09<Enter>
```

The hex representation for this ASCII data would be

```
094D4F560941482C30390D0A
```

where 09H is Tab, 0DH is Enter, and 0AH is Line Feed. When TYPE or an editor read the file, the Tab, Enter, and Line Feed characters automatically adjust the cursor on the screen.

Let's now examine the program in Figure 17–4, which reads and displays the file P17HANRD.ASM (from Figure 17–3), one sector at a time. The program performs much the same functions as DOS TYPE, where each line displays everything up to the Enter/Line Feed characters. Since lines in an ASCII file are of variable length, you have to scan for the end of each line before displaying it. Scrolling can be a problem. If you perform no special tests to determine whether you have reached the bottom of screen, the operation automatically displays new lines over old and, if the old line is longer, old characters still appear to the right. For proper scrolling, you have to count rows and test whether you are at the bottom of the screen.

The program reads a full sector of data into SECTOR. The procedure G10XFER transfers one byte at a time from SECTOR to DISAREA, where the characters are to be displayed. When a Line Feed is encountered, the routine displays the contents of DISAREA up to and including the Line Feed. (The display screen accepts Tab characters (09H) and automatically sets the cursor on the next location evenly divisible by eight.)

The program has to check for the end of a sector (to read another sector) and the end of the display area. For conventional ASCII files, such as .ASM files, each line is relatively short and is sure to end with Enter/Line Feed. Non-ASCII files, such as .EXE and .OBJ files, do not have lines, so the program has to check for the end of DISAREA to avoid crashing. The program is intended to display only ASCII files, but the test for the end is insurance against unexpected files.

These are the steps in G10XFER:

1. Initialize the address of SECTOR and the address of DISAREA.
2. If at the end of SECTOR, read the next sector. If at the end-of-file, exit; otherwise initialize the address of SECTOR.

```
TITLE       P17ASCRD (EXE)   Read an ASCII file
            .MODEL  SMALL
            .STACK  64
; --------------------------------------------------------
            .DATA
DISAREA  DB       120 DUP(' ')      ;Display area
ENDCDE   DW       00                ;End process indicator
HANDLE   DW       0                 ;File handle
OPENMSG  DB       '*** Open error ***'
PATHNAM  DB       'D:\17HANRED.ASM', 0
ROW      DB       00
SECTOR   DB       512 DUP(' ')      ;Input area
; --------------------------------------------------------
            .CODE
BEGIN    PROC     FAR               ;Main procedure
         MOV      AX,@data          ;Initialize
         MOV      DS,AX             ;  segment
         MOV      ES,AX             ;  registers
         MOV      AX,0600H
         CALL     Q10SCR            ;Clear screen
         CALL     Q20CURS           ;Set cursor
         CALL     E10OPEN           ;Open file
         CMP      ENDCDE,00         ;Valid open?
         JNE      A90               ;  no, exit
A20LOOP:                            ;  yes, continue
         CALL     R10READ           ;Read 1st disk sector
         CMP      ENDCDE,00         ;End of file, no data?
         JE       A90               ;  yes, exit
         CALL     G10XFER           ;Display and read
A90:
         MOV      AH,3EH            ;Request close file
         MOV      BX,HANDLE
         INT      21H
         MOV      AX,4C00H          ;Exit to DOS
         INT      21H
BEGIN    ENDP
;                 Open disk file:
;                 --------------
E10OPEN  PROC     NEAR
         MOV      AH,3DH            ;Request open
         MOV      AL,00             ;Read only
         LEA      DX,PATHNAM
         INT      21H
         JNC      E20               ;Test carry flag,
         CALL     X10ERR            ;  error if set
         RET
E20:
         MOV      HANDLE,AX         ;Save handle
         RET
E10OPEN  ENDP
;                 Transfer data to display line:
;                 ----------------------------
G10XFER  PROC     NEAR
         CLD                        ;Set left to right
         LEA      SI,SECTOR
G20:
         LEA      DI,DISAREA
G30:
         LEA      DX,SECTOR+512
         CMP      SI,DX             ;End of sector?
         JNE      G40               ;  no, bypass
         CALL     R10READ           ;  yes, read next
         CMP      ENDCDE,00         ;End of file?
```

Figure 17–4 Reading an ASCII File

```
                  JE      G80                  ; yes, exit
                  LEA     SI,SECTOR
         G40:
                  LEA     DX,DISAREA+80
                  CMP     DI,DX                ;End of DISAREA?
                  JB      G50                  ; no, bypass
                  MOV     [DI],0D0AH           ; yes, set CR/LF,
                  CALL    H10DISP              ; and display
                  LEA     DI,DISAREA
         G50:
                  LODSB                        ;[SI] to AL, INC SI
                  STOSB                        ;AL to [DI], INC DI
                  CMP     AL,1AH               ;End of file?
                  JE      G80                  ; yes, exit
                  CMP     AL,0AH               ;Line feed?
                  JNE     G30                  ; no, loop
                  CALL    H10DISP              ; yes, display
                  JMP     G20
         G80:
                  CALL    H10DISP              ;Display last line
         G90:     RET
         G10XFER  ENDP
         ;                 Display line:
         ;                 ------------
         H10DISP  PROC    NEAR
                  MOV     AH,40H               ;Request display
                  MOV     BX,01                ;Handle
                  LEA     CX,DISAREA           ;Calculate
                  NEG     CX                   ; length of
                  ADD     CX,DI                ; line
                  LEA     DX,DISAREA
                  INT     21H
                  CMP     ROW,22               ;Bottom of screen?
                  JAE     H20                  ; no, exit
                  INC     ROW
                  JMP     H90
         H20:
                  MOV     AX,0601H                 ;Scroll
                  CALL    Q10SCR
                  CALL    Q20CURS
         H90:     RET
         H10DISP  ENDP
         ;                 Scroll screen:
         ;                 -------------
         Q10SCR   PROC    NEAR                 ;AX set on entry
                  MOV     BH,1EH               ;Set color attribute
                  MOV     CX,0000              ;Scroll
                  MOV     DX,184FH
                  INT     10H
                  RET
         Q10SCR   ENDP
         ;                 Set cursor:
         ;                 ----------
         Q20CURS  PROC    NEAR
                  MOV     AH,02H               ;Request set
                  MOV     BH,00                ; cursor
                  MOV     DH,ROW
                  MOV     DL,00
                  INT     10H
                  RET
         Q20CURS  ENDP
         ;                 Read disk sector:
         ;                 ----------------
```

Figure 17–4   (continued)

```
R10READ   PROC    NEAR
          MOV     AH,3FH              ;Request read
          MOV     BX,HANDLE           ;Device
          MOV     CX,512              ;Length
          LEA     DX,SECTOR           ;Buffer
          INT     21H
          MOV     ENDCDE,AX
          RET
R10READ   ENDP
;                 Display disk error message:
;                 -------------------------
X10ERR    PROC    NEAR
          MOV     AH,40H              ;Request display
          MOV     BX,01               ;Handle
          MOV     CX,18               ;Length
          LEA     DX,OPENMSG
          INT     21H
          MOV     ENDCDE,01           ;Error indicator
          RET
X10ERR    ENDP
          END     BEGIN
```

Figure 17–4   (continued)

3. If at the end of DISAREA, force an Enter/Line Feed, display the line, and initialize DISAREA.
4. Get a character from SECTOR and store it in DISAREA.
5. If the character is end-of-file (1AH), exit.
6. If the character is Line Feed (0AH), display the line and go to step 2; otherwise go to step 3.

Try running this program under DEBUG with an appropriate drive number and ASCII file. After each disk input, display the contents of the input area and see how DOS has formatted your records. An enhancement to this program would be to prompt a user to enter the filename and extension via the keyboard.

USING FILE HANDLES FOR RANDOM PROCESSING

The preceding discussion on processing disk files sequentially is adequate for creating a file, for printing its contents, and for making changes to small files. Some applications, however, involve accessing a particular record on a file, such as information on a few employees or inventory parts.

To update a file with new data, a program that is restricted to sequential processing may have to read every record in the file up to the one that is required. For example, to access the 300th record in a file, sequential processing could involve reading through the preceding 299 records before delivering the 300th (although the system could begin at a specific record number).

The general solution is to use *random processing*, in which a program can directly access any given record in a file. Although a file is *created* sequentially, you may *access* records sequentially or randomly.

When a program first requests a random record, the operation uses the directory to locate the sector in which the record resides, reads the entire sector from disk into a buffer, and delivers the required record to the program.

In the next example, records are 128 bytes long and four to a sector. A request for random record number 21 causes the following four records to be read into the buffer:

record #20	record #21	record #22	record #23

When the program requests the next random record—say number 23—the operation first checks the buffer. Since the record is already there, it is transferred directly to the program. If the program requests a record number that is not in the buffer, the operation uses the directory to locate the record, reads the entire sector into the buffer, and delivers the record to the program. Accordingly, it is usually more efficient to request random record numbers that are close together in the file.

INT 21H, Function 42H: Move File Pointer

DOS maintains a file pointer that the open operation initializes to zero and subsequent sequential reads and writes increment for each record processed. You can use DOS function 42H (Move File Pointer) to set the file pointer anywhere within a file and then use other services for random retrieval or updating.

Set the file handle in the BX and the required offset as bytes in the CX:DX. For a move up to 65,535 bytes, set zero in the CX and the offset value in the DX. Also, set a method code in the AL that tells the operation the point from which to take the offset:

- 00   Take the offset from the start of the file.
- 01   Take the offset from the current location of the file pointer, which could be anywhere within the file, including at the start.
- 02   Take the offset from the end-of-file. You can use this method code for adding records to the end-of-file. Or you can determine the file size by setting the CX:DX to zero and using method code 02.

The following example moves the pointer 1,024 bytes from the start of a file:

```
MOV  AH,42H       ;Request move pointer

MOV  AL,00        ; to start of file

LEA  BX,HANDLE1   ;Set file handle

MOV  CX,00

MOV  DX,1024      ;1024-byte offset

INT  21H          ;Call DOS

JC   error
```

A valid operation clears the carry flag and delivers the new pointer location in the DX:AX. You may then perform a read or write operation for random processing. An invalid operation sets the carry flag and returns in the AX code 01 (invalid method code) or 06 (invalid handle).

Program: Reading a Disk File Randomly

The program in Figure 17–5 reads the file created in Figure 17–2. By keying in a relative record number that is within the bounds of the file, a user can request any record in the file to be displayed on the screen. If the file contains 24 records, then valid record numbers are 01 through 24. A number entered from the keyboard is in ASCII format and in this case should be only one or two digits.

The program is organized as follows:

C10OPEN   Opens the file and gets the file handle.

D10RECN   Accepts a record number from the keyboard and checks its length in the parameter list. There are three possible lengths:

00   End of processing requested

01   One-digit request, stored in the AL

02   Two-digit request, stored in the AX

The procedure has to convert the ASCII number to binary. Since the value is in the AX, the AAD instruction works well for this purpose. The system recognizes location 0 as the beginning of a file. The program deducts 1 from the actual number (so that a user request, for example, for record 1 becomes record 0), multiplies the value by 16 (the length of records in the file), and stores the result in a field called RECINDX.

As an example, if the entered number is ASCII 12, the AX would contain 3132. An AND instruction converts this value to 0102, AAD further converts it to 000C (12), and SHL effectively multiplies the number by 16 to get C0 (192). An improvement would be to validate the input number.

F10READ   Uses function 42H and the relative record location from RECINDX to set the file pointer and issues function 3FH to deliver the required record to the program in IOAREA.

G10DISP   Displays the retrieved record.

DISK SERVICES USING FILE CONTROL BLOCKS

We now cover the DOS FCB services for creating disk files and processing them sequentially and randomly. All of these services were introduced by the first version of DOS and are available under all versions.

Disk processing for the DOS FCB services involves defining a file control block (FCB) that defines the file and a disk transfer area (DTA) that defines records. You provide DOS with the DTA address for all disk input/output operations. Note that FCBs do not use file handles and do not use the error codes listed in Figure 17–1; they also do not clear or set the carry flag to indicate success or failure. (FCBs also exist in the PSP, which DOS installs immediately preceding programs loaded into memory for execution.)

```
TITLE       P17RANRD (EXE)  Read disk records randomly
            .MODEL  SMALL
            .STACK  64
; ----------------------------------------------------------
            .DATA
HANDLE      DW      ?                     ;File handle
RECINDX     DW      ?                     ;Record index
ERRCDE      DB      00                    ;Read error indicator
PROMPT      DB      'Record number? $'
IOAREA      DB      32 DUP(' ')           ;Disk record area
PATHNAM     DB      'D:\NAMEFILE.SRT',0
OPENMSG     DB      '*** Open error ***', 0DH, 0AH
READMSG     DB      '*** Read error ***', 0DH, 0AH
ROW         DB      00
COL         DB      00

RECDPAR     LABEL   BYTE                  ;Input parameter list:
MAXLEN      DB      3                     ;   maximum length
ACTLEN      DB      ?                     ;   actual length
RECDNO      DB      3 DUP(' ')            ;   record number

;----------------------------------------------------------
            .CODE
.386
BEGIN       PROC    FAR
            MOV     AX,@data              ;Initialize
            MOV     DS,AX                 ;   segment
            MOV     ES,AX                 ;   registers
            MOV     AX,0600H
            CALL    Q10SCRN               ;Clear screen
            CALL    Q20CURS               ;Set cursor
            CALL    C10OPEN               ;Open file
            CMP     ERRCDE,00             ;Valid open?
            JNZ     A90                   ;   no, exit
A20LOOP:
            CALL    D10RECN               ;Request record #
            CMP     ACTLEN,00             ;Any more requests?
            JE      A90                   ;   no, exit
            CALL    F10READ               ;Read disk record
            CMP     ERRCDE,00             ;Normal read?
            JNZ     A30                   ;   no, bypass
            CALL    G10DISP               ;   yes, display name,
A30:
            JMP     A20LOOP               ;   continue
A90:                                      ;
            MOV     AX,4C00H              ;Exit to DOS
            INT     21H
BEGIN       ENDP
;                   Open file:
;                   ---------
C10OPEN     PROC    NEAR
            MOV     AH,3DH                ;Request open
            MOV     AL,00                 ;Normal file
            LEA     DX,PATHNAM
            INT     21H
            JC      C20                   ;Error?
            MOV     HANDLE,AX             ;   no, save handle
            RET
C20:
            MOV     ERRCDE,01             ;   yes,
            LEA     DX,OPENMSG            ;   display
            CALL    X10ERR                ;   error message
            RET
```

Figure 17–5   Reading a Disk File Randomly

```
C10OPEN     ENDP
;                       Get record number:
;                       ------------------
D10RECN     PROC    NEAR
            MOV     AH,09H              ;Request display prompt
            LEA     DX,PROMPT
            INT     21H

            MOV     AH,0AH              ;Request input
            LEA     DX,RECDPAR          ;  of record number
            INT     21H
            CMP     ACTLEN,01           ;Check length 0, 1, 2
            JB      D40                 ;Length 0, terminate
            JA      D20
            XOR     AH,AH               ;Length 1
            MOV     AL,RECDNO
            JMP     D30
D20:
            MOV     AH,RECDNO           ;Length 2
            MOV     AL,RECDNO+1
D30:
            AND     AX,0F0FH            ;Clear ASCII 3s
            AAD                         ;Convert to binary
            DEC     AX                  ;Adjust (1st record is 0)
            SHL     AX,05               ;Multiply by 16
            MOV     RECINDX,AX          ;Save index
D40:
            MOV     COL,20
            CALL    Q20CURS
            RET
D10RECN     ENDP

;                       Read disk record randomly:
;                       -------------------------
F10READ     PROC    NEAR
            MOV     AX,4200H            ;Request set file pointer
            MOV     AL,00               ;Start of file
            MOV     BX,HANDLE           ;
            MOV     CX,00               ;
            MOV     DX,RECINDX
            INT     21H
            JC      F20                 ;Error condition?
                                        ;  yes, bypass
            MOV     AH,3FH              ;Request read
            MOV     BX,HANDLE
            MOV     CX,32               ;30 for name, 2 for CR/LF
            LEA     DX,IOAREA
            INT     21H
            JC      F20                 ;Error on read?
            CMP     IOAREA,1AH          ;EOF marker?
            JE      F30                 ;  yes, exit
            JMP     F90
F20:                                    ;  no,
            LEA     DX,READMSG          ;  invalid read
            CALL    X10ERR
F30:
            MOV     ERRCDE,01           ;Force end
F90:        RET
F10READ     ENDP
;                       Display name:
;                       ------------
G10DISP     PROC    NEAR
            MOV     AH,40H              ;Request display
            MOV     BX,01               ;Set handle
            MOV     CX,32               ;  and length
```

Figure 17–5   (continued)

```
                    LEA      DX,IOAREA
                    INT      21H
                    MOV      COL,00              ;Clear column
                    CMP      ROW,20              ;Bottom of screen?
                    JAE      G80                 ;  yes, bypass
                    INC      ROW                 ;  no, increment row
                    JMP      G90
          G80:
                    MOV      AX,0601H
                    CALL     Q10SCRN             ;Scroll
                    CALL     Q20CURS             ;Set cursor
          G90:      RET
          G10DISP   ENDP
          ;                  Scroll screen:
          ;                  ------------
          Q10SCRN   PROC     NEAR                ;AX set on entry
                    MOV      BH,1EH              ;Set color
                    MOV      CX,0000
                    MOV      DX,184FH            ;Request scroll
                    INT      10H
                    RET
          Q10SCRN   ENDP
          ;                  Set cursor:
          ;                  ----------
          Q20CURS   PROC     NEAR
                    MOV      AH,02               ;Request set
                    MOV      BH,00               ;  cursor
                    MOV      DH,ROW              ;  row
                    MOV      DL,COL              ;  column
                    INT      10H
                    RET
          Q20CURS   ENDP
          ;                  Display disk error message:
          ;                  --------------------------
          X10ERR    PROC     NEAR
                    MOV      AH,40H              ;DX contains address
                    MOV      DX,01               ;Handle
                    MOV      CX,20               ;Length
                    INT      21H                 ;  of message
                    INC      ROW
                    RET
          X10ERR    ENDP
                    END      BEGIN
```

Figure 17–5   (continued)

File Control Block

Since the FCB method does not support path names, its use is primarily for processing files in the current directory. The FCB, which you define in the data area, contains the following information about the file and its records (you initialize bytes 00–15 and 32–36, whereas DOS sets bytes 17–31):

0   *Disk drive.* For most FCB operations, 00 is the default drive, 01 is drive A, 02 is drive B, and so forth.

1–8   *Filename.* The name of the file, left adjusted with trailing blanks, if any.

9–11   *Filename extension.* A subdivision of filename for further identification, such as .DOC or .ASM, left adjusted if fewer than three characters. When you create a file, DOS stores its filename and extension in the directory.

12–13   *Current block number.* A block consists of 128 records. Read and write operations use the current block number and current record number (byte 32) to locate a particular record. The number is relative to the beginning of the file, where the first block is 0, the second is 1, and so forth. An open operation sets this entry to zero. DOS handles the current block number automatically, although you may change it for random processing.

14–15   *Logical record size.* An open operation initializes the record size to 128 (80H). After an open and before any read or write, you may change this entry to your own required record size.

16–19   *File size.* When a program creates a file, DOS calculates and stores its size (number of records × record size) in the directory. An open operation subsequently extracts the size from the directory and stores it in this field. Your program may read the field, but should not change it.

20–21   *Date.* DOS records the date in the directory when the file was created or last updated. An open operation extracts the date from the directory and stores it in this field.

22–31   *Reserved by DOS.*

32   *Current record number.* This entry is the current record number (0–127) within the current block. (See bytes 12–13.) The system uses the current block and record to locate records in the file. Although open initializes the record number to zero, you may set this field to begin sequential processing at any number between 0 and 127.

33–36   *Relative record number.* For random read/write, this entry must contain a relative record number. For example, to read record 25 (19H) randomly, set the entry to 19000000H. For random processing, the system automatically converts the relative record number to the current block and record. Because of the limit on the maximum file size (1,073,741,824 bytes), a file with a short record size can contain more records and may have a higher maximum relative record number than a file with a longer record size. If the record size is greater than 64, byte 36 always contains 00.

Preceding the FCB is an optional seven-byte extension, which may be used for processing files with special attributes. To use the extension, code the first byte with FFH, the second byte with the file attribute (described in Chapter 16), and the remaining five bytes with hex zeros.

USING FCBs TO CREATE DISK FILES

For each disk file referenced, a program using original DOS disk services defines an FCB. Disk operations require the address of the FCB in the DX register and use this address to access fields within the FCB. Operations include create file, set disk transfer area (DTA), write record, and close file.

INT 21H, Function 16H: Create File

On initialization, a program uses INT 21H, function 16H, to create a new file:

```
MOV   AH,16H        ;Request create
LEA   DX,FCBname    ; disk file
INT   21H           ;Call DOS
```

DOS searches the directory for a filename that matches the entry in the FCB. If one is found, DOS reuses the space in the directory, and if none is found, DOS searches for a vacant entry. The operation then initializes the file size to zero and opens the file. The open step checks for available disk space and sets one of the following return codes in the AL: 00H = space is available; FFH = no space is available. Open also initializes the FCB current block number to zero and sets a default value in the FCB record size of 128 (80H) bytes. Before writing a record, you may override this default with your own record size.

The Disk Transfer Area

The disk transfer area (DTA) is the start of the definition of your output record. Since the FCB contains the record size, the DTA does not require a delimiter to indicate the end of the record. Prior to a write operation, use FCB function 1AH to supply DOS with the address of the DTA. Only one DTA may be active at any time. The following code initializes the address of the DTA:

```
MOV   AH,1AH        ;Request set address
LEA   DX,DTAname    ; of DTA
INT   21H           ;Call DOS
```

If a program processes only one disk file, it needs to initialize the DTA only once for its entire execution. If a program processes more than one file, it must initialize the appropriate DTA immediately before each read or write.

INT 21H, Function 15H: Write Record

To write a disk record sequentially, use FCB function 15H:

```
MOV   AH,15H        ;Request write record
LEA   DX,FCBname    ; sequentially
INT   21H           ;Call DOS
```

The write operation uses the information in the FCB and the address of the current DTA. If the record is the size of a sector, the operation writes the record. Otherwise, the operation fills records into a buffer area that is the length of a sector and writes the buffer when it is full. For example, if each record is 128 bytes long, the operation fills the buffer with four records (4 × 128 = 512) and then writes the buffer into an entire disk sector.

On a successful write, DOS increments the FCB file size field (by adding the record size to it) and increments the current record number by 1. When the current record number exceeds 127, the operation sets it to 0 and increments the FCB current block number. (You could also change the current block and record number.) The write operation sets one of the following return codes in the AL: 00H = write was successful; 01H = disk is full; 02H = DTA is too small for the record.

INT 21H, Function 10H: Close File

When you have finished writing records for a file, you may write an end-of-file marker (1AH in the first byte of a special last record; not to be confused with function 1AH) and then use FCB function 10H to close the file:

```
MOV   AH,10H        ;Request close the
LEA   DX,FCBname    ; file
INT   21H           ;Call DOS
```

The close operation writes on disk any partial data still in the DOS disk buffer and updates the directory with the date and file size. One of the following codes is returned to the AL: 00H = close was successful; FFH = file was not in the correct position in the directory, perhaps caused by a user changing a diskette.

USING FCBs FOR SEQUENTIAL READING OF DISK FILES

A program that reads a disk file defines an FCB exactly like the one used to create the file. Sequential read operations include open file, set DTA, read record, and close file.

INT 21H, Function 0FH: Open File

Function 0FH opens an FCB file for input:

```
MOV   AH,0FH        ;Request open
LEA   DX,FCBname    ; the file
INT   21H           ;Call DOS
```

The open operation checks that the directory contains an entry with the filename and extension defined in the FCB. If the entry is not in the directory, the operation returns code FFH in the AL. If the entry is present, the operation returns code 00 in the AL and sets the actual file size, date, current block number (0), and record size (80H) in the FCB. After the open executes, you may override the default record size.

The Disk Transfer Area

The DTA defines an area for the input record, according to the format used to create the file. Use FCB function 1AH to set the address of the DTA, just as you do when you create a disk file.

INT 21H, Function 14H: Read Record

To read a disk record sequentially, use FCB function 14H:

```
MOV   AH,14H          ;Request read record
LEA   DX,FCBname      ; sequentially
INT   21H             ;Call DOS
```

The operation sets one of the following return codes in the AL: 00 = successful read; 01 = end of file, no data was read; 02 = DTA is too small for the record; 03 = end of file, record was read partially and filled out with zeros.

For a successful read, the operation uses the information in the FCB to deliver the disk record, beginning at the address of the DTA. An attempt to read past the last record of the file causes the operation to signal an end-of-file condition that sets the AL to 01H, for which you should test. It's a recommended practice to close an input file after fully reading it, because of the DOS limit on the number of files that may be open at one time.

USING FCBs FOR RANDOM PROCESSING

The requirements for random processing simply involve inserting the required record number in the FCB relative record field (bytes 33–36) and issuing a random read or write command. To locate a record randomly, the system automatically converts the relative record number to the current block (bytes 12–13) and current record (byte 32).

INT 21H, Function 21H: Read Record Randomly

The open operation and setting of the DTA are the same for both random and sequential processing. Consider a program that is to read relative record number 05 directly. Insert the number 05 into the FCB field for the relative record number, and request function 21H:

```
MOV   AH,21H          ;Request
LEA   DX,FCBname      ; random read
INT   21H             ;Call DOS
```

The read operation returns one of the following codes in the AL: 00 = successful read; 01 = end of file, no more data available; 02 = DTA too small for the record; 03 = record has been read partially and filled out with zeros.

A successful operation converts the relative record number to the current block and record. It uses this value to locate the required disk record and delivers it to the DTA. Faulty responses can be caused by an invalid relative record number or an incorrect address in the DTA or FCB.

INT 21H, Function 22H: Write Record Randomly

The create operation and setting of the DTA are the same for both random and sequential processing. With the relative record number initialized in the FCB, random write uses function 22H:

```
MOV   AH,22H           ;Request random

LEA   DX,FCBname       ; write

INT   21H              ;Call DOS
```

The write operation returns one of the following codes in the AL: 00 = successful write; 01 = disk full; 02 = DTA too small for the record.

RANDOM BLOCK PROCESSING

If a program has sufficient space, one random block operation can write an entire file from the DTA onto disk and can read the entire file from disk into the DTA. You still first open the file and initialize the DTA. You may then begin processing with any valid relative record number and any number of records, although the block must be within the file's range of records.

INT 21H, Function 28H: Write Block Randomly

For a random block write, initialize the required number of records in the CX register, set the starting relative record number in the FCB, and use function 28H:

```
MOV   AH,28H           ;Request random block write

MOV   CX,records       ;Set number of records

LEA   DX,FCBname       ;Address of FCB

INT   21H              ;Call DOS
```

The operation converts the FCB relative record number to the current block and record. It uses this value to determine the starting disk location and sets one of the following return codes in the AL: 00 = successful write of all records; 01 = no records written because of insufficient disk space; 02 = DTA too small for the record. The operation sets the FCB relative record field and the current block and record fields to the next record number.

INT 21H, Function 27H: Read Block Randomly

For a random block read, initialize the required number of records in the CX, and use FCB function 27H:

```
MOV   AH,27H           ;Request random block read

MOV   CX,records       ;Initialize number of records

LEA   DX,FCBname       ;Address of FCB

INT   21H              ;Call DOS
```

The read operation returns one of the following codes in the AL: 00 = successful read of all records; 01 = has read to end of file, last record is complete; 02 = DTA too small for the record, read not completed; 03 = end of file, has read a partial record.

The operation stores in the CX the actual number of records read and sets the FCB relative record field and current block and record fields for the next record.

ABSOLUTE DISK I/O

You can use DOS INT 25H and 26H for *absolute* reads and writes to process a disk directly, for example, in recovering a damaged file. In this case, you do not define file handles or FCBs, and you lose the advantages of directory handling and blocking or deblocking of records that you get with DOS INT 21H. Note that INT 21H, function 44H (covered in Chapter 18), provides a similar service and, according to Microsoft journals, has superseded INT 25H and 26H.

Since these operations treat all records as if they were the size of a sector, they directly access a whole sector or block of sectors. Disk addressing is in terms of relative record number (relative sector). To determine a relative record number on two-sided diskettes with nine sectors per track, count each sector from track 0, sector 1, as follows:

TRACK	SECTOR	RELATIVE RECORD NUMBER
0	1	0 (the first sector on the disk)
0	2	1
1	1	9
1	9	17
2	9	26

A convenient formula for determining the relative record number on diskettes with nine sectors is

$$\text{Relative record number} = (\text{track} \times 9) + (\text{sector} - 1)$$

Thus the relative record number for track 2, sector 9, is

$$(2 \times 9) + (9 - 1) = 18 + 8 = 26$$

Here is the required coding for disk partitions that are less than 32 MBs:

```
MOV   AL,drive#      ;0 for A, 1 for B, etc.

MOV   BX,addr        ;Transfer address

MOV   CX,sectors     ;Number of sectors to read/write

MOV   DX,sector#     ;Beginning relative sector number

INT   25H or 26H     ;DOS absolute read or write

POPF                 ;Pop flags

JC    [error]
```

Absolute disk read/write operations destroy all registers except the segment registers and use the carry flag to indicate a successful (0) or unsuccessful (1) operation. An unsuccessful operation returns one of the following nonzero codes to the AL:

10000000	Attachment failed to respond
01000000	Seek operation failed
00001000	Bad CRC read on diskette
00000100	Requested sector not found
00000011	Attempt to write on write-protected diskette
00000010	Other error

The INT operation pushes the flags onto the stack. Because the original flags are still on the stack upon returning from the operation, you should pop them after checking the carry flag.

Since DOS 4.0, you can use INT 25H and 26H to access disk partitions that exceed 32 megabytes. The AL and CX are still used the same way. The DX is not used, and the BX points to a 10-byte parameter block described as follows:

BYTES	DESCRIPTION
00H–03H	32-bit sector number
04H–05H	Number of sectors to read/write
06H–07H	Offset of buffer
08H–09H	Segment of buffer

KEY POINTS

- Many of the DOS disk services reference an ASCIIZ string that consists of a directory path followed by a byte of hex zeros.
- On errors, many of the DOS disk functions set the carry flag and return an error code in the AX.
- DOS maintains a file pointer for each file that a program is processing. The create and open operations set the value of the file pointer to zero, the file's starting location.
- The create and open functions return a file handle that you use for subsequent file accessing.
- Create function 3CH is used initially when writing a file and open function 3DH initially when reading a file.
- A program that has completed writing a file should close it so that DOS may update the directory.
- A program using original DOS INT 21H functions for disk I/O defines a file control block (FCB) for each file that it accesses.
- An FCB block consists of 128 records. The current block number, combined with the current record number, indicates the disk record to be processed. The entries in the FCB for the current block, record size, file size, and relative record number are stored in reversed-byte sequence.

- The disk transfer area (DTA) is the location of the record that is to be written or read. You have to initialize each DTA in a program prior to execution of a write or read operation.
- DOS INT 25H and 26H provide absolute disk read and write operations, but do not supply automatic directory handling, end-of-file operations, or record blocking and deblocking.

QUESTIONS

Of the following questions, the first 10 concern disk operations involving file handles, and the remainder involve FCB disk operations.

17–1. What are the error return codes for (a) file not found; (b) invalid handle?

17–2. Define an ASCIIZ string named PATH1 for a file named CUST.LST on drive C.

17–3. For the file in Question 17–2, provide the instructions to (a) define an item named CUSTHAN for the file handle; (b) create the file; (c) write a record from CUSTOUT (128 bytes); and (d) close the file. Test for errors.

17–4. For the file in Question 17–3, code the instructions to (a) open the file and (b) read records into CUSTIN. Test for errors.

17–5. Under what circumstances should you close a file that is used only for input?

17–6. Revise the code in Figure 17–4 so that a user at a keyboard can enter a filename, which the program uses to locate the file and to display its contents. Provide for any number of requests and for pressing only the Enter key to cause the input to end.

17–7. Write a program that allows a user to enter part numbers (3 characters), part descriptions (12 characters), and unit prices (xxx xx) on a terminal. The program is to use file handles to create a disk file containing this information. Remember to convert the price from ASCII to binary. Following is sample input data:

PART DESCRIPTION	PRICE
|023|Assemblers	|00315|
|024|Linkages	|00430|
|027|Compilers	|00525|
|049|Compressors	|00920|
|114|Extractors	|11250|
|117|Haulers	|00630|
|122|Lifters	|10520|
|124|Processors	|21335|
|127|Labelers	|00960|
|232|Bailers	|05635|
	999			00000	

17–8. Write a program that displays the contents of the file created in Question 17–7. It will have to convert the binary value for the price to ASCII format.

17–9. Use the file created in Question 17–7 for the following requirements: (a) The program reads the records into a table in memory; (b) a user can enter part number and quantity from the keyboard; (c) the program searches the table for part number; (d) if the part number is found, the program uses the table price to calculate the value of the part (quantity × price); (e) the program displays description and calculated value.

17–10. Revise the program in Question 17–8 so that it does random processing. Define a table of the valid part numbers. Allow a user to enter a part number, which the program locates in the table. Use the offset in the table to calculate the offset in the file, and use function 42H to move the file pointer. Display description and price. Allow the user to enter quantity sold; calculate and display amount of sale (quantity × price).

17–11. Provide the full DOS function operations for the following FCB operations: (a) create; (b) set DTA; (c) sequential write; (d) open; (e) sequential read.

17–12. A program uses the record size to which the FCB open operation defaults. (a) How many records would a sector contain? (b) How many records would a diskette contain, assuming three tracks with nine sectors per track? (c) If the file in part (b) is being read sequentially, how many physical disk accesses will occur?

CHAPTER 18 ————————————

Disk Processing:
II—DOS Operations for Supporting
Disks and Files

OBJECTIVE:

To examine the various operations involved in supporting the use of disk drives and files.

INTRODUCTION

This chapter introduces a number of useful operations involved in the handling of disk drives, the directory, the FAT, and disk files.

OPERATIONS HANDLING DISK DRIVES

0DH	Reset disk drive
0EH	Select default drive
19H	Get default drive
1BH, 1CH	Get drive information
1FH	Get default DPB
2EH	Set/reset disk verify
32H	Get DPB
36H	Get free disk space
4400H	Get device information

4401H	Set device information
4404H	Read control data from drive
4405H	Write control data to drive
4406H	Check input status
4407H	Check output status
4408H	Determine if removable media for device
440DH, Minor code 41H	Write disk sector
440DH, Minor code 61H	Read disk sector
440DH, Minor code 42H	Format track
440DH, Minor code 46H	Set media ID
440DH, Minor code 60H	Get device parameters
440DH, Minor code 66H	Get media ID
440DH, Minor code 68H	Sense media type
54H	Get verify state
59H	Get extended error

OPERATIONS HANDLING DISK FILES

29H	Parse filename
41H	Delete file
43H	Get/set file attribute
45H, 46H	Duplicate file handle
4EH, 4FH	Find matching file
56H	Rename file
57H	Get/set file date/time
5AH, 5BH	Create temporary/new file

OPERATIONS HANDLING THE DIRECTORY AND FAT

39H	Create subdirectory
3AH	Remove subdirectory
3BH	Change current directory
47H	Get current directory

Error codes cited in this chapter refer to the list in Figure 17–1.

OPERATIONS HANDLING DISK DRIVES

INT 21H, Function 0DH: Reset Disk Drive

Normally, closing a file properly writes all remaining records and updates the directory. Under special circumstances, such as between program steps or on an error condition, a program may need to reset a disk. DOS function 0DH flushes all file buffers (the operation does not automatically close the files and returns no values):

```
MOV  AH,0DH        ;Request reset disk

INT  21H           ;Call DOS
```

INT 21H, Function 0EH: Select Default Disk Drive

The main purpose of DOS function 0EH is to select a drive as the current default. Set the drive number in the DL, where 0 = drive A, 1 = B, and so forth:

```
MOV  AH,0EH        ;Request set default

MOV  DL,02         ; drive C

INT  21H           ;Call DOS
```

The operation returns the number of drives (all types, including RAM disks) to the AL. Because DOS requires at least two logical drives A and B, it returns the value 02 for a one-drive system. (Use INT 11H for determining the actual number of drives.)

INT 21H, Function 19H: Get Default Disk Drive

DOS function 19H determines the default disk drive:

```
MOV  AH,19H        ;Get default drive

INT  21H           ;Call DOS
```

The operation returns a drive number in the AL, where 0 = A, 1 = B, and so forth. You could move this number directly into your program for accessing a file from the default drive, although some operations assume that 1 = drive A and 2 = drive B.

INT 21H, Function 1BH: Get Information for Default Drive

This function returns information about the default drive:

```
MOV  AH,1BH        ;Request information

INT  21H           ;Call DOS
```

Since the operation changes the DS, you should PUSH it before the interrupt and POP it after. The operation has now been superseded by function 36H. A successful 1BH operation returns the following information:

AL Number of sectors per cluster
BX Pointer (DS:BX) to the first byte (media descriptor) in the FAT
CX Size of the physical sector, usually 512
DX Number of clusters on the disk

The product of the AL, CX, and DX gives the capacity of the disk. An unsuccessful 1BH operation returns FFH in the AL.

INT 21H, Function 1CH: Get Information for Specific Drive

This function returns information about a specific drive. Insert the required drive number in the DL, where 0 = default, 1 = A, and so forth:

```
MOV  AH,1CH        ;Request information

MOV  DL,drive      ;Device number

INT  21H           ;Call DOS
```

The operation is otherwise identical to function 1BH and is also superseded by function 36H.

INT 21H, Function 1FH: Get Default Drive Parameter Block (DPB)

The drive parameter block (DPB) is a data area containing the following low-level information about the data structure of the drive:

OFFSET	SIZE	CONTENTS
00H	Byte	Drive number (0 = A, etc.)
01H	Byte	Logical unit for driver
02H	Word	Sector size in bytes
04H	Byte	Sectors per cluster minus 1
05H	Byte	Sectors per cluster (power of 2)
06H	Word	First relative sector of the FAT
08H	Byte	Copies of the FAT
09H	Word	Number of root directory entries
0BH	Word	First relative sector of first cluster
0DH	Word	Highest cluster number plus 1
0FH	Word	Sectors occupied by each FAT
11H	Word	First relative sector of the directory
13H	Dword	Address of device driver
17H	Byte	Media descriptor
18H	Byte	Access flag (0 if disk was accessed)
19H	Dword	Pointer to next parameter block
1DH	Word	Last allocated cluster
1FH	Word	Number of free clusters

PUSH the DS before issuing this function, and POP it on returning from the function. The operation has no parameters. A valid operation clears the AL and returns an address in the DS:BX that points to the DPB for the default drive. For an error, the AL is set to FFH. See also function 32H.

INT 21H, Function 2EH: Set/Reset Disk Write Verification

This function allows you to verify disk write operations, that is, whether the data was properly written. The operation sets a switch that tells the system to verify the disk controller's cyclical redundancy check (CRC), a sophisticated form of parity checking. Loading 00 in the AL sets verify off and 01 sets verify on. The switch stays set until another operation changes it. Following is an example:

```
MOV   AH,2EH        ;Request verify (or MOV AX,2E01H)

MOV   AL,01         ;Set on

INT   21H           ;Call DOS
```

The operation does not return any value, since it simply sets a switch. The system subsequently responds to invalid write operations. Since a disk drive rarely records data incorrectly and the verification causes some delay, the operation is most useful where recorded data is especially critical. A related function, 54H, delivers the current setting of the verify switch.

INT 21H, Function 32H: Get Drive Parameter Block (DPB)

To get the DPB, load the drive number in the DX (where 0 = default, 1 = A, etc.). (See function 1FH; other than requesting a specific drive, this function is identical to 32H.)

INT 21H, Function 36H: Get Free Disk Space

This function delivers information about the space on a disk device. Load the drive number (0 = default, 1 = A, 2 = B, etc.) in the DL:

```
MOV  AH,36H       ;Request disk space

MOV  DL,0         ; for default drive

INT  21H          ;Call DOS
```

A successful operation returns the following:

        AX = Number of sectors per cluster
        BX = Number of available clusters
        CX = Number of bytes per sector
        DX = Total number of clusters on device

The product of AX, CX, and DX gives the capacity of the disk. For an invalid device number, the operation returns FFFFH in the AX. The operation does not set or clear the carry flag.

INT 21H, Function 44H: I/O Control for Devices

This elaborate service, IOCTL, communicates information between a program and an open device. The service also includes a number of operations not included here. Load a subfunction value in the AL to request one of a number of actions. A valid operation clears the carry flag. An error, such as invalid file handle, sets the carry flag and returns a standard error code to the AX. IOCTL subfunctions follow.

INT 21H, Function 4400H: Get Device Information

This operation returns information about a file or device:

```
MOV  AX,4400H     ;Request device information

MOV  BX,handle    ;Handle of file or device

INT  21H          ;Call DOS
```

A valid operation clears the carry flag and returns a value in the DX, where bit 7 = 0 means that the handle indicates a file, and bit 7 = 1 means a device. The other bits have this meaning:

FILE (BIT 7 = 0):

0–5 Drive number (0 = A, 1 = B, etc.)

6   1 = file not written to

DEVICE (BIT 7 = 1):

0   Standard console input

1   Standard console output

2   Null device

3   Clock device

4   Special device

5   0 = ASCII mode, 1 = binary mode

6   For input, 0 = end of file returned if device is read.

An error sets the carry flag and returns code 01, 05, or 06 in the AX.

INT 21H, Function 4401H: Set Device Information

This function loads the file handle in the BX and the bit setup in the DL for bits 0–7, as shown for subfunction 00H. The operation sets device information accordingly. An error sets the carry flag and returns code 01, 05, 06, or 0DH in the AX.

INT 21H, Function 4404H: Read Control Data from Drive

This operation reads control data from a block-device driver (disk drive). Load the drive (0 = default, 1 = A, etc.) in the BL, the number of bytes to read in the CX, and the address of the data area in the DX. A successful operation returns to the AX the number of bytes transferred. An error sets the carry flag and returns code 01, 05, or 0DH in the AX.

INT 21H, Function 4405H: Write Control Data to Drive

This operation writes control data to a block-device driver. The setup is otherwise the same as for function 4404H.

INT 21H, Function 4406H: Check Input Status

This service checks whether a file or device is ready for input. Load the handle in the BX. A valid operation returns one of the following codes in the AL:

- Device: 00H = not ready, FFH = ready
- File: 00H = EOF reached, FFH = EOF not reached

An error sets the carry flag and returns code 01, 05, or 06 in the AX.

INT 21H, Function 4407H: Check Output Status

This service checks whether a file or device is ready for output. A valid operation returns one of the following in the AL:

- Device: 00H = not ready, FFH = ready
- File: 00H = ready, FFH = ready

An error sets the carry flag and returns code 01, 05, or 06 in the AX.

INT 21H, Function 4408H: Determine if Removable Media for Device

This service determines whether the device contains removable media, such as diskette. Load the BL with the drive number (0 = default, 1 = A, etc.). A valid operation clears the carry flag and returns one of the following codes in the AX:

- 00H = removable device or 01H = fixed device

An error sets the carry flag and returns code 01 or 0FH (invalid drive number) in the AX.

INT 21H, Function 440DH, Minor Code 41H: Write Disk Sector

This operation writes data from a buffer to one or more sectors on disk. Load these registers:

```
MOV   AX,440DH      ;IOCTL for block device

MOV   BX,drive      ;Drive (0 = default, 1 - A, etc.)

MOV   CH,08H        ;Device category = 08H

MOV   CL,41H        ;Minor code = write track

LEA   DX,devblock   ;Address of device block

INT 21H             ;Call DOS
```

The DX points to a device block with the following format:

```
devblock  LABEL BYTE

specfunc  DB    0           ;Special functions (zero)

rwhead    DW    head        ;Read/write head

rwcyl     DW    cylinder    ;Cylinder

rwsect1   DW    sector      ;Starting sector

rwsects   DW    number      ;Number of sectors

rwbuffr   DW    buffer      ;Offset address of buffer

          DW    SEG _DATA   ;Address of data segment
```

The rwbuffr entry provides the address of the buffer in segment:offset (DS:DX) format, although coded in reverse-word sequence. The SEG operator indicates the definition of a segment, in this case the data segment, _DATA. The buffer identifies the data area to be written and should be the length of the number of sectors $\times$ 512, such as

```
WRBUFFER DB 1024 DUP (?) ;Output buffer
```

A successful operation clears the carry flag and writes the data. Otherwise, the operation sets the carry flag and returns error code 01, 02, or 05 in the AX.

INT 21H, Function 440DH, Minor Code 42H: Format Track

To use this function to format tracks, set these registers:

```
MOV  AX,440DH          ;Request disk service

MOV  BX,drive          ;Drive (0 = default, 1 = A, etc.)

MOV  CH,08             ;Device category (08)

MOV  CL,42H            ;Minor code = format track

LEA  DX,block          ;Address of block (DS:DX)

INT  21H              ;Call DOS
```

The DX points to a block with the following format:

```
blkname LABEL BYTE

specfun DB    0         ;Special function, code 0

diskhd  DW    ?         ;Disk head

cylindr DW    ?         ;Cylinder

tracks  DW    ?         ;Number of tracks
```

A successful operation clears the carry flag and formats the tracks. Otherwise, the operation sets the carry flag and returns error code 01, 02, or 05 in the AX.

INT 21H, Function 440DH, Minor Code 46H: Set Media ID

For this function to set the media ID, set these registers:

```
MOV    AX,440DH          ;Request disk service

MOV    BX,drive          ;Drive (0 = default, 1 = A, etc.)

MOV    CH,08             ;Device category (08)

MOV    CL,46H            ;Minor code = set media ID

LEA    DX,block          ;Address of block (DS:DX)

INT    21H              ;Call DOS
```

The DX points to a media block with the following format:

```
blkname LABEL BYTE

infolev DW    0         ;Information level = 0

serialn DD    ??        ;Serial number
```

```
volabel DB    11 DUP (?)      ;Volume label

filetyp DB    8 DUP (?)       ;Type of FAT
```

The filetyp field contains the ASCII value FAT12 or FAT16, with trailing blanks. A successful operation clears the carry flag and sets the ID. Otherwise, the operation sets the carry flag and returns error code 01, 02, or 05 in the AX. (See also function 440DH, minor code 66H.)

INT 21H, Function 440DH, Minor Code 60H: Get Device Parameters

For this function to get device parameters, set these registers:

```
MOV   AX,440DH        ;Request disk service

MOV   BX,drive        ;Drive (0 = default, 1 = A, etc.)

MOV   CH,08           ;Device category (08)

MOV   CL,60H          ;Minor code = get parameters

LEA   DX,block        ;Address of block (DS:DX)

INT   21H             ;Call DOS
```

The DX points to a device parameter block with the following format:

```
specfun DB     ?      ;Special functions (0 or 1)

devtype DB     ?      ;Device type

devattr DW     ?      ;Device attribute

cylindr DW     ?      ;Number of cylinders

medityp DB     ?      ;Media type

bytesec DW     ?      ;Bytes per sector

secclus DB     ?      ;Sectors per cluster

ressect DW     ?      ;Number of reserved sectors

fats    DB     ?      ;Number of FATs

rootent DW     ?      ;Number of root directory entries

sectors DW     ?      ;Total number of sectors

mediads DB     ?      ;Media descriptor

fatsecs DW     ?      ;Number of sectors per FAT

sectrak DW     ?      ;Sectors per track

heads   DW     ?      ;Number of heads
```

```
hidsect DD    ?              ;Number of hidden sectors

exsects DD    ?              ;Number of sectors if sectors field = 0
```

If the specfun field is 0, the information is about the default medium in the drive; if 1, the information is about the current medium. A successful operation clears the carry flag and delivers the data. Otherwise, the operation sets the carry flag and returns error code 01, 02, or 05 in the AX.

INT 21H, Function 440DH, Minor Code 61H: Read Disk Sector

This operation reads data from one or more sectors on disk to a buffer. Set the CL with minor code 61H; otherwise, technical details for the operation are identical to those for minor code 41H, which writes sectors. Figure 18–1, illustrates the function.

INT 21H, Function 440DH, Minor Code 66H: Get Media ID

For this function to get the media ID, set these registers:

```
MOV   AX,440DH       ;Request disk service

MOV   BX,drive       ;Drive (0 = default, 1 = A, etc.)

MOV   CH,08          ;Device category (08)

MOV   CL,66H         ;Minor code = get media ID

LEA   DX,block       ;Address of block (DS:DX)

INT   21H            ;Call DOS
```

The DX points to a media block with the following format:

```
blkname LABEL BYTE

infolev DW    0                    ;Information level = 0

serialn DD    ?                    ;Serial number

volabel DB    1 DUP (?)            ;Volume label

filetyp DB    8 DUP (?)            ;Type of FAT
```

A successful operation clears the carry flag and sets the ID. The filetyp field contains ASCII value FAT12 or FAT16, with trailing blanks. Otherwise, the operation sets the carry flag and returns error code 01, 02, or 05 in the AX. (See also function 440DH, minor code 46H.)

INT 21H, Function 440DH, Minor Code 68H: Sense Media Type

To use this function to get the media type, set these registers:

```
MOV   AX,440DH       ;Request disk service

MOV   BX,drive       ;Drive (0 = default, 1 = A, etc.)
```

```
MOV   CH,08           ;Device category (08)

MOV   CL,68H          ;Minor code = get media type

LEA   DX,block        ;Address of block (DS:DX)

INT   21H             ;Call DOS
```

The DX points to a two-byte media block to receive data in the following format:

```
default DB    ? ;01 for default value, 02 for other

medatyp DB    ? ;Disk-02 = 720K, 07 = 1.44MB, 09 = 2.88MB
```

A successful operation clears the carry flag and sets the type. Otherwise, the operation sets the carry flag and returns error code 01 or 05 in the AX.

Other function 44H IOCTL operations concerned with file sharing are outside the scope of this book.

INT 21H, Function 54H: Get Verify State

This service can determine the status of the disk write-verify flag. (See function 2EH for setting the switch.) The operation returns 00H to the AL for verify off or 01H for verify on. There is no error condition.

INT 21H, Function 59H: Get Extended Error

This operation provides additional information about errors after execution of INT 21H services that set the carry flag, FCB services that return FFH, and INT 24H error handlers. The operation returns the following:

- AX = Extended error code
- BH = Error class
- BL = Suggested action
- CH = Location

Also, the operation clears the carry flag and—watch for this—destroys the contents of the CL, DI, DS, DX, ES, and SI registers. PUSH all required registers prior to this interrupt, and POP them afterward.

Extended Error Code (AX).   Returns some 90 or more error codes; code 00 means that the previous INT 21H operation resulted in no error.

Error Class (BH).   Provides the following information:

01H	Out of resource, such as storage channel
02H	Temporary situation (not an error), such as a locked file condition that should go away
03H	Lack of proper authorization
04H	System software error, not this program
05H	Hardware failure

06H   Serious DOS error, not this program
07H   Error in this program, such as inconsistent request
08H   Requested item not found
09H   Improper file or disk format
0AH   File or item is locked
0BH   Disk error, such as CRC error or wrong disk
0CH   File or item already exists
0DH   Unknown error class.

Action (BL).   Provides information on the action to take:
01   Retry a few times; may have to ask user to terminate.
02   Pause first and retry a few times.
03   Ask user to reenter proper request.
04   Close files and terminate the program.
05   Terminate the program immediately; do not close files.
06   Ignore the error.
07   Request user to perform an action (such as change diskette) and retry the operation.

Location (CH).   Provides additional information on locating an error:
01   Unknown situation, can't help
02   Disk storage problem
03   Network problem
04   Serial device problem
05   Memory problem.

PROGRAM: READING DATA FROM SECTORS

The program in Figure 18–1 illustrates the use of IOCTL function 44H, subfunction 0DH, minor code 61H. The program reads data from a sector into a buffer in memory and displays each input byte as a pair of hex characters. RDBLOCK in the data segment arbitrarily specifies a head, cylinder, and starting sector, which you can change for your own purposes. RDBUFFR defines two addresses:

1. IOBUFFR is the offset address of the input buffer, which provides for one sector of data.
2. SEG _DATA uses the SEG operator to identify the address of the data segment for the IOCTL operation.

Major procedures in the code segment are:

B10READ   Uses the IOCTL operation to read the sector. The test for a valid read is made on returning from the procedure.

C10CONV   Converts each byte in IOBUFFR into two hex characters for displaying. Two XLAT instructions handle the conversion for each half-byte. The routine displays 16 rows of 32 pairs of characters.

```
TITLE       P18RDSCT (EXE)  Read disk sector
            .MODEL  SMALL
            .STACK  64
; ------------------------------------------------------
            .DATA
ROW      DB    00
COL      DB    00
XLATAB   DB    30H,31H,32H,33H,34H,35H,36H,37H,38H,39H
         DB    41H,42H,43H,44H,45H,46H
READMSG  DB    '*** Read error ***', 0DH, 0AH

RDBLOCK  DB    0              ;Block
RDHEAD   DW    0              ;  structure
RDCYLR   DW    0              ;
RDSECT   DW    8              ;
RDNOSEC  DW    1              ;
RDBUFFR  DW    IOBUFFR        ;
         DW    SEG _DATA      ;
IOBUFFR  DB    512 DUP(' ')   ;Disk sector area
;------------------------------------------------------
.386
            .CODE
MAIN     PROC  FAR
         MOV   AX,@data       ;Initialize
         MOV   DS,AX          ;  segment
         MOV   ES,AX          ;  registers
         CALL  Q10SCR         ;Clear screen
         CALL  Q20CURS        ;Set cursor
         CALL  B10READ        ;Get sector data
         JNC   A80            ;If valid read, bypass
         LEA   DX,READMSG     ;  invalid read
         CALL  X10ERR
         JMP   A90
A80:
         CALL  C10CONV        ;Convert and display
A90:
         MOV   AX,4C00H       ;Exit to DOS
         INT   21H
MAIN     ENDP

;              Read sector data:
;              -----------------
B10READ  PROC  NEAR
         MOV   AX,440DH       ;IOCTL for block device
         MOV   BX,01          ;Drive A
         MOV   CH,08          ;Device category
         MOV   CL,61H         ;Read sector
         LEA   DX,RDBLOCK     ;Address of block structure
         INT   21H
         RET
B10READ  ENDP
;              Display sector data:
;              ------------
C10CONV  PROC  NEAR
         LEA   SI,IOBUFFR
C20:
         MOV   AL,[SI]
         SHR   AL,04          ;Shift off right hex digit
         LEA   BX,XLATAB      ;Set table address
         XLAT                 ;Translate hex
         CALL  Q30DISPL
         INC   COL
         MOV   AL,[SI]
```

Figure 18–1 Reading Disk Sectors

```
                    AND      AL,0FH              ;Clear left hex digit
                    XLAT                         ;Translate hex
                    CALL     Q30DISPL
                    INC      SI
                    INC      COL
                    CMP      COL,64
                    JBE      C20
                    INC      ROW
                    MOV      COL,00
                    CALL     Q20CURS
                    CMP      ROW,16
                    JBE      C20
                    RET
C10CONV     ENDP
;                            Scroll screen:
;                            -------------
Q10SCR      PROC     NEAR
                    MOV      AX,0600H            ;Request scroll
                    MOV      BH,1EH              ;Set attribute
                    MOV      CX,0000
                    MOV      DX,184FH
                    INT      10H
                    RET
Q10SCR      ENDP
;                            Set cursor:
;                            ----------
Q20CURS     PROC     NEAR
                    MOV      AH,02H              ;Request set
                    MOV      BH,00               ;  cursor
                    MOV      DH,ROW              ;  row
                    MOV      DL,COL              ;  column
                    INT      10H
                    RET
Q20CURS     ENDP
Q30DISPL    PROC     NEAR
                    MOV      AH,02H              ;Request print
                    MOV      DL,AL               ;  character
                    INT      21H
                    RET
Q30DISPL    ENDP

;                            Display disk error message:
;                            --------------------------
X10ERR      PROC     NEAR
                    MOV      AH,40H              ;DX contains address
                    MOV      BX,01               ;Handle
                    MOV      CX,20               ;Length
                    INT      21H                 ;  of message
                    INC      ROW
                    RET
X10ERR      ENDP
                    END      MAIN
```

Figure 18–1   (continued)

You could enhance this program by allowing a user to request sectors via the keyboard.

OPERATIONS HANDLING THE DIRECTORY AND THE FAT

INT 21H, Function 39H: Create Subdirectory

This service creates a subdirectory, just as the DOS command MKDIR does. Load the DX with the address of an ASCIIZ string containing the drive and directory pathname—it's that simple:

```
ASCstrg DB     'd:\pathname' ,00H ;ASCIIZ string

        ...

        MOV  AH,39H           ;Request create subdirectory

        LEA  DX,ASCstrg       ;Address of ASCIIZ string (DS:DX)

        INT  21H
```

A valid operation clears the carry flag; an error sets the carry flag and returns code 03 or 05 in the AX.

INT 21H, Function 3AH: Remove Subdirectory

This service deletes a subdirectory, just as the DOS command RMDIR does. Load the DX with the address of an ASCIIZ string containing the drive and directory pathname (note that you cannot delete the current directory or a subdirectory containing files):

```
ASCstrg DB     'd:\pathname' ,00H ;ASCIIZ string

        ...

        MOV  AH,3AH           ;Request delete subdirectory

        LEA  DX,ASCstrg       ;Address of ASCIIZ string (DS:DX)

        INT  21H
```

A valid operation clears the carry flag; an error sets the carry flag and returns code 03, 05, or 10H in the AX.

INT 21H, Function 3BH: Change Current Directory

This service changes the current directory to one that you specify, just as the DOS command CHDIR does. Load the DX with the address of an ASCIIZ string containing the new drive and directory pathname:

```
ASCstrg DB     'd:\pathname' ,00H ;ASCIIZ string

        ...

        MOV  AH,3BH           ;Request change directory

        LEA  DX,ASCstrg       ;Address of ASCIIZ string (DS:DX)

        INT  21H
```

A valid operation clears the carry flag; an error sets the carry flag and returns code 03 in the AX.

INT 21H, Function 47H: Get Current Directory

DOS function 47H determines the current directory for any drive. Define a buffer space large enough to contain the longest possible pathname (64 bytes), and load its address in the SI. Identify the drive in the DL by 0 = default, 1 = A, 2 = B, and so forth:

```
            buffer DB    64 DUP(20H)    ;64-byte buffer space

                ...

            MOV  AH,47H         ;Request get directory

            MOV  DL,drive       ;Drive

            LEA  SI,buffer      ;Address of buffer (DS:DI)

            INT  21H
```

A valid operation clears the carry flag and delivers the name of the current directory (but not the drive) to the buffer as an ASCIIZ string, such as

ASSEMBLE\EXAMPLES0

A byte containing 00H identifies the end of the pathname. If the requested directory is the root, the value returned is only a byte of 00H. In this way, you can get the current pathname in order to access any file in a subdirectory. An invalid drive number sets the carry flag and returns error code 0FH in the AX.

INT 21H, Function 56H: Rename File or Directory

See the next section for this function.

PROGRAM: DISPLAYING THE DIRECTORY

The program in Figure 18–2 illustrates the use of two of the functions described in the preceding section. The procedures perform the following:

B10DRIV Uses function 19H to get the default drive in the AL register. The drive is returned as 0 (for A), 1 (for B), and so forth. To adjust the number to its alphabetic equivalent, simply add 41H, so that 00 becomes 41H (A), 01 becomes 42H (B), and so forth. The procedure then displays the drive letter followed by a colon and backslash (n:\).

C10PATH Uses function 47H to get the current directory pathname. The procedure tests immediately for the 00H ASCIIZ delimiter, since a default to the root directory would deliver only that character. Otherwise, the routine displays each character up to the 00H.

The program intentionally contains only features necessary to get it to work; a full program would include, for example, clearing the screen and setting colors.

OPERATIONS HANDLING DISK FILES

This section describes DOS operations that process disk files.

```
TITLE     P18GETDR (COM)  Get current directory
          .MODEL SMALL
          .CODE
          ORG    100H
BEGIN:    JMP    SHORT MAIN
; -------------------------------------------------------------
PATHNAM DB     64 DUP(' ')           ;Current pathname
; -------------------------------------------------------------
MAIN      PROC   NEAR
          CALL   B10DRIV               ;Get/display default drive
          CALL   C10PATH               ;Get/display path
          MOV    AH,10H                ;Pause until user
          INT    16H                   ;  presses a key
          MOV    AX,4C00H              ;Exit to DOS
          INT    21H
MAIN      ENDP

B10DRIV PROC   NEAR;
          MOV    AH,19H                ;Request default drive
          INT    21H
          ADD    AL,41H                ;Change hex no. to letter
          MOV    DL,AL                 ;  0=A, 1-B, etc.
          CALL   Q10DISP               ;Display drive number,
          MOV    DL,':'
          CALL   Q10DISP               ;  colon,
          MOV    DL,'\'
          CALL   Q10DISP               ;  backslash
          RET
B10DRIV ENDP

C10PATH PROC   NEAR;
          MOV    AH,47H                ;Request pathname
          MOV    DL,00
          LEA    SI,PATHNAM
          INT    21H
C20:
          CMP    BYTE PTR [SI],00H ;End of pathname?
          JE     C90                   ;  yes, exit
          MOV    AL,[SI]               ;Display pathname
          MOV    DL,AL                 ;  one byte at
          CALL   Q10DISP               ;  a time
          INC    SI
          JMP    C20                   ;Repeat
C90:      RET
C10PATH ENDP

Q10DISP PROC   NEAR                    ;DL set on entry
          MOV    AH,02H                ;Request display
          INT    21H
          RET
Q10DISP ENDP
          END    BEGIN
```

Figure 18–2 Get Current Directory

INT 21H, Function 29H: Parse Filename

This service converts a command line containing a file specification (filespec) of the form d:filename.ext into FCB format. The function can accept a filespec from a user for copying and deleting files.

Load the SI register (associated with the DS) with the address of the filespec to be parsed, the DI (associated with the ES) with the address of an area where the operation is to generate the FCB format, and the AL with a bit value that controls the parsing method:

```
MOV   AH,29H        ;Request parse filename

MOV   AL,code       ;Parsing method

LEA   DI,FCBname    ;Address of FCB (ES:DI)

LEA   SI,filespec   ;Address of filespec (DS:SI)

INT   21H           ;Call DOS
```

The codes for the parsing method are:

BIT	VALUE	ACTION
0	0	Filespec begins in the first byte location.
0	1	Scan past separators (such as blanks) to find the filespec.
1	0	Set drive ID byte in the generated FCB: missing drive = 00, A = 01, B = 02, and so forth.
1	1	Change drive ID byte in the generated FCB only if the parsed filespec specifies a drive. In this way, an FCB can have its own default drive.
2	0	Change filename in the FCB as required.
2	1	Change filename in the FCB only if the filespec contains a valid filename.
3	0	Change filename extension as required.
3	1	Change extension only if filespec contains a valid extension.
4–7	0	Must be zero.

For valid data, function 29H creates a standard FCB format for the filename and extension, with an eight-character filename filled out with blanks if necessary, a three-character extension filled out with blanks if necessary, and no period between them.

The operation recognizes standard punctuation and converts the wild cards * and ? into a string of one or more characters. For example, PROG12.* becomes PROG12bb???. The AL returns one of the following codes:

00H   No wild cards encountered

01H   Wild cards converted

FFH   Invalid drive specified

After the operation, the DS:SI contains the address of the first byte after the parsed filespec, and the ES:DI contains the address of the first byte of the FCB. For a failed operation, the byte at DI+1 is blank, although the operation attempts to convert almost anything you throw at it.

For this operation to work with file handles, you have to edit the FCB further, to delete blanks and enter the period between the filename and the extension.

INT 21H, Function 41H: Delete File

This function deletes a file (but not read-only) from within a program. Load the address in the DX of an ASCIIZ string containing the device path and filename, with no wild-card references:

```
ASCstrg DB    'd:\pathname',00H ;ASCIIZ string

        ...

        MOV  AH,41H            ;Request delete

        LEA  DX,ASCstrg        ;Address of ASCIIZ string (DS:DX)

        INT  21H               ;Call DOS
```

A valid operation clears the carry flag, marks the filename in the directory as deleted, and releases the file's allocated disk space in the FAT. An error sets the carry flag and returns code 02, 03, or 05 in the AX.

INT 21H, Function 43H: Get or Set File Attribute

You can use this operation either to get or set a file attribute in the directory. The operation requires the address of an ASCIIZ string containing the drive, path, and filename for the requested file. (Or use the default directory if no path is given.)

To get file attribute, load the AL with code 00. The following example gets a file's attribute:

```
ASCstrg DB    'd:\pathname',00H ;ASCIIZ string

        ...

        MOV  AH,43H            ;Request

        MOV  AL,00            ;  get attribute

        LEA  DX,ASCstrg        ;ASCIIZ string (DS:DX)

        INT  21H               ;Call DOS
```

A valid operation clears the carry flag and returns the current attribute to the CX (CH = 00 and CL = attribute):

BIT	ATTRIBUTE	BIT	ATTRIBUTE
0	Read-only file	3	Volume label
1	Hidden file	4	Subdirectory
2	System file	5	Archive file

An error sets the carry flag and returns code 02 or 03 to the AX.

To set file attribute, load the AL with code 01, and set the attribute bit(s) in the CX. You may change read-only, hidden, system, and archive files, but not the volume label or subdirectory. The following example sets hidden and archive attributes for a file:

```
MOV   AH,43H            ;Request

MOV   AL,01             ;  set attributes—

MOV   CX,22H            ;  hidden and archive

LEA   DX,ASCstrg        ;ASCIIZ string (DS:DX)

INT   21H               ;Call DOS
```

A valid operation clears the carry flag and sets the directory entry to the attribute in the CX. An invalid operation sets the carry flag and returns code 02, 03, or 05 to the AX.

INT 21H, Function 45H: Duplicate a File Handle

You can use this service to give a file more than one handle. The uses of old versus new handles are identical: the handles reference the same file, file pointer, and buffer area. One use is to request a file handle and use that handle to close the file. This action causes DOS to flush the buffer and update the directory. You can then use the original file handle to continue processing the file. An example of the use of function 45H is the following:

```
MOV   AH,45H        ;Request duplicate handle

MOV   BX,handle     ;Current handle to be duplicated

INT   21H
```

A successful operation clears the carry flag and returns a new file handle (the next one available) in the AX. An error sets the carry flag and returns error code 04 or 06 to the AX. (See also function 46H.)

INT 21H, Function 46H: Force Duplicate of a File Handle

This service is similar to function 45H, except that it can assign a specific file handle. You could use the service to redirect output, for example. Load the BX with the original handle and the CX with the second handle.

A successful operation clears the carry flag. An error sets the carry flag and returns error code 04 or 06 to the AX. Some combinations may not work; for example, handle 00 is always keyboard input, 04 is printer output, and 03 (auxiliary) cannot be redirected. (See also function 45H.)

INT 21H, Function 4EH: Find First Matching File

This operation is similar (and preferred) to the original function 11H. Use function 4EH to begin a search in a directory and 4FH to continue searching. You have to define a 43-byte buffer for the operation to return the located directory entry and issue function 1AH (set DTA) before using this service. For beginning the search, set the CX with the file attribute of the filename(s) to be returned— any combination of read only (bit 0), hidden (bit 1), system (bit 2), volume label (bit 3), directory (bit 4), or archive (bit 5). Load the DX with the address of an ASCIIZ string containing the pathname; the string may contain the wild-card characters ? and *:

```
DTAname DB    43 DUP(?)

ASCstrg DB    'ASCIIZ string',00H

        ...

        MOV   AH,1AH       ;Request set DTA

        LEA   DX,DTAname    ;Area for DTA (DS:DX)

        INT   21H          ;Call DOS

        MOV   AH,4EH        ;Request first match

        MOV   CX,00H        ;Normal attribute

        LEA   DX,ASCstrg    ;ASCIIZ string (DS:DX)

        INT   21H          ;Call DOS
```

An operation that locates a match between attribute bits clears the carry flag and fills the 43-byte (2BH) DTA with the following:

00H–14H	Reserved by DOS for subsequent search
15H	File attribute
16H–17H	File time
18H–19H	File date
1AH–1DH	File size: low word and then high word
1EH–2AH	Name and extension as an ASCIIZ string, followed by hex 00

An error sets the carry flag and returns code 02, 03, or 12H.

A unique use for function 4EH is to determine whether a reference is to a filename or to a subdirectory. For example, if the returned attribute is 10H, the reference is to a subdirectory. The operation also returns the size of the file. Thus you may use function 4EH to determine the size of a file and function 36H to check the space available for writing it.

INT 21H, Function 4FH: Find Next Matching File

This operation is similar to the original function 12H. First use function 4EH to begin the search in a directory and then function 4FH to continue searching. If you plan to use 4FH, do not change the contents of the DTA (see function 4EH for the value filled in the DTA):

```
        MOV   AH,4FH        ;Request next match

        INT   21H          ;Call DOS
```

A successful operation clears the carry flag and returns to the AX codes 00 (filename found) or 18 (no more files). An error sets the carry flag and returns code 02, 03, or 12H to the AX.

Figure 18–3 illustrates functions 4EH and 4FH.

INT 21H, Function 56H: Rename File or Directory

This service can rename a file or directory from within a program. Load the DX with the address of an ASCIIZ string containing the old drive, path, and name of the file or directory to be renamed. Load the DI (actually, ES:DI) with the address of an ASCIIZ string containing the new drive, path, and name, with no wild cards. Drive numbers, if used, must be the same in both strings. Since the paths need not be the same, the operation can both rename a file and move it to another directory on the same drive:

```
oldstrg DB     'd:\oldpath\oldname', 00H

newstrg DB     'd:\newpath\newname', 00H

        ...

        MOV  AH,56H            ;Request rename file/directory

        LEA  DX,oldstring      ;DS:DX

        LEA  DI,newstring      ;ES:DI

        INT  21H              ;Call DOS
```

A successful operation clears the carry flag; an error sets the carry flag and returns in the AX code 02, 03, 05, or 11H.

INT 21H, Function 57H: Get/Set a File's Date and Time

This service enables a program to get or set the date and time for an open file. The formats for time and date are the same as those in the directory:

BITS FOR TIME		BITS FOR DATE	
0BH–0FH	Hours	09H–0FH	Year (relative to 1980)
05H–0AH	Minutes	05H–08H	Month
00H–04H	Seconds	00H–04H	Day of month

(Seconds are in the form of the number of 2-second increments, 0–29.) Load the request (0 = get, 1 = set) in the AL and the file handle in the BX. For a set request, load the time in the CX and the date in the DX. Following is an example:

```
        MOV  AH,57H           ;Request date/time

        MOV  AL,01            ;Set

        MOV  BX,handle        ;File handle

        MOV  CX,time          ;New time

        MOV  DX,date          ;New date

        INT  21H
```

A valid operation clears the carry flag; get returns the time in the CX and date in the DX, whereas set changes the date and time entries for the file. An invalid operation sets the carry flag and returns in the AX error code 01 or 06.

INT 21H, Function 5AH: Create a Temporary File

This service would be useful for a program that creates temporary files, especially in networks, where the names of other files may be unknown and the program is to avoid accidentally overwriting them. The operation creates a file with a unique name within the path.

Load the CX with the required file attribute—any combination of read only (bit 0), hidden (bit 1), system (bit 2), volume label (bit 3), directory (bit 4), and archive (bit 5). Load the DX with the address of an ASCIIZ path—the drive (if necessary), the subdirectory (if any), a backslash, and 00H, followed by 13 bytes for the new filename:

```
ASCpath DB    'd:\pathname\', 00H, 13 DUP(20H)

        ...

        MOV   AH,5AH          ;Request create file
        MOV   CX,attribute    ;File attribute
        LEA   DX,ASCpath      ;ASCIIZ path
        INT   21H
```

A successful operation clears the carry flag, delivers the file handle to the AX, and appends the new filename to the ASCIIZ string, beginning at the 00H byte. An invalid operation sets the carry flag and returns code 03, 04, or 05 in the AX.

INT 21H, Function 5BH: Create a New File

This service creates a file only if the named file does not already exist; otherwise it is identical to function 3CH (create file). You could use function 5BH whenever you don't want to overwrite a file. A valid operation clears the carry flag and returns the file handle in the AX. An invalid operation (including finding an identical filename) sets the carry flag and returns code 03, 04, 05, or 50H in the AX.

PROGRAM: SELECTIVELY DELETING FILES

The program in Figure 18–3 illustrates the use of DOS functions 4EH and 4FH to find all filenames in the default directory and function 41H to delete selected files. The program consists of the following procedures:

MAIN	Calls procedures B10FIRST, C10NEXT, D10DISPL, and E10DELET.
B10FIRST	Sets the DTA for function 4EH and finds the first matched entry in the directory.
C10NEXT	Finds succeeding matched entries in the directory.
D10DISPL	Displays the names of the files and asks whether they are to be deleted.
E10DELET	Accepts a reply Y (yes) to delete the file, N (no) to keep it, or Enter to terminate processing, and deletes the files requested.

```
          TITLE     P18SELDL (COM)  Select and delete files
          CODESG    SEGMENT PARA 'Code'
                    .MODEL SMALL
                    .CODE
                    ORG    100H
          BEGIN:    JMP    MAIN
          ; -------------------------------------------------------------
          TAB       EQU    09
          LF        EQU    10
          CR        EQU    13
          CRLF      DB     CR, LF, '$'
          PATHNAM   DB     'F:\*.*', 00H
          DELMSG    DB     TAB, 'Erase ','$'
          ENDMSG    DB     CR, LF, 'No more directory entries', CR, LF, '$
          ERRMSG1   DB     'Invalid path/file', '$'
          ERRMSG2   DB     'Write-protected disk','$'
          PROMPT    DB     'Y = Erase, N = Keep, Ent = Exit', CR, LF, '$'
          DISKAREA  DB     43 DUP(20H)
          ; -------------------------------------------------------------
          MAIN      PROC   NEAR              ;Main procedure
                    CALL   Q10SCRN           ;Clear screen
                    CALL   Q20CURS           ;Set cursor
                    CALL   B10FIRST          ;  directory entry
                    CMP    AX,00H            ;If no entries,
                    JNE    A90               ;  exit
                    LEA    DX,PROMPT         ;Initial prompt
                    CALL   Q30LINE
          A20:
                    CALL   D10DISPL          ;Display filename
                    CALL   E10DELET          ;Delete if requested
                    CMP    AL,0FFH           ;Request for finish?
                    JE     A90               ;  yes, exit
                    LEA    DX,CRLF           ;Set cursor on
                    CALL   Q30LINE           ;  next line
                    CALL   C10NEXT           ;Get next directory entry
                    CMP    AX,00H            ;Any more entries?
                    JE     A20               ;  yes, loop
          A90:
                    MOV    AX,4C00H          ;Exit to DOS
                    INT    21H
          MAIN      ENDP
          ;
          B10FIRST  PROC   NEAR
                    MOV    AH,1AH            ;Get DTA for function
                    LEA    DX,DISKAREA       ;  calls
                    INT    21H
                    MOV    AH,4EH            ;Locate first directory
                    MOV    CX,00             ;  entry
                    LEA    DX,PATHNAM        ;Address of ASCIIZ string
                    INT    21H
                    JNC    B90               ;Valid operation?
                    PUSH   AX                ;  no,
                    LEA    DX,ERRMSG1        ;  display ending
                    CALL   Q30LINE           ;  message
                    POP    AX
          B90:      RET
          B10FIRST  ENDP

          C10NEXT   PROC   NEAR              ;Read directory entry
                    MOV    AH,4FH            ;Get next
                    INT    21H
                    CMP    AX,00H            ;More entries?
                    JE     C90               ;  yes, bypass
```

Figure 18–3   Select and Delete Files

```
                    PUSH    AX                      ;  no,
                    LEA     DX,ENDMSG               ;  display ending
                    CALL    Q30LINE                 ;  message
                    POP     AX
C90:                RET
C10NEXT     ENDP

D10DISPL    PROC    NEAR
                    LEA     DX,DELMSG               ;Display delete message
                    CALL    Q30LINE
                    LEA     SI,DISKAREA+1EH         ;Start of filename
D30:
                    MOV     DL,[SI]                 ;Get char for display
                    CALL    Q40CHAR
                    INC     SI                      ;Next character
                    CMP     BYTE PTR [SI],00H       ;Hex zero stopper?
                    JNE     D30                     ;  no, get next char
                    MOV     DL,'?'                  ;  yes, exit
                    CALL    Q40CHAR
                    RET
D10DISPL    ENDP
;
E10DELET    PROC    NEAR
                    MOV     AH,10H                  ;Accept 1-character
                    INT     16H                     ;  reply (y/n)
                    CMP     AL,0DH                  ;Enter character?
                    JE      E50                     ;  yes, exit
                    OR      AL,00100000B            ;Force lowercase
                    CMP     AL,'y'                  ;Delete requested?
                    JNE     E90                     ;  no , bypass
                    MOV     AH,41H                  ;  yes,
                    LEA     DX,DISKAREA+1EH         ;  address of filename
                    INT     21H                     ;  delete entry
                    JNC     E90                     ;Valid delete?
                    LEA     DX,ERRMSG2              ;  no, display
                    CALL    Q30LINE                 ;  warning message
E50:
                    MOV     AL,0FFH                 ;End-of-process indica
E90:                RET
E10DELET    ENDP

Q10SCRN     PROC    NEAR
                    MOV     AX,0600H                ;Request clear screen
                    MOV     BH,1EH                  ;Set attribute
                    MOV     CX,00
                    MOV     DX,184FH
                    INT     10II
                    RET
Q10SCRN     ENDP

Q20CURS     PROC    NEAR
                    MOV     AH,02H                  ;Request
                    MOV     BH,00                   ;  set cursor
                    MOV     DH,00                   ;Row 0
                    MOV     DL,10                   ;Column 10
                    INT     10H
                    RET
Q20CURS     ENDP

Q30LINE     PROC    NEAR
                    MOV     AH,09H                  ;Request display line
                    INT     21H                     ;DX set on entry
                    RET
Q30LINE     ENDP
```

Figure 18–3   (continued)

```
Q40CHAR    PROC    NEAR
           MOV     AH,02H                ;Request display
           INT     21H                   ;DL set on entry
           RET
Q40CHAR    ENDP
           END     BEGIN
```

Figure 18–3 (continued)

As a precaution during testing, use copied temporary files.

KEY POINTS

- Operations involved in handling disk drives include reset, select default, get drive information, get free disk space, and the extensive operation I/O control for devices.
- Operations involved in handling the directory and FAT include create subdirectory, remove subdirectory, change current directory, and get current directory.
- Operations involved in handling disk files (other than create, open, read, and write) include rename file, get/set attribute, find matching file, and get/set date/time.

QUESTIONS

Use DEBUG for the first three questions. Key in the A 100 command and the required instructions. Examine any values returned in the registers.

18–1. Operations involving disk drives:
  (a) Function 19H to determine the current default disk drive.
  (b) Function 1BH for information about the current default disk drive.
  (c) Function 1FH for information about the default DPB.
  (d) Function 36H to determine the amount of free disk space.
  (e) Function 4400H to get information on the device in use.
  (f) Function 4408H to determine whether any media in use are removable.
  (g) Function 440DH, minor code 60H, to get the device parameters.
  (h) Function 440DH, minor code 66H, to get the media ID.

18–2. Operations involving directories:
  (a) Function 39H to create a subdirectory. For safety, you could create it on a RAM disk or diskette. Use any name.
  (b) Function 56H to rename the subdirectory.
  (c) Function 3AH to remove the subdirectory.

18–3. Operations involving disk files:
  (a) Function 43H to get the attribute from a file on a diskette. (Use a copied file for this exercise.)
  (b) Function 56H to rename the file.
  (c) Function 43H to set the attribute to hidden.
  (d) Function 57H to get the file's date and time.
  (e) Function 41H to delete the file.

18–4. Write a small program from within DEBUG that simply executes DOS function 29H, parse filename. Provide for the filespec at 81H and the FCB at 5CH; both are in the PSP immediately before the program. Enter various filespecs, such as D:PROGA.DOC, PROGB, PROGC.*, and C:*.ASM. Check the results at offset 5CH after each execution of the

CHAPTER 19 —————————————

Disk Processing:
III—BIOS Disk Operations

OBJECTIVE

To examine the basic programming requirements for using the BIOS functions to read from, write to, format, and
verify disks.

INTRODUCTION

In Chapters 17 and 18, we examined the use of the DOS services for disk processing. You
can also code directly at the BIOS level for disk processing, although BIOS supplies no automatic use of the directory or blocking and deblocking of records. BIOS disk operation
INT 13H treats data as the size of a sector and handles disk addressing in terms of actual
track and sector numbers. BIOS disk operations involve resetting reading from , writing to,
verifying, and formatting the drive.

Most of the BIOS operations are for experienced software developers who are aware
of the potential danger in their misuse. Also, BIOS versions may vary according to the
processor used and even by computer model.

This chapter introduces the following BIOS INT 13H functions:

DISKETTE FUNCTIONS		HARD DISK FUNCTIONS	
00H	Reset diskette system	00H	Reset disk system
01H	Read diskette status	01H	Read disk status
02H	Read sectors	02H	Read sectors

03H	Write sectors	03H	Write sectors
04H	Verify sectors	04H	Verify sectors
05H	Format tracks	05H	Format tracks
08H	Get drive parameters	08H	Get drive parameters
15H	Get disk type	09H	Initialize drive
16H	Change of diskette status	0AH	Read extended sector buffer
17H	Set diskette type	0BH	Write extended sector buffer
18H	Set media type for format	0CH	Seek cylinder
		0DH	Alternate disk reset
		0EH	Read sector buffer
		0FH	Write sector buffer
		15H	Get disk type
		19H	Park disk heads

BIOS STATUS BYTE

Most of the BIOS INT 13H functions clear or set the carry flag on success or failure and return a status code to the AH register. BIOS maintains information in its data area about each device and its status. The *status byte* shown in Figure 19–1 reflects the indicator bits to be found in the BIOS data area at 40:41H for the Diskette Drive Data Area and at 40:74H for the Hard Disk Data Area. (See Chapter 25 for details.)

If an operation returns an error, a program's usual action is to reset the disk (function 00H) and to retry the operation three times. If there is still an error, display a message and give the user a chance to change the diskette if that's the solution to the problem.

```
Code            Status
00H   No error
01H   Bad command, not recognized by the controller
02H   Address mark on disk not found
03H   Writing on protected disk attempted
04H   Invalid track/sector
05H   Reset operation failed
06H   Diskette removed since last access
07H   Drive parameters wrong
08H   Direct memory access (DMA) overrun
      (data accessed too fast to enter)
09H   DMA across a 64K boundary attempted on read/write
10H   Bad CRC on a read encountered
      (error check indicated corrupted data)
20H   Controller failed (hardware failure)
40H   Seek operation failed (hardware failure)
80H   Device failed to respond (diskette: drive door open
      or no diskette; hard disk: time out)
AAH   Drive not ready
BBH   Undefined error
CCH   Write fault
```

Figure 19–1   INT 13H Status Codes

BASIC BIOS DISK OPERATIONS

This section covers the basic INT 13H disk functions, each requiring a function code in the AH register.

INT 13H, Function 00H: Reset Disk System

Use this operation after the preceding disk operation has reported a serious error. The operation performs a hard reset on the diskette or hard drive controller. That is, the next time the drive is accessed, it first resets to cylinder 0. For a diskette, set the DL to the drive number (0 = drive A, etc.), and for hard disk, set the DL to a value of 80H or higher (80H = the first drive, 81H = the second, etc.). An example of the use of function 00H is as follows:

```
MOV   AH,00H        ;Request reset disk

MOV   DL,80H        ;Hard disk

INT   13H           ;Call BIOS
```

A valid operation clears the carry flag. An error sets the carry flag and returns a status code in the AH. Function 0DH is a related operation.

INT 13H, Function 01H: Read Disk Status

This operation gives you another chance to examine the status of the most recent disk operation. (See status byte in Figure 19–1.) Set the DL to the usual code (0 = drive A, etc.) for diskette and a value of 80H or more (80H = the first drive, etc.) for hard disk. This operation returns to the AL the status code that the last disk operation would have returned to the AH. The operation, which should always be valid, clears the carry flag and returns its own status code, 00H, in the AH.

INT 13H, Function 02H: Read Sectors

This operation reads a specified number of sectors on the same track directly into memory. Initialize the following registers:

AL	Number of sectors, up to the maximum for a track
CH	Track number (numbers begin with 0)
CL	Bits 7–6 Track number (high two bits)
	Bits 5–0 Starting sector number (numbers begin with 1)
DH	Head (side) number (0 or 1 for diskette)
DL	Drive number for diskette (0 = A) or hard drive (80H or higher)
ES:BX	Address of an I/O buffer in the data area, which should be large enough for all the sectors to be read. (BX in this case is subject to the ES.)

The following example reads one sector into an area named INSECT:

```
INSECT  DB   512 DUP(?)      ;Area for input

        ...

        MOV  AH,02H          ;Request read
```

```
          MOV   AL,01              ;One sector

          LEA   BX,INSECT          ;Input buffer (ES:BX)

          MOV   CH,05              ;Track 05

          MOV   CL,03              ;Sector 03

          MOV   DH,00              ;Head 00

          MOV   DL,03              ;Drive 03 (D)

          INT   13H                ;Call BIOS
```

On return from a valid operation, the carry flag is cleared, and the AL contains the number of sectors that the operation has actually read. The contents of the DS, BX, CX, and DX registers are preserved. An error sets the carry flag and returns the status code in the AH; reset the drive (function 00H) and retry the operation.

For most situations, you specify only one sector or all sectors for a track. Initialize the CH and CL, and increment them to read the sectors sequentially. Once the sector number exceeds the maximum for a track, you have to reset it to 01 and either increment the track number on the same side of the disk or increment the head number for the next side.

Testing Whether a Diskette Is Ready

A program may issue a request for accessing a diskette that has not yet been inserted. A standard practice is to attempt the operation three times before displaying a message to the user. The example that follows uses INT 13H, function 02H, in an attempt to read a sector of data. Try using DEBUG to enter the instructions (but not the comments) and test the code with and without a diskette present in drive A. For an installed diskette, the operation should read the contents of the disk's boot record, 512 (200H) bytes read in, beginning at location DS:200H. The code is:

```
0100      MOV CX,03              ;Count for loop

0103      PUSH CX                ;Save count

0104      MOV AX,0201            ;Function code and sectors

0107      MOV BX,0200            ;Input address

010A      MOV CX,0001            ;Track and sector numbers

010D      MOV DX,0000            ;Head and drive numbers

0110      INT 13                 ;Call BIOS

0112      POP CX                 ;Restore count

0113      JNC 118                ;If no error, exit

0115      CLC                    ;If error,

0116      LOOP 103               ; try 3 times

0118      NOP
```

INT 13H, Function 03H: Write Sectors

This operation, the opposite of function 02H, writes a specified area from memory (512 bytes or a multiple of 512) onto designated formatted sectors. Load the registers and handle processing just as for function 02H. A valid operation clears the carry flag and delivers to the AL the number of sectors that were written. The contents of the DS, BX, CX, and DX registers are preserved. An error sets the carry flag and returns a status code in the AH; reset the drive and retry the operation.

USING BIOS TO READ SECTORS

Now let's examine the program in Figure 19–2, which uses BIOS INT 13H to read sectors from disk into memory. Note that there is no open operation or file handle. The major sections are:

CURADR	Contains the beginning track and sector (which the program increments).
ENDADR	Contains the ending track and sector. One way to enhance the program would be to prompt the user for the starting and ending track and sector.
C10ADDR	Calculates each disk address in terms of side, track, and sector. When the sector number reaches 10, the routine resets the sector to 01. If the side is 1, the program increments the track number; the side number is then changed, from 0 to 1 or from 1 to 0. This process works only for diskettes (because they are two sided) that contain nine sectors per track.
F10READ	Reads a sector and increments the sector number for a valid read operation.
G10DISP	Displays the currently read sector.

Try running this program under DEBUG. Trace through the instructions that initialize the segment registers. For the input operation, adjust the starting and ending sectors to the location of the disk's FAT. (See Chapter 16.) Use G (Go) to execute the program, and examine the FAT and directory entries in the input area.

As an alternative to DEBUG, your program could convert the ASCII characters in the input area to their hex equivalents and display the hex values just as DEBUG does. (See also the program in Figure 15–6.) In this way, you could examine the contents of any sector—even hidden ones—and could allow a user to enter changes and write the changed sector back onto disk.

Note that when DOS creates a file, it inserts records in available clusters, which may not be contiguous on disk. Thus, you can't expect BIOS INT 13H to read a file sequentially, although you could access the FAT entries for the location of the next cluster.

OTHER BIOS DISK OPERATIONS

The following describes additional BIOS INT 13H services for diskette and hard disk.

```
TITLE      P19BIORD (COM)  Read disk sectors via BIOS
           .MODEL   SMALL
           .STACK   64
;   -----------------------------------------------------------
           .DATA
CURADR    DW       0304H                 ;Beginning track/sector
ENDADR    DW       0501H                 ;Ending track/sector
ENDCDE    DB       00                    ;End process indicator
READMSG   DB       '*** Read error ***$'
RECDIN    DB       512 DUP(' ')          ;Input area
SIDE      DB       00
;   -----------------------------------------------------------
           .CODE
BEGIN     PROC     FAR
           MOV      AX,@data             ;Initialize
           MOV      DS,AX                ;  segment
           MOV      ES,AX                ;  registers
           MOV      AX,0600H             ;Request scroll
A20LOOP:
           CALL     Q10SCRN              ;Clear screen
           CALL     Q20CURS              ;Set cursor
           CALL     C10ADDR              ;Calculate disk address
           MOV      CX,CURADR
           MOV      DX,ENDADR
           CMP      CX,DX                ;At ending sector?
           JE       A90                  ;  yes, exit
           CALL     F10READ              ;Read disk record
           CMP      ENDCDE,00            ;Normal read?
           JNZ      A90                  ;  no , exit
           CALL     G10DISP              ;Display sector
           JMP      A20LOOP              ;Repeat
A90:       MOV      AX,4C00H
           INT      21H                  ;Exit to DOS
BEGIN     ENDP
;                   Calculate next disk address:
;
C10ADDR   PROC     NEAR
           MOV      CX,CURADR            ;Get track/sector
           CMP      CL,10                ;Past last sector?
           JNE      C90                  ;  no, exit
           MOV      CL,01                ;Set sector to 1
           CMP      SIDE,00              ;Bypass if side 0
           JE       C20
           INC      CH                   ;Increment track
C20:
           XOR      SIDE,01              ;Change side
           MOV      CURADR,CX
C90:       RET
C10ADDR   ENDP
;                   Read disk sector:
;                   ----------------
F10READ   PROC     NEAR
           MOV      AH,02H               ;Request read
           MOV      AL,01                ;Number of sectors
           LEA      BX,RECDIN            ;Address of buffer
           MOV      CX,CURADR            ;Track/sector
           MOV      DH,SIDE              ;Side
           MOV      DL,01                ;Drive B
           INT      13H
           CMP      AH,00                ;Normal read?
           JZ       F90                  ;  yes, exit
           MOV      ENDCDE,01            ;  no:
           CALL     X10ERR               ;  invalid read
```

Figure 19-2 Using INT 13H to Read Disk Sectors

```
F90:
              INC       CURADR                    ;Increment sector
              RET
F10READ ENDP
;                       Display sector:
;                       --------------
G10DISP  PROC  NEAR
              MOV       AH,40H                    ;Request display
              MOV       BX,01                     ;Handle
              MOV       CX,512                    ;Length
              LEA       DX,RECDIN
              INT       21H
              RET
G10DISP  ENDP
;                       Clear screen:
;                       ------------
Q10SCRN  PROC  NEAR
              MOV       AX,0600H                  ;Request scroll
              MOV       BH,1EH                    ;Set attribute
              MOV       CX,0000                   ;Full screen
              MOV       DX,184FH
              INT       10H
              RET
Q10SCRN  ENDP
;                       Set cursor:
;                       ----------
Q20CURS  PROC  NEAR
              MOV       AH,02H                    ;Request set
              MOV       BH,00                     ;  cursor
              MOV       DX,0000
              INT       10H
              RET
Q20CURS  ENDP
;                       Display disk error message:
;                       --------------------------
X10ERR   PROC  NEAR
              MOV       AH,40H                    ;Request display
              MOV       BX,01                     ;Handle
              MOV       CX,18                     ;Length of message
              LEA       DX,READMSG
              INT       21H
              RET
X10ERR   ENDP
         END       BEGIN
```

Figure 19–2   (continued)

INT 13H, Function 04H: Verify Sectors

This operation simply checks that the specified sectors can be read and performs a cyclical redundancy check (CRC). When an operation writes to a sector, the disk controller calculates and writes a CRC checksum immediately following the sector, based on the bits that are set. Function 04H reads the sector, recalculates the checksum, and compares it with the stored value. Note that the verification consists of recalculating the checksum rather than checking that the byte values in the sector agree with the output data in memory. You could use this function after a write (function 03H) to ensure more reliable output, although at a cost of more I/O time.

Load the registers just as for function 02H, but since the operation does not perform true verification of the written data, there is no need to set an address in the ES:BX. On returning from loading, the carry flag is cleared and the AL contains the number of sectors actually verified. The contents of the DS, BX, CX, and DX registers are preserved. An error sets the carry flag and returns a status code in the AH; reset the drive and retry the operation.

INT 13H, Function 05H: Format Tracks

Read/write operations require information on formatting to locate and process a requested sector. This operation formats tracks according to one of four different sizes. Prior to execution of the operation, use function 17H to set the diskette type and function 18H to set the media type. For formatting diskettes, initialize these registers:

AL	Number of sectors to format
CH	Track number (numbers begin with 0)
DH	Head (side) number (0 or 1 for diskette)
DL	Drive number for diskette (0 = A) or hard drive (80H or higher)
ES:BX	Segment:offset address that points to a group of address fields for a track. For each diskette sector on a track, there must be one four-byte entry of the form T/H/S/B, where

> Byte 0 T = track (cylinder) number
> 1 H = head (surface) number
> 2 S = sector number
> 3 B = bytes per sector (00H = 128, 01H = 256, 02H = 512, 03H = 1024)

For example, if you format track 03, head 00, and 512 bytes per sector, the first entry for the track is hex 03000102, followed by one entry for each remaining sector.

The operation clears or sets the carry flag and returns the status code in the AH.

INT 13H, Function 08H: Get Drive Parameters

This useful function returns information about a disk drive. Load the drive number in the DL (0 = A, 1 = B for diskette and 80H or higher for hard disk). A successful operation returns the following:

DL	Diskette type (01H = 360K, 02H = 1.2M, 03H = 720K, 04H = 1.44M)
CH	High cylinder/track number
CL	Bits 0–5 = high sector number
	Bits 6–7 = high-order two bits of cylinder number
DH	High head number
DL	Number of drives attached to the controller
ES:DI	For diskettes, segment:offset of an 11-byte diskette drive parameter table. Two relevant fields are:

> Offset 3—bytes per sector (00H = 128, 01H = 256, 02H = 512, 03H = 1024)
>
> Offset 4 sectors per track

You can use the DEBUG command D ES:offset (the offset in the DI) to display the values. The operation clears or sets the carry flag and returns the status code in the AH.

INT 13H, Function 09H: Initialize Drive

BIOS performs this function when you boot up your computer, according to a hard disk table in BIOS. The DL contains the drive number (80H or higher). The operation clears or sets the carry flag and returns the status in the AH. BIOS INT 41H and INT 46H are related operations.

INT 13H, Function 0AH: Read Extended Sector Buffer

The sector buffer on hard disks includes the 512 bytes of data plus 4 bytes for an error correction code (ECC), used for error checking and correcting the data. This function can read the whole sector buffer rather than just the data portion. To read an extended buffer, load these registers:

AL   Number of sectors (up to the maximum for the drive)
BX   Segment:offset address of the input buffer (as ES:BX)
CH   Cylinder/track number
CL   Bits 0–5 = high sector number
      Bits 6–7 = high-order two bits of cylinder number
DH   Head (side) number
DL   Drive number (80H or higher)

A successful operation returns to the AL the number of sectors transferred. The operation clears or sets the carry flag and returns a status code in the AH.

INT 13H, Function 0BH: Write Extended Sector Buffer

This function is similar to function 0AH, except that, rather than read the sector buffer, it writes it (including the ECC code) onto disk.

INT 13H, Function 0CH: Seek Cylinder

This function positions the read/write head on a hard disk at a specified cylinder (track), but does not transfer any data. To seek a cylinder, load these registers:

CH   Cylinder/track number
CL   Bits 0–5 = sector number
      Bits 6–7 = high-order two bits of cylinder number
DH   Head (side) number
DL   Drive (80H or higher)

The operation clears or sets the carry flag and returns a status code in the AH.

INT 13H, Function 0DH: Alternate Disk Reset

This operation is similar to function 00H, except that it is restricted to hard disks. Load the drive (80H or higher) in the DL. The read/write access arm is reset to cylinder 0. The operation clears or sets the carry flag and returns a status code in the AH.

INT 13H, Function 0EH: Read Sector Buffer

This operation is similar to function 0AH, except that it reads the 512-byte data portion of the sector and not the ECC bytes.

INT 13H, Function 0FH: Write Sector Buffer

This operation is similar to function 0BH, except that it writes the 512-byte data portion of the sector and not the ECC bytes.

INT 13H, Functions 10H: Test for Drive Ready; 11H: Recalibrate Hard Drive; 12H: ROM Diagnostics; 13H: Drive Diagnostics; and 14H: Controller Diagnostics

These functions perform internal diagnostics and report specified information for BIOS and for advanced utility programs. The operations clear or set the carry flag and return a status code in the AH.

INT 13H, Function 15H: Get Disk Type

This function returns information about a disk drive. Load the DL with the drive (0 = A, etc. for diskette or 80H or higher for hard disk). A valid operation returns one of the following codes in the AH:

00H	No drive/disk present
01H	Diskette drive that does not sense a change of diskette
02H	Diskette drive that senses a change of diskette
03H	Hard disk drive

For AH return code 03, the CX:DX pair contains the total number of disk sectors on the drive. The operation clears or sets the carry flag, and error codes are returned in the AH.

INT 13H, Function 16H: Change of Diskette Status

This function checks for a change of diskette for systems that can sense a change. Load the DL with the drive number (0 − A, etc.). The operation returns one of the following codes in the AH:

00H	No change of diskette (carry flag − 0)
01H	Invalid diskette parameter (carry flag = 1)
06H	Diskette changed (carry flag = 1)
80H	Diskette drive not ready (carry flag = 1)

Status codes 01H and 80H are errors that set the carry flag, whereas 06H is a valid status that also sets the carry flag. This is a potential source of confusion.

INT 13H, Function 17H: Set Diskette Type

This operation sets up the combination of drive and diskette. Use function 17H along with function 05H for disk formatting. Load the drive number (0 − A, etc.) in the DL and the diskette type in the AL. Diskette types are:

01H	3603K diskette in 360K drive
02H	360K diskette in 1.2M drive
03H	1.2M diskette in 1.2M drive
04H	720K diskette in 720K drive

The operation clears or sets the carry flag and returns the status in the AH.

INT 13H, Function 18H: Set Media Type for Format

Use this operation immediately before executing function 05H. To set the media type, load these registers:

CH	Number of tracks (low-order eight bits)
CL	Number of tracks (high two bits in bits 7–6), sectors per track (bits 5–0)
DL	Drive (0 = A, etc.)

A valid operation returns in the ES:DI a pointer to an 11-byte diskette parameter table. (See function 08H.) The operation clears or sets the carry flag and returns the status in the AH.

INT 13H, Function 19H: Park Disk Heads

This operation requires the drive number in the DL (80H and higher for hard disk). The operation clears or sets the carry flag and returns the status in the AH.

KEY POINTS

- BIOS INT 13H provides direct access to tracks and sectors.
- BIOS INT 13H does not supply automatic directory handling, end-of-file operations, or blocking and deblocking of records.
- The verify sector operation performs an elementary check of data written at some cost of processing time.
- A program should check for the status byte after each BIOS disk operation.

QUESTIONS

19–1. What are the two major disadvantages of using BIOS INT 13H? That is, why is the use of DOS interrupts usually preferred?

19–2. Under what circumstances would a programmer use BIOS INT 13H?

19–3. Most INT 13H operations return a status code. (a) Where is the code returned? (b) What does code 00H mean? (c) What does code 03H mean?

19–4. What is the standard procedure for an error returned by INT 13H?

19–5. Code the instructions to reset the diskette controller.

19–6. Code the instructions to read the diskette status.

19–7. Using memory address INDSK, drive A, head 0, track 6, and sector 3, code the instructions for BIOS INT 13H to read one sector.

19–8. Using memory address OUTDSK, drive B, head 0, track 8, and sector 1, code the instructions for BIOS INT 13H to write three sectors.

19–9. After the write in Question 19–8, how would you check for an attempt to write on a protected disk?

19–10. Based on Question 19–8, code the instructions to verify the write operation.

CHAPTER 20 ————————————

Printing

OBJECTIVE:

To describe the requirements for printing using the DOS and BIOS interrupts.

INTRODUCTION

Compared to screen and disk handling, printing appears to be a relatively simple process. There are only a few operations involved, all done either through DOS INT 21H or through BIOS INT 17H. The special commands to the printer include Form Feed, Line Feed, and Carriage Return.

A printer must understand a signal from the processor—for example, to eject to a new page, to feed one line down a page, or to tab across a page. The processor also must understand a signal from a printer indicating that it is busy or out of paper. Unfortunately, many types of printers respond differently to signals from a processor, and one of the more difficult tasks for software specialists is to interface their programs to such printers.

This chapter introduces the following interrupt operations:

DOS INT 21H FUNCTIONS	BIOS 17H FUNCTIONS
40H Print characters	00H Print character
05H Print character	01H Initialize port
	02H Get printer port status

COMMON PRINTER CONTROL CHARACTERS

Standard characters that control printing on all common printers for the PC include the following:

Decimal	Hex	Function
09	09H	Horizontal Tab
10	0AH	Line Feed (advance one line)
12	0CH	Form Feed (advance to next page)
13	0DH	Carriage Return (return to left margin)

Horizontal Tab. The Horizontal Tab (09H) control character causes the printer to place the current character at the next tab stop (usually, if set at all, every eight positions). The command works only on printers that have the feature and only when the printer tabs are set up. You can print blank spaces to get around a printer's inability to tab.

Line Feed. The Line Feed (0AH) control character advances a single line, and two successive line feeds cause a double space.

Form Feed. Initializing the paper when you power up a printer determines the starting position for the top of a page. The default length for a page is 11 inches, which provides 66 lines at 6 lines per inch. Neither the processor nor the printer automatically checks for the bottom of a page. On continuous forms, if your program continues printing down a page, it eventually prints over the perforation at the bottom of the page and onto the top of the next page. To control paging, count the lines as they print, and on reaching the maximum for a page (such as 60 lines), issue a Form Feed (0CH) command, and then reset the line count to 0 or 1.

At the end of printing, deliver a Line Feed or Form Feed command to force the printer to print the last line still in its buffer. Issuing a form feed at the end of printing also facilitates the user's tearing off the last page.

Carriage Return. The Carriage Return (0DH) control character resets the printer to its leftmost margin and programs normally accompany it with a Line Feed. On the keyboard, this character is known as Enter or Return.

DOS 21H, FUNCTION 40H: PRINT CHARACTERS

We have already used file handles in the chapters on screen handling and disk processing. For printing with DOS INT 21H, function 40H, load these registers:

AH   Function 40H
BX   File handle 04
CX   Number of characters to print
DX   Address of the text

The following example prints 25 characters from a data item named HEADING, beginning at the leftmost margin. The Carriage Return (0DH) and Line Feed (0AH) characters immediately following the text in HEADING cause the printer to reset the carriage and advance one line:

```
HEADING DB    'Industrial Bicycle Mfrs', 0DH, 0AH

        ...

        MOV   AH,40H        ;Request output

        MOV   BX,04         ;Handle 04 for printer

        MOV   CX,25         ;Send 25 characters

        LEA   DX,HEADING    ;Address of print area

        INT   21H           ;Call DOS
```

A successful operation prints the text, clears the carry flag, and returns in the AX the number of characters printed. An unsuccessful operation sets the carry flag and returns in the AX error code 05 (access denied) or 06 (invalid handle). An end-of-file marker (Ctrl-Z or 0AH) in the data also causes the operation to end.

PRINTING WITH PAGE OVERFLOW AND HEADINGS

The program in Figure 20–1 is similar to the one in Figure 9–2 that accepts names from a user at the keyboard and displays them down the screen. The former, however, directs the names to the printer instead of storing them on disk. Each printed page contains a heading followed by a double space and the entered names in the following format:

```
List of Employee Names      Page 01

Clancy Alderson

Janet Brown

David Christie

        ...
```

The program counts each line printed and, on nearing the bottom of a page, ejects the form to the top of the next page. The major procedures are the following:

D10INPT   Prompts for and accepts a name from the keyboard.
E10PRNT   If at the end of a page (60 lines), calls M10PAGE; prints the name (its length is based on the actual length in the keyboard input parameter list).
M10PAGE   Advances to a new page; prints the heading; resets line count and adds to page count.
P10OUT   Common routine, handles actual request to print.

```
            TITLE      P20PRTNM (EXE)  Accept entered names and print
                       .MODEL   SMALL
                       .STACK   64
            ; -------------------------------------------------------------
                       .DATA
            NAMEPAR    LABEL    BYTE                  ;Keyboard parameter list:
            MAXNLEN    DB       20                    ;   maximum length of name
            NAMELEN    DB       ?                     ;   actual length of name
            NAMEFLD    DB       20 DUP(' ')           ;   name entered
                                                      ;Heading line:
            HEADG      DB       'List of Employee Names    Page  '
            PAGECTR    DB       '01', 0AH, 0AH

            FFEED      DB       0CH                   ;Form feed
            LFEED      DB       0AH                   ;Line feed
            LINECTR    DB       01
            PROMPT     DB       'Name? '
            ; -------------------------------------------------------------
                       .CODE
            BEGIN      PROC     FAR
                       MOV      AX,@data              ;Initialize
                       MOV      DS,AX                 ;   segment
                       MOV      ES,AX                 ;   registers
                       CALL     Q10CLR                ;Clear screen
                       CALL     M10PAGE               ;Page heading
            A20LOOP:
                       MOV      DX,0000               ;Set cursor to 00,00
                       CALL     Q20CURS
                       CALL     D10INPT               ;Provide input of name
                       CALL     Q10CLR
                       CMP      NAMELEN,00            ;No name entered?
                       JE       A30                   ;   no name, exit
                       CALL     E10PRNT               ;   name, prepare printing
                       JMP      A20LOOP
            A30:
                       MOV      CX,01                 ;End of processing:
                       LEA      DX,FFEED              ;   one character
                       CALL     P10OUT                ;   for form feed,
                       MOV      AX,4C00H              ;   exit to DOS
                       INT      21H
            BEGIN      ENDP
            ;                   Accept input of name:
            ;                   --------------------
            D10INPT    PROC     NEAR
                       MOV      AH,40H                ;Request display
                       MOV      BX,01                 ;
                       MOV      CX,05                 ;   5 characters
                       LEA      DX,PROMPT             ;   prompt message
                       INT      21H
                       MOV      AH,0AH                ;Request keyboard
                       LEA      DX,NAMEPAR            ;   input
                       INT      21H
                       RET
            D10INPT    ENDP
            ;                   Prepare for printing:
            ;                   --------------------
            E10PRNT    PROC     NEAR
                       CMP      LINECTR,60            ;End of page?
                       JB       E20                   ;   no, bypass
                       CALL     M10PAGE               ;   yes, print heading
            E20:
                       MOV      CH,00
                       MOV      CL,NAMELEN            ;Set no. of characters
                       LEA      DX,NAMEFLD            ;Set address of name
```

Figure 20–1   Printing With Page and Overflow Headings

```
                    CALL      P10OUT              ;Print name
                    MOV       CX,01               ;One
                    LEA       DX,LFEED            ;  line feed
                    CALL      P10OUT
                    INC       LINECTR             ;Add to line count
                    RET
E10PRNT    ENDP
;                             Page heading routine:
;                             ---------------------
M10PAGE    PROC      NEAR
                    CMP       WORD PTR PAGECTR,3130H   ;First page?
                    JE        M30                 ;  yes, bypass
                    MOV       CX,01               ;
                    LEA       DX,FFEED            ;  no,
                    CALL      P10OUT              ;  form feed,
                    MOV       LINECTR,03          ;  reset line count
M30:
                    MOV       CX,36               ;Length of heading
                    LEA       DX,HEADG            ;Address of heading
M40:
                    CALL      P10OUT
                    INC       PAGECTR+1           ;Add to page count
                    CMP       PAGECTR+1,3AH       ;Page no. = hex 3A?
                    JNE       M50                 ;  no, bypass
                    MOV       PAGECTR+1,30H       ;  yes, set to ASCII
                    INC       PAGECTR             ;
M50:                RET
M10PAGE    ENDP
;                             Print routine:
;                             --------------
P10OUT     PROC      NEAR                         ;CX and DX set on entry
                    MOV       AH,40H              ;Request print
                    MOV       BX,04               ;Handle
                    INT       21H
                    RET
P10OUT     ENDP
;                             Clear screen:
;                             ------------
Q10CLR     PROC      NEAR
                    MOV       AX,0600H            ;Request scroll
                    MOV       BH,60H              ;Attribute
                    MOV       CX,0000             ;From 00,00
                    MOV       DX,184FH            ;  to 24,79
                    INT       10H
                    RET
Q10CLR     ENDP
;                             Set cursor row/col:
;                             -------------------
Q20CURS    PROC      NEAR                         ;DX set on entry
                    MOV       AH,02H              ;Request set cursor
                    MOV       BH,00               ;Page number 0
                    INT       10H
                    RET
Q20CURS    ENDP
                    END       BEGIN
```

Figure 20–1   (continued)

At the beginning of execution, it is necessary to print a heading, but not to eject to a new page. To this end, M10PAGE bypasses the form feed if PAGECTR contains 01, its initial value. PAGECTR is defined as

```
PAGECTR DB '01'
```

which generates an ASCII number, 3031H. The routine in M10PAGE increments PAGECTR by 1 so that it becomes, progressively, 3032, 3033, and so forth. The value is valid up to 3039 and then becomes 303A, which would print as a zero and a colon. If the rightmost byte of PAGECTR contains 3AH, the routine changes it to 30H and adds 1 to the leftmost byte, so that 303AH becomes 3130H, or decimal value 10.

Placing a test for the end of the page before (rather than after) printing a name ensures that the last page has at least one name under the title.

PRINTING ASCII FILES AND HANDLING TABS

A common procedure, performed, for example, by the video adapter, is to replace a Tab character (09H) with blanks through to the next location evenly divisible by 8. Thus tab stops could be at locations 8, 16, 24, and so forth, so that all locations between 0 and 7 tab to 8, those between 8 and 15 tab to 16, and so forth. Some printers, however, ignore Tab characters. DOS PRINT, for example, which prints ASCII files (such as assembly source programs), has to check each character that it sends to the printer. If the character is a Tab, the program inserts blanks to the next tab position.

The program in Figure 20–2 requests a user to enter the name of a file and prints the contents of the file. The program is similar to the one in Figure 17–3 that displays records, but goes a step further in replacing tab stops for the printer with blanks. You'll find the logic in G10XFER, after label G60. Following are three examples of tab stops, for print positions 1, 9, and 21, and the logic for setting the next tab position:

Present print location:	1	9	21
Binary value:	00000001	00001001	00010101
Clear rightmost 3 bits:	00000000	00001000	00010000
Add 8:	00001000	00010000	00011000
New tab location:	8	16	24

The program is organized as follows:

C10PRMP	Requests the user to enter a filename. Pressing only the Enter key indicates that the user is finished.
F10OPEN	Opens the requested disk file for input.
G10XFER	Checks the input data for end of sector, end of file, end of display area, Line Feed, and Tab. Basically, sends regular characters to the display area.
P10PRNT	Prints the display line and clears it to blanks.
R10READ	Reads a sector from the file.

Carriage Return, Line Feed, and Form Feed characters should work on all printers. You could modify the preceding program to count the lines printed and force a form feed when near the bottom of a page, at line 60 or so. (Some users prefer to use an editor program to embed Form Feed characters directly in their ASCII files, at the exact location where they want a page break, such as at the end of a procedure. The usual method is to

```
          TITLE     P20PRTAS (EXE)  Read and print disk records
                    .MODEL  SMALL
                    .STACK  64
          ; -------------------------------------------------------
                    .DATA
          PATHPAR   LABEL   BYTE              ;Parameter list for
          MAXLEN    DB      32                ;  input of
          NAMELEN   DB      ?                 ;  filename
          FILENAM   DB      32 DUP(' ')

          COUNT     DW      00
          DISAREA   DB      120 DUP(' ')      ;Display area
          ENDCDE    DW      00                ;End process indicator
          FFEED     DB      0CH
          HANDLE    DW      0
          OPENMSG   DB      '*** Open error ***'
          PROMPT    DB      'Name of file? '
          SECTOR    DB      512 DUP(' ')      ;Input area for file
          ; -------------------------------------------------------
                    .CODE
          BEGIN     PROC    FAR               ;Main procedure
                    MOV     AX,@data          ;Initialize
                    MOV     DS,AX             ;  segment
                    MOV     ES,AX             ;  registers
                    CALL    Q10SCR            ;Clear screen
                    CALL    Q20CURS           ;Set cursor
          A10LOOP:
                    MOV     ENDCDE,00         ;Initialize
                    CALL    C10PRMP           ;Request filename
                    CMP     NAMELEN,00        ;Any request?
                    JE      A90               ;  no, exit
                    CALL    E10OPEN           ;Open file, get handle
                    CMP     ENDCDE,00         ;Valid open?
                    JNE     A80               ;  no, request again
                    CALL    R10READ           ;Read 1st disk sector
                    CMP     ENDCDE,00         ;End of file, no data?
                    JE      A80               ;  yes, request next
                    CALL    G10XFER           ;Print/read
          A80:
                    JMP     A10LOOP           ;Repeat
          A90:      MOV     AX,4C00H          ;Exit to DOS
                    INT     21H
          BEGIN     ENDP
          ;                   Request file name:
          ;                   -----------------
          C10PRMP   PROC    NEAR
                    MOV     AH,40H            ;Prompt for filename
                    MOV     BX,01
                    MOV     CX,13
                    LEA     DX,PROMPT
                    INT     21H
                    MOV     AH,0AH            ;Accept filename
                    LEA     DX,PATHPAR
                    INT     21H
                    MOV     BL,NAMELEN        ;Insert
                    MOV     BH,00             ;  zero at end of
                    MOV     FILENAM[BX],0     ;  filename
          C90:      RET
          C10PRMP   ENDP
          ;                   Open disk file:
          ;                   --------------
          E10OPEN   PROC    NEAR
                    MOV     AH,3DH            ;Request open
                    MOV     AL,00             ;Read only
```

Figure 20–2   Printing an ASCII File

```
                LEA       DX,FILENAM
                INT       21H
                JNC       E20                 ;Test carry flag,
                CALL      X10ERR              ;  error if set
                JMP       E90
        E20:
                MOV       HANDLE,AX           ;Save handle
                MOV       AX,2020H
                MOV       CX,256              ;Clear sector
                LEA       DI,SECTOR           ;   area to blank
                REP STOSW
        E90:    RET
        E10OPEN ENDP
        ;                 Transfer data to print line:
        ;                 ---------------------------
        G10XFER PROC      NEAR
                CLD                           ;Set left to right
                LEA       SI,SECTOR           ;Initialize
        G20:
                LEA       DI,DISAREA
                MOV       COUNT,00
        G30:
                LEA       DX,SECTOR+512
                CMP       SI,DX               ;End of sector?
                JNE       G40                 ;  no, bypass
                CALL      R10READ             ;  yes, read next
                CMP       ENDCDE,00           ;End of file?
                JE        G80                 ;  yes, exit
                LEA       SI,SECTOR
        G40:
                MOV       BX,COUNT
                CMP       BX,80               ;At end of display area?
                JB        G50                 ;  no, bypass
                MOV       [DI+BX],0D0AH       ;  yes, set CR/LF
                CALL      P10PRNT
                LEA       DI,DISAREA          ;Reinitialize
                MOV       COUNT,00
        G50:
                LODSB                         ;[SI] to AL, INC SI
                MOV       BX,COUNT
                MOV       [DI+BX],AL          ;Character to print line
                INC       BX
                CMP       AL,1AH              ;End of file?
                JE        G80                 ;  yes, exit
                CMP       AL,0AH              ;Line feed?
                JNE       G60
                CALL      P10PRNT             ;Call print
                JMP       G20
        G60:
                CMP       AL,09H              ;Tab character?
                JNE       G70
                DEC       BX                  ;  yes, reset BX
                MOV       BYTE PTR [DI+BX],20H ;Clear tab to blank
                AND       BX,0FFF8H           ;Clear rightmost 3 bits
                ADD       BX,08               ;  and add 8
        G70:
                MOV       COUNT,BX
                JMP       G30
        G80:
                MOV       BX,COUNT            ;End of file
                MOV       BYTE PTR [DI+BX],0CH   ;Form feed
                CALL      P10PRNT             ;Print last line
        G90:    RET
        G10XFER ENDP
```

Figure 20–2   (continued)

```
;                       Print line:
;                       ----------
P10PRNT    PROC      NEAR
           MOV       AH,40H                  ;Request print
           MOV       BX,04
           MOV       CX,COUNT                ;Length
           INC       CX
           LEA       DX,DISAREA
           INT       21H
           MOV       AX,2020H                ;Clear display line
           MOV       CX,60
           LEA       DI,DISAREA
           REP STOSW
           RET
P10PRNT    ENDP
;                       Read disk sector:
;                       ----------------
R10READ    PROC      NEAR
           MOV       AH,3FH                  ;Request read
           MOV       BX,HANDLE               ;Device
           MOV       CX,512                  ;Length
           LEA       DX,SECTOR               ;Buffer
           INT       21H
           MOV       ENDCDE,AX
           RET
R10READ    ENDP
;                       Scroll screen:
;                       ------------
Q10SCR     PROC      NEAR
           MOV       AX,0600H                ;Request scroll
           MOV       BH,1EH                  ;Set attribute
           MOV       CX,0000
           MOV       DX,184FH
           INT       10H
           RET
Q10SCR     ENDP
;                       Set cursor:
;                       ----------
Q20CURS    PROC      NEAR
           MOV       AH,02H                  ;Request set
           MOV       BH,00                   ;   cursor
           MOV       DX,00
           INT       10H
           RET
Q20CURS    ENDP
;                       Display disk error message:
;                       -------------------------
X10ERR     PROC      NEAR
           MOV       AH,40H                  ;Request display
           MOV       BX,01                   ;Handle
           MOV       CX,18                   ;Length
           LEA       DX,OPENMSG              ;Error message
           INT       21H
           MOV       ENDCDE,01               ;Error indicator
           RET
X10ERR     ENDP
           END       BEGIN
```

Figure 20–2   (continued)

hold down the Alt key and press numbers on the numeric keypad—for example, 012 for
Form Feed.)

You could revise the program for DOS function 05H to send each character directly
to the printer, thereby eliminating the definition and use of the display area.

DOS 21H, FUNCTION 05H: PRINT CHARACTER

The original DOS function 05H provides print facilities. Load function 05H in the AH register, the character that you want to print in the DL, and issue INT 21H, as follows:

```
MOV  AH,05H          ;Request print character

MOV  DL,char         ;Character to print

INT  21H             ;Call DOS
```

These instructions are adequate for sending a single character to the printer. However, printing typically involves a full or partial line of text and requires stepping through a line formatted in the data area.

The following example illustrates printing a full line. It first initializes the address of HEADING in the SI register and sets the CX to the length of HEADING. The loop at P20 then extracts each character successively from HEADING and sends it to the printer. Since the first character in HEADING is a Form Feed and the last two characters are Line Feeds, the heading prints at the top of a new page and is followed by a double space. The code is as follows:

```
HEADING DB    0CH,'Industrial Bicycle Mfrs',0DH,0AH,0AH

        ...

        MOV  CX,27           ;Initialize length and

        LEA  SI,HEADING      ; address of heading

P20:

        MOV  AH,05H          ;Request to print

        MOV  DL,[SI]         ; character from heading

        INT  21H             ;Call DOS

        INC  SI              ;Next character in heading

        LOOP P20             ;Loop 27 times
```

If the printer is not on, DOS returns a message, "out of paper," repetitively. If you turn on the power, the program begins printing correctly. You can also press Ctrl+Break to cancel execution of the print operation.

SPECIAL PRINTER CONTROL CHARACTERS

We have already examined the use of a number of basic printer control characters, such as Form Feed and Carriage Return. Other commands suitable for many common printers are the following:

DECIMAL	HEX	ACTION
08	08	Backspace
11	0B	Vertical Tab
15	0F	Turn on condensed mode

14	0E	Turn on expanded mode
18	12	Turn off condensed mode
20	14	Turn off expanded mode

Some commands require a preceding Esc (escape) character (1BH). Some of these commands, depending on the printer, are:

1B	30	Set line spacing to 8 lines per inch
1B	32	Set line spacing to 6 lines per inch
1B	45	Set on emphasized printing mode
1B	46	Set off emphasized printing mode

You can send printer control characters in two different ways:

1. Define commands in the data area. The following sets condensed mode, sets 8 lines per inch, prints a title, and causes a carriage return and line feed:

```
HEADING DB 0FH, 1BH, 30H, 'Title ... ', 0DH, 0AH
```

2. Use immediate instructions to set condensed mode:

```
MOV  AH,05H    ;Request print

MOV  DL,0FH    ;Request condensed mode

INT  21H       ;Call DOS
```

All subsequent characters print in condensed mode until the program sends a command that resets the mode.

The foregoing commands do not necessarily work for all printer models. Check your manual for the printer's specific commands.

BIOS INT 17H FUNCTIONS FOR PRINTING

INT 17H provides facilities for printing at the BIOS level. Valid printer ports for INT 17H are 0 (the default), 1, and 2, for LPT1, LPT2, and LPT3, respectively. INT 17H provides three different functions, as specified in the AH register:

1. Issue function 02H first to determine the printer's status, via a selected port number. Include this status test before every attempt to print. If the printer is available, then
2. Issue function 01H to initialize the printer port, and
3. Issue function 00H operations to send characters to the printer.

The operations return the printer status to the AH, with one or more bits set to 1:

BIT	CAUSE
0	Time out
3	Input/output error
4	Selected

     5   Out of paper
     6   Acknowledged from printer
     7   Not busy

If the printer is already switched on and ready, the operation returns 90H (binary 10010000): the printer is not busy, but is selected, a valid condition. Printer errors are bit 5 (out of paper) and bit 3 (output error). If the printer is not switched on, the operation returns B0H, or binary 10110000, indicating "out of paper."

INT 17H, Function 00H: Print a Character

This operation causes printing of one character and allows for printer ports 0, 1, or 2. Load the character in the AL and the printer port number in the DX:

```
MOV   AH,00H      ;Request print

MOV   AL,char     ;Character to be printed

MOV   DX,00       ;Select printer port 0

INT   17H         ;Call BIOS
```

The operation returns the status to the AH register. The recommended practice is to use function 02H first to check the printer status.

INT 17H, Function 01H: Initialize the Printer Port

This operation selects a port, resets the printer, and initializes it for data:

```
MOV   AH,01H      ;Request initialize port

MOV   DX,00       ;Select printer port 0

INT   17H         ;Call BIOS
```

Since the operation sends a Form Feed character, you can use it to set the printer to the top-of-page position, although most printers do this automatically when turned on. The operation returns a status code in the AH.

INT 17H, Function 02H: Get Printer Port Status

The purpose of this operation is to determine the status of the printer:

```
MOV   AH,02H            ;Request read port

MOV   DX,00             ;Select printer port 0

INT   17H               ;Call BIOS

TEST  AH,00101001B      ;Ready?

JNZ   errormsg          ; no—display message
```

The operation returns the same printer port status as function 01H. When the program runs, if the printer is not initially turned on, BIOS is unable to return a message automatically—your program is supposed to test and act upon the printer status. If your program does not check the status, your only indication is the cursor blinking. If you turn on the printer at this point, some of the output data is lost. Consequently, before executing any BIOS print operations, check the port status; if there is an error, display a message. (The DOS operation performs this checking automatically, although its message, "out of paper," applies to various conditions.) When the printer is switched on, the message no longer appears, and printing begins normally with no loss of data.

At any time, a printer may run out of forms or may be inadvertently switched off. If you are writing a program for others to use, include a status test before every attempt to print.

KEY POINTS

- After printing is completed, use a Line Feed or Form Feed command to clear the printer buffer.
- DOS function 40H (the preferred choice) prints strings of characters, whereas DOS function 05H and BIOS function 17H print a single character at a time.
- DOS provides a message if there is a printer error; BIOS returns only a status code. When using BIOS INT 17H, check the printer status before printing.

QUESTIONS

20–1. Provide the printer control characters for (a) Horizontal Tab; (b) Form Feed; (c) Backspace; (d) Carriage Return.

20–2. Code a program using DOS function 40H for the following requirements: (a) Eject the forms to the next page; (b) print your name; (c) perform a carriage return and a line feed, and print your address; (d) perform a carriage return and a line feed, and print your city and state; (e) eject the forms.

20–3. Revise Question 20–2 to use DOS function 05H.

20–4. Code a heading line that sets condensed mode, defines a title (any name), provides for carriage return and form feed operations, and turns off condensed mode.

20–5. BIOS INT 17H for printing returns an error code. (a) Where is the code returned? (b) What does code 08H mean? (c) What does code 90H mean?

20–6. Revise Question 20–2 to use BIOS INT 17H. Include a test for the printer status.

20–7. Revise Question 20–2 so that the program performs parts (b), (c), and (d) five times.

20–8. Revise Figure 20–1 to run under DOS function 05H.

20–9. Revise Figure 20–2 so that it also displays printed lines.

CHAPTER 21 —————————

Other Input/Output Facilities

OBJECTIVE

To describe programming for the mouse, the IN and OUT
instructions, ports, and generating sound.

INTRODUCTION

This chapter describes the use of the mouse, accessing the the PC's ports, and generating
sound through the PC's speaker. The instructions that are introduced are:

- INT 33H for mouse handling
- IN and OUT for accessing ports

MOUSE FEATURES

The mouse is a commonly used pointing device, basically controlled by a driver that is normally installed by an entry in the CONFIG.SYS or AUTOEXEC.BAT file. The driver must
be installed for a program to respond to the mouse's actions.

All mouse operations within a program are performed by standard INT 33H functions
of the form

```
MOV  AX,function     ;Request mouse

...                  ;Parameter (if any)

INT  33H             ;Call mouse driver
```

Note that unlike other INT operations that use the AH register, INT 33H functions are loaded in the full AX register.

The first mouse instruction that a program issues is function 00H, which simply initializes the mouse driver for the program. Typically, you need issue this command just once, at the start of the program. The next instruction following function 00H should be function 01H, which causes the mouse pointer to appear on the screen. After that, you have a choice of a wide range of mouse operations.

Some Basic Mouse Definitions

- Mickey: A unit of measure for movement of the mouse, approximately 1/200 of an inch.
- Mickey count: The number of mickeys the mouse ball rolls horizontally or vertically. The mickey count is used by the mouse driver to move the pointer on the screen a certain number of pixels.
- Mouse pointer: In text mode, the pointer is a flashing block, in reverse video; in graphics mode, the pointer is an arrowhead.
- Pixel: The smallest addressable element on a screen. For text mode 03, for example, there are eight pixels per byte.
- Threshold speed: The speed in mickeys per second that the mouse must move to double the speed of the pointer on the screen. The default is 64 mickeys per second.

MOUSE FUNCTIONS

The following are the mouse functions available for INT 33H; relatively few of them are commonly used:

00H	Initialize the mouse
01H	Display the mouse pointer
02H	Conceal the mouse pointer
03H	Get button status and pointer location
04H	Set pointer location
05H	Get button-press information
06H	Get button-release information
07H	Set horizontal limits for pointer
08H	Set vertical limits for pointer
09H	Set graphics pointer type
0AH	Set text pointer type
0BH	Read mouse-motion counters
0CH	Install interrupt handler for mouse events

0DH	Turn on light pen emulation
0EH	Turn off light pen emulation
0FH	Set mickey-to-pixel ratio
10H	Set pointer exclusion area
13H	Set double-speed threshold
14H	Swap mouse-event interrupt
15H	Get buffer size for mouse driver state
16H	Save mouse driver state
17H	Restore mouse driver state
18H	Install alternative handler for mouse events
19H	Get address of alternative handler
1AH	Set mouse sensitivity
1BH	Get mouse sensitivity
1CH	Set mouse interrupt rate
1DH	Select display page for pointer
1EH	Get display page for pointer
1FH	Disable mouse driver
20H	Enable mouse driver
21H	Reset mouse driver
22H	Set language for mouse driver messages
23H	Get language number
24H	Get mouse information

COMMON MOUSE OPERATIONS

In this section, we examine the more common mouse operations required for most programs that use the device.

Function 00H: Initialize the Mouse

This is the first command for handling a mouse that a program issues; it needs to be issued only once. Simply load the AX with function 00H, and issue INT 33H. The operation requires no input parameters, but returns these values:

- AX = 0000H if no mouse support is available or FFFFH if support is available
- BX = number of mouse buttons (if support is available)

If mouse support is available, the operation *initializes the mouse driver* as follows:

- Sets the mouse pointer to the center of the screen
- Conceals the mouse pointer if it is visible
- Sets the mouse pointer display page to zero
- Sets the mouse pointer according to the screen mode:
  Text mode = rectangle, inverse color
  Graphics mode = arrow shape

- Sets the mickey-to-pixel ratio:

    Horizontal ratio = 8 to 8

    Vertical ratio = 16 to 8
- Sets the horizontal and vertical limits for the pointer to the minimum and maximum
- Enables light pen emulation mode
- Sets the double-speed threshold to 64 mickeys per second.

Function 01H: Display the Mouse Pointer

After issuing function 00H, use this operation to cause the mouse pointer to be displayed on the screen. The operation requires no input parameters and returns no values.

The mouse driver maintains a *pointer flag* that determines whether or not to display the pointer. It displays the pointer if the flag is zero and conceals it for any other value. Initially, the value is −1; function 01H increments the flag, thus causing the pointer to be displayed. (See also function 02H.)

Function 02H: Conceal the Mouse Pointer

The standard practice is to issue this function at the end of a program's execution, to cause the pointer to be concealed. The operation requires no input parameters and returns no values.

The pointer flag is displayed when it contains a zero value and is concealed for any other value. This function decrements the flag to force it to be concealed.

Function 03H: Get Button Status and Pointer Location

This function returns useful information about the mouse. It requires no input parameters, but returns these values:

- BX = Status of buttons, according to bit location, as follows:

    Bit 0 Left button, where 0 = up, 1 = down

    Bit 1 Right button, where 0 = up, 1 = down

    Bit 2 Center button, where 0 = up, 1 = down

    Bits 3–15 Reserved
- CX = Horizontal (x) coordinate
- DX = Vertical (y) coordinate

The horizontal and vertical coordinates are expressed in terms of *pixels*, even in text mode (8 per byte for video mode 03). The values are always within the minimum and maximum limits for the pointer.

Function 04H: Set Pointer Location

Use this operation to set the horizontal and vertical coordinates for the mouse pointer on the screen (the values for the location are in terms of pixels—8 per byte for video mode 03):

```
MOV   AX,04H           ;Request set mouse pointer

MOV   CX,horiz-locn    ;Horizontal location

MOV   DX,vertl-locn    ;Vertical location

INT   33H              ;Call mouse driver
```

The operation sets the pointer at the new location, adjusted as necessary if outside the minimum and maximum limits.

Illustrative Code

The following code illustrates the use of the mouse instructions covered to this point:

```
MOV    AX,00H          ;Request initialize mouse

INT    33H

CMP    AX,00H          ;Mouse available?

JE     exit            ; no-exit

MOV    AX,01H          ;Request show pointer

INT    33H             ;Call mouse driver

MOV    AX,04H          ;Request set pointer

MOV    CX,24           ;Horizontal location

MOV    DX,16           ;Vertical location

INT    33H             ;Call mouse driver

...

MOV    AX,02H          ;Request hide pointer

INT    33H             ;Call mouse driver
```

Function 05H: Get Button-Press Information

To use this function to return information about button presses, set the BX with the button number, where 0 = left, 1 = right, and 2 = center:

```
MOV   AX,05H           ;Request press information

MOV   BX,button-no     ;Button number

INT   33H              ;Call mouse driver
```

The operation returns the up-down status of all buttons and the press count and location of the requested button:

- AX = Status of buttons, according to bit location, as follows:
  Bit 0 Left button, where 0 = up, 1 = down
  Bit 1 Right button, where 0 = up, 1 = down

Bit 2 Center button, where 0 = up, 1 = down

Bits 3–15 Reserved

- BX = Button-press counter
- CX = Horizontal (x) coordinate of last button press
- DX = Vertical (y) coordinate of last button press

The operation resets the button-press counter to zero.

Function 06H: Get Button-Release Information

To use this function to return information about button releases, set the BX with the button number (0 = left, 1 = right, and 2 = center):

```
MOV   AX,06H          ;Request release information

MOV   BX,button-no    ;Button number

INT   33H             ;Call mouse driver
```

The operation returns the up-down status of all buttons and the release count and location of the requested button, as follows:

- AX = Status of buttons, according to bit location, as follows:

  Bit 0 Left button, where 0 = up, 1 = down

  Bit 1 Right button, where 0 = up, 1 = down

  Bit 2 Center button, where 0 = up, 1 = down

  Bits 3–15 Reserved
- BX = Button release counter
- CX = Horizontal (x) coordinate of last button release
- DX = Vertical (y) coordinate of last button release

The operation resets the button release counter to zero.

Function 07H: Set Horizontal Limits for Pointer

This operation sets the minimum and maximum horizontal limits for the pointer:

```
MOV   AX,07H        ;Request set horizontal limit

MOV   CX,min-locn   ;Minimum limit

MOV   DX,max-locn   ;Maximum limit

INT   33H           ;Call mouse driver
```

If the minimum value is greater than the maximum, the operation exchanges the values. The operation also moves the pointer to within the new area if necessary. See also functions 08H and 10H.

Function 08H: Set Vertical Limits for Pointer

This operation sets the minimum and maximum vertical limits for the pointer:

```
MOV   AX,08H           ;Request set vertical limit

MOV   CX,min-locn      ;Minimum limit

MOV   DX,max-locn      ;Maximum limit

INT   33H              ;Call mouse driver
```

If the minimum value is greater than the maximum, the operation exchanges the values. The operation also moves the pointer to within the new area if necessary. See also functions 07H and 10H.

Function 0BH: Read Mouse-Motion Counters

This operation returns the horizontal and vertical mickey count since the last call to the function (within the range $-32,768$ to $+32,767$). Returned values are:

- CX = Horizontal count (a positive value means travel to the right, negative means to the left)
- DX = Vertical count (a positive value means travel downwards, negative means upwards)

Function 0CH: Install Interrupt Handler for Mouse Events

Your program may need to determine automatically when some activity (or event) has occurred with the mouse. The purpose of function 0CH is to provide an event handler whereby the mouse software interrupts your program and calls the event handler, which performs its required function and returns to your program's point of execution on completion of the task.

Load the CX with an event mask to indicate the actions for which the handler is to respond and the ES:DX with the segment:offset address of the interrupt handler routine:

```
MOV   AX,0CH           ;Request interrupt handler

LEA   CX,mask          ;Address of event mask

LEA   DX,handler       ;Address of handler (ES:DX)

INT   33H              ;Call mouse driver
```

Define the event mask with bits set as required:

- 0 = mouse pointer moved
- 1 = left button pressed
- 2 = left button released
- 3 = right button pressed
- 4 = right button released
- 5 = center button pressed

- • 6 = center button released
- • 7–15 = reserved, define as 0

Define the interrupt handler as a FAR procedure. The mouse driver uses a far call to enter the interrupt handler with these registers set:

- • AX = The event mask as defined, except that bits are set only if the condition occurred
- • BX = Button state, where, if set, the bits mean the following:

0 left button down

1 right button down

2 center button down

- • CX = Horizontal (x) coordinate
- • DX = Vertical (y) coordinate
- • SI = Last vertical mickey count
- • DI = Last horizontal mickey count
- • DS = Data segment for the mouse driver

On the program's entry into the interrupt handler, push all registers and initialize the DS register to the address of your data segment. Within the handler, use only *BIOS*, not DOS, interrupts. On exit, pop all registers.

Function 10H: Set Pointer Exclusion Area

This operation defines a screen area in which the pointer is not displayed:

```
MOV   AX,10H          ;Request set exclusion area

MOV   CX,upleft-x     ;Upper left x coordinate

MOV   DX,upleft-y     ;Upper left y coordinate

MOV   SI,lowrgt-x     ;Lower right x coordinate

MOV   DI,lowrgt-y     ;Lower right y coordinate

INT   33H             ;Call mouse driver
```

To replace the exclusion area, call the function again with different parameters, or reissue function 00H or 01H.

Function 13H: Set Double-Speed Threshold

This operation sets the threshold speed at which the pointer motion on the screen is doubled. Load the DX with the new value (the default is 64 mickeys per second). (See also function 1AH.)

Function 1AH: Set Mouse Sensitivity

Sensitivity concerns the number of mickeys that the mouse needs to move before the pointer is moved. Function 1AH sets the horizontal and vertical mouse motion in terms of the number of mickeys per 8 pixels, as well as the threshold speed at which the pointer motion on the screen is doubled (see also functions 0FH, 13H, and 1BH):

```
MOV   AX,1AH        ;Request set mouse sensitivity

MOV   BX,horzon     ;Horizontal mickeys (default = 8)

MOV   CX,vertic     ;Vertical mickeys (default = 16)

MOV   DX,threshold ;Threshold speed (default = 64)

INT   33H           ;Call mouse driver
```

Function 1BH: Get Mouse Sensitivity

This operation returns the horizontal and vertical mouse motion in terms of number of mickeys per 8 pixels, as well as the threshold speed at which the pointer motion on the screen is doubled. (See function 1AH for the registers and values that are returned.)

Function 1DH: Select Display Page for Pointer

The page for video display is set with INT 10H, function 05H. For mouse operations, set the page number in the BX, and issue INT 33H, function 1DH.

Function 1EH: Get Display Page for Pointer

This operation returns the current video display page in the BX.

Function 24H: Get Mouse Information

This operation returns information about the version and type of mouse that is installed:

- BH = Major version number
- BL = Minor version number
- CH = Mouse type, where 1 = bus mouse, 2 = serial mouse, 3 = InPort mouse, 4 = PS/2 mouse, and 5 = HP mouse

MOUSE PROGRAM

The program in Figure 21–1 illustrates the use of a mouse. The screen displays the horizontal and vertical positions of the pointer as a user moves the mouse. The main procedures are:

BEGIN	Initializes the program, calls B10INIT, D10PTR, G10CONV, AND Q30DISP, and exits to DOS when the user presses the left button.
B10INIT	Issues INT 33H, function 00H, to initialize the mouse (or to indicate that no mouse driver is present) and issues function 01H to cause the mouse pointer to display.
D10PTR	Issues function 03H to check and exit if the user has pressed the left button. If not, the program converts the horizontal and vertical positions from pixel values to binary numbers (by shifting the values 3 bits to the right, effectively dividing by 8). If the location is the same as when it was previously checked, the routine repeats issuing function 03H; if the location has changed, control returns to the caller.

```
TITLE       P21MOUSE (EXE)  Handling the Mouse
            .MODEL SMALL
            .STACK 64
            .DATA
XBINARY     DW      0                       ;Binary X coordinate
YBINARY     DW      0                       ;Binary Y coordinate
ASCVAL      DW      ?                       ;ASCII field

;                   Screen display fields:
DISPDATA    LABEL   BYTE
XMSG        DB      'X = '                  ;X message
XASCII      DW      ?                       ;X ASCII value
            DB      ' '                     ;
YMSG        DB      'Y = '                  ;Y message
YASCII      DW      ?                       ;Y ASCII value

            .CODE
BEGIN       PROC    FAR
            MOV     AX,@data                ;Initialize
            MOV     DS,AX                   ;  DS register
            CALL    Q10CLEAR                ;Clear screen
            CALL    B10INIT                 ;Initialize mouse
            CMP     AX,00                   ;Mouse installed?
            JE      A90                     ;  no, exit
A10:
            CALL    D10PTR                  ;Get mouse pointer
            CMP     BX,01                   ;Button pressed?
            JE      A80                     ;  yes, exit
            CALL    Q20CURS                 ;Set cursor
            MOV     AX,XBINARY              ;
            CALL    G10CONV                 ;X to ASCII
            MOV     AX,ASCVAL               ;
            MOV     XASCII,AX               ;
            MOV     AX,YBINARY              ;
            CALL    G10CONV                 ;Y to  ASCII
            MOV     AX,ASCVAL               ;
            MOV     YASCII,AX               ;
            CALL    Q30DISP                 ;Display X and Y values
            JMP     A10                     ;Repeat
A80:
            CALL    H10HIDE                 ;Hide mouse pointer
A90:
            CALL    Q10CLEAR                ;Clear screen
            MOV     AX,4C00H                ;Exit to DOS
            INT     21H
BEGIN       ENDP
B10INIT     PROC    NEAR
            MOV     AX,00H                  ;Initialize mouse
            INT     33H
            CMP     AX,00                   ;Mouse installed?
            JE      B90                     ;  no, exit
            MOV     AX,01H                  ;Show pointer
            INT     33H
B90:
            RET                             ;Return to caller
B10INIT     ENDP

            .286
D10PTR      PROC    NEAR
D20:        MOV     AX,03H                  ;Get pointer location
            INT     33H
            CMP     BX,01                   ;Right button pressed?
            JE      D90                     ;  yes, means exit
            SHR     CX,03                   ;Divide pixel value
```

Figure 21-1   Using the Mouse

```
              SHR     DX,03              ;  by 8
              CMP     CX,XBINARY         ;Has pointer location
              JNE     D30                ;  changed?
              CMP     DX,YBINARY         ;
              JE      D20                ;  no, repeat operation
D30:                                     ;  yes,
              MOV     XBINARY,CX         ;  save new locations
              MOV     YBINARY,DX         ;
D90:
              RET                        ;Return to caller
D10PTR        ENDP

G10CONV       PROC    NEAR               ;AX = binary X or Y
              MOV     ASCVAL,2020H       ;Clear ASCII field
              MOV     CX,10              ;Set divide factor
              LEA     SI,ASCVAL+1        ;Load ASCVAL address
              CMP     AX,CX              ;Compare location to 10
              JB      G30                ;  lower, bypass
              DIV     CL                 ;  higher, divide by 10
              OR      AH,30H             ;Insert ASCII 3s
              MOV     [SI],AH            ;Store in rightmost byte
              DEC     SI                 ;Decr address of ASCVAL
G30:
              OR      AL,30H             ;Insert ASCII 3s
              MOV     [SI],AL            ;Store in leftmost byte
              RET                        ;Return to caller
G10CONV       ENDP
H10HIDE       PROC    NEAR
              MOV     AX,02H             ;Hide pointer
              INT     33H
              RET                        ;Return to caller
H10HIDE       ENDP

Q10CLEAR      PROC    NEAR
              MOV     AX,0600H           ;Request clear screen
              MOV     BH,30H             ;Colors
              MOV     CX,00              ;Full
              MOV     DX,184FH           ;  screen
              INT     10H
              RET                        ;Return to caller
Q10CLEAR      ENDP

Q20CURS       PROC    NEAR
              MOV     AH,02H             ;Set cursor
              MOV     BH,0               ;Page 0
              MOV     DH,0               ;Row
              MOV     DL,25              ;Column
              INT     10H
              RET                        ;Return to caller
Q20CURS       ENDP

Q30DISP       PROC    NEAR
              MOV     AH,40H             ;Request display
              MOV     BX,01              ;Screen
              MOV     CX,14              ;Number of characters
              LEA     DX,DISPDATA        ;Display area
              INT     21H
              RET                        ;Return to caller
Q30DISP       ENDP
              END     BEGIN
```

Figure 21–1   (continued)

G1OCONV   Converts the horizontal and vertical binary values to displayable ASCII characters. Note that with 8 pixels per byte, the horizontal value returned for screen column 79 (the rightmost location) is $79 \times 8 = 632$. The procedure divides this value by 8 to get, in this case, 79, the maximum case. Consequently, the conversion can correctly assume that values returned are within 0 through 79.

Q30DISP   Displays the horizontal and vertical values.

One way to improve this program would be to issue function 0CH to set an interrupt handler. In this way, the required instructions are automatically invoked whenever the mouse is active.

PORTS

A *port* is a device that connects a processor to the external world. Through a port, a processor receives a signal from an input device and sends a signal to an output device. Ports are identified by their addresses, in the range of 0H—3FFH, or 1,024 ports in all. Note that these addresss are not conventional memory addresses. You can use the IN and OUT instructions to handle I/O directly at the port level:

IN transfers data from an input port to the AL if a byte and to the AX if a word. The general format is

```
IN accum-reg,port
```

OUT transfers data to an output port from the AL if a byte and from the AX if a word. The general format is

```
OUT port,accum-reg
```

You can specify a port address statically or dynamically:

Statically.   Use an operand from 0 through 255 directly as

```
Input      IN AL,port#      ;Input one byte

Output     OUT port#,AX     ;Output one word
```

Dynamically. Use the contents of the DX register, 0 through 65,535, indirectly. This method is suitable for incrementing the DX to process consecutive port addresses. The following example uses port 60H:

```
MOV  DX,60H    ;Port 60H (keyboard)

IN   AL,DX     ;Get byte
```

Some of the major port addresses are:

020H–023H	Interrupt mask registers
040H–043H	Timer/counter
060H	Input from the keyboard
061H	Speaker (bits 0 and 1)
200H–20FH	Game controller
278H–27FH	Parallel printer adapter LPT3
2F8H–2FFH	Serial port COM2
378H–37FH	Parallel printer adapter LPT2
3B0H–3BBH	Monochrome display adapter
3BCH–3BFH	Parallel printer adapter LPT1
3C0H–3CFH	EGA/VGA
3D0H–3DFH	Color graphics adapter (CGA)
3F0H–3F7H	Disk controller
3F8H–3FFH	Serial port COM1

Although the recommended practice is to use DOS and BIOS interrupts, you may safely bypass BIOS when you access ports 21H, 40–42H, 60H, 61H, and 201H. For example, on bootup, a ROM BIOS routine scans the system for the addresses of the serial and parallel port adapters. If the serial port address is found, BIOS places them in its data area, beginning at memory location 40:00H; if the parallel addresses are found, BIOS places them in its data area, beginning at location 40:08H. Each location has space for four one-word entries. The BIOS table for a system with two serial ports and two parallel ports could look like this:

```
40:00   F803   COM1

40:02   F802   COM2

40:04   0000   unused

40:06   0000   unused

40:08   7803   LPT1

40:0A   7803   LPT2

40:0C   0000   unused

40:0E   0000   unused
```

To use BIOS INT 17H to print a character, insert the printer port number in the DX register:

```
MOV   AH,00H       ;Request print

MOV   AL,char      ;Character to print

MOV   DX,0         ;Printer port 0 = LPT1

INT   17H          ;Call BIOS
```

```
TITLE     P21PORT (COM)  Switch printer ports LPT1 & 2
BIOSDAT SEGMENT AT 40H             ;BIOS data area
        ORG      8H                ;Printer port addresses
PARLPRT DW       4 DUP(?)          ;4 words
BIOSDAT ENDS

CODESG  SEGMENT PARA 'code'
        ASSUME  DS:BIOSDAT,CS:CODESG
        ORG     100H
BEGIN:
        MOV     AX,BIOSDAT
        MOV     DS,AX

        MOV     AX,PARLPRT(0)      ;LPT1 address to AX
        MOV     BX,PARLPRT(2)      ;LPT2 address to BX
        MOV     PARLPRT(0),BX      ;Exchange addresses
        MOV     PARLPRT(2),AX      ;Exchange addresses
        MOV     AX,4C00H           ;Exit to DOS
        INT     21H
CODESG  ENDS
        END     BEGIN
```

Figure 21–2   Switching Printer Ports

Some programs allow for printing only via LPT1. If you have two printers attached, as LPT1 and LPT2, you could use the program in Figure 21–2 to reverse (toggle) their addresses in the BIOS table.

GENERATING SOUND

The PC generates sound by means of a built-in permanent magnet speaker. You can select one of two ways to drive the speaker or combine both ways: (1) Use bit 1 of port 61H to activate the Intel 8255A-5 Programmable Peripheral Interface (PPI) chip, or (2) use the gating of the Intel 8353-5 Programmable Interval Timer (PIT). The clock generates a 1.19318-Mhz signal. The PPI controls gate 2 at bit 0 of port 61H.

The program in Figure 21–3 generates a series of notes in ascending frequency. DURTION provides the length of each note, and TONE determines the frequency. The program initially accesses port 61H and saves the value that the operation delivers. A CLI instruction clears the interrupt flag to enable a constant tone. The interval timer generates a clock tick of 18.2 ticks per second that (unless you code CLI) interrupts execution of your program and causes the tone to wobble.

The contents of TONE determine its frequency; high values cause low frequencies and low values cause high frequencies. After the routine B10SPKR plays each note, it increases the frequency of TONE by means of a right shift of 1 bit (effectively halving its value). Since decreasing TONE in this example reduces how long it plays, the routine also increases DURTION by means of a left shift of 1 bit (effectively doubling its value).

The program terminates when TONE is reduced to 0. The initial values in DURTION and TONE have no technical significance. You can experiment with other values and try executing the program without the CLI instruction.

```
        TITLE     P21SOUND (COM)   Produce sound from speaker
        SOUNSG    SEGMENT PARA 'Code'
                  ASSUME    CS:SOUNSG,DS:SOUNSG,SS:SOUNSG
                  ORG       100H
        BEGIN:    JMP       SHORT MAIN
        ; --------------------------------------------------------
        DURTION DW          1000                ;Length of tone
        TONE    DW          256H                ;Frequency
        ; --------------------------------------------------------
        MAIN      PROC      NEAR
                  IN        AL,61H              ;Get port data
                  PUSH      AX                  ;  and save
                  CLI                           ;Clear interrupts
                  CALL      B10SPKR             ;Produce sound
                  POP       AX                  ;Reset
                  OUT       61H,AL              ;  port value
                  STI                           ;Reset interrupts
                  RET
        MAIN      ENDP

        B10SPKR PROC        NEAR
        B20:      MOV       DX,DURTION          ;Set duration of sound
        B30:
                  AND       AL,11111100B        ;Clear bits 0 & 1
                  OUT       61H,AL              ;Transmit to speaker
                  MOV       CX,TONE             ;Set length
        B40:
                  LOOP      B40                 ;Time delay
                  OR        AL,00000010B        ;Set bit 1 on
                  OUT       61H,AL              ;Transmit to speaker
                  MOV       CX,TONE             ;Set length
        B50:
                  LOOP      B50                 ;Time delay
                  DEC       DX                  ;Reduce duration
                  JNZ       B30                 ;Continue?
                  SHL       DURTION,1           ;  no, increase length
                  SHR       TONE,1              ;Reduce frequency
                  JNZ       B20                 ;Now zero?
                  RET                           ;  yes, return
        B10SPKR ENDP
        SOUNSG    ENDS
                  END       BEGIN
```

Figure 21–3   Generating Sound

You could use any variation of the logic to play a sequence of notes, in order, for example, to draw a user's attention. You could also revise the program as per Question 21–7.

KEY POINTS

- In text mode, the mouse pointer is a flashing block, in reverse video; in graphics mode, the pointer is an arrowhead.
- Mouse operations use INT 33H, with a function code loaded in the AX.
- The first mouse operation to execute is function 00H, which initializes the mouse driver.
- Function 01H is required to display the mouse pointer, 03H to get the button status, and 04H to get the pointer location.

- Through a port, a processor receives a signal from an input device and sends a signal to an output device. Ports are identified by their addresses, in the range 0H–3FFH, or 1,024 in all.
- The PC generates sound by means of a built-in permanent magnet speaker. You can select one of two ways to drive the speaker or combine both ways.

QUESTIONS

21–1. Explain these terms: (a) mickey; (b) mickey count; (c) mouse pointer.

21–2. Provide the INT 33H function for each of the following mouse operations:

   (a) Read mouse-motion counters

   (b) Get button-press information

   (c) Conceal the mouse pointer

   (d) Set pointer location

   (e) Get button-release information

   (f) Install interrupt handler for mouse events

21–3. What is the purpose of the mouse pointer flag?

21–4. Code the instructions for the following requirements:

   (a) Initialize the mouse

   (b) Display the mouse pointer

   (c) Get mouse information

   (d) Set the mouse pointer on the center row, to the far right

   (e) Get mouse sensitivity

   (f) Get button status and pointer location

   (g) Conceal the mouse pointer

21–5. Combine the requirements in Question 21–4 into a full program. You can run the program under DEBUG, although at times DEBUG may scroll the pointer off the screen.

21–6. Refer to Figure 21–2, and code the instructions to reverse the addresses for COM1 and COM2.

21–7. Revise the program in Figure 21–3 for the following requirements: Generate notes that decrease in frequency; initialize TONE to 01 and DURTION to a high value. On each loop, increase the value in TONE, decrease the value in DURTION, and end the program when DURTION equals 0.

PART F — Advanced Programming

CHAPTER 22 ⸻⸻⸻⸻

Writing Macros

```
                  OBJECTIVE:

  To explain the definition and use of macro instructions.
```

INTRODUCTION

For each symbolic instruction that you code, the assembler generates one machine-language instruction. But for each coded statement in a high-level language such as C or Pascal, the compiler may generate many machine-language instructions. In this regard, you can think of a high-level language as consisting of *macro* statements.

The assembler has facilities that programmers can use to define macros. You define a specific name for the macro, along with the set of assembly language instructions that the macro is to generate. Then, wherever you need to code the set of instructions, simply code the name of the macro, and the assembler automatically generates your defined instructions.

Macros are useful for the following purposes:

- To simplify and reduce the amount of repetitive coding.
- To reduce errors caused by repetitive coding.
- To streamline an assembly language program to make it more readable.

Examples of functions that may be implemented by macros are input/output operations that load registers and perform interrupts, conversions of ASCII and binary data, multiword arithmetic operations, string-handling routines, and performing division by subtraction.

A SIMPLE MACRO DEFINITION

For macros that you want to include with your program, you first must define them (or copy them from a macro library). A *macro definition* appears before any defined segment. Let's examine a simple macro definition that initializes the segment registers for an .EXE program:

```
INITZ MACRO                   ;Define macro
        MOV   AX,@data        ; } Body of
        MOV   DS,AX           ; } macro
        MOV   ES,AX           ; } definition
        ENDM                  ;End of macro
```

The name of this macro is INITZ, although any other unique valid name is acceptable. The *MACRO directive* on the first line tells the assembler that the instructions that follow, up to *ENDM* ("end macro"), are to be part of a macro definition. The ENDM directive ends the macro definition. The instructions between MACRO and ENDM comprise the *body* of the macro definition.

The names referenced in the macro definition—@data, AX, DS, and ES, must be defined elsewhere in the program or must otherwise be known to the assembler. You may subsequently use the macro instruction INITZ in the code segment where you want to initialize the registers. When the assembler encounters the macro instruction INITZ, it scans a table of symbolic instructions and, failing to find an entry, checks for macro instructions. Since the program contains a definition of the macro INITZ, the assembler substitutes the body of the definition, generating the instructions—the *macro expansion*. A program would use the macro instruction INITZ only once, although other macros are designed to be used any number of times, and each time the assembler generates the same macro expansion.

Figure 22–1 provides a listing of the assembled program. This particular assembler version lists the macro expansion with the number 1 to the left of each instruction to indicate that a macro instruction generated it. A macro expansion indicates only instructions for which object code is generated, so that directives like ASSUME or PAGE would not appear.

It's hardly worth bothering to define a macro that is to be used only once, but you could catalog such a macro in a library for use with all programs. A later section explains how to catalog macros in a library and how to include them automatically in any program.

USING PARAMETERS IN MACROS

To make a macro flexible, you can define names in it as dummy arguments. The following macro definition named PROMPT provides for the use of DOS function 09H to display any

```
                           page 60,132
                   TITLE   P22MACR1 (EXE)  Macro to initialize
                   ; ------------------------------------------------
                           INITZ  MACRO              ;Define macro
                           MOV    AX,@data
                           MOV    DS,AX
                           MOV    ES,AX
                           ENDM                      ;End macro
                   ; ------------------------------------------------
                           .MODEL SMALL
                           .STACK 64
                   ; ------------------------------------------------
                           .DATA
0000 54 65 73 74 20 6F     MESSGE  DB    'Test of macro instruction',13,10,'$'
     66 20 6D 61 63 72
     6F 20 69 6E 73 74
     72 75 63 74 69 6F
     6E 0D 0A 24
                   ; ------------------------------------------------
                           .CODE
0000               BEGIN   PROC   FAR
                           INITZ                     ;Macro instruction
0000 B8 ---- R    1        MOV    AX,@data
0003 8E D8        1        MOV    DS,AX
0005 8E C0        1        MOV    ES,AX
0007 B4 09                 MOV    AH,09H             ;Request display
0009 8D 16 0000 R          LEA    DX,MESSGE          ;Message
000D CD 21                 INT    21H
000F B8 4C00               MOV    AX,4C00H           ;Exit to DOS
0012 CD 21                 INT    21H
0014               BEGIN   ENDP
                           END    BEGIN
    -----------------------------------------------------------------
Macros:
          N a m e              Lines
INITZ . . . . . . . . . .      3

Segments and Groups:
          N a m e              Length  Align   Combine   Class
DGROUP . . . . . . . . . . .   GROUP
_DATA  . . . . . . . . . . .   001C    WORD    PUBLIC    'DATA'
STACK  . . . . . . . . . . .   0040    PARA    STACK     'STACK'
_TEXT  . . . . . . . . . . .   0014    WORD    PUBLIC    'CODE'

Symbols:
          N a m e              Type    Value   Attr
BEGIN  . . . . . . . . . . . . F PROC  0000    _TEXT     Length = 0014
MESSGE . . . . . . . . . . . . L BYTE  0000    _DATA
@CODE  . . . . . . . . . . . . TEXT    _TEXT
@FILENAME  . . . . . . . . . . TEXT    p22macr1
```

Figure 22–1   Simplified Assembled Macro Instruction

message. When using the macro instruction, the programmer has to supply the name of the message, which references a data area terminated by a dollar sign.

```
          PROMPT  MACRO MESSGE          ;Dummy argument

          MOV   AH,09H

          LEA   DX,MESSGE

          INT   21H

          ENDM                          ;End of macro
```

A *dummy argument* in a macro definition tells the assembler to match its name with any occurrence of the same name in the macro body. For example, the dummy argument MESSGE also occurs in the LEA instruction.

When using the macro instruction PROMPT, you would supply as a parameter the actual name of the message to be displayed, for example,

```
                        PROMPT MESSAGE2
```

In this case, MESSAGE2 has to be properly defined in the data segment. The parameter in the macro instruction matches the dummy argument in the original macro definition:

```
Macro definition: PROMPT   MACRO   MESSGE      (argument)
                                      |
Macro instruction:        PROMPT   MESSAGE2  (parameter)
```

The assembler has already matched the argument in the original macro definition with the LEA statement in the body of the macro. It now substitutes the parameter(s) of the macro instruction MESSAGE2 with the dummy argument in the macro definition, MESSGE. The assembler substitutes MESSAGE2 for the occurrence of MESSGE in the LEA instruction and would substitute it for any other occurrence of MESSGE.

The macro definition and macro expansion are shown in full in Figure 22–2. The program also defines the macro INITZ at the start and uses it in the code segment.

A dummy argument may contain any valid name, including a register name such as CX. You may define a macro with any number of dummy arguments, separated by commas, up to column 120 of a line. The assembler substitutes parameters of the macro instruction for dummy arguments in the macro definition, entry for entry, from left to right.

COMMENTS

You may code comments in a macro definition to clarify its purpose. A COMMENT directive or a semicolon indicates a comment line. The following example uses a semicolon to indicate a comment:

```
PROMPT   MACRO      MESSGE

;          This macro permits display of messages

         MOV   AH,09H

         LEA   DX,MESSGE

         INT   21H

         ENDM
```

Because the default is to list only instructions that generate object code, the assembler does not automatically display a comment when it expands a macro definition. If you want a comment to appear within an expansion, use the listing directive .LALL ("list all," including the leading period) prior to requesting the macro instruction:

```
                            page    60,132
                    TITLE   P22MACR2 (EXE)  Use of parameters
                    ; ------------------------------------------
                    INITZ   MACRO                    ;Define macro
                            MOV     AX,@data
                            MOV     DS,AX
                            MOV     ES,AX
                            ENDM
                                                     ;End macro
                    PROMPT  MACRO   MESSGE           ;Define macro
                            MOV     AH,09H
                            LEA     DX,MESSGE
                            INT     21H
                            ENDM                     ;End macro
                    ; ------------------------------------------
                            .MODEL SMALL
                            .STACK 64
                    ; ------------------------------------------
                            .DATA
0000 43 75 73 74 6F 6D   MESSG1  DB      'Customer name?', '$'
     65 72 20 6E 61 6D
     65 3F 24
000F 43 75 73 74 6F 6D   MESSG2  DB      'Customer address?', '$'
     65 72 20 61 64 64
     72 65 73 73 3F 24
                    ; ------------------------------------------
                            .CODE
0000                    BEGIN   PROC    FAR
                                INITZ
0000 B8 ---- R        1       MOV     AX,@data
0003 8E D8            1       MOV     DS,AX
0005 8E C0            1       MOV     ES,AX
                        PROMPT  MESSG2
0007 B4 09            1       MOV     AH,09H
0009 8D 16 000F R     1       LEA     DX,MESSG2
000D CD 21            1       INT     21H
000F B8 4C00                  MOV     AX,4C00H         ;Exit to DOS
0012 CD 21                    INT     21H
0014                    BEGIN   ENDP
                                END     BEGIN
```

Figure 22–2 Using Macro Parameters

```
        .LALL

PROMPT   MESSAGE1
```

A macro definition could contain a number of comments, some of which you may want to list and some to suppress. Still use .LALL to list them, but code double semicolons (;;) before comments that are always to be suppressed. (The assembler default is .XALL, which causes a listing only of instructions that generate object code.) On the other hand, you may not want to list any of the source code of a macro expansion, especially if the macro instruction is used several times in a program. In that case, code the listing directive .SALL ("suppress all"), which reduces the size of the printed program, although it has no effect on the size of the generated object module.

A listing directive holds effect throughout a program until another listing directive is encountered. You can place them in a program to cause some macros to list only the generated object code (.XALL), some to list both object code and comments (.LALL), and some to suppress listing both object code and comments (.SALL).

```
                              page    60,132
                       TITLE   P22MACR3 (EXE)  Use of .LALL & .SALL
                       ; ----------------------------------------------
                       INITZ   MACRO                      ;Define macro
                               MOV    AX,@data
                               MOV    DS,AX
                               MOV    ES,AX
                               ENDM                       ;End macro
                       ; ----------------------------------------------
                       PROMPT  MACRO MESSGE
                       ;       This macro displays any message
                       ;;      Generates code that calls DOS service
                               MOV    AH,09H      ;Request display
                               LEA    DX,MESSGE
                               INT    21H
                               ENDM
                       ; ----------------------------------------------
                               .MODEL SMALL
                               .STACK 64
                       ; ----------------------------------------------
                               .DATA
0000 43 75 73 74 6F 6D    MESSG1  DB      'Customer name?', 13, 10, '$'
     65 72 20 6E 61 6D
     65 3F 0D 0A 24
0011 43 75 73 74 6F 6D    MESSG2  DB      'Customer address?', 13, 10, '$'
     65 72 20 61 64 64
     72 65 73 73 3F 0D
     0A 24
                       ; ----------------------------------------------
                               .CODE
0000                   BEGIN   PROC    FAR
                               .SALL
                               INITZ
                               PROMPT MESSG1
                               .LALL
                               PROMPT MESSG2
                    1  ;       This macro displays any message
                    1  ;
000F B4 09          1          MOV    AH,09H            ;Request display
0011 8D 16 0011 R   1          LEA    DX,MESSG2
0015 CD 21          1          INT    21H
0017 B8 4C00                   MOV    AX,4C00H          ;Exit to DOS
001A CD 21                     INT    21H
001C                   BEGIN   ENDP
                               END    BEGIN
```

Figure 22–3　Listing and Suppression of Macro Expansions

The program in Figure 22–3 illustrates the preceding features. It defines the two macros, INITZ and PROMPT, described earlier. The code segment contains the listing directive .SALL to suppress listing the expansion of INITZ and the first expansion of PROMPT. For the second use of PROMPT, the listing directive .LALL causes the assembler to list the comment and the expansion of the macro. But note that in the macro definition for PROMPT, the comment in the macro expansion containing a double semicolon (;;) is not listed.

MASM 6.0 introduced the terms .LISTMACROALL, LISTMACRO, and .NOLIST-MACRO for .LALL, .XALL, and .SALL, respectively.

USING A MACRO WITHIN A MACRO DEFINITION

A macro definition may contain a reference to another defined macro. Consider a simple macro named DOS21 that loads a function in the AH register and issues INT 21H:

```
DOS21   MACRO  DOSFUNC
        MOV    AH,DOSFUNC
        INT    21H
        ENDM
```

To use this DOS21 macro to accept input from the keyboard, code

```
        LEA    DX,NAMEPAR
        DOS21 0AH
```

The generated code for DOS21 would load function 0AH into the AH and issue INT 21H for keyboard input. Now suppose you have another macro, named DISP, that loads INT 21H, function 02H, in the AH register to display a character:

```
DISP    MACRO  CHAR
        MOV    AH,02H
        MOV    DL,CHAR
        INT    21H
        ENDM
```

To display a question mark, for example, code the macro as DISP '?'. You could change DISP to take advantage of the DOS21H macro by referring to DOS21 within DISP's macro definition:

```
DISP    MACRO  CHAR
        MOV    DL,CHAR
        DOS21 02H
        ENDM
```

Now if you code the DISP macro as DISP '?', the assembler generates

```
        MOV    DL,'?'
        MOV    AH,02H
        INT    21H
```

THE LOCAL DIRECTIVE

Some macros require that you define data items and instruction labels within the macro definition. If you use the macro more than once in the same program, and the assembler defines the data item or label for each occurrence, the duplicate names would cause the assembler to generate an error message. To ensure that each generated name is unique, code the LOCAL directive immediately after the MACRO statement, even before comments. Its general format is

```
        LOCAL  dummy-1, dummy-2, ...    ;One or more dummy arguments
```

Figure 22–4 illustrates the use of LOCAL. The purpose of the program is to perform division by successive subtraction. The routine subtracts the divisor from the dividend and adds 1 to the quotient until the dividend is less than the divisor. The procedure requires two labels: COMP for the loop address and OUT for exiting the procedure on completion. Both COMP and OUT are defined as LOCAL and may have any valid names.

```
                              TITLE    P22MACR4 (EXE)  Use of LOCAL
                              ; ------------------------------------------------
                              INITZ    MACRO                           ;Define macro
                                       MOV     AX,@data
                                       MOV     DS,AX
                                       MOV     ES,AX
                                       ENDM                            ;End macro
                              DIVIDE   MACRO   DIVIDEND,DIVISOR,QUOTIENT
                                       LOCAL   COMP
                                       LOCAL   OUT
                              ;                AX = div'd, BX = divisor, CX = quotient
                                       MOV     AX,DIVIDEND      ;Set dividend
                                       MOV     BX,DIVISOR       ;Set divisor
                                       SUB     CX,CX            ;Clear quotient
                              COMP:
                                       CMP     AX,BX            ;Div'd < divisor?
                                       JB      OUT              ;  yes, exit
                                       SUB     AX,BX            ;Div'd - divisor
                                       INC     CX               ;Add to quotient
                                       JMP     COMP
                              OUT:
                                       MOV     QUOTIENT,CX      ;Store quotient
                                       ENDM                     ;End macro
                              ; ------------------------------------------------
                                       .MODEL SMALL
                                       .STACK 64
                              ; ------------------------------------------------
                                       .DATA
0000  0096                    DIVDND   DW      150              ;Dividend
0002  001B                    DIVSOR   DW      27               ;Divisor
0004  0000                    QUOTNT   DW      ?                ;Quotient
                              ; ------------------------------------------------
                                       .CODE
0000                          BEGIN    PROC    FAR
                                       .LALL
                                       INITZ
0000  B8 ---- R      1                 MOV     AX,@data
0003  8E D8         1                 MOV     DS,AX
0005  8E C0         1                 MOV     ES,AX
                                       DIVIDE DIVDND,DIVSOR,QUOTNT
              1 ;                AX = div'd, BX = divisor, CX = quotient
0007  A1 0000 R     1                 MOV     AX,DIVDND        ;Set dividend
000A  8B 1E 0002 R  1                 MOV     BX,DIVSOR        ;Set divisor
000E  2B C9         1                 SUB     CX,CX            ;Clear quotient
0010              1 ??0000:
0010  3B C3         1                 CMP     AX,BX            ;Div'd < divisor?
0012  72 05         1                 JB      ??0001           ;  yes, exit
0014  2B C3         1                 SUB     AX,BX            ;Div'd - divisor
0016  41            1                 INC     CX               ;Add to quotient
0017  EB F7         1                 JMP     ??0000
0019              1 ??0001:
0019  89 0E 0004 R  1                 MOV     QUOTNT,CX        ;Store quotient
001D  B8 4C00                         MOV     AX,4C00H         ;Exit to DOS
0020  CD 21                           INT     21H
0022                          BEGIN    ENDP
                                       END     BEGIN
```

Figure 22–4   Using LOCAL

In the macro expansion, the generated symbolic label for COMP is ??0000 and for OUT is ??0001. If you use the DIVIDE macro instruction again in the same program, the symbolic labels for the next macro expansion would become ??0002 and ??0003, respectively. In this way, the feature ensures that labels generated within a program are unique.

INCLUDES FROM A MACRO LIBRARY

Defining a macro such as INITZ or PROMPT and using it just once in a program is not very productive. The standard approach is to catalog your macros in a disk library under a descriptive name, such as MACRO.LIB. You simply have to gather all your macro definitions into one file and store the file on disk:

```
INITZ    MACRO
         ...
         ENDM
PROMPT   MACRO      MESSGE
         ...
         ENDM
```

To use any of the cataloged macros, instead of coding MACRO definitions at the start of the program, use an INCLUDE directive like this:

```
INCLUDE D:\MACRO.LIB
...
INITZ
```

The assembler accesses the file named MACRO.LIB on drive D and includes both macro definitions, INITZ and PROMPT, into the program. In this example, only INITZ is actually required. The assembled listing will contain a copy of the macro definitions, indicated by the letter C in column 30 of the LST file. Following each macro instruction will be the expansion of the macro, along with its generated object code, indicated by a plus (+) in column 31.

Since a MASM assembly (up to and including version 5.1) is a two-pass operation, you can use the following statements to cause INCLUDE to occur only on pass 1 (instead of both passes):

```
IF1

        INCLUDE D:\MACRO.LIB

ENDIF
```

IF1 and ENDIF are conditional directives. IF1 tells the assembler to access the named library only on pass 1 of the assembly. ENDIF terminates the IF logic. A copy of the macro definition no longer appears on the listing—a saving of both time and space. (MASM versions 6.0 and on do not need directives that refer to two passes.)

The program in Figure 22–5 contains the previously described IF1, INCLUDE, and ENDIF statements, although the assembler lists only the ENDIF in the LST file. The two macro instructions used in the code segment, INITZ and PROMPT, are both cataloged in

```
                                 page      60,132
                         TITLE   P22MACR5 (EXE)  Test of INCLUDE
                         ; ---------------------------------------
                                 .MODEL   SMALL
                                 .STACK   64
                         ; ---------------------------------------
                                 .DATA
0000 54 65 73 74 20 6F   MESSGE  DB       'Test of macro', '$'
     66 20 6D 61 63 72
     6F 24

                         ; ---------------------------------------
                                 .CODE
0000                     BEGIN   PROC     FAR
                                 INITZ
0000 B8 ---- R      1            MOV      AX,@data
0003 8E D8          1            MOV      DS,AX
0005 8E C0          1            MOV      ES,AX
                                 PROMPT   MESSGE
0007 B4 09          1            MOV      AH,09        ;Request display
0009 8D 16 0000 R 1              LEA      DX,MESSGE
000D CD 21          1            INT      21H
000F B8 4C00                     MOV      AX,4C00H     ;Exit to DOS
0012 CD 21                       INT      21H
0014                     BEGIN   ENDP
                                 END      BEGIN
```

Figure 22–5   Using the Library INCLUDE

MACRO.LIB. They were simply stored together as a disk file under that name by means of an editor program.

The placement of INCLUDE is not critical, but the directive must appear before any macro instruction that references the library entry.

The PURGE Directive

Execution of an INCLUDE statement causes the assembler to include all the macro definitions that are in the specified library. Suppose, however, that a library contains the macros INITZ, PROMPT, and DIVIDE, but a program requires only INITZ. The PURGE directive enables you to "delete" the unwanted macros PROMPT and DIVIDE from the current assembly:

```
        IF1
                INCLUDE D:\MACRO.LIB      ;Include full library
        ENDIF
        PURGE   PROMPT,DIVIDE            ;Delete unneeded macros
        ...
        INIT    CSEG,DATA,STACK          ;Use remaining macro
```

A PURGE operation facilitates only the assembly of a program and has no effect on macros stored in the library.

CONCATENATION

The ampersand (&) character tells the assembler to join (concatenate) text or symbols. The following MOVE macro provides for generating the MOVSB, MOVSW, or MOVSD instruction:

```
            MOVE   MACRO   TAG

                   REP  MOVS&TAG

                   ENDM
```

A user could code this macro instruction as MOVE B, MOVE W, or MOVE D. The assembler will concatenate the parameter with the MOVS instruction, to produce REP MOVSB, REP MOVSW, or REP MOVSD, respectively. (This example is somewhat trivial and is for illustrative purposes only.)

REPETITION DIRECTIVES

The repetition directives REPT, IRP, and IRPC cause the assembler to repeat a block of statements terminated by ENDM. (MASM 6.0 introduced the terms REPEAT, FOR, and FORC for REPT, IRP, and IRPC, respectively.) These directives do not have to be contained in a MACRO definition, but if they are, one ENDM is required to end the repetition and a second ENDM to end the MACRO definition.

REPT: Repeat

The REPT directive causes repetition of a block of statements up to ENDM according to the number of times in the expression entry:

```
            REPT      expression
```

The following example initializes the value N to 0 and then repeats the generation of DB N five times:

```
                   N =     0

                   REPT    5

                   N =     N + 1

                   DB      N

                   ENDM
```

The result is five generated DB statements, DB 1 through DB 5. A use for REPT could be to define a table or part of a table. The next example defines a macro that uses REPT for beeping the speaker five times:

```
        BEEPSPKR   MACRO
                   MOV     AH,02H        ;Request output
                   MOV     DL,07         ;Beep character
                    REPT   5             ;Repeat five times
                     INT   21H           ;Call DOS
                    ENDM                 ;End of REPT
                   ENDM                  ;End of MACRO
```

IRP: Indefinite Repeat

The IRP directive causes a repeat of a block of instructions up to ENDM. The general format is

```
IRP dummy,<arguments>
```

The arguments, contained in angle brackets, are any number of valid symbols, including string, numeric, or arithmetic constants. The assembler generates a block of code for each argument. In the following example, the assembler generates DB 3, DB 9, DB 17, DB 25, and DB 28:

```
IRP   N,<3,9,17,25,28>

DB    N
```

IRPC: Indefinite Repeat Character

The IRPC directive causes a repeat of the block of statements up to ENDM. The general format is

```
IRPC dummy,string
```

The assembler generates a block of code for each character in the string. In the following example, the assembler generates DW 3 through DW 8:

```
IRPC    N,345678
DW      N
ENDM
```

CONDITIONAL DIRECTIVES

Assembly language supports a number of conditional directives. We used IF1 earlier to include a library entry only during pass 1 of an assembly. Conditional directives are most useful within a macro definition, but are not limited to that purpose. Every IF directive must have a matching ENDIF to terminate a tested condition. One optional ELSE may provide an alternative action. Here is the general format for the IF family of conditional directives:

```
IFxx     (condition)  ⎫
...                    ⎪  conditional
ELSE     (optional)    ⎬
...                    ⎪  block
ENDIF    (end of IF)  ⎭
```

Omission of ENDIF causes the error message "Undetermined conditional." If a condition being examined is true, the assembler executes the conditional block up to the ELSE or, if no ELSE is present, up to the ENDIF. If the condition is false, the assembler executes the conditional block following the ELSE; if no ELSE is present, it does not generate any of the conditional block.

The following explains the various conditional directives:

- IF expression   If the expression evaluates to a nonzero value, the assembler assembles the statements within the conditional block.
- IFE expression   If the expression evaluates to a zero, the assembler assembles the statements within the conditional block.
- IF1 (no expression)   If the assembler is processing pass 1, it acts on the statements in the conditional block.
- IF2 (no expression)   If the assembler is processing pass 2, it acts on the statements in the conditional block.
- IFDEF symbol   If the symbol is defined in the program or is declared as EXTRN, the assembler processes the statements in the conditional block.
- IFNDEF symbol   If the symbol is not defined or is not declared as EXTRN, the assembler processes the statements in the conditional block.
- IFB <argument>   If the argument is blank, the assembler processes the statements in the conditional block. The argument requires angle brackets.
- IFNB <argument>   If the argument is not blank, the assembler processes the statements in the conditional block. The argument requires angle brackets.
- IFIDN <arg-1>,<arg-2>   If the argument-1 string is identical to the argument-2 string, the assembler processes the statements in the conditional block. The arguments require angle brackets.
- IFDIF <arg-1>,<arg-2>   If the argument-1 string is different from the argument-2 string, the assembler processes the statements in the conditional block. The arguments require angle brackets.

IF and IFE can use the relational operators EQ (equal), NE (not equal), LT (less than), LE (less than or equal), GT (greater than), and GE (greater than or equal) as, for example, in the statement

```
IF expression1 EQ expression2
```

Here's a simple example of the use of IFNB (if not blank). All INT 21H requests require a function in the AH register, and some requests also require a value in the DX. The macro DOS21 uses IFNB to test for a nonblank argument for the DX; if the result is true (the argument is nonblank), the assembler generates the MOV instruction that loads the DX:

```
DOS21   MACRO   DOSFUNC,DXADDRES
        MOV     AH,DOSFUNC
        IFNB    <DXADDRES>
        MOV     DX,OFFSET DXADDRES
        ENDIF
        INT     21H
        ENDM
```

Using DOS21 for simple keyboard input requires only loading the AH with a value, in this case, function 01H:

```
DOS21   01
```

The assembler generates MOV AH,01 and INT 21H. Input of a character string requires function 0AH in the AH and the input address in the DX. You could code the DOS21 macro as

```
DOS21   0AH,IPFIELD
```

The assembler then generates both the MOV and the INT 21H instructions.

The EXITM Directive

A macro definition may contain a conditional directive that tests for a serious condition. If the condition is true, the assembler is to exit from any further macro expansion. The EXITM directive serves this purpose:

```
IFxx  [condition]
...  (invalid condition)
EXITM
...
ENDIF
```

If the assembler encounters EXITM in an expansion of a macro instruction, it discontinues the macro expansion and resumes processing after ENDM. You can also use EXITM to end REPT, IRP, and IRPC directives, even if they are contained within a macro definition.

Macro Using IF and IFNDEF Conditions

The skeleton program in Figure 22–6 contains a macro definition named DIVIDE that generates a routine to perform division by successive subtraction. A user has to code the macro instruction with parameters for the dividend, divisor, and quotient, in that order. The macro uses IFNDEF to check whether the program actually contains their definitions. For any entry not defined, the macro increments a field named CNTR. Technically, CNTR could have any valid name and is for temporary use in a macro definition. After checking the three parameters, the macro checks CNTR for nonzero:

```
IF    CNTR

;    Macro expansion terminated

EXITM

ENDIF
```

If CNTR has been set to a nonzero value, the assembler generates the comment and exits (EXITM) from any further macro expansion. Note that an initial instruction clears CNTR to 0 and also that the IFNDEF blocks need only to set CNTR to 1 rather than increment it.

If the assembler passes all the tests safely, it generates the macro expansion. In the code segment, the second DIVIDE macro instruction contains an invalid dividend and quotient and generates only comments. A way to improve the macro would be to test whether the divisor is nonzero and whether the dividend and divisor have the same sign; for these purposes, use assembly instructions rather than conditional directives.

```
                              page      60,132
                     TITLE     P22MACR6 (EXE)  Test of IF and IFNDEF
                   ; --------------------------------------------------
                     INITZ     MACRO                        ;Define macro
                               MOV       AX,@data           ;Initialize
                               MOV       DS,AX              ;  segment
                               MOV       ES,AX              ;  registers
                               ENDM                         ;End macro
                     DIVIDE    MACRO     DIVIDEND,DIVISOR,QUOTIENT
                               LOCAL     COMP
                               LOCAL     OUT
                               CNTR      = 0
                   ;                     AX = div'nd, BX = div'r, CX = quot't
                               IFNDEF    DIVIDEND
                   ;                     Dividend not defined
                               CNTR      = CNTR +1
                               ENDIF
                               IFNDEF    DIVISOR
                   ;                     Divisor not defined
                               CNTR      = CNTR +1
                               ENDIF
                               IFNDEF    QUOTIENT
                   ;                     Quotient not defined
                               CNTR      = CNTR + 1
                               ENDIF
                               IF        CNTR
                   ;                     Macro expansion terminated
                               EXITM
                               ENDIF
                               MOV       AX,DIVIDEND        ;Set dividend
                               MOV       BX,DIVISOR         ;Set divisor
                               SUB       CX,CX              ;Clear quotient
                     COMP:
                               CMP       AX,BX              ;Div'd < divisor?
                               JB        OUT                ;  yes, exit
                               SUB       AX,BX              ;Div'd - divisor
                               INC       CX                 ;Add to quotient
                               JMP       COMP
                     OUT:
                               MOV       QUOTIENT,CX        ;Store quotient
                               ENDM
                   ; --------------------------------------------------
                               .MODEL    SMALL
                               .STACK    64
                               .DATA
0000  0096        DIVDND    DW        150                ;Dividend
0002  001B        DIVSOR    DW        27                 ;Divisor
0004  0000        QUOTNT    DW        ?                  ;Quotient
                   ; --------------------------------------------------
                               .CODE
0000              BEGIN     PROC      FAR
                               .LALL
                               INITZ
0000 B8 ---- R    1          MOV       AX,@data           ;Initialize
0003 8E D8        1          MOV       DS,AX              ;  segment
0005 8E   C0      1          MOV       ES,AX              ;  registers
                               DIVIDE    DIVDND,DIVSOR,QUOTNT
= 0000            1          CNTR      = 0
                  1 ;                   AX = div'nd, BX = div'r, CX = quot't
0007 A1 0000 R    1          MOV       AX,DIVDND          ;Set dividend
000A 8B 1E 0002 R 1          MOV       BX,DIVSOR          ;Set divisor
000E 2B C9        1          SUB       CX,CX              ;Clear quotient
0010              1 ??0000:
0010 3B C3        1          CMP       AX,BX              ;Div'd < divisor?
0012 72 05        1          JB        ??0001             ;  yes, exit
```

Figure 22–6 Using IF and IFNDEF

```
0014 2B C3          1              SUB     AX,BX              ;Div'd - divisor
0016 41             1              INC     CX                 ;Add to quotient
0017 EB F7          1              JMP     ??0000
0019               1 ??0001:
0019 89 0E 0004 R  1              MOV     QUOTNT,CX          ;Store quotient
                                   DIVIDE  DIDND,DIVSOR,QUOT
= 0000              1              CNTR    = 0
                   1 ;            AX = div'nd, BX = div'r, CX = quot't
                   1              IFNDEF DIDND
                   1 ;                    Dividend not defined
= 0001              1              CNTR    = CNTR +1
                   1              ENDIF
                   1              IFNDEF  QUOT
                   1 ;                    Quotient not defined
= 0002              1              CNTR    = CNTR + 1
                   1              ENDIF
                   1              IF      CNTR
                   1 ;                    Macro expansion terminated
                   1              EXITM
001D B8 4C00                      MOV     AX,4C00H           ;Exit to DOS
0020 CD 21                        INT     21H
0022                       BEGIN  ENDP
                                   END     BEGIN
```

Figure 22–6   (continued)

Macro Using IFIDN Condition

The skeleton program in Figure 22–7 contains a macro definition named MOVIF that generates MOVSB or MOVSW, depending on the parameter supplied. A user has to code the macro instruction with the parameter B (byte) or W (word) to indicate whether MOVS is to become MOVSB or MOVSW.

The first two statements of the macro definition are

```
MOVIF   MACRO   TAG

        IFIDN   <&TAG>,<B>
```

In the definition, the first IFIDN generates REP MOVSB if you code MOVIFB as a macro instruction. The second IFIDN generates REP MOVSW if you code MOVIFW as a macro instruction. If a user does not supply B or W, the assembler generates a comment and default to MOVSB. (The normal use of the ampersand (&) operator is for concatenation.)

The three examples in the code segment of MOVIF test for B, for W, and for an invalid condition. Don't attempt to execute the program as it stands, since the CX and DX registers need to contain proper values for the MOVS instructions. Admittedly, this macro is not very useful, since its purpose is to illustrate the use of conditional directives in a simple manner. By now, however, you should be able to develop some meaningful macros.

KEY POINTS

- A macro definition requires a MACRO directive, a block of one or more statements known as the body that the macro definition is to generate, and an ENDM directive to terminate the definition.

```
                              page    60,132
                      TITLE   P22MACR7 (EXE)  Tests of IFIDN
                      ; --------------------------------------------
                      INITZ   MACRO                       ;Define macro
                              MOV     AX,@data
                              MOV     DS,AX
                              MOV     ES,AX
                              ENDM                        ;End macro
                      MOVIF   MACRO   TAG                 ;Define macro
                              IFIDN   <&TAG>,<B>
                              REP MOVSB
                              EXITM
                              ENDIF
                              IFIDN   <&TAG>,<W>
                              REP MOVSW
                              ELSE
                      ;       No B or W tag, default to B
                              REP MOVSB
                              ENDIF
                              ENDM                        ;End macro
                      ; --------------------------------------------
                              .MODEL  SMALL
                              .STACK  64
                              .CODE
0000                  BEGIN   PROC    FAR
                              .LALL
                              INITZ
0000 B8 ---- R    1           MOV     AX,@data
0003 8E D8        1           MOV     DS,AX
0005 8E C0        1           MOV     ES,AX
                              MOVIF   B
                  1           IFIDN   <B>,<B>
0007 F3/ A4       1           REP MOVSB
                  1           EXITM
                              MOVIF   W
                  1           IFIDN   <W>,<W>
0009 F3/ A5       1           REP MOVSW
                  1           ENDIF
                              MOVIF
                  1           ELSE
                  1   ;       No B or W tag, default to B
000B F3/ A4       1           REP MOVSB
                  1           ENDIF
000D B8 4C00                  MOV     AX,4C00H            ;Exit to DOS
0010 CD 21                    INT     21H
0012                  BEGIN   ENDP
                              END     BEGIN
```

Figure 22–7 Using IFIDN

- A macro instruction is the use of the macro in a program. The code that a macro instruction generates is the macro expansion.
- The .SALL, .LALL, and .XALL directives control the listing of comments and the object code generated in a macro expansion.
- The LOCAL directive facilitates using names within a macro definition and must appear immediately after the macro statement.
- The use of dummy arguments in a macro definition allows a user to code parameters for more flexibility.
- A macro library makes macros available to other programs.
- Conditional directives enable you to validate macro parameters.

QUESTIONS

22–1. Under what circumstances would the use of macros be recommended?

22–2. Code the first and last lines for a simple macro named SETUP.

22–3. Distinguish between the body of a macro definition and the macro expansion.

22–4. What is a dummy argument?

22–5. Code the following statements: (a) Suppress all instructions that a macro generates; (b) list only instructions that generate object code.

22–6. Code two macro definitions that perform multiplication: (a) MULTBY is to generate code that multiplies a byte by a byte; (b) MULTWD is to generate code that multiplies a word by a word. Include the multiplicands and multipliers as dummy arguments in the macro definition. Test the execution of the macros with a small program that also defines the required data fields.

22–7. Store the macros defined in Question 22–6 in a macro library. Revise the program to INCLUDE the library entries during pass 1 of the assembly.

22–8. Write a macro named BIPRINT that uses BIOS INT 17H to print. The macro should include a test for the status of the printer and should provide for any defined print line with any length.

22–9. Revise the macro in Figure 22–6 so that it bypasses the division if the divisor is zero.

CHAPTER 23 ———————————————

Linking to Subprograms

```
┌─────────────────────────────────────────────────────────┐
│                      OBJECTIVE:                         │
│                                                         │
│   To cover the programming techniques involved in link- │
│   ing and executing separately assembled programs.      │
│                                                         │
└─────────────────────────────────────────────────────────┘
```

INTRODUCTION

Up to this chapter, the programs we have presented have consisted of one stand-alone assembled module. It is possible, however, to develop a program that consists of a main program linked with one or more separately assembled subprograms. The following are reasons for organizing a program into subprograms:

- To link between languages—for example, to combine the computing power of a high-level language with the processing efficiency of assembly language.
- To facilitate the development of large projects, in which different teams produce their modules separately.
- To overlay parts of a program during execution because of the program's large size.

Each program is assembled separately and generates its own unique object (.OBJ) module. The linker then links the object modules into one combined executable (.EXE) module. Typically, the main program is the one that begins execution, and it calls one or more subprograms. Subprograms in turn may call other subprograms.

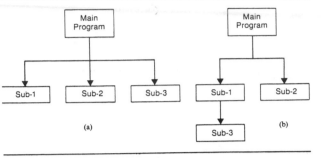

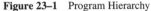

Figure 23–1   Program Hierarchy

Figure 23–1 shows two examples of a hierarchy of a main program and three sub-programs. In part (a), the main program calls subprograms 1, 2, and 3. In part (b), the main program calls subprograms 1 and 2, and only subprogram 1 calls subprogram 3.

There are numerous ways to organize subprograms, but the organization has to make sense to the assembler, to the linker, and for execution. You also have to watch out for situations in which, for example, subprogram 1 calls subprogram 2, which calls subprogram 3, which in turn calls subprogram 1. This process, known as recursion, can be made to work, but, if not handled carefully, can cause interesting execution bugs.

SEGMENTS

This section covers a number of options used for segments. The general format for the full SEGMENT directive is

| seg-name | SEGMENT | [align] [combine] ['class'] |

Align Type

The align operator tells the assembler to align the named segment beginning on a particular storage boundary:

BYTE   Byte boundary, for a segment of a subprogram that is to be combined with that of another program. Byte alignment is generally suitable for programs run on an 8088 processor.

WORD   Word boundary, for a segment of a subprogram that is to be combined with that of another program. Word alignment is generally suitable for programs run on 8086/80286 processors.

DWORD   Doubleword boundary, normally for the 80386 and later processors.

PARA   Paragraph boundary (divisible by 16, or 10H), the default and the most commonly used alignment for both main programs and subprograms.

PAGE   Page boundary (divisible by 256, or 100H).

Omitting the align operator from the first segment causes a default to PARA. Omitting it from succeeding segments causes a default to PARA if the name is unique; if it is not unique, the default is the alignment type of the previously defined segment of the same name.

Combine Type

The combine operator tells the assembler and linker whether to combine segments or to keep them separate. We have already used the STACK combine type. Other combine types relevant to this chapter are NONE, PUBLIC, and COMMON:

NONE	The segment is to be logically separate from other segments, although they all may end up to be physically adjacent. This type is the default for full segment directives.
PUBLIC	The linker is to combine the segment with all other segments that are defined as PUBLIC and have the same segment name and class. The assembler calculates offsets from the beginning of the first segment. In effect, the combined segment contains a number of sections, each beginning with a SEGMENT directive and ending with ENDS. This type is the default for simplified segment directives.
COMMON	If COMMON segments have the same name and class, the linker gives them the same base address. During execution, the second segment overlays the first one. The largest segment determines the length of the common area.

Class Type

We have already used the class names 'Stack,' 'Data,' and 'Code.' You can assign the same class name to related segments so that the assembler and linker group them together. That is, they are to appear as segments one after the other, but not combined into one segment unless the PUBLIC combine option is also coded. The class entry may contain any valid name, contained in single quotes, although the name 'Code' is recommended for the code segment.

The following two unrelated SEGMENT statements generate identical results, namely, an independent code segment aligned on a paragraph boundary:

```
CODESEG   SEGMENT   PARA NONE 'Code'

CODESEG   SEGMENT   'Code'
```

We explained fully defined segment directives in Chapter 4, but have used the simplified segment directives in subsequent chapters. Since full segment directives can provide tighter control when assembling and linking subprograms, most examples in this chapter use them.

Program examples in this and later chapters illustrate many of the Align, Combine, and Class options.

INTRASEGMENT CALLS

The CALL instructions used to this point have been *intrasegment* calls; that is, the called procedure is in the same code segment as that of the calling procedure. An intrasegment CALL is *near* if the called procedure is defined as or defaults to NEAR (that is, within 32K). The CALL operation pushes the IP register onto the stack and replaces the IP with the offset of the destination address. Thus a near CALL references a (near) procedure within the same segment.

Now consider an intrasegment CALL that consists of object code E8 2000, where E8 is the operation code and 2000 is the offset of a called procedure. The operation pushes the IP onto the stack and stores the 2000 as offset 0020 in the IP. The processor then combines the current address in the CS with the offset in the IP for the next instruction to execute. On exit from the called procedure, a (near) RET pops the stored IP off the stack and into the IP and returns to the instruction following the CALL:

```
          CALL   nearproc      ;Near call: push IP,

          ...                  ; link to nearproc

nearproc  PROC   NEAR

          ...

          RET                  ;Near return: pop IP, return

nearproc  ENDP
```

An intrasegment call may be near, as described, or far if the call is to a procedure defined as far within the same segment. RET is near if it appears in a NEAR procedure and far if it appears in a FAR procedure.

INTERSEGMENT CALLS

A CALL is classed as *far* if the called procedure is defined as FAR or as EXTRN, often in another segment. The CALL operation first pushes the contents of the CS register onto the stack and inserts a new segment address in the CS. It then pushes the IP onto the stack and inserts a new offset address in the IP. (The pushed CS and IP values provide the address of the instruction immediately following the CALL.) In this way, both addresses of the code segment and the offset are saved for the return from the called procedure. A call to another segment is always an *intersegment* far call:

```
          CALL   farproc       ;Far call: push CS,

          ...                  ; IP, link to farproc

farproc PROC   FAR

          ...

          RET                  ;Far return: pop IP, CS,

farproc ENDP                 ; return
```

Consider an intersegment CALL that consists of object code 9A 0002 AF04. Hex 9A is the operation code for an intersegment CALL. The operation pushes the current IP onto the

```
            EXTRN   SUBPROG:FAR
   MAINPROG PROC    FAR
            . . .
            CALL    SUBPROG
            . . .
   MAINPROG ENDP
- - - - - - - - - - - - - - - - - - - - - - - - - - -
            PUBLIC  SUBPROG
   SUBPROG  PROC    FAR
            . . .
            . . .
            RET
   SUBPROG  ENDP
```

Figure 23–2   Intersegment Call

stack and stores the new offset 0002 as 0200 in the IP. It then pushes the CS onto the stack and stores the new segment address AF04 as 04AF in the CS. The CS and IP values combine to establish the address of the first instruction to execute in the called subprogram:

Code segment:	04AF0H
Offset in IP:	+ 0200H
Effective address:	04CF0H

On exit from the called procedure, an intersegment (far) RET reverses the CALL operation, popping both the original IP and CS addresses back into their respective registers. The CS:IP pair now points to the address of the instruction following the original CALL, where execution resumes.

The difference then between a near and a far CALL is basically that a near CALL replaces only the IP offset, whereas a far CALL replaces both the CS segment address and the IP offset.

EXTRN AND PUBLIC ATTRIBUTES

Consider Figure 23–2, in which a main program (MAINPROG) calls a subprogram (SUBPROG). The requirement here is for an intersegment CALL.

The CALL in MAINPROG has to know that SUBPROG exists outside MAINPROG (or else the assembler generates an error message that SUBPROG is an undefined symbol). The directive EXTRN SUBPROG:FAR notifies the assembler that any reference to SUBPROG is to a FAR label that in this case is defined externally, in another assembly. Because the assembler has no way of knowing the address at execution time, it generates "empty" object code operands in the far CALL (zeros for the offset and hyphens for the segment), which the linker subsequently is to fill:

```
        9A 0000 ---- E       ;CALL subprogram
```

SUBPROG in its turn contains a PUBLIC directive that tells the assembler and linker that another module has to know the address of SUBPROG. In a later step, when both MAINPROG and SUBPROG are successfully assembled into object modules, they may be linked as follows:

```
    LINK Prompt                 Reply

Object Modules [.OBJ]:     D:MAINPROG+D:SUBPROG

Run File [filespec.EXE]:   D:COMBPROG (or any valid name)

List File [NUL.MAP]:       CON

Libraries [.LIB]:          [Enter]
```

The linker matches EXTRNs in one object module with PUBLICs in the other and inserts any required offset addresses. It then combines the two object modules into one executable module. If unable to match references, the linker supplies error messages; watch for these before attempting to execute the module.

The EXTRN Directive

The EXTRN directive tells the assembler that the named item—a data item, procedure, or label—is defined in another assembly. (MASM 6.0 introduced the term EXTERN.) EXTRN has the following format:

```
EXTRN name:type [, ... ]
```

You can define more than one name up to the end of the line or code additional EXTRN statements. The other assembly module in its turn must define the name and identify it as PUBLIC. The type entry may be ABS (a constant), BYTE, DWORD, FAR, NEAR, WORD, or a name defined by an EQU and must be valid in terms of the actual definition of a name:

- BYTE, WORD, and DWORD identify data items that one module references but another module defines.
- NEAR and FAR identify a procedure or instruction label that one module references but another module defines.

THE PUBLIC Directive

The PUBLIC directive tells the assembler and linker that the address of a specified symbol defined in the current assembly is to be available to other modules. The general format for PUBLIC is

```
PUBLIC symbol [, ... ]
```

You can define more than one symbol up to the end of the line or code additional PUBLIC statements. The symbol entry can be a label (including PROC labels), a variable, or a number. Invalid entries include register names and EQU symbols that define values greater than two bytes.

The calling of far procedures and the use of EXTRN and PUBLIC should offer little difficulty, although considerable care is required for making data defined in one module known in other modules.

Let's now examine three different ways of making data known between programs: using EXTRN and PUBLIC, defining common data in subprograms, and passing parameters.

USE OF EXTRN AND PUBLIC FOR A LABEL

The program in Figure 23–3 consists of a main program, P23MAIN1, and a subprogram, P23SUB1, both using full segment directives. The main program defines segments for the stack, data, and code. The data segment defines QTY and PRICE. The code segment loads the AX with PRICE and the BX with QTY and then calls the subprogram. An EXTRN in the main program defines the entry point to the subprogram as P23SUB1.

The subprogram contains a PUBLIC statement (after the ASSUME) that makes P23SUB1 known to the linker as the entry point for execution. This subprogram simply multiplies the contents of the AX (price) by the BX (quantity) and develops the product in the DX:AX pair as 002E 4000H.

Since the subprogram does not define any data, it does not need a data segment; it could, but only the subprogram itself would recognize the data.

As well, the subprogram does not define a stack segment, because it references the same stack addresses as the main program. Consequently, the stack defined in the main program is available to the subprogram. Since the linker requires the definition of at least one stack for an .EXE program, the stack in the main program serves this purpose.

Now let's examine the symbol tables following each assembly. Note that the symbol table for the main program shows P23SUB1 as Far and External. The symbol table for the subprogram shows P23SUB1 as F (for Far) and Global. The term *global* implies that the name is known to other subprograms outside P23SUB1.

The link map at the end of the listing shows the organization of the program in memory. Note that there are two code segments, one for each assembly, but at different starting addresses, since their combine types are NONE. These appear in the sequence that you enter when linking, with the main program normally first. In the current example, the code segment for the main program starts at offset 00090H and the code segment for the subprogram at 000B0H.

A trace of program execution disclosed that the CS register for P23MAIN1 contained 0F20[0] and the instruction CALL P23SUB1 generated

```
9A 0000 220F (expect your segment value to differ)
```

The machine code for an intersegment CALL is 9AH. The operation pushes the IP register onto the stack and loads 0000 in the IP. It then pushes the CS containing 0F20[0] onto the stack and loads 0F22[0] (from the CALL operand) in the CS. (We'll show the register contents in normal, not reversed, byte order.)

The next instruction to execute is CS:IP, or 0F22[0] plus 0000. What is at 0F220? It's the entry point to P23SUB1 at its first executable instruction, which you can calculate. The main program began with the CS register containing 0F20[0]. According to the map, the main code segment offset begins at offset 00090H and the subprogram offset begins at offset 000B0H, 20H bytes apart. Adding the main program's CS value plus 20H supplies the effective address of the subprogram's code segment:

```
                        TITLE     P23MAIN1 (EXE)  Call subprogram
                                  EXTRN  P23SUB1:FAR
                        ; ------------------------------------------------
0000                    STACKSG   SEGMENT PARA STACK 'Stack'
0000 0040[????]                   DW      64 DUP(?)
0080                    STACKSG   ENDS
                        ; ------------------------------------------------
0000                    DATASG    SEGMENT PARA 'Data'
0000 0140               QTY       DW      0140H
0002 2500               PRICE     DW      2500H
0004                    DATASG    ENDS
                        ; ------------------------------------------------
0000                    CODESG    SEGMENT PARA 'Code'
0000                    BEGIN     PROC    FAR
                                  ASSUME  CS:CODESG,DS:DATASG,SS:STACKSG
0000 B8 ---- R                    MOV     AX,DATASG
0003 8E D8                        MOV     DS,AX
0005 A1 0002 R                    MOV     AX,PRICE      ;Set up price
0008 8B 1E 0000 R                 MOV     BX,QTY        ;  and quantity
000C 9A 0000 ---- E               CALL    P23SUB1       ;Call subprogram
0011 B8 4C00                      MOV     AX,4C00H      ;Exit to DOS
0014 CD 21                        INT     21H
0016                    BEGIN     ENDP
0016                    CODESG    ENDS
                                  END     BEGIN
```

Segments and Groups:
```
              N a m e        Length   Align    Combine   Class
CODESG . . . . . . . . .  .  0016     PARA     NONE      'CODE'
DATASG . . . . . . . . .  .  0004     PARA     NONE      'DATA'
STACKSG  . . . . . . . .  .  0080     PARA     STACK     'STACK'
```
Symbols:
```
              N a m e        Type     Value    Attr
BEGIN  . . . . . . . .  .  . F PROC   0000     CODESG      Length = 0016
P23SUB1  . . . . . . .  .  . L FAR    0000     External
PRICE  . . . . . . . .  .  . L WORD   0002     DATASG
QTY  . . . . . . . . .  .  . L WORD   0000     DATASG
```

```
    -----------------------------------------------------------------------
                        TITLE     P23SUB1 Called subprogram
                        ; --------------------------------
0000                    CODESG    SEGMENT PARA 'Code'
0000                    P23SUB1   PROC    FAR
                                  ASSUME  CS:CODESG
                                  PUBLIC  P23SUB1
0000 F7 E3                        MUL     BX           ;AX = price, BX = qty
0002 CB                           RET                  ;DX:AX = product
0003                    P23SUB1   ENDP
0003                    CODESG    ENDS
                                  END     P23SUB1
```

Segments and Groups:
```
              N a m e        Length   Align    Combine   Class
CODESG . . . . . . . .  .  . 0003     PARA     NONE        'CODE'
```
Symbols:
```
              N a m e        Type     Value    Attr
P23SUB1  . . . . . . . .  .  F PROC   0000     CODESG  Global Length=0003
    -----------------------------------------------------------------------
```

```
    Link Map
    Object Modules: P23MAIN1+P23SUB1

    Start  Stop   Length  Name              Class
    00000H 0007FH 00080H  STACKSG           STACK
```

Figure 23–3 Using EXTRN and PUBLIC

```
00080H 00083H 00004H DATASG          DATA
00090H 000A5H 00016H CODESG          CODE <-- Note: 2 code
000B0H 000B2H 00003H CODESG          CODE <--    segments

Program entry point at 0009:0000
```

Figure 23–3   (continued)

CS address for P23MAIN1:	0F200H
Size of P23MAIN1:	+00020H
CS address for P23SUB1:	0F220H

The program loader determines this address just as we have and substitutes it in the CALL operand. P23SUB1 multiplies the two values in the AX and BX, with the product in the DX:AX, and makes a far return to P23MAIN1 (because RET is in a FAR procedure).

USE OF PUBLIC IN THE CODE SEGMENT

Figure 23–4 provides a variation of Figure 23–3. There is one change in the main program, P23MAIN2, and one change in the subprogram, P23SUB2, both involving the use of PUBLIC in the SEGMENT directive for both code segments:

```
CODESG SEGMENT PARA PUBLIC 'Code'
```

Interesting results appear in the link map and the CALL object code. In the symbol table following each assembly, the combine type for CODESG is PUBLIC, whereas in Figure 23–3 it was NONE. Also, the link map at the end now shows only one code segment. The fact that both segments have the same name (DATASG), class ('Code'), and PUBLIC attribute caused the linker to combine the two logical code segments into one physical code segment. Further, a trace of machine execution showed that the CALL is far; that is, even though the call is within the same segment, it is to a FAR procedure:

```
9A 2000 200F (expect your segment address to differ)
```

This far CALL stores 2000H in the IP as 0020H and 200FH in the CS register as 0F20[0]. Because the subprogram shares a common code segment with the main program, the CS register is set to the same starting address, 0F20H. But the CS:IP for P23SUB2 now provide the following:

CS address for P23MAIN2 and P23SUB2:	0F200H
IP offset for P23SUB2:	+ 0020H
Effective address of P23SUB2:	0F220H

The code segment of the subprogram therefore presumably begins at 0F220H. Is this correct? The link map doesn't make the point clear, but you can infer the address from the listing of the main program, which ends at offset 0015H. (The map shows 16H, which is the next available location.) Since the code segment for the subprogram is defined as

```
                         TITLE       P23MAIN2 (EXE)  Call subprogram
                                     EXTRN  P23SUB2:FAR
                         ; ------------------------------------------------
0000                     STACKSG     SEGMENT PARA STACK 'Stack'
0000 0040[????]                      DW       64 DUP(?)
0080                     STACKSG     ENDS
                         ; ------------------------------------------------
0000                     DATASG      SEGMENT PARA 'Data'
0000 0140                QTY         DW       0140H
0002 2500                PRICE       DW       2500H
0004                     DATASG      ENDS
                         ; ------------------------------------------------
0000                     CODESG      SEGMENT PARA PUBLIC 'Code'
0000                     BEGIN       PROC     FAR
                                     ASSUME  CS:CODESG,DS:DATASG,SS:STACKSG
0000 B8 ---- R                       MOV      AX,DATASG
0003 8E D8                           MOV      DS,AX
0005 A1 0002 R                       MOV      AX,PRICE      ;Set up price
0008 8B 1E 0000 R                    MOV      BX,QTY        ; and quantity
000C 9A 0000 ---- E                  CALL     P23SUB2       ;Call subprogram
0011 B8 4C00                         MOV      AX,4C00H      ;Exit to DOS
0014 CD 21                           INT      21H
0016                     BEGIN       ENDP
0016                     CODESG      ENDS
                                     END      BEGIN

Segments and Groups:
        N a m e                   Length   Align   Combine   Class
CODESG . . . . . . . . . .        0016     PARA    PUBLIC    'CODE'
DATASG . . . . . . . . . .        0004     PARA    NONE      'DATA'
STACKSG . . . . . . . .           0080     PARA    STACK     'STACK'
Symbols:
        N a m e                   Type     Value   Attr
BEGIN . . . . . . . . . .         F PROC   0000    CODESG      Length = 0016
P23SUB2 . . . . . . . .           L FAR    0000    External
PRICE . . . . . . . . . .         L WORD   0002    DATASG
QTY . . . . . . . . . .           L WORD   0000    DATASG

-----------------------------------------------------------------------

                         TITLE     P23SUB2 Called subprogram
                         ; -------------------------------
0000                     CODESG    SEGMENT PARA PUBLIC 'Code'
0000                     P23SUB2   PROC    FAR
                                   ASSUME  CS:CODESG
                                   PUBLIC  P23SUB2
0000 F7 E3                         MUL     BX         ;AX = price, BX = qty
0002 CB                            RET                ;DX:AX = product
0003                     P23SUB2   ENDP
0003                     CODESG    ENDS
                                   END     P23SUB2
Segments and Groups:.
        N a m e                   Length   Align   Combine   Class
CODESG . . . . . . . . . .        0003     PARA    PUBLIC    'CODE'
Symbols:
        N a m e                   Type     Value   Attr
P23SUB2 . . . . . . . .           F PROC   0000    CODESG   Global Length=0003

-----------------------------------------------------------------------

    Link Map
    Object Modules: P23MAIN2+P23SUB2
```

Figure 23–4 Code Segment Defined as PUBLIC

```
ie segment
```

Figure 23–4B (continued)

PARA, it begins on a paragraph boundary (evenly divisible by 10H, so that the rightmost digit is 0):

```
┌──────────────────────────────┬──────────────┐
│ main program ....(unused)     │  subprogram  │
└──────────────────────────────┴──────────────┘
  |             |                 |
  0F200        141F0             0F220
```

The linker sets the subprogram at the first paragraph boundary immediately following the main program, at offset 00020H. Therefore, the code segment of the subprogram begins at 0F200H plus 0020H, or 0F220H.

Now let's examine this same program defined with simplified segment directives.

SIMPLIFIED SEGMENT DIRECTIVES

Figure 23–5 shows the previous program now defined with simplified segment directives. Figure 23–4 defines the code segments as PUBLIC, whereas Figure 23–5 defaults to PUBLIC, so that both examples generate one code segment. However, the use of simplified segment directives causes some significant differences. First, the linker has rearranged the segments (as shown in the map) in sequence of code, data, and stack, although this has no effect on program execution. Second, the subprogram's code segment (_TEXT) aligns on a word (rather than paragraph) boundary. A trace of machine execution showed the following object code for the CALL:

```
9A 1600 170F (expect your segment address to differ)
```

This time, the new offset value is 16H, and the segment address is 0F17H. Because the subprogram shares a common code segment with the main program, the CS register is set to the same starting address, 0F17(0), for both. The address of P23SUB3 may therefore be calculated as follows:

CS address for P23MAIN3 and P23SUB3:	F170H
IP offset for P23SUB3:	+ 016H
Effective address of P23SUB3:	F186H

You can infer the address from the listing of the main program, which ends at offset 0015H. (The map shows 16H, which is the next available location.) Since the map shows the main code segment beginning at 00000H, the next word boundary following 0015H is at 00016H, where P23SUB3 begins.

```
                         TITLE      P23MAIN3 (EXE)  Call subprogram
                                    .MODEL  SMALL
                                    .STACK  64
                                    EXTRN   P23SUB3:FAR
                    ; --------------------------------------------------
                                    .DATA
0000 0140           QTY        DW      0140H
0002 2500           PRICE      DW      2500H
                    ; --------------------------------------------------
                                    .CODE
0000                BEGIN      PROC    FAR
0000 B8 ---- R                 MOV     AX,@data
0003 8E D8                     MOV     DS,AX
0005 A1 0002 R                 MOV     AX,PRICE       ;Set up price
0008 8B 1E 0000 R              MOV     BX,QTY         ;  and quantity
000C 9A 0000 ---- E            CALL    P23SUB3        ;Call subprogram
0011 B8 4C00                   MOV     AX,4C00H       ;Exit to DOS
0014 CD 21                     INT     21H
0016                BEGIN      ENDP
                               END     BEGIN

Segments and Groups:
        N a m e                    Length  Align    Combine    Class
DGROUP  . . . . . . . . . . GROUP
 _DATA  . . . . . . . . . . 0004    WORD     PUBLIC     'DATA'
 STACK  . . . . . . . . . . 0040    PARA     STACK      'STACK'
 _TEXT  . . . . . . . . . .+.0016   WORD     PUBLIC     'CODE'
Symbols:
        N a m e                    Type    Value    Attr
BEGIN   . . . . . . . . . . F PROC  0000    _TEXT      Length = 0016
P23SUB3 . . . . . . . . . . L FAR   0000    External
PRICE   . . . . . . . . . . L WORD  0002    _DATA
QTY     . . . . . . . . . . L WORD  0000    _DATA


-----------------------------------------------------------------------

                         TITLE      P23SUB3 Called subprogram
                                    .MODEL SMALL
                                    .CODE
0000                P23SUB3    PROC    FAR
                               PUBLIC P23SUB3
0000 F7 E3                     MUL     BX         ;AX = price, BX = qty
0002 CB                        RET                ;DX:AX = product
0003                P23SUB3    ENDP
                               END     P23SUB3
Segments and Groups:
        N a m e                    Length  Align    Combine    Class
DGROUP  . . . . . . . . . . GROUP
 _DATA  . . . . . . . . . . 0000    WORD     PUBLIC     'DATA'
 _TEXT  . . . . . . . . . . 0003    WORD     PUBLIC     'CODE'
Symbols:
        N a m e                    Type    Value    Attr
P23SUB3 . . . . . . . . F PROC     0000    _TEXT      Global  Length=0003


-----------------------------------------------------------------------

    Link Map
    Object Modules: P23MAIN3+P23SUB3
    Start   Stop    Length Name              Class
    00000H 00018H 00019H _TEXT               CODE   <-- code segment 1st
    0001AH 0001DH 00004H _DATA               DATA
    00020H 0005FH 00040H STACK               STACK

    Program entry point at 0000:0000
```

Figure 23–5   Using Simplified Segment Directives

COMMON DATA IN SUBPROGRAMS

A common programming requirement is to process data in one module that is defined in another module. Let's modify the preceding examples so that, although the main program still defines QTY and PRICE, the subprogram (rather than the main program) inserts their values into the BX and AX. Figure 23–6 gives the revised coding, with the following changes:

- The main program, P23MAIN4, defines QTY and PRICE as PUBLIC. The data segment is also defined with the PUBLIC attribute. Note in the symbol table the global attribute for QTY and PRICE.
- The subprogram, P23SUB4, defines QTY and PRICE as EXTRN and as WORD. This definition informs the assembler of the length of the two fields. The assembler can generate the correct operation code for the MOV instructions, but the linker will have to complete the operands. (Note in the symbol table that PRICE and QTY are now classed as external.)

The assembler lists the MOV instructions in the subprogram as

```
A1 0000 E        MOV   AX,PRICE

8B 1E 0000 E     MOV   BX,QTY
```

Object code A1 means move a word from memory to the AX, whereas 8B means move a word from memory to the BX. (AX operations often require fewer bytes.) For P23SUB4, the assembler has no way of knowing the locations of QTY and PRICE, so it has stored zeros in the operands for both MOVs. Tracing through program execution reveals that the linker has completed the object code operands as follows:

```
A1 0200

8B 1E 0000
```

The object code is now identical to that generated for the three preceding programs, where the MOV instructions are in the calling program. This is a logical result because the operands in all three programs reference the same data segment address in the DS register and the same offset values.

The main program and the subprogram may define other data items, but only those defined as PUBLIC and EXTRN are known in common to them.

DEFINING DATA IN BOTH PROGRAMS

In the previous example, P23MAIN4 defined QTY and PRICE, whereas P23SUB4 did not define any data. The reason P23SUB4 can reference P23MAIN4's data is because it has preserved the address of the data segment in the DS register, which still points to P23MAIN4's data segment. (The only segment address changed was that of the code segment.) But programs are not always so simple, and subprograms often have to define their own data, as well as reference data in the calling program.

```
                             TITLE     P23MAIN4 (EXE)  Call subprogram
                             EXTRN     P23SUB4:FAR
                             PUBLIC    QTY,PRICE
                        ; ------------------------------------------
0000                    STACKSG   SEGMENT PARA STACK 'Stack'
0000 0040[????]                   DW      64 DUP(?)
0080                    STACKSG   ENDS
                        ; ------------------------------------------
0000                    DATASG    SEGMENT PARA PUBLIC 'Data'
0000 0140               QTY       DW      0140H
0002 2500               PRICE     DW      2500H
0004                    DATASG    ENDS
                        ; ------------------------------------------
0000                    CODESG    SEGMENT PARA PUBLIC 'Code'
0000                    BEGIN     PROC    FAR
                                  ASSUME  CS:CODESG,DS:DATASG,SS:STACKSG
0000 B8 ---- R                    MOV     AX,DATASG
0003 8E D8                        MOV     DS,AX
0005 9A 0000 ---- E               CALL    P23SUB4        ;Call subprogram
000A B8 4C00                      MOV     AX,4C00H       ;Exit to DOS
000D CD 21                        INT     21H
000F                    BEGIN     ENDP
000F                    CODESG    ENDS
                                  END     BEGIN
```

Segments and Groups:

Name	Length	Align	Combine	Class
CODESG	000F	PARA	PUBLIC	'CODE'
DATASG	0004	PARA	PUBLIC	'DATA'
STACKSG	0080	PARA	STACK	'STACK'

Symbols:

Name	Type	Value	Attr	
BEGIN	F PROC	0000	CODESG	Length = 000F
P23SUB4	L FAR	0000	External	
PRICE	L WORD	0002	DATASG	Global
QTY	L WORD	0000	DATASG	Global

```
                             TITLE     P23SUB4 Called subprogram
                             EXTRN     QTY:WORD, PRICE:WORD
                        ; ------------------------------------
0000                    CODESG    SEGMENT PARA PUBLIC 'CODE'
0000                    P23SUB4   PROC    FAR
                                  ASSUME CS:CODESG
                                  PUBLIC P23SUB4
0000 A1 0000 E                    MOV     AX,PRICE
0003 8B 1E 0000 E                 MOV     BX,QTY
0007 F7 E3                        MUL     BX             ;DX:AX = product
0009 CB                           RET
000A                    P23SUB4   ENDP
000A                    CODESG    ENDS
                                  END     P23SUB4
```

Segments and Groups:

Name	Length	Align	Combine	Class
CODESG	000A	PARA	PUBLIC	'CODE'

Symbols:

Name	Type	Value	Attr	
P23SUB4	F PROC	0000	CODESG	Global Length=000A
PRICE	.V WORD	0000	External	
QTY	.V WORD	0000	External	

Figure 23–6 Common Data in Subprograms

```
Link Map
Object Modules: P23MAIN4+P23SUB4

Start  Stop    Length Name                      Class
00000H 0007FH  00080H STACKSG                   STACK
00080H 00083H  00004H DATASG                    DATA
00090H 000A9H  0001AH CODESG                    CODE

Program entry point at 0009:0000
```
                                                                            Figure 23-6   (continued)

In a variation on the preceding program, Figure 23–7 defines QTY in P23MAIN5, but defines PRICE in P23SUB5. From inside P23MAIN5, PRICE does not exist, although P23SUB5 has to know the location of both items. P23SUB5's code segment has to retrieve QTY right away, while the DS register still contains the address of P23MAIN5's data segment. P23SUB5 then pushes the DS onto the stack and loads the DS with the address of its own data segment. P23SUB5 can now get PRICE and perform the multiplication of QTY and PRICE.

Before returning to P23MAIN5, P23SUB5 has to pop the DS off the stack so that P23MAIN5 can access its own data segment. (Technically, this is not really necessary in the current example, because P23MAIN5 happens to return to DOS immediately, but we'll do it as a standard practice.)

As a final note, you could make both data segments PUBLIC, with the same name and class. In that case, the linker would combine them, and P23SUB5 wouldn't have to push and pop the DS, because the programs would use the same data segment and DS address. We'll leave this variation as an exercise for you to revise and trace under DEBUG. P23SUB5's code segment could look like this:

```
EXTRN   QTY,WORD

ASSUME CS:CODESG,DS:DATASG

PUBLIC P23SUB5

MOV     AX,PRICE      ;PRICE in own data segment

MOV     BX,QTY        ;QTY in P23MAIN5

MUL     BX            ;Product in DX:AX

RET
```

PASSING PARAMETERS

Another way of making data known to a called subprogram is by *passing parameters*, in which a program passes data physically via the stack. In this case, ensure that each PUSH references a word (or doubleword on advanced systems), in either memory or a register.

The Stack Frame

The stack frame is the portion of the stack that the calling program uses to pass parameters and that the called subprogram uses for accessing the parameters. The called subprogram

```
                        TITLE     P23MAIN5 (EXE)  Call subprogram
                        EXTRN   P23SUB5:FAR
                        PUBLIC QTY
                      ; --------------------------------------------
0000                    STACKSG   SEGMENT PARA STACK 'Stack'
0000 0040[????]         DW      64 DUP(?)
0080                    STACKSG   ENDS
                      ; --------------------------------------------
0000                    DATASG    SEGMENT PARA 'Data'
0000 0140               QTY       DW      0140H
0002                    DATASG    ENDS
                      ; --------------------------------------------
0000                    CODESG    SEGMENT PARA 'Code'
0000                    BEGIN     PROC    FAR
                        ASSUME  CS:CODESG,DS:DATASG,SS:STACKSG
0000 B8 ---- R          MOV     AX,DATASG
0003 8E D8              MOV     DS,AX
0005 9A 0000 ---- E     CALL    P23SUB5     ;Call subprogram
000A B8 4C00            MOV     AX,4C00H    ;Exit to DOS
000D CD 21              INT     21H
000F                    BEGIN     ENDP
000F                    CODESG    ENDS
                        END     BEGIN
```

Segments and Groups:

N a m e	Length	Align	Combine	Class
CODESG	000F	PARA	NONE	'CODE'
DATASG	0002	PARA	NONE	'DATA'
STACKSG	0080	PARA	STACK	'STACK'

Symbols:

N a m e	Type	Value	Attr	
BEGIN	F PROC	0000	CODESG	Length = 000F
P23SUB5	L FAR	0000	External	
QTY	L WORD	0000	DATASG	Global

```
-------------------------------------------------------------------
                        TITLE     P23SUB5 Called subprogram
                        EXTRN    QTY:WORD
                      ; --------------------------------------------
0000                    DATASG    SEGMENT PARA 'Data'
0000 2500               PRICE     DW      2500H
0002                    DATASG    ENDS
                      ; --------------------------------------------
0000                    CODESG    SEGMENT PARA 'CODE'
0000                    P23SUB5   PROC    FAR
                        ASSUME  CS:CODESG
                        PUBLIC P23SUB5
0000 8B 1E 0000 E       MOV     BX,QTY      ;Get QTY from CALLMUL
0004 1E                 PUSH    DS          ;Save CALLMUL's DS
                        ASSUME  DS:DATASG
0005 B8 ---- R          MOV     AX,DATASG   ;Set up own DS
0008 8E D8              MOV     DS,AX       ;Price from
000A A1 0000 R          MOV     AX,PRICE    ;  own data segment
000D F7 E3              MUL     BX          ;DX:AX = product
000F 1F                 POP     DS          ;Restore CALLMUL's DS
0010 CB                 RET
0011                    P23SUB5   ENDP
0011                    CODESG    ENDS
                        END     P23SUB5
```

Segments and Groups:

N a m e	Length	Align	Combine	Class
CODESG	0011	PARA	NONE	'CODE'
DATASG	0002	PARA	NONE	'DATA'

Figure 23–7 Defining Data in Both Programs

```
Symbols:
        N a m e             Type    Value   Attr
P23SUB5 . . . . . . . .     F PROC  0000    CODESG  Global Length=0011
PRICE . . . . . . . . .     L WORD  0000    DATASG
QTY . . . . . . . . . .     V WORD  0000    External


------------------------------------------------------------------------

    Link Map
    Object Modules: P23MAIN5+P23SUB5

    Start  Stop   Length Name                Class
    00000H 0007FH 00080H STACKSG             STACK
    00080H 00081H 00002H DATASG              DATA
    00090H 00091H 00002H DATASG              DATA
    000A0H 000AEH 0000FH CODESG              CODE
    000B0H 000C0H 00011H CODESG              CODE

    Program entry point at 000A:0000
```

Figure 23–7 (continued)

may also use the stack frame for temporary storage of local data. The BP register acts as a frame pointer. For passing parameters, we'll make use of both the BP and SP registers.

In Figure 23–8, the calling program P23MAIN6 pushes both PRICE and QTY prior to calling the subprogram P23SUB6. Initially, the SP contained the size of the stack, 80H. Each word pushed onto the stack decrements the SP by 2. After the CALL, the stack frame appears as follows:

. . .	1200	200F	4001	0025
	78	7A	7C	7E

1. A PUSH loaded PRICE (2500H) onto the stack frame at offset 7EH.
2. A PUSH loaded QTY (0140H) onto the stack frame at offset 7CH.
3. CALL pushed the contents of the CS (0F20H for this execution) onto the stack frame at 7AH. Since the subprogram is PUBLIC, the linker combines the two code segments, and the CS address is the same for both.
4. CALL also pushed the contents of the IP register, 0012H, onto the stack frame at 78H.

The called program requires the use of the BP to access the parameters in the stack frame. Its first action is to save the contents of the BP for the calling program, so it pushes the BP onto the stack. In this example, the BP happens to contain zero, which PUSH stores in the stack at offset 76H:

0000	1200	200F	4001	0025
76	78	7A	7C	7E

The program then inserts the contents of the SP (0076H) into the BP because the BP (but not the SP) is usable as an index register. Since the BP now also contains 0076H, PRICE is in the stack at BP + 8 (offset 7EH), and QTY is at BP + 6 (offset 7CH). We know these relative locations because we pushed three words (six bytes) onto the stack after QTY was pushed. The routine transfers PRICE and QTY from the stack to the AX and BX, respectively, and performs the multiplication.

```
                         TITLE      P23MAIN6 (EXE)  Passing parameters
                         EXTRN    P23SUB6:FAR
                    ; ------------------------------------------------
0000             STACKSG   SEGMENT PARA STACK 'Stack'
0000 0040[????]             DW     64 DUP(?)
0080             STACKSG   ENDS
                    ; ------------------------------------------------
0000             DATASG    SEGMENT PARA 'Data'
0000 0140        QTY       DW     0140H
0002 2500        PRICE     DW     2500H
0004             DATASG    ENDS
                    ; ------------------------------------------------
0000             CODESG    SEGMENT PARA PUBLIC 'Code'
0000             BEGIN     PROC   FAR
                           ASSUME CS:CODESG,DS:DATASG,SS:STACKSG
0000 B8 ---- R             MOV    AX,DATASG
0003 8E D8                 MOV    DS,AX
0005 FF 36 0002 R          PUSH   PRICE
0009 FF 36 0000 R          PUSH   QTY
000D 9A 0000 ---- E        CALL   P23SUB6        ;Call subprogram
0012 B8 4C00               MOV    AX,4C00H       ;Exit to DOS
0015 CD 21                 INT    21H
0017             BEGIN     ENDP
0017             CODESG    ENDS
                           END    BEGIN
```

Segments and Groups:

Name	Length	Align	Combine	Class
CODESG	0017	PARA	PUBLIC	'CODE'
DATASG	0004	PARA	NONE	'DATA'
STACKSG	0080	PARA	STACK	'STACK'

Symbols:

Name	Type	Value	Attr	
BEGIN	F PROC	0000	CODESG	Length = 0017
P23SUB6	L FAR	0000	External	
PRICE	L WORD	0002	DATASG	
QTY	L WORD	0000	DATASG	

```
--------------------------------------------------------------------
                         TITLE      P23SUB6  Called subprogram
0000             CODESG    SEGMENT PARA PUBLIC 'Code'
0000             P23SUB6   PROC   FAR
                           ASSUME CS:CODESG
                           PUBLIC P23SUB6
0000 55                    PUSH   BP
0001 8B EC                 MOV    BP,SP
0003 8B 46 08              MOV    AX,[BP+8]      ;Get price
0006 8B 5E 06              MOV    BX,[BP+6]      ;Get quantity
0009 F7 E3                 MUL    BX             ;DX:AX = product
000B 5D                    POP    BP
000C CA 0004               RET    4
000F             P23SUB6   ENDP
000F             CODESG    ENDS
                           END
```

Segments and Groups:

Name	Length	Align	Combine	Class
CODESG	000F	PARA	PUBLIC	'CODE'

Symbols:

Name	Type	Value	Attr	
P23SUB6	F PROC	0000	CODESG	Global Length=000F

Figure 23–8 Passing Parameters

```
Link Map
Object Modules: P23MAIN6+P23SUB6

Start  Stop    Length Name            Class
00000H 0007FH  00080H STACKSG         STACK
00080H 00083H  00004H DATASG          DATA
00090H 000BEH  0002FH CODESG          CODE

Program entry point at 0009:0000
```
                                                  Figure 23–8   (continued)

Before returning to the calling program, the routine pops the BP (returning the zero address to the BP), which increments the SP by 2, from 76H to 78H.

The last instruction, RET, is a far return to the calling program, which performs the following:

- Pops the word now at the top of the stack frame (1200H) to the IP and increments the SP by 2, from 78H to 7AH.
- Pops the word now at the top (0F20) onto the CS and increments the SP by 2, from 7AH to 7CH.

Because of the two passed parameters at offsets 7CH and 7EH, the RET instruction is coded as

```
                    RET     4
```

The 4, known as a *pop-value*, contains the number of bytes in the passed parameters (two one-word parameters in this case). The RET operation adds the pop-value to the SP, correcting it to 80H. In effect, because the parameters in the stack are no longer required, the operation discards them and returns correctly to the calling program. Note that the POP and RET operations increment the SP, but don't actually erase the contents of the stack.

If you follow the general rules discussed in this chapter, you should be able to link a program consisting of more than two assembly modules and to make data known in all the modules. But watch out for the size of the stack: For large programs, defining 64 words could be a wise precaution, because of the many PUSH and CALL operations.

Chapter 24 covers some important concepts on memory management and executing overlay programs. Chapter 26 provides additional features of segments, including defining more than one code or data segment in the same assembly module and the use of GROUP to combine these into a common segment.

LINKING PASCAL AND ASSEMBLY LANGUAGE PROGRAMS

This section explains how to link a Pascal program to an assembly language subprogram. The simple Pascal program in Figure 23–9 links to an assembly language subprogram whose purpose is just to set the cursor. The Pascal program is compiled to produce an .OBJ module, and the assembly language program is assembled to produce an .OBJ module. The linker then combines these two .OBJ modules into one .EXE executable module.

The Pascal program defines two items named temp_row and temp_col and accepts entries for row and column from the keyboard into these variables. The program defines the name of the assembly language subprogram as set_curs and defines the two parameters as

```
program p23pascal ( input, output );

  procedure set_curs( const row: integer;
                      const col: integer ); extern;
  var
        temp_row:       integer;
        temp_col:       integer;

  begin
        write( 'Enter cursor row: ' );
        readln( temp_row );

        write( 'Enter cursor column: ' );
        readln( temp_col );

        set_curs( temp_row, temp_col );
        write( 'New cursor location' );
  end.

----------------------------------------------------------------

TITLE     23SETCUR  Assembler subprogram called by Pascal
          PUBLIC SET_CURS
;
;     SET_CURS: Set cursor on screen at passed location
;     Passed:   const row         Row and column where
;               const col         cursor is to be set
;     Returned: Nothing
;
CODESEG   SEGMENT PARA PUBLIC 'CODE'
SET_CURS PROC     FAR
          ASSUME  CS:CODESEG
          PUSH    BP                ;Caller's BP register
          MOV     BP,SP             ;Point to parameters passed

          MOV     SI,[BP+8]  ;SI points to row
          MOV     DH,[SI]    ;Move row to DH

          MOV     SI,[BP+6]  ;SI points to column
          MOV     DL,[SI]    ;Move column to DL

          MOV     AH,02H     ;Request set cursor
          MOV     BH,0       ;Video page
          INT     10H

          POP     BP         ;Return to caller
          RET     4
SET_CURS ENDP
CODESEG  ENDS
          END
```

Figure 23–9 Linking Pascal to Assembler

extern. It sends the addresses of temp_row and temp_col as parameters to the subprogram to set the cursor to that location. The Pascal statement that "calls" the name of the subprogram and passes the parameters is

```
set_curs( temp_row, temp_col );
```

Values pushed onto the stack are the calling program's stack pointer, the return segment pointer, the return offset, and the addresses of the two passed parameters. The following shows the offsets for each entry in the stack:

00   Caller's stack pointer
02   Caller's return segment pointer
04   Caller's return offset
06   Address of second parameter
08   Address of first parameter

Since the assembly language subprogram has to use the BP register, you have to push the BP onto the stack to save its address for the return to the Pascal calling program. Note that the steps in the called subprogram are similar to those in the program in Figure 23–7.

The SP register normally addresses entries in the stack. But since you cannot use the SP to act as an index register, the step after pushing the BP is to move the address in the SP to the BP. This step enables you to use the BP as an index register to access entries in the stack frame.

The next step is to access the addresses of the two parameters in the stack frame. The first passed parameter, the row, is at offset 08H in the stack frame and can be accessed by BP + 08H. The second passed parameter, the column, is at offset 06H and can be accessed by BP + 06H.

Each of the two addresses in the stack frame has to be transferred to one of the available index registers: BX, DI, or SI. This example uses [BP+08] to move the address of the row to the SI and then uses [SI] to move the contents of the passed parameter to the DII register.

The column is transferred to the DL register in a similar way. Then the subprogram uses the row and column in the DX register for INT 10H to set the cursor. On exit, the subprogram pops the BP. The RET instruction requires an operand value that is two times the number of parameters—in this case, 2×2, or 4. Values are automatically popped off the stack and control transfers back to the calling program.

If you change a segment register, be sure to PUSH it on entry into and POP it on exit from the subprogram. The recommended practice for a Pascal call is to preserve the DI, SI, BP, DS, and SS registers. You can also use the stack to pass values from a subprogram to a calling program. Although the subprogram in Figure 23–9 doesn't return values, Pascal would expect a subprogram to return them as a single word in the AX or as a pair of words in the DX:AX.

This trivial program produces a module larger than 20K bytes. A compiler language typically generates considerable overhead regardless of the size of the source program.

Do not assume that other Pascal versions necessarily follow the conventions we have used here. The appropriate standard is that described in the compiler manual, usually in a section whose title begins with "Interfacing . . ." or "Mixed Languages . . .".

LINKING C AND ASSEMBLY LANGUAGE PROGRAMS

The problem with describing the linkage of C to assembly language programs is that versions of C have different conventions. (For precise requirements, refer to your C manual.) Some points of interest are the following:

- For versions of C that are sensitive to uppercase and lowercase, the name of the assembly language module should be in the same case as the C program's reference.

- Most versions of C pass parameters onto the stack in a sequence that is the *reverse* of that of other languages. Consider, for example, the C statement

```
Adds (m, n);
```

The statement pushes n and then m onto the stack in that order and calls Adds. On return from the called module, the C module (not the assembly language module) adds 4 to the SP to discard the passed parameters. The typical procedure in the called assembly language module for accessing the two passed parameters is as follows:

```
PUSH    BP

MOV     BP,SP

MOV     DH,[BP+4]

MOV     DL,[BP+6]

 . . .

POP     BP

RET
```

- Some versions of C require that an assembly language module that changes the DI and SI registers should push them on entry into and pop them on exit from the assembly subprogram.
- The assembly language module should return values, if required, as one word in the AX or two words in the DX:AX pair.
- For some versions of C, an assembly language program that sets the DF flag should clear it (CLD) before returning.

Linking Microsoft C with Microsoft Assembler

Naming conventions. In Microsoft C and assembler, the assembly language modules must use a naming convention for segments and variables that is compatible with that in C. All assembler references to functions and variables in the C module must begin with an underscore (_). Further, since C is *case sensitive*, the assembly language module should use the same case (upper or lower) for any variable names in common with the C module.

Registers. The assembly language module must preserve the original values in the BP, SP, CS, DS, SS, DI, and SI registers.

Passing parameters. There are two methods of passing parameters:

1. By *reference*, either as near (an offset in the default segment) or as far (an offset in another segment). The called assembly module can directly alter the value defined in the C module.
2. By *value*, in which the C caller passes a copy of the variable on the stack. The called assembly module can alter the passed value, but has no access to the original C value. If there is more than one parameter, C pushes them onto the stack from right to left.

Compatibility of data types.   The following lists shows the types of C variables and their equivalent assembler types:

C DATA TYPE	MASM 5.X TYPE	MASM 6.X TYPE
char	DB	BYTE
unsigned short/int	DW	WORD
int, short	DW	SWORD
unsigned long	DD	DWORD
long	DD	SWORD

Returned values.   The called assembly module uses the following registers for any returned values:

C DATA TYPE	REGISTER
char	AL
short, near, int (16 bit)	AX
short, near, int (32 bit)	EAX
long, far (16 bit)	DX:AX
long, far (32 bit)	EDX:EAX

On return from the called module, issue RET with no pop value.

Compiling and Assembling.   Use the same memory model for both languages. The assembly .MODEL statement indicates the C convention, such as .MODEL SMALL,C. Also, use the appropriate assembly switch to preserve the case of (nonlocal) names.

Linking Turbo C with Turbo Assembler

Language Interfaces.   Turbo C provides two ways of interfacing with Turbo Assembler—by separate modules and by inline code:

1. *Separate modules*. For this conventional method, you code the C and assembly programs separately. Use TCC to compile the C module, TASM to assemble the assembly module, and TLINK to link them.
2. *Inline Assembly Code*. To compile the C module, you request TCC.EXE (the command version of Turbo C). Simply insert assembly statements, preceded by the keyword asm, in the source code, as, for example,

```
asm  INC WORD PTR FLDX
```

Segments.   The code segment must be named _TEXT. The data segments (two if required) are named _DATA for data that is to be initialized on entry to a block and _BSS for uninitialized data.

Naming conventions.   The Turbo Assembler modules must use a naming convention for segments and variables that is compatible with that of Turbo C. All assembler references to functions and variables in the C module must begin with an underscore (_). Further, since C is case sensitive, the assembly module should use the same case (upper or lower) for any variable names in common with the C module.

Registers.   The assembly module may freely use the AX, BX, CX, DX, ES, and flags registers. It may also use the BP, SP, CS, DS, SS, DI, and SI registers, provided that it saves (pushes) and restores (pops) them.

Passing parameters.   Turbo C passes parameters by value. If there is more than one parameter, Turbo C pushes them onto the stack from right to left.

Return.   The assembly program simply uses RET (with no pop-value) to return to the C module. The C module pops the stack on reentry to it.

Example of a C Program

The program in Figure 23–10 illustrates linking a Turbo C program with an assembly module. The program performs the same actions as the Pascal program in the previous section: The C program accepts values from the keyboard for row and column and passes them to the assembler subprogram. The assembler subprogram in its turn sets the cursor and returns to the C module.

KEY POINTS

- The align operator tells the assembler to align the named segment, beginning on a particular storage boundary.
- The combine operator tells the assembler and linker whether to combine segments or to keep them separate.
- You can assign the same class name to related segments so that the assembler and linker group them together.
- An intrasegment CALL is near if the called procedure is defined as or defaults to NEAR (within 32K). An intrasegment call may be far if the call is to a far procedure within the same segment.
- An intersegment CALL calls a procedure in another segment and is defined as FAR or as EXTRN.
- In a main program that calls a subprogram, define the entry point as EXTRN; in the subprogram, define the entry point as PUBLIC.
- If two code segments are to be linked into one segment, define them with the same name, the same class, and the PUBLIC combine type.
- It is generally easier (but not necessary) to define common data in the main program. The main program defines the common data as PUBLIC, and the subprogram (or subprograms) defines the common data as EXTRN.

```
#include <stdio.h>

int main (void)
{
    int temp_row, temp_col;

    printf ("Enter cursor row: ");
    scanf ("%d", &temp_row);

    printf ("Enter cursor column: ");
    scanf ("%d", &temp_col);

    set_curs (temp_row, temp_col);
    printf ("New cursor location\n");
}
;-------------------------------------------------------------
;
; Use small memory model for C: near code, near data
; Use 'standard' segment names  and group directive

_DATA        segment word 'DATA'
row          equ     [bp+4]          ;Parameters
col          equ     [bp+6]          ;  (arguments)
_DATA        ends


_TEXT        SEGMENT BYTE PUBLIC 'CODE'
DGROUP       GROUP   _DATA
             ASSUME  CS:_TEXT, DS:DGROUP, SS:DGROUP

             PUBLIC  _set_curs
_set_curs PROC       NEAR
             PUSH    BP              ;Caller's BP register
             MOV     BP, SP          ;Point to parameters

             MOV     AH, 02H         ;Request set cursor
             MOV     BX, 0           ;Video page
             MOV     DH, ROW         ;Row from BP+4
             MOV     DL, COL         ;Column from BP+6
             INT     10H             ;Call BIOS

             POP     BP              ;Restore BP
             RET                     ;Return to caller
_set_curs ENDP
_TEXT        ENDS
             END
```

Figure 23–10   Linking C to Assembler

QUESTIONS

23–1. Provide four reasons for organizing a program into subprograms.

The next three questions refer to the general format for the SEGMENT directive:

```
seg-name SEGMENT [align] [combine] ['class']
```

23–2. (a) For the SEGMENT directive's align option, what is the default? (b) What is the effect of the BYTE option? (That is, what action does the assembler take?)

23–3. (a) For the SEGMENT directive's combine option, what is the default? (b) When would you use the PUBLIC option? (c) When would you use the COMMON option?

23–4. (a) What should the code segment's class option be for the SEGMENT directive? (b) Two segments have the same class, but not the PUBLIC combine option. What is the effect? (c) Two segments have the same class, and both have the PUBLIC combine option. What is the effect?

23–5. Distinguish between an intrasegment call and an intersegment call.

23–6. A program named MAINPRO is to call a subprogram named SUBPRO. (a) What statement in MAINPRO informs the assembler that the name SUBPRO is defined outside its own assembly? (b) What statement in SUBPRO is required to make its name known to MAINPRO?

23–7. Assume that MAINPRO in Question 23–6 has defined variables named QTY as DB, VALUE as DW, and PRICE as DW. SUBPRO is to divide VALUE by QTY and is to store the quotient in PRICE. (a) How does MAINPRO inform the assembler that the three variables are to be known outside this assembly? (b) How does SUBPRO inform the assembler that the three variables are defined in another assembly?

23–8. Combine Questions 23–6 and 23–7 into a working program and test it.

23–9. Revise Question 23–8 so that MAINPRO passes all three variables as parameters. Note, however, that SUBPRO is to return the calculated price intact in its parameter.

23–10. Expand Question 23–9 so that MAINPRO accepts quantity and value from the keyboard, subprogram SUBCONV converts the ASCII amounts to binary, subprogram SUBCALC calculates the price, and subprogram SUBDISP converts the binary price to ASCII and displays the result.

CHAPTER 24 ───────────

DOS Memory Management

```
┌─────────────────────────────────────────────────────┐
│                     OBJECTIVE:                        │
│                                                       │
│  To describe the boot procedure, DOS initialization, the │
│  program segment prefix, the environment, memory con- │
│  trol, the program loader, and resident programs.     │
└─────────────────────────────────────────────────────┘
```

INTRODUCTION

This chapter describes DOS organization in detail. The operations introduced are DOS INT 2FH, function 4A01H, multiplex interrupt; and these INT 21H functions:

25H	Set interrupt address
31H	Keep program
3306H	Get DOS version
34H	Get address of DOS busy flag
35H	Get interrupt address
48H	Allocate memory
49H	Free allocated memory
4AH	Modify allocated memory block
4BH	Load or execute a program
51H	Get segment address of current PSP
52H	Get address of internal DOS list
58H	Get/set memory allocation strategy

MAIN DOS PROGRAMS

The four major DOS programs are the boot record, IO.SYS, MSDOS.SYS, and COM-MAND.COM:

1. The *boot record* is on track 0, sector 1, of any disk that you format with FORMAT /S. When you initiate the computer, the system automatically loads the boot record from disk into memory. The boot record, in turn, loads IO.SYS from disk into memory.

2. *IO.SYS* is a low-level interface to the BIOS routines in ROM. On initiation, it determines the status of the devices and equipment associated with the computer and sets interrupt table addresses for interrupts up to 20H. IO.SYS also handles input/output between memory and external devices such as a video monitor or disk. It then loads MSDOS.SYS.

3. *MSDOS.SYS* is a high-level interface to programs that sets interrupt table addresses for interrupts 20H through 3FH. It manages the directory and files on disk, blocking and deblocking of disk records, INT 21H functions, and a number of other services. It then loads COMMAND.COM.

4. *COMMAND.COM* handles the various commands such as DIR and CHKDSK and runs all requested .COM, .EXE, and .BAT programs. It is responsible for loading executable programs from disk into memory.

Figure 24–1 shows a map of memory after the DOS system programs have been loaded. Details vary by system.

```
 Beginning                 Contents
  Address

  F0000H  System ROM area
  E0000H  ROM BIOS
  D0000H  ROM BIOS
  C0000H  ROM BIOS
  B0000H  Video buffers
  A0000H  Video buffers
  xxxx0H  Transient portion of COMMAND.COM, at top of RAM
          ...
          User programs
          Resident programs (if any)
  xxxx0H  Resident portion of COMMAND.COM
  xxxx0H  MSDOS.SYS and IO.SYS
  00500H  DOS communication area
  00400H  BIOS data area
  00000H  Interrupt address table

 Note: Conventional memory is from 00000H to A0000H (640K).
       Upper memory area is from A0000H up to FFFF0H (one meg).
       High memory area (HMA) is 64K from FFFF0H through FFFFFH.
       Extended memory is above HMA.
```

Figure 24–1   Map of Memory

HIGH-MEMORY AREA

The processor uses a number of address lines to access memory. For the 80286 and later, line number A20 can address a 64K space known as the *high-memory area* (HMA), from FFFF:10H through FFFF:FFFFH, just above the DOS limit of one megabyte.

When the computer runs in real (8086) mode, it normally disables the A20 line so that addresses that exceed this limit wrap around to the beginning of memory. Enabling the A20 line permits addressing locations in the HMA. Since DOS 5.0, you can ask CONFIG.SYS to relocate DOS from low memory to the HMA, thereby freeing space for user programs. You can use INT 21H, function 3306H (Get DOS version), to determine the presence of DOS in the HMA:

```
MOV   AX,3306H      ;Request DOS version

INT   21H           ;Call DOS
```

The operation returns the following:

- BL = Major version number (as the 7 in version 7.1)
- BH = Minor version number (as the 1 in version 7.1)
- DL = Revision number in the three low bits (2–0)
- DH = DOS version flags, where bit 4 = 1 means in HMA

DOS INT 2FH (multiplex interrupt), among its many services, also provides a check (via function 4A01H) for available space in the HMA:

```
MOV   AX,4A01H   ;Request space in HMA

INT   2FH        ;Call DOS
```

The operation returns the following:

- BX = Number of free bytes available in the HMA (zero if DOS is not loaded high)
- ES:DI = Address of the first free byte in the HMA (FFFF:FFFF if DOS is not loaded high)

COMMAND.COM

The system loads the three portions of COMMAND.COM into memory either permanently during a session or temporarily as required. The following describes the three parts:

1. The *resident portion* of COMMAND.COM immediately loads MSDOS.SYS (and its data areas), where it resides during processing. The resident portion handles errors for disk I/O and the following interrupts:

   INT 22H   Terminate address

   INT 23H   Ctrl+Break handler

   INT 24H   Error detection on disk read/write or bad memory image of the FAT

   INT 27H   Terminate but stay resident (TSR)

2. The *initialization portion* of COMMAND.COM immediately follows the resident portion and contains the setup for AUTOEXEC files. When the system starts up, the initialization portion takes control and determines the segment address at which the system is to load programs for execution. None of the initialization routines is required again during a session. Consequently, your first request to load a program from disk causes DOS to overlay the initialization portion of COMMAND.COM wherever it resides in memory.

3. The *transient portion* of COMMAND.COM is loaded into a high area of memory. "Transient" implies that DOS may overlay this area with other requested programs if necessary. The transient portion displays the familiar screen prompt and accepts and executes requests. It contains a relocation loader facility that loads .COM and .EXE files from disk into memory for execution. When you request execution of a program, the transient portion constructs a program segment in the lowest available memory location. It creates the PSP at 00H, loads your requested executable program at offset 100H, sets exit addresses, and gives control to your loaded program.

Normal termination of a program causes a return to the resident portion of COMMAND.COM. If the executed program overlaid the transient portion of COMMAND.COM, the resident portion reloads it into memory.

PROGRAM SEGMENT PREFIX

DOS loads .COM and .EXE programs for execution into a program segment and creates a PSP at offset 00H and the program itself at offset 100H of the segment. The PSP contains the following fields, according to relative position:

00–01H	An INT 20H instruction (CD20H) to facilitate the return to DOS
02–03H	The segment address of the last paragraph of memory allocated to the program, as xxxx0. For example, 640K is indicated as 00A0H, meaning A0000[0].
04–09H	Reserved by DOS
0A–0DH	Terminate address (segment address for INT 22H)
0E–11H	Ctrl+Break exit address (segment address for INT 23H)
12–15H	Critical error exit address (segment address for INT 24H)
16–17H	Reserved by DOS
18–2BH	Default file handle table
2C–2DH	Segment address of program's environment
2E–31H	Reserved by DOS
32–33H	Length of the file handle table
34–37H	Far pointer to the handle table
38–4FH	Reserved by DOS
50–51H	Call to DOS function (INT 21H and RETF)
52–5BH	Reserved by DOS
5C–6BH	Parameter area 1, formatted as a standard unopened FCB (#1)

6C–7FH   Parameter area 2, formatted as a standard unopened FCB (#2); overlaid if the FCB at 5CH is opened

80–FFH   Buffer for a default DTA

PSP 18–2BH: Default File Handle Table

Each byte in the 20-byte default file handle table refers to an entry in a DOS table that defines the related device or driver. Initially, the table contains 0101010002FF . . . FF, where the first 01 refers to the keyboard, the second 01 to the screen, and so forth:

TABLE	DEVICE	HANDLE	DEVICE
01	Console	0	Keyboard (standard input)
01	Console	1	Screen (standard output)
01	Console	2	Screen (standard error)
00	COM1 (serial port)	3	Auxiliary
02	Printer	4	Standard printer
FF	Unassigned	5	Unassigned

The table of 20 handles explains why DOS allows a maximum of 20 files open at one time. Normally, the word at PSP offset 32H contains the length of the table (14H, or 20), and 34H contains its segment address in the form IP:CS, where the IP is 18H (the offset in the PSP) and the CS is the segment address of the PSP.

Programs that need more than 20 open files have to release memory (INT 21H, function 4AH) and use function 67H (set maximum handle count):

```
MOV    AH,67H          ;Request handles

MOV    BX,count        ;New number (20 to 65,535)

INT    21H             ;Call DOS
```

The amount of memory required is one byte per handle, rounded up to the next byte paragraph plus 16 bytes. The operation creates the new handle table outside the PSP and updates PSP locations 32H and 34H. An invalid operation sets the carry flag and sets an error code in the AX.

PSP 2C–2DH: Segment Address of Environment

Every program loaded for execution has a related *environment* that DOS stores in memory, beginning on a paragraph boundary before the program segment. The default size is 160 bytes, with a maximum of 32K. The environment contains such DOS commands as COMSPEC, PATH, PROMPT, and SET that are applicable to the program.

PSP 5C–6BH: Standard Unopened FCB #1

DOS formats this area with a dummy or real FCB #1, based on the characters (if any) that you enter following a request for the name of a program that is to be executed, such as MASM D:PROGRAM1.ASM. FCB #1 contains the *first* (or only) filename entered.

PSP 6C–7FH: Standard Unopened FCB #2

DOS also formats this area with a dummy or real FCB #2, based on the characters (if any) that you enter when you request the name of a program that is to be executed. FCB #2 contains the *second* (if any) filename entered.

PSP 80–FFH: Default DTA Buffer

This portion of the PSP is called a *default buffer* for the DTA. DOS initializes this area with the full text (if any) that a user keys in following the requested program name. The first byte contains the number of keys (if any) pressed immediately after the entered program name that is entered, followed by any actual characters entered. After that is any "garbage" left in memory from a previous program.

The following four examples should clarify the contents and purpose of FCB #1, FCB #2, and the DTA.

Example 1:   Command with No Operand. Suppose that a user causes a program named CALCIT.EXE to execute by keying in CALCIT [Enter]. When DOS constructs the PSP for this program, it sets up FCB #1, FCB #2, and the default DTA as follows:

```
5CH FCB #1:    00 20 20 20 20 20 20 20 20 20 20 20 ...

6CH FCB #2:    00 20 20 20 20 20 20 20 20 20 20 20 ...

80H DTA:       00 0D ...
```

FCB #1 and FCB #2:   These are both dummy FCBs. Their first byte, 00H, refers to the default drive number. The subsequent bytes for filename and extension are blank, since the user entered no text following the keyed program name.

DTA: The first byte contains the number of bytes keyed in after the name CALCIT, not including the Enter character. Since no keys other than Enter were pressed, the number is zero. The second byte contains the Enter character, 0DH, that was pressed.

Example 2:   Command with Text Operand. Suppose that a user wants to execute a program named COLOR and passes a parameter "BY" that tells the program to set the color to blue (B) on a yellow (Y) background. The user types the program name followed by the parameter: COLOR BY. DOS then sets the following in the PSP:

```
5CH FCB #1:    00 42 59 20 20 20 20 20 20 20 20 20 ...

6CH FCB #2:    00 20 20 20 20 20 20 20 20 20 20 20 ...

80H DTA:       03 20 42 59 0D ...
```

FCB #1:   DOS has set up FCB #1 with 00H as the default drive and 4259H (BY) as the filename. Note that DOS doesn't know whether the filename is valid.

DTA: The bytes at 80H mean a length of 3, followed by a space, "BY," and the Enter character. Other than the length, this field contains exactly what was typed.

Example 3:   Command with a Filename Operand. Programs like DOS DEL allow users to enter a filename after the program name. If a user keys in, for example, DEL D:CALCIT.OBJ [Enter], the PSP contains the following:

```
5CH FCB #1:    04 43 41 4C 43 49 54 20 20 4F 42 4A ...
                  C  A  L  C  I  T        O  B  J

6CH FCB #2:    00 20 20 20 20 20 20 20 20 20 20 20 ...

80H DTA:       0D 20 44 3A 43 41 4C 43 49 54 2E 4F 42 4A 0D ...
                     D  :  C  A  L  C  I  T  .  O  B  J
```

FCB #1:   The first character indicates the drive number (04 = D), followed by the name of the file, CALCIT, that the program is to reference. Then come two blanks that complete the eight-character filename and, finally, the extension, OBJ.

DTA: The length of 13 (0DH) is followed by exactly what was typed, including the Enter character.

Example 4:   Command With Two Filename Operands. Consider entering a command followed by two parameters, such as

```
COPY A:FILEA.ASM D:FILEB.ASM
```

DOS sets the FCBs and DTA with the following:

```
5CH FCB #1:    01 46 49 4C 45 41 20 20 20 41 53 4D ...
                  F  I  L  E  A        A  S  M

6CH FCB #2:    04 46 49 4C 45 42 20 20 20 41 53 4D ...
                  F  I  L  E  B        A  S  M

80H DTA:       10 20 41 3A 46 49 4C 45 41 2E 41 53 4D 20 etc...
                     A  :  F  I  L  E  A  .  A  S  M      etc...
```

FCB #1:   The first byte, 01, refers to drive A, followed by the filename.
FCB #2:   The first byte, 04, refers to drive D, followed by the filename.
DTA: The bytes contain the number of characters entered (10H), a space (20H), A:FILEA.ASM D:FILEB.ASM, and the Enter character (0DH).

Accessing the PSP

By determining the address of the PSP, you can access its data in order to process specified files or to take special action. An .EXE program can't always assume that its code segment immediately follows the PSP. DOS function 51H delivers to the BX register the segment address of the current PSP. The following code gets the address of the PSP and saves it in the ES register:

```
MOV   AH,51H          ;Request address of PSP
INT   21H             ;Call DOS
MOV   ES,BX           ;Save PSP address in ES
```

You may now use the ES to access data in the PSP:

```
            CMP   ES:BYTE PTR[80H],0   ;Check PSP buffer

            JE    EXIT                 ; zero, no data
```

To locate the DTA for a .COM program, simply set 80H in the SI, DI, or BX register, and access the contents:

```
            MOV   SI,80H               ;Address of DTA

            CMP   BYTE PTR[SI],0        ;Check buffer (DS:SI)

            JE  EXIT                   ; zero, no data
```

Extended Example Using the PSP

The partial .COM program in this section sets the attribute of a requested file to normal (00H). A user would key in the program name followed by the name of the file, such as P24ATTRB d:filename.ext. The program scans the DTA for the Enter character and replaces it with a byte of hex zeros, creating an ASCIIZ string. A user could also type in the directory path. Following is the coded program:

```
        TITLE   P24ATTRB (.COM) 'Set file attribute to normal'
        CODESG  SEGMENT PARA
                ASSUME CS:CODESG
                ORG    100H
        BEGIN:  MOV    AL,0DH          ;Search character (Enter)
                MOV    CX,21           ;Number of bytes
                MOV    DI,82H          ;Start address in PSP
                REPNZ SCASB            ;Scan for Enter
                JNZ    ***             ;Not found, error
                DEC    DI              ;Found:
                MOV    BYTE PTR [DI],0 ;Replace with 00H
                MOV    AH,43H          ;Request
                MOV    AL,01           ; set attribute
                MOV    CX,00           ; to normal
                MOV    DX,82H          ;ASCIIZ string in PSP
                INT    21H             ;Call DOS
                JC     ***             ;Write error?...
                ...
        CODESG  ENDS
                END    BEGIN
```

MEMORY BLOCKS

DOS allows any number of programs to be loaded and to stay resident. Examples include RAMDISK, MOUSE, and SIDEKICK. DOS sets up one or two *memory blocks* for each loaded program. Immediately preceding each memory block is an *arena header* (or *memory control record*) beginning on a paragraph boundary and containing the following fields:

00–00H   Code, where 4DH ('M') means more blocks to follow and 5AH ('Z') means zero blocks to follow (the last block). (This is a useful interpretation, but not necessarily the original intention.)

01–02H   Segment address of the owner's PSP. 0800H means that the segment belongs to MSDOS.SYS, and 0000H means that it is released and available.

03–04H   Length of the memory block, in paragraphs

05–07H   Reserved

08–0FH   Filename of owner, in ASCIIZ format (since DOS 4.0).

A forward linked list connects memory blocks. The *first* memory block, set up and owned by MSDOS.SYS, contains DOS file buffers, FCBs used by file handle functions, and device drivers loaded by DEVICE commands in CONFIG.SYS.

The *second* memory block is the resident portion of COMMAND.COM with its own PSP. A few special programs such as FASTOPEN and SHARE may be loaded before COMMAND.COM.

The *third* memory block is the master environment containing the COMSPEC command, PROMPT commands, PATH commands, and any strings set by SET.

Succeeding blocks include any resident (TSR) programs and the currently executing program. Each of these programs has two blocks; the *first* is a copy of the environment, and the *second* is a program segment with the PSP and the executable module.

INT 21H, Function 52H: Get Address of Internal DOS List

The arena header for the first memory block, which belongs to MSDOS.SYS, can be located by means of an undocumented feature: INT 21H, function 52H. The DOS table of addresses begins with these entries:

00H   DD   Address of first drive parameter block
04D   DD   Address of list of DOS file tables
08H   DD   Address of CLOCK$ device driver
0CH   DD   Address of CON device driver

Function 52H returns the segment address of the list of DOS file tables (the second entry) in the ES and an offset in the BX. ES:[BX-4] therefore points to the preceding entry, a doubleword in IP:CS format that contains the address of the first arena header.

To find subsequent memory blocks in the chain:

1. Use the address of the arena header for the memory block.
2. Add 1 to the segment address of the arena header to get the start of its memory block. (The arena header is 10H bytes long.)
3. Add the length of the memory block from offsets 03–04H of the arena header. You now have the segment address of the next arena header.

To determine the paragraphs of memory available to DOS for the last program, find the arena header containing "Z" in byte 0, and perform the preceding calculations. The last block has available to it all remaining higher memory.

Example of Tracing Memory Blocks

If you use DEBUG to trace through memory blocks on your own system, you can use DEBUG's H (Hex) command for hexadecimal arithmetic. Use it like this:

```
H value1,value2
```

The H command returns the sum and the difference of the two values.

For the following example, DEBUG displayed the required memory contents. Watch out for reversed-byte sequence. The trace proceeded as follows:

1. Function 52H returned 02CC[0] in the ES and 0026H in the BX. Since we want the four bytes to the left at 0022H, use D 02CC:22 to display the address of the arena header for the first memory block in IP:CS format. This turns out to be 00 00 56 0B. The address is therefore 0B56[0].

2. Use D B56:0 to display the first arena header:

```
4D 08 00 AE 05 ...
```

The 4D ("M") means more memory blocks follow, 0800 (0008H) tells us that the memory block belongs to MSDOS.SYS, and AE05 (05AEH) is the length of the memory block.

3. Locate the second arena header (COMMAND.COM):

Location of first arena header:	B56[0]
Add 1 paragraph:	+ 1[0]
Add length of its memory block:	+ 5AE[0]
Location of next arena header:	1105[0]

Use D 1105:0 to display the second arena header:

```
4D 06 11 64 01 ...
```

You could also examine the contents of COMMAND.COM at this point.

4. Locate the third arena header, the master environment:

Location of previous arena header:	1105[0]
Add 1 paragraph:	+ 1[0]
Add length of its memory block:	+ 164[0]
Location of next arena header:	126A[0]

Use D 126A:0 to display the third arena header: 4D ... .

You could follow the same procedure to examine the contents of the master environment and locate any remaining memory blocks. Note that succeeding programs have *two* memory blocks each: one for their environment and one for their program segment. The last arena header has 5AH ("Z") in its first byte. If you display from within DEBUG, this is its own memory block, since DEBUG would be the last program loaded in memory.

Handling Upper Memory Blocks

Since DOS 5.0, CONFIG.SYS may contain a DOS=UMB (upper memory block) statement for allocating memory to programs above conventional memory, between the 640K and the one-megabyte boundaries. The statement causes DOS to establish a dummy arena header 16 bytes before the 640K boundary and marked as owned. Its size field contains a value large enough to bypass any video buffers and ROM routines.

In this way, it is possible to step up from the last arena header in conventional memory to locate memory blocks in upper memory. Within upper memory, other arena headers marked as owned are also used to bypass any areas already used by ROM or video.

MEMORY ALLOCATION STRATEGY

DOS uses a number of strategies to determine where to load a program in memory. INT 21H, function 58H, provides services for this purpose.

Function 5800H: Get Memory Allocation Strategy

This operation allows queries to the memory allocation strategy:

```
MOV  AX,5800H        ;Request get strategy

INT  21H             ;Call DOS
```

The operation clears the carry flag and returns the strategy in the AX:

- 00H = First fit (the default): Search from the lowest address in conventional memory for the first available block that is large enough to load the program.
- 01H = Best fit: Search for the smallest available block in conventional memory that is large enough to load the program.
- 02H = Last fit: Search from the highest address in conventional memory for the first available block.
- 40H = First fit, high only: Search from the lowest address in upper memory for the first available block.
- 41H = Best fit, high only: Search for the smallest available block in upper memory.
- 42H = Last fit, high only: Search from the highest address in upper memory for the first available block.
- 80H = First fit, high: Search from the lowest address in upper memory for the first available block. If none is found, search conventional memory.
- 81H = Best fit, high: Search for the smallest available block in upper memory. If none is found, search conventional memory.
- 82H = Last fit, high: Search from the highest address in upper memory for the first available block. If none is found, search conventional memory.

Best fit and last fit strategies are appropriate to multitasking systems, which could have fragmented memory because of programs running concurrently. When a program finishes processing, its memory is released to the system.

Function 5801H: Set Memory Allocation Strategy

This operation allows changes to the memory allocation strategy. To set a strategy, set the AL with code 01 and the BX with the strategy code. An error sets the carry flag and returns 01 (invalid function) in the AX.

Function 5802H: Get Upper Memory Link

This operation indicates whether a program can allocate memory from the upper memory area (above 640K). The operation clears the carry flag and returns one of the following codes to the AL:

- 00H = Area is not linked, cannot allocate
- 01H = Area is linked, can allocate

Function 5803H: Set Upper Memory Link

This operation can link or unlink the upper memory area and, if the area is linked, can allocate memory from it:

```
MOV   AX,5803H        ;Request
MOV   BX,linkflag     ; link/unlink
INT   21H             ; upper memory area
```

The link flag parameter has the following meaning:

- 00H = unlink the area
- 01H = link the area

A successful operation clears the carry flag and allows a program to allocate memory from it. An error sets the carry flag and returns to the AX code 01 (CONFIG.SYS did not contain DOS=UMB) or 07 (memory links damaged).

PROGRAM LOADER

On loading .COM and .EXE programs, DOS performs the following:

1. Sets up memory blocks for the program's environment and for the program segment
2. Creates a program segment prefix at location 00H of the program segment and loads the program at 100H.

Other than these steps, the load and execute steps differ for .COM and .EXE programs. A major difference is that the linker inserts a special header record in an .EXE file when storing it on disk, and the DOS loader uses this record for loading.

Loading and Executing a .COM Program

Since the organization of a .COM file is relatively simple, DOS needs to know only that the file extension is .COM. As described earlier, a program segment prefix precedes .COM and

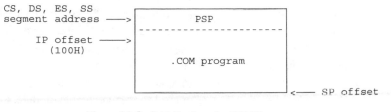

Figure 24–2   Initialization of a .COM Program

.EXE programs loaded in memory. The first two bytes of the PSP contain the INT 20H instruction (return to DOS). On loading a .COM program, DOS

- Sets the four segment registers with the address of the first byte of the PSP.
- Sets the stack pointer (SP) to the end of the 64K segment, offset FFFEH (or to the end of memory if the segment is not large enough), and pushes a zero word on the stack.
- Sets the instruction pointer to 100H (the size of the PSP) and allows control to proceed to the address generated by CS:IP, the first location immediately following the PSP. This is the first byte of your program, and it should contain an executable instruction. Figure 24–2 illustrates this initialization.

Loading and Executing an .EXE Program

The linker stores on disk an .EXE module that consists of two parts: a *header record* containing control and relocation information; and the actual *load module*.

The header is a minimum of 512 bytes and may be longer if there are many relocatable items. The header contains information about the size of the executable module, where it is to be loaded in memory, the address of the stack, and relocation offsets to be inserted into incomplete machine addresses. In the following, the term *block* refers to a 512-byte area in memory.

- 00–01H   Hex 4D5A ('MZ') identifies an .EXE file.
- 02–03H   Number of bytes in the last block of the .EXE file.
- 04–05H   Size of the file, including the header, in 512-byte block increments. For example, if the size is 1,025, this field contains 2 and 02–03H contains 1.
- 06–07H   Number of relocation table items (see 1CH).
- 08–09H   Size of the header, in 16-byte (paragraph) increments, to help DOS locate the start of the executable module following the header. The minimum number is 20H (32) ($32 \times 16 = 512$ bytes).
- 0A–0BH   Minimum count of paragraphs that must reside above the end of the program when it is loaded.
- 0C–0DH   High/low loader switch. When linking, you decide whether the program is to load for execution at a low (the usual) or a high memory address. The value 0000H indicates high. Otherwise, this location contains the maximum count of paragraphs that must reside above the end of the loaded program.
- 0E–0F   Offset location in the executable module of the stack segment.

- 10–11H   Offset that the loader is to insert in the SP register when transferring control to the executable module. The value is the defined size of the stack.
- 12–13H   Checksum value—the sum of all the words in the file (ignoring overflows), used as a validation check for possible lost data.
- 14–15H   Offset (usually, but not necessarily, 00H) that the loader is to insert in the IP register when transferring control to the executable module.
- 16–17H   Offset in the executable module of the code segment. The loader inserts the offset in the CS register. If the code segment is first, the offset would be zero.
- 18–19H   Offset of the relocation table (see the item at 1CH).
- 1A–1BH   Overlay number: zero (the usual) means that the .EXE file contains the main program.
- 1CH–end   Relocation table containing a variable number of relocation items, as identified at offset 06–07H. Positions 06–07H of the header indicate the number of items in the executable module that are to be relocated. Each relocation item, beginning at header 1CH, consists of a two-byte offset value and a two-byte segment value.

The system constructs memory blocks for the environment and the program segment. Following are the steps that DOS performs when loading and initializing an .EXE program:

- Reads the formatted part of the header into memory.
- Calculates the size of the executable module (total file size in position 04H minus header size at position 08H) and reads the module into memory at the start segment.
- Reads the relocation table items into a work area and adds the value of each item to the start segment value.
- Sets the DS and ES registers to the segment address of the PSP.
- Sets the SS register to the address of the PSP, plus 100H (the size of the PSP), plus the SS offset value (at 0EH). Also, sets the SP register to the value at 10H, the size of the stack.
- Sets the CS to the address of the PSP, plus 100H (the size of the PSP), plus the CS offset value in the header (at 16H) to the CS. Also, sets the IP with the offset at 14H. The CS:IP pair provides the starting address of the code segment and, in effect, program execution. Figure 24–3 illustrates this initialization.

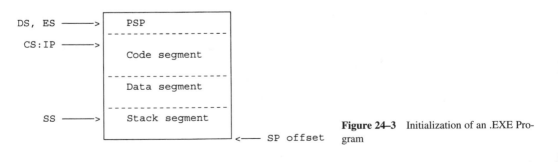

Figure 24–3   Initialization of an .EXE Program

After the preceding, DOS is finished with the .EXE header and discards it. The CS and SS registers are set correctly, but your program has to set the DS (and ES) for its own data segment:

```
MOV   AX,datasegname     ;Set DS and ES registers
MOV   DS,AX              ;  to address
MOV   ES,AX              ;  of data segment
```

Example of Loading an .EXE Program

Consider the following Map that the linker generated for an .EXE program:

```
Start    Stop   Length  Name      Class

00000H  0003AH  003BH   CSEG         Code
00040H  0005AH  001BH   DSEG         Data
00060H  0007FH  0020H   STACK       Stack

Program entry point at 0000:0000
```

The map provides the *relative* (not actual) location of each of the three segments. Note that some linkers arrange these segments in alphabetic sequence by name. According to the map, the code segment (CSEG) is to start at 00000H—its relative location is the beginning of the executable module, and its length is 003BH bytes. The data segment, DSEG, begins at 00040H and has a length of 001BH. This is the first address following CSEG that aligns on a paragraph boundary (a boundary evenly divisible by 10H). The stack segment, STACK, begins at 00060H, the first address following DSEG that aligns on a paragraph boundary.

DEBUG can't display a header record after a program is loaded for execution, because DOS replaces the header record with the PSP. However, there are various utility programs on the market (or you can write your own) that allow you to view the hex contents of any disk sector. The header for the program we are examining contains the following relevant information, according to hex location (the contents of fields are in reverse-byte sequence):

00H   Hex 4D5A ("MZ")
02H   Number of bytes in last block: 5B00H
04H   Size of file, including header, in 512-byte blocks: 0200H (0002 × 512 = 1,024 bytes)
06H   Number of relocation table items following formatted portion of header: 0100H—that is, 0001
08H   Size of header, in 16-byte increments: 2000H (0020H = 32, and 32 × 16 = 512 bytes)
0CH   Load in low memory: FFFFH
0EH   Offset location of stack segment: 6000H, or 0060H
10H   Offset to insert in SP: 2000H, or 0020H
14H   Offset for IP: 0000H
16H   Offset for CS: 0000H
18H   Offset for the relocation table: 1E00H, or 001EH

When DEBUG loaded this program, the registers contained the following values:

```
SP = 0020    DS = 138F    ES = 138F

SS = 13A5    CS = 139F    IP = 0000
```

For .EXE modules, the loader sets the DS and ES to the address of the PSP and sets the CS, IP, SS, and SP to values from the header record. Let's now see how the loader initializes these registers.

CS Register

According to the DS register, when the program loaded, the address of the PSP was 138F[0]H. Since the PSP is 100H bytes long, the executable module follows immediately at 139F[0]H, which the loader inserts in the CS register:

Start address of PSP (see DS):	138F0H
Length of PSP:	+ 100H
Address of code segment	139F0H

The CS provides the starting address of the code portion (CSEG) of the program. You can use the DEBUG display command D CS:0000 to view the machine code of a program in memory. The code is identical to the hex portion of the assembler .LST printout, other than operands that .LST tags as R.

SS Register

The loader used the value 60H in the header (at 0EH) for setting the address of the stack in the SS register:

Start address of PSP (see DS):	138F0H
Length of PSP:	+ 100H
Offset of stack (see location 0EH in header):	+ 60H
Address of stack:	13A50H

SP Register

The loader used 20H from the header (at 10H) to initialize the stack pointer to the length of the stack. In this example, the stack was defined as 16 DUP(?), that is, 16 two-byte fields = 32, or 20H. The SP points to the current top of the stack.

DS Register

The loader uses the DS register to establish the starting point for the PSP at 138F[0]. Because the header does not contain a starting address for the DS, your program has to initialize it:

```
0004 B8 ---- R        MOV   AX,DSEG

0007 8E D8            MOV   DS,AX
```

The assembler left unfilled the machine address of DSEG, which becomes an entry in the relocation table in the header, discussed earlier. DEBUG shows the completed instruction as

```
B8 A313
```

A313 is loaded into the DS as 13A3. The DS address is calculated as follows:

CS address:	139F0H
Plus offset for the DS:	40H
DS address:	13A30H

We now have these values at the start of execution:

REGISTER	ADDRESS	MAP OFFSET
CS	139F[0]H	00H
DS	13A3[0]H	40H
SS	13A5[0]H	60H

As an exercise, trace any of your linked .EXE programs with DEBUG, and note the changed values in the registers:

INSTRUCTION	REGISTERS CHANGED
MOV AX,DSEG	IP and AX
MOV DS,AX	IP and DS
MOV ES,AX	IP and DS

The DS now contains the correct address of the data segment. You can use D DS:00 to view the contents of DSEG and use D SS:00 to view the contents of the stack.

ALLOCATING AND FREEING MEMORY

DOS services allow you to *allocate, release,* and *modify the size of* an area of memory. The most likely uses for these services are with resident programs and programs that load other programs for execution. Under DOS, which was designed as a single-user environment, a program that needs to load another program for execution has to release some of its memory space.

INT 21H, Function 48H: Allocate Memory

To allocate memory for a program, request function 48H, and set the BX with the number of required paragraphs:

```
        MOV   AH,48H        ;Request allocate memory
        MOV   BX,paragraphs ;Number of paragraphs
        INT   21H           ;Call DOS
```

A successful operation clears the carry flag and returns in the AX the segment address of the allocated memory block. The operation begins at the first memory block and steps through each block until it locates a space large enough for the request, usually at the high end of memory.

An unsuccessful operation sets the carry flag and returns in the AX an error code (07 = memory block destroyed or 08 = insufficient memory) and in the BX the size, in paragraphs, of the largest block available. A memory block destroyed means that the operation found a block in which the first byte was not 'M' or 'Z'.

INT 21H, Function 49H: Free Allocated Memory

Function 49H frees allocated memory; it is commonly used to release a resident program. Load in the ES the segment address of the block to be returned:

```
MOV    AH,49H            ;Request free allocated memory

LEA    ES,seg-address    ;Address of block for paragraphs

INT    21H               ;Call DOS
```

A successful operation clears the carry flag and stores 00H in the second and third bytes of the memory block, meaning that it is no longer in use. An unsuccessful operation sets the carry flag and returns in the AX an error code (07 = memory block destroyed and 09 = invalid memory block address).

INT 21H, Function 4AH: Modify Allocated Memory Block

Function 4AH can increase or decrease the size of a memory block. Initialize the BX with the number of paragraphs to retain for the program and the ES with the address of the PSP:

```
MOV    AH,4AH            ;Request modify allocated memory

MOV    BX,paragraphs     ;Number of paragraphs

LEA    ES,PSP-address    ;Address of PSP

INT    21H               ;Call DOS
```

A program can calculate its own size by subtracting the end of the last segment from the address of the PSP. You'll have to ensure that you use the last segment if your linker rearranges segments in alphabetic sequence.

A successful operation clears the carry flag. An unsuccessful operation sets the carry flag and returns in the AX an error code (07 = memory block destroyed, 08 = insufficient memory, and 09 = invalid memory block address) and returns in the BX the maximum possible size (if an attempt to increase the size was made). A wrong address in the ES can cause error 07.

LOADING OR EXECUTING A PROGRAM FUNCTION

Let's now examine how to get an executing program to load, and in turn, execute a subprogram. Function 4BH enables a program to load a subprogram into memory for execution. Load these registers:

- AL = Function code for one of the following:

00H = Load and execute

01H = Load program

03H = Load overlay

05H = Set execution state (not covered in this text)

- ES:BX = Address of a parameter block
- DX = Address of the path name for the called subprogram, an ASCIIZ string in uppercase letters

The code to load the subprogram is as follows:

```
MOV     AH,4BH              ;Request load

MOV     AL,code             ;Function code

LEA     BX,para-block       ;Address of parameter block

LEA     DX,path             ;Address of path name

INT     21H                 ;Call DOS
```

An invalid operation sets the carry flag and returns an error code in the AX.

AL = 00H: Load and Execute

This operation loads an .EXE or .COM program into memory, establishes a program segment prefix for it, and transfers control to it for execution. Since all registers, including the stack, are changed, the operation is not for novices. The parameter block addressed by the ES:BX has the following format:

OFFSET	PURPOSE
00H	Address of environment-block segment to be passed at PSP+2CH. A zero address means that the loaded program is to inherit the environment of its parent.
02H	Doubleword pointer to command line for placing at PSP+80H.
06H	Doubleword pointer to default FCB #1 for passing at PSP+5CH.
0AH	Doubleword pointer to default FCB #2 for passing at PSP+6CH.

The doubleword pointers have the form offset:segment address.

AL = 01H: Load Program

This operation loads an .EXE or .COM program into memory and establishes a program segment prefix for it, but does not transfer control to it for execution. The parameter block addressed by the ES:BX has the following format:

OFFSET	PURPOSE
00H	Address of environment-block segment to be passed at PSP+2CH. If the address is zero, the loaded program is to inherit the environment of its parent.

02H	Doubleword pointer to command line for placing at PSP+80H.
06H	Doubleword pointer to default FCB #1 for passing at PSP+5CH.
0AH	Doubleword pointer to default FCB #2 for passing at PSP+6CH.
0EH	Starting stack address
12H	Starting code segment address

The doubleword pointers have the form offset:segment address.

AL = 03H: Load Overlay

This operation loads a program or block of code, but does not establish a PSP or begin execution of the program or block. Thus the requested code could be a program overlay. The parameter block addressed by the ES:BX has the following format:

OFFSET	PURPOSE
00H	Word segment address where file is to be loaded
02H	Word relocation factor to apply to the image

An error sets the carry flag and returns an error code in the AX, described in Figure 18–1.

Program: Load and Execute

The program in Figure 24–4 requests DOS to perform the DIR command for drive D. The program first uses function 4AH to reduce its memory requirements to its actual size—the difference between its last (dummy) segment ZNDSEG and the start of its PSP. Note that at this point, the ES still contains the address of the PSP, as loaded on entry. (The ASSUME statements preceding and following MOV BX,SEG ZNDSEG appear to be required for MASM 5.1, but not for some other assemblers.) The module is 80 bytes in size, so that the PSP (10H paragraphs) and the program (8 paragraphs) total 18H paragraphs.

Function 4BH with code 00 in the AL handles the loading and execution of COM-MAND.COM. The program displays the directory entries for drive D.

INT 21H, Function 4DH: Get Subprogram Return Value

This operation retrieves the return value that the last subprogram delivered when it terminated by function 4CH or 31H. The returned values are:

- AH = Subprogram's termination method, where

    00H = Normal termination

    01H = Terminated by Ctrl+C

    02H = Critical device error

    03H = Terminated by function 31H (keep program)

- AL = Return value from the subprogram

```
TITLE      P24EXDOS (EXE) DOS function 4BH to execute DIR
; ----------------------------------------------------------------
SSEG       SEGMENT PARA STACK 'Stack'
           DW      32(?)
SSEG       ENDS
; ----------------------------------------------------------------
DSEG       SEGMENT PARA 'Data'
PARAREA    LABEL   BYTE                 ;Parameter block for load/exec:
           DW      0                    ;  address of envir. string
           DW      OFFSET DIRCOM        ;  pointer to command line
           DW      DSEG
           DW      OFFSET FCB1          ;  pointer to default FCB1
           DW      DSEG
           DW      OFFSET FCB2          ;  pointer to default FCB2
           DW      DSEG
DIRCOM     DB      17,'/C DIR D:',13,0
FCB1       DB      16 DUP(0)
FCB2       DB      16 DUP(0)
PROGNAM    DB      'D:COMMAND.COM',0
DSEG ENDS
; ----------------------------------------------------------------
CSEG       SEGMENT PARA 'Code'
           ASSUME  CS:CSEG,DS:DSEG,SS:SSEG,ES:DSEG
BEGIN      PROC    FAR
           MOV     AH,4AH               ;Reduce allocated memory
           ASSUME  CS:ZNDSEG
           MOV     BX,SEG ZNDSEG        ;Ending segment
           ASSUME  CS:CSEG
           MOV     CX,ES                ;  minus start of
           SUB     BX,CX                ;  program segment
           INT     21H
           JC      E10ERR               ;Not enough space?
           MOV     AX,DSEG
           MOV     DS,AX                ;Set DS and ES
           MOV     ES,AX
           MOV     AH,4BH               ;Request load
           MOV     AL,00                ;  and execute
           LEA     BX,PARAREA           ;  COMMAND.COM
           LEA     DX,PROGNAM
           INT     21H
           JC      E20ERR               ;Execute error?
           MOV     AL,00                ;OK, no error code
           JMP     X10XIT
E10ERR:
           MOV     AL,01                ;Error code 1
           JMP     X10XIT
E20ERR:
           MOV     AL,02                ;Error code 2
           JMP     X10XIT
X10XIT:
           MOV     AH,4CH               ;Request
           INT     21H                  ;  exit to DOS
BEGIN      ENDP
CSEG       ENDS

ZNDSEG     SEGMENT                      ;Dummy segment
ZNDSEG     ENDS
           END     BEGIN
```

Figure 24–4   Execution of DIR from within a Program

PROGRAM OVERLAYS

The program in Figure 24–5 uses the same service as that in Figure 24–4, but this time just to load a program into memory without executing it. The process consists of a main program, P24CALLV, and two subprograms, P24SUB1 and P24SUB2.

P24CALLV is the main program, with these segments:

```
STACKSG SEGMENT PARA STACK 'Stack1'

DATASG  SEGMENT PARA 'Data1'

CODESG  SEGMENT PARA 'Code1'

ZENDSG  SEGMENT                          ;Dummy (empty) segment
```

P24SUB1 is linked with and called by P24CALLV. Its segments are:

```
DATASG   SEGMENT PARA 'Data2'

CODESG   SEGMENT PARA 'Code2'
```

P24CALLV's segments are linked first—that's why their class names differ: 'Data1', 'Data2', 'Code1', 'Code2', and so forth. Here's the link map for P24CALLV+P24SUB1:

```
Start   Stop    Length Name            Class

00000H 0007FH 00080H STACKSG          Stack1

00080H 000C2H 00043H DATASG           Data1

000D0H 0016DH 0009EH CODESG           Code1

00170H 00170H 00000H ZENDSG

00170H 00185H 00016H DATASG           Data2

00190H 001AFH 00020H CODESG           Code2
```

P24SUB2 is also called by P24CALLV, but is linked separately. Its segments are:

```
DATASG   SEGMENT   PARA   'Data'

CODESG   SEGMENT   PARA   'Code'
```

P24SUB2's link map looks like this:

```
Start    Stop    Length Name           Class

00000H 00015H 00016H DATASG            Data

00020H 0003EH 0001FH CODESG            Code
```

When P24CALLV+P24SUB1 is loaded into memory for execution, P24CALLV calls and executes P24SUB1 in normal fashion. The near CALL initializes the IP correctly,

```
TITLE       P24CALLV (EXE)  Call subprogram and overlay
            EXTRN   P24SUB1:FAR
; --------------------------------------------------------------
STACKSG     SEGMENT PARA STACK 'Stack1'
            DW      64 DUP(?)
STACKSG     ENDS
; --------------------------------------------------------------
DATASG      SEGMENT PARA 'Data1'
PARABLK     LABEL   WORD                    ;Parameter block
            DW      0                       ;
            DW      0                       ;
FILENAM     DB      'F:\P24SUB2.EXE',0
ERRMSG1     DB      'Modify mem error'
ERRMSG2     DB      'Allocate error  '
ERRMSG3     DB      'Seg call error  '
DATASG      ENDS
; --------------------------------------------------------------
CODESG      SEGMENT PARA 'Code1'
BEGIN       PROC    FAR
            ASSUME  CS:CODESG,DS:DATASG,SS:STACKSG
            MOV     AX,DATASG
            MOV     DS,AX
            CALL    Q10SCR                  ;Scroll screen
            CALL    P24SUB1                 ;Call subprogram 1

            MOV     AH,4AH                  ;Shrink memory
            ASSUME  CS:ZENDSG
            MOV     BX,SEG ZENDSG           ;Address of end program
            ASSUME  CS:CODESG
            MOV     CX,ES                   ;Address of PSP
            SUB     BX,CX                   ;Size of this program
            INT     21H
            JC      A30ERR                  ;If error, exit

            MOV     AX,DS                   ;Initialize ES for
            MOV     ES,AX                   ;  this service
            MOV     AH,48H                  ;Allocate memory for overlay
            MOV     BX,40                   ;40 paragraphs
            INT     21H
            JC      A40ERR                  ;If error, exit
            MOV     PARABLK,AX              ;Save segment address

            MOV     AH,4BH                  ;Load subprogram 2
            MOV     AL,03                   ;  with no execute
            LEA     BX,PARABLK
            LEA     DX,FILENAM
            INT     21H
            JC      A50ERR                  ;If error, exit
            MOV     AX,PARABLK              ;Exchange two words
            MOV     PARABLK+2,AX            ;  of PARABLK
            MOV     PARABLK,20H             ;Set CS offset to 20H
            LEA     BX,PARABLK
            CALL    DWORD PTR [BX]          ;Call subprogram 2
            JMP     A90
A30ERR:
            CALL    Q20SET                  ;Set cursor
            LEA     DX,ERRMSG1
            CALL    Q30DISP                 ;Display message
            JMP     A90
A40ERR:
            CALL    Q20SET                  ;Set cursor
            LEA     DX,ERRMSG2
            CALL    Q30DISP                 ;Display message
            JMP     A90
```

Figure 24–5 Calling a Subprogram and Overlay

```
A50ERR:
            CALL    Q20SET              ;Set cursor
            LEA     DX,ERRMSG3
            CALL    Q30DISP             ;Display message
            JMP     A90
A90:
            MOV     AH,4CH              ;Exit
            INT     21H
BEGIN       ENDP
;                   Video screen services:
;                   ---------------------
Q10SCR      PROC    NEAR
            MOV     AX,0600H            ;Request scroll
            MOV     BH,1EH              ;Set attribute
            MOV     CX,0000
            MOV     DX,184FH
            INT     10H
            RET
Q10SCR      ENDP

Q20SET      PROC    NEAR
            MOV     AH,02H              ;Request set
            MOV     BH,00               ;  cursor
            MOV     DH,12
            MOV     DL,00
            INT     10H
            RET
Q20SET      ENDP
Q30DISP     PROC    NEAR                ;DX set on entry
            MOV     AH,40H              ;Request display
            MOV     BX,01               ;Handle
            MOV     CX,16               ;Length
            INT     21H
            RET
Q30DISP     ENDP
CODESG      ENDS

ZENDSG      SEGMENT                     ;Dummy (empty) segment
ZENDSG      ENDS
            END     BEGIN


------------------------------------------------------------


TITLE       P24SUB1  Called subprogram
; ----------------------------------
DATASG      SEGMENT PARA 'Data2'
SUBMSG      DB      'Subprogram 1 reporting'
DATASG      ENDS

CODESG      SEGMENT PARA 'Code2'
P24SUB1     PROC    FAR
            ASSUME  CS:CODESG,DS:DATASG
            PUBLIC  P24SUB1
            PUSH    DS                  ;Save caller's DS
            MOV     AX,DATASG           ;Initialize DS
            MOV     DS,AX
            MOV     AH,02H              ;Request set
            MOV     BH,00               ;  cursor
            MOV     DH,05
            MOV     DL,00
            INT     10H
            MOV     AH,40H              ;Request display
            MOV     BX,01               ;Handle
            MOV     CX,22               ;Length
```

Figure 24–5   (continued)

```
                LEA        DX,SUBMSG
                INT        21H
                POP        DS                    ;Restore DS for caller
                RET
  P24SUB1       ENDP
  CODESG        ENDS
                END
```
- -
```
  TITLE         P24SUB2 Called overlay subprogram
  ; -----------------------------------------------
  DATASG        SEGMENT PARA 'Data'
  SUBMSG        DB         'Subprogram 2 reporting'
  DATASG        ENDS

  CODESG        SEGMENT PARA 'Code'
  P24SUB2       PROC       FAR
                ASSUME     CS:CODESG,DS:DATASG
                PUSH       DS                    ;Save caller's DS
                MOV        AX,CS                 ;Set address of first
                MOV        DS,AX                 ;  segment in DS
                MOV        AH,02H                ;Request set
                MOV        BH,00                 ;  cursor
                MOV        DH,10
                MOV        DL,00
                INT        10H
                MOV        AH,40H                ;Request display
                MOV        BX,01                 ;Handle
                MOV        CX,22                 ;Length
                LEA        DX,SUBMSG
                INT        21H
                POP        DS                    ;Restore caller's DS
                RET
  P24SUB2       ENDP
  CODESG        ENDS
                END
```

Figure 24–5 (continued)

but since P24SUB1 has its own data segment, it has to push P24CALLV's DS and establish its own DS address. P24SUB1 sets the cursor, displays a message, pops the DS, and returns to P24CALLV.

To overlay P24SUB2 on P24SUB1, P24CALLV has to *shrink* its own memory space, since DOS has given it all available memory. P24CALLV's highest segment is ZENDSG, which is empty. P24CALLV subtracts the address of its PSP (still in the ES) from the address of ZENDSG. The difference is 270H (27H paragraphs), calculated as the size of the PSP (100H) plus the offset of ZENDSG (170H), which is delivered to DOS by function 4AH.

DOS function 48H then allocates memory to allow space for P24SUB2 to be loaded (overlaid) on top of P24SUB1, arbitrarily set to 40H paragraphs. The operation returns the loading address in the AX register, which P24CALLV stores in PARABLK. This is the first word of a parameter block to be used by function 4BH.

Function 4BH with code 03 in the AL loads P24SUB2 into memory. Note the definition in the data segment: F:\P24SUB2.EXE,0. Function 4BH references CS and PARABLK—the first word contains the segment address where the overlay is to be loaded and the second word is an offset, in this case, zero. A diagram may help make these steps clearer:

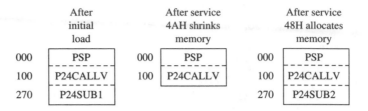

The far CALL to P24SUB2 requires a reference defined as IP:CS, but PARABLK is in the form CS:IP. The CS value is therefore moved to the second word, and 20H is stored in the first word for the IP, since the link map shows that value as the offset of P24SUB2's code segment. The next instructions load the address of PARABLK in the BX and call P24SUB2:

```
LEA   BX,PARABLK        ;Address of PARABLK

CALL  DWORD PTR [BX]    ;Call P24SUB2
```

Note that P24CALLV doesn't reference P24SUB2 by name in its code segment and so doesn't require an EXTRN statement specifying P24SUB2. Since P24SUB2 has its own data segment, it first pushes the DS onto the stack and initializes its own address. But P24SUB2 wasn't linked with P24CALLV. As a result, the instruction MOV AX,DATASG would set the AX only with the offset address of DATASG, 0[0]H, and not its segment address. We know that CALL set the CS with the address of the first segment, which (according to the map) happens to be the address of the data segment. Moving the CS to the DS gives the correct address in the DS. Note that if P24SUB2's code and data segments were in a different sequence, the coding would have to be somewhat different.

P24SUB2 sets the cursor, displays a message, pops the DS, and returns to P24CALLV. DEBUG was indispensable in developing this program.

RESIDENT PROGRAMS

A number of popular commercial and shareware programs are designed to *reside* in memory while other programs run, and you can activate their services through special keystrokes. You load resident programs after DOS is loaded and before activating other normal processing programs. They are almost always .COM programs and are also known as "terminate but stay resident" (TSR) programs.

The easy part of writing a resident program is getting it to reside. Instead of normal termination, you exit by means of INT 21H, function 31H (keep program). The operation requires the size of the program in the DX register:

```
MOV  AH,31H          ;Request TSR

MOV  DX,prog-size    ;Size of program

INT  21H
```

When you execute the initialization routine, DOS reserves the memory block where the program resides and loads subsequent programs higher in memory.

The not-so-easy part of writing a resident program involves activating it after it is resident, since it is not a program internal to DOS, as are CLS, COPY, and DIR. A common approach is to modify the interrupt services table so that the resident program interrupts all keystrokes, acts on a special keystroke or combination, and passes on all other keystrokes. The effect is that a resident program typically, but not necessarily, consists of the following parts:

1. A section that redefines locations in the interrupt services table.
2. An initialization procedure that executes only the first time the program runs and that performs the following:
   - Replaces the address in the interrupt services table with its own address.
   - Establishes the size of the portion of the program that is to remain resident.
   - Uses an interrupt that tells DOS to terminate executing the current program and to attach the specified portion of the program in memory.
3. A procedure that remains resident and that is activated, for example, by special keyboard input or, in some cases, by the timer clock.

In effect, the initialization procedure sets up all the conditions to make the resident program work and then allows itself to be erased. The organization of memory now appears as follows:

- Rest of available memory
- Initialization portion of program   (overlaid by next program)
- Resident portion of program   (stays in memory)
- COMMAND.COM
- IO.SYS and MSDOS.SYS
- Interrupt services table

A resident program may use two INT 21H functions for accessing the interrupt services table, since there is no assurance that more advanced computers will have the interrupt table located in the same memory locations.

INT 21H, Function 35H: Get Interrupt Address

To retrieve the address of a particular interrupt, load the AL with the required interrupt number:

```
MOV  AH,35H        ;Request interrupt address

MOV  AL,int#       ;Interrupt number

INT  21H
```

The operation returns the address of the interrupt in the ES:BX as segment:offset. For conventional memory, a request for the address of INT 09H returns 00H in the ES and 24H (36) in the BX.

INT 21H, Function 25H: Set Interrupt Address

To set a new interrupt address, load the required interrupt number in the AL and the new address in the DX:

```
MOV  AH,25H        ;Request interrupt address

MOV  AL,int#       ;Interrupt number

LEA  DX,newaddr    ;New address for interrupt

INT  21H
```

The operation replaces the present address of the interrupt with the new address. In effect, then, when the specified interrupt occurs, processing links to your (resident) program, rather than to the normal interrupt address.

Example of a Resident Program

The resident program in Figure 24–6 named P24TSTNM beeps when you use the numeric keypad when NumLock is on. Its purpose is to warn you that you are entering a number rather than, say, pressing an arrow key to move the cursor. This program has to intercept INT 09H, keyboard input, to check for the key pressed.

The following points about the resident program are of interest:

BIODATA defines the BIOS data segment beginning at 40[0]—in particular, the keyboard flags byte, called here KBSTAT, which reflects the status of the keyboard. Bit 5 on (1) means that NumLock is on.

CODESG begins the code segment of P24TSTNM. The first executable instruction, JMP INITZE, transfers execution past the resident portion to the INITZE procedure near the end. This routine first uses CLI to prevent any further interrupts that may happen to occur at this time. It then uses DOS function 35H to locate the address of INT 09H in the interrupt services table. The operation returns the address in the ES:BX, which the INITZE routine stores in INT9SAV. Next, function 25H sets the program's own address for INT 09H in the interrupt table, TESTNUM, the entry point to the resident program. In effect, the program saves INT 09H's address and replaces it with its own address. The last step establishes the size of the resident portion (all the code up to INITZE) in the DX and uses DOS function 31H (terminate but stay resident) to exit. The code from INITZE to the end gets overlaid by the next program that is loaded for execution.

TESTNUM is the name of the resident procedure that is activated when a user presses a key. The system transfers execution to the address of INT 09H in the interrupt service table, which has been changed to the address of TESTNUM. Since the interrupt may happen, for example, while the user is in DOS or an editor or word processing program, P24TSTNM has to save the registers that it uses. The program accesses the keyboard flag to determine whether NumLock is on and whether the numeric keypad was pressed (a keyboard scan code between 71 and 83, inclusive). If so, the program beeps the speaker. (The use of the speaker is explained in Chapter 21, under the section "Generating Sound.") Final instructions involve restoring the pushed registers—in reverse sequence—and jumping

```
        TITLE   P24TSTNM (COM)  Resident program: checks NumLock on
        BIODATA SEGMENT AT 40H              ;BIOS data area
                ORG     17H
        KBSTAT  DB      ?                    ;Keyboard status byte
        BIODATA ENDS
        ;       ----------------------------------------------
        CODESG  SEGMENT PARA
                ASSUME  CS:CODESG,DS:BIODATA
                ORG     100H
        BEGIN:
                JMP     INITZE               ;Jump to initialization
        SAVINT9 DD      ?
        TESTNUM:
                PUSH    AX                   ;Save registers
                PUSH    CX
                PUSH    DS

                MOV     AX,BIODATA           ;Segment address of
                MOV     DS,AX                ;  BIOS data area
                MOV     AL,KBSTAT            ;Get keyboard flag
                TEST    AL,00100000B         ;NumLock state?
                JZ      EXIT                 ;No, exit

                IN      AL,60H               ;Get keystroke from port
                CMP     AL,71                ;Scan code < 71?
                JL      EXIT                 ;  yes, exit
                CMP     AL,83                ;Scan code > 83?
                JG      EXIT                 ;  yes, exit
                                             ;Must be from numeric keypad
                MOV     AL,10110110B         ;Set frequency
                OUT     43H,AL
                MOV     AX,1000
                OUT     42H,AL
                MOV     AL,AH
                OUT     42H,AL
                IN      AL,61H               ;Turn on speaker
                MOV     AH,AL
                OR      AL,03
                OUT     61H,AL
                MOV     CX,5000              ;Set duration
        PAUSE:
                LOOP    PAUSE
                MOV     AL,AH                ;Turn off speaker
                OUT     61H,AL
        EXIT:
                POP     DS                   ;Restore registers
                POP     CX
                POP     AX
                JMP     CS:SAVINT9           ;Resume INT 09H
        ;       Initialization routine
        ;       ----------------------
        INITZE:
                CLI                          ;Prevent further interrupts
                MOV     AH,35H               ;Get address of INT 09H
                MOV     AL,09                ;  in ES:BX
                INT     21H
                MOV     WORD PTR SAVINT9,BX  ;  and save it
                MOV     WORD PTR SAVINT9+2,ES

                MOV     AH,25H
                MOV     AL,09                ;Set new address for INT 09H
                MOV     DX,OFFSET TESTNUM    ;  in TESTNUM
                INT     21H
```

Figure 24–6 Resident Program

```
                MOV     AH,31H               ;Request stay resident
                MOV     DX,OFFSET INITZE  ;Set size of resident portion
                STI                          ;Restore interrupts
                INT     21H
        CODESG  ENDS
                END     BEGIN
```

Figure 24–6   (continued)

to INT9SAV, which contains the original INT 09H address. We now release control back to the interrupt.

The next example should help make the procedure clear. First we explain a conventional operation without a TSR intercepting the interrupt:

1. A user presses a key, and the keyboard sends interrupt 09H to BIOS.
2. BIOS uses the address of INT 09H in the interrupt services table to locate its BIOS routine.
3. Control then transfers to the BIOS routine.
4. The routine gets the character and (if it's a standard character) delivers it to the keyboard buffer.

Next is the procedure for the resident program:

1. A user presses a key, and the keyboard sends INT 09H to BIOS.
2. BIOS uses the address of INT 09H in the interrupt services table to locate its BIOS routine.
3. But the table now contains the address of TESTNUM, the resident program, to which control transfers.
4. If NumLock is on and the character is a numeric keypad number, TESTNUM beeps the speaker.
5. TESTNUM exits by jumping to the original saved INT 09H address, which transfers control to the BIOS routine.
6. The BIOS routine gets the character and (if it's a standard character) delivers it to the keyboard buffer.

Since this program is intended to be illustrative, you can modify or expand it for your own purposes. A few commercial programs that also replace the table address of interrupt 09H do not allow concurrent use of a resident program such as this one.

INT 21H, Function 34H: Get Address of DOS Busy Flag

Although this interrupt is used internally by DOS, some TSRs use it when requesting a DOS interrupt to check whether another interrupt is currently active. Since DOS is not reentrant (that is, you cannot enter DOS while it is active), the TSR has to wait until DOS is no longer busy, as indicated by the DOS busy flag, inDOS.

```
        MOV     AH,34H              ;Request busy

        INT     21H                 ;Call DOS

        CMP     ES:BYTE PTR[BX],0 ;Test if flag is zero

        JE      ...
```

The service returns the address of inDOS in the ES:BX. The flag contains the number of DOS functions currently active, where 0 means none. You may enter DOS only if inDOS is 0.

KEY POINTS

- The boot record is on track 0, sector 1, of any disk that you use FORMAT /S to format. When you initiate the system, it automatically loads the boot record from disk into memory. The boot record then loads IO.SYS from disk into memory.

- IO.SYS is a low-level interface to the BIOS routines in ROM. On initiation, IO.SYS determines the status of all devices and equipment associated with the computer and sets interrupt table addresses for interrupts up to 20H. IO.SYS also handles I/O between memory and external devices.

- MSDOS.SYS is a high-level interface to programs that is loaded into memory after IO.SYS. Its operations include setting interrupt table addresses for interrupts 20H through 3FH, managing the directory and files on disk, handling blocking and deblocking of disk records, and handling INT 21H functions.

- COMMAND.COM handles the various DOS commands and runs requested .COM, .EXE, and .BAT files. It consists of a small resident portion, an initialization portion, and a transient portion. COMMAND.COM is responsible for loading executable programs from disk into memory.

- The .EXE module that the linker creates consists of a header record containing control and relocation information and the actual load module.

- On loading either a .COM or an .EXE program, DOS sets up memory blocks for the program's environment and for the program segment. Preceding each memory block is a 16-byte arena header beginning on a paragraph boundary. DOS also creates a PSP at location 00H of the program segment and loads the program at 100H

- On loading a .COM program, DOS sets the segment registers wiht the address of the PSP, sets the stack pointer to the end of the segment, pushes a zero word onto the stack, and sets the intruction pointer to 100H (the size of the PSP). Control then proceeds to the address generated by CS:IP, the first location immediatley following the PSP.

- On loading an .EXE program, DOS reads the header record into memory, calculates the size of the executable module, and reads the module into memory at the start segment. It adds the value of each relocation table item to the start segment value. It sets the DS and ES to the segment address of the PSP; sets the SS to the address of the PSP, plus 100H, plus the SS offset value; sets the SP to the size of the stack, and sets the CS to the address of the PSP, plus 100H, plus the CS offset value in the header. DOS also sets the IP with the offset at 14H. The CS:IP pair provide the starting address of the code segment for program execution.

- Useful fields within the PSP include parameter area 1 at 5CH, parameter area 2 at 6CH, and default disk transfer area at 80H.

- Load resident programs before activating other normal processing programs. Exit by means of INT 21H, function 31H, which requires the size of the program in the DX.

QUESTIONS

24–1. (a) Where is the boot record located? (b) What is its purpose?

24–2. What is the purpose of IO.SYS (IBMBIO.COM)?

24–3. What is the purpose of MSDOS.SYS (IBMDOS.COM)?

24–4. Where, generally, are the following portions of COMMAND.COM located in memory and what is their purpose? (a) Resident; (b) transient.

24–5. (a) Where is the program segment prefix located? (b) What is its size?

24–6. A user types in the instruction FUDGE C:ALF.DOC to request execution of a FUDGE program. Show the hex contents in the program's PSP at (a) 5CH, parameter area 1 (FCB #1), and (b) 80H, the default DTA.

24–7. Your program has to determine what PATH commands are set for its environment. Explain where the program may find its own environment. (*Note*: The request is for the program's environment, not the DOS master environment.)

24–8. A .COM program is loaded for execution with its PSP beginning at location 2BA1[0]H. What address does DOS store in each of the following registers (ignore reverse-byte notation): (a) CS; (b) DS; (c) ES; (d) SS.

24–9. A link map for an .EXE program shows the following:

START	STOP	LENGTH	NAME	CLASS
00000H	0002FH	00030H	STACK	STACK
00030H	0005BH	0002CH	CODESG	CODE
00060H	0007CH	0001DH	DATASG	DATA

DOS loads the program with the PSP beginning at location 1A25[0]H. Showing calculations where appropriate, state the contents of each of the registers at the time of loading (ignore reverse-byte notation): (a) CS; (b) DS; (c) ES; (d) SS; (e) SP.

24–10. An arena header begins at location EB6[0] and contains the following: 4D C00E 0A00 ... . (a) What does the 4D (M) mean to DOS? (b) How would the contents differ if this were the last memory block? (c) What is the memory location of the next arena header? Show calculations.

24–11. (a) Resident programs commonly intercept keyboard input. Where and what exactly is this intercepted address? (b) In what two significant ways does the coding for terminating a resident program differ from the coding for terminating a normal program?

CHAPTER 25 ————————————

BIOS Data Areas and Interrupts

OBJECTIVE:

To describe the BIOS data areas and interrupt services.

INTRODUCTION

BIOS contains an extensive set of input/output routines and tables that indicate the status of the system's devices. DOS and user programs can request BIOS routines for communication with devices attached to the system. The method of interfacing with BIOS is software interrupts. This chapter examines the data areas (or tables) that BIOS supports, the interrupt procedure, and the various interrupt services.

The chapter covers the following BIOS interrupts:

00H	Divide by zero	0FH	LPT1 control
01H	Single step	10H	Video display
02H	Nonmaskable interrupt	11H	Equipment determination
03H	Break point	12H	Memory size determination
04H	Overflow	13H	Disk input/output
05H	Print screen	14H	Communications input/output

08H	System timer	16H	Keyboard input
09H	Keyboard interrupt	17H	Printer output
0BH	COM1 control	18H	ROM BASIC entry
0CH	COM2 control	19H	Bootstrap loader
0DH	LPT2 control	1AH	Read and set
0EH	Diskette control	1BH	Get control on keyboard break

THE BOOT PROCESS

On the PC, ROM resides beginning at location FFFF0H. Turning on the power causes a "cold boot." The processor enters a reset state, sets all memory locations to zero, performs a parity check of memory, and sets the CS register to FFFF[0]H and the IP register to zero. The first instruction to execute is therefore at FFFF:0, the entry point to BIOS. BIOS also stores the value 1234H at 40[0]:72H to signal a subsequent Ctrl+Alt+Del ("warm reboot") not to perform the preceding power-on self-test.

BIOS checks the various ports to identify and initialize devices that are attached, including INT 11H (equipment determination) and INT 12H (memory size determination). Then, beginning at location 0 of memory, BIOS establishes the interrupt service table that contains addresses of interrupt routines.

Next, BIOS determines whether a disk containing DOS is present and, if so, it executes INT 19H to access the first disk sector containing the bootstrap loader. This program is a temporary operating system to which the BIOS routine transfers control after loading it into memory. The bootstrap has only one task: to load the first part of the real operating system into memory. The DOS files IO.SYS, MSDOS.SYS, and COMMAND.COM are then loaded from disk into memory.

THE BIOS DATA AREA

BIOS maintains its own 256-byte (100H) data area in lower memory beginning at segment address 40[0]H. A worthwhile exercise is to use DEBUG to examine these fields. They are next listed by offset.

Serial Port Data Area

00H–07H   Four words, addresses of up to four serial ports

Parallel Port Data Area

08H–0FH   Four words, addresses of up to four parallel ports

System Equipment Data Area

10H–11H   Equipment status, a primitive indication of the status of installed devices. You can issue INT 11H, which returns the following in the AX:

BIT	DEVICE
15,14	Number of parallel ports attached
11–9	Number of RS232 serial adapters
7,6	Number of diskette devices: Bit 00 = 1, 01 = 2, 10 = 3, and 11 = 4
5,4	Initial video mode. Bit values are:
	00 = unused
	01 = 40 × 25 color
	10 = 80 × 25 color
	11 = 80 × 25 monochrome
2	Pointing device (mouse); 1 = installed
1	1 = math coprocessor is present
0	1 = diskette drive is present

Miscellaneous Data Area

12H   Manufacturer's test flags

Memory Size Data Area

13H–14H   Amount of memory on system board, in kilobytes

15H–16H   Amount of expansion memory, in kilobytes

Keyboard Data Area 1

17H–17H   First byte of current shift status:

BIT	ACTION	BIT	ACTION
7	Insert active	3	Alt pressed
6	CapsLock active	2	Ctrl pressed
5	NumLock active	1	Left shift pressed
4	Scroll Lock active	0	Right shift pressed

18H–18H   Second byte of current shift status:

BIT	ACTION	BIT	ACTION
7	Insert pressed	3	Ctrl/NumLock pressed
6	CapsLock pressed	2	SysReq pressed
5	NumLock pressed	1	Left Alt pressed
4	Scroll Lock pressed	0	Left Ctrl pressed

19H   Alternate keyboard entry for ASCII characters.

1AH–1BH   Pointer to keyboard buffer head

1CH–1DH   Pointer to keyboard buffer tail
1EH–3DH   Keyboard buffer (32 bytes)

Diskette Drive Data Area

3EH   Disk seek status. Bit number 0 refers to drive A, 1 to B, 2 to C, and 3 to D. A bit value of 0 means that the next seek is to reposition to cylinder 0 to recalibrate the drive.

3FH   Disk motor status. If bit 7 = 1, a write operation is in progress. Bit number 0 refers to drive A, 1 to B, 2 to C, and 3 to D; a bit value of 0 means that the motor is on.

40H   Motor count for time-out until motor is turned off

41H   Disk status, indicating an error on the last diskette drive operation:

00H	No error	09H	Attempt to make DMA across 64K boundary
01H	Invalid drive parameter	0CH	Media type not found
02H	Address mark not found	10H	CRC error on read
03H	Write-protect error	20H	Controller error
04H	Sector not found	40H	Seek failed
06H	Diskette change line active	80H	Drive not ready
08H	DMA overrun		

42H–48H   Diskette drive controller status

Video Data Area 1

49H   Current video mode, indicated by a 1-bit:

BIT	MODE	BIT	MODE
7	Monochrome	3	80 × 25 color
6	640 × 200 monochrome	2	80 × 25 monochrome
5	320 × 200 monochrome	1	40 × 25 color
4	320 × 200 color	0	40 × 25 monochrome

4AH–4BH   Number of columns on screen
4CH–4DH   Size of video page buffer
4EH–4FH   Starting offset of video buffer
50H–5FH   Eight words for current starting location for each of eight pages, numbered 0–7
60H–61H   Starting and ending line of cursor
62H   Currently active display page
63H–64H   Port address of active display, where monochrome is 3B4H and color is 3D4H
65H   Current setting of video mode register
66H   Current color palette

System Data Area

67H–68H	Data-edge time count
69H–6AH	Cyclical redundancy check (CRC) register
6BH	Last input value
6CH–6DH	Lower half of timer
6EH–6FH	Higher half of timer
70H	Timer overflow (1 if timer has passed midnight)
71H	Ctrl+Break keys set bit 7 to 1
72H–73H	Memory reset flag. If contents are 1234H, Ctrl+Alt+Del keys cause a "warm" (rather than "cold") reboot

Hard Disk Data Area

74H	Status of last hard disk operation (details in Chapter 19)
75H	Number of hard disks attached

Time-Out Data Area

78H–7BH	Time-out for parallel ports (LPT1–LPT4)
7CH–7FH	Time-out for serial ports (COM1–COM4)

Keyboard Data Area 2

80H–81H	Offset address for start of keyboard buffer
82H–83H	Offset address for end of keyboard buffer

Video Data Area 2

84H	Number of rows on screen (minus 1)
85H	Character height, in scan lines
86H–8AH	Miscellaneous video information

Diskette/Hard Disk Data Area

8BH–95H	Controller and error status

Keyboard Data Area 3

96H	Keyboard mode state and type flags

BIT	ACTION	BIT	ACTION
7	Read ID in progress	3	Right Alt pressed
6	Last code was ACK	2	Right Ctrl pressed
5	Force NumLock if read ID and KBX	1	Last scan code was E0
4	101/102 keyboard installed	0	Last scan code was E1

97H	Keyboard LED Flags (bit 0 = ScrollLock, 1 = NumLock, and 2 = CapsLock)

Real-Time Clock Data Area

98H–A7H   Status of wait flags

Save Pointer Data Area

A8H–ABH   Pointers to various BIOS tables

Miscellaneous Data Area 2

ACH–FFH   Reserved by DOS

INTERRUPT SERVICES

An interrupt is an operation that suspends execution of a program so that the system can take special action. We have already used a number of interrupts for video display, disk I/O, printing, and resident programs. The interrupt routine executes and normally returns control to the interrupted procedure, which then resumes execution. BIOS handles interrupts 00H–1FH, and DOS handles interrupts 20H–3FH.

Interrupt Service Table

When the computer powers up, BIOS and DOS establish an interrupt service table in memory locations 000H–3FFH. The table provides for 256 (100H) interrupts, each with a related four-byte offset:segment address in the form IP:CS. The operand of an interrupt instruction such as INT 05H identifies the type of request. Since there are 256 entries, each four bytes long, the table occupies the first 1,024 bytes of memory, from 00H through 3FFH. Each address in the table relates to a BIOS or DOS routine for a specific interrupt type. Thus bytes 0–3 contain the address for interrupt 0, bytes 4–7 for interrupt 1, and so forth:

INT 00H	INT 01H	INT 02H	INT 03H	INT 04H	INT 05H	INT 06H	...
IP:CS	IP:CS	IP:CS	IP:CS	IP:CS	IP:CS	IP:CS	...
00H	04H	08H	0CH	10H	14H	18H	...

Executing an Interrupt

An interrupt pushes onto the stack the contents of the flags register, the CS, and the IP. For example, the table address of INT 05H (which prints the screen when a user presses Ctrl+PrtSc) is 0014H (05H × 4 = 14H). The operation extracts the four-byte address from location 0014H and stores two bytes in the IP and two in the CS. The address in the CS:IP then points to the start of a routine in the BIOS area, which now executes. The interrupt returns via an IRET (Interrupt Return) instruction, which pops the IP, CS, and flags from the stack and returns control to the instruction following the INT.

External and Internal Interrupts

An *external* interrupt is caused by a device that is external to the processor. The two lines that can signal external interrupts are the nonmaskable interrupt (NMI) line and the interrupt request (INTR) line. The NMI line reports memory and I/O parity errors. The processor always acts on this interrupt, even if you issue CLI to clear the interrupt flag in an attempt to disable external interrupts. The INTR line reports requests from external devices, namely, interrupts 05H through 0FH, for the timer, keyboard, serial ports, fixed disk, diskette drives, and parallel ports.

An *internal* interrupt occurs as a result of the execution of an INT instruction or a divide operation that causes an overflow, execution in single-step mode, or a request for an external interrupt, such as disk I/O. Programs commonly use internal interrupts, which are nonmaskable, to access BIOS and DOS procedures.

BIOS INTERRUPTS

This section covers BIOS interrupts 00H through 1BH. There are other operations not covered that can be executed only by BIOS.

INT 00H: Divide by Zero.   Invoked by an attempt to divide by zero. Displays a message and usually hangs the system. Program developers are familiar with this error because erasing a segment register may accidentally cause it.

INT 01H: Single Step. Used by DEBUG and other debuggers to enable single-stepping through program execution.

INT 02H: Nonmaskable Interrupt. Used for serious hardware conditions, such as parity errors, that are always enabled. Thus a program issuing a CLI (clear interrupt) instruction does not affect these conditions.

INT 03II.   Break Point. Used by debugging programs to stop execution. DEBUG's Go and Proceed commands set this interrupt at the appropriate stopping point in the program; DEBUG undoes single-step mode and allows the program to execute normally up to INT 03H, whereupon DEBUG resets single-step mode.

INT 04H: Overflow. May be caused by an arithmetic operation, although usually no action takes place.

INT 05H: Print Screen. Causes the contents of the screen to print. Issuing INT 05H activates the interrupt internally, and pressing the Ctrl+PrtSc keys activates it externally. The operation enables interrupts and saves the cursor position. No registers are affected. Address 50:00 in the BIOS data area contains the status of the operation.

INT 08H: System Timer. A hardware interrupt that updates the system time and (if necessary) date. A programmable timer chip generates an interrupt every 54.9254 milliseconds, about 18.2 times a second.

INT 09H: Keyboard Interrupt. Caused by pressing or releasing a key on the keyboard; described in detail in Chapter 11.

INT 0BH, INT 0CH: Serial Device Control. Control the COM1 and COM2 ports, respectively.

INT 0DH, INT 0FH: Parallel Device Control. Control the LPT2 and LPT1 ports, respectively.

INT 0EH: Diskette Control. Signals diskette activity, such as completion of an I/O operation.

INT 10H: Video Display. Accepts a number of functions in the AH for screen mode, setting the cursor, scrolling, and displaying; described in detail in Chapter 10.

INT 11H: Equipment Determination. Determines the optional devices on the system and returns the value at BIOS location 40:10H to the AX. (At power-up time, the system executes this operation and stores the AX in location 40:10H; see the earlier section, "BIOS Data Area," for details.)

INT 12H: Memory Size Determination. Returns in the AX the size of memory on the system board, in terms of contiguous kilobytes such that 640K memory is 0280H, as determined during power-on.

INT 13H: Disk Input/Output. Accepts a number of functions in the AH for disk status, read sectors, write sectors, verify, format, and get diagnostics; covered in Chapter 19.

INT 14H: Communications Input/Output. Provides byte stream I/O (that is, one bit at a time) to the RS232 communication port. The DX should contain the number of the RS232 adapter (0–3 for COM1, 2, 3, and 4, respectively). A number of functions are established through the AH register.

Function 00H: Initialize Communications Port. Set the following parameters in the AL, according to bit number:

BAUD RATE	PARITY	STOP BIT	WORD LENGTH
7–5	4–3	2	1–0
000 = 110	00 = none	0 = 1	10 = 7 bits
001 = 150	01 = odd	1 = 2	11 = 8 bits
010 = 300	10 = none		
011 = 600	11 = even		
100 = 1,200			
101 = 2,400			
110 = 4,800			
111 = 9,600			

The operation returns the status of the communications port in the AX. (See function 03H for details.) Here's an example that sets COM1 to 1,200 baud, no parity, one stop bit, and eight-bit data length:

```
MOV   AH,00H          ;Request initialize port
MOV   AL,10000011B    ;Parameters
MOV   DX,00           ;COM1 serial port
INT   14H             ;Call BIOS
```

Function 01H: Transmit Character. Load the AL with the character that the routine is to transmit and the DX with the port number. On return, the operation sets the port status in the AH. (See function 03H.) If the operation is unable to transmit the byte, it also sets bit 7 of the AH, although the normal purpose of this bit is to report a time-out error. Make sure to execute function 00H before using this service.

Function 02H: Receive Character. Load the port number in the DX. The operation accepts a character from the communications line into the AL. It also sets the AH with the port status (see function 03) for error bits 7, 4, 3, 2, and 1. Thus a nonzero value in the AX indicates an input error. Make sure to execute function 00H before using this service.

Function 03H: Return Status of Communications Port. Load the port number in the DX. The operation returns the line status in the AH and modem status in the AL:

AH (LINE STATUS)	AL (MODEM STATUS)
7 Time out	7 Received line signal detect
6 Trans shift register empty	6 Ring indicator
5 Trans hold register empty	5 Data set ready
4 Break detect	4 Clear to send
3 Framing error	3 Delta receive line signal detect
2 Parity error	2 Trailing edge ring detector
1 Overrun error	1 Delta data set ready
0 Data ready	0 Delta clear to send

Other INT 14H functions are 04H (extended initialize) and 05H (extended communications port control).

INT 15H: System Services. This rather elaborate operation provides for a large number of functions in the AH, such as the following:

21H	Power-on self-testing
43H	Read system status
84H	Joystick support
88H	Determine extended memory size
89H	Switch the processor to protected mode
C2H	Mouse interface

For example, with function code 88H in the AH, the operation returns in the AX the number of kilobytes of extended memory. (For example, 0580H means 1408K bytes.) Since the operation exits without resetting interrupts, use it like this:

```
MOV  AH,88H      ;Request extended memory
INT  15H         ;  from BIOS
STI              ;Restore interrupts
```

INT 16H: Keyboard Input. Accepts a number of functions in the AH for basic keyboard input; covered in Chapter 10.

INT 17H: Printer Output. Provides a number of functions for printing via BIOS; discussed in Chapter 20.

INT 18H: ROM BASIC Entry. Called by BIOS if the system starts up with no disk containing the DOS system programs.

INT 19H: Bootstrap Loader. If a disk(ette) device is available with the DOS system programs, reads track 0, sector 1, into the boot location in memory at 7C00H and transfers control to this location. If there is no disk drive, transfers to the ROM BASIC entry point via INT 18H. It is possible to use this operation as a software interrupt; it does not clear the screen or initialize data in ROM BIOS.

INT 1AH: Read and Set Time. Reads or sets the time of day according to a function code in the AH:

- 00H = Read system timer clock. Returns the high portion of the count in the CX and the low portion in the DX. If the time has passed 24 hours since the last read, the operation sets the AL to a nonzero value.
- 01H = Set system timer clock. Load the high portion of the count in the CX and the low portion in the DX.
- 02H–07H.   These functions handle the time and date for real-time clock services.

To determine how long a routine executes, you could set the clock to zero and then read it at the end of processing.

INT 1BH: Get Control on Keyboard Break.   When Ctrl+Break keys are pressed, causes ROM BIOS to transfer control to its interrupt address, where a flag is set.

KEY POINTS

- ROM resides beginning at location FFFF0H. Turning on the power causes a "cold boot." The processor enters a reset state, sets all memory locations to zero, performs a parity check of memory, and sets the CS register to FFFF[0]H and the IP register to zero. The first instruction to execute is therefore at FFFF:0, or FFFF0, the entry point to BIOS.
- On boot-up, BIOS checks the various ports to identify and initialize devices that are attached. BIOS then establishes an interrupt service table, beginning at location 0 of memory, that contains addresses for interrupts that occur. Two operations that BIOS performs are equipment and memory size determination. If a disk containing DOS is present, BIOS accesses the first disk sector containing the bootstrap loader. This program loads DOS files IO.SYS, MSDOS.SYS, and COMMAND.COM from disk into memory.
- BIOS maintains its own data area in lower memory, beginning at segment address 40[0]H. Relevant data areas include those of the serial port, parallel port, system equipment, keyboard, diskette drive, video control, hard disk, and real-time clock.

- The operand of an interrupt instruction such as INT 12H identifies the type of request. For each of the 256 possible types, the system maintains a four-byte address in the interrupt services table at locations 0000H through 3FFH. Thus bytes 0–3 contain the address for interrupt 0, bytes 4–7 for interrupt 1, and so forth.
- BIOS interrupts range from 00H through 1FH and include divide by zero, print screen, timer, video control, diskette control, video display I/O, equipment and memory size determination, disk I/O, communications I/O, keyboard input, printer output, and bootstrap loader.

QUESTIONS

25–1. Distinguish between an external and an internal interrupt.

25–2. Distinguish between an NMI line and an INTR line.

25–3. (a) What is the memory location of the entry point to BIOS? (b) On power-up, how does the system direct itself to this address?

25–4. On bootup, BIOS performs interrupts 11H, 12H, and 19H. What is their purpose?

25–5. What is the beginning location of the BIOS data area?

25–6. The following binary values were noted in the BIOS data area. For each item, identify the field and explain the significance of the 1-bits.

    (a) 10–11H: 10000010 00100101   (b) 17H: 11100001

    (c) 18H: 00000011   (d) 96H: 00001100

25–7. The following hex values were noted in the BIOS data area. For each item, identify the field and explain the significance of the value.

    (a) 00–03H: F8 03 F8 02   (h) 08–0BH: 78 03 00 00

    (c) 13–14H: 80 02   (d) 15–16H: 00 08

    (e) 4A–4BH: 50 00   (f) 60–61H: 0E 0D

    (g) 84H: 18

25–8. Identify the following BIOS interrupts: (a) Divide by zero; (b) print screen; (c) keyboard interrupt; (d) video display; (e) disk I/O; (f) keyboard input; (g) printer output; (h) get equipment status; (i) memory size determination; (j) communications I/O.

CHAPTER 26 ─────────

DOS Interrupts

OBJECTIVE:

To describe the various DOS interrupt functions.

INTRODUCTION

The two DOS modules, IO.SYS and MSDOS.SYS, facilitate using BIOS. Since these modules provide much of the additional required testing, the DOS operations are generally easier to use than their BIOS counterparts and are generally more machine independent.

IO.SYS is a low-level interface to BIOS that facilitates reading data from external devices into memory and writing data from memory onto external devices.

MSDOS.SYS contains a file manager and provides a number of services. For example, when a user program requests INT 21H, the operation delivers information to MSDOS.SYS via the contents of registers. To complete the request, MSDOS.SYS may translate the information into one or more calls to IO.SYS, which in turn calls BIOS. The following shows the relationships involved:

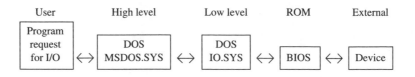

DOS INTERRUPTS

Interrupts 20H through 3FH are reserved for DOS operations, as described in the following sections.

INT 20H: Terminate Program. Ends execution of a .COM program, restores addresses for Ctrl+Break and critical errors, flushes register buffers, and returns control to DOS. This function would normally be placed in the main procedure and, on exit from it, the CS should contain the address of the PSP. The preferred termination is INT 21H, function 4CH.

INT 21H: DOS Function Request. The main DOS operation, which requires a function in the AH and is described in detail later.

INT 22H: Terminate Address. Copies the address of this interrupt into the program's PSP (at offset 0AH) when DOS loads a program for execution. On program termination, DOS transfers control to the address of the interrupt. Your programs should not issue this interrupt.

INT 23H: Ctrl+Break Address. Designed to transfer control to a DOS routine (via PSP offset 0EH) when you press Ctrl+Break or Ctrl+C. The routine ends execution of a program or a batch file. A program could also change this address to that of its own routine to perform special action without ending the program. Your programs should not issue this interrupt.

INT 24H: Critical-Error Handler. Used by DOS to transfer control (via PSP offset 12H) when it recognizes a critical error (often in a disk or printer operation). Your programs should not issue this interrupt.

INT 25H: Absolute Disk Read. Reads the contents of one or more disk sectors; covered in Chapter 17, but superseded by INT 21H, function 440DH, minor code 61H.

INT 26H: Absolute Disk Write. Writes data from memory to one or more disk sectors; covered in Chapter 17, but superseded by INT 21H, function 440DH, minor code 41H.

INT 27H: Terminate but Stay Resident. Causes a .COM program on exit to remain in memory; superseded by INT 21H, function 31H.

INT 2FH: Multiplex Interrupt. Involves communication between programs, such as communicating the status of a print spooler, the presence of a device driver, or DOS commands such as ASSIGN or APPEND. Chapter 24 describes function 4A01H, which checks the high-memory area for available space.

INT 33H: Mouse Handler. Provides services for handling a mouse. (See Chapter 21.)

DOS INT 21H SERVICES

Following are the DOS function requests for INT 21H, which require a function code in the AH register:

00H   Terminate program. Basically the same as INT 20H and also superseded by
       INT 21H, function 4CH.
01H   Keyboard input with echo. (See Chapter 11.)
02H   Display character. (See Chapter 9.)
03H   Communications input. Reads a character from the serial port into the AL.
       This is a primitive service, and BIOS INT 14H is preferred.
04H   Communications output. The DL contains the character to transmit. BIOS
       INT 14H is preferred.
05H   Printer output. (See Chapter 20.)
06H   Direct keyboard and display. (See Chapter 11.)
07H   Direct keyboard input without echo. (See Chapter 11.)
08H   Keyboard input without echo. (See Chapter 11.)
09H   Display string. (See Chapter 9.)
0AH   Buffered keyboard input. (See Chapter 11.)
0BH   Check keyboard status. (See Chapter 11.)
0CH   Clear keyboard buffer and invoke input. (See Chapter 11.)
0DH   Reset disk drive. (See Chapter 18.)
0EH   Select default disk drive. (See Chapter 18.)
0FH   Open FCB file. (See Chapter 17.)
10H   Close FCB file. (See Chapter 17.)
11H   Search for first matching disk entry. Obsolete and superseded by function 4EH.
12H   Search for next matching disk entry. Obsolete and superseded by function 4FH.
13H   Delete FCB file. Obsolete and superseded by function 41H.
14H   Read FCB sequential record. (See Chapter 17.)
15H   Write FCB sequential record. (See Chapter 17.)
16H   Create FCB file. (See Chapter 17.)
17H   Rename FCB file. Obsolete and superseded by function 56H.
19H   Determine default disk drive. (See Chapter 18.)
1AH   Set disk transfer area. (See Chapter 17.)
1BH   Get information for default drive. (See Chapter 18.)
1CH   Get information for specific drive. (See Chapter 18.)
1FH   Get default drive parameter block. (See Chapter 18.)
21H   Read FCB record randomly. (See Chapter 17.)
22H   Write FCB record randomly. (See Chapter 17.)
23H   Get FCB file size. Obsolete and superseded by function 42H.
24H   Set random FCB record field. (See Chapter 17.)
25H   Set interrupt table address. (See Chapter 24.) The example that follows illus-
       trates the use of this function. When a user presses the Ctrl+Break or Ctrl+C
       keys, the normal procedure is for the program to terminate and return to DOS.
       You may want your program to provide its own routine to handle this situa-
       tion. The example uses INT 21H, function 25H, to set the address for
       Ctrl+Break in the interrupt table (INT 23H) for its own routine, C10BRK.
       The routine could reinitialize the program or do whatever is necessary. The
       code is as follows:

```
            MOV   AH,25H              ;Request set table address

            MOV   AL,23H              ; for interrupt 23H

            LEA   DX,C10BRK           ;New address

            INT   21H                 ;Call DOS

            ...

      C10BRK:                         ;Ctrl+Break routine

            ...

            IRET                      ;Interrupt return
```

26H   Create new program segment prefix. Superseded by function 4B00H.

27H   Read disk block randomly. (See Chapter 17.)

28H   Write disk block randomly. (See Chapter 17.)

29H   Parse filename. (See Chapter 18.)

2AH   Get system date. Returns these binary values:

AL = day of week (Sunday = 0)

CX = year (1980–2099)

DH = month (01–12)

DL = day (01–31)

2BH   Set system date. Set the following binary values:

CX = year (1980–2099)

DH = month (01–12)

DL = day (01–31)

On return, the AL indicates valid (00H) or invalid (FFH).

2CH   Get system time. Returns these binary values:

CH = hours, in 24-hour format (00–23, where midnight = 00)

CL = minutes (00–59)

DH = seconds (00–59)

DL = hundredths of a second (00–99)

2DH   Set system time. Set the following binary values:

CH = hours, in 24-hour format (00–23, where midnight = 00)

CL = minutes (00–59)

DH = seconds (00–59)

DL = hundredths of a second (00–99)

On return, the AL indicates valid (00H) or invalid (FFH).

2EH   Set/reset disk verification. (See Chapter 18.)

2FH   Get address of current disk transfer area (DTA). (See Chapter 17, and see function 1AH for setting the address.)

30H   Get version number of DOS. Returns these values:

AL = major number, such as 7 for version 7.11

AH = minor number, such as hex B (11) for version 7.11

BH = manufacturer number or version flag. If version flag is 08H, DOS runs in ROM.

BL:CX = zero or 24-bit user serial number (manufacturer dependent)
See also function 3306H.

31H   Terminate but stay resident. (See Chapter 24.)

32H   Get drive parameter block (DPB). (See Chapter 18.)

3300H Get Ctrl+C state. If the Ctrl+C flag is off (0), DOS checks for Ctrl+C only
       while handling character I/O functions 01H–0CH. If the flag is on (1), DOS
       checks while handling other functions as well. To get the state, set sub-
       function 00H in the AL. The value returned in the DL is 00H = checking
       disabled or 01H = checking enabled.

3300H Check Ctrl+C state. If the Ctrl+C flag is off (0), DOS checks for Ctrl+C
       only while handling character I/O functions 01H–0CH. If the flag is on (1),
       DOS checks while handling other functions as well. To set the state, set sub-
       function 01H in the AL, and set the state in the DL as 00H = set checking
       off or 01H = set checking on.

3305H Get startup drive (available since DOS 5). The operation returns in the DL
       the drive (1 = A, etc.) used to load DOS.

3306H Get DOS version (available since DOS 5). The operation returns:
       BL = major version number, such as 7 for version 7.11
       BH = minor version number, such as hex B (11) for version 7.11
       DL = revision number in bits 2–0
       DH = DOS version flag (indicates whether DOS is running in conventional
           memory, high-memory area, or ROM)
       Although the DOS SETVER command can fake the DOS version number,
       function 3306H delivers the true version.

34H   Get DOS busy flag (inDOS) address. (See Chapter 24.)

35H   Get interrupt table address. (See Chapter 24.)

36H   Get free disk space. (See Chapter 18.)

38H   Get/set country-dependent information. Supports a number of functions
       concerning information specific to various countries, such as the symbol and
       format for the country's currency, separators for thousands and decimal
       places, and separators for the date and time . Load the DX for the operation:
       DX = FFFFH: Set the country code that DOS is to use until further notice.
       DX = any other value: Get the country code currently in use.

39H   Create subdirectory (MKDIR). (See Chapter 18.)

3AH   Remove subdirectory (RMDIR). (See Chapter 18.)

3BH   Change current directory (CHDIR). (See Chapter 18.)

3CH   Create file with handle. (See Chapter 17.)

3DH   Open file with handle. (See Chapter 17.)

3EH   Close file with handle. (See Chapter 17.)

3FH   Read file/device. (See Chapters 9 and 17.)

40H   Write file/device with handle. (See Chapters 9, 17, and 20.)

41H   Delete file from directory. (See Chapter 18.)

42H   Move file pointer. (See Chapter 17.)

43H   Check/change file attribute. (See Chapter 18.)

44H	I/O control for devices. Supports an extensive set of subfunctions for checking devices and reading and writing data, listed in the following functions:
4400H	Get device information. (See Chapter 18.)
4401H	Set device information. (See Chapter 18.)
4404H	Read control data from drive. (See Chapter 18.)
4405H	Write control data to drive. (See Chapter 18.)
4406H	Check input status. (See Chapter 18.)
4407H	Check output status. (See Chapter 18.)
4408H	Determine if removable media for device. (See Chapter 18.)
440DH,	Minor Code 41H Write disk sector. (See Chapter 18.)
440DH,	Minor Code 61H Read disk sector. (See Chapter 18.)
440DH,	Minor Code 42H Format track. (See Chapter 18.)
440DH,	Minor Code 46H Set media ID. (See Chapter 18.)
440DH,	Minor Code 60H Get device parameters. (See Chapter 18.)
440DH,	Minor Code 66H Get media ID. (See Chapter 18.)
440DH,	Minor Code 68H Sense media type. (See Chapter 18.)
45H	Duplicate a file handle. (See Chapter 18.)
46H	Force duplicate of handle. (See Chapter 18.)
47H	Get current directory. (See Chapter 18.)
48H	Allocate memory block. (See Chapter 24.)
49H	Free allocated memory block. (See Chapter 24.)
4AH	Set allocated memory block size. (See Chapter 24.)
4BH	Load/execute a program. (See Chapter 24.)
4CH	Terminate program. (See Chapter 4.) This is the standard operation for terminating a program.
4DH	Retrieve return code of a subprocess. (See Chapter 24.)
4EH	Find first matching directory entry. (See Chapter 18.)
4FH	Find next matching directory entry. (See Chapter 18.)
50H	Set address of program segment prefix (PSP). Load the BX with the offset address of the PSP for the current program. No values are returned.
51H	Get address of program segment prefix (PSP). Returns the offset address of the PSP for the current program. (See Chapter 24.)
52H	Get address of internal DOS list (undocumented, see Chapter 24).
54H	Get verify state. (See Chapter 18.)
56H	Rename a file. (See Chapter 18.)
57H	Get/set file date and time. (See Chapter 18.)
5800H	Get memory allocation strategy. (See Chapter 24.)
5801H	Set memory allocation strategy. (See Chapter 24.)
5802H	Get upper memory link. (See Chapter 24.)
5803H	Set upper memory link. (See Chapter 24.)
59H	Get extended error code. (See Chapter 18.)
5AH	Create a temporary file. (See Chapter 18.)
5BH	Create a new file. (See Chapter 18.)

5CH   Lock/unlock file access. Used for networking and multitasking environments.

5DH   Set extended error. Load the DX with the offset address of a table of information on errors The table is to be retrieved by the next execution of function
59H (get extended error code: see function 59H in Chapter 18 for details.)

5EH   Local area network services. A subfunction in the AL specifies the service:
00H   Get machine name
02H   Set printer setup
03H   Get printer setup

5FH   Local area network services. A subfunction in the AL specifies the service:
02H   Get assign-list entry
03H   Make network connection
04H   Cancel network connection

62H   Get address of PSP. (See function 51H for an identical operation.)

65H   Get extended country information. Supports a number of subfunctions concerning information specific to various countries.

66H   Get/set global code page.

67H   Set maximum handle count. (See Chapter 24.)

68H   Commit file. (See Chapter 18.)

6CH   Extended open file. Combines functions 3CH (create file), 3DH (open file),
and 5BH (create unique file). (See Chapter 18.)

KEY POINTS

- Interrupts 20H through 3FH are reserved for DOS operations.
- DOS INT 21H handles such operations as keyboard input, display output, printer output, reset disk, open/close file, delete file, read/write sequential record, read/write random record, terminate but stay resident, create subdirectory, and terminate program.

QUESTIONS

26–1. What interrupts are reserved for DOS?

26–2. Identify the functions for the following DOS INT 21H services: (a) communications input;
(b) get system time; (c) get DOS version; (d) terminate but stay resident; (e) get address of
interrupt table; (f) create subdirectory; (g) get free disk space; (h) get address of PSP.

26–3. Identify the following INT 21H, functions: (a) 05H; (b) 0AH; (c) 0FH; (d) 16H; (e) 35H;
(f) 3CH; (g) 3DH; (h) 3FH; (i) 40H.

CHAPTER 27

Operators and Directives

> OBJECTIVE:
>
> To describe in detail the assembly language operators and directives.

INTRODUCTION

The various assembly language features at first tend to be somewhat overwhelming. But once you have become familiar with the simpler and more common features described in earlier chapters, you should find the descriptions in this chapter more easily understood and a handy reference. Here, we describe the various type specifiers, operators, and directives. The assembly language manual contains a few other marginally useful features.

TYPE SPECIFIERS

Type specifiers can provide the size of a data variable or the relative distance of an instruction label. Type specifiers that give the size of a data variable are BYTE, WORD, DWORD, FWORD, QWORD, and TBYTE. Those that give the distance of an instruction label are NEAR, FAR, and PROC. A near address, which is simply an offset, is assumed to be in the current segment; a far address, which consists of a segment:offset address, can be used to access another segment.

The PTR and THIS operators, as well as the COM, EXTRN, LABEL, and PROC directives, use type specifiers.

OPERATORS

An operator provides a facility for changing or analyzing operands during an assembly. Operators are divided into various categories:

- Calculation operators: Arithmetic, index, logical, shift, and structure field name.
- Macro operators: Various types, covered in Chapter 22.
- Record operators: MASK and WIDTH, covered later in this chapter under the RECORD directive.
- Relational operators: EQ, GE, GT, LE, LT, and NE.
- Segment operators: OFFSET, SEG, and segment override.
- Type (or attribute) operators: HIGH, HIGHWORD, LENGTH, LOW, LOWWORD, PTR, SHORT, SIZE, THIS, and TYPE.

Since a knowledge of these categories is not necessary, we'll simply cover the operators in alphabetic sequence.

Arithmetic Operators

Arithmetic operators include the familiar arithmetic signs and perform arithmetic during an assembly. In most cases, you could perform the calculation yourself, although the advantage of using these operators is that every time you change the program and reassemble it, the assembler automatically recalculates the values of the arithmetic operators. Following is a list of the operators, together with an example of their use and the effect obtained:

SIGN	TYPE	EXAMPLE	EFFECT
+	Addition	FLD1+25	Adds 25 to address of FLD1
+	Positive	+FLD1	Treats FLD1 as positive
−	Subtraction	FLD2-FLD1	Calculates difference between two offset addresses
−	Negation	−FLD1	Reverses sign
*	Multiplication	value*3	Multiplies value by 3
/	Division	value/3	Divides value by 3
MOD	Remainder	value1 MOD value2	Delivers remainder for value1/value2

Except for addition (+) and subtraction (−), all operators must be integer constants. The following related examples of integer expressions are illustrative:

```
value1 = 12 * 4          ;48

value1 = value1 / 6      ;48 / 6 = 8

value1 = -value1 - 3     ;(-8) - (3) = -11
```

HIGH and HIGHWORD Operators

The HIGH operator returns the high (leftmost) byte of an expression, and HIGHWORD (since MASM 6.0) returns the high word of an expression. (See also the LOW operator.) Here is an example:

```
        EQUVAL  EQU   1234H

        . . .

        MOV   CL,HIGH EQUVAL      ;Load 12H in CL
```

INDEX Operators

For a direct memory reference, one operand of an instruction specifies the name of a defined variable, as shown by COUNTER in the instruction ADD CX,COUNTER. During execution, the processor locates the specified variable in memory by combining the offset value of the variable with the data segment address in the DS.

For indirect addressing of memory, an operand references a base or index register, constants, offset variables, and variables. The index operator, which uses square brackets, acts like a plus (+) sign. A typical use of indexing is to reference data items in tables. You can use the following operations to reference indexed memory:

- [Constant], i.e., an immediate number or name in square brackets. For example, load the fifth entry of TABLEA into the CL (note that TABLEA[0] is the first entry):

```
        TABLEA  DB   25 DUP(?)        ;Defined table

        . . .

        MOV   CL,TABLEA[4]     ;Get fifth entry from TABLEA
```

- Base register BX as [BX] in association with the DS segment register, and base register BP as [BP] in association with the SS segment register. For example, use the offset address in the BX (combined with the segment address in the DS register), and move the referenced item to the DX:

```
        MOV DX,[BX]            ;Base register DS:BX
```

- Index register DI as [DI] and index register SI as [SI], both in association with the DS segment register. For example, combine the address in the DS with the offset address in the SI, and move the referenced item to the AX:

```
        MOV AX,[SI]           ;Index register DS:SI
```

- Combined index registers. For example, move the contents of the AX to the address determined by adding the DS address, the BX offset, the SI offset, and the constant 4:

```
        MOV [BX+SI+4],AX     ;Base + index + constant
```

The preceding example could also be coded as [BX+SI]+4. You may combine these operands in any sequence, but don't combine two base registers [BX+BP] or two index registers [DI+SI]. Only the index registers must be in square brackets.

LENGTH Operator

The LENGTH operator returns the number of entries defined by a DUP operator. The following MOV instruction returns the length 10 to the DX:

```
TABLEA   DW    10 DUP(?)

            . . .

         MOV  DX,LENGTH TABLEA
```

If the referenced operand does not contain a DUP entry, the operator returns the value 01. (See also the SIZE and TYPE operators.)

Logical Operators

The logical operators perform logical operations on the bits in an expression:

OPERATOR	USED AS	EFFECT
AND	expression1 AND expression2	ANDs the bits
OR	expression1 OR expression2	ORs the bits
XOR	expression1 XOR expression2	Exclusive ORs the bits
NOT	NOT expression1	Reverses the bits

Here are two examples:

```
         MOV  AL,00111100B AND 01010101B    ;00010100B

         MOV  BL,NOT 01010101B              ;10101010B
```

LOW and LOWWORD Operators

The LOW operator returns the low (rightmost) byte of an expression, and LOWWORD (since MASM 6.0) returns the low word of an expression. (See also the HIGH operator.) Here is an example:

```
EQUVAL   EQU   1234H

            . . .

         MOV  CL,LOW EQUVAL        ;Load 34H in CL
```

OFFSET Operator

The OFFSET operator returns the offset address (that is, the relative address within the data segment or code segment) of a variable or label. The general format is

```
OFFSET variable or label
```

The following MOV returns the offset address of TABLEA:

```
MOV DX,OFFSET TABLEA
```

Note that LEA doesn't require OFFSET to return the same value:

```
LEA DX,TABLEA
```

MASK Operator

See "RECORD directive" in the section entitled "Directives."

PTR Operator

The PTR operator can be used on data variables and instruction labels. It uses the type specifiers BYTE, WORD, FWORD, DWORD, QWORD, and TBYTE to specify a size in an ambiguous operand or to override the defined type (DB, DW, DF, DD, DF, or DT) for variables. It also uses the type specifiers NEAR, FAR, and PROC to override the implied distance of labels. The general format for PTR is

```
type PTR expression
```

The type is the new attribute, such as BYTE. The expression is a variable or constant. Following are examples of the PTR operator (watch out for FLDW, where the bytes are in reverse sequence):

```
FLDB DB    22H
     DB    35H
FLDW DW    2672H              ;Stored as 7226
     . . .
     MOV   AH,BYTE PTR FLDW   ;Move first byte (72)
     ADD   BL,BYTE PTR FLDW+1 ;Add second byte (26)
     MOV   BYTE PTR FLDW,05   ;Move 05 to first byte
     MOV   AX,WORD PTR FLDB   ;Move two bytes (2235) to AX
     CALL  FAR PTR[BX]        ;Call far procedure
```

A feature that performs a similar function to PTR is the LABEL directive, described later.

SEG Operator

The SEG operator returns the address of the segment in which a specified variable or label is placed. Programs that combine separately assembled segments would most likely use this operator. The general format is

```
SEG variable or label
```

The following MOV instructions return the address of the segment in which the referenced names are defined:

```
MOV  DX,SEG FLDW   ;Address of data segment

MOV  DX,SEG A20    ;Address of code segment
```

Segment Override Operator

This operator, coded as a colon (:), calculates the address of a label or variable relative to a particular segment. The general format is

$$\left[\text{segment:expression}\right]$$

The named segment can be any of the segment registers or a segment or group name. The expression can be a constant, an expression, or a SEG expression. These next examples override the default DS segment register:

```
MOV   BH,ES:10H        ;Access from ES plus offset 10H

MOV   CX,SS:[BX]       ;Access from SS plus offset in BX
```

An instruction may have a segment override operator apply to only one operand.

SHL and SHR Operators

The operators SHL and SHR shift an expression during an assembly. The general formats are

$$\left[\begin{array}{l}\text{expression SHL   count}\\ \text{expression SHR   count}\end{array}\right]$$ *count ⇒ # bits positions to shift*

In the following example, the SHR operator shifts the bit constant three bits to the right:

```
MOV   BL,01011101B SHR 3    ;Load 00001011B
```

Most likely, the expression would reference a symbolic name rather than a constant value.

SHORT Operator

The purpose of the SHORT operator is to modify the NEAR attribute of a JMP destination that is within +127 and −128 bytes. The format is

$$\left[\text{JMP SHORT label}\right]$$

The assembler reduces the machine code operand from two bytes to one. This feature is useful for near jumps that branch forward, since otherwise the assembler initially doesn't know the distance of the jump address and may assume two bytes for a far jump.

SIZE Operator

The SIZE operator returns the product of LENGTH times TYPE and is useful only if the referenced variable contains the DUP entry. The general format is

$$\left[\text{SIZE variable}\right]$$

See "TYPE Operator" for an example.

THIS Operator

The THIS operator creates an operand with segment and offset values that are equal to those of the current location counter. The general format is

The type specifier can be BYTE, WORD, DWORD, FWORD, QWORD, or TBYTE for variables and NEAR, FAR, or PROC for labels. You typically use THIS with the EQU, or equals sign (=) directive. The following example defines FLDA:

```
FLDA    EQU    THIS BYTE
```

The segment is the same as if you used the LABEL directive

```
FLDA    LABEL BYTE
```

TYPE Operator

The TYPE operator returns the number of bytes, according to the definition of the referenced variable. However, the operation always returns 1 for a string variable and 0 for a constant.

DEFINITION	NUMBER OF BYTES FOR NUMERIC VARIABLE
DB	1
DW	2
DD	4
DF	6
DQ	8
DT	10
STRUC	Number of bytes defined by STRUC
NEAR	label FFFFH
FAR	label FFFEH

The general format of TYPE is

```
TYPE variable or label
```

The following examples illustrate the TYPE, LENGTH, and SIZE operators:

```
FLDB    DB    ?    ;Define one byte
TABLEA  DW    20 DUP(?)   ;Define 20 words
        ...
        MOV   AX,TYPE FLDB     ;AX = 0001H
        MOV   AX,TYPE TABLEA   ;AX = 0002H
        MOV   CX,LENGTH TABLEA ;CX = 000AH (10)  0014H (20)
        MOV   DX,SIZE TABLEA   ;DX = 0014H (20)  0028H (40)
```

Since TABLEA is defined as DW, TYPE returns 0002H, LENGTH returns 000AH based on the DUP entry, and SIZE returns type times length, or 14H (20). 0014H
                                                                    28H (40)

WIDTH Operator

See "RECORD Directive" in the following section.

DIRECTIVES

This section describes most of the assembly language directives. Chapter 4 covered in detail the directives for defining data (DB, DW, etc.), and Chapter 22 covered the directives for macro instructions, so they aren't repeated here. Directives are divided into various categories:

- Code labels: ALIGN, EVEN, LABEL, and PROC.
- Conditional assembly: IF, ELSE, and others, covered in Chapter 21.
- Conditional errors: .ERR, .ERR1, and others.
- Data allocation: ALIGN, EQU, EVEN, LABEL, and ORG. DB, DW, DD, DF, DQ, and DT, covered in Chapter 4.
- Listing control: .CREF, .LIST, PAGE, SUBTTL (SUBTITLE), TITLE, .XCREF, and .XLIST, covered in this chapter. .LALL, .LFCOND, .SALL, .SFCOND, .TFCOND, and .XALL, covered in Chapter 22.
- Macros: ENDM, EXITM, LOCAL, MACRO, and PURGE, covered in Chapter 21.
- Miscellaneous: COMMENT, INCLUDE, INCLUDELIB, NAME, &OUT, and .RADIX.
- Processor: .8086, .286, .286P, .386, .386P, .8087, .287, .387, etc.
- Repeat blocks: IRP, IRPC, and REPT, covered in Chapter 22.
- Scope: COMM, EXTRN, and PUBLIC.
- Segment: .ALPHA, ASSUME, .DOSSEG, END, ENDS, GROUP, SEGMENT, and .SEQ.
- Simplified segment: .CODE, .CONST, .DATA, .DATA?, DOSSEG, .EXIT, .FARDATA, .FARDATA?, .MODEL, and .STACK.
- Structure/Record: ENDS, RECORD, STRUCT, TYPEDEF, UNION.

Since a knowledge of these categories is not necessary, we'll cover the directives (other than macro-related ones) in alphabetic sequence.

ALIGN Directive

MASM 5.0 introduced the ALIGN directive to force the assembler to align the next data item or instruction according to a given value. The general format is

$$\left[\; \texttt{ALIGN number} \;\right]$$

The number must be a power of 2, such as 2, 4, 8, or 16. For the statement ALIGN 4, the assembler advances its location counter to the next address that is evenly divisible by 4. If the location counter is already at the required address, it is not advanced. The assembler fills unused bytes with zeros for data and NOPs for instructions. Note that ALIGN 2 has the same effect as EVEN.

Alignment is no advantage on the 8088 processor, which accesses only one byte at a time, but can speed up more advanced processors.

.ALPHA Directive

The .ALPHA directive, placed at or near the start of a program, tells the assembler to arrange segments in alphabetic sequence. It overrides the assembler option /S. (See also the .SEQ directive.)

ASSUME Directive

ASSUME tells the assembler to associate segment names with the CS, DS, ES, and SS segment registers. The general format is

```
ASSUME  seg-reg:seg-name [, ... ]
```

Valid segment register entries are CS, DS, ES, and SS, plus FS and GS on the 80386 and later processors. Valid segment names are those of segment registers, NOTHING, GROUPs, and a SEG expression. One ASSUME statement may assign up to four segment registers, in any sequence. The simplified segment directives automatically generate an ASSUME.

In the following ASSUME statement, CODESG, DATASG, and STACK are the names the program has used to define the segments:

```
ASSUME   CS:CODESG,DS:DATASG,SS:STACK,ES:DATASG
```

Omission of a segment reference is the same as coding NOTHING. Use of the keyword NOTHING also cancels any previous ASSUME for a specified segment register:

```
ASSUME   ES:NOTHING
```

Suppose that you neither assign the ES register nor use NOTHING to cancel it. Then, to reference a data item in the data segment, an instruction operand may use the segment override operator (:) to reference the ES register, which must contain a valid address:

```
MOV  AX,ES:[BX]       ;Use indexed address

MOV  AX,ES:FLDW       ;Move contents of FLDW
```

.CODE Directive

This simplified segment directive defines the code segment. Its general format is

```
.CODE [name]
```

All executable code must be placed in this segment. For TINY, SMALL, and COMPACT models, the default segment name is _TEXT. The MEDIUM and LARGE memory models permit multiple code segments, which you distinguish by means of the name operand. (See also the .MODEL directive.)

COMM Directive

Defining a variable as COMM gives it both the PUBLIC and EXTRN attributes. In this way, you would not have to define the variable as PUBLIC in one module and EXTRN in another. The general format is

```
COMM [NEAR/FAR] label:size[:count]
```

- COMM is coded within a data segment.
- NEAR or FAR attributes may be coded or allowed to default to one or the other, depending on the memory model.
- Label is the name of the variable. Note that the variable cannot have an initial value.
- Size can be any of the type specifiers BYTE, WORD, DWORD, QWORD, and TBYTE, or an integer specifying the number of bytes.
- Count indicates the number of elements for the variable. The default is 1.

The following example defines FLDCOM with the COMM attribute:

```
COMM NEAR FLDCOM:WORD
```

COMMENT Directive

This directive is useful for multiple lines of comments. The general format is

```
COMMENT delimiter [comments]

    [comments]

delimiter [comments]
```

The delimiter is the first nonblank character, such as % or +, following COMMENT. The comments terminate on the line on which the second delimiter appears. This next example uses a plus sign as a delimiter:

```
COMMENT + This routine scans
          the input stream
          for invalid
        + characters.
```

.CONST Directive

This simplified segment directive defines a data (or constant-data) segment with the 'const' class. (See also the .MODEL directive.)

.CREF Directive

This directive (the default) tells the assembler to generate a cross-reference table. It would be used following an .XCREF directive that caused suppression of the table.

.DATA and .DATA? Directives

These simplified segment directives define data segments. .DATA defines a segment for initialized near data; .DATA? defines a segment for uninitialized near data, usually used when linking to a high-level language. For a stand-alone assembly program, you may also define uninitialized near data in a .DATA segment (See, in addition, the .FARDATA and .MODEL directives.)

DOSSEG Directive

There are a number of ways to control the sequence in which the assembler arranges segments. (Some versions arrange them alphabetically.) You may code the .SEQ or .ALPHA directives at the start of a program, or you may enter the /S or /A assembler options at assembly time. The DOSSEG (.DOSSEG since MASM 6.0) directive tells the assembler to ignore all other requests and to adopt the DOS segment sequence—basically, code, data, and stack. Code this directive at or near the start of the program, primarily to facilitate the use of CODEVIEW for stand-alone programs.

END Directive

The END directive is placed at the end of a source program. The general format is

$$\text{END [start-address]}$$

The optional start-address indicates the location in the code segment (usually the first instruction) where execution is to begin. The system loader uses this address to initialize the CS register. If your program consists of only one module, define a start-address. If it consists of a number of modules, only one (usually the first) has a start-address.

ENDP Directive

This directive indicates the end of a procedure, defined by PROC. The general format is

$$\text{label ENDP}$$

The label is the same as the one that defines the procedure.

ENDS Directive

This directive indicates the end of a segment (defined as SEGMENT) or a structure. Its general format is

$$\text{label ENDS}$$

The label is the same as the one that defines the segment or structure.

EQU Directive

The EQU directive is used to redefine a data name or variable with another data name, variable, or immediate value. The directive should be defined in a program before it is referenced. The formats for numeric and string data differ:

```
Numeric equate:   name EQU expression
String equate:    name EQU <string>
```

The assembler replaces each occurrence of the name with the operand. Since EQU is used for simple replacement, it takes no additional storage in the generated object program.

Examples of the use of EQU with numeric data are:

```
COUNTER DW    0
SUM     EQU   COUNTER       ;Another name for COUNTER
TEN     EQU   10            ;Numeric value
        ...
        INC   SUM           ;Increment COUNTER
        ADD   SUM,TEN       ;Add 10 to COUNTER
```

Examples of the use of EQU with string data are:

```
PRODMSG EQU   <'Enter product number:'>
BYPTR   EQU   <BYTE PTR>
        ...
MESSGE1 DB    PRODMSG          ;Replace with string
        ...
        MOV   SAVE,BYPTR [BX]  ;Replace with string
```

The angle brackets make it easier to indicate a string operand.

.ERR Directives

These conditional error directives can be used to help test for errors during an assembly:

DIRECTIVE	ERROR FORCED
.ERR	When encountered
.ERR1	During pass 1 of an assembly
.ERR2	During pass 2 of an assembly
.ERRE	By true (0) expression
.ERRNZ	By false (not 0) expression
.ERRDEF	By defined symbol
.ERRNDEF	By not defined symbol
.ERRB	By blank string
.ERRNB	By not blank string
.ERRIDN[I]	By identical strings
.ERRDIF[I]	By different strings

You could use the preceding directives in macros and in conditional assembly statements. In the following conditional assembly statements, the assembler displays a message if the condition is not true:

```
IF      condition

        ...

ELSE    .ERR

        %OUT [message]

ENDIF
```

Since MASM 6.0, it is no longer necessary to refer to pass 1 (.ERR1) or pass 2 (.ERR2) of an assembly.

EVEN Directive

EVEN tells the assembler to advance its location counter if necessary so that the next defined data item or label is aligned on an even storage boundary. This feature makes processing more efficient on processors that access 16 or 32 bits at a time. (See also the ALIGN directive.)

In the following example, BYTELOCN is a one-byte field on an even boundary. The assembler's location counter starts at 0017. EVEN causes the assembler to advance the location counter one byte to 0018:

```
0016      BYTELOCN  DB   ?

0017                EVEN        (advances location counter)

[0017               NOP]

0018      WORDLOCN  DW   ?
```

EXTRN Directive

The EXTRN (or EXTERN since MASM 6.0) directive informs the assembler and linker about data variables and labels that the current assembly references, but that another module (linked to the current one) defines. The general format is

```
EXTRN   name:type [, ... ]
```

The name entry is an item defined in another assembly and declared in it as PUBLIC. The type specifier can refer to either of the following:

- Data items: ABS (a constant), BYTE, WORD, DWORD, FWORD, QWORD, TBYTE. Code the EXTRN in the segment in which the item occurs.
- Distance: NEAR or FAR. Code NEAR in the segment in which the item occurs, and code FAR anywhere.

In the next example, the calling program defines CONVAL as PUBLIC and as a DW. The called subprogram identifies CONVAL (in another segment) as EXTRN and FAR. The code is as follows:

Calling program:

```
DSEG1   SEGMENT

        PUBLIC CONVAL

        ...

CONVAL  DW      ?

        ...

DSEG1   ENDS
```

Called subprogram:

```
                        EXTRN   CONVAL:FAR

          DSEG2         SEGMENT

                        . . .

                        MOV     AX,CONVAL

                        . . .

          DSEG2         ENDS
```

See Chapter 23 for examples of EXTRN.

.FARDATA and .FARDATA? Directives

These simplified segment directives define data segments. .FARDATA defines a segment for initialized far data, and .FARDATA? defines a segment for uninitialized far data. For a stand-alone assembly program, you may also define uninitialized far data in a .FARDATA segment. (See also the .DATA and .MODEL directives.)

GROUP Directive

A program may contain several segments of the same type (code, data, or stack). The purpose of the GROUP directive is to collect them all under one name, so that they reside within one segment, usually a data segment. The general format is

```
     [ name     GROUP   seg-name [, seg-name], ...  ]
```

The following GROUP combines SEG1 and SEG2 in the same assembly module:

```
          GROUPX    GROUP      SEG1, SEG2

          SEG1      SEGMENT    PARA 'Data'

                    ASSUME     DS:GROUPX

                    . . .

          SEG1      ENDS

          SEG2      SEGMENT    PARA 'Data'

                    ASSUME     DS:GROUPX

                    . . .

          SEG2      ENDS
```

The effect of using GROUP is similar to giving the segments the same name and the PUBLIC attribute.

INCLUDE Directive

You may have sections of assembly code or macro instructions that various programs use. If so, you may store these in separate disk files available for use by any program. Consider a routine that converts ASCII code to binary is stored on drive D in a file named CON-VERT.LIB. To access the file, insert an INCLUDE statement such as

```
INCLUDE D:CONVERT.LIB
```

at the location in the source program where you would normally code the ASCII conversion routine. The assembler then locates the file on disk and includes the statements in your own program. (If the assembler cannot find the file, it issues an error message and ignores the INCLUDE.)

For each included line, the assembler prints a C in column 30 of the .LST file and begins the source code in column 33.

Chapter 22 gives a practical example of INCLUDE and explains how to use the directive for only pass 1 of an assembly.

LABEL Directive

The LABEL directive enables you to redefine the attribute of a data variable or instruction label. The general format is

```
[ name    LABEL    type-specifier ]
```

For labels, you may use LABEL to redefine executable code as NEAR, FAR, or PROC, such as for a secondary entry point into a procedure. For variables, you may use the type specifiers BYTE, WORD, DWORD, FWORD, QWORD, or TBYTE, or a structure name, to redefine data items and the names of structures, respectively. For example, LABEL enables you to define a field as both DB and DW. The following illustrates the use of BYTE and WORD types:

```
REDEFB    LABEL    BYTE

FIELDW    DW       2532H

REDEFW    LABEL    WORD

FIELDB    DB       25H

          DB       32H

          . . .

          MOV      AL,REDEFB      ;Move 1st byte

          MOV      BX,REDEFW      ;Move 2 bytes
```

The first MOV instruction moves only the first byte of FIELDW. The second MOV moves the two bytes beginning at FIELDB. The PTR operator performs a similar function.

.LIST Directive

The .LIST directive (the default) causes the assembler to list the source program. You may use the .XLIST directive anywhere in an assembly source program to discontinue listing it. A typical situation is where statements are common to other programs and you don't need another listing. .LIST resumes the listing. Code both of these directives with no operand.

.MODEL Directive

This simplified segment directive creates default segments and the required ASSUME and GROUP statements. Its general format is

```
[.MODEL memory-model]
```

The memory models are

TINY	Since MASM 6.0, used for .COM programs.
SMALL	All data in one segment and all code in one segment.
MEDIUM	All data in one segment, but code in more than one segment.
COMPACT	Data in more than one segment, but code in one segment.
LARGE	Both data and code in more than one segment, but no array may exceed 64K.
HUGE	Both data and code in more than one segment, and arrays may exceed 64K.

The .STACK directive defines the stack, .CODE defines the code segment, and any or all of .DATA, .DATA?, .FARDATA, and .FARDATA? may define data segments. Here is an example:

```
.MODEL  SMALL
.STACK  120
.DATA
        [data items]
.CODE
        [instructions]
END
```

ORG Directive

The assembler uses a *location counter* to account for its relative position in a data or code segment. Consider a data segment with the following definitions:

OFFSET	NAME	OPERATION	OPERAND	LOCATION COUNTER
00	FLDA	DW	2542H	02
02	FLDB	DB	36H	03
03	FLDC	DW	212EH	05
05	FLDD	DD	00000705H	09

Initially, the location counter is set to 00. Since FLDA is two bytes, the location counter is incremented to 02 for the location of the next item. Since FLDB is one byte, the location counter is incremented to 03, and so forth. You may use the ORG directive to change the contents of the location counter and, accordingly, the location of the next defined items. The general format is

$$\left[\text{ORG expression}\right]$$

The expression must form a two-byte absolute number and must not be a symbolic name. Suppose the following data items are defined immediately after FLDD in the previous definition:

OFFSET	NAME	OPERATION	OPERAND	LOCATION COUNTER
		ORG	0	00
00	FLDX	DB	?	01
01	FLDY	DW	?	02
03	FLDZ	DB	?	04
		ORG	$+5	09

The first ORG resets the location counter to 00. The variables that follow—FLDX, FLDY, and FLDZ—redefine these memory locations as FLDA, FLDB, and FLDC, respectively:

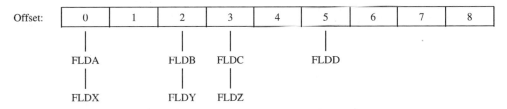

An operand containing a dollar symbol ($), as in the second ORG, refers to the current value in the location counter. The operand $+5 therefore sets the location counter to 04 + 5, or 09, which is the same setting as after the definition of FLDD.

A reference to FLDC is to a one-word field at offset 03, and a reference to FLDZ is to a one-byte field at offset 03:

```
MOV   AX,FLDC        ;One word

MOV   AL,FLDZ        ;One byte
```

You may use ORG to redefine memory locations in the preceding manner. But be sure that you reset the location counter to the correct value and that you account for all redefined memory locations. Also, the redefined variables should not contain defined constants—these would overlay constants on top of the original ones. ORG cannot appear within a STRUC definition.

%OUT Directive

This directive tells the assembler to direct a message to the standard output device (usually the screen). (Since MASM 6.0, the name is ECHO.) The general format is

$$\left[\text{%OUT message}\right]$$

The ".ERR Directives" section gives an example.

PAGE Directive

The PAGE directive at the start of a source program specifies the maximum number of lines to list on a page and the maximum number of characters on a line. Its general format is

```
[ PAGE  [[length],width] ]
```

The following example sets 60 lines per page and 132 characters per line:

```
PAGE  60,132
```

The number of lines per page may range from 10 to 255, and the number of characters per line may range from 60 to 132. Omission of a PAGE statement causes the assembler to assume PAGE 50,80. To force a page to eject at a specific line, such as at the end of a segment, code PAGE with no operand.

PROC Directive

A procedure is a block of code that begins with the PROC directive and terminates with ENDP. A typical use is for a subroutine within the code segment. Although technically, you may enter a procedure in line or by a JMP instruction, the normal practice is to use CALL to enter and RET to exit. The CALL operand may be a NEAR or FAR type specifier, and RET assumes the same type.

A procedure that is in the same segment as the calling procedure is a NEAR procedure and is accessed by an offset:

```
[ proc-name  PROC [ NEAR] ]
```

An omitted operand defaults to NEAR. If a called procedure is external to the calling segment, it must be declared as PUBLIC, and you should use CALL to enter it.

For an .EXE program, the main PROC that is the entry point for execution must be FAR. Also, a called procedure under a different ASSUME CS value must have the FAR attribute:

```
PUBLIC  proc-name

proc-name  PROC     FAR
```

A far label may be in another segment, which CALL accesses by a segment address and offset.

Processor Directives

These directives define the processors that the assembler is to recognize. The normal placement of processor directives is at the start of a source program, although you could code them inside a program at a point where you want a processor enabled or disabled. A reference to the 8086 also assumes the 8088, and .486 was introduced by MASM 6.0.

- .8086 enables the 8086 and 8087 coprocessor (the default mode).
- .186, .286, .386, and .486 enable all the instruction sets up to and including the named processor and its associated coprocessor. That is, the directive permits instructions of earlier processors. (For example, .386 enables .387, .286, .186, and .8086.)

- .186P, .286P, .386P, and .486P enable all the instruction sets just cited, plus the processor's privileged instructions.

PUBLIC Directive

The purpose of the PUBLIC directive is to inform the assembler and linker that the identified symbols in an assembly are to be referenced by other modules linked with the current one. The general format is

```
PUBLIC  symbol [, ... ]
```

The symbol can be a label, a number (up to two bytes), or a variable. See the "EXTRN Directive" section and Chapter 23 for examples.

RECORD Directive

The RECORD directive enables you to define patterns of bits. One purpose is to define switch indicators either as one bit or as multibit. The general format is

```
record-name RECORD field-name:width[=exp] [, ... ]
```

The record name and the field names may be any unique valid identifiers. Following each field name is a colon (:) and a width—the number of bits. The range of the width entry is 1 to 16 bits:

NUMBER OF DEFINED BITS	DEFAULT SIZE
1–8	8
9–16	16

Any length up to 8 becomes 8 bits, and lengths 9 to 16 become 16 bits, with the contents right adjusted if necessary. The following example defines RECORD:

```
BITREC  RECORD  BIT1:3,BIT2:7,BIT3:6
```

BIT1 defines the first 3 bits of BITREC, BIT2 defines the next 7, and BIT3 defines the last 6. The total is 16 bits, or one word. You may initialize values in RECORD as follows:

```
BITREC2 RECORD  BIT1:3=101B,BIT2:7=0110110B,BIT3:6=011010B
```

Suppose that a definition of RECORD is at the start of the data segment. Within the data segment, there should be another statement that allocates storage for the record. Define a unique valid name, the record name, and an operand consisting of angle brackets (the less-than and greater-than symbols):

```
DEFBITS BITREC <>
```

The allocation for DEFBITS generates object code AD9AH (stored as 9AAD) in the data segment. The angle brackets may also contain entries that redefine BITREC.

The program in Figure 27–1 defines BITREC as RECORD, but without initial values in the record fields. In this case, an allocation statement in the data segment initializes each field as shown within angle brackets.

```
                      TITLE     P27RECOR (COM)  Test of RECORD Directive
0000                  CODESG    SEGMENT PARA 'Code'
                                ASSUME CS:CODESG,DS:CODESG,SS:CODESG
0100                            ORG    100H
0100 EB 02            BEGIN:    JMP    SHORT MAIN
                      ; ----------------------------------------------------------
                      BITREC    RECORD BIT1:3,BIT2:7,BIT3:6    ;Define record
0102 AD9A             DEFBITS   BITREC <101B,0110110B,011010B> ;Init. record
                      ; ----------------------------------------------------------
0104                  MAIN      PROC   NEAR
0104                  A10:                                     ;Width:
0104 B7 10                      MOV    BH,WIDTH BITREC         ;  of record (16)
0106 B0 07                      MOV    AL,WIDTH BIT2           ;  of field  (07)
0108                  B10:                                     ;Shift count:
0108 B1 0D                      MOV    CL,BIT1                 ;  hex 0D
010A B1 06                      MOV    CL,BIT2                 ;      06
010C B1 00                      MOV    CL,BIT3                 ;      00
010E                  C10:                                     ;Mask:
010E B8 E000                    MOV    AX,MASK BIT1            ;  hex E000
0111 BB 1FC0                    MOV    BX,MASK BIT2            ;      1FC0
0114 B9 003F                    MOV    CX,MASK BIT3            ;      003F
0117                  D10:                                     ;Isolate BIT2:
0117 A1 0102 R                  MOV    AX,DEFBITS              ;  get record
011A 25 1FC0                    AND    AX,MASK BIT2            ;  clear BIT1 & 3
011D B1 06                      MOV    CL,BIT2                 ;  get shift 06
011F D3 E8                      SHR    AX,CL                   ;  shift right
0121                  E10:                                     ;Isolate BIT1:
0121 A1 0102 R                  MOV    AX,DEFBITS              ;  get record
0124 B1 0D                      MOV    CL,BIT1                 ;  get shift 13
0126 D3 E8                      SHR    AX,CL                   ;  shift right
0128 B8 4C00                    MOV    AX,4C00H                ;Exit to DOS
012B CD 21                      INT    21H
012D                  MAIN      ENDP
35 012D               CODESG    ENDS
36                              END    BEGIN
```

```
-----------------------------------------------------------------------------
Structures and Records:
            N a m e                    Width   # fields
                                       Shift   Width  Mask   Initial
BITREC . . . . . . . . . . . .         0010    0003
  BIT1 . . . . . . . . . . .           000D    0003   E000   0000
  BIT2 . . . . . . . . . . .           0006    0007   1FC0   0000
  BIT3 . . . . . . . . . . .           0000    0006   003F   0000
Segments and Groups:
            N a m e                    Length  Align  Combine Class
CODESG . . . . . . . . . . .           012D    PARA   NONE    'CODE'
Symbols:
            N a m e                    Type    Value  Attr
A10  . . . . . . . . . . . .         L NEAR    0104   CODESG
B10  . . . . . . . . . . . .         L NEAR    0108   CODESG
BEGIN  . . . . . . . . . . .         L NEAR    0100   CODESG
BIT1 . . . . . . . . . . . .           000D
BIT2 . . . . . . . . . . . .           0006
BIT3 . . . . . . . . . . . .           0000
C10  . . . . . . . . . . . .         L NEAR    010E   CODESG
D10  . . . . . . . . . . . .         L NEAR    0117   CODESG
DEFBITS  . . . . . . . . . .         L WORD    0102   CODESG
E10  . . . . . . . . . . . .         L NEAR    0121   CODESG
MAIN . . . . . . . . . . . .         N PROC    0104   CODESG  Length = 0029
```

Figure 27–1   Using the RECORD Directive

Record-specific operators are WIDTH, shift count, and MASK. The use of these operators permits you to change a RECORD definition without having to change the instructions that reference it.

WIDTH operator. The WIDTH operator returns a width as the number of bits in a RECORD or in a RECORD field. For example, in Figure 27–1, following A10 are two examples of WIDTH. The first MOV returns the width of the entire RECORD BITREC (16 bits); the second MOV returns the width of the record field BIT2 (7 bits). In both cases, the assembler has generated an immediate operand for WIDTH.

Shift count. A direct reference to a RECORD field, such as

```
MOV CL,BIT2
```

does not refer to the contents of BIT2. (Indeed, that would be rather difficult.) Instead, the assembler generates an immediate operand that contains a *shift count* to help you isolate the field. The immediate value represents the number of bits that you would have to shift BIT2 to right adjust it. In Figure 27–1, the three examples following B10 return the shift count for BIT1, BIT2, and BIT3.

MASK operator. The MASK operator returns a mask of 1-bits representing the specified field and, in effect, defines the bit positions that the field occupies. For example, the MASK for each of the fields defined in BITREC is

FIELD	BINARY	HEX
BIT1	1110000000000000	E000
BIT2	0001111111000000	1FC0
BIT3	0000000000111111	003F

In Figure 27–1, the three instructions following C10 return the MASK values for BIT1, BIT2, and BIT3. The instructions following D10 and E10 isolate BIT2 and BIT1, respectively, from BITREC. D10 gets the record into the AX register and uses a MASK of BIT2 to AND it :

```
Record:          101 0110110 011010

AND MASK BIT2:   000 1111111 000000

Result:          000 0110110 000000
```

The effect is to clear all bits except those of BIT2. The next two instructions cause the AX to shift six bits so that BIT2 is right-adjusted:

```
0000000000110110    (0036H)
```

The example following E10 gets the record into the AX, and because BIT1 is the leftmost field, the routine simply uses its shift factor to shift right 13 bits:

```
0000000000000101    (0005H)
```

SEGMENT Directive

An assembly module consists of one or more segments, part of a segment, or even parts of several segments. The general format for a segment is

```
seg-name   SEGMENT [align] [combine] ['class']
           ...
seg-name   ENDS
```

All operands are optional. The following subsections describe the entries for align, combine, and class.

Align.   The align operand indicates the starting boundary for a segment:

```
BYTE        Next address
WORD        Next even address (divisible by 2)
DWORD       Next doubleword address (divisible by 4)
PARA        Next paragraph (divisible by 10H)
PAGE        Next page address (divisible by 100H)
```

PARA is commonly used for all types of segments. BYTE and WORD can be used for segments that are to be combined within another segment, usually a data segment. DWORD is normally used with 80386 and later processors.

Combine.   The combine operands NONE, PUBLIC, STACK, and COMMON indicate the way the linker is to handle a segment:

- NONE (default): The segment is to be logically separate from other segments, although it may end up physically adjacent to them. The segment is presumed to have its own base address.
- PUBLIC: LINK loads PUBLIC segments of the same name and class adjacent to one another. One base address is presumed for all such PUBLIC segments.
- STACK: LINK treats STACK the same as PUBLIC. There must be at least one STACK defined in a linked .EXE program. If there is more than one stack, the SP is set to the start of the first stack.
- COMMON: If COMMON segments have the same name and class, the linker gives them the same base address. During execution, the second segment overlays the first one. The largest segment determines the length of the common area.
- AT paragraph-address: The paragraph must be defined previously. The entry facilitates defining labels and variables at fixed offsets within fixed areas of memory, such as the interrupt table in low memory or the BIOS data area at 40[0]H. For example, the code in ROM defines the location of the video display buffer as

```
VIDEO_RAM SEGMENT AT 0B800H
```

The assembler creates a dummy segment that provides, in effect, an image of memory locations.

'class'. The class entry can help the linker associate segments with different names, identify segments, and control their order. Class may contain any valid name, contained in single quotes. The linker uses the name to relate segments that have the same name and class. Typical examples are 'Data' and 'Code'. If you define a class as 'Code', the linker expects that segment to contain instruction code. Also, the CODEVIEW debugger expects that class for the code segment.

The linker combines the following two segments with the same name (CSEG) and class ('Code') into one physical segment under the same segment register:

```
            ---------------------------------
Assembly    CSEG    SEGMENT PARA PUBLIC 'Code'
module 1            ASSUME  CS:CSEG

                    ...

            CSEG    ENDS
            ---------------------------------
Assembly    CSEG    SEGMENT PARA PUBLIC 'Code'
module 2            ASSUME  CS:CSEG

                    ...

            CSEG    ENDS
            ---------------------------------
```

Since you may want to control the ordering of segments within a program, it is useful to understand how the linker handles the process. The original order of the segment names provides the basic sequence, which you may override by means of the PUBLIC attribute and class names. The following example links two object modules (both modules contain a segment named DSEG1 with the PUBLIC attribute and identical class names):

Before linking the .OBJ modules:

```
module 1    SSEG    SEGMENT    PARA STACK

module 1    DSEG1   SEGMENT    PARA PUBLIC 'Data'

module 1    DSEG2   SEGMENT    PARA

module 1    CSEG    SEGMENT    PARA 'Code'

module 2    DSEG1   SEGMENT    PARA PUBLIC 'Data'

module 2    DSEG2   SEGMENT    PARA

module 2    CSEG    SEGMENT    PARA 'Code'
```

After linking the .OBJ modules into one .EXE module:

```
module 1        CSEG    SEGMENT     PARA 'Code'

module 2        CSEG    SEGMENT     PARA 'Code'

module 1 + 2    DSEG1   SEGMENT     PARA PUBLIC 'Data'

module 1        DSEG2   SEGMENT     PARA

module 2        DSEG2   SEGMENT     PARA

module 1        SSEG    SEGMENT     PARA STACK
```

You may nest segments, provided that one nested segment is completely contained within the other. In the following example, SEG2 is completely contained within SEG1:

```
┌─── SEG1   SEGMENT
│
│           . . .                   SEG1 begins
│    ┌─ SEG2   SEGMENT
│    │
│    │       . . .                  SEG2 area
│    └─ SEG2   ENDS
│
│           . . .                   SEG1 resumes
└─── SEG1   ENDS
```

The .ALPHA, .SEQ, and DOSSEG directives and the assembler options /A and /S can also control the order of segments. (To combine segments into groups, see the GROUP directive.)

.SEQ Directive

This directive (the default), placed at or near the start of a program, tells the assembler to leave segments in their original sequence. It overrides the assembler option /A. (See also the .ALPHA directive.)

.STACK Directive

This simplified segment directive defines the stack. Its general format is

$$\left[\text{.STACK [size]} \right]$$

The default stack size is 1,024 bytes, which you may override. (See also the .MODEL directive.)

STRUC Directive

The STRUC directive (STRUCT since MASM 6.0) facilitates defining related fields within a structure. Its general format is

```
struc name   STRUC

             . . .

      [ defined fields ]

             . . .

struc-name   ENDS
```

A structure begins with its name and the directive STRUC and terminates with the name and the directive ENDS. The assembler stores the defined fields one after the other from the start of the structure. Valid entries are DB, DW, DD, DQ, and DT definitions with optional field names.

In Figure 27–2, STRUC defines a parameter list named PARLIST for use with DOS INT 21H, function 0AH, to input a name via the keyboard. A subsequent statement allocates storage for the structure, making it addressable within the program:

```
PARAMS   PARLIST   <>
```

The angle brackets (less-than and greater-than symbols) in the operand are empty in this example, but you may use them to redefine (or override) data within a structure.

Instructions may reference a structure directly by its name. To reference fields within a structure, instructions must qualify them by using the allocate name of the structure (PARAMS in the example), followed by a period that connects it with the field name, as, for example,

```
MOV  AL, PARAMS.ACTLEN
```

You may also use the allocate statement (PARAMS in Figure 27–2) to redefine the contents of fields within a structure.

SUBTTL Directive

The SUBTTL directive (SUBTITLE since MASM 6.0) causes a subtitle of up to 60 characters to print on line 3 of each page of an assembly source listing. You may code SUBTTL any number of times. The general format is

```
SUBTTL  text
```

TEXTEQU Directive

The general format for this directive (introduced by MASM 6.0) is

```
TEXTEQU [text-item]
```

The operand text-item can be a literal string, a constant preceded by %, or a string that a macro function has returned.

TITLE Directive

The TITLE directive causes a title of up to 60 characters to print on line 2 of each page of a source listing. You may code TITLE once, at the start. The general format is

```
TITLE text
```

```
                                    TITLE    P27DSTRU (COM)  Defining a structure
          0000                      CODESG   SEGMENT PARA 'Code'
                                             ASSUME CS:CODESG,DS:CODESG,SS:CODESG
          0100                               ORG      100H
          0100 EB 2C                BEGIN:   JMP      SHORT MAIN
                                    ; --------------------------------------------
                                    PARLIST  STRUC                     ;Parameter list
          0000 19                   MAXLEN   DB       25               ;
          0001 00                   ACTLEN   DB       ?                ;
          0002 0019[20]             NAMEIN   DB       25 DUP(' ') ;
          001B                      PARLIST  ENDS

          0102 19                   PARAMS   PARLIST <>               ;Allocate storage
          0103 00
          0104 0019[20]
          011D 57 68 61 74 20 69 PROMPT   DB       'What is the name?'
               73 20 74 68 65 20
               6E 61 6D 65 3F
                                    ; --------------------------------------------
          012E                      MAIN     PROC     NEAR
          012E B4 40                         MOV      AH,40H           ;Request display
          0130 BB 0001                       MOV      BX,01
          0133 B9 0011                       MOV      CX,17            ;Length of prompt
          0136 8D 16 011D R                  LEA      DX,PROMPT        ;Address of prompt
          013A CD 21                         INT      21H
          013C B4 0A                         MOV      AH,0AH           ;Accept keyboard
          013E 8D 16 0102 R                  LEA      DX,PARAMS        ;  input
          0142 CD 21                         INT      21H
          0144 A0 0103 R                     MOV      AL,PARAMS.ACTLEN
                                    ;          ...                     ;Length of input
          0147 B8 4C00                       MOV      AX,4C00H         ;Exit to DOS
          014A CD 21                         INT      21H
          014C                      MAIN     ENDP
          014C                      CODESG   ENDS
          42                                 END      BEGIN
          --------------------------------------------------------------------
```

```
Structures and Records:
          N a m e                 Width    # fields
                                  Shift    Width    Mask      Initial
PARLIST . . . . . . . . . .  001B    0003
   MAXLEN . . . . . . . . . .  0000
   ACTLEN . . . . . . . . . .  0001
   NAMEIN . . . . . . . . . .  0002
Segments and Groups:
          N a m e                 Length   Align    Combine   Class
CODESG . . . . . . . . . .  014C    PARA     NONE      'CODE'
Symbols:
          N a m e                 Type     Value    Attr
BEGIN  . . . . . . . . . . . L NEAR   0100     CODESG
MAIN . . . . . . . . . . . . N PROC   012E     CODESG    Length = 001E
PARAMS . . . . . . . . . . . L 0102   CODESG
PROMPT . . . . . . . . . . . L BYTE   011D     CODESG
```

Figure 27–2 Using a Structure

.XCREF Directive

This directive (named .NOCREF since MASM 6.0) tells the assembler to suppress the cross-reference table. The general format is

```
.XCREF   [name [,name] ...]
```

Omitting the operand causes suppression of all entries in the table. You may also suppress the cross-reference of particular items. Here are examples of .XCREF and .CREF:

```
.XCREF                    ;Suppress cross-reference

...

.CREF                     ;Restore cross-reference

...

.XREF FIELDA,FIELDB       ;Suppress cross-reference of FIELDA and FIELDB.
```

.XLIST Directive

You may use the .XLIST directive (named .NOLIST since MASM 6.0) anywhere in a source program to discontinue printing an assembled program. A typical situation would be where the statements are common to other programs and you don't need another listing. The .LIST directive (the default) resumes the listing. Code both of these directives with no operand.

CHAPTER 28 ——————————

The PC Instruction Set

OBJECTIVE:

To explain machine code and to provide a description of the PC instruction set.

INTRODUCTION

This chapter explains machine code and provides a list of symbolic instructions with an explanation of their purpose.

Many instructions have a specific purpose, so that a one-byte machine language instruction code is adequate. The following are examples:

MACHINE CODE	SYMBOLIC INSTRUCTION	COMMENT
40	INC AX	;Increment AX
50	PUSH AX	;Push AX
C3	RET (short)	;Short return from procedure
CB	RET (far)	;Far return from procedure
FD	STD	;Set direction flag

None of these instructions makes a direct reference to memory. Instructions that specify an immediate operand, an eight-bit register, two registers, or a reference to memory are more complex and require two or more bytes of machine code.

```
General, Base, and Index Registers
   Bits       w = 0      w = 1              Bits for
   000        AL         AX/EAX      Segment Registers
   001        CL         CX/ECX          000        ES
   010        DL         DX/EDX          001        CS
   011        BL         BX/EBX          010        SS
   100        AH         SP              011        DS
   101        CH         BP              100        FS
   110        DH         SI              101        GS
   111        BH         DI
```

Figure 28–1   Register Notation

Machine code has a special provision for indicating a particular register and another provision for referencing memory by means of an addressing mode byte.

REGISTER NOTATION

Instructions that reference a register may contain three bits that indicate the particular register and a w-bit that indicates whether the width is a byte (0) or a word (1). Also, only certain instructions may access the segment registers. Figure 28–1 shows the complete register notations. For example, the bit value 000 means AH if the w bit is 0 and AX if it is 1.

Here's the symbolic and machine code for a MOV instruction with a one-byte immediate operand:

```
MOV   AH,00      10110 100 00000000
                 |  |||
                 w reg = AH
```

In this case, the first byte of machine code indicates a width of one byte (w = 0) and refers to the AH register (100). Here's a MOV instruction that contains a one-word immediate operand, along with its generated machine code:

```
MOV   AX,00      10111 000 00000000 00000000
                 |  |||
                 w reg = AX
```

The first byte of machine code indicates a width of one word (w = 1) and refers to the AX register (000). For other instructions, w and reg may occupy different positions.

ADDRESSING MODE BYTE

The *mode* byte, when it is present, occupies the second byte of machine code and consists of the following three elements:

mod   A two-bit mode, where the values 00, 01, and 10 refer to memory locations
      and 11 refers to a register

reg   A three-bit reference to a register

r/m   A three-bit reference to a register or memory, where r specifies which regis-
      ter and m indicates a memory address

Also, the first byte of machine code may contain a d-bit that indicates the direction
of flow. Here's an example of adding the AX to the BX:

```
ADD    BX,AX      00000011  11 011 000
                            dw mod reg r/m
```

In the example, d = 1 means that mod (11) and reg (011) describe the first operand and r/m
(000) describes the second operand. Since w = 1, the width is a word. Therefore, the instruction is to add the AX (000) to the BX (011).

The second byte of the object code indicates most modes of addressing memory. The
next section examines the addressing mode in more detail.

Mod Bits

The two *mod bits* distinguish between addressing of registers and memory. The following
explains their purpose:

00   r/m bits give the exact addressing option; there is no offset byte.

01   r/m bits give the exact addressing option; there is one offset byte.

10   r/m bits give the exact addressing option; there are two offset bytes.

11   r/m specifies a register. The w-bit (in the operation code byte) determines
      whether a reference is to an 8-, 16-, or 32-bit register.

Reg Bits

The three reg bits, in association with the w-bit, determine the actual 8- or 16-bit register.

R/M Bits

The three *r/m (register/memory) bits*, in association with the mod bits, determine the addressing mode, as shown in Figure 28–2.

```
r/m    mod=00    mod=01 or 10    mod=11    mod=11
                                 w=0       w=1
000    BX+SI     DS:[BX+SI+disp]  AL        AX
001    BX+DI     DS:[BX+DI+disp]  CL        CX
010    BP+SI     SS:[BP+SI+disp]  DL        DX
011    BP+DI     SS:[BP+DI+disp]  BL        BX
100    SI        DS:[SI+disp]     AH        SP
101    DI        DS:[DI+disp]     CH        BP
110    Direct    SS:[BP+disp]     DH        SI
111    BX        DS:[BX+disp]     BH        DI
```

Figure 28–2   The r/m Bits

TWO-BYTE INSTRUCTIONS

The following example of a two-byte instruction adds the BX to the AX:

```
ADD  AX,BX  0000 0011   11 000 011
                 ||     ||  |||  |||
                 dw    mod reg r/m
```

d = 1	reg plus w describe the first operand, and mod plus r/m plus w describe the second operand
w — 1	The width is a word
mod = 11	The second operand is a register
reg = 000	The first operand is the AX register
r/m = 011	The second operand is the BX register

The next example multiplies the AL by the BL:

```
MUL  BL 11110110   11 100 011
        |      ||  |||  |||
        w    mod reg r/m
```

The processor assumes that the multiplicand is in the AL if it is a byte, the AX if it is a word, and the EAX if it is a doubleword. The width (w = 0) is a byte, mod (11) references a register, and the register (r/m = 011) is the BL (011). Reg = 100 is not meaningful here.

THREE-BYTE INSTRUCTIONS

The following MOV generates three bytes of machine code:

```
MOV  mem-word,AX     10100011 dddddddd dddddddd
                        ||
                        dw
```

A move from the accumulator (AX or AL) needs to know only whether the operation is byte or word. In this example, w = 1 means a word, and the 16-bit AX is understood. (The use of AL in the second operand would cause the w bit to be zero.) Bytes 2 and 3 contain the offset to the memory location. The use of the accumulator register is often more efficient (because of the shorter instruction length required for it and its faster execution) than the use of other registers.

FOUR-BYTE INSTRUCTIONS

The following example of a four-byte instruction multiplies the AL by a memory location:

```
MUL  mem-byte  11110110   00 100 110 x--x x--x
                  |       ||  |||  |||
                  w      mod reg r/m
```

For this instruction, although reg is 100, the multiplicand is assumed to be in the AL. Mod = 00 indicates a memory reference, and r/m = 110 means a direct reference to memory. The machine instruction also contains two subsequent bytes that provide the offset to the memory location.

The next example illustrates the LEA instruction, which specifies a word address:

```
LEA  DX,mem    10001101  00 010 110 x--x x--x
                         ||  |||  |||
               LEA    mod reg r/m
```

Reg = 010 designates the DX register. Mod = 00 and r/m = 110 indicate a direct reference to a memory address. The two subsequent bytes provide the offset to this location.

INSTRUCTION SET

This section covers the instruction set in alphabetic sequence, although closely related instructions are grouped together for convenience. In addition to the preceding discussion of mode byte and width bit, the following abbreviations are relevant:

addr	Address of a memory location
addr-high	Rightmost byte of an address
addr-low	Leftmost byte of an address
data	Immediate operand (8-bit if w = 0, 16-bit if w = 1)
data-high	Rightmost byte of an immediate operand
data-low	Leftmost byte of an immediate operand
disp	Displacement (offset value)
reg	Reference to a register

The 80286 and later processors support a number of specialized instructions not covered here: ARPL, BOUND, CLTS, ENTER, LAR, LEAVE, LGDT, LIDT, LLDT, LMSW, LSL, LTR, SGDT, SIDT, SLDT, SMSW, STR, VERR, and VERW. Instructions unique to the 80486 and later are BSWAP, XADD, CMPXCHG, INVD, WBINVD, AND INVLPG, also not covered here.

AAA: ASCII Adjust after Addition

Operation. Corrects the sum of two ASCII bytes in the AL. If the rightmost four bits of the AL have a value greater than 9, or if the AF flag is set to 1, AAA adds 1 to the AH and sets the AF and CF flags. Otherwise, the AF and CF are cleared. AAA always clears the leftmost four bits of the AL.
Flags. Affects AF and CF. (OF, PF, SF, and ZF are undefined.)
Source code. AAA (no operand)
Object code. 00110111

AAD: ASCII Adjust before Division

Operation. Corrects for division of ASCII values. Use AAD before dividing into an unpacked BCD value in the AX. (Strip out ASCII 3s.) AAD corrects the dividend to a binary value in the AL for a subsequent binary divide. It multiplies the AH by 10, adds the product to the AL, and clears the AH.

Flags. Affects PF, SF, and ZF. (AF, CF, and OF are undefined.)

Source code. AAD (no operand)

Object code. |11010101|00001010|

AAM: ASCII Adjust after Multiplication

Operation. Corrects the product generated by multiplying two unpacked BCD values. AAM divides the AL by 10 and stores the quotient in the AH and the remainder in the AL.

Flags. Affects PF, SF, and ZF. (AF, CF, and OF are undefined.)

Source code. AAM (no operand)

Object code. |11010100|00001010|

AAS: ASCII Adjust after Subtraction

Operation. Corrects the difference of two ASCII bytes in the AL. If the rightmost four bits have a value greater than 9, or if the CF flag is 1, AAS subtracts 6 from the AL, subtracts 1 from the AH, and sets the AF and CF flags. Otherwise, the AF and CF are cleared. AAS always clears the leftmost four bits of the AL.

Flags. Affects AF and CF. (OF, PF, SF, and ZF are undefined.)

Source code. AAS (no operand)

Object code. 00111111

ADC: Add with Carry

Operation. Typically used in multiword binary addition to carry an overflowed 1-bit into the next stage of arithmetic. ADC adds the contents of the CF flag (0/1) to the first operand, and then adds the second operand to the first, just like ADD. (See also SBB.)

Flags. Affects AF, CF, OF, PF, SF, and ZF.

Source code. ADC {register/memory},{register/memory/immediate}

Object code. Three formats:

- Reg/mem with register: |000100dw|modregr/m|
- Immed to accumulator: |0001010w|---data--|data if w=1|
- Immed to reg/mem: |100000sw|mod010r/m|---data---|data if sw=01|

ADD: Add Binary Numbers

Operation. Adds binary values from memory, register, or immediate to a register, or adds values in a register or immediate to memory. Values may be byte, word, or doubleword (80386 and later).

Flags. Affects AF, CF, OF, PF, SF, and ZF.

Source code. ADD {register/memory},{register/memory/immediate}

Object code. Three formats:

- Reg/mem with register: |000000dw|modregr/m|
- Immed to accumulator: |0000010w|-- data--|data if w=1|
- Immed to reg/mem: |100000sw|mod000r/m|---data ---|data if sw=01|

AND: Logical AND

Operation. Performs a logical AND operation on bits of two operands. Both operands are bytes, words, or doublewords (80386 and later), which AND matches bit for bit. If both matched bits are 1, the 1-bit in the first operand is set to 1; otherwise, the bit is cleared. (See also OR, XOR, and TEST.)

Flags. Affects CF. (0), OF (0), PF, SF, and ZF. (AF is undefined.)

Source code. AND {register/memory},{register/memory/immediate}

Object code. Three formats:

- Reg/mem with register: `|001000dw|modregr/m|`
- Immed to accumulator: `|0010010w|---data--|data if w=1|`
- Immed to reg/mem: `|100000sw|mod 100 r/m|---data--|data if w=1|`

BSF and BSR: Bit Scan (80386 and later)

Operation. Scans a bit string for the first 1-bit. BSF scans from right to left, and BSR scans from left to right. The second operand's register (16 or 32 bits) contains the string to be scanned. The operation returns the position of the bit (if any) in the first operand's register.

Flags. Affects ZF.

Source code. `BSF/BSR register,{register/memory}`

Object code. BSF: `|00001111|10111100|modregr/m|`
                    BSR: `|00001111|10111101|modregr/m|`

BT/BTC/BTR/BTS: Bit Test (80386 and later)

Operation. Copies a specified bit into the CF flag. The first operand contains the bit string being tested, and the second indicates its position. BTC complements the bit by reversing its value in the first operand. BTR resets the bit by clearing it to zero. BTS sets the bit to 1. References are to 16-and 32-bit values.

Flags. Affects CF.

Source code. BT/BTC/BTR/BTS {register/memory},{register/immediate}

Object code. Two formats:

- Immed to reg: `|00001111|10111010|mod***r/m|`
- Reg/mem to reg: `|00001111|10***010|modregr/m|`
  (`*** means BT` = 100, BTC = 111, BTR = 110, BTS = 101)

CALL: Call a Procedure

Operation. Calls a near or far procedure. The assembler generates a near CALL if the called procedure is NEAR and a far CALL if the called procedure is FAR. For near, CALL pushes the IP (the address of the next instruction) onto the stack. It then loads the IP with the destination offset address. For far, CALL pushes the CS onto the stack and loads an intersegment pointer onto the stack. It then pushes the IP onto the stack and loads the IP with the destination offset address. A subsequent near or far RET reverses these steps on return.

Flags. Affects none.

Source code. CALL {register/memory}

Object code. Four formats:
- Direct within segment: |11101000|disp-low |disp-high|
- Indirect within segment: |11111111|mod010r/m|
- Indirect intersegment: |11111111|mod011r/m|
- Direct intersegment: |10011010|offset-low|offset-high|seg-low|seg-high|

CBW: Convert Byte to Word

Operation. Extends a one-byte signed value to a word by duplicating the sign (bit 7) of the AL through the bits in the AH. (See also CWD, CWDE, and CDQ.)
Flags. Affects none.
Source code. CBW (no operand)
Object code. 10011000

CDQ: Convert Doubleword to Quadword (80386 and later)

Operation. Extends a 32-bit signed value to a 64-bit value by duplicating the sign (bit 31) of the EAX through the EDX. (See also CBW, CWD, and CWDE.)
Flags. Affects none.
Source code. CDQ (no operand)
Object code. 10011001

CLC: Clear Carry Flag

Operation. Clears the CF flag so that, for example, an ADC does not add a 1-bit. (See also STC.)
Flags. CF (becomes 0).
Source code. CLC (no operand)
Object code. 11111000

CLD: Clear Direction Flag

Operation. Clears the DF flag, to cause string operations such as MOVS to process from left to right. (See also STD.)
Flags. DF (becomes 0).
Source code. CLD (no operand)
Object code. 11111100

CLI: Clear Interrupt Flag

Operation. Clears the IF flag, to disable maskable external interrupts. (See also STI.)
Flags. IF (becomes 0).
Source code. CLI (no operand)
Object code. 11111010

CMC: Complement Carry Flag

Operation. Complements the CF flag: reverses the CF bit value—0 becomes 1 and 1 becomes 0.

Flags. CF (reversed).
Source code. CMC (no operand)
Object code. `11110101`

CMP: Compare

Operation. Compares the contents of two data fields. CMP internally subtracts the second operand from the first and sets or clears flags, but does not store the result. Both operands are byte, word, or doubleword (80386 and later). CMP may compare register, memory, or immediate to a register or compare register or immediate to memory. (See also CMPS.)
Flags. Affects AF, CF, OF, PF, SF, and ZF.
Source code. CMP {register/memory},{register/memory/immediate}
Object code. Three formats:

- Reg/mem with reg: `|001110dw|modregr/m|`
- Immed to accumulator: `|0011110w|---data--|data if w=1|`
- Immed to reg/mem: `|100000sw|mod111r/m|---data----|data if sw=0|`

CMPS/CMPSB/CMPSW/CMPSD: Compare String

Operation. Compares strings of any length in memory. A REPn prefix normally precedes these instructions, along with a maximum value in the CX. CMPSB compares bytes, CMPSW compares words, and CMPSD (80386 and later) compares doublewords. The DS:SI registers address the first operand, and the ES:DI registers address the second. If the DF flag is 0, the operation compares from left to right and increments the SI and DI; if the DF is 1, it compares from right to left and decrements the SI and DI. REPn decrements the CX by 1 for each repetition. The operation terminates when the compared value is found (REPNE), when it is not found (REPE), or when the CX is decremented to 0; the DI and SI are advanced past the byte that caused termination. The last compare sets/clears the flags, not the contents of the CX.
Flags. Affects AF, CF, OF, PF, SF, and ZF.
Source code. [REPnn] CMPSB/CMPSW/CMPSD (no operand)
Object code. `1010011w`

CWD: Convert Word to Doubleword

Operation. Extends a one-word signed value to a doubleword in the DX:AX by duplicating the sign (bit 15) of the AX through the DX, typically to generate a 32-bit dividend. (See also CBW, CWDE, and CDQ.)
Flags. Affects none.
Source code. CWD (no operand)
Object code. `10011001`

CWDE: Convert Word to Extended Doubleword (80386 and later)

Operation. Extends a one-word signed value to a doubleword in the EAX by duplicating the sign (bit 15) of the AX, typically to generate a 32-bit dividend. (See also CBW, CWD, and CDQ.)

Flags. Affects none.
Source code. CWDE (no operand)
Object code. `10011000`

DAA: Decimal Adjust after Addition

Operation. Corrects the result of adding two packed BCD items in the AL. If the rightmost four bits have a value greater than 9, or if the AF flag is 1, DAA adds 6 to the AL and sets the AF. If the AL contains a value greater than 99H, or if the CF flag is 1, DAA adds 60H to the AL and sets the CF. Otherwise, the AF and CF are cleared. (See also DAS.)
Flags. Affects AF, CF, PF, SF, and ZF. (OF is undefined.)
Source code. DAA (no operand)
Object code. `00100111`

DAS: Decimal Adjust after Subtraction

Operation. Corrects the result of subtracting two packed BCD items in the AL. If the rightmost four bits have a value greater than 9, or if the AF flag is 1, DAS subtracts 60H from the AL and sets the CF flag. Otherwise, the AF and CF are cleared. (See also DAA.)
Flags. Affects AF, CF, PF, SF, and ZF. (OF is undefined.)
Source code. DAS (no operand)
Object code. `00101111` (no operand)

DEC. Decrement by 1

Operation. Decrements 1 from a byte, word, or doubleword (80386 and later) in a register or memory. (See also INC.)
Flags. Affects AF, OF, PF, SF, and ZF.
Source code. DEC {register/memory}
Object code. Two formats:

- Register: `|01001reg|`
- Reg/memory: `|1111111w|mod001r/m|`

DIV: Unsigned Divide

Operation. Divides an unsigned dividend by an unsigned divisor. DIV treats a leftmost 1-bit as a data bit, not a minus sign. Division by zero causes a zero-divide interrupt. (See also IDIV). Here are the divide operations for byte, word, and doubleword:

Size	Dividend (Operand 1)	Divisor (Operand 2)	Quotient	Remainder	Example
16-bit	AX	8-bit reg/memory	AL	AH	DIV BH
32-bit	DX:AX	16-bit reg/memory	AX	DX	DIV CX
64-bit	EDX:EAX	32 bit reg/memory	EAX	EDX	DIV ECX

Flags. Affects AF, CF, OF, PF, SF, and ZF. (all undefined.)
Source code. DIV {register/memory}
Object code. |1111011w|mod110r/m|

ESC: Escape

Operation. Facilitates the use of coprocessors such as the 80x87 to perform special operations. ESC provides the coprocessor with an instruction and operand for execution. Note that as of version 6.1, MASM no longer supports ESC; instead, it generates the full required object code for coprocessor instructions.
Flags. Affects none.
Source code. ESC immediate,{register/memory}
Object code. |11011xxx|modxxxr/m| (x-bits are not important)

HLT: Enter Halt State

Operation. Causes the processor to enter a halt state while waiting for an interrupt. HLT terminates with the CS and IP registers pointing to the instruction following the HLT. When an interrupt occurs, the processor pushes the CS and IP onto the stack and executes the interrupt routine. On return, an IRET instruction pops the stack, and processing resumes following the original HLT.
Flags. Affects none.
Source code. HLT (no operand)
Object code. 11110100

IDIV: Signed (Integer) Divide

Operation. Divides a signed dividend by a signed divisor. IDIV treats the leftmost bit as the sign (0 = positive, 1 = negative). Division by zero causes a zero-divide interrupt. (See CBW and CWD to extend the length of a signed dividend, and see also DIV.) Here are the divide operations for byte, word, and doubleword:

Size	Dividend (Operand 1)	Divisor (Operand 2)	Quotient	Remainder	Example
16-bit	AX	8-bit reg/memory	AL	AH	IDIV BH
32-bit	DX:AX	16-bit reg/memory	AX	DX	IDIV CX
64-bit	EDX:EAX	32-bit reg/memory	EAX	EDX	IDIV ECX

Flags. Affects AF, CF, OF, PF, SF, and ZF.
Source code. IDIV {register/memory}
Object code. |1111011w|mod111r/m|

IMUL: Signed (Integer) Multiply

Operation. Multiplies a signed multiplicand by a signed multiplier. IMUL treats a leftmost bit as the sign (0 = positive, 1 = negative). (See also MUL.) Here are the multiply operations for byte, word, and doubleword:

Size	Multiplicand (Operand 1)	Multiplier (Operand 2)	Product	Example
8-bit	AL	8-bit register/memory	AX	IMUL BL
16-bit	AX	16-bit register/memory	DX:AX	IMUL BX
32-bit	EAX	32-bit register/memory	EDX:EAX	IMUL ECX

Flags. Affects CF and OF. (AF, PF, SF, and ZF are undefined.)
Source code. IMUL {register/memory} (all processors)
Object code. |1111011w|mod101r/m| (first format)

Three other IMUL formats are available for advanced processors:

- IMUL register,immediate (80286 and later)
- IMUL register,register,immediate (80286 and later)
- IMUL register,{register/memory} (80386 and later)

IN: Input Byte or Word

Operation. Transfers from an input port a byte to the AL or a word to the AX. Code the port as a fixed numeric operand (as IN AX,port#) or as a variable in the DX (as IN AX,DX). Use the DX if the port number is greater than 256. The 80286 and later processors also support an INS (Input String) instruction. (See also OUT.)
Source code. IN {AL/AX},{portno/DX}
Flags. Affects none.
Object code. Two formats:

- Variable port: |1110110w|
- Fixed port: |1110010w|--port--|

INC: Increment by 1

Operation. Increments by 1 a byte, word, or doubleword (80386 and later) in a register or memory, coded, for example, as INC CX. (See also DEC.)
Flags. Affects AF, OF, PF, SF, and ZF.
Source code. INC {register/memory}
Object code. Two formats:

- Register: |01000reg|
- Reg/memory: |1111111w|mod000r/m|

INT: Interrupt

Operation. Interrupts processing and transfers control to one of the 256 interrupt (vector) addresses beginning at segment 0, offset 0. INT performs the following: (1) pushes the flags onto the stack and resets the IF and TF flags; (2) pushes the CS onto the stack and places the high order word of the interrupt address in the CS; and (3) pushes the IP onto the stack and fills the IP with the low-order word of the interrupt address. For the 80386 and later, INT pushes a 16-bit IP for 16-bit segments and a 32-bit IP for 32-bit segments. IRET returns from the interrupt routine.

Flags. Clears IF and TF.

Source code. INT number

Object code. |1100110v|--type--| (if v = 0 type is 3)

INTO: Interrupt on Overflow

Operation. Causes an interrupt (usually harmless) if an overflow has occurred (the OF is set to 1) and performs an INT 04H. The interrupt address is at location 10H of the interrupt service table. (See also INT.)

Flags. Affects IF and TF.

Source code. INTO (no operand)

Object code. 11001110

IRET/IRETD: Interrupt Return

Operation. Provides a far return from an interrupt routine. IRET performs the following procedure: (1) pops the word at the top of the stack into the IP, increments the SP by 2, and pops the top of the stack into the CS; (2) increments the SP by 2 and pops the top of the stack into the flags register. This procedure undoes the steps that the interrupt originally took and performs a return. For the 80386 and later, use IRETD (doubleword) to pop a 32-bit IP. (See also RET.)

Flags. Affects all.

Source code. IRET

Object code. 11001111 (no operand)

JA/JNBE: Jump if Above or Jump if not Below/Equal

Operation. Used after a test of unsigned data. If the CF flag is 0 (no carry) and the ZF flag is 0 (a nonzero condition), the instruction adds the operand offset to the IP and performs a jump. The jump must be short (−128 to 127 bytes), except for the 80386 and later, on which it may be near (within 32K).

Flags. Affects none.

Source code. JA/JNBE label

Object code. |01110111|--disp--|

JAE/JNB: Jump if Above/Equal or Jump if Not Below

Operation. Used after a test of unsigned data. If the CF flag is 0 (no carry), the instruction adds the operand offset to the IP and performs a jump. The jump must be short (−128 to 127 bytes), except for the 80386 and later, on which it may be near (within 32K).

Flags. Affects none.

Source code. JAE/JNB label

Object code. |01110011|--disp--|Z

JB/JNAE: Jump if Below or Jump if Not Above/Equal

Operation. Used after a test of unsigned data. If the CF flag is 1 (carry), the instruction adds the operand offset to the IP and performs a jump. The jump must be short (−128 to 127 bytes), except for the 80386 and later, on which it may be near.
Flags. Affects none.
Source code. JB/JNAE label
Object code. |01110010|--disp--|

JBE/JNA: Jump if Below/Equal or Jump if Not Above

Operation. Used after a test of unsigned data. If the CF flag is 1 (carry) or the AF flag is 1, the instruction adds the operand offset to the IP and performs a jump. The jump must be short (−128 to 127 bytes), except for the 80386 and later, on which it may be near.
Flags. Affects none.
Source code. JBE/JNA label
Object code. |01110110|--disp--|

JC: Jump if Carry

Operation. See JB/JNAE (identical operations).

JCXZ/JECXZ: Jump if CX/ECX Is Zero

Operation. Jumps to a specified address if the CX or the ECX (80386 and later) contains zero. This operation could be useful at the start of a loop, although limited to a short jump.
Flags. Affects none.
Source code. JCXZ/JECXZ label
Object code. |11100011|--disp--|

JE/JZ: Jump if Equal or Jump if Zero

Operation. Used after a test of signed or unsigned data. If the ZF flag is 1 (zero condition), the instruction adds the operand offset to the IP and performs a jump. The jump must be short (−128 to 127 bytes), except for the 80386 and later, on which it may be near.
Flags. Affects none.
Source code. JE/JZ label
Object code. |01110100|--disp--|

JG/JNLE: Jump if Greater or Jump if Not Less/Equal

Operation. Used after a test of signed data. If the ZF flag is 0 (nonzero condition) and the SF flag equals the OF (both 0 or both 1), the instruction adds the operand offset to the IP and performs a jump. The jump must be short (−128 to 127 bytes), except for the 80386 and later, on which it may be near.
Flags. Affects none.
Source code. JG/JNLE label
Object code. |01111111|--disp--|

JGE/JNL: Jump if Greater/Equal or Jump if Not Less

Operation. Used after a test of signed data. If the SF flag equals the OF (both 0 or both 1), the instruction adds the operand offset to the IP and performs a jump. The jump must be short (−128 to 127 bytes), except for the 80386 and later, on which it may be near.
Flags. Affects none.
Source code. JGE/JNL label
Object code. |01111101|--disp--|

JL/JNGE: Jump if Less or Jump if Not Greater/Equal

Operation. Used after a test of signed data. If the SF flag is not equal to the OF, the instruction adds the operand offset to the IP and performs a jump. The jump must be short (−128 to 127 bytes), except for the 80386 and later, on which it may be near.
Flags. Affects none.
Source code. JL/JNGE label
Object code. |01111100|--disp--|

JLE/JNG: Jump if Less/Equal or Jump if Not Greater

Operation. Used after a test of signed data. If the ZF flag is 1 (zero condition) or if the SF flag is not equal to the OF, the instruction adds the operand offset to the IP and performs a jump. The jump must be short (−128 to 127 bytes), except for the 80386 and later, on which it may be near.
Flags. Affects none.
Source code. JLE/JNG label
Object code. |01111110|--disp--|

JMP: Unconditional Jump

Operation. Jumps to a designated address under any condition. A JMP address may be short (−128 to +127 bytes), near (within 32K), or far (to another segment). A short JMP replaces the IP with a destination offset address. A far jump (such as JMP FAR PTR label) replaces the CS:IP with a new segment address.
Flags. Affects none.
Source code. JMP {register/memory}
Object code. Five formats:

- Direct within seg short: |11101011|--disp---|
- Direct within segment: |11101001|disp-low |disp-high|
- Indirect within segment: |11111111|mod100r/m|
- Indirect intersegment: |11111111|mod101r/m|
- Direct intersegment: |11101010|offset-low|offset-high|seg-low seg-high|

JNC: Jump if No Carry

Operation. See JAE/JNB (identical operations).

JNE/JNZ: Jump if Not Equal or Jump if Not Zero

Operation. Used after a test of signed data. If the ZF flag is 0 (nonzero condition), the instruction adds the operand offset to the IP and performs a jump. The jump must be short (-128 to 127 bytes), except for the 80386 and later, on which it may be near.
Flags. Affects none.
Source code. JNE/JNZ label
Object code. |01110101|--disp--|

JNO: Jump if No Overflow

Operation. Jumps if an operation caused no overflow. If the OF flag is 0, the instruction adds the operand offset to the IP and performs a jump. The jump must be short (-128 to 127 bytes), except for the 80386 and later, on which it may be near. (See also JO.)
Flags. Affects none.
Source code. JNO label
Object code. |01110001|--disp--|

JNP/JPO: Jump if No Parity or Jump if Parity Odd

Operation. Jumps if an operation caused no (or odd) parity—that is, if an operation set an odd number of bits on in the low-order eight bits. If the PF flag is 0 (odd parity), the instruction adds the operand offset to the IP and performs a jump. The jump must be short (-128 to 127 bytes), except for the 80386 and later, on which it may be near. (See also JP/JPE.)
Flags. Affects none.
Source code. JNP/JPO label
Object code. |01111011|--disp--|

JNS: Jump if No Sign

Operation. Jumps if an operation set the sign to positive. If the SF flag is 0 (positive), JNS adds the operand offset to the IP and performs a jump. The jump must be short (-128 to 127 bytes), except for the 80386 and later, on which it may be near. (See also JS.)
Flags. Affects none.
Source code. JNS label
Object code. |01111001|--disp--|

JO: Jump if Overflow

Operation. Jumps if an operation caused an overflow. If the OF flag is 1 (overflow), JO adds the operand offset to the IP and performs a jump. The jump must be short (-128 to 127 bytes), except for the 80386 and later, on which it may be near. (See also JNO.)
Flags. Affects none.
Source code. JO label
Object code. |01110000|--disp--|

JP/JPE: Jump if Parity or Jump if Parity Even

Operation. Jumps if an operation caused even parity—that is, if an operation set an even number of bits on in the low-order eight bits. If the PF flag is 1 (even parity), the instruction adds the operand offset to the IP and performs a jump. The jump must be short (-128 to 127 bytes), except for the 80386 and later, on which it may be near. (See also JNP/JPO.)
Flags. Affects none.
Source code. JP/JPE label
Object code. `|01111010|--disp--|`

JS: Jump if Sign

Operation. Jumps if an operation set the sign to negative. If the SF flag is 1 (negative), JS adds the operand offset to the IP and performs the jump. The jump must be short (-128 to 127 bytes), except for the 80386 and later, on which it may be near. (See also JNS.)
Flags. Affects none.
Source code. JS label
Object code. `|01111000|--disp--|`

LAHF: Load AH from Flags

Operation. Loads the rightmost eight bits of the flags register into the AH. (See also SAHF.)
Flags. Affects none.
Source code. LAHF (no operand)
Object code. `10011111`

LDS/LES/LFS/LGS/LSS: Load Segment Register

Operation. Initializes a far address and offset of a data item so that succeeding instructions can access it. The first operand references any of the general, index, or pointer registers. The second operand references four bytes in memory containing an offset and a segment address. The operation loads the segment address in the segment register and the offset address in the first operand's register. For example, LDS means load data segment register. LFS, LGS, and LSS are supported by the 80386 and later.
Flags. Affects none.
Source code. LDS/LES/LFS/LGS/LSS register,memory
Object code.
```
LDS: |11000101|mod reg r/m|
LES: |11000100|mod reg r/m|
LFS: |00001111|10110100|mod reg r/m|
LGS: |00001111|10110101|mod reg r/m|
LSS: |00001111|10110010|mod reg r/m|
```

LEA: Load Effective Address

Operation. Loads a near (offset) address into a register.
Flags. Affects none.
Source code. LEA register,memory
Object code. `10001101`

LES/LFS/LGS: Load Extra Segment Register

Operation. See LDS.

LOCK: Lock Bus

Operation. Prevents 80x87 or other coprocessors from changing a data item at the same time as the processor. LOCK is a one-byte prefix that you may code immediately before any instruction. The operation sends a signal to the coprocessor to prevent it from using the data until the next instruction is completed.

Flags. Affects none.

Source code. LOCK instruction

Object code. 11110000

LODS/LODSB/LODSW/LODSD: Load Byte, Word, or Doubleword String

Operation. Loads the accumulator register with a value from memory. Although LODS is a string operation, it does not require a REP prefix. The DS:SI registers address a byte (if LODSB), word (if LODSW), or doubleword (if LODSD) and load it from memory into the AL, AX, or EAX, respectively. If the DF flag is 0, the operation adds 1 (if byte), 2 (if word), or 4 (if doubleword) to the SI; otherwise it subtracts 1, 2, or 4.

Flags. Affects none.

Source code. LODSB/LODSW/LODSD (no operand)

Object code. 1010110w

LOOP/LOOPW/LOOPD: Loop until Complete

Operation. Controls the execution of a routine a specified number of times. The CX should contain a count before starting the loop. LOOP appears at the end of the loop and decrements the CX by 1. If the CX is nonzero, LOOP transfers to its operand address, which points to the start of the loop (adds the offset in the IP); otherwise LOOP drops through to the next instruction. The offset must be a short jump.

For the 80386 and later, LOOP uses the CX in 16-bit mode and the ECX in 32-bit mode. LOOPW can specify the 16-bit CX, and LOOPD can specify the 32-bit ECX.

Flags. Affects none.

Source code. LOOP label

Object code. |11100010|--disp--|

LOOPE/LOOPZ: Loop while Equal or Loop while Zero

Operation. Controls the repetitive execution of a routine. LOOPE and LOOPZ are similar to LOOP, except that they transfer to the operand address if the CX is nonzero and the ZF flag is 1 (zero condition). (See also LOOPNE/LOOPNZ.)

For the 80386 and later, LOOPE and LOOPZ use the CX in 16-bit mode and the ECX in 32-bit mode. LOOPEW and LOOPZW can specify the 16-bit CX, and LOOPED and LOOPZD can specify the 32-bit ECX.

Flags. Affects none.
Source code. LOOPE/LOOPZ label
Object code. |11100001|--disp--|

LOOPNE/LOOPNZ: Loop while Not Equal or Loop while Not Zero

Operation. Controls the repetitive execution of a routine. LOOPNE and LOOPNZ are similar to LOOP, except that they transfer to the operand address if the CX is nonzero and the ZF flag is 0 (nonzero condition). (See also LOOPE/LOOPZ.)

For the 80386 and later, LOOPNE and LOOPNZ use the CX in 16-bit mode and the ECX in 32-bit mode. LOOPNEW and LOOPNZW can specify the 16-bit CX, and LOOPNED and LOOPNZD can specify the 32-bit ECX.

Flags. Affects none.
Source code. LOOPNE/LOOPNZ label
Object code. |11100000|--disp--|

LSS: Load Stack Segment Register

Operation. See LDS.

MOV: Move Data

Operation. Transfers data between two registers or between a register and memory, and transfers immediate data to a register or memory. The referenced data defines the number of bytes (1, 2, or 4) moved; the operands must agree in size. MOV cannot transfer between two memory locations (use MOVS), from immediate data to a segment register, or from a segment register to a segment register. (See also MOVSX/MOVZX.)

Flags. Affects none.
Source code. MOV {register/memory},{register/memory/immediate}
Object code. Seven formats:

- Reg/mem to/from reg: |100010dw|modregr/m|
- Immed to reg/mem: |1100011w|mod000r/m|---data---|data if w=1|
- Immed to register: |1011wreg|---data--|data if w=1|
- Mem to accumulator: |1010000w| addr-low| addr-high |
- Accumulator to mem: |1010001w| addr-low| addr-high |
- Reg/mem to seg reg: |10001110|mod0sgr/m| (sg = seg reg)
- Seg reg to reg/mem: |10001100|mod0sgr/m| (sg = seg reg)

MOVS/MOVSB/MOVSW/MOVSD: Move String

Operation. Moves data between memory locations. Normally used with the REP prefix and a length in the CX, MOVSB moves bytes, MOVSW moves words, and MOVSD (80386 and later) moves doublewords. The first operand is addressed by the ES:DI, the second by the DS:SI. If the DF flag is 0, the operation moves data from left to right into the first operand's destination and increments the DI and SI by 1, 2, or 4. If the DF is 1, the operation moves data from right to left and decrements the DI and SI. REP decrements the CX by 1 for each repetition. The operation terminates when the CX is decremented to 0; the DI and SI are advanced past the last byte moved.

Flags. Affects none.

Source code. [REP] MOVSB/MOVSW/MOVSD (no operand)

Object code. 1010010w

MOVSX/MOVZX: Move with Sign Extend or Zero Extend (80386 and later)

Operation. Copies an 8- or 16-bit source operand into a 16- or 32-bit destination operand. MOVSX fills the sign bit into leftmost bits, and MOVZX fills zero bits.

Flags. Affects none.

Source code. MOVSX/MOVZX {register/memory},{register/memory/ immediate}

Object code. MOVSX: |00001111|1011111w|modregr/m|

MOVZX: |00001111|1011011w|modregr/m|

MUL: Unsigned Multiply

Operation. Multiplies an unsigned multiplicand by an unsigned multiplier. MUL treats a leftmost 1-bit as a data bit, not a negative sign. (See also IMUL.) Here are the multiply operations for byte, word, and doubleword:

Size	Multiplicand (Operand 1)	Multiplier (Operand 2)	Product	Example
8-bit	AL	8 bit register/memory	AX	MUL BL
16-bit	AX	16-bit register/memory	DX:AX	MUL BX
32-bit	EAX	32-bit register/memory	EDX:EAX	MUL ECX

Flags. Affects CF and OF. (AF, PF, SF, and ZF are undefined.)

Source code. MUL {register/memory}

Object code. |1111011w|mod100r/m|

NEG: Negate

Operation. Reverses a binary value from positive to negative and from negative to positive. NEG provides the two's complement of the specified operand by subtracting the operand from zero and adding 1. Operands may be a byte, word, or doubleword (80386 and later) in a register or memory. (See also NOT.)

Flags. Affects AF, CF, OF, PF, SF, and ZF.

Source code. NEG {register/memory}

Object code. |1111011w|mod011r/m|

NOP: No Operation

Operation. Used to delete or insert machine code or to delay execution for purposes of timing. NOP simply performs a null operation by executing XCHG AX,AX.

Flags. Affects none.
Source code. NOP (no operand)
Object code. `10010000`

NOT: Logical NOT

Operation. Changes 0-bits to 1-bits and vice versa. The operand is a byte, word, or doubleword (80386 and later) in a register or memory. (See also NEG.)
Flags. Affects none.
Source code. NOT {register/memory}
Object code. `|1111011w|mod 010 r/m|`

OR: Logical OR

Operation. Performs a logical OR operation on bits of two operands. Both operands are bytes, words, or doublewords (80386 and later), which OR matches bit for bit. If either matched bit is 1, the bit in the first operand is set to 1; otherwise the bit is unchanged. (See also AND and XOR.)
Flags. Affects CF. (0), OF (0), PF, SF, and ZF. (AF is undefined.)
Source code. OR {register/memory},{register/memory/immediate}
Object code. Three formats:

- Reg/mem with register: `|000010dw|modregr/m|`
- Immed to accumulator: `|0000110w|---data--|data if w=1|`
- Immed to reg/mem: `|100000sw|mod001r/m|---data----|data if w=1|`

OUT: Output Byte or Word

Operation. Transfers a byte from the AL or a word from the AX to an output port. The port is a fixed numeric operand (as OUT port#,AX) or a variable in the DX (as OUT DX,AX). Use the DX if the port number is greater than 256. The 80286 and later processors also support an OUTS (Out String) instruction. (See also IN.)
Flags. Affects none.
Source code. OUT {portno/DX},{AL/AX}
Object code. Variable sort: `|1110111w|`
              Fixed port: `|1110011w|--port--|`

POP: Pop Word off Stack

Operation. Pops a word or doubleword (80386 and later) previously pushed on the stack to a specified destination—a memory location, general register, or segment register (except the CS—use RET for this). The SP points to the current (double)word at the top of the stack; POP transfers it to the specified destination and increments the SP by 2 or 4. (See also PUSH.)
Flags. Affects none.
Source code. POP {register/memory}
Object code. Three formats:

- Register: |01011reg|
- Segment reg: |000sg111| (sg implies segment reg)
- Reg/memory: |10001111|mod 000 r/m|

POPA: Pop All General Registers (80286 and later)

Operation. Pops the top eight words from the stack into the DI, SI, BP, SP, BX, DX, CX, and AX, in that order, and increments the SP by 16. Normally, a PUSHA has pushed the registers. For the 80386 and later, POPAD handles doublewords and increments the SP by 32. The SP value is discarded rather than loaded.
Flags. Affects none.
Source code. POPA/POPAD (no operand)
Object code. 0110 0001

POPF: Pop Flags off Stack

Operation. Pops the top word from the stack to the flags register and increments the SP by 2. Normally a PUSHF has pushed the flags. For the 80386 and later, POPFD handles doublewords and increments the SP by 4.
Flags. Affects all.
Source code. POPF/POPFD (no operand)
Object code. 10011101

PUSH: Push onto Stack

Operation. Pushes a word or doubleword (80386 and later) onto the stack for later use. The SP register points to the current (double)word at the top of the stack. PUSH decrements the SP by 2 or 4 and transfers a (double)word from the specified operand to the new top of the stack. The source may be a general register, segment register, or memory. (See also POP and PUSHF.)
Flags. Affects none.
Source code. PUSH {register/memory} (all processors)
PUSH immediate (80286 and later)
Object code. Three formats:

- Register: |01010reg|
- Segment reg: |000sg110| (sg implies segment reg)
- Reg/memory: |11111111|mod110r/m|

PUSHA: Push All General Registers (80286 and later)

Operation. Pushes the AX, CX, DX, BX, SP, BP, SI, and DI, in that order, onto the stack and decrements the SP by 16. For the 80386 and later, PUSHAD handles doublewords and decrements the SP by 32. Normally, a POPA later pops the registers.
Flags. Affects none.
Source code. PUSHA/PUSHAD (no operand)
Object code. 0110 0000

PUSHF: Push Flags onto Stack

Operation. Pushes the contents of the flags register onto the stack for later use. PUSHF decrements the SP by 2 and transfers the flags to the new top of the stack. For the 80386 and later, PUSHFD handles doublewords and decrements the SP by 4. (See also POPF and PUSH.)

Flags. Affects none.

Source code. PUSHF (no operand)

Object code. `10011100`

RCL/RCR: Rotate Left through Carry and Rotate Right through Carry

Operation. Rotates bits through the CF flag. The operation rotates bits left or right in a byte, word, or doubleword (80386 and later) in a register or memory. The operand may be an immediate constant or a reference to the CL. On the 8088/86, the constant may be only 1; a larger rotate must be in the CL. On later processors, the constant may be up to 31. For RCL, the leftmost bit enters the CF, and the CF bit enters bit 0 of the destination; all other bits rotate left. For RCR, bit 0 enters the CF, and the CF bit enters the leftmost bit of the destination; all other bits rotate right. (See also ROL and ROR.)

Flags. Affects CF and OF.

Source code. RCL/RCR {register/memory},{CL/immediate}

Object code. RCL: `|110100cw|mod010r/m|` (if c = 0, shift is 1;
          RCR: `|110100cw|mod011r/m|` if c = 1, shift is in CL)

REP: Repeat String

Operation. Repeats a string operation a specified number of times. REP is an optional repeat prefix coded before the string instructions MOVS and STOS (and before INS and OUTS). Load the CX with a count prior to execution. For each execution of the string instruction, REP decrements the CX by 1 and repeats the operation until the CX is 0. (See also REPE/REPZ/REPNE/REPNZ.)

Flags. See the associated string instructions.

Source code. REP string-instruction

Object code. `11110010`

REPE/REPZ/REPNE/REPNZ: Repeat String Conditionally

Operation. Repeats a string operation a specified number of times or until a condition is met. REPE, REPZ, REPNE, and REPNZ are optional repeat prefixes coded before the string instructions SCAS and CMPS. Load the CX with a count prior to execution. For REPE/REPZ (repeat while equal/zero), the operation repeats while the ZF is 1 (equal/zero condition) and the CX is not equal to zero. For REPNE/REPNZ (repeat while not equal/zero), the operation repeats while the ZF is 0 (unequal/nonzero condition) and the CX is not equal to zero. While the conditions are true, the operation decrements the CX by 1 and executes the string instructions.

Flags. See the associated string instruction.
Source code. REPE/REPZ/REPNE/REPNZ string-instruction
Object code. REPNE/REPNZ: 11110010
           REPE/REPZ: 11110011

RET/RETN/RETF: Return from a Procedure

Operation. Returns from a procedure previously entered by a near or far CALL. The assembler generates a near RET if it is within a procedure labeled NEAR and a far RET if it is within a procedure labeled FAR. For near, RET moves the word at the top of the stack to the IP and increments the SP by 2. For far, RET moves the words at the top of the stack to the IP and CS and increments the SP by 4. Any numeric operand (a pop value coded as RET 4) is added to the SP.

    RETN and RETF were introduced by MASM 5.0. You can code a near or far return explicitly and can code the procedure without PROC or ENDP directives. Use CALL NEAR/FAR PTR label to call the procedure.

Flags. Affects none.
Source code. RET/RETN/RETF [pop-value]
Object code. Four formats:

- Within a segment: |11000011|
- Within a segment with pop value: |11000010|data-low|data-high|
- Intersegment: |11001011|
- Intersegment with pop value: |11001010|data-low|data-high|

ROL/ROR: Rotate Left and Rotate Right

Operation. Rotates bits left or right in a byte, word, or doubleword (80386 and later) in a register or memory. The operand may be an immediate constant or a reference to the CL. On the 8088/86, the constant may be only 1; a larger rotate must be in the CL. On later processors, the constant may be up to 31. For ROL, the leftmost bit enters bit 0 of the destination; all other bits rotate left. For ROR, bit 0 enters the leftmost bit of the destination; all other bits rotate right. (See also RCL and RCR.) The rotated bit also enters the CF.

Flags. Affects CF and OF.
Source code. ROL/ROR {register/memory},{CL/immediate}
Object code. ROL: |110100cw|mod000r/m| (if c=0 count=1;
              ROR: |110100cw|mod001r/m| if c=1 count is in CL)

SAHF: Store AH Contents in Flags

Operation. Stores bits from the AH in the rightmost bits of the flags register. (See also LAHF.)
Flags. Affects AF, CF, PF, SF, and ZF.
Source code. SAHF (no operand)
Object code. 10011110

SAL/SAR: Shift Algebraic Left or Shift Algebraic Right

Operation. Shifts bits to the left or right in a byte, word, or doubleword in a register or memory. The operand may be an immediate constant or a reference to the CL. On the 8088/86, the constant may be only 1; a larger shift must be in the CL. On later processors, the constant may be up to 31.

SAL shifts bits to the left a specified number and fills 0 bits in vacated positions to the right. SAL acts exactly like SHL. SAR is an arithmetic shift that considers the sign of the referenced field. SAR shifts bits to the right a specified number and fills the sign bit (0 or 1) to the left. All bits shifted off are lost.

Flags. Affects CF, OF, PF, SF, and ZF. (AF is undefined.)

Source code. SAL/SAR {register/memory},{CL/immediate}

Object code. SAL: |110100cw|mod100r/m| (If c=0 count=1;
             SAR: |110100cw|mod111r/m| if c=1 count in CL)

SBB: Subtract with Borrow

Operation. Typically used in multiword binary subtraction to carry an overflowed 1-bit into the next stage of arithmetic. SBB first subtracts the contents of the CF from the first operand and then subtracts the second operand from the first, just like SUB. (See also ADC.)

Flags. Affects AF, CF, OF, PF, SF, and ZF.

Source code. SBB {register/memory},{register/memory/immediate}

Object code. Three formats:

- Reg/mem with register: |000110dw|modregr/m|
- Immed from accumulator: |0001110w|---data--|data if w=1|
- Immed from reg/mem: |100000sw|mod011r/m|---data---Zdata if sw501Z

SCAS/SCASB/SCASW/SCASD: Scan String

Operation. Scans a string in memory for a specified value. For SCASB load the value in the AL, for SCASW load it in the AX, and for SCASD load it in the EAX. The ES:DI pair references the string in memory that is to be scanned. The operations are normally used with a REPE/REPNE prefix, along with a count in the CX. If the DF flag is 0, the operation scans memory from left to right and increments the DI. If the DF is 1, the operation scans memory from right to left and decrements the DI. REPn decrements the CX for each repetition. The operation terminates on an equal (REPNE) or an unequal (REPE) condition or when the CX is decremented to 0. The *last* compare clears or sets flags, not the contents of the CX.

Flags. Affects AF, CF, OF, PF, SF, and ZF.

Source code. [REPnn] SCASB/SCASW/SCASD (no operand)

Object code. 1010111w

SETnn: Set Byte Conditionally (80386 and later)

Operation. Sets a specified byte based on a condition. This is a group of 30 instructions, including SET(N)E, SET(N)L, SET(N)C, and SET(N)S, that parallel conditional jumps.

If a tested condition is true, the operation sets the byte operand to 1, otherwise to 0. An example is

```
CMP  AX,BX    ;Compare contents of AX to BX

SETE CL       ;If equal, set CL to 1, else to 0
```

Flags. Affects none.
Source code. SETnn {register/memory}
Object code. |00001111|1001cond|mod000r/m|
                (cond varies according to condition tested)

SHL/SHR: Shift Logical Left or Shift Logical Right

Operation. Shifts bits left or right in a byte, word, or doubleword in a register or memory. The operand may be an immediate constant or a reference to the CL. On the 8088/86, the constant may be only 1; a larger shift must be in the CL. On later processors, the constant may be up to 31. SHL and SHR are logical shifts that treat the sign bit as a data bit.

SHL shifts bits to the left a specified number and fills 0 bits in vacated positions to the right. SHL acts exactly like SAL. SHR shifts bits to the right a specified number and fills 0 bits to the left. All bits shifted off are lost.

Flags. Affects CF, OF, PF, SF, and ZF. (AF is undefined.)
Source code. SHL/SHR {register/memory},{CL/immediate}
Object code. SHL: |110100cw|mod100r/m| (If c = 0, count = 1;
             SHR: |110100cw|mod101r/m| if c = 1, count in CL)

SHLD/SHRD: Shift Double Precision (80386 and later)

Operation. Shifts multiple bits into an operand. The instructions require three operands. The first operand is a 16-or 32-bit register or memory location containing the value to be shifted. The second is a register (same size as the first operand) containing the bits to be shifted into the first operand. The third operand is the CL or an immediate constant containing the shift value.
Flags. Affects CF, OF, PF, SF, and ZF. (AF is undefined.)
Source code. SHLD/SHRD {register/memory},register,{CL/immediate}
Object code. |00001111|10100100|modregr/m|

STC: Set Carry Flag

Operation. Sets the CF flag to 1. (See CLC for clear CF.)
Flags. Sets CF.
Source code. STC (no operand)
Object code. 11111001

STD: Set Direction Flag

Operation. Sets the DF flag to 1 to cause string operations such as MOVS to process from right to left. (See CLD for clear DF.)

Flags. Sets DF.
Source code. STD (no operand)
Object code. `11111101`

STI: Set Interrupt Flag

Operation. Sets the IF flag to 1 to enable maskable external interrupts after execution of the next instruction. (See CLI for clear IF.)
Flags. Sets IF.
Source code. STI (no operand)
Object code. `11111011`

STOS/STOSB/STOSW/STOSD: Store String

Operation. Stores the contents of the accumulator in memory. When used with a REP prefix along with a count in the CX, the operation duplicates a string value a specified number of times; this is suitable for such actions as clearing an area of memory. For STOSB load the value in the AL, for STOSW load the value in the AX, and for STOSD load the value in the EAX. The ES:DI pair references a location in memory where the value is to be stored. If the DF flag is 0, the operation stores in memory from left to right and increments the DI. If the DF is 1, the operation stores from right to left and decrements the DI. REP decrements the CX for each repetition and terminates when it becomes 0.
Flags. Affects none.
Source code. [REP] STOSB/STOSW/STOSD (no operand)
Object code. `1010101w`

SUB: Subtract Binary Values

Operation. Subtracts binary values in a register, memory, or immediate from a register, or subtracts values in a register or immediate from memory. Values may be byte, word, or doubleword (80386 and later). (See also SBB.)
Flags. Affects AF, CF, OF, PF, SF, and ZF.
Source code. SUB {register/memory},{register/memory/immediate}
Object code. Three formats:

- Reg/mem with register: `|001010dw|modregr/m|`
- Immed from accumulator: `|0010110w|---data--|data if w=1|`
- Immed from reg/mem: `|100000sw|mod101r/m|---data----|data if sw=01|`

TEST: Test Bits

Operation. Tests a field for a specific bit configuration such as AND, but does not change the destination operand. Both operands are bytes, words, or doublewords (80386 and later) in a register or memory; the second operand may be immediate. TEST uses AND logic to set flags, which you may test with JE or JNE.
Flags. Clears CF and OF and affects PF, SF, and ZF. (AF is undefined.)
Source code. TEST {register/memory},{register/memory/immediate}
Object code. Three formats:

- Reg/mem and register: `|1000010w|modregr/m|`
- Immed to accumulator: `|1010100w|---data--|data if w=1|`
- Immed to reg/mem: `|1111011w|mod000r/m|---data----|data if w=1|`

WAIT: Put Processor in Wait State

Operation. Allows the main processor to remain in a wait state until an external interrupt occurs, in order to synchronize it with a coprocessor. The main processor waits until the coprocessor finishes executing and resumes processing on receiving a signal in the TEST pin.

Flags. Affects none.

Source code. WAIT (no operand)

Object code. `10011011`

XCHG: Exchange

Operation. Exchanges data between two registers (as XCHG AH,BL) or between a register and memory (as XCHG CX,word).

Flags. Affects none.

Source code. XCHG {register/memory},{register/memory}

Object code. Two formats:

- Reg with accumulator: `|10010reg|`
- Reg/mem with reg: `|1000011w|mod reg r/m|`

XLAT/XLATB: Translate

Operation. Translates bytes into a different format, such as ASCII to EBCDIC. You define a table, load its address in the BX, and then load the AL with a value that is to be translated. The operation uses the AL value as an offset into the table, selects the byte from the table, and stores it in the AL. (XLATB is a synonym for XLAT.)

Flags. Affects none.

Source code. XLAT [AL] (AL operand is optional)

Object code. `11010111`

XOR: Exclusive OR

Operation. Performs a logical exclusive OR on bits of two operands. Both operands are bytes, words, or doublewords (80386 and later), which XOR matches bit for bit. If both matched bits are the same, the bit in the first operand is cleared to 0; if the matched bits are different the bit in the first operand is set to 1. (See also AND and OR.)

Flags. Affects CF (0), OF (0), PF, SF, and ZF. (AF is undefined.)

Source code. XOR {register/memory},{register/memory/immediate}

Object code. Three formats:

- Reg/mem with register: `|001100dw|mod reg r/m|`
- Immed to reg/mem: `|1000000w|mod 110 r/m|---data----|data if w=1|`
- Immed to accumulator: `|0011010w|---data----|data if w=1|`

APPENDIX A ———————————

Conversion between Hexadecimal and Decimal

This appendix provides the steps in converting between hexadecimal and decimal formats. The first section shows how to convert hex A7B8 to decimal 42,936, and the second section shows how to convert 42,936 back to hex A7B8.

CONVERTING HEXADECIMAL TO DECIMAL

To convert hex number A7B8 to a decimal number, start with the leftmost hex digit (A), continuously multiply each hex digit by 16, and accumulate the results. Since multiplication is in decimal, convert hex digits A through F to decimal 10 through 15. The steps proceed as follows:

First digit: A (10)	10
Multiply by 16	$\times$ 16
	160
Add next digit, 7	+ 7
	167
Multiply by 16	$\times$ 16
	2,672
Add next digit, B (11)	+ 11
	2,683

Multiply by 16	× 16
	42,928
Add next digit, 8	+ 8
Decimal value	42,936

You can also use a conversion table. For A7B8H, think of the rightmost digit (8) as position 1, the next digit to the left (B) as position 2, the next digit (7) as position 3, and the leftmost digit (A) as position 4. Refer to Table A–1, and locate the value for each hex digit:

For position 1 (8), column 1 =	8
For position 2 (B), column 2 =	176
For position 3 (7), column 3 =	1,792
For position 4 (A), column 4 =	40,960
Decimal value	42,936

CONVERTING DECIMAL TO HEXADECIMAL

To convert decimal number 42,936 to hexadecimal, first divide 42,936 by 16; the remainder becomes the rightmost hex digit, 6. Next divide the new quotient, 2,683, by 16; the remainder, 11 or B, becomes the next hex digit to the left. Develop the hex number from the remainders of each step of the division. Continue in this manner until the quotient is zero. The steps proceed as follows:

OPERATION	QUOTIENT	REMAINDER	HEX	
42,936/16	2,683	8	8	(rightmost)
2,683/16	167	11	B	
167/16	10	7	7	
10/16	0	1	A	(leftmost)

You can also use Table A–1 to convert decimal to hexadecimal. For decimal number 42,936, locate the number that is equal to or next smaller than it. Note the equivalent hex number and its position in the table. Subtract the decimal value of that hex digit from 42,936, and locate the difference in the table. The procedure works as follows:

	DECIMAL	HEX
Starting decimal value	42,936	
Subtract next smaller number	−40,960	A000
Difference	1,976	
Subtract next smaller number	−1,792	700
Difference	184	
Subtract next smaller number	−176	B0
Difference	8	8
Final hex number		A7B8

TABLE A-1 HEXADECIMAL-DECIMAL CONVERSION TABLE

Hex	Dec (8)	Dec (7)	Dec (6)	Dec (5)	Dec (4)	Dec (3)	Dec (2)	Dec (1)
0	0	0	0	0	0	0	0	0
1	268,435,456	16,777,216	1,048,576	65,536	4,096	256	16	1
2	536,870,912	33,554,432	2,097,152	131,072	8,192	512	32	2
3	805,306,368	50,331,648	3,145,728	196,608	12,288	768	48	3
4	1,073,741,824	67,108,864	4,194,304	262,144	16,384	1,024	64	4
5	1,342,177,280	83,886,080	5,242,880	327,680	20,480	1,280	80	5
6	1,610,612,736	100,663,296	6,291,456	393,216	24,576	1,536	96	6
7	1,879,048,192	117,440,512	7,340,032	458,752	28,672	1,792	112	7
8	2,147,483,648	134,217,728	8,388,608	524,288	32,768	2,048	128	8
9	2,415,919,104	150,994,944	9,437,184	589,824	36,864	2,304	144	9
A	2,684,354,560	167,772,160	10,485,760	655,360	40,960	2,560	160	10
B	2,952,790,016	184,549,376	11,534,336	720,896	45,056	2,816	176	11
C	3,221,225,472	201,326,592	12,582,912	786,432	49,152	3,072	192	12
D	3,489,660,928	218,103,808	13,631,488	851,968	53,248	3,328	208	13
E	3,758,096,384	234,881,024	14,680,064	917,504	57,344	3,584	224	14
F	4,026,531,840	251,658,240	15,728,640	983,040	61,440	3,840	240	15
	8	7	6	5	4	3	2	1

APPENDIX B

ASCII Character Codes

The term ASCII stands for "American Standard Code for Information Interchange." Table B–1 lists the representations of the entire 256 ASCII character codes (00H through FFH), along with their hexadecimal representations. The categories are:

00–1FH	Control codes for screens, printers, and data transmission, that are intended to cause an action.
20–7FH	Character codes for numbers, letters, and punctuation. Note that 20H is the standard space or blank.
80–FFH	Extended ASCII codes, foreign characters, Greek and mathematic symbols, and graphic characters for drawing boxes.

Here are the control codes from 00H through 1FH; those in parentheses do not print:

HEX	CHARACTER	HEX	CHARACTER	HEX	CHARACTER
00	(Null)	01	Happy face	02	Happy face
03	Heart	04	Diamond	05	Club
06	Spade	07	(Beep)	08	(Back space)
09	(Tab)	0A	(Line feed)	0B	(Vertical tab)
0C	(Form Feed)	0D	(Return)	0E	(Shift out)
0F	(Shift in)	10	(Data line esc)	11	(Dev ctl 1)
12	(Dev ctl 2)	13	(Dev ctl 3)	14	(Dev ctl 4)
15	(Neg acknowledge)	16	(Synch idle)	17	(End tran block)

18	(Cancel)	19	(End of medium)	1A	(Substitute)
1B	(Escape)	1C	(File separator)	1D	(Group separator)
1E	(Record separator)	1F	(Unit separator)		

00		20		40	@	60	`	80	Ç	A0	á	C0	└	E0	α
01	☺	21	!	41	A	61	a	81	ü	A1	í	C1	┴	E1	ß
02	☻	22	"	42	B	62	b	82	é	A2	ó	C2	┬	E2	Γ
03	♥	23	#	43	C	63	c	83	â	A3	ú	C3	├	E3	π
04	♦	24	$	44	D	64	d	84	ä	A4	ñ	C4	─	E4	Σ
05	♣	25	%	45	E	65	e	85	à	A5	Ñ	C5	┼	E5	σ
06	♠	26	&	46	F	66	f	86	å	A6	ª	C6	╞	E6	µ
07		27	'	47	G	67	g	87	ç	A7	°	C7	╟	E7	τ
08		28	(	48	H	68	h	88	ê	A8	¿	C8	╚	E8	Φ
09		29	)	49	I	69	i	89	ë	A9	⌐	C9	╔	E9	Θ
0A		2A	*	4A	J	6A	j	8A	è	AA	¬	CA	╩	EA	Ω
0B		2B	+	4B	K	6B	k	8B	ï	AB	½	CB	╦	EB	δ
0C		2C	,	4C	L	6C	l	8C	î	AC	¼	CC	╠	EC	∞
0D		2D	-	4D	M	6D	m	8D	ì	AD	¡	CD	═	ED	φ
0E		2E	.	4E	N	6E	n	8E	Ä	AE	«	CE	╬	EE	ε
0F		2F	/	4F	O	6F	o	8F	Å	AF	»	CF	╧	EF	∩
10	►	30	0	50	P	70	p	90	É	B0	░	D0	╨	F0	≡
11	◄	31	1	51	Q	71	q	91	æ	B1	▒	D1	╤	F1	±
12	↕	32	2	52	R	72	r	92	Æ	B2	▓	D2	╥	F2	≥
13	‼	33	3	53	S	73	s	93	ô	B3	│	D3	╙	F3	≤
14	¶	34	4	54	T	74	t	94	ö	B4	┤	D4	╘	F4	⌠
15	§	35	5	55	U	75	u	95	ò	B5	╡	D5	╒	F5	⌡
16	▬	36	6	56	V	76	v	96	û	B6	╢	D6	╓	F6	÷
17	↨	37	7	57	W	77	w	97	ù	B7	╖	D7	╫	F7	≈
18	↑	38	8	58	X	78	x	98	ÿ	B8	╕	D8	╪	F8	°
19	↓	39	9	59	Y	79	y	99	Ö	B9	╣	D9	┘	F9	·
1A		3A	:	5A	Z	7A	z	9A	Ü	BA	║	DA	┌	FA	·
1B		3B	;	5B	[	7B	{	9B	¢	BB	╗	DB	█	FB	√
1C	∟	3C	<	5C	\	7C	|	9C	£	BC	╝	DC	▄	FC	^{n}
1D	↔	3D	=	5D	]	7D	}	9D	¥	BD	╜	DD	▌	FD	^{2}
1E	▲	3E	>	5E	^	7E	~	9E	₧	BE	╛	DE	▐	FE	■
1F		3F	?	5F	_	7F	⌂	9F	ƒ	BF	┐	DF	▀	FF	

TABLE B-1 ASCII CHARACTER SET

APPENDIX C

Reserved Words

The assembler recognizes some words as having a specific meaning; you may use these words only under prescribed conditions. Words that the assembler reserves may be classed into four categories:

- Register names, such as AX and AH
- Symbolic instructions, such as ADD and MOV
- Directives (commands to the assembler), such as PROC and END
- Operators, such as DUP and SEG.

If used to define a data item, many of the reserved words that follow may confuse the assembler or cause an assembly error.

Register Names

AH, AL, AX, BH, BL, BP, BX, CH, CL, CS, CX, DH, DI, DI, DL, DS, DX, EAX, EBP, EBX, ECX, EDI, EDX, EIP, ES, ES, ESI, FS, GS, IP, SI, SP, SS

Symbolic Instructions

AAA, AAD, AAM, AAS, ADC, ADD, AND, ARPL, BOUND, BSF, BSR, BTn, CALL, CBW, CDQ, CLC, CLD, CLI, CLTS, CMC, CMP, CMPSn, CWDn, DAA, DAS, DEC, DIV, ENTER, ESC, IILT, IDIV, IMUL, IN, INC, INSw, INT, INTO, IRET, JA, JAE, JB,

JBE, JCXZ, JE, JECXZ, JG, JGE, JL, JLE, JMP, JNA, JNAE, JNB, JNBE, JNE, JNG, JNGE, JNL, JNLE, JNO, JNP, JNS, JNZ, JO, JP, JPE, JPO, JS, JZ, LAHF, LAR, LDS, LEA, LEAVE, LES, LFS, LGDT, LGS, LIDT, LLDT, LMSW, LOCK, LODSn, LOOP, LOOPE, LOOPNE, LOOPNZ, LOOPZ, LSL, LSS, LSS, LTR, MOV, MOVSn, MOVSX, MOVZX, MUL, NEG, NOP, NOT, OR, OUTn, POP, POPA, POPAD, POPF, POPFD, PUSH, PUSHAD, PUSHF, PUSHFD, RCL, RCR, REN, REP, REPE, REPNE, REPNZ, REPZ, RET, RETF, ROL, ROR, SAHF, SAL, SAR, SBB, SCASn, SETnn, SGDT, SHL, SHLD, SHR, SHRD, SIDT, SLDT, SMSW, STC, STD, STI, STOSn, STR, SUB, TEST, VERR, VERRW, WAIT, XCHG, XLAT, XOR

Directives

ALIGN, .ALPHA, ASSUME, .CODE, COMM, COMMENT, .CONST, .CREF, .DATA, .DATA?, DB, DD, DF, DOSSEG, DQ, DT, DW, ELSE, END, ENDIF, ENDM, ENDP, ENDS, EQU, .ERRnn, EVEN, EXITM, EXTRN, .FARDATA, .FARDATA?, GROUP, IF, IF1, IF2, IFB, IFDEF, IFDIF, IFE, IFIDN, IFNB, IFNDEF, INCLUDE, INCLUDELIB, IRP, IRPC, LABEL, .LALL, .LFCOND, .LIST, LOCAL, MACRO, .MODEL, NAME, ORG, OUT, PAGE, PROC, PUBLIC, PURGE, .RADIX, RECORD, REPT, .SALL, SEGMENT, .SEQ, .SFCOND, .STACK, STRUC, SUBTTL, .TFCOND, TITLE, .XALL, .XCREF, .XLIST

Operators

AND, BYTE, COMMENT, CON, DUP, EQ, FAR, GE, GT, HIGH, LE, LENGTH, LINE, LOW, LT, MASK, MOD, NE, NEAR, NOT, NOTHING, OFFSET, OR, PTR, SEG, SHL, SHORT, SHR, SIZE, STACK, THIS, TYPE, WHILE, WIDTH, WORD, XOR

APPENDIX D

Assembler and Link Options

This appendix covers the rules for assembling, linking, generating cross-reference files, and converting .EXE programs to .COM. The Microsoft assembler version is MASM, Borland's is TASM, and SLR System's is OPTASM, all of which are similar. Since version 6.0, the Microsoft assembler uses the ML command, which can perform an assembly and link in one command. Examples in this appendix use disk drive D; users of other drives can substitute the appropriate letter and path.

ASSEMBLING A PROGRAM

You can use a command line to request an assembly, although MASM also provides for prompts.

Assembling with a Command Line

The general format for using a command line to assemble is

```
MASM/TASM [options] source[,object][,listing][,crossref]
```

- Options are explained later.
- Source identifies the source program. The assembler assumes the extension .ASM, so you need not enter it. You may also key in the disk drive or path (or both.)

- Object provides for a generated OBJ file. The drive or path and the filename may be the same as or different from the source.
- Listing provides for a generated .LST file that contains the source and object code. The drive or path and the filename may be the same as or different from the source.
- Crossref provides for a generated file containing symbols for a cross-reference listing. The extension is .CRF for MASM and .XRF for TASM. The drive or path and the filename may be the same or different.

This example spells out all the files:

```
MASM D:name.ASM,D:name.OBJ,D:name.LST,D:name.CRF
```

The following shortcut command allows for defaults for the object, listing, and cross-reference files, all with the same name:

```
MASM D:filename,D:,D:,D:
```

This next example requests a cross-reference, but no listing, file:

```
MASM D:filename,D:,,D:
```

Assembling with Prompts

You can also key in just the name of the assembler with no command line, although TASM and MASM (through version 5.1) respond differently. TASM displays the general format for the command line and an explanation of the options, whereas MASM displays a list of prompts to which you are to reply:

```
Source filename [.ASM]:

Object filename [source.OBJ]:

Source listing  [NUL.LST]:

Cross-reference [NUL.CRF]:
```

- Source filename identifies the name of the source file. Key in the drive or path (if it's not the default) and the name of the source file, without the extension ASM.
- Object filename provides for the object file. The prompt assumes the same filename, although you could change it. To get an object file on drive D, type D: and press Enter.
- Source listing provides for an assembler listing, although the prompt assumes that you do not want one. To get a listing on drive D, type D: and press Enter.
- Cross-reference provides for a cross-reference listing, although the prompt assumes that you do not want one. To get one on drive D, type D: and press Enter.

For the last three prompts, just press Enter if you want to accept the default.

Assembler Options

Assembler options for MASM, TASM, and OPTASM include the following:

/A	Arrange source segments in alphabetic sequence.
/C	Create a cross-reference file.
/D	MASM: Produce listing files on both pass 1 and pass 2 to locate phase errors. For TASM, /Dsymbol means define a symbol.
/E	Accept 80x87 coprocessor instructions and generate a linkage to BASIC, C, or FORTRAN for emulated floating-point instructions.
/H	Display assembler options with a brief explanation. Enter /H (for help) with no filenames or other options.
/L	Create a normal listing file.
/ML	Make all names case sensitive.
/MU	Convert all names to uppercase.
/MX	Make public and external names case sensitive.
/N	Suppress generation of the symbol table.
/R	Provide real math coprocessor support.
/S	Leave source segments in original sequence.
/T	(Terse) Display diagnostics at the end of the assembly only if an error is encountered.
/V	(Verbose) At the end of the assembly, display the number of lines and symbols processed. (Not with OPTASM.)
/Wn	Set the level of warning messages: 0 = display only severe errors; 1 = display severe errors and serious warnings (the default); 2 = display severe errors, serious warnings, and advisory warnings.
/Z	Display source lines on the screen for errors.
/ZD	Include information on line numbers in the object file for CodeView, Turbo-Debugger, or SYMDEB.
/ZI	Include information on line-numbers and symbolic information in the object file for CodeView, TurboDebugger, or SYMDEB.

You may request options in either prompt or command-line mode. For prompts, you could code MASM/A/V [Enter], for example, and then key in the usual filename. Or you may key in options in any prompt line—for example, as

```
source filename [.ASM]: /A/V filename or filename /A/V [Enter]
```

The /A/V options tell the assembler to write segments in alphabetic sequence and to display additional diagnostics at the end of the assembly.

Additional Turbo Assembler Features

Turbo Assembler lets you assemble multiple files, each with its own options, in one command line. You can also use DOS wild cards (* and ?). To assemble all source programs in the current directory, key in TASM *. To assemble all source programs named

PROG1.ASM, PROG2.ASM, and so on, key in TASM PROG?. You can key in groups (or sets) of filenames, with each group separated by a semicolon. The following command assembles PROGA and PROGB with the /C option and PROGC with the /A option:

```
TASM /C PROGA PROGB; /A PROGC
```

Microsoft Version 6.x

The command line for Microsoft assemblers since version 6.0 is

```
ML [options] filenames [[options] filenames] ... [/link options]
```

The assembler allows you to assemble any number of programs into one executable module. One useful option is ML -?, which displays the complete command-line syntax and options.

Tables

Following an assembler .LST listing are a segments and groups table and a symbols table.

Segment and Group Table.   This table has the following heading:

```
Name          Length     Align  Combine    Class
```

The *name* column gives the names of all segments and groups, in alphabetic sequence. The *length* column give the size, in hex, of each segment. The *align* column gives the alignment type, such as BYTE, WORD, or PARA. *Combine* lists the defined combine type, such as STACK for a stack, NONE where no type is coded, PUBLIC for external definitions, or a hex address for AT types. The *class* column lists the segment class names, as coded in the SEGMENT statement.

Symbol Table.   A symbol table has the following heading:

```
Name          Type       Value      Attribute
```

The *name* column lists the names of all defined items, in alphabetic sequence. The *type* column gives the type, as follows:

- L NEAR or L FAR: A near or far label
- N PROC or F PROC: A near or far procedure
- BYTE, WORD, DWORD, FWORD, QWORD, TBYTE: A data item
- ALIAS: An alias (or nickname) for another symbol
- NUMBER: An absolute label
- OPCODE: An equate for an instruction operand
- TEXT: An equate for text

The *value* column gives the hex offset from the beginning of a segment for names, labels, and procedures. The *attribute* column lists a symbol's attributes, including its segment and length.

CROSS-REFERENCE FILE

A .CRF or .XRF file is used to produce a cross-reference listing of a program's labels, symbols, and variables, However, you have to use CREF for Microsoft or TCREF for Borland to convert the listing to a sorted cross-reference file. You can key in CREF or TCREF with a command line or use prompts.

Using a Command Line

The general format for using a command line is

```
CREF/TCREF xreffile,reffile
```

The command line contains references to the original cross-reference file (.CRF or .XRF) and to a generated .REF file. The following example using CREF writes a cross-reference file named ASMPROG.REF on drive D:

```
CREF/TCREF D:ASMPROG,D:
```

Using Prompts

You can key in just CREF or TCREF with no command line. TCREF simply displays the general format for the command and an explanation of its options, whereas CREF displays these prompts:

```
Cref filename [.CRF]:

List filename [cross-ref REF]·
```

For the first prompt, key in the name of the file, without a .CRF extension. For the second prompt, you can key in the drive and/or path only and accept the default file name.

LINKING A PROGRAM

Microsoft's linker is LINK, and Borland's is TLINK. LINK and TLINK accept a command line to request linking; LINK also provides for prompts.

Linking with a Command Line

The general format for using a command line to link is

```
LINK/TLINK [options] objfile,exefile[,mapfile][,libraryfile]
```

- Options are described later.
- Objfile identifies the object file generated by the assembler. The linker assumes the extension .OBJ, so you need not enter it. You can also key in the drive or path.
- Exefile provides for generating an .EXE file. The filename and drive or path may be the same as or different from the source.

- Mapfile provides for generating a file with an extension .MAP that indicates the relative location and the size of each segment and any errors that LINK has found. A typical error is the failure to define a stack segment. Entering CON tells the linker to display the map on the screen (instead of writing it on disk) so that you can view it immediately for errors.
- Libraryfile provides for the libraries option.

To link more than one object file into an executable module, combine them in one line like this:

```
LINK D:PROGA+D:PROGB+D:PROGC
```

Linking Using Prompts

You can key in just the name of the linker with no command line, although TLINK and LINK respond differently. TLINK displays the general format for the command and an explanation of options, whereas LINK displays a list of prompts. Here are the LINK prompts to which you are to reply:

```
Object Modules [.OBJ]:

Run File [EXASM1.EXE]:

List File [NUL.MAP]:

Libraries [.LIB]:
```

- Object Modules asks for the name(s) of the object module(s) to be linked; it defaults to .OBJ if you omit the extension.
- Run File requests the name of the file that is to execute and allows a default to the object module filename. You just need to key in the drive and/or path.
- List File provides for the map file, although the default is NUL.MAP (that is, no map). The reply CON tells the linker to display the map on the screen, a convenient choice.
- Libraries asks for the library option, which is outside the scope of this text.

For the last three prompts, just press Enter to accept the default. The following example tells the linker to produce .EXE and .CON files:

```
Object Modules [.OBJ]: D:ASMPROG [Enter]

Run File [ASMPROG.EXE]: D: [Enter]

List File [NUL.MAP]: CON [Enter]

Libraries [.LIB]: [Enter]
```

Debugging Options

If you intend to use CodeView, TurboDebugger, or SYMDEB, use the assembler's /ZI option for assembling. For linking, use DOS LINK's /CO option, in either command-line or prompt mode, or Turbo TLINK's /V option:

```
LINK /CO filename ...

TLINK /V filename ...
```

Converting Turbo Object Files to .COM Programs

Borland's TLINK allows you to convert an object program directly to .COM format, provided that the source program was originally coded according to .COM requirements. Use the /T option:

```
TLINK /T objfile,comfile,CON
```

CROSS-REFERENCE LISTING

The assembler generates an optional .CRF or .XRF file that you can use to produce a cross-reference listing of a program's labels, symbols, and variables. The program that performs this function is CREF for Microsoft or TCREF for Borland. You can key in CREF or TCREF with a command line or by means of prompts.

Use of a Command Line

```
CREF/TCREF d:xreffile,d:reffile
```

- Xreffile identifies the cross-reference file generated by the assembler. The program assumes the extension, so you need not enter it.
- Reffile provides for generating a .REF file. The drive, subdirectory, and filename may be the same as or different from those of the source.

Use of a Prompt

You can key in TCREF or CREF with no command line, although they respond differently. TCREF displays the general format for the command and an explanation of options, whereas CREF displays prompts. Here are the CREF prompts to which you reply:

```
Cross-reference [.CRF]:

Listing [filename.REF]:
```

For the first prompt, key in the name of the .CRF file, such as D:EXASM1. For the second prompt, you can key in drive number only and accept the default file name. This choice causes CREF to write a cross-reference file named EXASM1.REF on drive D.

EXE2BIN OPTIONS

The DOS EXE2BIN program converts .EXE modules generated by MASM into .COM modules, provided that the source program was originally coded according to .COM requirements. Enter the following command:

```
EXE2BIN D:filename D:filename.COM
```

The first operand is the name of the .EXE file, which you key in without an extension. The second operand is the name of the .COM file; you may change the name, but be sure to code a .COM extension. Delete the .OBJ and .EXE files

APPENDIX E ————————————

The DOS Debug Program

The DEBUG program on the DOS disk is useful for writing very small programs, for debugging assembly language programs, and for examining the contents of a file or memory. You may enter one of two commands to start DEBUG:

1. To create a file or examine memory, key in DEBUG with no filespec.
2. To modify or debug a program (.COM or .EXE) or to modify a file, key in DEBUG with a filespec, such as DEBUG D:PROGC.COM.

DOS loads DEBUG into memory, and DEBUG displays a hyphen (-) as a prompt. The memory area for your program is known as a *program segment*. The CS, DS, ES, and SS registers are initialized with the address of the program segment prefix (PSP), and your work area begins at PSP + 100H.

A reference to a memory address may be in terms of a segment and offset, such as DS:120, or an offset only, such as 120. You may also make direct references to memory addresses, such as 40:417, where 40[0]H is the segment and 417H is the offset. DEBUG assumes that all numbers entered are hexadecimal, so you do not key in the trailing H. The F1 and F3 keys work for DEBUG just as they do for DOS; that is, F1 duplicates the previous command one key at a time, and F3 duplicates the entire previous command. Also, DEBUG does not distinguish between uppercase and lowercase letters.

Following is a description of each DEBUG command, in alphabetic sequence.

A (Assemble).   Translates assembly source statements into machine code. The operation is especially useful for writing small assembly language programs and for examining small segments of code. The default starting address for code is CS:0100H, and the general format for the command is

```
A [address]
```

The following example creates an assembly language program consisting of five statements. You code the assembly statements (but not the comments); on the left, DEBUG generates the code segment (shown here as xxxx:) and an offset beginning at 0100H:

```
           A (or A 100) [Enter]        Explanation

xxxx:0100  MOV CX,[10D] [Enter]        Get contents at 10D

xxxx:0104  ADD CX,1A [Enter]           Add immediate value

xxxx:0107  MOV [10D],CX [Enter]        Store CX in 10D

xxxx:010B  JMP 100 [Enter]             Jump back to start

xxxx:010D  DW 2500 [Enter]             Define constant

           [Enter]                     End of command
```

Since DEBUG sets the IP to 100H because of the size of the PSP, the statements begin at 100H. The last Enter key (that's two in a row) tells DEBUG to end the program. You can now use the U (unassemble) command to see the machine code and the T (trace) command to execute it.

You may change any of the preceding instructions, provided that the length of the new instruction is the same as that of the old one. For example, to change the ADD at 104H to SUB, enter

```
           A 104 [Enter]

xxxx:0104  SUB CX,1A [Enter] [Enter]
```

When you reexecute the program, the IP is still incremented. Use the register (R) command to reset it to 100H. Use Q to quit.

Note that you can use DB and DW to define data items.

C (Compare).   Compares the contents of two blocks of memory. The default register is the DS, and the general format is

```
C [range] [address]
```

You may code the command one of two ways: (1) a starting address (compare from), a length, and a starting address (compare to); or (2) a starting address and an ending address (compare from) and a starting address (compare to). These examples compare bytes beginning at DS:050 to bytes beginning at DS:300:

```
C 050 L30 300    Compare using a length of 30H

C 050 080 300    Compare using a range
```

The operation displays the addresses and contents of unequal bytes.

D (Display or Dump).   Displays the contents of a portion of memory in hex and ASCII. The default register is the DS, and the general format is

```
                 D [address] or D [range]
```

You may specify a starting address or a starting address with a range. Omission of a range or length causes a default to 80H. Examples of the D command sre:

```
D 200       Display 80H bytes beginning at DS:200H

D           Display 80H bytes beginning from last display

D CS:150    Display 80H bytes beginning at CS:150H

D DS:20 L5  Display 5 bytes beginning at DS:20H

D 300 32C   Display the bytes from 300H through 32CH
```

E (Enter).   Enters data or machine instructions. The default register is the DS, and the general format is

```
                 E address [list]
```

The operation allows two options: to replace bytes with those in a list or to provide sequential editing of bytes. Examples of the first option follow:

```
E 105 13 3A 21     Enter three bytes beginning at DS:105H

E CS:211 21 2A     Enter two bytes beginning at CS:211H

E 110 'anything'   Enter a character string beginning at DS:110H
```

For the second option, key in the address that you want displayed:

```
E 12C              Show contents of DS:12CH
```

The operation waits for your input. Enter one or more bytes of hex values, separated by a space, beginning at DS:12CH. Character strings accept either single or double quotes.

F (Fill).   Fills a range of memory locations with values in a list. The default register is the DS. The general format is

```
                 F range list
```

These examples fill locations in memory beginning at DS:214H with bytes containing repetitions of 'SAM':

```
F 214 L21 'SAM'    Use a length of 21H

F 214 234 'SAM'    Use a range, 214H through 234H
```

G (Go).   Executes a machine language program that you are debugging through to a specified breakpoint. Be sure to examine the machine code listing for valid IP addresses, because an invalid address may cause unpredictable results. Also, set break points only in your own program, not in DOS or BIOS. The operation executes through interrupts and pauses, if necessary, to wait for keyboard input. The default register is the CS. The general format is

```
G [=address] address [address ...]
```

The entry =address provides an optional starting address. The other entries provide up to 10 break-point addresses. The following example tells DEBUG to execute through location 11A:

```
G 11A
```

H (Hexadecimal).   Shows the sum and difference of two hex values, coded as H value value. The maximum length is four hex digits. For example, H 14F 22 displays the result 171 (sum) and 12D (difference).

I (Input).   Inputs and displays one byte from a port. Code this as I portaddress.

L (Load).   Loads a file or disk sectors into memory. There are two general formats:

1. Load a named file:

```
L [address]
```

Use the address parameter to cause L to load beginning at a specific location. Omission of the address causes L to load at CS:100. To load a file, note that it should be already named (see N):

```
N filespec    Name the file

L             Load the file at CS:100H
```

To reload a file, simply issue L with no address.

2. Load data from sectors:

```
L [address [drive start number]]
```

- Address provides the memory location for loading the data. (The default is CS:100.)
- Drive identifies the disk drive, where 0 = A, 1 = B, etc.
- Start specifies the hex number of the first sector to load. (This is a relative number, where cylinder 0, track 0, sector 1, is relative sector 0.)
- Number gives the hex number of consecutive sectors to load.

The following example loads beginning at CS:100 from drive 0 (A), starting at sector 20H for 15H sectors:

```
L 100 0 20 15
```

The L operation returns to the BX:CX the number of bytes loaded. For an .EXE file, DEBUG ignores the address parameter (if any) and uses the load address in the .EXE header. It also strips off the header; to preserve it, first rename the file with a different extension.

M (Move).   Moves (or copies) the contents of memory locations. The default register is the DS, and the general format is

```
M range address
```

These examples copy the bytes beginning at DS:050H through 150H into the address beginning at DS:400H:

```
M DS:50 L100 DS:400      Use a length

M DS:50 150 DS:400       Use a range
```

N (Name).   Names a program or a file that you intend to read from or write onto disk. Code the command as N filespec, such as

```
N D:SAM.COM
```

The operation sets the name at CS:80 in the PSP. The first byte at CS:80 contains the length (0AH), followed by the space and the filespec. You may then use L (Load) or W (Write) to read or write the file.

O (Output).   Sends a byte to a port. Code this as O portaddress byte.

P (Proceed).   Executes a subroutine call (CALL), loop (LOOP), interrupt (INT), or repeat string instruction (REP) through to the next instruction. The general format is

```
P [=address] [value]
```

where =address is an optional starting address and value is an optional number of instructions to proceed through. Omission of =address causes a default to the CS:IP register pair. For example, if your trace of execution is at an INT 21H operation, just key in P to execute through that operation.

Q (Quit).   Exits DEBUG. The operation does not save files; use W for that purpose.

R (Register).   Displays the contents of registers and the next instruction. The general format is

```
R [registername]
```

The following examples illustrate the use of this command:

R	Displays all registers
R DX	Displays the DX. DEBUG gives you an option:

    1. Press Enter; no change occurs to the contents of the DX.

    2. Enter one to four hex characters to change the contents of the DX.

R IP	Displays the IP. You key in another value to change its contents.
R F	Displays the current setting of each flag as a two-letter code. You can change any number of flags, in any sequence:

FLAG	SET	CLEAR
overflow	ov	nv
direction	dn	up
sign	ng ($-$)	pl ($+$)
zero	zr	nz
carry	cy	nc

S (Search). Searches memory for characters in a list. The default register is the DS, and the general format is

```
S range list
```

If the characters are found, the operation delivers their addresses; otherwise it does not respond. The following example searches for the word "VIRUS" beginning at DS:300 for 2000H bytes:

```
S 300 L 2000 "VIRUS"
```

This example searches from CS:100 through CS:400 for a byte containing 51H:

```
S CS:100 400 51
```

T (Trace). Executes a program in single-step mode. Note that you should normally use P (Proceed) to trace through INT instructions. The default register is the CS:IP pair, and the general format is

```
T [=address] [value]
```

The optional entry =address tells DEBUG where to begin the trace, and the optional value gives the number of instructions to trace. Omission of the operands causes DEBUG to execute the next instruction and to display the registers. Here are two examples:

```
T           Executes the next instruction
                              •
T 10        Executes the next 16 (10H) instructions
```

U (Unassemble). Unassembles machine instructions. The default register is the CS:IP pair, and the general format is

```
U [address] or U [range]
```

The area specified should contain valid machine code, which the operation displays as symbolic instructions. Here are three examples:

```
U 0100          Unassemble 32 bytes beginning at CS:100

U               Unassemble 32 bytes since last U, if any

U 100 140       Unassemble from 100H through 140H
```

Note that DEBUG does not properly translate some conditional jump instructions, although they still execute correctly.

W (Write).   Writes a file from DEBUG. The file should first be named if it wasn't already loaded. The default register is the CS, and the general format is

```
W [address [drive start-sector number-of-sectors]]
```

Write program files only with a .COM extension, since W does not support the .EXE format. (To modify an .EXE program, you may change the extension temporarily.) The following example uses W with no operands and has to set the size of the file in the BX:CX pair (first ensure that the BX is zero):

```
N filespec      Name the file

R CX            Request CX register

length          Insert file size

W               Write the file
```

If you modify a file and make no change to its length or name, DEBUG can still correctly write the file back to its original disk location. You may also write the file directly to disk sectors, although this practice requires considerable care.

See the DOS manual for these commands:

- XA: Allocate expanded memory.
- XD: Deallocate expanded memory.
- XM: Map logical pages onto physical pages.
- XS: Display expanded memory status.

APPENDIX F

Keyboard scan codes and ASCII Codes

In the following lists, keys are grouped rather arbitrarily into categories. For each category, the columns show the format for a normal key (not combined with another key) and the formats when the key is combined with the Shift, Ctrl, and Alt keys. Under the columns headed "Normal," "Shift," "Ctrl," and "Alt" are two hex bytes as they appear when a keyboard operation delivers them to the AH and AL registers. For example, pressing the letter "a" the normal delivers 1EH in the AH for the scan code and 61H in the AL for the ASCII character. When shifted to uppercase ("A"), the letter delivers 1EH and 41H, respectively. Scan codes 85H and higher are for the enhanced 101-key keyboard.

LETTERS	NORMAL		SHIFT		CTRL		ALT	
a and A	1E	61	1E	41	1E	01	1E	00
b and B	30	62	30	42	30	02	30	00
c and C	2E	63	2E	43	2E	03	2E	00
d and D	20	64	20	44	20	04	20	00
e and E	12	65	12	45	12	05	12	00
f and F	21	66	21	46	21	06	21	00
g and G	22	67	22	47	22	07	22	00
h and H	23	68	23	48	23	08	23	00
i and I	17	69	17	49	17	09	17	00
j and J	24	6A	24	4A	24	0A	24	00

	NORMAL		SHIFT		CTRL		ALT	
k and K	25	6B	25	4B	25	0B	25	00
l and L	26	6C	26	4C	26	0C	26	00
m and M	32	6D	32	4D	32	0D	32	00
n and N	31	6E	31	4E	31	0E	31	00
o and O	18	6F	18	4F	18	0F	18	00
p and P	19	70	19	50	19	10	19	00
q and Q	10	71	10	51	10	11	10	00
r and R	13	72	13	52	13	12	13	00
s and S	1F	73	1F	53	1F	13	1F	00
t and T	14	74	14	54	14	14	14	00
u and U	16	75	16	55	16	15	16	00
v and V	2F	76	2F	56	2F	16	2F	00
w and W	11	77	11	57	11	17	11	00
x and X	2D	78	2D	58	2D	18	2D	00
y and Y	15	79	15	59	15	19	15	00
z and Z	2C	7A	2C	5C	2C	1A	2C	00
Spacebar	39	20	39	20	39	20	39	20

FUNCTION KEYS	NORMAL		SHIFT		CTRL		ALT	
F1	3B	00	54	00	5E	00	68	00
F2	3C	00	55	00	5F	00	69	00
F3	3D	00	56	00	60	00	6A	00
F4	3E	00	57	00	61	00	6B	00
F5	3F	00	58	00	62	00	6C	00
F6	40	00	59	00	63	00	6D	00
F7	41	00	5A	00	64	00	6E	00
F8	42	00	5B	00	65	00	6F	00
F9	43	00	5C	00	66	00	70	00
F10	44	00	5D	00	67	00	71	00
F11	85	00	87	00	89	00	8B	00
F12	86	00	88	00	8A	00	8C	00

NUMERIC KEYPAD	NORMAL		SHIFT		CTRL		ALT	
Ins and 0	52	00	52	30	92	00		
End and 1	4F	00	4F	31	75	00	00	01
Dn Arrow and 2	50	00	50	32	91	00	00	02
PgDn and 3	51	00	51	33	76	00	00	03
Lt Arrow and 4	4B	00	4B	34	73	00	00	04
5 (keypad)	4C	00	4C	35	8F	00	00	05
Rt Arrow and 6	4D	00	4D	36	74	00	00	06
Home and 7	47	00	47	37	77	00	00	07
Up Arrow and 8	48	00	48	38	8D	00	00	08
PgUp and 9	49	00	49	39	84	00	00	09
+ (gray)	4E	2B	4E	2B	90	00	4E	00

	NORMAL		SHIFT		CTRL		ALT	
− (gray)	4A	2D	4A	2D	8E	00	4A	00
Del and .	53	00	53	2E	93	00		
* (gray)	37	2A	37	2A	96	00	37	00

TOP ROW	NORMAL		SHIFT		CTRL		ALT	
' and ~	29	60	29	7E			29	00
1 and !	02	31	02	21			78	00
2 and @	03	32	03	40	03	00	79	00
3 and #	04	33	04	23			7A	00
4 and $	05	34	05	24			7B	00
5 and %	06	35	06	25			7C	00
6 and ^	07	36	07	5E	07	1E	7D	00
7 and &	08	37	08	26			7E	00
8 and *	09	38	09	2A			7F	00
9 and (	0A	39	0A	38			80	00
0 and)	0B	30	0B	29			81	00
− and _	0C	2D	0C	5F	0C	1F	82	00
= and +	0D	3D	0D	2B			83	00

OPERATION KEYS	NORMAL		SHIFT		CTRL		ALT	
Esc	01	1B	01	1B	01	1B	01	00
Backspace	0E	08	0E	08	0E	7F	0E	00
Tab	0F	09	0F	00	94	00	A5	00
Enter	1C	0D	1C	0D	1C	0A	1C	00

PUNCTUATION	NORMAL		SHIFT		CTRL		ALT	
[and {	1A	5B	1A	7B	1A	1B	1A	00
] and }	1B	5D	1B	7D	1B	1D	1B	00
; and :	27	3B	27	3A			27	00
' and "	28	27	28	22			28	00
\ and |	2B	5C	2B	7C	2B	1C	2B	00
, and <	33	2C	33	3C			33	00
, and >	34	2E	34	3E			34	00
/ and ?	35	2F	35	3F			35	00

Following are the duplicate keys for the enhanced keyboard (the first two entries are ASCII characters, and the rest are cursor keys):

KEY	NORMAL		SHIFT		CTRL		ALT	
Slash (/)	E0	2F	E0	2F	95	00	A4	00
Enter	E0	0D	E0	0D	E0	0A	A6	00
Home	47	E0	47	E0	77	E0	97	00
End	4F	E0	4F	E0	75	E0	9F	00
PageUp	49	E0	49	E0	84	E0	99	00
PageDown	51	E0	51	E0	76	E0	A1	00
Down Arrow	50	E0	50	E0	91	E0	A0	00

Left Arrow	4B	E0	4B	E0	73	E0	9B	00
Right Arrow	4D	E0	4D	E0	74	E0	9D	00
Up Arrow	48	E0	48	E0	8D	E0	98	00
Ins	52	E0	52	E0	92	E0	A2	00
Del	53	E0	53	E0	93	E0	A3	00

Control keys also have identifying scan codes, although BIOS doesn't deliver them to the keyboard buffer. Here are their scan codes:

CapsLock	3A
NumLock	45
ScrollLock	46
Shift (Left)	2A
Shift (Right)	36
Alt	38
Ctrl	1D
PrtScreen	37

Answers to Selected Questions

CHAPTER 1

1–1. (a) 0110; (c) 10110.

1–2. (a) 00100010; (c) 00100000.

1–3. (a) 11101010; (c) 11000100.

1–4. (a) 00111000; (c) 00000010.

1–5. (a) 51; (c) 5D.

1–6. (a) 23C8; (c) 8000.

1–7. (a) 13; (c) 59; (e) FFF.

1–8. (a) 01010000; (c) 00100011.

1–10. ROM (read-only memory) is permanent, performs startup procedures, and handles input/output. RAM (random-access memory) is temporary and is the area where programs and data reside when executing.

1–12. (a) A section of a program, up to 64K in size, containing code, data, or the stack.

1–13. (a) Stack, data, and code.

1–15. (a) AX, BX, CX, DX, DI, SI; (c) AX and DX; (e) flags.

1–17. (a) MOV CH,25.

CHAPTER 2

2–4. (a) The program segment prefix (PSP).

2–5. (a) CS = the address of the code segment; IP = the offset address of the first instruction, usually zero.

2–7. (a) DOS defines the stack for a .COM program.

2–8. (a) Two bytes (a word).

2–9. (a) 5A302.

2–10. (a) 5B37A.

CHAPTER 3

3–1. The commands are identified at the beginning of the chapter.

3–2. (a) D DS:264; (c) E DS:200 A8 B3 64.

3–3. (a) B82946.

3–4. E CS:101 54.

3–5. (a)
```
MOV     AX,3004
ADD     AX,3000
NOP
```
(c) Use R and IP to reset the IP to 100.

3–6. The product is 0612H.

3–8. Use the N command to name the program, set the length in the BX:CX, and use the W command to write the program.

CHAPTER 4

4–3. Name (of a data item) and label (of an instruction).

4–4. (d) Invalid because it starts with a number; (e) valid only if it refers to the AX register.

4–6. (a) TITLE.

4–8. (a) Causes alignment of a segment on a boundary, such as a paragraph.

4–9. (a) Provides a section of related code, such as a subroutine.

4–10. (a) END; (c) ENDS.

4–11. The END directive tells the assembler that there are no more instructions to assemble; instructions to cause control to return to the operating system are MOV AX,4C00H and INT 21H.

4–12. ASSUME SS:STKSEG,DS:DATSEG,CS:CDSEG.

4–15. (a) 4; (c) 10; (e) 1.

4–16. TITLE1 DB 'RGB Electronics'

4–17. (a) FLDA   DD 73H
(c) FLDC   DW ?
(e) FLDE   DW 17, 19, 21, 26, 31

4–18. (a) ASCII 3238; (b) hex 1C.

4–19. (a) 28; (c) 3A732800.

CHAPTER 5

5–1. MASM/TASM C:DISCOUNT, C:, C:, C:.

5–3. (a) DEBUG C:DISCOUNT.EXE

5–4. (a) Assembly language source program; (c) assembled listing file with source and object code; (e) assembled object file.

5–5. `MOV AX,DATSEG`
`MOV DS,AX`

5–6. Partial coding:

```
MOV   AL,40H          ;Load 40H

SHL   AL,1            ;Shift left (double)

MOV   BL,22H          ;Multiply AL

MUL   BL             ; by 22H
```

5–8. The data segment should contain these data items:

```
FIELDA DB   40H

FIELDB DB   22H

FIELDC DW   ?
```

CHAPTER 6

6–2. (a) The first MOV moves immediate value 325AH; the second MOV moves the contents of locations 325AH and 325BH into the AX.

6–4. Move the contents to the CX of the memory location pointed to by the sum of the offset addresses in the BX, plus the SI, plus 4 (technically by DS:[BX+SI+4]).

6–5. (a) The processor cannot move data directly from one memory location to another.

6–7. (a) `MOV AX,320`
(c) `ADD BX,40H`
(e) `SHL FLDB,1 (or SAL)`

6–8. Use XCHNG.

6–9. Use LEA.

6–11. (a) Pushes the flags, IP, and CS onto the stack, replaces the IF and TF flags, and stores the interrupt address in the CS:IP.

CHAPTER 7

7–1. 64K.

7–4. It uses the high area of the .COM program or, if insufficient space there, uses the end of memory.

7–5. (a) EXE2BIN SAMPLE SAMPLE.COM.

CHAPTER 8

8–1. (a) Within -128 and $+127$ bytes.

8–2. (a) Within -128 and $+127$ bytes. (b) The operand is a one-byte value allowing for 00H through 7FH (0 through $+128$) and 80H through FFH (-128 through -1).

8–3. (a) 64B; (c) 5EA.

8–4. Here is one of many possible solutions:

```
          MOV   AX,00

          MOV   BX,01

          MOV   CX,12

          MOV   DX,00

B20:

          ADD   AX,BX     ;Number is in the AX

          MOV   BX,DX

          MOV   DX,AX

          LOOP  B20
```

8–5. (a) CMP DX,CX   (c) JCXZ address   (e) CMP BX,AX
         JA address   or CMP CX,0   JLE or JNG
                           JZ address

8–6. (a) OF (1); (c) ZF (1); (e) DF (1).

8–8. The first (main) PROC must be FAR because DOS links to its address for execution. A NEAR attribute means that the address is within this particular segment.

8–10. Three (one for each CALL).

8–11. (a) 1001 1010; (c) 1111 1011; (e) 0000 0000.

8–13. (a) 5CDCH; (c) CDC8H; (e) 3737H; (g) 72B9H.

CHAPTER 9

9–1. (a) Row = 00 and column = 00.

9–3.
```
MOV AX,060BH      ;Request
MOV  BH,attribute ; clear
MOV  CX,0C00H     ; screen
MOV  DX,164FH
INT  10H
```

9–4.
```
MSSGE  DB   'What is the date (mm/dd/yy)?',07H,'$'
          MOV  AH,09H         ;Request display
          LEA  DX,MSSGE       ; of date
          INT  21H
```

9–5.
```
DATEPAR LABEL BYTE
    MAXLEN  DB    9              ;Space for slashes and Enter
    ACTLEN  DB    ?
    DATEFLD DB    9 DUP(' ')
            ...
            MOV   AH,0AH         ;Request input
            LEA   DX,DATEPAR     ; of date
            INT   21H
```

9–8. (a) 00.

CHAPTER 10

10–1. (a) 0000 0001; (c) 0111 1000.

10–2. (a) 1011 0101; (c) 1000 1100.

10–3.
```
(a) MOV   AH,00H       ;Request set mode
    MOV   AL,02        ;80-column monochrome
    INT   10H
(c) MOV   AH,060AH     ;Request scroll 10 lines
    MOV   BH,07         ;Normal video
    MOV   CX,0000       ;Entire screen
    MOV   DX,184FH
    INT   10H
```

10–4. Eight colors for background and 16 for foreground.

10–5.
```
MOV   AH,09H          ;Request display
MOV   AL,04           ;Diamond
MOV   BH,00           ;Page number 0
MOV   BL,01011010B    ;Light green on magenta
MOV   CX,05           ;Five times
INT   10H
```

10–11. First set graphics mode; then use INT 10H, function 0BH, to set the background color.

10–12. First set graphics mode, then read the dot like this:
```
MOV   AH,0DH          ;Request read dot
MOV   CX,13           ;Column
MOV   DX,12           ;Row
INT   10H
```

CHAPTER 11

11–1. (a) Location 40:17H (417H).

11–2. (a) Keyboard input with echo. Requires two interrupts if an extended function.

11–4. (a) 48H; (c) 47H.

11–6. Use INT 16H, function 00H or 10H, for input and testing for the scan code, and use INT 10H for setting the cursor.

11–8. On any press or release of a key.

11–10. (a) Location 40:1EH (41EH).

CHAPTER 12

12–1. (a) ES:DI and DS:SI.

12–4. (a)
```
        JCXZ    label2
label1: MOV     AX,[SI]
        MOV     [DI],AX
        INC     DI
        INC     DI
        INC     SI
        INC     SI
        LOOP    label1
label2: ...
```

12–5. Set the DF for a right-to-left move. For MOVSB, initialize at NAME1+9 and NAME2+9. For MOVSW, initialize at NAME1+8 and NAME2+8.

12–6. (a)
```
CLD                     ;Left to right
MOV  CX,20              ;Initialize
LEA  SI,CONAME          ; to move
LEA  DI,PRLINE          ; 20 bytes
REP  MOVSB              ;Move string
```
(c)
```
CLD
LEA  SI,CONAME+2        ;Start at 3rd byte
LODSW                   ;Load 2 bytes
```
(e)
```
CLD                     ;Left to right
MOV  CX,20              ;20 bytes
LEA  SI,CONAME          ;Initialize
LEA  DI,PRLINE          ; address
REPE CMPSB              ;Compare string
```

12–7. Here is one solution:

```
H10SCAS PROC NEAR
        CLD                     ;Left to right
        MOV  CX,10              ;10 bytes
        LEA  DI,NAME1           ;Initialize address
        MOV  AL,'e'             ; and scan character
H20:
        REPNE SCASB             ;Scan
        JNE  H30                ;Found?
        CMP  BYTE PTR[DI],'r'   ;Yes, next byte
        JNE  H20                ; equals 'r'?
        MOV  AL,03
H30:    RET
H10SCAS ENDP
```

12–8. PATTERN DB   03H,04H,05H,0B4H
           DISPLAY DB   80 DUP(' '),'$'

```
        CLD                          ;Left to right
        MOV   CX,20                  ;20 bytes
        LEA   SI,PATTERN             ;Initialize
        LEA   DI,DISPLAY             ; address
        REP MOVSW                    ;Move pattern
```

Then use INT 21H, function 09H, to display the variable DISPLAY.

CHAPTER 13

13–1. (a) 127 and 255.

13–3. (a) MOV   AX,DATAY
```
            ADD   AX,DATAX           ;Add DATAX
            MOV   DATAY,AX           ; to DATAY
```
(b) See Figure 13–2 for multiword addition.

13–4. STC sets the carry flag. The sum is 0148H, plus 0237H, plus 1.

13–5. (a) MOV   AX,DATAX
```
            MUL   DATAY              ;Product is in the DX:AX
```
(c) See Figure 13–4 for multiplying a doubleword by a word.

13–7. (a) MOV   AX,DATAX
```
            MOV   BL,25              ;Divide DATAX
            DIV   BL                 ; by 23
```

CHAPTER 14

14–1. (a) ADD generates 6CH, and AAA generates 0102H.
(c) SUB generates 02H, and AAS has no effect.

14–2.
```
        LEA   SI,UNPAK               ;Initialize address
        MOV   CX,04                  ; and 4 loops
    B20:
        OR    [SI],30H               ;Insert ASCII 3
        INC   SI                     ;Increment for next byte
        LOOP B20                     ;Loop 4 times
```

14–3. Use Figure 14–2 as a guide, but initialize the CX to 03.

14–4. Use Figure 14–3 as a guide, but initialize the CX to 03.

14–5. (a) Convert decimal 46,328 to binary:

	Decimal	Hex
$8 \times 1 =$	8	8
$2 \times 10 =$	20	14
$3 \times 100 =$	300	12C
$6 \times 1000 =$	6000	1770
$4 \times 10000 =$	40000	9C40
		B4F8

CHAPTER 15

15–2. TABLEX DW 50 DUP (' ').

15–3. (a) ITEMNO DB '06','10','14','21','24'
(c) ITPRICE DW 9395,8225,9067,8580,1385

15–4. A possible organization is into the following procedures:

SUBROUTINE	PURPOSE
B10READ	Display prompt, accept item number.
C10SRCH	Search table, display message if invalid item.
D10MOVE	Extract description and price from table.
E10CONV	Convert quantity from ASCII to binary.
F10CALC	Calculate value (quantity × price).
G10CONV	Convert value from binary to ASCII.
K10DISP	Display description and value on screen.

15–5. The following routine copies the table. Refer to Figure 15–7 for sorting table entries.

```
SORTAB   DB   5 DUP(9 DUP(?))
         ...
         LEA SI,ITDESC     ;Initialize
         LEA DI,SORTAB     ; table address and
         MOV CX,45         ; number of characters
         CLD               ;Left to right
         REP MOVSB         ;Move string
```

15–6. The intention is to use XLAT for translation.

CHAPTER 16

16–1. 512.

16–4. (a) A group of sectors (1, 2, 4, or 8) that DOS treats as a unit of storage space on a disk.

16–5. (a) 40 cylinders × 9 sectors × 2 sides × 512 bytes = 368,640.

16–7. (a) Side 0, track 0, sector 1.

16–8. In the directory, the first byte of filename is set to E5H.

16–11. (a) Positions 28–31 of the directory; (b) 0B4AH, stored as 4A0B.

16–12. (a) The first byte (media descriptor) contains F8H.

CHAPTER 17

17–1. (a) 02.

17–3. (b)
```
         MOV  AH,3CH        ;Request create
         MOV  CX,00         ;Normal file
         LEA  DX,PATH1      ;ASCIIZ string
         INT  21H           ;Call DOS
         JC   error         ;Exit if error
         MOV  CUSTHAN,AX    ;Save handle
```

17–4. (a)
```
        MOV    AH,3DH          ;Request open
        MOV    AL,00           ;Read only
        LEA    DX,PATH1        ;ASCIIZ string
        INT    21H             ;Call DOS
        JC     error           ;Exit if error
        MOV    CUSTHAN,AX      ;Save handle
```

17–5. Where a program opens many files.

17–7. Use Figure 17–2 as a guide for creating a disk file and Figure 14–5 for conversion from ASCII to binary.

17–8. Use Figure 17–3 as a guide for reading the file and Figure 14–6 for conversion from binary to ASCII.

17–10. See Figure 17–4 for the use of function 42H.

17–11. All the functions involve INT 21H: (a) 16H; (c) 15H; (e) 14H.

17–12. (a) 4; (b) 108 (9 sectors × 3 tracks × 4 records/track); c) one access per sector, or 27 in all.

CHAPTER 18

All the questions for this chapter are exercises involving the use of DEBUG.

CHAPTER 19

19–2. Most likely as a developer of disk utility programs.

19–3. (a) In the AH.

19–5. Use INT 13H and function 00H.

19–6. Use INT 13H and function 01H.

19–8.
```
        MOV    AH,03H          ;Request write
        MOV    AL,03           ;3 sectors
        LEA    BX,OUTDSK       ;Output area
        MOV    CH,08           ;Track 08
        MOV    CL,01           ;Sector 01
        MOV    DH,00           ;Head #0
        MOV    DL,01           ;Drive B
        INT    13H
```

19–9. The status byte in the AH contains 00000011.

CHAPTER 20

20–1. (a) 09.

20–3. (a)
```
        MOV    AH,05H          ;Request print
        MOV    DL,0CH          ;Form feed
        INT    21H
```

```
(b)          LEA   SI,NAMEFLD      ;Initialize name
             MOV   CX,length       ; and length
      B20:
             MOV   AH,05H          ;Request print
             MOV   DL,[SI]         ;Character from name
             INT   21H             ;
             INC   SI              ;Next character in name
             LOOP  B20             ;Loop length times
```

(c) You could code a line feed (0AH) in front of the address. The solution is similar to part (b). (e) Issue another form feed (0CH).

20–4. HEADNG DB 13, 10, 15, 'Title', 12

20–5. (a) In the AH.

20–7. The CX is not available for looping because the loop that prints the name uses the CX. You could use the BX like this:

```
             MOV   BX,05           ;Set 5 loops
      C20:
             ...
             DEC   BX              ;Decrement loop count
             JNZ   C20             ;Loop if still nonzero
```

CHAPTER 21

21–1. (a) Unit of measure for mouse movement in increments of 1/200 of an inch.

21–2. All these functions are identified near the beginning of the chapter.

21–3. Note the effect of functions 01H and 02H on the flag.

21–6. Note that the figure reverses the parallel ports, LPT1 and LPT2.

CHAPTER 22

22–1. The introduction to this chapter gives three reasons.

22–2. The statements include MACRO and ENDM.

22–5. (a) SALL.

22–6. (a)
```
MULTBY MACRO   MULTPR,MULTCD
       MOV     AL,MULTCD
       MUL     MULTPR
       ENDM
```

22–7. To include the macro in pass 1, code the following:

```
IF1

       INCLUDE library-name

ENDIF
```

22–8. The macro definition could begin with

```
BIPRINT MACRO PRTLINE,PRLEN
```
PRTLINE and PRLEN are dummy arguments for the address and length, respectively, of the line to be printed. See Chapter 20 for using BIOS INT 17H to print.

22–9. Note that you cannot use a conditional IF to test for a zero divisor. A conditional IF works only during assembly, whereas the test must occur during program execution. Code assembly instructions such as these:

```
CMP  DIVISOR,00        ;Zero divisor?
JNZ  (bypass)          ;No, bypass
CALL (error message routine)
```

CHAPTER 23

23–1. The introduction to this chapter gives reasons.

23–2. (a) PARA.

23–3. (a) NONE.

23–4. (a) 'code'.

23–6. (a) EXTRN SUBPRO:FAR

23–7. (a) PUBLIC QTY,VALUE,PRICE

23–8. Use Figure 23–6 as a guide.

23–9. Use Figure 23–8 as a guide for passing parameters. However, this question involves pushing three variables onto the stack. The called program therefore has to access [BP+10] for the third entry (PRICE) in the stack. You can define your own standard for returning PRICE through the stack. Watch also for the pop value in the RET operand.

23–10. This program involves material from Chapters 9 (screen I/0), 13 (binary multiplication), 14 (conversion between ASCII and binary), and 23 (linkage to subprograms). Be careful of the stack.

CHAPTER 24

24–1. (a) In sector 1, track 0.

24–2. Acts as a low-level interface to the BIOS routines in ROM.

24–4. (a) Following MSDOS.SYS.

24–5. (a) The first 256 bytes of a program when loaded in memory for execution.

24–6. 5CH: 03 41 4C 46 20 20 20 20 20 44 4F 43
      80H: 0A 20 43 3A 41 4C 46 2E 44 4F 43 0D

24–8. (a) 2BA1.

24–9. (a) 1A25[0] + 100H (PSP) + 30H = 1A38[0].

24–10. (a) It means the start of a memory block (not the last one).

24–11. (a) INT 09H, in the interrupt services table at 24H.

CHAPTER 25

25–1. The section on interrupts at the start of this chapter discusses these types.

25–2. The section on interrupts at the start of this chapter discusses these lines.

25–3. (a) FFFF[0]H.

25–5. At 40[0]H.

25–6. (a) Equipment status; (c) second byte of shift status.

25–7. (a) The addresses (in reverse-byte sequence) of COM1 and COM2.

25–8. (a) INT 00H.

CHAPTER 26

26–1. Interrupts 20H through 3FH.

26–2. (a) 03H; (c) 30H or 3306H.

26–3. (a) Printer output; (c) buffered keyboard input.

Index

2